375

Edwin Saulx Bodes

Trinity - 1955

From the library
of Julia Saulx

THE MAKING OF THE MODERN MIND

REVISED EDITION

A Survey of the Intellectual Background of the Present Age

JOHN HERMAN RANDALL, JR.
Columbia University

HOUGHTON MIFFLIN COMPANY
BOSTON · NEW YORK · CHICAGO · DALLAS · ATLANTA · SAN FRANCISCO
The Riverside Press Cambridge

COPYRIGHT, 1940
BY JOHN HERMAN RANDALL, JR.
COPYRIGHT, 1926, BY JOHN HERMAN RANDALL, JR.

ALL RIGHTS RESERVED INCLUDING THE RIGHT TO REPRODUCE
THIS BOOK OR PARTS THEREOF IN ANY FORM

The Riverside Press
CAMBRIDGE · MASSACHUSETTS
PRINTED IN THE U.S.A.

TO
FREDERICK JAMES EUGENE WOODBRIDGE
Philosopher, Teacher, and Friend

FOREWORD

WHAT the following pages attempt was stated in the Foreword to the first edition: "This book aims, by entering sympathetically into the spirit of the past, to make the thought of the present more intelligible. Covering so vast a field, it can of course lay little claim to originality; but it does rest, so far as possible, upon a first-hand acquaintance with the words of those who have expressed the intellectual currents of their times. This explains the abundance of quotation, in which the men of the past themselves give voice to their beliefs; for it has seemed best to try to look at the development of thought with the eyes of those who participated in it."

In the years since I first set down these words, I have, I trust, learned much, above all from those many students of ideas who have taken the trouble to instruct my ignorance. I wish to thank them here collectively for their generous help. If I have not always been able to incorporate their suggestions, it is not that I have failed to agree. Were I to start the enterprise afresh, I am far from sure I should express quite the same judgments. Yet careful consideration has suggested little it seemed imperative to alter. Except for some things I have found out about the birth of modern science, I have been content to leave without major changes the earlier portion of my story. It is the history men have lived rather than the history scholars have discovered that has dictated the thoroughgoing revision of the chapters of Book IV, dealing with the past hundred years.

Of those hundred, the fifteen since the book was first written have not been the least momentous. They have brought the intellectual currents of a century to a more unified and a more tragic focus. The problems of 1940 force a fresh perspective, which has called for emphasis throughout. And in science, philosophy, and religion new movements of ideas have awakened sharp debate: they demand interpretation. These changes and additions have increased Book IV by some forty pages. Among other major new topics, this book now treats the recent revolution in physical theory, its reaction on 19th century mechanistic science, and the changed conception of the nature and function of the scientific enterprise it has induced; the most recent developments in the science of man; the new philosophies of nature and of science; the rise of Protestant neo-orthodoxy; and the social ideals and methods of the world that has been with us since the incidence of the depression and the advent of Hitler.

In that earlier Foreword I tried to indicate something of my immense indebtedness to other minds. It was there stated: "I wish to acknowledge my deep obligation above all to Dean F. J. E. Woodbridge, of Columbia University, whose wisdom and insight have been my key to the understanding both of history and of philosophy; to Professor John Dewey, who has done so much to place the development of modern philosophy in its proper perspective; and to Professor John J. Coss, of Columbia University, to whose suggestion and sympathetic encouragement this work owes its existence. Special thanks are due to those who have furnished helpful advice and criticism. Dr. Harry Elmer Barnes has given unstintingly of his vast store of information and his refreshingly original points of view; Professor Sterling P. Lamprecht (now of Amherst College) and Professor Horace L. Friess, of Columbia University, have been fertile with valuable suggestions; Dr. Felix Adler, Professor James Gutmann, of Columbia University, and Professor Morris R. Cohen, of the College of the City of New York, have read the manuscript and furnished helpful criticism. Professor Austin P. Evans, of Columbia University, has given the first book the benefit of his knowledge of the Middle Ages. Professor Edwin A. Burtt (now of Cornell University) has contributed much to my understanding of the rise of modern science. The staff of the course in Contemporary Civilization at Columbia University have checked the work by their teaching experience. The intellectual companionship of my father, John Herman Randall, has meant more to me than I can ever hope to express. It is impossible to put into words my debt to my wife."

From all these friends and mentors I have continued to learn through the years. It is with sorrow that I must record the passing of three of my teachers. Dr. Adler and Professor Coss are no longer among the living; and Professor Woodbridge, the wisest man I have ever known, has joined Socrates in that Platonic heaven to which the circumstances of time are wholly irrelevant.

J. H. R., Jr.

CONTENTS

INTRODUCTION 3

Book I

THE INTELLECTUAL OUTLOOK OF MEDIEVAL CHRISTENDOM

CHAPTER I. THE COMING OF AGE OF THE WESTERN PEOPLES . 9
History a human achievement — The historical setting of Western civilization — The twelfth-century renaissance.

CHAPTER II. THE WORLD AS THE SCENE OF THE DRAMA OF SALVATION 17
The Christian epic and its setting — The educated classes and the average man — The world of the common man — The unseen world — The ordered universe of Thomas and Dante — The divine governance of the world.

CHAPTER III. THE CHIEF END OF MAN — THE ENJOYMENT OF ETERNAL LIFE 38
The richness of the Christian tradition — Hebrew righteousness — Gospel love — Hellenistic love of wisdom — Platonism — Oriental religious asceticism — The medieval system — Medieval virtues and vices — Life eternal.

CHAPTER IV. THE EMBODIMENT — THE CITY OF GOD . . . 58
The functional ideal of society — The organization of religious society — The saintly ideal — The monastic life — Saint Bernard, the Monk — Saint Francis, the Mendicant Friar — The church as the City of God and the Body of Christ — The ideal of organized spiritual power.

CHAPTER V. THE EMBODIMENT — LAY SOCIETY 82
Feudal society — The knightly ideal — The peasant's lot — The economic ideals of the guild system — The vocation of the scholar — The method of scholastic science — The scientific ideal of the Aristotelian-Thomistic system — The ideal of a unified Christendom — Dante's universal monarchy.

Book II

THE NEW WORLD OF THE RENAISSANCE

CHAPTER VI. THE NEW INTERESTS OF THE MODERN AGE — THE NATURAL MAN 111
The gradual growth of the humanistic spirit — Humanism in the

CONTENTS

Middle Ages — The discovery of the humanity of the classics — The heritage of Rome and Greece — The revolt from the Christian ethic — The humanistic spirit — The diverging streams of humanism — The modernity and the tragedy of Erasmus — The ideal of the gentleman — The new ethic of industry and thrift.

CHAPTER VII. THE RELIGIOUS REACTION — THE REVOLT FROM THE MEDIEVAL CHURCH 143
The compromise of the Reformation — The spirit of reform in the Middle Ages — The religious revolt — The gospel of Luther — The Calvinistic system — The Catholic reformation — The moral revolt — The Puritan life — The Puritan spirit and industrialism — The political revolt — The Reformation and the Renaissance — The outcome of the Reformation.

CHAPTER VIII. THE REVOLT FROM FEUDALISM AND A UNIFIED CHRISTENDOM 172
The rise of national cultures and sentiment — The emergence of centralized national states — The birth of modern political theory — The theory of absolute monarchy — The emergence of middle-class constitutionalism — The theory of mercantilism, paternalistic nationalism in economics — Irresponsible national sovereignty — The restraining force of international law.

CHAPTER IX. THE NEW INTERESTS OF THE MODERN AGE — THE WORLD OF NATURE 203
Medieval interest in nature — The expansion of Europe — The discovery of Arabian science — Natural science in the high Middle Ages — The anti-scientific bias of humanism — The attack on the barrenness and irrelevance of scholasticism — The revival of Alexandrian mathematical science — The direct appeal to nature — The new method — The Baconian spirit.

CHAPTER X. THE NEW SCENE OF HUMAN LIFE 226
The Copernican revolution — The simplicity and uniformity of Nature — The appeal to the observation of Nature — The Cartesian revolution — The foundation of dynamics — The mechanical interpretation of Nature — The infinite worlds — The reign of law.

Book III

THE ORDER OF NATURE — THE DEVELOPMENT OF THOUGHT IN THE SEVENTEENTH AND EIGHTEENTH CENTURIES

CHAPTER XI. THE NEWTONIAN WORLD-MACHINE 253
The success of the mathematical interpretation of Nature — The mathematical synthesis of Newton — The method of Newtonian science — The rise of the experimental method — The problem of knowledge and the new ideal of science — The empiricists' attack on tradition — The scientific ideals of the age of reason.

CHAPTER XII. THE RELIGION OF REASON 282
The spread of the humanistic spirit — The growth of religious

rationalism — The Religion of Reason, or Natural Religion — The place of Revelation — The Deistic attack on Revelation — The critique of prophecy and miracles — The rationalistic attack on Deism — The arguments of natural theology — Skepticism and atheism.

CHAPTER XIII. THE SCIENCE OF MAN — THE SCIENCES OF HUMAN NATURE AND OF BUSINESS 308

The creation of the social sciences — The deductive, mechanical method — The science of human nature — The omnipotence of environment — The science of society — Political economy — Social physics and laisser-faire — Adam Smith and commerce — The dismal science of the factory system.

CHAPTER XIV. THE SCIENCE OF MAN — THE SCIENCE OF GOVERNMENT 334

The decline of absolute monarchy — The theory of absolutism founded on reason — The theory of modern constitutionalism — The Whig apologetic of John Locke — The theory of the American Constitution — Democracy on the basis of natural rights: Rousseau — Jeffersonian democracy — Jacksonian democracy — The utilitarian method.

CHAPTER XV. THE MORALITY OF REASONABLENESS — HUMANITARIANISM 365

The rational science of morality — The humanitarian ideal — The argument for toleration — Cosmopolitanism and pacifism — The idea of progress.

Book IV

THE GROWING WORLD — THOUGHT AND ASPIRATION IN THE LAST HUNDRED YEARS

CHAPTER XVI. THE ROMANTIC PROTEST AGAINST THE AGE OF REASON 389

The social basis of intellectual complexity and change, and the demand for its organization — Reaction against the age of reason — Emphasis on the less rational side of human nature — The natural no longer equivalent to the reasonable — Tradition found truly natural — Emphasis on faith, as a support to religion — Faith as a support to revolutionary tendencies — The rational justification of faith — Emphasis on the individual personality and its expression — Nature interpreted in personal terms — The Romantic science of the individual — Interest in human history and tradition.

CHAPTER XVII. THE CONFLICT OF SOCIAL IDEALS TO 1848 . . 427

The philosophy of conservatism — Acceptance of the Romantic protest against rationalism — The appeal to faith — The worship of tradition — The philosophy of liberalism and individualism — Utilitarianism — The worship of progress — Liberal nationalism and internationalism — The new philosophy of industrial society — Benevolent industrialism — Social democracy.

CONTENTS

CHAPTER XVIII. THE WORLD CONCEIVED AS A PROCESS OF GROWTH AND EVOLUTION 458
The two scientific revolutions — Eighteenth-century ideas of progress and evolution — The idea of growth and development in human society — The spread of naturalistic uniformitarianism — The method of mechanistic analysis universalized and broadened — Basic generalizations unifying the fields of physics and chemistry — The newer concepts of physics — Mechanistic explanations in biology — Mechanistic analysis in psychology — Experimental analysis applied to the origin of present forms — The development of the solar system — The development of the earth — The development of the forms of life — The effect of the notion of development on scientific ideals.

CHAPTER XIX. THE SCIENCE OF MAN IN THE GROWING WORLD . 497
The search for an adequate method — The persistence of the eighteenth-century mechanical ideal — The historical method of the romanticists — The evolutionary and biological methods — The influence of psychology and experimentalism — The development of psychology — The problem of the elements of human behavior — The problem of the functioning of the integrated personality — Psychoanalysis — The contemporary view of human nature — The schools of sociology — The achievement of a critical method in anthropology — The creation of a realistic, genetic, and experimental economics — Investigation in jurisprudence and political science — The need for popularizing the social sciences.

CHAPTER XX. RELIGION IN THE GROWING WORLD 533
Causal factors in the religious development of the present — Opposition to the new world as conflicting with religious traditions — Protestant fundamentalism — Catholic opposition to modern tendencies — The reaction of Pius IX — Catholic modernism — The Catholic renaissance — Liberal Protestantism — Definite abandonment of parts of the religious tradition — The new faith of the liberals — Monistic evolutionary theologies — Æsthetic naturalism — Ethical religion and the social gospel — Beyond modernism and liberalism — Naturalism with vision — Effects of religious changes on the churches.

CHAPTER XXI. PHILOSOPHIC REACTIONS TO THE GROWING WORLD OF MECHANISM AND NATURALISM 577
The picture of the mechanistic world generalized from science — Disillusionment — Pessimism in the face of the alien world — Consolation sought in art and beauty — Promethean defiance of the mechanistic world — Escape from the alien world into philosophic idealism — Glorification of the growing world — Faith in the inevitability of progress — Confidence in creative evolution — A new evolutionary ethics — Worship of the future — The new naturalism — New philosophies of nature and of science — Naturalism, Greek and Baconian.

CHAPTER XXII. SOCIAL IDEALS IN THE GROWING WORLD . . 622
Contrasting types of social ideal — Middle-class ideals — Social ideals of an individualistic industrialism — Liberal ideals of social

legislation and social reform — Religious and humanitarian ideals for an industrial society — Working-class ideals — Social ideals of organized labor — Industrial democracy — Collectivistic visions and programs — Non-democratic and authoritarian methods — Ideals of international relations — Patriotic nationalism — Cosmopolitanism — Internationalism and pacifism.

INDEX 685

THE MAKING OF THE MODERN MIND

THE MAKING OF
THE MODERN MIND

INTRODUCTION

THE visitor to Rome who leaves the Corso and wanders westward toward the Tiber, through the maze of narrow streets that swarm with the youth and age of the capital of modern Italy, takes inexhaustible delight in tracing on this ever-changing palimpsest in stone the work of the successive generations of Romans whose descendants are to-day in possession of their dwellings. Leave the tram-line, dodge that big Fiat, turn a corner, and there before you is a picturesque and dilapidated pile framed in the pillars of an old amphitheater, erected in the age when this was the Campus Martius, the pleasure-ground of the subjects of Hadrian. Between the columns are walls of great blocks of travertine, quarried from some Imperial edifice, and built here into a gloomy fortress in the days when the feudal families of the Orsini and the Colonna were at swords' points over the election of a Leo or a Gregory as Pope. Above is a fine Renaissance cornice from the time of Bramante and Michelangelo; while here and there the stucco of the Ottocento is peeling off under the hard usage of the red shirts of Garibaldi and the black shirts of Mussolini. Cross a crowded piazza, thread that narrow way between two palaces famed in story, and there is a Fascist celebration before the tomb of Vittorio Emanuele in the church of Santa Maria Rotonda, better known as that Pantheon erected by Hadrian to commemorate the conquest by Roman legions of all the Oriental gods. For century after century the men of one age have adapted to their purposes the buildings of another, sometimes preserving them almost entire, merely altering the use, sometimes adding new stones and new forms, sometimes tearing down and building up again with the old material. And still the life goes on, teeming with new activity, oblivious of what went before, the round of birth and hope and failure and death, under emperor or baron, pope, king, or dictator. Of a truth Rome is the Eternal City, eternally old in its forms and walls, eternally new in its hopes and aspirations — a fitting symbol of the humanity that has for so long looked upon it as its center.

For the history of human civilization is just such a story of labors and edifices, continually modified and enlarged and adapted to the new streams of life — a story of old walls outgrown, torn down, rebuilded in new forms, of the sacrilegious hands of rude barbarians clumsily laid upon ancient monuments, of old churches piously preserved by the faithful, of palaces demolished for the passage of the tram-car, of slums razed for a broad boulevard, of modern parliaments sitting in the halls of Renaissance despots, of Communist headquarters in the casinos of Roman nobles. If the persistence of the past into the present is not everywhere so palpable as in the city of the Popes, it is none the less true that the ideas and beliefs, the aims and ideals of the California fruit-grower or the Pennsylvania coal-miner, the sheep-rancher of Queensland or the cultured clubman of Buenos Aires, are just such a mosaic of bits and pieces gathered from here and there along the journey through the ages, set into new patterns to serve the needs and the taste of America or Australia. A ramble through the mind of the modern man would reveal the same juxtaposition of beliefs that have endured unchanged for centuries, with ideas gleaned from the morning paper, all put together in a structure with a shaky enough foundation and with many a makeshift to fill the gaps, yet somehow strong enough to answer the demands made on it and to give shelter until it can be improved. A man to-day will believe that the mercury atom can be changed into an atom of gold, and that Jesus of Nazareth rose from the dead and now sits at the right hand of God, that it is glorious to die on the field of battle for one's country, and that all disputes between nations should be settled in a world court, that the unions should be smashed and that the world should be made safe for democracy; and he will believe these things with as little sense of their origin and their meaning and their relevance to his own life as the Roman boy playing in the streets displays toward the embodied past about him.

It is fascinating to explore the mind of the present generation, to unravel the many threads that enter into its tangled fabric and trace them back to their first appearance in the loom of history, far more fascinating even than a walk through Rome. But it is more; it is of the utmost importance, for one who wishes to understand the life about him, to comprehend its intellectual forces, to discern the probable drift of the current, and perchance to take his place at the oar. Ideas are much more lasting than anything else in man's civilization, and those which find themselves in modern minds have roots going back into the immemorial past. It is through the mind that man attaches himself to his remote predecessors, far more than through any physical persistence, even of racial stock. Especially is this true in America, which, despite its relatively new background, is as much a part of European civilization as Rome herself. To understand, appreciate, and judge the science, the religion, the art, the moral ideals of to-day, it is imperative to understand those great achievements in the past of mankind that have created the home in which man's spirit now moves.

But the chief need for disentangling men's beliefs and tracing their lineage is due to the fact, so overwhelmingly important and so little heeded by the vast majority, that ideas are not like the eternal gods of Olympus, unchanging and ever young; like all things human they are born and grow and mature, and may even die. Ideas are living, and all that lives has an environment in which it must exist and to which it must be adapted. Men are prone to regard the body of their beliefs as they do the hills to which they lift up their eyes, as fixed and immutable, and all departures therefrom as in the very nature of the case absurd. Or they treat them as coins of tested gold, always able to pass current in any land or age. Christianity, science, democracy, private property, these must always have been and must be destined to endure forever. The revolutionary changes which all are willing to recognize in the domain of material things, few can discern in the more intangible realm of the spirit. Not that it is difficult to comprehend that men once believed otherwise than they do to-day, but that it is almost impossible to realize that they really *believed* these seeming absurdities, believed them just as tenaciously and just as sincerely, and perhaps with just as little evidence, as men now hold their most cherished convictions. A tracing of the history of the birth and growth of these convictions should make it easier to achieve a sense of the relevance of ideas to their setting, of their validity in the terms of the environment which developed them, and of their utility only so long as that environment still nurtures them.

If men's minds are a mosaic or a palimpsest of belief upon belief, it is of the highest importance that they understand the life-history of those beliefs, why they are there, and whether they are justified in being there or should be discarded. What have been the great waves of thought and aspiration that have left these successive deposits? What did they mean when they were at the flood, what of value for to-day have they left, what must men seek out anew for themselves in the never-ending task of rebuilding civilization? When one has reached an understanding of what materials are furnished by the world around about him, and what resources he can hope for inside himself, it still remains for him to appraise the past as it is left to operate in the present, to understand it, to appropriate it, and to become its master.

BOOK I
THE INTELLECTUAL OUTLOOK OF MEDIEVAL CHRISTENDOM

CHAPTER I

THE COMING OF AGE OF THE WESTERN PEOPLES

History a Human Achievement

It is customary to regard the course of history as a great river, with its source in some small rivulet of the distant past, taking its rise on the plains of Asia, and flowing slowly down through the ages, gathering water from new tributaries on the way, until finally in our own days it broadens majestically over the whole world. Men have even personified this flow, made of it a being that develops of its own volition, following its own laws to the achievement of some preconceived goal. They have spoken of the "dialectic of ideas," and regarded men and whole civilizations as the passive instruments employed by this great Being in the working-out of its purposes. The observer not already committed to faith in such an interpretation finds it difficult to discern any such steady sweep in the course of human events, and above all he feels that to look upon humanity as a passive tool to which things are done and with which ends are accomplished, is a falsification of the cardinal fact that it is men who have made history and not history which has made men. Men have built up civilization, men have patiently and laboriously found out every way of doing things and toilingly worked out every idea that is to-day a part of our heritage from the past — men working at every turn, to be sure, under the influences of their environment and with the materials at hand, individual men and races and not even some such being as "humanity." The complex of beliefs and ideals by which the modern world lives and with which it works is not a gift from the gods, as ancient myth had it, but an achievement of a long succession of generations.

Nor has this achievement been a steady and continuous acquisition, like the rolling-up of a great snowball. Whole nations and races have painfully worked out ideas and then disappeared, leaving little mark upon the minds of subsequent ages. What has remained has been seized upon by another group, worked over and amalgamated with the rest of its beliefs, and then taken and distorted by still further peoples. Many fresh starts have been made, much of value has been irretrievably lost, much that is worthless or even positively harmful has been preserved. It is now possible with all the sources and the indefatigable energy of modern scholarship to go back into the distant past and reconstruct much of what those early civilizations really were like, to see them as completed wholes. Such an endeavor always impresses us with the wonder that so much had been already found out, and that the Egyptians of the fourth millennium B.C. or the contemporary Babylonians were after all so much like ourselves — were, in a word, so human. But it is no part of an analysis of how men to-day come to believe as they do, to undertake any such task. Our own civilization is a composite of what our ancestors were able to glean from these vanished cultures and what they were able to add to the materials they discovered ready-made for them, and a better understanding of the whole can be gained from starting with the Western peoples and seeing just how they made their own the treasures of the past.

The Historical Setting of Western Civilization

When we speak to-day of civilization in a eulogistic sense, we mean that body of beliefs and practices that prevails in Europe and in those portions of the globe peopled by men of European stock. For certain purposes, this is synonymous with Christendom; for others, with those lands touched by the Industrial Revolution. This is the civilization that, thanks to the possession of applied science and hence of machine-guns and battleships, has managed to obtain a superficial hold upon the whole globe. It is very young, as civilizations go, claiming a continuous history of less than a thousand years; but in that time it has undergone more changes than any of the other civilizations of the world. Although it has been in possession of science for more than three centuries, it is only in the last hundred years that it has shown any distinctive advantages over other cultures. As late as the end of the eighteenth century, the Emperor of China saw nothing to learn from the West, and it is in many minds still an open question whether he was not then right. But this is the civilization that is our own heritage, that to which we and perhaps the whole world are committed; and before we undertake to examine the circumstances of its growth, it is interesting to see it in its proper historical perspective.

Western civilization is the product of those generations of men, chiefly in northwestern Europe, who lived after the ancient Roman Empire had entered upon a social and intellectual disintegration. It represents a fusion of the ideas of the Hellenistic world with the customs and the temper of mind of the barbarian invaders of the Empire. For many and complex reasons, in which the barbarian invasions were at most but a contributory factor, and probably more a result than a cause, the material and intellectual civilization of Rome declined. The center of intellectual life shifted more and more to the East, to Greek and Hellenistic Constantinople; while in the West many factors, among which was the Moslem conquest of a large part of the Mediterranean basin, forced the center of power farther and farther north, where it seems established, by the time of Charlemagne, in France and western Germany. The population of these regions was for the most part not of that stock that had produced ancient civilization, but a mixture of the earlier Gauls whom the Romans had civilized at the opening of the Christian era and of a much smaller number of Teutonic invaders from the east. Even in Roman Italy, Spain, and southern France the newer "barbarians" formed an appreciable part of the inhabitants. This northward shift meant that the Western peoples, gradually emerging out of an amalgamation of these elements, were on the whole of a stock that had been introduced to civilization more recently than the Mediterranean peoples. Moreover, they were living in a region still very sparsely settled, under social conditions still resembling those of pioneer settlers; while even in the South social life was growing more and more crude. In Italy and Spain and southern France there was probably little break in the continuity of ancient culture, although even here the economic basis suffered a period of decline; but in the North, from the days of the first Roman conquest onward, the main problem was to build up an organized social life in a comparatively undeveloped region and to assimilate as rapidly as possible the culture of the Mediterranean world. The influx of new barbarians, who captured the government, delayed a process that had advanced remarkably under Roman rule; for a time there was probably a distinct relapse. We can form some idea of the situation by comparing it to what prevailed in America at the beginning of the nineteenth century. Northwestern Europe corresponded to what was then the Mississippi Valley and the western United States, Italy and the South to the Atlantic seaboard, possessing a much higher culture, and Constantinople and the East to Europe, the seat of civilized life. It is because Western Europe was essentially a pioneer society, struggling to develop a new country, and in the process having little time to devote to the things of the mind, that there lies whatever of truth exists in the term "Dark Ages" as applied to that period. In northwestern Europe the period was "dark," not because of any lack of energy or power in its inhabitants, not because of any lack of promise of a rich life to come, but because those lands were then, as the American frontier later, devoting their very considerable energies to tasks that had to be done before a cultivated society could there hope to exist.

The center of Western life had thus shifted to regions occupied by men whom from this time on we can call the Western peoples, primarily concerned with developing a sparsely settled country. For the few who had the leisure, the monks and some city-dwellers and nobles, there was available as high a culture as the declining Roman Empire had known; but side by side with these there were great masses of uneducated and rude dwellers upon the land too busy for such refinements. Similarly Colonial America contained in the seaboard cities highly refined groups, and farther inland vigorous and intelligent but uneducated pioneers. For the most part these Western peoples could neither develop nor assimilate much of a culture, although wherever the influence of the Church was felt learning and art flourished quite respectably. They were forced to live for some five hundred years the lives of quarrelsome pioneer settlers, in the woods and extending clearings of Western Europe, about as far removed from the intellectual currents of the day as the Californian or Australian of a couple of generations back. Had there been factories or surplus capital anywhere in the world desiring a market, these Westerners might well have been assigned the rôle of "backward peoples," and writers would have been found in abundance to prove that races, so incapable of learning from the Hellenistic world that after centuries only the externals of a rude Christianity marked their attainment, could never furnish more than a brown or a yellow man's burden for the great Eastern cultures. They would have misread the true situation, but it is naturally difficult for us to realize that our ancestors began with so little, and developed so slowly; and it is far from conducive to the pride of race to recognize that the intellectual riches to which they finally won their way lay for hundreds of years almost forgotten and overlooked. The riches of Greece and the Orient, which the Romans made their own in four or five centuries at most, and which Semitic civilizations assimilated without much difficulty, it took the Western peoples, under much harder conditions, to be sure, fully twice as long to build into their lives. It was not until the twelfth century that they had reached a position where they could begin to comprehend the meaning of the ancient ideas, and it was not until the sixteenth that they stood upon the intellectual level of the men of Alexandria or Constantinople or Rome of over a thousand years before, and could rightly claim to be civilized in the sense that the Hindus or the Chinese were civilized centuries before the Christian era. Perhaps it is with races as with individuals, and those whose infancy is most prolonged are for that very reason able to continue learning when others have reached the limits of their powers and their natural resources.

That by the thirteenth century the fully amalgamated peoples of the West had created a society of magnificent form and beauty, a society that carries a strong appeal to many a heart to-day because of its possession of priceless things we seem to have lost, is of course not to be gainsaid; yet for all its beauty it was still quite crude and ignorant and new, a pioneer society just struggling out of a long past of bitter toil for a bare subsistence, both physical and spiritual. If we take the eleventh century as marking the end of those "Dark Ages" in which the Western peoples were fighting to assure themselves of the physical basis of life, we must recognize that Western Europe was still an outpost of human life. In the primeval forests of France there dwelt a few million hardy tillers of the soil, in the clearings of England barely a million. Wild beasts still roamed the streets of the few tiny hamlets and market towns. Art there was, to be sure, of a rather "primitive" and wholly delightful type, but learning and the refinements of urban existence were about as remote as they were from the frontier settlements of the Mississippi Valley in the days of Washington. Far away to the eastward was Constantinople, the heir of Greece and Rome, in all its unchanging and unprogressive life much more cultivated and "civilized" than anything in the West. But the true successors of ancient learning were not even in the Eastern Empire, but in Bagdad, the seat of the Arabian Caliphate, the home of Greek science and of an active intellectual interest, whither Hellenistic philosophy and knowledge of nature had been carried when Christian fanaticism drove it from Constantinople. In the newly Moslemized land of Spain, at Cordova and Granada, the continuing Hellenistic culture had been fostered by the conquering Mohammedans, and learned Moors from their rich cities and well-stocked libraries looked northward with disdain upon the simpler agricultural folk of France and Germany. But to discover real civilizations, grounded in a long and continued life of material well-being and spiritual energy, one must turn even farther east than the upstart Semitic blends of ancient cultures in Mesopotamia, to India and to China, by whose standards almost everything in Europe was poor and meager indeed.

The Twelfth-Century Renaissance

Gradually Europe erected the foundations for a cultural life of its own. Agriculture slowly built up a surplus that found expression in an increased demand for other than local wares. Market towns grew up for the exchange of local commodities and for the distribution of the luxury goods from the East. With the rise of a town population, with increased leisure and widened interests, there came an intellectual curiosity that expressed itself in an examination of the accepted beliefs and an eager groping after other wisdom. The quickening of the religious life began with the founding of the great monastery of Cluny in the tenth century and led to the reforms that changed the Church from the largely local institution of the Dark Ages, with here and there an abbey whose inmates found time from their labors of clearing the forest and tilling the land to pore over old manuscripts, to the all-embracing system of the Papacy and the scores of new foundations where men had leisure to satisfy their curiosity. This greatly increased the number of those with intellectual interests and indirectly furnished a fertile soil for the new tendencies in thought. A lay culture of song and romance grew up in feudal castles and in rich merchants' homes in the towns. Europe's first great adventure of expansion in the crusades brought many into contact with the much higher civilization of the Saracens and Moors, and the conquest of Constantinople in 1204 brought a first-hand experience of Greece. But while events are significant, it is important to recognize that no single contact or institution, but rather the slow but steady growth of medieval society, particularly in its economic life, was the real cause of the coming of age of the Western peoples.

From the beginning of the twelfth century through the close of the thirteenth, the men of Western Europe built up a rounded and fairly homogeneous civilization. It is this body of beliefs and practices that is generally meant when we refer to the cultural life of the Middle Ages; it is hardly too much to say that for the first time the peoples who now control the entire globe had developed what might fairly be called a "civilization" or "culture." There is, of course, no definite period or even moment, from the twelfth-century renaissance to the present day, when the forces of change ceased to operate, when economic and intellectual growth gave place to anything as static as the life that China, India, and the East in general have enjoyed for long ages in their history. Human energy and human intelligence have worked ever since at the increasingly rapid transformation of their heritage, a process that has never been so swift as to-day. Yet there are certain broad and general characteristics of the medieval world and viewpoint that remained relatively fixed and stable for several centuries. These ideas and ideals are in a very real sense the underlying stratum of modern Christendom. Many of them remained basic in the beliefs of the vast majority of men until the last generation; some of them are accepted as fundamental to-day. And even at those points where the modern Englishman or Frenchman would feel the medieval mind most alien, the intervening changes and the contemporary formulation of the differences can scarcely be understood save in the light of what went before. It is very often the best way of understanding ideas and beliefs to realize what they are reactions against.

Starting, then, with the world of the thirteenth century, we shall endeavor to picture what the scene of human life looked like and felt like to our predecessors. We shall try to discern what has remained relatively permanent and what has passed away, and we shall dwell upon the main features of the successive discoveries that have transformed that medieval world into the universe in which we are at home.

SELECTED READING LISTS

The following bibliographies are for use in guiding further reading; more exhaustive lists will be found in the books cited.

On the Material Basis of Medieval Civilization: General Surveys: Lynn Thorndike, *H. of Medieval Europe;* C. Stephenson, *Medieval History;* E. M. Hulme, *The Middle Ages;* G. B. Adams, *Civilization during the M.A.;* A. L. Guérard, *French Civilization, from its Origins to the Close of the M.A.* Brief outlines of economic development: H. Heaton, *Economic H. of Europe;* F. L. Nussbaum, *H. of the Econ. Institutions of Modern Europe;* N. S. B. Gras, *Int. to Econ. H.* Fuller: H. Pirenne, *Ec. and Soc. H. of Med. Europe;* J. W. Thompson, *Ec. and Soc. H. of the M.A., Ec. and Soc. H. of Europe in the Later M.A.;* A. Dopsch, *Ec. and Soc. Foundations of Med. Civilization.* H. Sée, *Histoire économique et sociale de la France;* J. Kulischer, *Allgemeine Wirtschaftsgeschichte des Mittelalters und der Neuzeit.* The *Cambridge Medieval History* and the *Histoire Générale* of Lavisse et Rambaud contain much material. Eileen Power, *Medieval People;* G. G. Coulton, *Life in the M.A.;* P. Boissonade, *Life and Work in Med. Europe;* A. Luchaire, *Social France at the Time of Philip Augustus.* C. G. Crump and E. F. Jacob, *The Legacy of the M.A.;* Munro and Sellery, *Med. Civilization.*

Feudalism and the Manorial System: Articles "Feudalism," "Land Tenure," "Manorial System," in *Encyc. of the Soc. Sciences; Camb. Med. Hist.,* II, c. 20, III, c. 18. C. Seignobos, *The Feudal Régime.* C. Petit-Dutaillis, *The Feudal Monarchy in France and England;* F. Funck-Brentano, *The M.A.* (*Nat. H. of France*). Munroe Smith, *Dev. of Eur. Law,* B. III; R. W. and A. J. Carlyle, *H. of Med. Pol. Theory in the West,* III, pt. I. N. Neilson, *Med. Agrarian Economy;* N. S. B. Gras, *H. of Agriculture;* G. G. Coulton, *The Med. Village.*

Commerce and the Towns: C. Day, *H. of Commerce;* S. Baldwin, *Business in the M.A.;* Pirenne, Thompson. H. Sée, *Modern Capitalism.* E. Lipson, *Ec. H. of England,* L. F. Salzman, *English Trade in the M.A., English Industries in the M.A.* H. Pirenne, *Med. Cities;* M. V. Clarke, *The Med. City State;* C. Stephenson, *Borough and Town.* L. Mumford, *Culture of Cities.*

Byzantine Civilization: Gibbon, *Decline and Fall of the Roman Empire,* is still the most interesting account; recent is J. B. Bury, *H. of the Later Roman Empire, H. of the Eastern Roman Empire.* S. Runciman, *Byz. Civilization;* R. Byron, *The Byz. Achievement.* Histories of the Byz. Empire by C. Diehl, N. H. Baynes, and E. A. Foord.

Muslim Civilization: Classic estimate by Gibbon in *Decline and Fall,* L, LI. T. W. Arnold and A. Guillaume, *Legacy of Islam.* Amir Ali, *H. of the Saracens;* Chapman, *H. of Spain;* R. P. A. Dozy, *Spanish Islam;* S. Lane-Poole, *The Moors in Spain.* G. Sarton, *Int. to the H. of Science,* I; E. G. Browne, *Arabian Medicine;* C. H. Haskins, *Studies in the H. of Med. Science, The Renaissance of the 12th Cent.* D. E. O'Leary, *Arabic Thought;* T. J. de Boer, *H. of Philosophy in Islam.* J. E. Sandys, *H. of Classical Scholarship,* I, chs. 22, 23.

CHAPTER II

THE WORLD AS THE SCENE OF THE DRAMA OF SALVATION

The Christian Epic and its Setting

IN *The Garden of Epicurus*, Anatole France has strikingly contrasted the world of the Middle Ages with the world of to-day.

We have some trouble in picturing the state of mind of a man of olden times who firmly believed that the earth was the center of the world and that all the stars turned round it. He felt under his feet the souls of the damned writhing in flames, and perhaps he had seen with his own eyes and smelled with his own nostrils the sulphurous fumes of Hell escaping from some fissures in the rocks. Lifting his head he contemplated the twelve spheres, that of the elements, containing the air and fire, then the spheres of the Moon, of Mercury, of Venus, which Dante visited on Good Friday of the year 1300, then those of the Sun, of Mars, of Jupiter, and of Saturn, then the incorruptible firmament from which the stars were hung like lamps. Beyond, his mind's eye discerned the Ninth Heaven to which saints were rapt, the Primum Mobile or Crystalline, and finally the Empyrean, abode of the blessed, toward which, he firmly hoped, after his death two angels robed in white would bear away, as it were a little child, his soul washed in baptism and perfumed with the oil of the last sacraments. In those days God had no other children than men, and all his creation was ordered in a fashion at once childlike and poetic, like an immense cathedral. Thus imagined, the universe was so simple that it was represented in its entirety with its true shape and motions in certain great painted clocks run by machinery.

We are done with the twelve heavens and the planets under which men were born lucky or unlucky, jovial or saturnine. The solid vault of the firmament is shattered. Our eye and our thought plunge into the infinite abysses of heaven. Beyond the planets we discover no longer the Empyrean of the elect and the angels, but a hundred million rolling suns, escorted by their cortege of obscure satellites invisible to us. In the midst of this infinity of worlds our own sun is but a bubble of gas and our earth but a drop of mud. . . .

Worlds die, since they are born. They are born and die without end. And creation, ever imperfect, undergoes incessant change. Stars are extinguished without our being able to say whether these daughters of light, in thus dying, begin as planets a fruitful existence, and whether the planets themselves dissolve to become stars once more. We know only that there is no more rest in the spaces of heaven than on earth, and that the law of work and effort rules the infinity of worlds.

There are stars which are extinguished before our eyes, others flicker like the dying flame of a candle. The heavens, which men once thought incorruptible, know nothing of eternity save the eternal flow of things.[1]

But the most important fact about what appears to our more sophisticated minds as the bandbox universe of the Middle Ages, was its essential purpose as the scene of the great drama God had prepared for the human race. However limited the man of the Middle Ages may have been in his knowledge of the great world, one thing he never doubted: that the earth and the heavens and all things therein had been created solely that he might work out his life and destiny. And the story of that creation, the stirring scenes that had already taken place, the vividly imagined pictures of what was yet to occur, were familiar to him in legend and tale, and filled his thoughts just as they covered the walls of his great cathedrals in stone or fresco. How the average intelligent man regarded the purpose of history and his own prospects has been beautifully put into words by Santayana, following in large part the narration of the Bishop Bossuet, whose *Discourse on Universal History* was written at the end of the seventeenth century when most leaders of thought had already outgrown it.

There was in the beginning, so runs the Christian story, a great celestial King, wise and good, surrounded by a court of winged musicians and messengers. He had existed from all eternity, but had always intended, when the right moment should come, to create temporal beings, imperfect copies of himself in various degrees. These, of which man was the chief, began their career in the year 4004 B.C., and they would live on an indefinite time, possibly, that chronological symmetry might not be violated, until A.D. 4004. The opening and close of this drama were marked by two magnificent tableaux. In the first, in obedience to the word of God, sun, moon, and stars, and earth with all her plants and animals, assumed their appropriate places, and Nature sprang into being with all her laws. The first man was made out of clay, by a special act of God, and the first woman was fashioned from one of his ribs, extracted while he lay in a deep sleep. They were placed in an orchard where they could often see God, its owner, walking in the cool of the evening. He suffered them to range at will and eat of all the fruits he had planted save that of one tree only. But they, incited by a devil, transgressed this single prohibition, and were banished from that paradise with a curse upon their head, the man to

[1] From *The Garden of Epicurus*, by Anatole France. Reprinted by permission of the publishers, Dodd, Mead & Company.

live by the sweat of his brow and the woman to bear children in labour. These children possessed from the moment of conception the inordinate natures which their parents had acquired. They were born to sin and to find disorder and death everywhere within and without them.

At the same time God, lest the work of his hands should wholly perish, promised to redeem in his good season some of Adam's children and restore them to a natural life. This redemption was to come ultimately through a descendant of Eve, whose foot should bruise the head of the serpent. But it was to be prefigured by many partial and special redemptions. Thus, Noah was to be saved from the deluge, Lot from Sodom, Isaac from the sacrifice, Moses from Egypt, the captive Jews from Babylon, and all faithful souls from heathen forgetfulness and idolatry. For a certain tribe had been set apart from the beginning to keep alive the memory of God's judgments and promises, while the rest of mankind, abandoned to its natural depravity, sank deeper and deeper into crimes and vanities. The deluge that came to punish these evils did not avail to cure them. "The world was renewed and the earth rose again above the bosom of the waters, but in this renovation there remained eternally some trace of divine vengeance. Until the deluge all nature had been exceedingly hardy and vigorous, but by that vast flood of water which God had spread out over the earth, and by its long abiding there, all saps were diluted; the air, charged with too dense and heavy a moisture, bred ranker principles of corruption. The early constitution of the universe was weakened, and human life, from stretching, as it had formerly done, to near a thousand years, grew gradually briefer. Herbs and roots lost their primitive potency and stronger food had to be furnished to man by the flesh of other animals. ... Death gained upon life and men felt themselves overtaken by a speedier chastisement. As day by day they sank deeper in their wickedness, it was but right they should daily, as it were, stick faster in their woe. The very change in nourishment made manifest their decline and degradation, since as they became feebler they became also more voracious and blood-thirsty."

Henceforth there were two spirits, two parties, or, as Saint Augustine called them, two cities in the world. The City of Satan, whatever its artifices in art, war, or philosophy, was essentially corrupt and impious. Its joy was but a comic mask and its beauty the whitening of a sepulchre. It stood condemned before God and before man's better conscience by its vanity, cruelty, and secret misery, by its ignorance of all that it truly behoved a man to know who was destined to immortality. Lost, as it seemed, within this Babylon, or visible only in its obscure and forgotten purlieus, lived on at the same time the City of God, the society of all the souls God predestined to salvation; a city which, however humble and inconspicuous it seemed on earth, counted its myriad transfigured citizens in heaven, and had its destinies, like its foundations, in eternity. To this City of God belonged, in the first place, the patriarchs and the prophets who, throughout their plaintive and ardent lives, were faithful to what echoes still remained of a primeval revelation, and waited patiently for the greater revelation to come. To the same city belonged the magi who followed a star till it halted over the stable in Bethlehem; Simeon, who divined the present salvation of Israel; John the Baptist, who bore witness to the same and made straight its path; and Peter, to whom not flesh and blood, but the spirit of the Father in heaven, revealed the Lord's divinity. For salvation had indeed come with the fullness of time, not, as the carnal Jews imagined it, in the form of an earthly restoration, but through the incarnation of the Son of God in the Virgin Mary, his death upon a cross, his descent into hell, and his resurrection at the third day according to the Scriptures. To the same city belonged finally all those who, believing in the reality and efficacy of Christ's mission, relied on his merits and followed his commandment of unearthly love.

All history was henceforth essentially nothing but the conflict between these two cities; two moralities, one natural, the other supernatural; two philosophies, the one rational, the other revealed; two beauties, the one corporeal, the other spiritual; two glories, the one temporal, the other eternal; two institutions, one the world, the other the Church. These, whatever their momentary alliances or compromises, were radically opposed and fundamentally alien to one another. Their conflict was to fill the ages until, when wheat and tares had long flourished together and exhausted between them the earth for whose substance they struggled, the harvest should come; the terrible day of reckoning when those who had believed the things of religion to be imaginary would behold with dismay the Lord visibly coming down through the clouds of heaven, the angels blowing their alarming trumpets, all generations of the dead rising from their graves, and judgment without appeal passed on every man, to the edification of the universal company and his own unspeakable joy or confusion. Whereupon the blessed would enter eternal bliss with God their master and the wicked everlasting torments with the devil whom they served.

The drama of history was thus to close upon a second tableau: long-robed and beatified cohorts passing above, amid various psalmodies, into an infinite luminous space, while below the damned, howling, writhing, and half transformed into loathsome beasts, should be engulfed in a fiery furnace. The two cities, always opposite in essence, should thus be finally divided in existence, each bearing its natural fruits and manifesting its true nature.[2]

The Educated Classes and the Average Man

Before examining in more detail the medieval beliefs about the scene of human life and its goal and purpose, it is important to remember the great gulf that existed between the ideas of the average man and of those who were conversant with the best

[2] From *Reason in Religion*, by George Santayana. Reprinted by permission of the publishers, Charles Scribner's Sons.

available knowledge. Such a gulf always exists, and in spite of our elaborate school systems is perhaps as great to-day as ever; but several circumstances made it at least superficially wider in the Middle Ages. The vast majority of men were rude, hard-working agricultural laborers, who had never been outside their native valley save on some fighting expedition with their lord. Quite unable to read, and with no books or manuscripts available for them had they been able, they were forced to depend upon the hearsay reports of pilgrims or merchants for all they knew of the outside world. Practically their only contact with any knowledge whatsoever was the village priest; and of all the clerics it was precisely these who were themselves least educated and least able to teach. They were both too busy and too poor to pore over manuscripts, and they were despised by the higher and educated prelates and the monks alike. The familiarity which practically every farmer or factory worker has to-day with events and sometimes the outside of ideas through newspapers, magazines, and moving pictures, to say nothing of schooling, had no substitute six hundred years ago. Moreover, even the educated class was proportionately much smaller than it is to-day; for though we read of thousands attending the universities of Paris and Bologna, until the fourteenth century the large and important universities numbered scarcely a dozen. Nearly all were of the clergy, though this order included what to-day would be the political, legal, and teaching professions; that is, they were set apart from the rest of the community, mingling little with it, and thoroughly committed to the pastoral belief that learning was their special province, not to be entered upon by the laity without dangerous consequences. The fact that all books pretending to scholarship, and most documents, were in the Latin tongue, unintelligible to the mass of even the Italian people, was but an additional mark of this divergence of function. The Bible itself, so basic for the whole of medieval life, was available only in the Latin Vulgate of Saint Jerome; its translation into the vernacular was the forerunner of the Reformation, and was one of the chief counts against the early reformers of the fourteenth and fifteenth centuries, Wyclif and Hus. Until the coming of the mendicant friars, the Dominicans and the Franciscans, in the beginning of the thirteenth century, there was in most lands little preaching that the masses could understand;

much of the popularity of these orders was due to their missions to the people and their willingness to share their knowledge with all.

The upper classes, of course, were not entirely cut off from the available store of learning. During the later Middle Ages the feudal lords could read and write, after a fashion, and for their amusement there developed a great body of romances and songs, fascinating tales of travel and adventure, which furnishes the glory of the early literature of every European country. The wealthy burghers of the towns also were fairly well educated; indeed, it was probably among the scions of the merchant families, the municipal secretaries and officials required by complex commercial life, that the only really profound lay learning was to be discovered. Dante of Florence, son of a notary, represents this town culture as it flourished in the busy cities of northern Italy in the thirteenth century, and a similar class existed in Germany, France, and Flanders. It was among these men that the newly discovered literatures of antiquity first found enthusiasts: they were the original humanists of the Renaissance. For this reading public there early developed a large literature of popular science that mixed pleasure with edification, and naturally ran to the marvelous and the strange. But the widely read *Romaunt of the Rose*, translated into many tongues, by Chaucer into English; the *Image of the World*, the *Romance of Sidrach*, the *Treasure* of Dante's master Bruneto Latini, the *Properties of Things* of Bartholomew the Englishman, and their many imitators, are really no closer to the best scientific knowledge of the day than are the many magazines of "popular science" of the present. Compared with the sanity and the wisdom of the great encyclopedias of Albert the Great or Saint Thomas, they smack of the ventures of the contemporary pseudo-scientific journalist.

The World of the Common Man

If we turn to the beliefs of the vast majority of common men about the world, we shall find that, so far as they reflected upon the scene into which God had placed them for their mortal life, their ideas were a mixture of shrewd observation of those things which could come within their own limited observation and affected their daily labors, fantastic tales and legends about whatever was more remote in space or in time, and implicit belief, so far as they sought any explanations further than those to be gained by common experience, in the words of the Bible distorted by the popular imagination. For such an uneducated common man the world had of course been created in six days by the God of ancient Hebrew tradition, with all its furniture complete, and whatsoever changes had since occurred were limited to the works of men. It was a great flat plain, surrounded, so he had heard, on all sides by a vast body of water. Above it stretched the dome of the heavens, across which the sun and moon and planets moved and around which the angels carried stars like lamps. The movements of these heavenly bodies he knew much better than the modern man; he lived in the open, and after sundown could afford little artificial illumination, and so he had plenty of opportunity to become familiar with the courses of the stars. He had the farmer's interest in their influence upon the weather, to say nothing of what he might know of the science of astrology, which, coming down from immemorial antiquity, and cultivated most extensively in the lands of the infidels, was relied upon to guide enterprises, regulate planting and the cure of men's bodies, and furnish predictions about the future. The Eastern metaphors of the Old Testament he for the most part took literally, and probably sympathized with the ancient bishop who wrote:

The heaven is not a sphere, but a tent or tabernacle; "it is He ... that stretcheth out the heavens as a curtain and spreadeth them out as a tent to dwell in"; the Scripture says that it has a top, which a sphere has not, and it is also written: "The sun was risen upon the earth when Lot came unto Zoar." The earth is flat, and the sun does not pass under it at night, but travels through the northern parts "as if hidden by a wall; the sun goeth down and hasteth to his place where he ariseth." [3]

Seizing upon such expressions, the monk Kosmas endeavored, in a work that, written in the sixth century, had great popularity among even the educated till the twelfth, to picture the world as a tabernacle, oblong in shape, filled with water above the firmament, whence fell the rain.

But all men who had access to the twelfth and thirteenth century books of popular science knew better than this. The earth is easily proved to be round; and about it turn the heavens and the planets.

On the second day [runs a manual of the tenth century] God made the heaven, which is called the firmament, which is visible and corporeal; and yet we may never see it, on account of its great elevation and the thickness of the clouds, and on account of the weakness of our eyes. The heaven encloses in its bosom all the world, and it ever turns about us, swifter than any mill-wheel, all as deep under the earth as it is above. It is all round and entire and studded with stars. Truly the sun goes by God's command between heaven and earth, by day above and by night under the earth. She is ever running about the earth, and so light shines under the earth by night, as it does above our heads by day.... The sun is very great: as broad she is, from what books say, as the whole compass of the earth; but she appears to us very small, because she is very far from our sight. Everything, the further it is, the less it seems.... The moon and all the stars receive light from the great Sun. The sun is typical of our Saviour, Christ, who is the sun of righteousness, as the bright stars are typical of the believers in God's congregation, who shine in good converse.[4]

The heavens are so far above the earth that a great stone falling from them would take a hundred years to arrive. Indeed, most educated men were familiar with the main lines of the Greek astronomy possessed by the learned, embedded in a mass of legend. Thus, in *Sidrach* shooting stars are the path of the winds, or moisture sighed by the earth reaching the upper regions of the air, or perhaps the good angels striking back with fire the fallen angels who are seeking to reënter Heaven.

Of geography the average man knew only from travelers' tales, but he was quite willing then, as indeed often to-day, to believe anything of distant lands, peopled by still stranger inhabitants. It must not, of course, be forgotten that practically all of these "medieval" tales of wonders were drawn from the books of the ancients, Romans like Pliny and the post-classical Greeks, and are as typical of the average beliefs of the ancient civilizations as of the Middle Ages. The point is not that they represented a step backward, but rather the highest point that all save a few men had ever reached.

Satyrs be somewhat like men, and have crooked noses, and horns in the forehead, and are like to goats in their feet. Saint Anthony saw such an one in the wilderness... These wonderful beasts be divers; for some of them be called Cynocephali, for they have heads as hounds, and seem by the working, beasts rather than men; and some be called Cyclops, and have that name because each of them hath but one eye, and that in the middle of the forehead; and some be all headless and noseless, and their eyes be in the shoulders; and some have plain faces without nostrils, and the nether lips of them stretch so, that they veil therewith their faces when they be in the heat of the sun. Also in Scythia be some with so great and large ears, that they spread their ears and cover all their bodies with them, and these be called Panchios. ... And others there be in Ethiopia, and each of them have only one foot, so great and so large that they beshadow themselves with the foot when they lie gasping on the ground in strong heat of the sun; and yet they be so swift that they be likened to hounds in swiftness of running, and therefore among the Greeks they be called Cynopodes. Also some have the soles of their feet turned backward behind the legs, and in each foot eight toes, and such go about and stare in the desert of Lybia.[5]

Nor were the wonders of beasts and plants less strange.

Avicenna saith that the bear bringeth forth a piece of flesh imperfect and evil shapen, and the mother licketh the lump, and shapeth the members with licking. ... For the whelp is a piece of flesh little more than a mouse, having neither eyes nor ears, and having claws some-deal bourgeoning, and so this lump she licketh, and shapeth a whelp with licking. And it is wonder to tell a thing, that Theophrastus saith and telleth that bear's flesh stewed that time of their sleeping vanisheth if it be laid up, and is no token of meat found in the almory, but a little quantity of humour.[6]

Also there is another thing said that is full wonderful: among the Ethiopians in some countries elephants be hunted in this wise: there go in the desert two maidens all naked and bare, with open hair of the head: and one of them beareth a vessel, and the other a sword. And these maidens begin to sing alone: and the beast hath liking when he heareth their song, and cometh to them, and licketh their teats, and falleth asleep anon for liking of the song, and then the one maid sticketh him in the throat or in the side with a sword, and the other taketh his blood in a vessel, and with that blood the people of the same country dye cloth, and done colour it therewith.[7]

The Dragon is the most greatest of all serpents, and oft he is drawn out of his den, and riseth up into the air, and the air is moved by him, and also the sea swelleth against his venom, and he hath a crest with a little mouth, and draweth breath at small pipes and straight, and reareth his tongue, and hath teeth like a saw, and hath strength, and not only in teeth, but also in his tail, and grieveth both with biting and with stinging, and hath not so much venom as other serpents. Oft four or five of them fasten their tails together, and rear up their heads, and sail over sea and over rivers to get good meat. Between elephants and dragons is everlasting fighting. ... And at the last after long fighting the elephant waxeth feeble for great blindness, in so much that he falleth upon the dragon, and slayeth in his dying the dragon that him slayeth. The cause why the dragon desireth his blood, is coldness of the elephant's blood, by the which the dragon desireth to cool himself. Jerome saith, that the dragon is a full thirsty beast, insomuch that never he may have water enough to quench his great thirst; and openeth his mouth therefore against the wind, to quench the burning of his thirst in that wise. Therefore, when he seeth ships sail in the sea in great wind, he flieth against the sail to take their cold wind, and overthroweth the ship sometimes for greatness of body, and strong rese against the sail. And when the shipmen see the dragon come nigh, and know his coming by the water that swelleth ayenge him, they strike the sail anon, and scape in that wise.[8]

The wonders of a land grew marvelously with its distance. To Bartholomew the Englishman,

England is the most island of Ocean, and is beclipped all about by the sea, and departed from the roundness of the world, and hight sometimes Albion: and had that name of white rocks, which were seen on the sea cliffs. And by continuance of time, lords and noble men of Troy, after that Troy was destroyed, went from thence, and were accompanied with a great navy, and fortuned to the cliffs of the foresaid island, and that by revelation of their feigned goddess Pallas, as it is said, and the Trojans fought with giants long time that dwelled therein, and overcame the giants, both with craft and with strength, and conquered the island, and called the land Britain, by the name of Brute that was prince of that host.

In describing the England of his day he is on firmer ground.

England is a strong land and a sturdy, and the plenteousest corner of the world, so rich a land that never it needeth the help of any land, and every other land needeth help of England. England is full of mirth and of game, and men oft times able to mirth and game, free men of heart and with tongue, but the hand is more free and more better than the tongue.[9]

France too he knows well.

This land of France is a rank country, and plentiful of trees, of vines, of corn, and of fruits, and is noble by the affluence of rivers and of fountains. . . . In France be many noble and famous cities, but among all Paris beareth the prize; for as sometime the city of Athens, mother of liberal arts and of letters, nurse of philosophers, and well of all sciences, made it solemn in science and in condition among Greeks, so doth Paris in this time, not only in France, but also all the other deal of Europe. For as mother of wisdom she receiveth all that cometh out of every country of the world, and helpeth them in all that they need, and ruleth

THE DRAMA OF SALVATION

all peaceably, and as a servant of soothness, she sheweth herself detty to wise men and unwise. This city is full good and mighty of riches, it rejoiceth in peace: there is good air of rivers according to philosophers, there be fair fields, meads, and mountains to refresh and comfort the eyen of them that be weary in study, there be convenable streets and houses, namely for studiers. And nevertheless the city is sufficient to receive and to feed all others that come thereto, and passeth all other cities in these things, and in such other like.[10]

But India is a long way off.

As among all countries and lands India is the greatest and most rich: so among all lands India is most wonderful. For as Pliny saith, India aboundeth in wonders. In India be many huge beasts bred, and more greater hounds than in other lands. Also there be so high trees that men may not shoot to the top with an arrow, as it is said. And that maketh the plenty and fatness of the earth and temperateness of weather, of air, and of water. Fig trees spread there so broad, that many great companies of knights may sit at meat under the shadow of one tree. Also there be so great reeds and so long that every piece between two knots beareth sometimes three men over the water. Also there be men of great stature, passing five cubits in height, and they never spit, nor have never headache nor toothache, nor sore eyes, nor they be not grieved with passing heat of the sun, but rather made more hard and sad therewith.... Also among some nations of India be women that bear never child but once, and the children wax white-haired anon as they are born. And there be satyrs and other men wondrously shapen. Also in the end of East India, about the rising of Ganges, be men without mouths, and they be clothed in moss and in rough hairy things, which they gather off trees, and live commonly by odour and smell at the nostrils. And they nother eat nother drink, but only smell odour of flowers and of wood apples, and live so, and they die anon in evil odour and smell. And other there be that live full long, and age never, but die as it were in middle age. Also some be hoar in youth, and black in age. Pliny rehearseth these wonders, and many other mo.[11]

We have dwelt upon these ancient tales because nothing reveals so clearly the difference between the notions of men in ancient times and during the Middle Ages, and those widely held by at least large numbers to-day, than that they were then implicitly believed by the average man, while like accounts, though perhaps still prevalent amongst the least intelligent, would probably in their crudest forms be rejected by most educated city-dwellers and progressive farmers now. It is true that we all have our own curious misconceptions of foreign lands and peoples, but it is doubtful whether they are quite as erroneous and quite as widespread to-day as they were everywhere before, let us say, the eighteenth century. This is the measure in which a "scientific" viewpoint has spread through all classes.

To the man of six hundred years ago, anything might happen in this world. Nothing was too strange or too contrary to nature for him to credit on respected authority. Why should he reject such strange narrations when he was prepared for almost any miraculous event to occur in his daily life? Above and beneath him swarmed a myriad of intelligences, demons or angels, strange descendants of ancient gods, ever ready at the behest of God or Satan — it was always difficult to tell which, as witness the voices of Joan of Arc — to work wonders for the edification or damnation of men. Holy men were daily the vehicles of God's power in the performance of miracles to strengthen the piety of the faithful, the Devil and his cohorts waged a never-ending war of temptation upon the purest of heart. This faith in the miraculous grows out of an attitude of mind that colored everything in the Middle Ages, from the chance event to the cosmic sweep of Providence, the desire to understand, that is, to find a meaning and a significance in things. Modern science does not seek meanings and purposes in the world; it endeavors to describe *how* events occur, not *why*.

We sometimes speak [says Santayana] as if superstition or belief in the miraculous was disbelief in law and was inspired by a desire to disorganize experience and defeat intelligence. No supposition could be more erroneous. Every superstition is a little science, inspired by the desire to understand, to foresee, or to control the real world. . . . Moral and individual forces are more easily intelligible than mechanical universal laws. . . . The ground of the miracle is immediately intelligible: we see the mercy or the desire to vindicate authority, or the intention of some other sort that inspired it. A mechanical law, on the contrary, is only a record of the customary but reasonless order of things. A merely inexplicable event, manifesting no significant purpose, would be no miracle. What surprises us in the miracle is that, contrary to what is usually the case, we can see a real and a just ground for it.[12]

And so the Middle Ages, in their very eagerness to understand the world about them, saw purposes everywhere, discovered intelligences at work in every event, and found the ultimate

[12] From *Reason in Religion*, by George Santayana. Reprinted by permission of the publishers, Charles Scribner's Sons.

reason for the universe in the will of God, which, however inscrutable in its details, gave at least the promise of rationality and meaning to things.

The Unseen World

Living naturally in such a world, it is no wonder that men peopled the earth with minds and spiritual powers and expected the unexpected to possess significance. Nor is it less natural that in the exuberance of their being these powers should seek to express themselves in the marvelous. The lives of the saints, so dear to the Middle Ages, so bound up with local pride, so eagerly put into stone and celebrated in festival, abound in works of wonder; indeed, such miracles are the prerequisite of canonization. The Devil and his demons were very real and very close, and the powers of God and his angels needed constantly to be drawn upon to combat them. The relics of the saints, the blessings of the Church, the virtues of prayer and supplication and offering, were a most helpful stay in times of trouble. From the tooth of Saint Peter, the blood of Saint Basil, the hair of Saint Denys, and the vesture of the Virgin in Roland's great sword Durendal, or the body of Saint Mark which Venetian sailors stole to bring home to their jeweled cathedral on the lagoons, to the house of the Virgin Mary that miraculously flew across the sea to Loretto, they could invoke a supernatural power against man and devil. So greatly were they sought that Saint Louis of France could console himself by claiming his crusade gloriously successful, despite the fact that he never saw the Holy Land, because he had brought home a fragment of the true cross.

Gregory the Great tells a tale of a holy man that is typical of what, throughout the Middle Ages, men thought took place daily.

In Campania, upon Mount Marsicus, a venerable man called Martin lived for many years the solitary life, shut up in a very small cave. Many of us knew him, and were witnesses of his deeds. I myself have heard much of him both from Pope Pelagius, my predecessor, and from other religious men who related anecdotes of him. His first miracle was this: hardly had he established himself in the cleft of the mountain, when from the very rock which was hollowed out to make his narrow cave burst forth a stream of water just sufficient to supply the daily need of the servant of God, and there was never too much or too little. ... But the ancient enemy of mankind envies the man's strength, and labored with his wonted skill to drive him forth from the cave. For he entered into the beast that is his friend — the serpent — and sought to make the monk afraid, and drive him from his dwelling. He came at twilight, and stretched himself out before the holy man while he was praying, and lay down with him when he went to rest. The holy man was entirely unafraid. He would hold to the serpent's mouth his hand or his foot, and say to him, "If thou hast leave to smite me, I do not say thee nay." After these things had taken place continuously for three years, on a certain day the ancient enemy of mankind, vanquished by such great endurance, groaned; and the serpent let himself glide over the steep mountain-side to a precipice. And the flame that went out from him burned all the trees in that place. Almighty God constrained him to burn the mountainside, and so compelled him to show forth the great virtue of the man from whom he had departed, conquered.[13]

Such evil spirits dwelt in Hell, a grim reality whose precise location popular imagination left vague, but knew to be very close indeed, waiting for every soul who failed in his duties toward God. The Hebrew Gehenna had been much embroidered upon, embellished with the details of all the infernal regions, classical and barbarian. Heaven, on the other hand, was quite remote, far beyond the firmament and the outermost stars, though the power of God could reach to every corner of his creation. Men were frequently accorded glimpses of this hereafter, as a reward or a warning, and their experiences were always narrated with the proper humility of trembling and horror. To the peasant or townsman, it was a far greater certainty than Ethiopia or India, or even Rome. It must not be thought that such a man, or even the average monk, lived his life much more circumspectly because of this world to come, or that the surety of such punishments and rewards operated as a controlling motive. Of course, he took the precaution of absolution, and his intentions were doubtless of the best; but Hell and Heaven were rather inevitabilities, like old age or death, about which after all little can be done; and it does not pay to worry too much. Other-worldliness for the most part expressed itself in the mass of customs and accepted ideas that men followed, rather than as an ever-present incentive to action.

Such was the world in which the average man lived. All in all, it was perhaps not so different from the world in which many, at least in the country, are living to-day. "Enlightenment" proceeds slowly and in spots. To the anthropologist it is obvious that the outstanding traits of the minds that dwelt in such a world are simply the universal and widespread characteristics of human belief wherever it has not felt the pruning of scientific verification. This "primitive mentality," so called because it can now be observed at its purest among the most backward of present-day tribes, was deeply impressed upon the beliefs of the Middle Ages, determining the nature of the intellectual interests of even the most intelligent; in those beliefs that go back to that time, modern man finds himself most akin to the primitive savage because farthest from the skeptical testing of the scientist. The universal characteristics of such a frame of mind, whether it be found in the South Seas or in the Middle Ages or in the modern backwoods farmer, are abundance of belief and explanation for every event that makes an impression, confident certainty of the truth of these beliefs, and intense dislike of calling these fanciful beliefs into question or subjecting them to any testing. In short, such a mind "understands" the meaning of all things but possesses exact knowledge about only those details of daily technique where error would spell disaster.

The Ordered Universe of Thomas and Dante

When we turn to the world of the learned, of the educated classes amongst the clergy or in the towns, we find a world more harmonized and ordered, less picturesque and more rational, possessed of knowledge of many facts, and of much sanity, and yet very close to the everyday experience of the common man. The same traits characteristic of primitive belief are controlling in the minds of the greatest doctors of the medieval period — a wealth of untested explanation, a passion for certainty, and a dislike of the doubting and tentative spirit that was to give birth to science.

The best knowledge of the Middle Ages was but common sense systematized and glorified, a thing we are apt to forget as we forget that our "scientific" and "naturalistic" temper of mind is a tremendous achievement, anything but natural to the human race, and all too superficial in the very best of us. Scholastic science is an easy and natural development of common and universal habits of thought, and from the ideas of the most illiterate peasant to the highest reaches of Saint Thomas' philosophy is a shorter step than from the knowledge of the intelligent constructor of a radio set to the mathematical physics that makes it possible. It stays close to things as they seem to us, to human experience, and its glory lies in its careful observance of the distinctive qualities that make things differ from each other, just as its shortcomings lie in the failure to discover underlying relationships and hidden causes. It has the same passion of the common man for intelligibility, for understanding the meaning and the significance of everything. It is not too much to say that in the vast encyclopedias of Thomas and the schoolmen everything that came within their observation, and much that did not, but was only inherited from past speculation, received its appropriate explanation, until a Thomas could truly believe that he understood the universe — a hope which modern man, like Faust before the sign of the Macrocosm, knows to be but a vision and a dream.

We get this sense of completeness, of finitude, from the medieval universe as Dante has preserved it for us in all its simplicity. Dante relied on a combination of the ideas of Ptolemy, a Hellenistic astronomer of Alexandria who systematized Greek views, and Aristotle, who wrote much earlier. Ptolemy was above all a mathematician interested in calculating the positions of the heavenly bodies, and his *Almagest* was the astronomical Bible of the Middle Ages. He calculated the orbits of the planets about the earth by geometrical means. Aristotle, who was no mathematician, placed the planets, not in imaginary orbits, but in actual crystalline spheres which revolved concentrically about the earth. Dante relied on the one for his mathematics and on the other for his picture. The outcome was a series of twelve heavens, one within the other, revolving at slightly varying rates about the earth fixed in the center. Starting from within, there came in order the sphere of the air, fire, the moon, Mercury, Venus, the sun, Mars, Saturn, Jupiter, the firmament of the fixed stars, the Crystalline, to account for precession, and the Primum Mobile, which moved all the rest. Outside this was located the Empyrean or Heaven, where dwelt the saints in glory, and the celestial throne. To account for accurate observations, Ptolemy had given the planets orbits combined of two circular motions, with a consequent epicycloid motion; but this was difficult to harmonize with Aristotle's solid spheres. The orbits had to be circular, inasmuch as they were made by a perfect God and the circle is the most perfect of all figures. The distance and size of the moon were measured fairly accurately; and the method for discovering that of the sun was used, though an error of instruments made the estimate about one twentieth of the true distance. The inconceivably great distance of the fixed stars, assumed by Ptolemy, was not favored by the Middle Ages.

At the center of this orderly universe lay the earth. Its size was approximately known, and its shape. Three quarters of its sphere were covered by water; for half its circumference, in the Northern Hemisphere, stretched the continents of Europe, Africa, and Asia. In the center of this land lay Jerusalem. Somewhere in the East lay the Garden of Eden, the scene of man's transgression. Dante located it at the antipodes of Jerusalem, but some favored the island of Ceylon, or some other remote island or mountain. Wherever it was, it was surrounded by a wall of fire, and at present inhabited only by Enoch and Elijah. Monks often visited it, perhaps the most famous journey being that of the Irish Saint Brandon. Somewhere beneath the earth was Hell. Dante gave it definite shape, and order: it was a huge funnel, with the tormented sinners ranged around its sides in circles appropriate to their sin. At the very tip, in the center of the entire universe, farthest removed from God in the Empyrean, lay Satan himself.

Such was the universe, tidy, ordered, neatly arranged throughout. Nor must it be overlooked that just as this world of matter was but a tiny bubble in the illimitable realm of spirit that is God's mind, so its whole duration was but a moment in eternity. According to the computation of Dante, Christ was born fifty-two hundred years after the creation. Since the whole existence of earth was to be complete in seven thousand years, in 1300 there were but five hundred years left. The universe was old; as Dante says, "We have come to the last age of the world." During this brief period there was no growth, no development, no change outside human affairs; the world had been created for the one purpose of furnishing the background for the drama of Man's salvation, and as such it was fixed and immutable till the last trump.

The Divine Governance of The World

But far more striking than the mere difference in size or even complexity was the overwhelming reality of this divine purpose. The world was governed throughout by the omnipotent will and omniscient mind of God, whose sole interests were centered in man, his trial, his fall, his suffering and his glory. Worm of the dust as he was, man was yet the central object in the whole universe. About him revolved the heavens, for him were made land and sea and all that dwelt therein. He was the lord of creation, made in the very image of God himself. For his sake, despite his unworthiness, Almighty God had taken on flesh in Bethlehem and bled upon the cross that he might be saved from his own folly and pride. And when his destiny was completed, the heavens would be rolled up as a scroll and he would dwell with the Lord forever. Only those who rejected God's freely offered grace and with hardened hearts refused repentance would be cut off from this eternal life. With such a conviction it was inevitable that seekers after the meaning of things should scrutinize every object and event of this the background of humanity's struggles to discover its bearing upon the fundamental purpose of things. Everything must possess significance, not in and for itself, but for man's pilgrimage. There must be a reason for everything, a purpose it served in the divine scheme. That one of God's creatures should exist apart from the course of Providence, that a single stone should fall unknown and unplanned by the Maker of Heaven and Earth, was an intolerable thought. If no other purpose could be discerned, it was enough that God's creatures existed to make manifest his greatness and lead the soul of man to glorify him. The whole soul of the Middle Ages as it looked upon the world about it cried out with Saint Augustine:

> I asked the earth, and it answered me, "I am not He"; and whatsoever are in it confessed the same. I asked the sea and the deeps, and the living creeping things, and they answered, "We are not thy God, seek above us." I asked the moving air; and the whole air with his inhabitants answered, "Anaximines was deceived, I am not God." I asked the heavens, sun, moon, stars, "Nor," say they, "are we the God whom thou seekest." And I replied unto all the things which encompass the door of my flesh, "Ye have told me of my God, that ye are not He; tell me something of Him." And they cried out with a loud voice, "He made us." [14]

Of course it was not given to mortal reason to decipher the hieroglyph of the universe in detail; but the important fact is that this was the fundamental aim of all wisdom and learning, coloring the whole intellectual life and all but excluding any interest in prediction and control, in "natural science" as we know it. From this follows the intense faith in the intelligibility of the world that makes the medieval scholar, whether mystic seeking wisdom by intuition and vision, or rationalist seeking it by dialectic, reject our modern agnosticisms and romanticisms. From this follows his search for the meaning of everything, his belief in allegory throughout nature and in every written book, his science of the functions and purposes of objects. Hugo of Saint Victor, chief of the twelfth century mystics, who attempted a complete interpretation of the symbolism of all creation, puts the matter briefly when he says, "The spirit was created for God's sake, the body for the spirit's sake, and the whole world for the body's sake, so that the spirit might be subject to God, the body to the spirit, and the world to the body." [15] Whether the mystic sought symbolism in nature or in history, or the scholastic sought the form and end of all things, there was this same hierarchical order of importance leading up to God, supreme reality, supreme end, supreme genus. And since such was the use of learning, it mattered little, after all, whether nature be exactly described or history accurately written. Without inquiring too closely as to the literal basis of the tales of wonder and marvels that delighted the masses, the scholar could discern in them the fundamental moral and spiritual truths which he had most deeply at heart. To such a mind it was meaningless to inquire whether the pelican really nourished her young with her own blood, or there really existed a phœnix who rose from the ashes, so long as these creatures, whether of God directly or of God through man's imagination, made manifest the Saviour who shed his blood upon the cross and rose the third day. Indeed, a knowledge of natural history for its own sake would have been regarded as almost blasphemous, taking men's thoughts away from its essential meaning for man. Hence it was inevitable that, when men wrote or builded works of their own, they should weave into the fabric all the rich meaning and symbol they looked for around them, and the intricate allegories of a *Divine Comedy* or the loving care displayed on the elaboration of a bible in stone like Chartres Cathedral merely added to the treasures of nature.

The world was a great allegory, whose essential secret was its meaning, not its operation or its causes; it was a hierarchical order, extending from lowest to highest, from stones and trees through man to the choirs upon choirs of angels, just as society ranged from serf through lord and king to pope; and it was inspired throughout by the desire to fulfill its divine purpose. The power that moved all things was Love; that love of God which kept all things eternally aspiring to be themselves, the love of the flame for fire that caused it to strain upward, the love of the stone that is its hardness, of the grass that is its greenness, of the beasts that is their bestiality, of the bad man for evil that is his nature, and of the good man for God that is his home. From the highest heaven to the lowest clod, aspiration to fulfill the will of God, to blend with the divine purpose, was the cosmic force that made the world go round. And highest and lowest could truly say, "In his will is our peace."

REFERENCES

1. Anatole France, *The Garden of Epicurus*, 1–5.
2. George Santayana, *Reason in Religion*, 92–97.
3. J. L. E. Dreyer, *Planetary Systems from Thales to Kepler*.
4. James Harvey Robinson, *Readings in European History*, I, 441.
5. Bartholomew of England, *On the Properties of Things*, ed. by Steele as *Medieval Lore*, 156, 157.
6. *Ibid.*, 169.
7. *Ibid.*, 155.
8. *Ibid.*, 149–51.
9. *Ibid.*, 84–86.
10. *Ibid.*, 91, 92.
11. *Ibid.*, 94–96.
12. Santayana, *Reason in Religion*, 22, 23.
13. Gregory's *Dialogues*, in Robinson, *Readings in European History*, I, 92.
14. Augustine, *Confessions*, Everyman ed., 208, 209.
15. Hugo of St. Victor, cited in H. O. Taylor, *The Medieval Mind*, II, 91.

SELECTED READING LISTS

General Outlook: Henry Osborn Taylor, *The Medieval Mind*, esp. Bk. I, The Groundwork, and Bk. II, The Early Middle Ages, is a mine of material; also his *Classical Heritage of the Middle Ages*. Brief chapters in F. S. Marvin, *The Living Past*, and F. M. Stawell and F. S. Marvin, *The Making of the Western Mind*. Excellent summary in C. H. Grandgent, *Dante*. K. Vossler, *Medieval Culture*, the world of Dante. R. L. Poole, *Illustrations of Medieval Thought*, chs. I, II; H. von Eicken, *Geschichte und System der mittelalterlichen Weltanschauung;* A. E. Berger, *Die Kulturaufgaben der Reformation*.

Medieval Science: For popular ideas, see R. R. Steele, *Medieval Lore* (Bartholomew the Englishman); selections in J. H. Robinson, *Readings in Eur. History*,

I, and full excerpts in C. V. Langlois, *La connaissance de la nature et du monde au moyen âge*. For the world of the learned, the Temple Classics ed. of *Dante*, with full notes, is helpful. Good surveys of medieval science by C. Singer, in F. S. Marvin, *Science and Civilization*, ch. v, and W. C. D. Dampier-Whetham, *History of Science*. Lynn Thorndike, *H. of Magic and Experimental Science*, a monumental mass of learning; G. Sarton, *Int. to the H. of Science*. C. H. Haskins, *Studies in the H. of Med. Science*, *The Renaissance of the 12th Cent.*, *Studies in Med. Culture*, C. Singer, *From Magic to Science*, *Studies in the H. and Method of Science*. R. McKeon, *Experimental Science in the M.A.*, in *Essays in Honor of John Dewey*; P. Duhem, *Système du Monde*, *Études sur Léonard de Vinci*. A. Berry, *Short H. of Astronomy*; J. L. E. Dreyer, *Planetary Systems from Thales to Kepler*. Histories of Medicine by F. H. Garrison and V. Robinson; cf. L. Thorndike, *op. cit.*, also *Science and Thought in the 15th c*. J. K. Wright, *The Geographical Lore of the Time of the Crusades*.

The Medieval Attitude and Primitive Thought: G. Santayana, *Three Philosophical Poets*, Dante; and *Reason in Religion*. J. H. Robinson, *The Mind in the Making;* Franz Boas, *The Mind of Primitive Man;* L. Lévy-Bruhl, *Primitive Mentality;* W. I. Thomas, *Source-Book for Social Origins*, Pt. II. V. Rydberg, *Magic in the Middle Ages;* H. A. Guerber, *Myths and Legends of the Middle Ages.* For the symbolic science of the early Middle Ages, see Taylor, McKeon; E. Brehaut, *Isidore of Seville;* E. Male, *Religious Art in France in the 13th century*.

CHAPTER III

THE CHIEF END OF MAN — THE ENJOYMENT OF ETERNAL LIFE

The Richness of the Christian Tradition

What was the will of God for man, and how was he to order his life to attain his chief end? When we turn from the physical environment of the medieval man to his moral dwelling-place, we find ourselves in the presence of some of those beliefs that have remained a part of the foundation of the intellectual life to this very day. The twelve heavens and the celestial hierarchies, the daily miracles and the science of purposes, have gone, and to recount them is to realize the contrast with modern knowledge; but Christian righteousness and Christian love are with us yet, the oldest stones in our modern edifice. The barbarians appropriated them first, long before they discovered the science of Greece, and we have kept them long after we have outgrown that science. And yet, just because they have been so basic and so living, they have been adapted by each successive age to its own conditions of life, and have again and again furnished the principles appropriate to a new social order. There is no one Christian way of life, there is no "Christian" ideal; the moral tradition of the Western world is so complex and contains from its very sources such conflicting tendencies that no single path has remained undisputed, and no single age has been able to display a unified and all-embracing goal. Yet so rich and variegated was the Christian heritage from the ancient world that the barbarian peoples found in it the fullest scope for their changing needs, and no type of human demand, no character or temperament, has been unable to secure some measures of satisfaction in its broad confines. This diversity has been its chief source of weakness: it explains why Christianity has never been able to remake society in its image, nor to stamp a permanent character upon civilization, like Islam; but it has also been its chief strength, in that from its conflicting elements have come flexibility, adaptation, and what we like to call moral progress. The fact that the West has never crystallized into the stable societies of India or China, however great their achievements in themselves, must be in large part attributed to the essential nature of its moral tradition. Saint Paul the missionary, Saint Augustine the bishop, Saint Benedict the monk, Gregory the Pope, Saint Francis the brother of man and beast, Saint Louis the crusader, Luther the reformer, Cromwell the Puritan, Fox the Quaker, Wesley the preacher, Voltaire the humanitarian, Parker the democrat, Lincoln the emancipator, Macdonald the socialist — it is difficult to imagine wider divergencies of ideal, and yet each of these typical figures was nourished upon the tradition of Christian ethics.

Though succeeding generations have emphasized now one and now another of the tendencies embodied in the Christian heritage, they were all present in the Middle Ages, and, despite the varied ideals for the different walks of life, the thirteenth century did manage to achieve its own synthesis and to create a moral world that was the product of its own needs. We shall endeavor to disentangle the chief of these tendencies, and to sketch the outlines of this medieval structure; then we shall turn to the more specialized ideals for the component parts of medieval society.

Hebrew Righteousness

From the Hebrew people there entered into the Christian tradition the fundamental conviction that God has given man a supernaturally revealed law wherein all man's duties are made known. What the law enjoins is right, what it forbids is wrong. Morality is summed up as essentially righteousness, obedience to this supreme law of God. The Old Testament enshrines the history of the development of this conception from the dim days when the Lord was a tribal God and exacted sacrifices and burnt-offerings like any other Oriental deity, to the moral grandeur of the prophets, when he has become the Lord of Heaven and Earth and the universal Father of men, when he cannot will other than righteousness and demands only the sacrifice of a contrite heart. Two divergent tendencies are embodied in the Jewish Scriptures, the tendency to interpret this law as an elaborate and fixed body of ritual and ceremonial usages, and a complete social code suitable for the simple agricultural society of Palestine, developed by a priestly class and obeyed to the letter because it was God's will; and the tendency to penetrate beneath this levitical code to the enduring principles of right and justice and mercy, which found expression in the simplifying and universalizing exhortations of the prophets. The one results in a settled, stable, formalistic order of minute observance, the other in a flaming hatred of injustice, in a revolutionary zeal for the oppressed, at times narrow, fierce, cruel, fanatical, intolerant, at times broad, merciful, understanding, universal in its sympathies and scope. The prophetic strain reacted again and again upon the practices embodied in the levitical law. Just before the fall of Jerusalem and the captivity in Babylon there appeared the formulation of the old law modified by the prophets, in the Book of Deuteronomy.

The code of ancient Israel had been the bloody and cruel one of Semitic nomads. The Lord was a jealous tribal God who led to the merciless slaughter of other nations, a God who held the entire group responsible for the failings of a member, visiting the iniquity of the fathers upon the children unto the third and fourth generation. But he insisted on fierce justice within Israel, and forbade under severe penalties the crude coarse crimes of the Decalogue. As the Jews developed a more settled and civilized life in Palestine, the early prophets, Elijah and Elisha, looked back to the austerity and simplicity of the desert and raised a bitter cry against the new vices of a richer community, the greed of land and wealth, the selfish luxury of the rich and the harsh oppression of the poor, and sacrifice to the gods of the plain rather than to Jehovah. With Amos and Hosea social wrongs and injustices come more and more to the fore. God cares not for ceremonial observances if the heart be full of iniquity. "I hate, I despise your fast days. Though ye offer me burnt offerings and meat offerings, I will not accept. But let judgment run down as waters and righteousness as a mighty stream." [1] "I desire mercy and not sacrifice, and the knowledge of God more than burnt offerings." [2] Ezekiel repudiates the old idea of collective responsibility, proclaiming, "The son shall not bear the iniquity of the father, neither shall the father bear the iniquity of the son: the righteousness of the righteous shall be upon him, and the wickedness of the wicked shall be upon him." [3] And Micah and Isaiah upheld the universal reach of God's law of justice, rejecting the Lord God of battles for universal brotherhood and peace. "Out of Zion shall go forth the law, and the word of the Lord from Jerusalem, and he shall judge among the nations, and shall rebuke many people; and they shall beat their swords into ploughshares, and their spears into pruning hooks; nation shall not lift up sword against nation, neither shall they learn war any more."⁴ And Micah sums up the whole law of righteousness in the noble words, "He hath showed thee, O man, what is good; and what doth the Lord require of thee, but to do justly, and to love mercy, and to walk humbly with thy God?"⁵

While the revolutionary zeal of the prophets for the poor and oppressed and their denunciations of the rich were written into the Old Testament and became the natural expression of later generations of Christian idealists, they were of course not embodied in the Deuteronomic code under which later Israel lived. This code remained a mixture of the more savage and the more elevated ideals; the bloodthirsty war ethics of the ancient East, with its injunctions, "Thou shalt save nothing alive that breatheth, thou shall smite them and utterly destroy them, thou shalt make no covenant with them, nor show mercy unto them";⁶ and the fierce duty of exterminating all idolators and misbelievers, not only made the Israelites the most ferocious and savage of the warriors of antiquity, but handed on the fires of warfare and intolerant persecution to Islam and to Christianity. The medieval *Directorium Inquisitorum* followed Deuteronomy word for word, and many a mass of victory to this day has exulted with the Psalmist, "I have pursued mine enemies and overtaken them: neither did I turn again till they were consumed. I have wounded them that they were not able to rise: they are fallen under my feet. Thou hast also given me the necks of mine enemies, that I might destroy them that hate me. Then did I beat them small as the dust before the wind: I did cast them out as the dirt in the streets."⁷ But at the same time this code insisted on justice for the lowly and help for the poor. By many provisions it was sought to prevent the alienation of land. The poor were protected from creditors, their wages promptly paid, their goods secured, sheaves were left at harvest for the gleaners, widows were especially favored, rest ordained for all, even slaves, and interest on loans, sought then only by those in distress, was prohibited. The whole ordering of human relations was much more humane than that prevailing in either Greece or Rome.

The record of this moral development was a fundamental part

of the Christian tradition. It has remained in the Scriptures to furnish both texts and inspiration to this day. If we ask what the Middle Ages took from it, it is clear that the fundamental notion of morality as essentially obedience to divine law, and the corresponding conception of God's will as essentially the making of righteousness to prevail, an attitude so widely removed from the moral ideas of Greece and Rome, had become the very core of the moral life. Although the Middle Ages did not seek to observe much of the old ceremonial law or social code, partly because of Paul's insistence that with the coming of Christ that law was abrogated, partly because of the medieval habit of seeking a spiritual rather than a literal meaning in the Scriptures — it was only the simple-minded and the more literal-minded Puritans of the Reformation who sought to embody in their own life the old Jewish theocracy — the idea remained potent, and developed into the moral duty of observing the ceremonial prescriptions of the Church. Nor has Christendom ever lost the prophetic insistence that the heart of morality is righteousness, and that righteousness demands a hatred of injustice and a zeal for the oppressed. The core of Hebrew morality is the conviction that in every man there dwells a holy, precious thing, never to be violated by others, expressing itself in this very refusal to violate and in respect for its fellows. To this negative ideal of non-violation is the positive counterpart of mercy. Justice and mercy, these are the will of God. It is a stern and austere code, more ready to burst into the flame of indignation than the warm glow of love; but it appealed to the barbarians, and came into its own in the Protestantism of the Northern nations.

Gospel Love

With the Gospels Christianity received a whole new stream of life. Jesus of Nazareth stands in many respects, so far as his ethical teachings are concerned, in the line of the prophets. In his words there rings the same scorn for the ceremonial law of the scribes and the Pharisees, the same sympathy for the poor and the outcast, the same hatred of oppression, the same conviction of the universal fatherhood of God and brotherhood of man, the same insistence on the doing of the divine will. But the core of the Gospels is a new emphasis, the all-embracing love of God for man and of man for man in God. Less negative and less austere than the older ethics of non-violation, it makes the inner life, the attitude of mind and heart, the all-important thing; "for the kingdom of God is within you." God is no longer the Lord of hosts to be feared and obeyed in shaking and terror; he is throughout conceived as the loving father of mankind, patient, long-suffering, forgiving, who asks only that men shall do his bidding from love of his goodness. In filling himself with the divine spirit, man becomes like God, united in his love with all other men. Not prayer and fasting, but purity of heart, the purity that rejects all evil deeds and evil thoughts and seeks to be of good-will to all men — this is the following of God's commandment. To Jesus every man was infinitely precious in virtue of his kinship with the heavenly father. In the face of injustice and oppression — and it was to those suffering such that Jesus, like all the prophets, appealed — a man aware of this relation will seek to cast out evil in his own heart and purify himself for membership in the fellowship of the spirit, the Kingdom of God.

When we go beyond this central teaching of inward attitude and universal love, the precise definition of the "message of Jesus" becomes a task for interpretation in the light of one's own ideals even more than for historical scholarship. Nor does it matter here, for we are seeking, not what Jesus meant, but what the Christian tradition has found there; and it has found many and diverse lights. There is obviously a revolutionary leaven; if this Kingdom of God is to be made real upon earth, if the mighty are to be cast down and those of low degree exalted, if there are to be no riches and no selfishness, then must man indeed bring about a new heaven and a new earth. Again and again men aflame with the vision of a new and better society have interpreted the gospel in this wise, never more earnestly than to-day; and none can deny that there is much to confirm them in the sayings of Jesus. If the Kingdom of God is above all within, and not of this world, if we are to render unto Cæsar those things that are of Cæsar and concern ourselves only with those things that are of God, if the powers that be are ordained of God, so that whosoever resisteth the power, resisteth the ordinance of God, and they that resist shall receive to themselves damnation — then is the existing order sanctified, and the path of love, though it be hard, is to be that of Saint Francis, not that of the social revolutionary. Quite naturally this has been the orthodox interpretation, favored by kings and bishops and men of great possessions. Or if the Kingdom lie not on earth, but in the world to come, then the whole machinery of the medieval Church is a very plausible way to its attainment. For all these views the Gospels furnish an authority, and all of them have entered into the Christian tradition.

It was Paul who stamped the conservative brand upon the Christian ideal; but from Paul also there came the insistence on the mutual duties of the different classes, the reminder that the powers that be are servants of God and accountable to him, the conception of wealth as essentially a stewardship, granted that it might be exercised in love for the brethren. This side of Paul's doctrine especially appealed to the hierarchical society of the Middle Ages, just as his personal religion was beloved of the individualists of the Reformation.

Hellenistic Love of Wisdom

But Hebrew and Gospel ideals are only a part of the heritage the West received; fully as important in determining the complex ideal of Christendom was the legacy of Greece. Christianity grew up in the Hellenistic world, dominated throughout by Greek science and Greek conceptions of life. So soon as it ceased to be the possession of a few obscure bands of men the process of Hellenistic assimilation began. Despite the loss of the essentially civic and political setting of Athenian ideals, Alexandria and Antioch retained many of the beliefs characteristic of the earlier Greek world. Through the early fathers of the Church they entered deep into the spirit of the Western world, to be renewed again and again as men went back to a first-hand contact with the writers of classical Athens.

Perhaps most important of all was the Greek faith in intelligence and science. The Greeks were preëminently interested in knowing, something the Romans cared very little about: they could be moved strongly by nothing which they did not understand. Where the Romans observed human life and sought to order it, the Greeks searched heaven and earth for the reasons of things. It was from Greek science, as we shall see, that the modern world took its birth. Aristotle invented the sciences,

Greeks at Alexandria carried them to the point where the Renaissance took them up again. Greeks invented the philosophic interpretations of the universe by which all thoughtful men of antiquity ordered their lives. When the Christian cult came into prominence, it was Greeks who elaborated it, endeavored to understand it, adjusted it to their philosophies, and formulated the theological conceptions of the Christian epic. Greek councils decided upon its dogmas. The Latin fathers were on the whole little interested in this endeavor to build an intelligible Christian system; for them, Christianity was a human, ethical thing, a path to salvation, not a cosmic picture of the structure of the world. Tertullian, who rejected reason entirely, and believed because it was absurd, and Arnobius, who saw no profit in knowledge of any sort, were typical of the Western Church. It is significant that Clement, Origen, and Athanasius, at Alexandria, developed the doctrine of the Trinity, while Cyprian, Ambrose, and Augustine in the West centered their minds on the moral struggle in man, on sin and grace, and on the characteristically Roman task of organizing the Church. In philosophy, the East was Platonic, and sought the supreme reason by dialectic; the West was Stoic, and believed nothing much mattered so long as you kept your soul untouched.

This Greek love of understanding was embodied in the Christian tradition more in the form of its intricate speculative doctrine than in an active faith in intelligence. At first it led to an insistence on orthodoxy, right doctrine, because it was holy, catholic, and apostolic, rather than because it was right. The faith of the early Church, faith in Christ and in Christ's ideal, became in Greek minds belief in a body of truths that could not be understood by many, and in the West were hardly understood at all. Into the Athanasian Creed was written, "Whosoever will be saved, before all things, it is necessary that he hold the Catholic faith, which faith, except every one who do keep entire and unviolated, without doubt he shall perish everlastingly." [8] It is difficult to realize to-day what a new and what an important thing this insistence on the virtue of correct belief was. No other religion of the world had ever made any such demand upon its adherents. Unbelief, doubt, even honest error, became for the first time sinful. It is needless to point to the long history of the warfare of intellectual investigation and authoritative doctrine in the Christian Church to emphasize its momentous consequences for ill. But it must not be forgotten that the presence of such a body of complex beliefs was the original incentive to the barbarian in the twelfth century to seek to understand, and that through all its rigid crystallizations there has shone the Greek spirit of knowing and comprehending. It enshrines the duty of knowledge, even if it be on authority; it is the starting-point of investigation.

Platonism

When the thirteenth century discovered the glory of Aristotle, its greatest minds took delight in his belief that the life of intellectual contemplation was so far superior to all other earthly pursuits that it alone was worthy to be ascribed to God himself. But while Thomas and Dante accepted this fundamental Aristotelian ideal, and adopted many of the virtues and the classifications of his work on *Ethics*, that preëminently sensible manual for a prudent gentleman of means hardly suited their temper, and it remained for the Renaissance to make a cult of his beloved "high-minded man." It was rather from Platonic sources that Greek ideas came to the Christian tradition, and that, too, after they had dwelt for near a thousand years in the half-Oriental schools of Alexandria, and there lost most of that delight in the natural beauty of man and his human life that constitutes for many to-day the chief charm of Plato. But Christianity as a great and comprehensive system has always been fundamentally Neo-Platonic in its philosophy, and for long stretches of time in its values. The Middle Ages, though their thinkers knew far more of the writings of Aristotle than they did of those of Plato, were none the less better Platonists than Aristotelians; and in spite of subsequent changes these Platonic elements have been written large into the life of the West.

The fundamental note of Platonism is the contrast it sees between the things of the senses and the things of the mind, between the body and the spirit. The first are ever-changing, impermanent, transitory; the second immutable, everlasting, eternal. True knowledge is of these things of the mind, the ideas, as Plato called them, or the forms of things, as they became for Aristotle. All things of the senses possess meaning and value only as they shadow forth these ideas; human life itself achieves significance in the measure that the mind forsakes the sense realm and communes with the intelligible world. Thus can man make himself immortal, by rising to the realm of imperishable things and dwelling with them in eternity. The Neo-Platonists, chief of whom was Plotinus, put these ideas in the single all-embracing mind of God, from whose perfect fullness of being the realms of existence stretched down by stages to the lowest world of matter. Man, a dweller in these two realms, can forsake his true blessedness to immerse himself in the things of the senses, in which case he becomes like them and perishes in nothingness; or he can turn his inward eye upward and in the spiritual beauty of God's mind find eternal life.

Oriental Religious Asceticism

Plato himself saw the spiritual glory of the intelligible in the whole world of life and art that was Athens, but his Orientalized successors turned more and more away from the setting of human life to the higher realm. Even Plato at times was touched by this asceticism, and in the beautiful dialogue of *Phædo* called the entire aim of man the seeking of death — death to the body and immortal being for the soul.

For Plato, and for his Greek followers in general, this process of attaining man's true blessedness was an entirely natural turning from one part of experience to another, a rational discrimination of that aspect of life which possessed true worth. But for the many Oriental religions that flourished among the Hellenized inhabitants of the eastern part of the Empire, religions which the decay of their original civic and national status had transformed into cults offering private salvation to individual participants, the forsaking of the flesh and the dwelling in the spirit became a supernatural process involving a complete transformation of man's nature under the influence of mystical union with a Saviour. With the second generation, Christianity had become just such a mystery cult offering private salvation to the followers of its Lord. Almost from the very outset, therefore, it combined the general philosophic dualism of matter and spirit, so basic in all the Platonic philosophizing, with the more Oriental conception of man's chief need as a magical transformation of his nature that would permit him to forsake the flesh for the spirit. With Paul this fundamental dualism had already entered deeply into Christianity; for him existence was one long struggle of the spirit against the flesh, the higher against the lower nature, and the victory of the spirit could come only through the supernatural union of the soul with Christ by faith in his power to save man from the body of this death.

The succeeding fathers of the church worked out the detailed body of Christian theology increasingly under the influence of Neo-Platonic conceptions. They explained, as the fruit of original sin inherited from Adam, man's need for a miraculous transformation; they formulated the Christology or theory of Christ's nature and work definitely promulgated at the Councils of Nicæa and Chalcedon; and they elaborated the doctrine of the means whereby man could be saved through the transformation of his nature by divine grace, that power which stills the natural appetites and liberates man from the sin and death which of himself he can never overcome. The perfected form of this theory of grace is due to Augustine, whose whole thought was colored by his own moral struggle against the lusts of the flesh, and his long search for some means of conquering this natural man of instincts and passions. After tasting of most of the means of salvation offered in the Hellenistic world, he found power and victory in the grace of the Christians, and, when he came to interpret his experience intellectually in philosophic terms, he naturally made this living reality of grace the core of his doctrine of salvation and of the Church through which it must come. The whole elaborate mechanism of the medieval Church with its disciplines and sacraments, which Augustine largely formulated, was at bottom the instrument of giving by supernatural or magical means this power of grace to all men, and thus gaining for them both moral perfection in this life and immortality in eternity.

From this orientalized Platonic source the Christian tradition gained its fundamental dualism, a notion quite unknown to the Hebrews. The natural life of man with its desires and pleasures became something to be shunned as evil and degraded, something to be forsaken for higher things. Man's true nature was of a different quality, his destiny lay in another realm. It is easy to see how from this belief sprang the other-worldliness of the Middle Ages, expressing itself, not only in the vision of this world as a vale of tears and temptations, the vestibule to a real existence to come, but even more in the ascetic ideal which made withdrawal and contemplation preferable to action. However far from attainment by rude fighters and ruder peasants, the ideal of the holy monk was regarded by all classes as the only really perfect life for man. It is this dualism running through all of man's actions that has left its impress on the commonly accepted moral codes of the West to this day, and seems even yet to make impossible that whole-hearted and simple enjoyment of the goods of a natural existence that men now envy in the Greeks of old. It is not that men have ever refrained from action or from these pleasures, but that they have never been able to rid themselves of the notion that there is something essentially wrong about them. Thus the ideal to which men give allegiance has become meager even when intense, and the life they lead tainted with a sense of disgrace and shame. On the one hand, ecstatic rapture and bliss, on the other, hypocrisy and concealment — these things the West owes to its heritage of Neo-Platonism.

The Medieval System

Out of these elements, Hebrew righteousness, the love of the Gospels, Greek faith in the mind, and Hellenistic asceticism, the fathers of the ancient Church moulded an organic whole. This body of beliefs the barbarians found ready-made for them, a thing of life and beauty which they were drawn to reverence, but which for centuries they were unable to understand. When the slow growth of their social life brought them to the place where they could really assimilate it, they found in it a vehicle admirably adapted to express their own aspirations and energies. By the thirteenth century this Christian scheme of things had really taken root in the soil of the Western mind; and it is this great medieval synthesis that makes such an appeal to those weary of the cross-currents and confusion of to-day. Though its elements were diverse and its structure complex, there does seem in it — at least to modern eyes looking backward — a kind of monumental unity, like that of the great cathedrals that were its supreme expression. Builded during centuries, in changing styles and tastes, intricate, infinitely variegated, embracing the arts, not only of architecture, but of sculpture, of color, of music, of poetry in their overlaid symbolism, and of drama in their mighty services, Durham or Lincoln, Chartres or Rheims, stand preeminently for one thing — the union of all men's energies in the service of God. We find the same architectonic grandeur in the great *Summa* of Thomas Aquinas, ordering all man's knowledge under the wisdom of God, and in the intensely human *Divine Comedy* that seems to spring from the whole of human life, complete in its errors as in its aspiration.

The Christian ideals were embodied in a visible institution, the Church, which undertook to administer authoritatively the moral life of the community. Since the Church was the sole ark of salvation and the supreme authority in all things of faith and morals, conformity with its regulations was the framework within which men's varying aims were sought. The Church was of necessity one, holy, apostolic, and catholic — one in its faith and love, holy in the possession of the magic grace necessary to salvation, apostolic in its tradition and infallibility, catholic in its universal spread. The core of its authority and power over men's lives lay in its possession of this power of grace and in its administration of grace through the sacraments. The grace of God was doubly essential, both to that conquest of man's higher nature over his lower nature that made possible a moral life on earth, and to that change of his substance that freed him from the extinction of death. It was contained only in the sacraments of the Church, and was there visibly embodied, in a real and magical as well as in a symbolic sense. The efficacy of the sacraments in conveying the power of God lay not in the character of either the administrant or the partaker; indeed, the only absolutely necessary one, baptism, could be given, not only by any layman, but even by an infidel. They worked *ex opere operato*, not *ex opere operantis* — by virtue of the rite itself, not by virtue of the holiness of the priest. Though, to be sure, the presence of fervent faith and good-will in the participant conferred a double grace, only his contempt, or positive disbelief, or mortal sin, prevented their efficacy. Normally, however, the administration of the sacraments involved a combination of divine grace and human merit.

The seven sacraments were baptism, confirmation, the mass or Eucharist, penance, extreme unction, ordination, and matrimony. The first five were intended to secure the spiritual perfection of every man, the last two for certain classes, "for the governance and increase of the Church." Three, baptism, confirmation, and

THE ENJOYMENT OF ETERNAL LIFE

ordination, impressed upon the soul an indelible character, and hence were given but once. The observance of the five universal rites was incumbent upon all the faithful, but for the moral life the sacrament of penance was most important. In the words of Pope Eugene IV:

The material of penance consists in the acts of penitence, which are divided into three parts. The first of these is contrition of the heart, wherein the sinner must grieve for the sins he has committed, with the resolve to commit no further sins. Second comes confession with the mouth, to which it pertains that the sinner should make confession to his priest of all the sins he holds in his memory. The third is satisfaction for sins according to the judgment of the priest, and this is made chiefly by prayer, fasting, and almsgiving.... The minister of this sacrament is the priest, who has authority to absolve either regularly or by the commission of a superior. The benefit of this sacrament is absolution from sins.[9]

By baptism man was freed from the original sin inherited from Adam, but the corruption of his nature endured, finding expression in acts of pride and disobedience to God's law. To wipe out these mortal sins — no special grace was required to absolve from venial sins — penance is necessary. The satisfaction begun in this life may continue in Purgatory, the realm where those already forgiven purify themselves. This satisfaction consists primarily in good works, which can be commuted into money payments and applied by the Church. These commutations or indulgences cannot of themselves free from eternal punishment; they are efficacious only after genuine repentance, and merely substitute one kind of satisfaction for another. Moreover, by a beautiful application of the spirit of Christian love, it was believed that Christ and the saints have laid up a treasure of superfluous merits which they can employ for the satisfaction due by others. This store could be drawn upon by the direct intercession of the saints — there was many a touching story of such love for the lowest sinner who had repented — or through the Pope, at whose disposal they were.

It is obvious that this system if sincerely and nobly administered could flower in a very beautiful moral life and a much-needed moral guidance, and at its best it certainly did. But it is also easy to see how it could degenerate into mere formalism and superstitious faith in magic. Again and again reformers called men back to the spirit rather than the letter, until with the Protestants the external and institutional side was subordinated to the heart and conscience of the individual. What the Protestants attempted to accomplish by breaking the organic system of the Church and placing all responsibility upon the individual, the Catholics undertook in their great Reformation dating from the Council of Trent, in the sixteenth century. After the initial force of both these great spiritual movements had passed away, it can hardly be decided which system, in its actual effect upon the moral life of its adherents, has been most fruitful. If in losing the rich symbolism of the Catholic sacramental system the Protestant has also lost the temptation to forget the spiritual meaning in the external form, he has run the perhaps greater danger of giving up entirely the inward grace with the outward sign. The medieval Church knew the weakness of the average man, and in its humanity did not call upon him to perform the impossible. And for him whose spirit soared there were illimitable reaches into which to fly.

Medieval Virtues and Vices

But important as was this great machinery for the administration of men's lives, and often as it came to seem a supreme end in and by itself, it was after all only the means to the attainment of a certain kind of life. Out of the elements already enumerated the Church erected a set of ideals of universal scope, to be applied flexibly to the different stations to which men were called. The schoolmen delighted in ordering and ranking the virtues, and the poets and builders in giving them vesture of concrete form. In the moral scheme of the *Divine Comedy* we have perhaps the most representative and certainly the most enduring of these attempts at a discrimination of values.

From classical Greece came the four cardinal virtues of Prudence, Justice, Fortitude, and Temperance. To them were added the three theological virtues — so called because they have God as their object, and are poured into men by God alone — the Faith, Hope, and Love of Paul, completing the tale of seven. And the greatest of these was Love. The cardinal virtues, however, scarcely corresponded to their Greek namesakes. Prudence becomes the search for truth and the thirst for a fuller knowledge of God; Justice overflows the strict bounds of giving every man his due and becomes virtually a part of love; Fortitude includes the bravery of the soldier, but culminates in patience, longsuffering, and martyrdom; and Temperance, when honored in the observance, is moderation in fasting and ascetic practices. Faith is, of course, faith in the Christian doctrine; it includes intelligence and science, and its opposites are infidelity, heresy, apostasy, blasphemy, and spiritual blindness. Hope is hope in salvation, opposed to desperation and presumption alike. But Love fills the whole moral life, ranging from joy and delight to sympathy for the sufferings of others. With Dante all vice is due to some defect in love. In the scheme of the *Purgatorio*, where the repentant as they climb the mount toward the Earthly Paradise are successively purified of the seven deadly sins, these are derived from love of an evil object, or from too little or too much vigor in love. Perverted love gives rise to Pride, Envy, and Wrath; defective love, to Sloth; and excessive love to Avarice, Gluttony, and Lust. It is significant that the sin most easily pardoned, highest on the Mount of Purgatory, the outermost Circle of Hell, is that love of man for woman that, transcending its proper limits, becomes lust; and the eternal punishment of Paolo and Francesca, the very type of love that is too strong, is only that everlasting continuance of love that cuts them off from participation in other spiritual joys. On the other hand, the most heinous offense is pride, expressing itself in the greatest crime of a feudal society based on the mutual performance of obligations — treachery, in which "is forgotten that love which nature makes, and also that which afterwards is added, giving birth to special trust." [10] In the lowest pit of Hell, frozen deep in the ice of Cocytus, farthest removed from the light and warmth of the divine love that is God, lies Satan, supreme example of Pride refusing obedience to the will of the Most High, and with him the arch-traitors Judas, Brutus, and Cassius. Here is no monkish asceticism; nor did the aberrations of the anchorite striving after perfect purity ever obscure the great and saving life-stream of Christian love. It is no accident that that purest flower of the monastic ideal, Saint Francis of Assisi, lived all his life bathed in the spirit of eternal joy in God's great world and in his fellow men. And over the very gate of Hell was written, "Justice moved my high Maker; Divine Power made me, Wisdom Supreme, and Primal Love" [11]

— love of the good which is life, and hatred of the evil which is death. This is terrible, this is tragic, but, if we may judge by what experience offers to man, it is true.

When we look at the list of Christian virtues, the all-embracing love, the hatred of pride in every form that became humility, meekness, obedience, gentleness, compassion, resignation, and renunciation of the world, certain traits are at once apparent. These are ideals which can be reached by every man in every walk of life, however hard to the spirit the actual attainment. They are individual, in the sense that, though they lead to social coöperation, they can be practiced without the setting of an appropriate society. They are not civic and patriotic, like the ideals of the Greek and Roman moralists, depending for their existence upon a highly developed community life. They are not the ideals of a single class, though they are quite compatible with an aristocratically ordered society; at its best the Aristotelian ethics or the Platonic path was founded upon a slave basis and served a leisure class. These virtues are both individual and universal. Yet at the same time they do seem in their content the virtues of the humbler mass of society. Nearly all those types of excellence held most dear by the aristocratic Greek and Roman are despised, and in their places the servile qualities exalted. It is easy to see how the Roman should find such ideals wholly alien to him, and how the virtues of the pagans should seem to a sincere Christian but splendid vices, shot through and through with pride. Moreover, forged as they were in the decaying society of the ancient world, they are full of the spirit of defeat and renunciation, appropriate to a society where the best is no longer possible. Like the Stoicism of Marcus Aurelius, they are touched with the spirit that sees the highest excellence of man, not, with the Greeks, in living well, but rather in bearing misfortune nobly. It is strange that the Western barbarians, so exuberantly full of life and energy, should have made such a moral world their own; it is not strange that they should have permeated it with elements expressing their own needs, and that Christianity should betray such an amazing divergence between its professed principles and its real ideals.

Life Eternal

What is most characteristic of this whole scheme of Christian values is the way in which it catches up the manifold desires and strivings of men and sweeps them all on toward one all-embracing aspiration, the yearning for eternal life. Many and diverse were the contents poured into this ideal, from the crudest and basest of hopes to the highest and most exalted of longings; but the vision shone forth for every man as of an existence infinitely worth while, embracing all the joys of human experience in an ordered harmony. For the masses the whole practice of virtue was directed to the attainment of a future life that was but a prolongation of the delights of this corporeal world. The world to come, for those not doomed to the everlasting punishment of earthly wickedness, was to be a life meager and poor, judged by our modern sophistication, but not more meager than the uninspired pictures of present-day "spiritualists." Even the most imaginative visions of a Dante could find no colors in which to paint a satisfying eternity. The furniture of Hell lay only too ready at hand in the world of men; but in Paradise the poet could discern only a play of radiant light, and wisely filled that part of his journey with the doctrines of holy faith. Poor creature of time and mundane limits, the mind of man shrinks back abashed before the task of portraying a bliss that shall endure without end. Wisest of all, the mystics knew that Heaven is not a stretching-out of time, that with the cessation of time and matter pure spirit drops all its vestment of humanity, and loses itself in a sea of being. For the greatest souls of the Middle Ages, whether they sought it through pure faith and intuition or by the more painful path of dialectic reasoning, Paradise was either a present reality to which the spirit could here and now lift itself, or an infinite nothingness. The sum of their wisdom lay in their conviction that this is life eternal, to know God. The saddest words of the whole *Inferno*, "Without hope we live in desire," were uttered by the virtuous philosophers and poets of antiquity whose only punishment was that they could never expect to look upon the face of God. Through divine faith and love alone could all human striving reach its final goal, this peace that passeth understanding.

But the catalogues of the schoolmen, even the genius of a Dante, mean little unless the concrete realization of these ideals in the complex, variegated world of the Middle Ages be before our eyes. Therefore let us turn to the embodiment of the medieval values in the vast organism of medieval society.

REFERENCES

1. Amos, V, 22–24.
2. Hosea, VI, 6.
3. Ezekiel, XVIII, 20.
4. Isaiah, II, 3, 4; also Micah, IV, 2, 3.
5. Micah, VI, 8.
6. Deuteronomy, XX, 16, 17; VII, 2.
7. Psalms, XVIII, 37–43.
8. *Athanasian Creed*, quoted in P. Schaff, *The Creeds of Christendom*, II.
9. Pope Eugene IV, *Statement for the Armenians*, quoted in Robinson, *Readings in European History*, I, 352, 353.
10. Dante, *Inferno*, Canto XI, v. 61, 62, 63.
11. *Ibid.*, Canto III, v. 4, 5, 6.

SELECTED READING LISTS

General Surveys of the Christian Tradition: H. L. Friess and H. W. Schneider, *Religion in Various Cultures;* Clemen, *Religions of the World;* Reinach, *Orpheus*. *H. of Christianity in the Light of Modern Knowledge*, a *Collective Work*. Articles "Christianity," "Religious Institutions: Christian," in *Enc. Soc. Sciences*. Interpretation by a former Catholic, G. Santayana, *Reason in Religion;* by a liberal Protestant, W. Rauschenbusch, *Christianity and the Social Crisis;* by agnostics, C. Guignebert, *Christianity, Past and Present;* J. H. Robinson, *The Mind in the Making;* H. E. Barnes, *The Twilight of Christianity*. The classic Protestant work on Christian doctrine is A. Harnack, *H. of Dogma;* brief outline by H. B. Workman, *Christian Thought to the Reformation;* fuller in A. C. McGiffert, *H. of Christian Thought*. Summaries of the Christian ideals in P. V. Myers, *History as Past Ethics*, and P. Monroe, *H. of Education*. E. Troeltsch, *Social Teachings of the Christian Churches*.
Hebrew Ideals: E. R. Bevan and C. Singer, *Legacy of Israel*. C. H. Cornill, *Prophets of Israel, H. of the People of Israel*, conservative, compare with Reinach, *Orpheus*. A. Lods, *Israel;* A. L. Sachar, *H. of the Jews*. G. F. Moore, *The Literature of the Old Testament*. Lazarus, *Principles of Jewish Ethics*, emphasizing the priestly strain. Interpretation in F. Adler, *Ethical Philosophy of Life*, Bk. I, chs. II, IV.
The Gospel of Jesus: A. Harnack, *What is Christianity?* liberal Protestant; A. Loisy, *The Gospel and the Church*, answer by a Catholic modernist. Social interpretations in V. Simkhovitch, *Towards an Understanding of Jesus;* C. A. Ellwood, *Reconstruction of Religion;* H. F. Ward, *The Ancient Lowly*. Classic lives of Jesus by D. F. Strauss, E. Renan; by S. J. Case (liberal Protestant); J. Klausner (Jewish): Nathaniel Schmidt, *The Prophet of Nazareth*. F. C. Conybeare, *Myth, Magic, and Morals;* J. M. Robertson, *Pagan Christs;* G. S. Hall, *Jesus Christ in the Light of Psychology*, radical views.
The Rise of the Christian System: *Epistles* of Paul; I. Edman, *The Mind of Paul;* H. A. A. Kennedy, *St. Paul and the Mystery Religions;* F. A. Spencer, *Beyond Damascus*. Apostolic Fathers, ed. K. Lake. Irenaeus, *Against Heresies;* Origen, *De Principiis;* Cyprian. Brief survey, K. Lake, *Landmarks in the History of Early Christianity*. A. C. McGiffert, *Apostolic Age;* Harnack, *H. of Dogma, Expansion of Christianity*. A. C. Flick, *Rise of the Med. Church;* C. Dawson, *Making of Europe;* L. Duchesne, *Early H. of the Christian Church;* F. Lot, *End of the Ancient World;* H. Moss, *Birth of the M.A.* S. J. Case, *The Social Origins of Christianity, The Social Triumph of the An-*

cient Church, Makers of Christianity, I. K. Kautsky, Foundations of Christianity; M. Beer, Social Struggles in Antiquity, in the M.A. (Marxian).

Influence of Hellenistic Beliefs: For the "Platonism" of Greek thought, see of Plato's dialogues esp. the *Phaedo, Symposium, Phaedrus*, Bks. VI and VII of the *Republic*, and the *Timaeus*. Works by W. Pater, A. E. Taylor, Paul Shorey, Paul Elmer More. F. M. Cornford, *Plato's Cosmology*. Plotinus, *Enneads*, S. MacKenna tr. Works by T. Whittaker, W. R. Inge, C. Bigg. Harnack, appendix to vol. I, *Platonism*. See Inge in Livingstone, *Legacy of Greece;* E. Hatch, *Influence of Greek Thought and Usages upon the Christian Church*, an overemphasis. For the Oriental religions: F. Cumont, *Oriental Religions in Roman Paganism, The Mysteries of Mithra;* T. R. Glover, *Conflict of Religions in the Early Roman Empire;* S. Dill, *Roman Society from Nero to Marcus Aurelius;* W. R. Halliday, *Pagan Background of Christianity;* S. Angus, *The Religious Quests of the Graeco-Roman World, The Mystery-Religions and Christianity*. W. Pater, *Marius the Epicurean*. Philo Judaeus, *Creation of the World, Allegories of the Sacred Laws;* see J. Drummond, E. Bréhier.

The Medieval System: Augustine, *Confessions, City of God, Enchiridion, On Nature and Grace, The Correction of the Donatists*. Lives by J. McCabe, Rebecca West, J. J. F. Poujoulat, L. Bertrand. E. Gilson, *Int. to the Study of St. Augustine*. Thomas Aquinas, *Summa Theologica, Summa contra Gentiles*, tr. Dominicans. Studies by E. Gilson, M. Grabmann. E. Gilson, *Les moralistes chrétiens: St.-Thomas d'Aquin*. Dante, Temple ed. and notes; see E. G. Gardner, J. B. Fletcher, G. Santayana (in *Three Phil. Poets*), Karl Vossler. Modern interpretation of the medieval synthesis in Henry Adams, *Mont-Saint-Michel and Chartres*.

Christian Mysticism: Thomas à Kempis, *Imitation of Christ; Sermons* of Johann Tauler; Albertus Magnus, *On Union with God;* Bernard of Clairvaux, *On the Love of God;* Henry Suso, *Eternal Wisdom; Theologia Germanica*. E. Underhill, *Mysticism;* C. A. Bennett, *A Phil. Study of Mysticism*.

CHAPTER IV
THE EMBODIMENT — THE CITY OF GOD

It is not our purpose here to sketch the outlines and the history of medieval institutions, or to attempt the difficult task of determining to what extent ideals of life were actually attained in the rude, fierce, and lustful society of Europe. These institutions, when still with us, are altered almost beyond recognition; it is as ideas and beliefs that they have exerted their fullest influence, directly or by opposition, to the present day. Against the background of these ideas we shall attempt to understand the mind of modern man. Hence our endeavor shall be to discern how the pure white light of Christian love and obedience to the will of God was caught up and refracted by the many facets of barbarian society, even as the sun shone through the great rose window of a thirteenth-century cathedral; to seek out not only the professed ideals that served men's aspirations at their highest, but even more the actual ideals which in spite of all obstacles they sought to attain in church and guild and feudal order. In reality, complexity and confusion mark medieval civilization; nothing was ever simple or pure. But this need not deter us from gazing at what men in their hearts admired, even though ignorance and the heavy hand of tradition and the refractory material of human passions made its attainment rare.

THE FUNCTIONAL IDEAL OF SOCIETY

The fundamental note in medieval civilization is the complete harmony between the individual and the social. Society is a great hierarchy of ascending orders, in which every man has his God-appointed function and recognized obligations, and at the same time his rights and privileges. Each man is a member of some estate or group, and each estate is an essential organ of the whole, discharging a function at once peculiar to itself and necessary to the full life of Christendom. Only through his participation in this group life can the individual attain his own ends, and conversely, only with the aid of every individual and every group can society afford the appropriate setting for the fullest life of its individual members. All men exist in and for each other, and are bound to each other by an intricate network of mutual obligations.

The spirit of this group life is well expressed by Saint Thomas:

> Man is called by nature to live in society; for he needs many things which are necessary to his life, and which by himself he cannot procure for himself. Whence it follows that man naturally becomes part of a group, to procure him the means of living well. He needs this assistance for two reasons. First, in order that he may obtain the elementary necessities of life; this he does in the domestic circle of which he is a part. Every man receives from his parents life and nourishment and education; and the reciprocal aid of the family members facilitates the mutual provision of the necessities of life. But there is a second reason why the individual is helped by the group, of which he is a part, and in which alone he finds his adequate well-being. And this is, that he may not only *live*, but live the *good life* — which is enabled by the opportunities of social intercourse. Thus civil society aids the individual in obtaining the material necessities, by uniting in the same city a great number of crafts, which could not be so united in the same family. And civil society also assists him in the moral life.[1]

The sources of this fundamental social principle are many. Basic were the very conditions of barbarian existence, which made the union of men for mutual support a bitter necessity. The vassal needed the military protection of his lord, as the lord needed fighting men; and hence feudalism flourished. The merchant needed the protection of his guild and his city, the craftsman needed the support of his fellows, while monk and priest alike needed a strong church to maintain their own existence. In such conditions the freedom of the individual from all social bonds would have meant only the freedom of the outlaw, a hunted thing. But about this necessity there gathered many ideal values. The great unified purpose of Christianity, to attain eternal life, the love of God which united all men in the one mystic body of Christ, found in such a society a fertile soil. The explicit teaching of Paul on the body and its members, "For as we have many members in one body, and all members have not the same office, so we, being many, are one body in Christ, and every one members one of another.... And whether one member suffer, all the members suffer with it; or one member be honored, all the members rejoice with it";[2] — provided an appropriate statement of the functional unity of such a diversified life.

From Plato, too, the Plato of the *Republic*, that vision of an idealized Spartan community, came the same principle; it has been well said that the Middle Ages were full of a spontaneous Platonism, inspired by a mind *naturaliter Platonica*. Plato's three classes, of guardians, warriors, and workers correspond to the medieval clergy, baronage, and commons; the control of the guardians over civic society in the light of the Idea of the Good finds its counterpart in the control of the clergy in the light of divine revelation. Even the Platonic communism for the guardians is repeated in the monasteries; while the Platonic creed of "Do thine own duty," that from such perfect functioning Justice may arise, is but the Christian "doing my duty in that state of life to which it has pleased God to call me." The chief difference between the Greek Utopia and the Christian world is that in the former the good of the state was supreme over the development and well-being of the members, whereas in the latter, society's sole aim is the life and salvation of all men. Christianity, drawing upon the Stoic teachings of the equality of man — though not the similarity of men — and the single society of all humanity, was both more democratic in spirit and more universal than Platonism.

As we look abroad upon medieval civilization, then, we shall expect throughout diversity of gifts and function combined with unity of aim and life. We shall not attempt to evaluate the calling of any man in itself, without reference to the other members of the body of Christ. We shall not look for the one perfect type of humanity, the "high-minded man" of Aristotle or the "universal man" of the Renaissance. Knight or peasant, monk or doctor, each in his own way does God's bidding, each can attain perfection in his station. "Certainly, a lowly peasant who serves God is better than a proud philosopher who, to the neglect of his own soul, studies the course of the heavens.... Learning, when considered in itself, or knowledge upon any subject, is not to be disparaged; for it is good, and ordained of God.... But he is really great who is great in charity; he is really great who is little in his own eyes, and cares not for the honor of high positions; he is really wise who counts all earthly things as dung that he may win Christ; he is really learned who does the Will of God, and forsakes his own will." [3] Hence we must be prepared for a multiplicity of ideals, quite impossible of combination in one man, yet all evoking admiration. The doughty warrior is as needful and as much a servant of God as the cloistered monk. It is perhaps in appreciating monasticism that it is most necessary for us to bear in mind this fundamental division of function. The monk is no selfish individualist, in theory at least; he is "a necessary organ of Christian society, discharging his function of prayer and devotion for the benefit not of himself solely, or primarily, but rather of every member of that society. He prays for the sins of the whole world, and by his prayer he contributes to the realization of the end of the world, which is the attainment of salvation." [4] He is serving the Christian God for all mankind, just as to-day the erudite scholar or the patient investigator serves our god of Scientific Truth.

The Organization of Religious Society

The Middle Ages, as we have already seen, knew two societies, the *civitas Dei* and the *civitas terrena*, the City of God and the Earthly City. Faithful Christians dwelt in both. Just where the boundaries lay, the Middle Ages, for all their searching and their struggles back and forth, were never able to decide; the powers of the two cities were in eternal conflict in the soul of every man. But for ordinary purposes the distinction was clear enough; the City of God was the Church, and wielded the sword of the spirit, the Earthly City was lay society, and exercised the secular sword. In the thirteenth century the spiritual power, under an Innocent III, was unquestionably supreme, then the economic growth of the nations proved too much for it, and, shattered and riven, it has since been largely at the beck and call of temporal monarchs.

But within the very structure of the Church itself there dwelt a diversity of ideals. Those who devoted themselves to the service of God as her immediate ministers formed two great classes, the regular clergy, consecrated and set apart to display God's love in contemplation, study, and works of charity; and the secular clergy, dwelling in the world and administering the great system of moral and spiritual guidance that was the Church. On the one hand, the saint, the monk, the holy man, on the other the bishop, the prelate, the Pope — surely a wide difference! Within the ranks of each branch, too, there was plenty of choice; the monk could imitate the ascetic hermit, Saint Anthony, in his continual fasting and self-torment, or follow the sane and prudent rule of Saint Benedict, and spend his days in tilling the fields, or copying manuscripts, and praying. He could set up as a stern reformer, causing kings and cardinals to tremble, with that irascible mystic Saint Bernard, or he could wander over the countryside with Saint Francis and share his joyous poverty. The priest could be the simple servitor of his parish, or the proud warrior bishop — a secular prince in his own right — or the great cardinal and minister of state, or the imperious and haughty Pope himself. He would probably fall far short of attaining these ideals, to be sure; he might have more sympathy with Chaucer's high-living, fox-hunting monk, or his dainty, sweet-tongued friar, or even take his place in the gallery of Boccaccio's care-free rascals. But such frailties, though human, were not universal; above all, they were not what society approved as best.

The Saintly Ideal

Though sainthood flowered in many diverse forms, it was the saintly ideal that was honored most highly by the citizens of the City of God, even when they felt no urge toward it themselves. Not only monks, but the priests of the Church and the lords of this world, were measured by its standard. The secular clergy were in principle held to the same saintliness as the monks, though allowance was made for the dangers of a life spent in the cure of souls. But always the cloister was looked upon as the safest abiding-place: the life of the layman, merchant, or knight, was fraught with instant peril; that of the secular clergy, especially when they held high office, was also perilous. Nothing is more revealing of the medieval temper than the election of Pope Celestine V. After wrangling for two years the College of Cardinals selected for the most difficult and complex post in Christendom, facing, in the height of the thirteenth century, problems so thorny as to tax the wisest statesmanship, an ignorant, superstitious peasant, an old man of eighty who had spent his entire life as a secluded and ascetic hermit in the crags of the Apennines; and they called him to his inevitable failure and disgrace because they believed that the power of a saintly life could work miracles. The records are full of fighters and rulers, merchants and bishops, who, impelled by the call of what seemed to them higher things, laid off the pomp and glory of this world for the simple habit of the monk of God.

The Monastic Life

Christian monasticism was rooted deep in the traditions of the past and in the conditions of medieval life. It originated in the most Oriental of the Hellenistic tendencies of the ancient Church, upon the Egyptian deserts where monastic communities had long lived. The East has always known monasticism and asceticism, and several strains in Christianity made for its assimilation. Christian asceticism was bred originally, not of renunciation of the world, but of an indifference to the things of Cæsar in view of the imminent approach of the Kingdom of God. The early communities of the Church were simple and austere, both to preserve the all-important spirit of Christian love — a thing most difficult in a luxurious life — and to train the soul in holiness and virtue — the root meaning of "asceticism" is "training" — that thereby the coming of the Kingdom might be hastened. This asceticism had the twofold value of steeling the Christian soul for the demands to be made upon it, and of withdrawing its energies from less important channels that they might be poured whole-heartedly into the things supremely needful. With this concentration of attention upon the fundamentals, that disregard of mere pleasure natural to all who feel the call to perform an important mission, there was soon combined the Oriental and Neo-Platonic dualism that despised the body and all its desires. From Paul, from the Gnostics, from the Platonism of the Alexandrians and of Augustine, this mortification of the flesh and renunciation of the world came to have a value in itself, entirely apart from its original worth as discipline, training, and concentration. This Oriental dualism was strongest in Egypt; pagan Plotinus, Christian Origen, and Saint Anthony, most famous of ascetics, were all Copts, that is, Egyptians. The deserts of the Thebaid were early peopled by Christian hermits who had withdrawn from all human contact to reach God.

But the life of the anchorite, even where the Egyptian climate permitted a solitary man to sustain himself, soon degenerates into insane austerities that can only craze and brutalize, and develops the most pathological of visions. Saint Simeon Stylites, perched for thirty years on top of his pillar, even the marvelous devil-fighting Anthony, have always been aberrations of the Christian ideal, not of its essence. The Church gathered these hermits together and forced them to submit to a communal existence that forbade extraordinary austerities and never let them forget that their asceticism had value only as it trained soldiers of the Lord. Pachomius first, and then Saint Basil, in the fourth century, laid down the great *regula* or rule of the Eastern monasteries, enjoining chastity and freedom from all ties of kinship, labor directed toward a useful end, and obedience to a superior.

To these motives of the monastic ideal the West also responded, but with less of fanaticism and more of the sense of peace and joy. The Christian communities, full of the spirit of apostolic love and already living in eternal life, turned aside without regret from the exhausted and sophisticated civilization of Rome to something purer and more worth while. For centuries, as the civic spirit decayed and the luxury of a parasitic economic class made obsolete the old virtues, men had been searching for something that would give them supreme, never-ending blessedness. Stoics, Epicureans, Platonists — none had been able to stave off the disillusion of a jaded palate. This blessedness the Christians had found. So long as the persecutions lasted, no man needed to seek the crucifixion of the flesh; soldiers and athletes of Christ found their discipline in training for the martyr's crown. But when Christianity became respectable, the universal laxity of morals, particularly that bane of the fathers, sexual promiscuity, crept into the fold with the new "converts." Then it was that multitudes turned away from such a world in quiet disdain and sought out for themselves a purer and a more temperate life. Those whom death had not daunted now fled from luxury and looseness to seek the highest. The athlete of Christ went forth from the community as from a bed of ease.

With the barbarian conquests and the general breakdown of civilized society, a new motive entered that persisted through the long ages to modern times. Monasteries were not only refuges from the temptations and the ugliness of this world; they were also strongholds of quiet in the midst of a sea of force, fighting, and indiscriminate struggle for existence. Those who refused to mould Christian love to the call of the war trumpet, those who from weakness had failed to hold their own amidst the buffets, those who were drawn toward the contemplative life of study and reflection, all alike found an oasis in the monastery. Thus the monasteries naturally absorbed all that was left of intellectual life, and, incidentally, became the sole repositories of ancient learning. But the monks must not be thought of as cowards. During the rudest portion of the dark ages they undertook the dangerous task of converting the barbarians to Christianity and civilization. The annals of Saint Columba, the apostle to Scotland, and Saint Boniface, the great German missionary, are as stirring as any of the tales of the Jesuits in North America; their task was the same, amid similar conditions. Nor did the monks stop with conversion. They became the pioneers in the new land, teaching the barbarians all they learned, from agricultural methods to Christian philosophy. Until the rise of the universities in the twelfth century, the monasteries were almost the sole seats of education. All that we boast of the pioneer spirit that has made America was the possession of the monks, under much greater obstacles.

For such men, renunciation of the world was the renunciation of the Pilgrim fathers, of the Oregon Trail. Even for those who pursued the *vita contemplativa*, and loved Christ with a love that culminated in mystic union, life was no barren mortification, it was the fruition of fulfilled desire, ecstasy, not asceticism. To us it may seem strange that Saint Francis did not miss our motor cars and our steam engines; we are not enamored of the dowry of his Lady Poverty. But even to-day we may be able to conceive that a richer life filled the great Abbey of Cluny, even the sparer Grande Chartreuse, than the mining-camp world from which it had withdrawn.

Rome took this mighty force and made of it a characteristically organized army, with a power of obedience and command, a force and energy aimed at a great purpose and controlled from the papal chair. From the great convent of Monte Cassino, south of Rome, Saint Benedict of Nursia sent forth the *regula* that was to furnish the law of the Western monks. To the minutest detail of his daily life the monk's existence was regulated, and yet the twofold prescription of seven hours daily of manual labor and two hours of literary study left the way flexibly open for his civilizing mission.

The fundamental ideal of monasticism as it lived in the Middle Ages, whatever it may have been earlier or become later, was the provision of a body of men consecrated and set apart to realize in their lives the Christian community of selfless love and humble service to all mankind. By clearing and draining the wilderness, tilling the soil, and making the desert to blossom as the rose; by introducing new ideas for the peasant, new processes for the craftsman, new styles for the architect; by caring for the poor, the sick, the wayfarer; by teaching and by training the young; by cultivating the quiet and hidden glory of the *vita contemplativa;* above all, by serving to all mankind as the perfect examplar of the principles of Christ applied to communal existence — the monks, in selfless love and humility to God and man, were to provide for the City of God an inexhaustible source of spiritual energy and power, the special vehicle for the influx into human life of Divine love and moral purity. What the Church should give in its vast and far-flung ramifications to all men, the monks should give to the Church. For this great boon men would in loving gratitude undertake to provide for this supremely important estate the wherewithal to perform their function. It is hardly too much to say that, in spite of all the abuses of a rebellious humanity, the monks fulfilled their task. In successive waves there did come from them an ever-overflowing fountain of moral energy, that gave the Middle Ages most of what they possessed of spiritual value. Some new reformer, when the fires of faith burned low, would always arise to recall men to their dimmed vision. Cluny in the tenth century, the Cistercians and Carthusians in the twelfth, the Franciscans and Dominicans in the thirteenth, Luther and Erasmus and the Reformation — all these movements renewing men's faith in the Christian principle came from the monks.

From this fundamental function spring the concomitants of the monastic way of life. The monks, that they may the better serve God and man, must be freed from all particular ties to take unto themselves the universal bonds of love. Hence the vows of poverty, chastity, and obedience. Chastity meant more than physical continence, with its assisting regimen of diet and fasting: it meant the breaking of the ties of love for father or mother, or child or sister, that all men might be the better served. Poverty meant absolute freedom from the bonds of things, rejection of all material interests, the better to serve man's true interests with no remorse. Obedience meant complete self-effacement, complete surrender to the will of God as interpreted by those in authority, the better to accomplish the Christian's tasks. It is true that these three vows meant the negation of the three great obligations of the ordinary man, the family, industrial life, and the state; they meant often disregard of the ecclesiastical hierarchy, save only the Pope. But they freed men only for the fuller service; they were the necessary discipline of the chosen regiment of God. Renunciation of what others enjoy, the supreme blessedness of bringing God closer to man in visible incarnation, of bringing man to God through act and example — this constituted the particular goal of the monk in the motley of the Middle Ages. This was the service of the saint.

To the modern mind the task which the monk set himself seems an impossible concentration of human energies. Only the very strongest of motives could enable a man to repress so much of what is natural and human, the desire for human relationships, the love of the natural goods of life, above all the strong and imperious sexual urges. It is no wonder that the records are full of the sad rebellions of outraged instincts, that the impurity complex flourished with its pathological concern with sex and its distorted fear of the most beneficent forces of life. It was no accident that the monastic orders were continually needing new "reforms" to restore them to their pristine austerity. For the average man, even the average monk of the Age of Faith, the repression was too much. So soon as society had a richer and more wholesome life to offer, the cloister proved impossible; and of all medieval institutions it first displayed widespread signs of decay. The very respect shown the monasteries heaped lands and riches upon them, and they acquired an economic function in medieval society that clashed sadly with their spiritual aim. Worldly motives increasingly drew their inmates; they took care of the surplus population which agriculture could not support, and came to furnish a good living with none of the responsibilities of parenthood. All these facts help to explain how from the thirteenth century onward it was upon the monk's head that were heaped the criticisms bred of the sense that society had outgrown its older institutions. To the townsman of the fourteenth or fifteenth centuries the monks were the worst example of the leisure class, the medieval counterpart of modern absentee landlords and capitalists.

But the monk at his best, not the self-seeking ascetic, but the integral and necessary member of the great body of Christ, flourished in innumerable ways, each differing from the others as the stars in glory. We can look more closely only at two great figures, supreme examples of two important types, Saint Bernard of Clairvaux and Saint Francis of Assisi. The one stands out as the leader of the ecclesiastical reforms of the early twelfth century, the age of the crusades, the other, as the expression of the very soul of the thirteenth century, the age of Thomas and Dante, the age that built the cathedrals.

Saint Bernard — The Monk

Bernard, strange figure of dramatic contradictions, equally full of the divine wrath and of the love of God, ascetic, mystic, orator, statesman, impelled at the age of twenty to lead his brothers and relatives from the life of the feudal nobility into the austerities of Citeaux, soon found too much ease even there, and, we may suspect, too little scope for his fiery will; and with twelve companions went forth to found a new abbey in the remote valley of Clairvaux, from those fastnesses to sway Christendom for a quarter of a century as rarely holy man before or since. Thenceforth, urged alike by his great zeal for making holiness to prevail and by the entreaties of his fellow men, he was ever roaming the world he had forsworn, electing and rebuking Popes, stemming both heresy and cruel fanaticism, preaching the Crusade and giving the Templars a rule, crushing the rationalism of Abélard, interfering in the remotest parts of Christendom wherever his watchful eye saw God's holy Church prostituted to selfish ends, writing letters, sermons, treatises, hymns; and yet ever sighing for the peace and obscurity of his cloister and the quiet that would allow him to pursue the mystic path to the face of God. Prizing above all things the contemplative life, his restless energies would allow him no peace so long as a single money-changer lurked in the house of God: he is the living refutation of monastic quietism. It was with true insight that Dante selected this monk as the revealer in the highest heaven of Paradise of the inmost mysteries of the vision of divine love.

For the keynote of Saint Bernard's life was the love of God

and man, even as it was the core of Saint Francis' being. But these two greatest exemplars of Christian saintliness stand for the two opposite poles of the Christian spirit, that inner bifurcation of temper that springs from the Gospels themselves. Both were on fire with an all-consuming love; but the love of Saint Bernard is that love of the good whose necessary counterpart is the hatred of evil, the primal love that must needs create a hell to vindicate the glories of heaven; while the love of Saint Francis is the love that, understanding all things, forgives all things. The one is the source of the reforming, even revolutionary zeal of the prophet, seeking to make all things new; the other is the tender and merciful compassion of the saint that solaces the disconsolate and comforts the weary while leaving the world to wag its way. The one is dualistic, absolutistic, profoundly social; the other is monistic, aware of the infinitely complex causes of things, individual. In Jesus the two loves seem to have been blended into one whole; in Bernard, love took form in wrath and stern rebuke, in Francis, in humility and obedience. Both are magnificent, but both are incomplete. Control and consolation are alike needed in the world of man.

The love of God made Bernard fearless in his wrath. To the great haughty giant, William, the well-nigh sovereign Duke of Aquitaine, who boasted that with his armed retainers at his back he feared neither God nor man, he commanded that he reinstate the bishops whom he had expelled. When words proved of no avail, Bernard proceeded to the mass, and with the consecrated host in his hand advanced toward the Duke with terrible authority:

We have besought you, and you have spurned us. This united multitude of the servants of God, meeting you elsewhere, has entreated you, and you have despised them. Behold, here comes to you the Virgin's Son, the Head and Lord of the Church which you persecute! Your Judge is here, at whose name every knee shall bow, of things in heaven, and things on earth, and things under the earth! Your Judge is here, into whose hands your soul is to pass! Will you spurn Him, also? Will you despise Him, as you have despised His servants? [5]

The dread count, at the head of his army, fell to the ground, then, lifted up, meekly did the monk's bidding. To the King Bernard wrote:

It is a fearful thing to fall into the hands of the living God, even for thee, O King.[6]

And to the very Pope himself he could say:

Remember, first of all, that the holy Roman Church, over which thou art chief, is the mother of churches, not their sovereign mistress; that thou thyself art not the lord of bishops, but one among them, a brother of those delighting in God, and a partaker with those that fear him. For the rest, regard thyself as under obligation to be the figure of justice, the mirror of holiness, the exemplar of piety, the restorer of its freedom to truth, the defender of the faith, the teacher of nations, the guide of Christians, the friend of the Bridegroom, the bridesman of the Bride, the regulator of the clergy, the pastor of the people, the master of the foolish, the refuge of the oppressed, the advocate of the poor, the hope of the suffering, the protector of orphans, the judge of widows, eyes to the blind, a tongue to the dumb, the staff of the aged, an avenger of crimes, a terror to evil-doers, and a glory to the good, a rod for the powerful, a hammer for tyrants, the father of kings, the director of laws, the superintendent of canons, the salt of the earth, the light of the world, the priest of the Most High, the vicar of Christ, the anointed of the Lord. Remember what I say, and the Lord give thee understanding.[7]

Yet bitter as was his hatred of the infidel and the heretic, those who of their own free will rejected the love of God, it was their good he sought, not their destruction. When the fanaticism of the Crusades awoke men's baser passions, and a German monk preached "Death to the Jews" along the Rhine, the Archbishop of Mainz called him to quell the popular outburst. "The Church triumphs more abundantly over the Jews," he wrote, "in every day convincing and converting them, than if it were to give them all on the instant to be consumed by the sword."[8] Against the intolerant leader he exploded, "Oh, monstrous doctrine! Oh, what infernal counsel! contrary to prophets, hostile to apostles, practically subversive of all piety and grace! — a sacrilegious harlot of a doctrine, impregnated with the very spirit of falsehood, conceiving anguish, and bringing forth iniquity!"[9] Letters proving futile, he betook himself to Mainz, met the monk Rudolf and broke his spirit, and dispersed the mob in confusion, by the force of his own fiery will. Even to the heretical sects who were teaching doctrines he regarded as shameful and of the devil his spirit was compassionate. "They are to be overcome,"

THE CITY OF GOD

he said, "not with weapons, but with arguments; to be led back to the faith by instruction and persuasion." [10]

This indignation at iniquity was but the reverse of the shield whose face was the mystic love of God. Bernard's eloquence here finds its true theme.

I should call love undefiled because it keeps nothing of its own. Indeed it has nothing of its own, for everything which it has is God's. The undefiled law of the Lord is love, which seeks not what profits itself but what profits many. . . . It is not irrational to speak of God as living by law, that law being love. Indeed in the blessed highest Trinity what preserves that highest ineffable unity, except love?

Yet because we are of the flesh and are begotten through the concupiscence of the flesh, our yearning love must begin from the flesh; yet if rightly directed, advancing under the leadership of grace, it will be consummated in spirit. For that which is first is not spiritual, but that which is natural; then that which is spiritual. First man loves himself for his own sake. For he is flesh, and is able to understand nothing beyond himself. When he sees that he cannot live by himself alone, he begins, as it were from necessity, to seek and love God. Thus, in this second stage, he loves God, but only for his own sake. Yet as his necessities lead him to cultivate and dwell with God in thinking, reading, praying, and obeying, God little by little becomes known and becomes sweet. Having thus tasted how sweet is the Lord, he passes to the third stage, where he loves God for God's sake. Whether any man in this life has perfectly attained the fourth stage, where he loves himself for God's sake, I do not know. Let those say who have knowledge; for myself I confess it seems impossible. Doubtless it will be so when the good and faithful servant shall have entered into the joy of his Lord, and shall be drunk with the flowing richness of God's house. Then oblivious to himself he will pass to God and become one spirit with Him.[11]

This final consummation of the soul's union with God, Bernard, with the whole Christian tradition, symbolized by the marriage of the Bride with the Bridegroom, drawing upon the burning phrases of the *Song of Songs*. In the holy union of man and wife the ascetic monk found the only adequate shadowing forth of perfect spiritual joy.

O love [he cries], headlong, vehement, burning, impetuous, that canst think of nothing beyond thyself, detesting all else, despising all else, satisfied with thyself! Thou dost confound ranks, carest for no usage, knowest no measure. In thyself dost thou triumph over apparent opportuneness, reason, shame, council and judgment, and leadest them into captivity. Everything which the soul-bride utters resounds of thee and nothing else; so hast thou possessed her heart and tongue.[12]

Saint Francis — The Mendicant Friar

That love which proved the imperious master of Bernard burned deeper and perhaps purer in the life of Francis of Assisi. He who has become the most saintly of all the saints, the most Christlike of Christians, shone by no intellectual force: he taught nothing new, he never had an original thought. He lived untouched by the stirring events of his day, in them but not of them. Clerical corruption and its rebuking were not for him, nor the putting down of heresy or schism. Politics, war, the vexed problems of changing social relations, meant nothing to him. Of theological learning, of Augustine and scholasticism, he possessed not a trace; he had not even any sense of the organization of the medieval hierarchy. He went through life with a childlike wonder and joy, a freshness and a spontaneity that brooked no knowledge or deliberation. He struck men's imaginations, not their minds; he was the very incarnation of the Gospel ideal. If the function of the monasteries was to bring God's fullness nearer to mortal man, it was the supreme accomplishment of Francis that he visibly embodied it. Not what he did, but what he was: this was the repetition of Bethlehem, this *was* the love of God made flesh once more among men. Francis had only to *be* to prove the reality of the Christian faith.

We have seen how Bernard's love and faith were essentially dualistic, the type of the prophetic strain in Christianity. Francis was monistic to the very core of his being: he beheld only God. He never saw the world as it exists; for him it was always as it really is in God's purpose, made whole and perfect. From the day when he rode forth from Assisi singing French songs of joy that he was to take part in the romantic quest of chivalry, he never lost the childlike innocence that imagines that what men admire as best really is the way of the world. When Roland and King Arthur claimed his allegiance, he sought to imitate the perfect knight, down to the last detail; when Christ was his master, it was not otherwise. In very truth he was Parsifal, the pure fool.

Seeing only God in all things, it was natural that Francis should love every man, every beast of the field and bird of the air, that he should rejoice in that fellowship with nature that is bred of and breeds pantheism of the spirit. This is God's world, and man and beast are God's holy creatures. Hence ascetic dualism, renunciation, withdrawal from the world, scourging the unjust and fighting sin, were quite incomprehensible to him. Thus quite naturally he dwelt among men, trusting in their bounty, taking no thought for the morrow; and all his ministry to the poor and the sick was filled with the spirit of joy, not the fierce joy that comes from the conscious doing of God's will, but the simple joy in men and women, in the very beauty of his life with Lady Poverty. In the order of mendicant friars that grew up about him this preaching and service in the market-place became the dominant note; where the earlier monasteries had been as remote as possible, the Franciscans placed their houses in cities, and were ever wandering from town to town. But Francis had no fixed purpose of changing the *vita contemplativa* into the *vita activa;* his love of the world would not permit another existence. He was not active, like Bernard; he did actually nothing of any importance. His acts were of value chiefly as expressions of what he was, as symbols of that reality that could do so much for man.

The story of Saint Francis' life, how he was born in Assisi a merchant's son, how he passed a gay youth, enjoying merriment and fine raiment, but kept by an innate delicacy and love of chivalry and its trappings from anything coarse or base, how he dreamed of becoming a fine knight; then how he turned to the poor and the lepers, was disowned by his indignant father, and, still singing joyous French songs, dwelt in the little church of the Portiuncula with his companions — all this is as well known as the gospel story itself. Many a painter, too, from Giotto down, has tried his hand at the portrayal of those poetic moments in his life when the fullness of his spirit poured itself out without stint or limit: at Saint Peter's in Rome, where, offended that the Prince of the Apostles was being honored with such mean offerings, he flung down his whole purse and went to ask alms in a beggar's garb; before the Bishop, when he returned not only his money but all his garments to his father, and renounced earthly parents for his Heavenly Father; at the conversion of his first disciple, when opening the Scriptures after prayer he read, "If thou wouldst be perfect, go, sell all that thou hast, and give to the poor, and thou shalt have treasure in heaven," which they obeyed to the letter; or those innumerable incidents, of which his sermon to the birds is but one, in which love for God's creatures filled his heart.

Poverty, a high-born lady, poor and beautiful, he had seen in a vision, in the midst of a desert, and worthy to be wooed by the King. To the brethren he said, " Best beloved brothers and my children, do not be ashamed to go for alms, because the Lord made Himself poor for us in this world after whose example we have chosen the truest poverty." [13] Holy obedience, too, he loved, though he could on occasion stand up to cardinal or pope and gain his will. He resigned the headship of his order in part that he might have a superior to obey in all humility. But the virtue he elevated highest was joy. His life was one long pæan of praise.

Drunken with the love and pity of Christ, the blessed Francis would sometimes act like this, for the sweetest melody of spirit within him often boiling outward gave sound in French, and the strain of the divine whisper which his ear had taken secretly, broke forth in a glad French song. He would pick up a stick, and holding it over his left arm, would with another stick in his right hand make as if drawing a bow over a violin, and with fitting gestures would sing in French of the Lord Jesus Christ.[14]

Francis' spirit shines forth best of all in the one work he left, the Lauds, or Canticle of Brother Sun.

Most High, omnipotent, good Lord, thine is the praise, the glory, the
    honor and every benediction;
To Thee alone, Most High, these do belong, and no man is worthy to
    name Thee.
Praised be Thou, my Lord, with all thy creatures, especially my lord
    Brother Sun that dawns and lightens us;
And he, beautiful and radiant with great splendor, signifies thee,
    Most High.
Be praised, my Lord, for Sister Moon, and the stars that thou hast
    made bright and precious and beautiful.
Be praised, my Lord, for Brother Wind, and for the air and cloud and
    the clear sky and for all weathers through which thou givest
    sustenance to thy creatures.
Be praised, my Lord, for Sister Water, that is very useful and humble
    and precious and chaste.
Be praised, my Lord, for Brother Fire, through whom thou dost illumine
    the night, and comely is he and glad and bold and strong.
Be praised, my Lord, for Sister, Our Mother Earth, that doth cherish
    and keep us, and produces various fruits with colored flowers
    and the grass.

Be praised, my Lord, for those who forgive for love of thee, and endure
    sickness and tribulation; blessed are they who endure in peace;
    for by Thee, Most High, shall they be crowned.
Be praised, my Lord, for our bodily death, from which no living man
    can escape; woe unto those who die in mortal sin.
Blessed are they that have found thy most holy will, for the second
    death shall do them no hurt.
Praise and bless my Lord, and render thanks, and serve Him with great
    humility.[15]

THE CHURCH AS THE CITY OF GOD AND THE BODY OF CHRIST

If the monks were an order set apart to realize the ideal of individual saintliness, the medieval social ideal of an all-embracing Christian commonwealth was the special province of the Church in her secular organization. Saint Augustine's City of God, eternally at war with the city of this world, had conquered at last; under Gregory the Seventh and his successors, from the middle of the eleventh to the end of the thirteenth century, the Church freed itself from the divided and secular control of the earlier period of the *Landeskirche* — that time when the great Archbishops of Rheims and Mainz and Milan were practically independent and hereditary feudal lords — and achieved, with unity, a dominion over all the energies of men.

Depositary of the truth, and only depositary of the truth, by divine revelation, the Church, under the guidance of the papacy, seeks to realize the truth in every reach of life, and to control, in the light of Christian principle, every play of human activity. Learning and education, trade and commerce, war and peace, are all to be drawn into her orbit. By the application of Christian principle a great synthesis of human life is to be achieved, and the *lex Christi* is to be made a *lex animata in terris*.

This was the greatest ambition that has ever been cherished. . . . The City of God which the great medieval popes were seeking to establish was a city of this world, if not of this world only. It was a fusion of the actual Church, reformed by papal direction and governed by papal control, with actual lay society, similarly reformed and similarly governed. Logically this meant a theocracy, and the bull of Boniface VIII, "We proclaim, declare, and pronounce that it is altogether necessary to salvation for every human being to be subject to the Roman pontiff," was its necessary outcome. But a theocracy was only a means, and a means that was never greatly emphasized in the best days of the papacy. It was the end that mattered; and the end was the moulding of human life into conformity with divine truth. The end may appear fantastic, unless one remembers the plenitude of means which stood at the command of the medieval Church. The seven sacraments had become the core of her organization. Central among the seven stood the sacrament of the Mass, in which bread and wine were transubstantiated into the divine body and blood of our Lord. By that sacrament men could touch God; and by its mediation the believer met the supreme object of his belief. Only the priest could celebrate the great mystery; and only those who were fit could be admitted by him to participation. The sacrament of penance, which became the antechamber, as it were, to the Mass, enabled the priest to determine the terms of admission. Outside the sacraments stood the Church courts, exercising a large measure of ethical and religious discipline over all Christians; and in reserve, most terrible of all weapons, were the powers of excommunication and interdict, which could shut men and cities from the rites of the Church and the presence of the Lord. Who shall say, remembering these things, that the aims of the medieval Church were visionary or impracticable?[16]

We shall see in the next chapter how the Church took unto herself all the estates of the realm, all the members of the Body of Christ, consecrating and idealizing the institutions of medieval society. The knightly class she first attempted to control through the Truce of God, imposing limitations upon private warfare; then in chivalry she enlisted the fighting instincts of feudal society under her own banner, making the initiation into knighthood almost an eighth sacrament, an ordination, and directing barbarian pugnacity and commercial imperialism into the channels of the Crusades, the greatest common enterprise of a united Christendom. In trade and commerce she sought to transmute competition and greed into Christian love and service, making of every guild a religious organization; while the learning of the great universities was made to serve Christian ends. Upon the whole of society she stamped the conception of a wise and beneficent organized spiritual power to which men in every walk of life owed supreme obligations and which in turn should regulate and elevate their natural pursuits. It is this marvelous capacity for taking up into one whole all the varied and divergent desires of a complex civilization and directing them toward a single common end, that is the spiritual glory of the Middle Ages and their Church, and it is just this idea of a unified spiritual power that sets them off most sharply from the present day.

[16] From *Unity of Western Civilization*, by F. S. Marvin. Reprinted by permission of the publishers, Oxford University Press.

The Ideal of Organized Spiritual Power

Though this vision dawned upon the monk Hildebrand who became Pope Gregory VII in 1073, it was Innocent III, *Dominus Dominantium*, greatest of popes, to whom at the beginning of the thirteenth century it was given in some measure to realize it. A high-spirited, imperious Roman noble, a scholar and a preacher, bred upon the canon law that was the legal formulation of the supreme claims of the Church to regulate society, he truly believed that to him as the apostolic successor of Peter God had said, "I have set thee over the nations and over the kingdoms, to root out, and to pull down, and to destroy, and to throw down, and to build and to plant." [17] The heir of Bernard's reforming zeal, he ruled his Church with an iron hand. To the clergy he thundered:

The lust of the flesh pertaineth to voluptuousness, the lust of the eyes to riches, the pride of life to honors; and by these three bonds are we clergy especially bound. ... To us the prophet spoke: "Be ye clean that bear the vessels of the Lord." Foul to speak of, most foul to do; there are some who worship the son of Venus by night in the bedchamber and in the morning offer up the Son of the Virgin on the altar. ... And also the rope of avarice holds us so tight that many of us do not blush to buy and sell and practice usury; from the prophet even unto the priest they are given to covetousness, and from the least of them even unto the greatest of them, every one dealeth falsely. And the rope of pride holds us so fast that we had rather appear proud than humble, and we walk head high, with eyes uplifted and neck erect; ... and we are far from imitating Him who said, "Learn of me, for I am meek and lowly in spirit." [18]

This was the proud ruler who accepted the realm of England from King John as a papal fief; who crowned Otto of Brunswick Emperor and saw his cause prosper until insubordination brought excommunication, then chose and established Frederick; to whom the King of Aragon freely did homage as vassal; who rated the kings of Castile, Leon, and Portugal like schoolboys and warned and admonished those of Norway, Hungary, and Armenia. Under him — and the greedy Venetians who plundered Constantinople during the Fourth Crusade — the schismatic Greeks professed obedience to the Roman See. Of him Saint Francis sought authorization for his order; to him came ceaselessly Saint Dominic to serve and obey. He it was who assembled the great Lateran Council, the chief œcumenical council of the Church in the Middle Ages, and before it preached a new crusade for a united Christendom. Even in his death he vindicated the divine governance of the world by a fitting expiation of his necessary pride. In Perugia, where he died, his body being left alone unwatched in the church, "During the night," tells the pious Jacques de Vitry, "thieves stripped it of its precious vestments and left it almost naked and stinking in the church. And I with my own eyes have seen how brief, vain, and deceitful is the glory of this world." [19]

But there was another side to the medieval ideal of an organized spiritual power guiding all men toward a single goal. Attractive as it now seems to many gazing afar from the warring nationalisms and selfish struggle of class against class for the goods of this world, we cannot forget that modern history is in large part a revolt against precisely this side of the Middle Ages. If Western Europe seems in the last four hundred years to have sacrificed, in the name of liberty, a precious heritage of unity in aspiration and action, it can only be understood as a long, slow, and painful reaction against the medieval sacrifice of liberty to unity. The thirteenth century knew liberty, of course; the knight, the craftsman, perhaps even the serf, enjoyed almost as much of its fruits as the average worker to-day, all things considered. Even in thought, before the Reformation caused in Catholics and Protestants alike a tightening of doctrinal orthodoxy, there were within the broad frame of the Christian tradition as great divergences of philosophy and opinion as have ever existed. But the very conception of such a spiritual power necessarily implies that it shall act in certain ways; and these ways are not the ways approved by the theories widely held to-day, even though they be tolerated in practice by most men, including some of the most intelligent. Of course it is a commonplace that the inquisitorial powers which the Church formerly exercised have now been largely taken over by the national State. Such governments, though not claiming in theory to be spiritual powers, in practice often attempt the same strict control of beliefs and ideals as well as of actions. In spite of our professions, we moderns, in political and social matters at least, really believe as much in the medieval conception of doctrinal unity as did the Holy Office.

Such a conception, accepted in the Middle Ages in theory as

well as in practice, implies that the power is in possession of the truth, and that any attempt to seek it elsewhere, any doubt or questioning save upon its established axioms, is to be discouraged. It implies that there is but one way of life that can be permitted to men, and that the errant must be warned back as much for his own sake as for the safety of others. It implies that liberty is only perfect obedience to perfect law, and that the body of that perfect law is known. It implies a despotism that may or may not be benevolently paternalistic. It forbids the free search of the spirit for new truth and new light, and makes forever impossible the glorious adventuring of the untrammeled mind, that human striving immortalized in *Faust* that forever links the possibility of the attainment of truth with the possibility of error. As in Dante's great work, it elevates into cosmic terms petty and transitory human likes and hatreds. In Santayana's words, "It shows how desperate at heart is the folly of an egotistic or anthropocentric philosophy. This philosophy begins by assuring us that everything is obviously created to serve our needs; it then maintains that everything serves our ideals; and in the end it reveals that everything serves our blind hatreds and superstitious qualms." [20] It is overweening in its pride, blind in its intolerance, cruel in its self-righteousness. Aiming at a common purpose, it inevitably divides and digs chasms; and the unity it achieves is often such as to make the very word an abomination to the eyes and a stench in the nostrils.

There is no need here either to belabor the Inquisition once more or to reverence the earnest, upright, and sincere character of those who steeled themselves to practice it. Granted the presuppositions of the Church, that she was indeed the sole vehicle of a divinely revealed, and hence immutable, authoritative, and necessary truth, the expediency of the methods of the Inquisition may be questioned, but their logic and their morality are irrefutable. The most merciful love is then truly the extirpation of heresy root and branch, with fire and sword; and the blows fall upon the simple, pious, and evangelical love of the Waldensians and upon the destructive asceticism of the Albigensian Cathari alike. It is both the unforgivable sin and the greatest of tragedies that men should wreak intolerable wrong

[20] From *Three Philosophical Poets*, by George Santayana. Reprinted by permission of the publishers, Harvard University Press.

upon other men while earnestly and sincerely serving what they believe to be most high.

Saint Dominic, inseparably linked with Saint Francis, yet never loved and seldom admired, stands for this side of Christian faith, the great contrast with the Christian love of him of Assisi. He was a scholar and a theologian, a man of boundless energy and of compassion withal, much given to tears, who was touched to the quick by the prevalence of heresies in the brilliant, restless civilization of the south of France. He devoted his life to the founding of an order that should be the weapon of the Pope in support of right doctrine. He believed himself in preaching and exhortation, and did not found the Inquisition or take part in the bloody Albigensian crusade. But correct faith was his priceless jewel, and its keeping was soon given to the *Domini canes*, the hounds of the Lord. It is a sufficient commentary on the glory and the weakness of the doctrinal ideal in the Christian tradition that the "Preaching Friars" soon gained control of the universities and in Albertus Magnus and Saint Thomas lifted the torch of Christian knowledge to its highest point, and that into their dread keeping were given the terrible powers of the Inquisition.

The unity of the City of God and the Body of Christ is magnificent, but it can be purchased at too great price: amidst all its baser, more material shortcomings, the modern world carried this lesson from the Middle Ages.

REFERENCES

1. Thomas Aquinas, *Commentary on Nicomachean Ethics*, Lib. I.
2. Romans, XII, 4, 5. Corinthians, XII, 26.
3. Thomas à Kempis, *The Imitation of Christ*, chs. II, III.
4. Ernest Barker, *Unity in the Middle Ages*, in F. S. Marvin, *Unity of Western Civilization*, 110.
5. R. S. Storrs, *Bernard of Clairvaux*, 168, cited.
6. Bernard, *Ep. 170 ad Ludovicum* (cited by Taylor, *Medieval Mind*, I, 416).
7. Bernard, *Opera*, I, *De consideratione*, Paris, 1839; cited by Storrs, 175.
8. Cited by Storrs, 179.
9. *Epistola ccclxv*, cited by Storrs, 179, 180.
10. *Ibid.*, 181.
11. Bernard, *Ep. 11 ad Guigonem;* cited by Taylor, I, 421.
12. Bernard, *Sermo lxxix in Cantica;* Taylor, I, 427.
13. Francis, *Speculum Perfectionis*, 18.
14. *Ibid.*, 93.
15. *Ibid.*, 120.
16. Barker, in F. S. Marvin, *Unity of Western Civilization*, 101.
17. Jeremiah, I, 10.
18. Henry Dwight Sedgwick, *Italy in the Thirteenth Century*, I, 77, 78.

THE CITY OF GOD

19. Paul Sabatier, *Life of St. Francis of Assisi*, ch. 12.
20. George Santayana, *Three Philosophical Poets*, ch. III, "Dante," 115.

SELECTED READING LISTS

Medieval Social Ideal: E. Barker, *Unity in the Middle Ages*, in F. S. Marvin, *Unity of Western Civilization*, emphasizing collectivism; cf. M. De Wulf, *Philosophy and Civilization in the Middle Ages*, ch. X, for the individualistic strain. Augustine, *City of God;* Troeltsch, ch. 2; Henry Adams.

The Medieval Church: A. L. Guérard, *French Civilization*, Pt. II, Bk. i; C. Guignebert, *Christianity, Past and Present;* H. E. Barnes, *H. of Western Civilization*, ch. xix. *Cam. Med. Hist.*, I, chs. iv–vi, xvii–xxi. A. C. Flick, *The Rise of the Medieval Church*, *The Decline of the Med. Church*. Church histories by Fisher, A. H. Newman, W. Moeller, Protestants, and Alzog, Catholic. Critical estimate by Lecky, *H. of Rationalism*, Pt. I, ch. iv, Pt. II; G. G. Coulton, *Five Centuries of Religion*. On the social work of the Church, E. L. Cutts, *Parish Priests and their People in the M.A.*; G. A. Prévost, *L'Église et les campagnes au. M.A.*; Queen, *Social Work in the Light of History*.

The Papacy and the Inquisition: W. O. Ault, *Europe in the M.A.*, c. 23; H. D. Sedgwick, *Italy in the 13th c.*; *Cam. Med. H.*, VI, c. 1, 16. S. Baldwin, *Organization of Med. Christianity;* S. R. Packard, *Europe and the Church under Innocent III.* H. C. Lea, *H. of the Inquisition in the M.A.*, esp. I, III, c. 8; Catholic defenses, by E. Vacandard and A. L. Maycock.

The Monastic Ideal: H. O. Taylor, *Classical Heritage of the M.A.*, c. 7; A. Harnack, *Monasticism;* H. B. Workman, *Evolution of the Monastic Ideal*. *Cam. Med. Hist.*, I, c. 18; II, c. 16; V, c. 20. The classic work is Montalembert, *Monks of the West from St. Benedict to St. Bernard;* criticism in Guignebert, G. G. Coulton, *Five Centuries of Religion*. Jerome, lives of *Paul the first Hermit*, of *St. Anthony*, Nicene Fathers ed. *Life of St. Columban*, Trans. and Reprints U. of P., ii, 7; Benedictine Rule in E. F. Henderson, *Select Documents of the M.A.*; E. C. Butler, *Benedictine Monasticism*. Arts. "Cluniac Movement," "Dominican Friars," in *En. Soc. Sciences*. Taylor, *Medieval Mind*, Bk. III, c. 18, Bernard, c. 19, Francis. Lives of Bernard by R. S. Storrs, E. Vacandard. Lives of Francis by Paul Sabatier (a classic), Le Monnier, L. Salvatorelli. Francis' *Works*, tr. P. Robinson; *Speculum Perfectionis*, ed. P. Sabatier. Lives of Dominic by J. Guiraud, Bede Jarrett. Interpretations by William James, *Varieties of Religious Experience*, chs. 11–13; G. Flaubert, *Temptation of St. Anthony*.

CHAPTER V

THE EMBODIMENT — LAY SOCIETY

WITH such an aim and such an instrument for bringing beliefs and institutions into line with this aim, the thirteenth century found appropriate expression for its restless energies. The basic social institution, agriculture, embracing the vast majority of the population, was ordered on the manorial system, a thing that seems to owe nothing to the Christian tradition and little to any theory whatever. It enabled the peasants to support the knightly class, also an almost universal phenomenon, and certainly far removed from the ancient Hebrew democracy, the non-resistant love of the Gospels, or the renunciation of the Neo-platonists. The rising towns with their trade, their growing craftsmanship, and the new class of burghers devoted to business — the novel and disruptive force in late medieval society — had similarly little to do with Christian salvation. Nor did it seem that the restless curiosity of the universities, all the more intense that it was limited to the matters of common observation and repute to work upon, could easily be assimilated by a system that had again and again denounced the snares of learning.

And yet the miracle was achieved. All these forces were taken up and accorded their appropriate place in the Christian Commonwealth. Their roots in the natural desires and needs of that growing society, their branches were drawn to the heaven of the Son of God. From one point of view the medieval synthesis was a great supernatural structure leading men away from the world into which they are born; from another, and perhaps deeper, it was the natural flowering of a social life of peculiar richness, and singularly free from the distortions, the blindnesses, the one-sidedness of our later age.

FEUDAL SOCIETY

Since Europe lived by farming, the relation of men to the land was the very foundation of society. Just because it was so basic, it stretched back into the immemorial past, and by the thirteenth century had become a complex mass of customs and usages whose authority lay primarily in the fact that to men it seemed they had always been so — though of course they had undergone a constant modification as social conditions had changed. Most unchanging of all were the relations of that unit of medieval society, the vil or manor. The self-contained estate of serfs attached to the soil, owing agricultural and military services of various kinds to the lord, and in return receiving the right to protection and to land, is a very natural institution, growing up in such distant places as Mexico, Japan, Madagascar, and Abyssinia; for a rude and primitive society it appears to be far more natural than the independent farm. In Western Europe it goes back to the days of the late Roman *villa*. With the break-up of Charlemagne's empire this type of relation was gradually made the chief social bond between the various manors as well. The origins of feudalism are complex and vague; something like it, in the subordination of man to man and land to land, for the sake of protection, existed in Roman Gaul, and the barbarians brought with them the clannish idea of the personal bond uniting leaders and followers. The conquest created a privileged class which soon merged with those who by luck, cunning, or prowess rose to power. Since land was the only form of wealth, and since money was almost non-existent, the leaders naturally gave it with its fruits to those whose service they wished to reward or secure, for their support in arms and followers. Thus the lords of the manor held their estates, and with them, in the absence of much central authority, an almost complete sovereignty, in return for military and other services; for their own part, they received protection and various other rights.

In theory, feudal society should have been a symmetrical pyramid, every landholder with an overlord, who, in his turn, with his peers, would be bound to one higher still, until at the apex stood the king, who held his rights from God under the guidance of the Church. The tie should have been a mutual loyalty and obligation, of service performed in return for service. In reality, there was no feudal *system;* the lord might hold land from his vassals, or from a mixture of warring overlords and ecclesiastics. The oath of loyalty never prevented war either between barons or between vassal and overlord. Every one grabbed what land and power he could, and observed a mass of irrational customs. The theory of feudalism was formulated only when its force had waned, as a rationalization of the existent disorder. "As a matter of fact, the essence of the régime which prevailed in the Early Middle Ages was neither 'the confusion of property and authority,' nor 'the delegation of property as a reward for service.' It was, at first, chaos roughly organized; later on, confusion perpetuated by custom." [1]

But this does not alter the significance of the fundamental principles involved. It was recognized that property and its attendant authority — for of course they have always been confused — should be, even if they often were not, not an absolute possession or a sacred right, but the condition of the performance of service. The king owed obligations to his vassals and the lords to their serfs just as much as vassals and serfs to their lords. This merged naturally into the Christian ideal of property as essentially a stewardship for the brethren. The bond of economic society thus became essentially a personal relation of faith and trust and mutual obligation, and by this standard all mere force and custom could be judged. The peasant and the lord took their place in the Christian Commonwealth, and the way was paved for the emergence of the knightly class, bound together by a strict code of honor, united by contract and not by compulsion, hallowed by the double brotherhood of soldiers and Christians.

The Knightly Ideal

The ideal of the knight is a part of the medieval mind that has in its fundamentals remained with Europe to this day. In its modern form of the gentleman it still exerts an incalculable influence. Like all medieval ideals, it is a class ideal; it does not stretch beyond the pale, even where the normal and unrebuked indifference and cruelty to the peasants, those beasts of another blood, is tempered by Christian chivalry. But as lived by the great Crusaders, as idealized in chivalry and the romances, before the artificiality of the troubadours and the degeneration of its natural basis, it is a priceless part of our heritage.

The knight or chevalier was the possessor of at least enough land to support the full equipment of a horseman. His steed lifted him above the common man to a fighting class in which, theoretically, all riders were equals in a brotherhood of arms.

This gave him the right to fight his peers, a privilege which the absence of window-glass and the consequent cold and dark houses made a pleasant form of exercise, more exciting than his other occupation, hunting. Plundering and robbing, too, was profitable; so was the business of defeating other knights and collecting ransoms. There were not enough external foes to keep these gentlemen busy, so that private warfare occupied most of their attention. The Church first tried to limit it, to protect its own lands and later the peasants. The Truce of God enjoined a peaceful week-end, and finally limited the open season for human game to Monday, Tuesday, and Wednesday of certain weeks only. This was not very successful; then she had the happy inspiration of sending the trouble-makers off to the Holy Land with as many of the worse elements in society as could be prevailed upon to accompany them for the sake of booty and the love of God.

Out of these rather unpromising materials the Middle Ages developed the order of chivalry and all the knightly virtues. It sought a blend between the barbarian warrior and the Christian saint, and though this reached its consummate expression in the foundation of the great crusading Orders of the Templars, Hospitallers, and Teutonic Knights, which added the monastic to the knightly vows, in some measure chivalry became itself an order, blessed, sanctified, and inspired by the Church. Knighthood was made, not the hereditary appurtenance of land, but a personal distinction, to be won by high and low alike — within the class of nobles — only after long training, proved worth, and religious ordination.

The knight was first and last a warrior. Hence valor, personal and physical, was his prime quality. The reckless courage of Roland, who from pride and confidence refused to blow his mighty war-horn for Charlemagne when the Moors ambushed the rear guard of the Frankish army, and thus doomed his fellows to destruction, had its counterpart in many of the great fighters, like Godfrey of Bouillon and Richard the Lion-Hearted; it was forever making impossible anything like sound military tactics. The French knights lost to the English bowmen at Crécy from the very defects of their chief virtue. Of equal importance was loyalty; for the performance of the numerous vows of medieval society, the very structure of feudal obligations, depended upon it. To secure the performance of service from the ordinary man, the full force of faith in the magical efficacy of a vow blessed by the Church, or made on some holy relic, was always invoked; but the knight was expected to keep his word, though the wise took precautions. Roland expresses this feudal loyalty admirably as he goes into battle:

> And for his lord great evil a good man must endure,
> And bear great heat, moreover, and likewise bitter cold.
> And flesh and blood of his body to lose he must be bold.
>
> Smite with the lance. With Durendal the battle will I try,
> The good blade the king gave me. And if I hap to die,
> He that shall have it hereafter, shall say about the sword,
> That it was a good vassal's who was faithful to his lord.[2]

The traitor, not to country but to his overlord, is the object of chief execration. Ganelon in the *Song of Roland*, who betrays the hero; Sir Modred the rebel against King Arthur; King John of England, false to his brother in Palestine — these are the favorite villains. Not only are traitors placed in the lowest circle of Dante's Hell, but traitors to their lords are placed below traitors to kin, country, and hospitality. The heinousness of Satan's sin is that he rebelled against his suzerain. According to the typically feudal atonement theory of Anselm, Adam's fall lay in his violation of God's trust in him, and his wanton desertion to the side of the traitorous Lucifer.

In the great medieval poems, the tragedy is typically the conflict between two loyalties, and the inevitable disaster it must bring. Tristram is destroyed between loyalty to his king and to his lady Iseult; Paolo owes allegiance both to his brother and lord and to his love Francesca; Hagen, in the *Niebelungenlied*, is driven by allegiance to his lord's wife to murder treacherously his friend and guest Siegfried; saddest of all, the good and noble Lancelot, very model of a perfect knight, is crushed between what he owes Arthur and what he owes his lady Guinevere. Touching are the words of Rüdiger in the *Niebelungenlied*. To him Queen Kriemhild appeals, that he should slay her enemies, his guests: "Bethink thee, Rüdiger, of thy great fealty, of thy constancy, and of thine oaths, that thou wouldst ever avenge mine injuries and all my woes." Sadly he replies, "There's no denying that I swore to you, my lady, for your sake I'd risk both life and honor, but I did not swear that I would lose my soul. 'Twas I that bade the highborn lordings to this feast." Again friendship and hospitality are pitted against feudal fealty. "Woe is me, most wretched man, that I have lived to see this day. I must give over all my honors, my fealty, my courtesy, that God did bid me use. . . . I shall act basely and full evil, whatever I do or leave undone. But if I give over both, then will all people blame me. Now may he advise me, who hath given me life." [3]

The third of the knightly virtues was largesse or bounty, most useful and prime means of winning men in those days. Such liberality was necessary to secure retainers, and largely their reward. Perhaps most characteristic of all was honor, dignity, or self-respect, the mark of the superior class, not to display which set the knight below the level of his comrades. He must stand on his rights as a man, resenting every insult and returning blow for blow. From this sprang the long stupidities of outraged "honor," of the duel and the feud, also pride and cruelty to inferiors. To these warrior virtues, however, were added the more Christian traits of magnanimity, fairness, justice, and that courtesy that is the offspring of mingled pride and humility. From courtesy sprang both the romance of the knight-errant, wandering abroad to succor the distressed, and the artificial codes of knightly love that in its later days supplanted the earlier fighting chivalry.

For illustrations of the perfect knight we might turn to the valorous, pure, and humble Godfrey of Bouillon, who shared the simplicity and childlike faith of the First Crusade, in his setting of Homeric heroes; or better still to that medieval gentleman and saint, Louis IX of France, wise and firm ruler, dispensing patriarchal justice under the oak tree at Vincennes, simple and pious, brave and courteous fighter. "He was the most loyal man of his time," writes his vassal the Sire de Joinville, "and kept faith even with the Saracens, and to his own disadvantage." [4] Romance is full of such figures, hardly surpassing reality — Lancelot, Galahad, King Arthur himself. But it will suffice to use that brush of Chaucer that never painted men as they were not.

> A Knight ther was, and that a worthy man,
> That from the tyme that he first began

88 THE OUTLOOK OF MEDIEVAL CHRISTENDOM

> To ryden out, he loved chivalrye,
> Trouthe and honour, freedom and curteisye.
> Full worthy was he in his lordes werre,
> And therto hadde he riden (no man ferre)
> As wel in Cristendom as hethenesse,
> And ever honoured for his worthinesse ...
> At mortal batailles hadde he been fiftene,
> And foughten for our faith at Tramissene
> In listes thryes, and ay slain his fo.
> This ilke worthy knight had been also
> Somtyme with the lord of Palatye,
> Ageyn another hethen in Turkye:
> And evermore he hadde a sovereyn prys.
> And though that he were worthy he was wys,
> And of his port as meke as is a mayde.
> He never yet no vileinye ne sayde
> In al his lyf, unto no maner wight.
> He was a verray parfit gentil knight.[5]

THE PEASANT'S LOT

Thus the knight and Crusader took his place in the Christian tradition beside the monk and saint. He was the goal of the upper, landholding class. If we turn to the peasant and his aspirations, the darkest side of the Middle Ages is revealed. For him, strictly speaking, there could be no ideal; Christian resignation was his lot, and human contempt. Where the manorial system did not extend, the fate of the sturdy yeoman was not so bad, and we have touching pictures of the simple joys of the countryside, Umbrian peasants singing at the harvest, English serfs dancing about the maypole on the village green. Insecurity, the great dread of the modern worker, did not haunt him; though families were occasionally broken up, his land at least was nearly always guaranteed him. But even to a sympathetic Franciscan friar, amelioration of his lot seemed out of the question.

A servant woman is ordained to learn the wife's rule, and is put to office and work of travail, toiling, and slubbering. And is fed with gross meat and simple, and is clothed with clothes, and kept low under the yoke of thraldom and serfage; and if she conceive a child, it is thrall or it be born, and is taken from the mother's womb to serfage.... A bond servant woman is bought and sold like a beast.... Also a bond servant [serf] suffereth many wrongs, and is beat with rods, and constrained and held low with diverse and contrary charges and travails among wretchedness and woe. Never is he suffered to rest or to take breath. And therefore among all wretchedness and woe the condition of bondage and thraldom is most wretched. It is one property of bond serving women, and of them that be of bond condition, to grudge and to be rebel and unbuxom to their lords and ladies, as saith Rabanus. And when they be not held low with dread, their hearts swell, and wax stout and proud, against the commandments of their sovereigns. Dread maketh bond men and women meek and low, and goodly love maketh them proud and stout and despiteful.[6]

The Economic Ideals of the Guild System

Leaving the countryside and turning to the towns, we find here a new estate with its own vows and obligations. The rise of the urban civilization, first primarily commercial and later more and more industrial, was the outstanding social force in the later Middle Ages; from it can be traced practically everything that, beginning with the renaissance of the twelfth century, created modern times. The story of how the merchants and craftsmen fought or bought off the lords, sometimes, as in the republics of northern Italy, bringing them into the town, incarcerating them in their fortress mansions, and denying them all political power, has been often told. Let us rather see how commerce and industry were, under the guidance of the Church, brought into the Christian Commonwealth.

In theory medieval business was a coöperative enterprise for the good of all, controlled and regulated by moral principles toward a religious end. These theories the canonist writers developed in great detail. Though here as throughout practice fell far short of profession, as the innumerable fines for the violation of guild regulations evince, many facts in the economic situation aided the Christian attempt to curtail competition in the interests of brotherly community. When commerce gradually revived after the Dark Ages, coöperation was absolutely essential, coöperation against the local lord and against the perils of the journey. It was the communal enterprise of the early merchant guilds that alone made trade possible; the Hanseatic League of the thirteenth century only represents this necessary group action at its highest. The great fleets sent out to the East and West by Venice and Genoa had to travel as a single body. Naturally this entailed careful regulation and mutual confidence; any one violating the carefully built-up standards of fairness would become a traitor to his fellows. Hence the loathing with which the conforming merchants regarded "forestalling" — buying outside the regular market — "engrossing" — cornering the market — and "regrating" — retailing at higher than market price; these were all individual revolts against practices necessary for the common end of the community, equivalent to "scabbing" in a union.

This habit of expecting group control of business naturally carried over into the crafts and was perpetuated by custom; unfair prices, goods of poor quality, unjust working conditions, reacted on the welfare of the whole town. Moreover, we must remember that the scale of industry was small, relations predominantly personal, production for the local market whose demand was constant and fairly well known. This made it much less difficult to attempt an intelligent direction of economic enterprise than after the commercial revolution of the fifteenth century, less necessary to give up in despair, and trust to luck and laisser-faire. When these principles and standards had become consecrated by custom — was not the law of custom the law of God? — it is not hard to see how the rules of the canonists could come to form the background of economic life. Examples, too, of just such group-regulated industry were present in the great monastic establishments, while the most important form of property, land and its rent, had from time out of mind been subject to like customary restrictions. From customary rent to customary prices and wages was an easy step.

The first great principle, then, of the business enterprise of the towns, was that industry was under group control, and that interference on the part of the group was entirely justified. Property had no absolute rights apart from the well-being of the group. When little land was held outright, by allodial tenure, it was natural that manufactured goods should be similarly regarded. Thomas defends private property on utilitarian grounds; on the whole it causes less confusion and fewer quarrels, and tends to order and peace. But "man ought to possess external things, not as his own but as common, so that, to wit, he is ready to communicate to others in their need." [7] If the owner refuses to exercise this stewardship, the group must enforce it.

The second great principle is that value is something objective, a definite amount being contributed to an article by a definite amount of labor. To a science that regarded every quality as something objective inhering in the substance of a thing, as greenness in grass or wetness in water, this was a natural doctrine, just as our theory of value is in accord with our psychological view of such qualities. Hence everything has its just price, in practice based on a combination of cost of production and custom. The buyer should offer no less, the seller take no more. The rule for prices was also the rule for wages. These rules were soon enforced by the municipality in its assizes of bread and ale, maximum prices for the necessities of life, and its Statutes of Laborers. Hence, also, since the usurer does no work, and loans are unproductive of new value, he who takes interest is profiting by the misfortune of his neighbor; and so all interest is prohibited. So long as industry did not need credit, this prohibition worked; but soon recourse was had to Jews, who were almost forced to become money-lenders in the absence of any other permissible pursuit. Philippe-Auguste granted them the rate of forty-six per cent in the thirteenth century. This rule soon broke down, and the "Lombards," or Italians, who lent for nothing, but exacted damages for all delay in repayment, became the bankers of Europe.

With fixed prices and wages it becomes imperative to enforce standards of workmanship, as our trade-unions are just discovering; hence the guilds developed a minute regulation of all articles. This affected the very spirit of craftsmanship, and coupled with the comparative lack of division of labor gives some basis to those who see in medieval industry a loving workmanship that has been quite lost. We can perhaps regard the great cathedrals, fundamentally municipal enterprises born of civic pride as much as of the specifically religious spirit — the blending is most significant — as the highest and most enduring expression of this temper. The care with which the last details, even where they could not hope to be seen, were painstakingly elaborated, and the willingness of the workmen to find their fame in their work — most of the architects even are quite unknown — is a tribute to the success of this medieval ideal of craftsmanship.

Of course, all this implied in return a grant of monopoly that soon degenerated into a selfish spirit of privilege. The late Middle Ages saw the guilds grow hereditary and exclusive; they split into masters' and journeymen's guilds, and the municipal enforcement of guild regulations, that had existed from the very beginning, was carried over by the seventeenth-century despots into a national mercantilistic control. But the significant thing is not that in practice there was little altruism; it is that the whole of business was regarded as essentially a social function subject to social control. Merchants and craftsmen had definite obligations to their fellows and to their customers; their profession was as definitely an order in an integrated society as knighthood, the Church, or the monastic bodies, and entrance to it was similarly accorded only after proved ability and appropriate initiation.

The Vocation of The Scholar

Clergy, secular and regular, serfs, knights, merchants, craftsmen — these were the chief estates of medieval society. One further class remains, far smaller in extent, yet perhaps most important of all, the scholars. What were the functions, the obligations, the ideals of the medieval scientist? He occupied a somewhat anomalous position. Nominally a part of the Church, at first merely a clerk in orders, later usually a Dominican or Franciscan monk, he was really no more a fundamental part of the apparatus of salvation than the knight or the merchant. To the saintly soul, monk or friar or bishop, he was always somewhat suspect, always too prone to fall into some pitfall of the pride of intellect. The Western Church throughout its history has been more interested in the governance of God's kingdom than in the things of the mind; it has been political rather than intellectual. In this it but inherited the spirit of ancient Rome, which never cared for science and never produced a single scientist of note. The twelfth-century renaissance of intellectual interest came from the learned Arabs, and it brought the science of Greece. The scholasticism of Thomas and his successors, imposing as it is, always remained somewhat alien to the heart of the Middle Ages. It really sprang from the curiosity of the Western peoples come to maturity in the enlightened civilization of the towns, an independent force which the Church endeavored to mould and fit into the great scheme of the Christian Commonwealth, but could never wholly make her own. From Abélard in the eleventh century to the later Ockamites whose speculation merged directly into modern scientific ideas, scholasticism was always reaching out beyond the medieval synthesis to the modern world. The great Aristotelian-Thomistic system was logically driven to assimilate the Cartesian science of the seventeenth century and reach its fullest development in the very different structure of Spinoza.

Scholasticism developed in the great University of Paris, the chief of those vast congregations of eager, alert, and irrepressible minds that sprang up with the towns in the twelfth century to supplement the unsatisfying education offered to the curious by the earlier monastic and cathedral schools. It began innocently enough, in the desire to grasp and understand the heritage of Christian doctrine that came from the schools of Alexandria and the age of the Fathers. Saint Anselm, who in the eleventh century believed that he might understand, marks the first stage; on his heels came Abélard seeking to understand that he might believe. These truths are; why? *"Deus homo; cur Deus homo?"*[8] they asked. This desire to comprehend, elaborate, systematize, defend, is the scientific spirit already at work upon its inherited beliefs; once aroused, its questionings can never be satisfied. The scholastics thought they were harmonizing old truths; in reality they were forging new ones. The transition to the most advanced doctrines of to-day proceeded by easy and gradual stages. At first men seized upon the few scraps of ancient learning they found to hand, and in Aristotle's logic discovered a free knowledge and a potent instrument of criticism. From the Arabs of Spain and the East they demanded the rest of Aristotle; in these writings, which they purified of the accretions gathered by centuries of sojourn in Persian and Mohammedan lands, they found the best science of the classic age of Greece. With this Thomas remained content; his successors soon pushed on to the better science of Hellenistic Alexandria, found there the investigation of nature itself, and the way was open for a Galileo, a Descartes, a Newton. But these later adventures are unintelligible without an understanding of the synthesis that Thomas made of Aristotle in the interests of the Christian system.

This intellectual interest had to fight against much opposition. Knowledge was no part of the saintly ideal. We can understand why Saint Francis had no place for it: Jesus was not a philosopher. It was not till the theological concern of the Dominicans had given them control of the universities that the Franciscans were driven to imitate their learning. But we might expect the keen mind of Saint Bernard to think otherwise. Not so; he was clearly aware of what Abélard was doing and why he detested it. "Peter Abélard is trying to make void the merit of Christian faith, when he deems himself able by human reason to comprehend God altogether. He ascends to the heavens and descends even to the abyss! Nothing may hide from him in the depths of hell or in the heights above! The man is great in his own eyes — this scrutinizer of Majesty and fabricator of heresies."[9] "He sees nothing as an enigma, nothing as in a glass darkly, but looks on everything face to face."[10] Bernard was a mystic; he sought God by the less painful and perilous path of intuition and vision. "If once you had tasted true food, how quickly you would leave these Jew makers of books to gnaw their crusts by themselves."[11]

Adam of Saint Victor, one of the great mystical school of the twelfth century, sums up the common attitude to this searching:

Of the Trinity to reason
Leads to license or to treason
   Punishment deserving.
What is birth or what procession,
Is not mine to make profession,
   Save with faith unswerving.
	Digne loqui de personis
	Vim transcendit rationis,
	   Excedit ingenia.
	Quid sit gigni, quid processus,
	Me nescire sum professus,
	   Sed fide non dubia.

Thus professing, thus believing,
Never insolently leaving
   The highway of our faith,
Duty weighing, law obeying,
Never shall we wander straying
   Where heresy is death.
	Qui sic credit, non festinet,
	Et a via non declinet
	   Insolenter regia.
	Servet fidem, formet mores,
	Nec attendat ad errores,
	   Quos damnat Ecclesia.[12]

But Thomas finally made clear to the thirteenth century that this path of reason, though perilous, led to God as surely as the mystic's feeling, and that it had joys of its own beyond compare.

The prime author and mover of the universe is intelligence. Therefore the final cause of the universe must be the good of the intelligence, and that is truth. Truth then must be the final end of the whole universe; and about the consideration of that end wisdom must primarily be concerned.... Of all human pursuits, the pursuit of wisdom is the most perfect, the most sublime, the most useful, and the most agreeable. The most perfect, because in so far as a man gives himself up to the pursuit of wisdom, to that extent he enjoys already some portion of true happiness. "Blessed is the man that shall dwell in wisdom" (Eccles. xiv, 22). The most sublime, because thereby man comes closest to the likeness of God, "who hath made all things in wisdom" (Ps. ciii, 24). The most useful, because by this same wisdom we arrive at the realm of immortality. "The desire of wisdom shall lead to an everlasting life" (Wisdom, vi, 21). The most agreeable, because "her conversation hath no bitterness, nor her company any weariness, but gladness and joy" (Wisdom viii, 16).[13]

If, then, the final happiness of man does not consist in those exterior advantages which are called goods of fortune, nor in goods of the body, nor in goods of the soul in its sentient part, nor in the intellectual part in respect of the moral virtues, nor in the virtues of the practical intellect, called art and prudence, it remains that the final happiness of man consists in the contemplation of truth. This act alone in man is proper to him, and is in no way shared by any other being in this world. This is sought for its own sake, and is directed to no other end beyond itself. By this act man is united in likeness with pure spirits, and even comes to know them in a certain way. For this act also man is more self-sufficient, having less need of external things. Likewise to this act all other human activities seem to be directed as toward their end. For to the perfection of contemplation there is requisite health of body, and all artificial necessaries of life are means to health. Another requisite is rest from the disturbing forces of passion: that is attained by means of the moral virtues and prudence. Likewise rest from exterior troubles, which is the whole aim of civil life and government. Thus, if we look at things rightly, we may see that all human occupations seem to be ministerial to the service of the contemplators of truth.[14]

To be noted in this magnificent statement is that the aim is not the patient and never-ending search for truth, the careful investigation of nature that is the goal of modern science, but rather the contemplation of a truth static, fixed, complete, and perfect for all eternity. The product, not the process, gives the joy. This notion, drawn like so many of Thomas' views and arguments from Aristotle, expresses the very inmost spirit of this medieval science. It explains why its method is dialectical rather than investigatory, drawing the consequences from truth already known rather than seeking new truths. It explains its willingness to start from premises based on authority. "The philosopher" — Aristotle — found this truth; why question his achievement? It explains also the cardinal relation of faith to reason; the goal can be handed to men without the process. And it explains, finally, that curious contrast between the theory and the practice of science that, lasting to the present day, has given rise to most of the philosophic puzzles and skepticisms of the modern age.

The Method of Scholastic Science

It is important to examine the method of this medieval science, since it was upon method that the Renaissance launched its chief attack. Its starting-point was not the observation and establishment of a fact, but the agreement upon some accepted belief. This belief could be accepted upon the authority of the Scriptures, the writings of the Fathers, or the Church: Augustine had laid down the rule that "Greater is the authority of the Scriptures than all the powers of the human mind." Hence, where the Bible contradicted observation, observation had to go. Next to the Bible came the authority of Aristotle, which was accepted save in those cases where it specifically contradicted Christian doctrine, as in denying a creation to the world. Then came "natural reason," glorified common sense, especially sound when it was backed up by the opinions of the ancients. This expressed itself in a number of accepted axioms, such as, "From nothing nothing can come," and, "There must be at least as much of reality in the cause as in the effect," axioms that lasted in modern science till the criticism of Hume and Kant. As men's interests enlarged, natural reason had to be more and more relied upon, especially since from Abélard on the scholastics delighted in lining up authorities on both sides of any moot question. All the great *Summæ* were based on this analysis of contradictory authorities.

Thomas, in proceeding against the Gentiles or infidels, puts the method of appealing to authority succinctly:

> It is difficult to proceed against each particular error, ... because some [of the Gentiles], as Mohammedans and Pagans, do not agree with us in recognizing the authority of any scripture available for their conviction, as we can argue against the Jews from the Old Testament, and against heretics from the New. But these receive neither: hence it is necessary to have recourse to natural reason, which all are obliged to assent to. But in the things of God natural reason is often at a loss.[15]

It might seem that this reverence for authority would stifle thought; in reality, on the leading minds it placed few fetters. Thomas argued as far as he could from natural reason, appealing to authority only to confirm an argument; in the nature of the case his knowledge of the manifold divergencies of his sources necessitated the appeal to reason. The interpretation of authorities, also, could take place in the freest way, thanks to the medieval habit of seeing hidden meanings in all things. Dante expounds the principles of interpretation:

It should be known that writings may be taken and should be expounded chiefly in four senses. The first is called the literal, and it is the one that extends no further than the letter as it stands; the second is called the allegorical, and is the one that hides itself under the mantle of these tales, and is a truth hidden under beauteous fiction. ... The third sense is called moral, and this is the one that lecturers should go intently noting throughout the Scriptures for their own behoof and that of their disciples. ... The fourth sense is called the anagogical, that is to say "above the sense"; and this is when a scripture is spiritually expounded which even in the literal sense, by the very things it signifies, signifies again some portion of the supernal things of eternal glory.

Thus: "When Israel came out of Egypt, the house of Jacob out of a barbarous people, Judea became his sanctification, Israel his power." For should we consider the *letter* only, the exit of the children of Israel from Egypt in the time of Moses is what is signified to us; if the *allegory*, our redemption accomplished through Christ is signified to us; if the *moral* sense, the conversion of the mind from the grief and misery of sin to the state of grace is signified to us; if the *anagogical*, the exit of the holy soul from the slavery of this corruption to the liberty of eternal glory is signified.[16]

Nor was this method of interpretation a new thing. Augustine himself accepted Christianity only after he had been assured by Ambrose, with all the authority of the Church behind him, that the crude and immoral Bible stories did not have to be believed literally. Insistence on the letter of Holy Writ came into fashion only with the unimaginative Protestants; it has always been something provincial in the great Christian tradition. With such an attitude, it is easy to see how authorities could be bent to any position, and the mind left free.

The second principle of scientific method is the relation of reason and faith. Here Thomas had to combat both the mystics, who scorned reason, and the later upholders of the doctrine of the twofold truth, that what was true in theology had no relation to what was true in science. Against both forms of irrationalism he was adamant. "The natural dictates of reason must certainly be quite true: it is impossible to think of their being otherwise. Nor again is it permissible to believe that the tenets of faith are false, being so evidently confirmed by God. Since therefore falsehood alone is contrary to truth, it is impossible for the truth of faith to be contrary to principles known by natural reason." [17] But not all truths are accessible to reason, as a process, though they conform to its test. Some, like the Trinity, are as unreachable to the greatest intellect as the reasonings of a philosopher are to the plain man. It is of great advantage for even the truths of God known by natural reason to be proposed to men with fixed certainty, to be believed on faith; thus they are accessible to all, not the few scholars alone; they are known without long and laborious search, and without the everpresent risk of error. How much the more is it advantageous for things that cannot be searched out by reason to be proposed as tenets of faith! Thus the mind is led upward and onward to desire something that transcends its present powers, Christian humility is enforced, and yet the mind shares in some fashion in these fundamental truths. Of these mysteries we are convinced by the testimony of miracles and the answer of our own minds.

The third principle of scientific method is its dialectical nature. Starting with accepted principles, from them a complete system is to be deduced, a great chain of reasoning ultimately dependent upon its axioms. The test of truth is not experimental verification, it is its inclusion in such a system. The Renaissance changed the axioms to mathematical truths, but it kept the systematic and dialectical nature of the goal even when it supplemented it by an appeal to nature. In Newton's *Principia Mathematica* is its highest development; to the present day physicists insist on these selfsame principles, though the experimental sciences demur.

The Scientific Ideal of the Aristotelian-Thomistic System

Operating with this method, Thomas built up a great system of genuine science. It is not inspired by the aims of modern science, to predict the future and control nature; it seeks understanding rather than description, contemplation rather than control. Its goal was wisdom, a comprehension of the meaning and significance of things, above all of the chief end of man, the meaning of human life and of all creation as related to it; and hence its object was that which alone gave purpose to existence, God. Our science tells us how to do an infinitely greater number of things, it picks apart the cog-wheels of nature; but it is not wise, it does not discriminate what is worth doing, and before the greatest problem of all, what meaning can man give to his life in this vast world, it gives a despairing "Nescio," if not an "I don't care." The ambition of Thomas may have been overweening, and his answer born of hope and fear; but it was a worthy ambition, and one to which men must return. That we have dropped the search for a purpose is in large part due to the too easy finding of purposes in all things that marked scholasticism. Again, reaction explains the defects of the modern mind.

Athenian science was primarily interested in living. It was biological, not mathematical; hence it was most wise in the study of man and his works, and least successful in the sticks and stones that failed to interest it. Aristotle's ethics and politics are a marvel, his physics is rightly a subject for ridicule. Thomas largely accepted both. What the Greek wanted to know was not how things originated, but what they could do. What were stones and trees and men and cities good for? To know a cart was not to be able to make it, it was to be able to use it aright; to know man was not physiology, it was the good life. The purposes, in Aristotle's phrase the "forms" of things, what they could become — this was the object of science. The raw material was their "matter," the finished achievement the "form." To know a pine tree was to know what constituted the perfect pine tree, to know a stone was to know the perfect doorstep The modern scientist would comprehend a clock by dissecting it and watching the wheels go round; Thomas would seek to understand time, and how the clock marked it. It is obvious that both forms of knowledge are essential; without a knowledge of its operation we could never make a clock, but without a knowledge of its purpose we would never think of making it, or be able to use it after it had been made.

To our modern way of thinking, the mistake of Aristotle and Thomas was not in looking for purposes, but in making them too simple and rigid. They saw the whole of existence as an infinite number of types striving to realize themselves each in a single definite way, and when these prefigured goals were not reached they saw failure, error. To them the world was a work of reason, and must be interpreted, as we interpret the actions of a man, by its motives. We may smile with Molière when he ridicules such knowledge by making his chorus sing that opium puts men to sleep because of its dormitive virtue, the nature of which is to make the senses slumber; but this is important knowledge. After all, the *use* of opium is that it is a narcotic, no matter by what mechanism; the *use* of the body is the mind, whatever the body's origin. And what is true of particular organs or substances is true of the whole body of nature: its *use* is to serve the good, to make life, happiness, and virtue possible. Where Aristotle and Thomas made their great assumption was in reading these uses, so complex and so human, into a simple scheme objective and absolute for the whole world. They read into the cause and goal of the universe that which alone justifies it for man, its service of the good. Where they seem to go beyond the warrant of experience, to the physics of to-day, is in interpreting the causes that actually produce change in the world on the analogy of human aspiration, and seeing all moving and living things as drawn onward by what may be said to be love for their unrealized ideals. To the modern scientist, who prefers to enumerate the successive steps in this process, the goal is uncertain and the force of love smacks of magic. But this faith that the world can not only be made to serve man's purposes, but actually does so, that things can not only be perfected, but that the whole course of nature draws toward perfection, was precisely what the Middle Ages meant by faith in God. They studied the universe to discern how God moves the world by the love of his perfection; the modern physicist tries to give man God's knowledge of how to do it, but he has overlooked the knowledge of what is best to do. Which is to say, modern science is physics, while medieval science was something at once less potent and more important, ethics. With ethics alone, man may love the good, but never find it; with physics alone he may gain the whole world, and lose his own soul. The sum of medieval wisdom, and it is true wisdom, lies in the words of Saint Francis: "Suppose that you have enough subtlety and science to know all things, that you are acquainted with all languages, the course of the stars and all the rest, what have you to be proud of? A single demon in hell knows more than all the men on earth put together.

But there is one thing of which the demon is incapable, and which is the glory of man: to be faithful to God." [18]   The physicist elaborating a new poison gas, or the economist tracing the inevitable working of the law of supply and demand, may well ponder these words.

This interest in the purposes of things is fundamental in all the medieval scientists. A word must be said about the chief problem of this science, a problem whose ramifications are as broad as man's interests. Since Aristotle's thought revolved about logic, and his logic was the earliest known of his works, it naturally was formulated in logical terms, as the issue between *nominalism* and *realism;* that is, between the relative importance of the individual and the group of which it is a member. Which is the more important, the controlling element, "man" with his qualities and functions of humanity, or "men"? Which is supreme, the group, Church, or guild, or its individual members? The early Middle Ages, being Platonist, answered, Man, the Church. They held that the class, the universal, exists by itself apart from the members, the particulars; they held that it preceded them in time, that it is more real, that it made them, and was the source of their being. This naturally accorded with the hierarchical group organization of society, and glorified the Church, the guild, the order; it explained how God could be three in one, how all men could be lost in the type-man Adam and saved in Christ. It led man upward through the more and more general logical classes, to that Supreme Being that was the most real, that was the first thing, that was the cause of all things, God. It made the end of life the release from the bonds of individuality and the return to true reality or the great all that is God. It was aristocratic, contemplative, mystic. But it seemed also to merge into pantheism, into a denial of all distinctions between the perfect God and the imperfect world, between good and evil, and to make the moral life and the struggle to realize ideals a meaningless farce. Hence there was soon a reaction to the opposite view, nominalism, which predicated reality of the individual, and regarded the class or the group as a mere symbol or name. This meant an interest primarily in the world of concrete things, in this world, in the life of good works and good citizenship. It meant individualism rather than group control, democracy rather than an ordered hierarchy, worldliness and industrialism rather than the contemplation of God, nationalism rather than universality, freedom rather than unity. The Church could not adopt either view; with Thomas she attempted to follow the compromise of Aristotle in what is sometimes called moderate realism, sometimes conceptualism. The universal exists and is important, but it exists only in the particular; the group exists for its members, and is nothing apart from them, no end in itself, and yet the members are in a real sense constituted by the group of which they are a part. This is the essence of the medieval theory of society, as we have seen; and it stands in marked contrast with the nominalistic tendencies of the later scholastics, who deprecated group control for the good of the members, and merged naturally into the Protestant individualism of the Reformation. It is significant that these nominalists were mostly English Franciscans; Catholic theology and Catholic organization did not desert moderate realism.

But however disruptive of the medieval synthesis some of the tendencies of scholasticism, nay, the substance of scholasticism itself, may have been, in the thirteenth century this had not yet appeared, and the scholar was absorbed into his appointed place in the Christian scheme of things as one of the chief glories of the faith. He had effected a genuine harmony of all the knowledge available, Christian or pagan, and he had ordered it under the common social purpose. The *Summæ* of Saint Thomas are in their way as marvelous creations as the cathedrals or the *Divine Comedy* — lacking the ornament of the former and the perfect pictures of the latter, they yet have an architectonic and imaginative glory of their own, building all the wisdom of the ages bit by bit into the massive walls, cementing the whole together with a beautiful and faultless logic, rising in the towers to a hymn of praise to the Truth that is God. Never before or since has science been wrought into so complete an expression of an age; never has there been effected such a harmony of knowledge and aspiration.

The Ideal of a Unified Christendom

We have passed in review the various orders of medieval society; it remains but for us to contemplate that society as a whole. For the crowning achievement of the Middle Ages was that within the limits of the West it was able to rise to the ideal of a united Christendom, and bring all mankind within the scope of its aim. For European civilization at the height of the Middle Ages constituted under the Church one great fairly homogeneous society, with uniform and universal institutions and common aspirations. It was, to be sure, the uniformity bred of a low stage of economic development, in which every fief or manor or town was largely isolated, self-contained, and hence very similar to every other one. What differentiation was present was vertical rather than horizontal; there were everywhere different estates rather than different states. The richly articulated life of the modern world was not present; from Scotland to Naples, from Spain to Prussia, there was much the same feudalism, the same agriculture, the same towns, the same guilds — and everywhere the Church. Life went on its customary way in manor hall or serf's cottage, in cloister or in market-place, from one end of Europe to the other. With such a uniformity of simple elements, it was easy for the culture of the Church to spread over Christendom with little regional or national differentiation. When the economic unit grew from the manor and town to the nation, bringing with it a much more complex life and a much richer scope for the mind, this facile unity of the Middle Ages gave way to national economy, national cultures, national religions. It remains to be seen whether the infinitely more complex uniformity of modern industrial life can reëstablish such a unity again, this time upon a much higher level of attainment.

Illustrative is the matter of language, perhaps more than any other factor the basis of the present national state. In the Middle Ages dialects varied from village to village. In the absence of any language covering a large region, national culture was impossible, and a universal language a necessity. The Church carried Latin from Hungary to Greenland, and with this, the only possible culture was universal. One other tongue, vulgar Latin, Romance in its North-French form, became almost as widespread, as the language of the knightly class. It was the vehicle of the lay culture, the *chansons* and romances, the tongue of courts. The Normans carried it to England, to Sicily, to Jerusalem. We have seen how Saint Francis, that chivalric nature, delighted in its syllables. It still forms the basis of the *lingua franca* of the Levant. With it the knight could adventure in any land, just as the monk was sure of understanding whithersoever he journeyed.

Classes might quarrel, knights might fight, towns might compete with other towns; yet over this whole great amorphous body of Christendom there stretched a common aim and a common life. We have already seen how it was the Church which provided the bonds. One other medieval institution likewise strove to express this ideal of a united Christendom. Formed several centuries before the Papacy reached its full power, the Holy Roman Empire seemed always a backward-looking thing; its yearning for the glories of the Cæsars and the blessings of the *Pax Romana* never lost an anachronistic flavor. Yet this attempt to revive universal empire fascinated many a mind, and caused many a struggle for what proved a lost ideal.

The German Emperor and the Roman Pontiff fought for the supremacy for three weary centuries; but this everlasting medieval struggle was not between universality and particularity. It was between clerical and lay control of society; and the Kaiser had not finally acknowledged defeat before the rising national monarchs took up his cause and won the victory. The very arguments used by Imperial legists were turned against both Pope and Emperor by the kings of France and England. Kings, too, claimed a divine right; and, supported by the growing commercial classes, they gained the day. Thereafter the cause of liberty was to be waged, not by the secular against the spiritual power, but by the churches against the kings. But this struggle is of the coming age. Whether Church should be free and supreme, and Emperor rule by the authority of the Pope, or whether Emperor and Pope were alike the vicegerents of God upon earth, no one seriously questioned the universal sway of the Pope in things spiritual, and in the realms of the Empire no one denied an all-embracing unity under the Kaiser.

Dante's Universal Monarchy

We can find in Dante's *De Monarchia* the most appealing expression of this ideal of a united Christendom, and the best contrast to the competing nationalisms of the modern age. Never was more faithful son of the Church; yet Dante was also the apostle of an idealized Empire. Fascinated by the dream of world-peace, inspired, like all the Imperialists, by the renewed vision of the achievement of the organizing power of ancient Rome that came with the great revival of the study of Roman law at the University of Bologna, he conceived the magnificent ideal of Pope and Emperor as the two heirs of the Roman State ruling the world for the same end, each by his own means and in his own sphere.

Man may be considered with regard to either of his essential parts, body or soul. If considered in regard to the body alone, he is perishable; if in regard to the soul alone, he is imperishable. . . . If man holds a middle place between the perishable and the imperishable, then, inasmuch as every man shares the nature of the two extremes, man must share both natures. And inasmuch as every nature is ordained for a certain ultimate end, it follows that there exists for man a twofold end. . . . One end is for that in him which is perishable, the other for that which is imperishable. Ineffable Providence has thus designed two ends to be contemplated of man: first, the happiness of this life, which consists in the activity of his natural powers, . . . and then the blessedness of life everlasting, which consists in the enjoyment of the countenance of God, to which man's natural powers may not attain unless aided by divine light. . . . Wherefore a twofold directive agent was necessary to man, in accordance with the twofold end: the Supreme Pontiff to lead the human race to life eternal by means of revelation, and the Emperor to guide it to temporal felicity by means of philosophic instruction. And since none or few — and these with exceeding difficulty — could attain this port, were not the waves of seductive desire calmed, and mankind made free to rest in the tranquillity of peace, therefore this is the goal which he whom we call the guardian of the earth and Roman Prince should most urgently seek; then would it be possible for life on this mortal threshing-floor to pass in freedom and peace.[19]

Never was the plea for a world-state placed on higher grounds.

The proper function of the human race, taken in the aggregate, is to actualize continually the entire capacity possible to the intellect, primarily in speculation, then through its extension and for its sake, secondarily in action. . . . It is plain that amidst the calm and tranquillity of peace the human race accomplishes most freely and easily its given work. . . . Whence it is manifest that universal peace is the best of those things that are ordained for our beatitude. And hence to the shepherds sounded from on high the message, not of riches, nor pleasures, nor honors, nor length of life, nor health, nor beauty; but the message of peace. Likewise "Peace be unto you" was the salutation of the Saviour of men. . . .[20]

Wherefore to abolish these wars and their causes needs must all the earth and whatsoever is given to the generations of men for a possession be a monarchy, that is one single princedom having one prince; who, possessing all things and not being able to desire more, shall keep the kings contented within the boundaries of their kingdoms, so that there shall be peace between them, in which peace the cities may have rest, and in this rest the districts may love one another, and in this love the households may receive whatsoever they need, and when they have received this, man may live in felicity, which is that whereto man was born. ...[21] Thus it becomes obvious that for the well-being of the world there is needed a Monarchy, or Empire.[22]

Dante recounts in famous words the argument for an international tribunal.

Between any two princes, of whom the one is in no way subject to the other, disputes may arise, either by their own fault or by that of their subjects. Judgment must therefore be given between them. And since neither can have cognizance of the other because neither is subject to the other (for an equal cannot control an equal), there must be a third of ampler jurisdiction, to control both by the ambit of his power.[23]

Such universal jurisdiction as Dante claimed for the Emperor was, in fact, both claimed and exercised by the Pope. Innocent III, who gave the French possessions of King John of England to the King of France, proudly defended his right to arbitrate.

It belongs to our office to correct all Christian men for every mortal sin, and if they despise correction, to coerce them by ecclesiastical censure. And if any shall say, that kings must be treated in one way, and other men in another, we appeal in answer to the law of God, wherein it is written, "Ye shall judge the great as the small, and there shall be no acceptance of persons among you." But if it is ours to proceed against criminal sin, we are especially bound so to do when we find a sin against peace.[24]

In thus extolling the necessity of a universal monarchy Dante expresses what we may consider as the entire social ideal of the Middle Ages:

It is of the intention of God that all things should represent the divine likeness in so far as their peculiar nature is able to receive it. ... The human race, therefore, is ordered well, nay, is ordered for the best, when according to the utmost of its power it becomes like unto God. But the human race is most like unto God when it is most one, for the principle of unity dwells in him alone. Wherefore it is written, "Hear, O Israel, the Lord our God is one." But the human race is most one when all are united together.[25]

Unity, that unity that caught up in its generous embrace all men and all peoples, nay, all creatures upon earth and every slightest fact, and carried them upward upon the wings of the spirit to the supreme unity of God himself — such unity may well stand as the supreme ideal of the Middle Ages.

LAY SOCIETY

REFERENCES

1. A. L. Guérard, *French Civilization — From its Origins to the Close of the Middle Ages*, 214.
2. *Song of Roland*, Leonard Bacon tr., 55.
3. *Niebelungenlied*, D. B. Shumway tr., 291.
4. F. W. Cornish, *Chivalry*, 148.
5. Chaucer, *Prologue to Canterbury Tales*.
6. Bartholomew of England, in *Medieval Lore*, 54, 55.
7. Thomas Aquinas, *Summa Theologica*, II, ii, 66, i.
8. Title of one of Anselm's chief works.
9. Bernard, *Ep. 191*, quoted in Taylor, *Medieval Mind*, I, 416.
10. Bernard, quoted in Henry Adams, *Mont-Saint-Michel and Chartres*, 315.
11. *Ibid.*, 315.
12. *Ibid.*, 315.
13. Thomas Aquinas, *Summa Contra Gentiles*, Bk. I, chs. 1 and 2; tr. by Rickaby as *Of God and His Creatures*.
14. *Ibid.*, ch. 37.
15. *Ibid.*, ch. 2.
16. Dante, *Convivio*, Second Treatise, ch. 1.
17. Thomas Aquinas, *Summa Contra Gentiles*, I, ch. 7.
18. Francis, quoted in P. Sabatier, *Life*, ch. XVII.
19. Dante, *De Monarchia*, Bk. III, ch. 16.
20. *Ibid.*, Bk. I, ch. 4.
21. Dante, *Convivio*, Fourth Treatise, ch. 4.
22. Dante, *De Monarchia*, Bk. I, ch. 5.
23. *Ibid.*, Bk. I, ch. 10.
24. Innocent III, quoted in A. J. Carlyle, *Medieval Political Theory in the West*, II, 219.
25. Dante, *De Monarchia*, Bk. I, ch. 8.

SELECTED READING LISTS

General: In addition to books listed under Chapters I and II: Henry Adams; Guérard, Pt. II, Bk. II; Taylor, Bk. IV; E. Power; Coulton, *Life in the M.A.*; Boissonade; Luchaire; J. Evans, *Life in Med. France;* L. F. Salzman, *English Life in the M.A.*; C. V. Langlois, *La Société Française au 13ᵉ siècle, La Vie en France au M.A.*

Chivalry: F. W. Cornish, *Chivalry; Cam. Med. Hist.*, VI, c. 24; E. Prestage, ed., *Chivalry:* O. Cartellieri, *The Court of Burgundy. Song of Roland, Niebelungenlied, Parzival.* Chaucer, *Canterbury Tales; Aucassin and Nicolette;* chronicles of Joinville and Froissart; Malory, *Morte d'Arthur.* Coulter, *Medieval Garner.* G. Saintsbury, *Flourishing of Romance.* See also Myers and P. Monroe. For the peasant, E. Power; Coulton, *Medieval Village;* Davis, *Life on a Med. Barony;* K. W. D. Fedden, *Manor Life in Old France.*

Medieval Economic Ideals: R. H. Tawney, *Religion and the Rise of Capitalism*, pp. 3–62; A. P. Evans, *Problem of Control in Med. Industry*, in *Pol. Sci. Quart.*, 1921; L. H. Haney, *Hist. of Econ. Thought.* G. O'Brien, *Med. Econ. Theory;* V. Brants, *L'Économie politique du M.A.* Arts. "Guilds," "Just Price," "Law Merchant," "Usury," *En. Soc. Sciences.* Bede Jarrett, *Social Theories of the Middle Ages.* Tr. of documents in A. J. Monroe, *Early Economic Thought.*

Scholastic Science and the Universities: On the universities: *Cam. Med. H.*, VI, c. 17; C. H. Haskins, *Rise of the Universities;* H. Rashdall, *Universities of Europe in the M.A.* On the thought of the Schools: Taylor, *Med. Mind*, II, chs. 39, 40; E. Gilson, *La philosophie au M.A.* (by far the best survey); Gilson, *Spirit of Med. Philosophy;* W. Turner, *H. of Phil.* R. McKeon, *Selections from Med. Philosophers*, with excellent introductions. Standard accounts, M. De Wulf, *H. of Med. Phil.*, B. Geyer, in Ueberweg, *Ges. der Phil.*, II. De

Wulf, *Phil. and Civil. in the M.A., Med. Phil.* For the earlier period, R. L. Poole, *Illustrations of the H. of Med. Thought and Learning.* Anselm, *Cur Deus Homo?* J. McCabe, *Abelard.* Gilson, *St. Bonaventura.* On Aristotelianism: Aristotle, *De Anima, Organon, Physics, Metaphysics.* Brief accounts by A. E. Taylor, W. D. Ross, Mure. Hantz, *The Biological Motivation of A.'s Phil.*; C. W. Shute, *Aristotle's Psychology;* W. Barrett, *A.'s Analysis of Movement;* E. H. Johnson, *The Argument of A.'s Metaphysics;* P. Duhem, *Système du Monde*, I, c. iv; Wicksteed and Cornford ed. of the *Physics.* Thomas Aquinas, *Summa Theologica, Summa contra Gentiles.* Studies by Gilson (best), M. Grabmann, M. C. D'Arcy, A. D. Sertillanges. Dante, Temple ed., esp. *Convivio.* Santayana, *Three Phil. Poets;* P. H. Wicksteed, *Dante and Aquinas.* Criticism in John Dewey, *Reconstruction in Phil.*, chs. ii, iii.

Political Ideals: G. H. Sabine, *A History of Political Theory*, Pt. II; W. A. Dunning, *H. of Political Theories*, I; C. H. McIlwain, *Growth of Political Thought in the West;* O. Gierke, *Pol. Theories in the M.A.*; R. W. and A. J. Carlyle, *H. of Med. Pol. Theory in the West.* Augustine, *City of God;* N. H. Baynes, *Political Ideas of St. Augustine's De Civitate Dei;* Gilson, *St. Augustine*, c. 4; J. N. Figgis, *Pol. Aspects of St. Augustine's City of God.* Thomas Aquinas, *Summa Theol.*, Prima Secundae, qq. 90–108; B. Rolland-Gosselin, *La doctrine politique de S. Thomas d'Aquin.* Dante, *De Monarchia*, Oxford ed. with int., "*The Pol. Theory of Dante*," by W. H. V. Reade. *Social and Political Ideas of Some Great Med. Thinkers*, ed. F. J. C. Hearnshaw.

Roman Law: *Cam. Med. Hist.*, V, c. 21; Taylor, c. 34; Rashdall, c. 4. Munroe Smith, *Development of European Law*, Bk. iii. C. G. Crump and E. F. Jacob, *Legacy of the M.A.*; P. Vinogradoff, *Roman Law in Med. Europe;* J. Declareuil, *Rome the Law-Giver.* E. Barker, *The Conception of Empire*, in C. Bailey, *Legacy of Rome.*

BOOK II
THE NEW WORLD OF THE RENAISSANCE

CHAPTER VI

THE NEW INTERESTS OF THE MODERN AGE — THE NATURAL MAN

The Gradual Growth of the Humanistic Spirit

It is, of course, impossible to speak of *the* Renaissance, as though it were a single age or a single force, and had a definite date, like the French Revolution. Moreover, dramatic and painfully beautiful as were the life and the products of the Italy of the fifteenth and sixteenth centuries, the age of the humanists and of the noontide of Italian art does not mark one of the major intellectual events of the Western peoples. The earlier renaissance of the twelfth and thirteenth centuries was a much more unmistakable rebirth of the mind, while the forces at work in the Middle Ages, which in the sixteenth century were clearly revealed as disruptive of the old order, did not produce their fundamental revolution in men's ways of thinking until the seventeenth and eighteenth. Nevertheless, though the old forms and the old beliefs persisted relatively unchanged, that period which we loosely call the Renaissance was marked by the increasing prevalence of attitudes and interests that had hitherto played but a minor rôle in the life of Western Europe. These growing interests burst the bonds of the narrow if intricately carved medieval world and left men toying with the fragments. It was for the next age to seek the broad foundations upon which those fragments could be builded into a new structure. Ordered and precise Versailles was then to succeed Rheims.

If, then, the central feature of the period of the Renaissance is an outgrowing, a freeing from ties that have proved to be bonds, it is evident that we have to do with new forces arising within an old order, with stresses and strains, with unstable attempts to effect some kind of adjustment between traditional allegiances and modern appeals. The age of the Renaissance and the Reformation was above all others an age of compromise. If in the joy of widened vistas many were intoxicated by the beauty and the lusts of life at its richest, many more were caught half-hesitant, reluctant, like Bruno, both to leave the Father's house and not to venture into the glorious world. What was best in the Renaissance and Reformation could not last; it was the noble enthusiasm of youth, and what was needed was the hard and painful work of maturity. Nor could what was worst endure; it was the incongruous compromise between elements neither of which was clearly understood, the Christian tradition and the natural, pagan view of man's life and its scene. The Western peoples were leaving the old world; eagerly they snatched at the treasures of Greece and Rome as they moved onward to the new. But not till the turn of the seventeenth century did any man realize the nature of that new world, and not till the nineteenth did its features impress the average man. Only in Mr. Shaw's plays do the Saint Joans of history talk wisely of the Protestantism and Nationalism they are ushering in.

The ordered society of the Middle Ages allowed the forces that had created it to develop until they naturally outgrew the fixed and narrow framework through which they functioned. The gradual accumulation of a surplus and a greater store of physical objects, the growth of an urban population, and the increasing desire for knowledge, led men to take more and more interest in themselves and in their environment. Eagerly they turned to the literature of Greece and Rome, which revealed to them men who had had similar interests, and eventually led them on to investigate the actual world in which they were living. The complex hierarchy of medieval society, with its fixed group control, proved increasingly inadequate to satisfy the new needs and demands of human nature, and to organize men's diversified and changing activities. The forces centered in the individual members broke down the nicely adjusted binding ties, and in every field of human endeavor, in religion, in science, in art, in economic life, in political control, more and more emphasis was laid on the growth and expression of the potentialities of the individual elements and less and less on the organization of these elements into wholes, toward which the individual members felt a diminishing sense of responsibility. The typical ideal of the period, individuality and self-sufficiency, served as the ground of a new attempt to order the world, an order that became more mathematical and mechanical than hierarchical and organic.

We have spoken of new forces at work within the old forms. These forces were many rather than simple, but they all bore a close relation to the fundamental force which we have already seen bringing the barbarians out of their pioneering ignorance and building the thirteenth century. This is the economic growth of European society that made the towns and was now making the nations. It is trade and commerce and material riches that can alone explain the possibility of the rich and diversified civilization of Medicean Florence or the France of Francis I or the Germany of Luther or the Netherlands of Erasmus, just as these things had founded Periclean Athens and Imperial Rome. We can even explain many of the contrasts between these cultures in terms of the varying relations between the old agricultural classes and the new merchants and bankers, though we should be on our guard lest we assume too facile an explanation of the peculiar forms life took in Florence or in London. No one would seek in economics the source of Petrarch's delight in landscape, or Luther's combats with a personal devil, however unintelligible the import of these things without it.

It is not for us to narrate here the well-known story of the tremendous economic changes that, gathering momentum slowly in the town life of the Middle Ages, have rushed on with ever greater speed through finance, commerce, agriculture, and industry, and are working greater transformations to-day than ever before. But the significance of this growth must be kept in mind if we are to understand the making of the modern world. Expanding commerce demanded a money economy in place of the crude barter and exchange of goods of the early Middle Ages. German mines supplied a wealth of silver, and America poured in her golden hoard. Kings and nobles grew rich, merchants even richer. Banks and bankers, with the mechanism of credit, were soon developed in the Italian and German towns. Rich bankers, like the Fuggers, put their wealth into extensive enterprises in mining, manufacturing, in sheep-raising and wheat-growing, and created a full-fledged capitalism. The great merchants and commercial companies needed a far larger production than guild methods could afford. Commerce, seeking new worlds to conquer, found India and America, and simultaneously trade changed from luxuries to staples. Towns proved too small as units; trade must be national in scope to hold colonial empires.

In the face of these startling transformations, the old city guilds, with their traditional regulations and their spirit of serving a small community, proved totally inadequate. As they decayed or were legislated out of existence, the new class of bankers and capitalistic merchants rose to power. The Church was superseded as leader in urban society by the bourgeoisie, the great middle class. Needing firm and stable government against their rivals in other lands, as well as freedom from the stupid interference of the feudal nobility, these commercial classes built up strong centralized monarchies. The economic support which they could give the national monarchs, especially the mobile subventions and taxes in money, enabled the latter to build up standing armies, to cut loose from reliance on feudal levies, and to consolidate the national domain and establish the "king's peace" and the "king's law." The nobles were crushed and their lands taken, the Church was plundered and dispossessed in their greed for more. Art and learning they bent to their glorification, and the lower classes they held in subjection. With the magnified power of money and commerce, those who lived by commerce and money became more and more a political and social power. No longer was the aim of society the service of God in Christian love, but national prosperity for the middle class.

This rapid growth involved fundamental readjustments in every institution of society; it also demanded thoroughgoing intellectual reconstruction. The changes that came over the mind of Europe during this period, its new knowledge and new ideals, were conditioned by a multitude of other factors, but every new belief, every changed view of man and his destiny, was worked out by men living in such a society and powerfully influenced at every turn by the forces of this society. Only against this background is it possible to understand the new aspirations of the European nations, their achievements and their errors. But if the roots of the new world of the Renaissance are to be sought in economic conditions, its justification and its meaning are to be found in the new spirit and knowledge, that destroyed monasticism and Aristotelian science as capitalism was destroying feudalism and the guilds.

This new spirit consisted at bottom in an increasing interest in human life as it can be lived upon earth, within the bourne of time and space, and without necessary reference to any other destiny in the beyond or the hereafter. It meant the decay of that Oriental dualism in which the flesh for so many long years had lusted against the spirit, and the growth in its stead of the conviction that the life of flesh and spirit merged into one living man is not evil, but good. It meant that when society offered more than a rude mining-camp existence of blood and toil, the monastic temper declined, and gave way to a new and vital perception of the dignity of man, of the sweetness and glory of being a rational animal.

It happened that those who felt the call of human experience had a great literature to which they could turn, a literature written by peoples who had been stirred by the same passion for the free life of man in its natural setting. The frenzied zeal with which they did find in this literature a confirmation of their own inward stirrings in the face of a rich urban society, has left an indelible impress on the form taken by this interest in the natural man. But if the manuscripts of Greece and Rome had perished every one beneath the monk's missal, the outcome would not have been essentially different. Men would still have turned to man and nature, and if the modern world might not so soon have come into being, it is quite possible that men would not have wandered down so many blind alleys. Of a truth the Renaissance discovered the humanities, but it found them in Florence or Augsburg or Paris, not in ancient books. The books had always been there; they were discovered when men had grown fit to appreciate them. The polished and urbane Cicero, he who had taken the intellectual world of Greece and translated it from the idiom of free and heaven-questioning Athens into the Roman tongue of the market-place and the law-court, he who had dropped from the already fundamentally anthropomorphic wisdom of Hellas all that led the mind away from the passions and the will of the mortal life of man, became naturally the idol of those whose days were passed in palace or piazza; and his conception of culture as essentially *Studia humanitatis ac litterarum*, the study of humanity and letters, was acclaimed by those dissatisfied with Aquinas' "truths of God."

Humanism in the Middle Ages

This interest in humanity had indeed lived strong and clear from the ages before the barbarians were conquered by Christianity. The Homeric life of their pagan epics has the true savor of human existence, and we can be sure that it was never lost under the imprint of the saintly ideal. The most that the Christian tradition could do was to make it disreputable, especially among the clerical class gifted with the power of literary expression. Throughout the later Middle Ages there existed a stream of vulgar songs extolling a frank enjoyment of life and its pleasures, all the freer in their animal exuberance in that they lived *sub rosa*, as it were, beyond the pale. Not only ribald soldiers, but the selfsame clerks who later rose to write *summæ* and hymns to the Virgin, enlivened their student days at the great universities with lauds to wine, women, and song. Who can read these songs of the "Wandering Clerks" and believe that the age of the Crusades lay crushed under the terrifying fear of Hell? In the most thoughtful the note is "Gaudeamus igitur"; for the most part it is:

> We in our wandering,
> Blithesome and squandering,
>   Tara, tantara, teino!
> Eat to satiety,
> Drink to propriety,
>   Tara, tantara, teino!
> Laugh till our sides we split,
> Rags on our hides we fit;
>   Tara, tantara, teino!
>
> Jesting eternally,
> Quaffing infernally,
>   Tara, tantara, teino!
> Brother catholical,
> Man apostolical,
>   Tara, tantara, teino!
> Clasped on each other's breast,
> Brother to brother pressed,
>   Tara, tantara, teino![1]

So soon as ever a lay and vernacular literature arose, it portrayed the same pagan enjoyment of the goods of life, high and low. The troubadours of gay Provence, whose delight in life as well as unnatural flight from it stirred stern Dominic to wrath and the Pope to the bloody Albigensian crusade, turned Christian chivalry into a glorification of human love; at the court of the Emperor Frederick II, at the very time Francis was singing and begging his way through Umbria, these joyous songsters lived and reveled amidst surroundings as rich, as learned, and as cruel as those of any Renaissance despot. The "sweet new style" Dante and the other North Italian poets took from them symboled heavenly things in the most earthly of guises. It is significant that the most frank and realistic of these poems sprang from the bourgeois culture of the towns; the obscene French *fabliaux* rose to the level of the shrewd delight in all sorts and conditions of men as they really are, with a special love for rogues and scoundrels and the foibles of the clergy, that marks the motley crew of Chaucer and the rogues' gallery of Boccaccio. In sober Aquinas there is already the blend between this sense of the worth-whileness and dignity of all that is specifically human, and the antique humanism of Aristotle. Thomas has hardly a trace of asceticism; his whole treatment of the flesh and its impulses is inspired by the Aristotelian principle of maintaining the supremacy of the most characteristically human part of man, his reason. For this reason, and this alone, is carnality to be regulated. Though the head of scholasticism reached to heaven, its feet were firmly planted on the solid ground of a humanistic appreciation of man's life as an organic union of soul with body.

Indeed, from the twelfth century onward such an attitude and such interests became increasingly respectable, and the thirteenth century merged almost imperceptibly into what we call the humanistic revival in its narrower sense. Art tells the same story as literature; the earlier virgins and saints on Chartres, with their childlike, beatific countenances, pass into realistic portraits, and the conventional Byzantine madonnas are transformed into Italian peasant girls.

The Discovery of the Humanity of the Classics

It was but natural that these interests should turn men more and more to the records of the past. The interest in the ancient literatures really dates from the founding of the universities in the twelfth century; the early students had as intense a love for the classics as the fourteenth-century scholars. Abélard's pupil, John of Salisbury, collected the Latin poets and delighted to read them. The discovery of Aristotle and the consequent preoccupation with science, with man's destiny rather than with his life, only postponed the later revival. Europe was learning from the past, taking what she fancied. In Dante the two interests are equally vivid; he is full of ancient Rome, and pagan and Christian symbols serve him alike throughout his masterpiece. Petrarch, seventeen when Dante died, is the vanguard of the changed emphasis. Distrustful of Aristotle, disdainful alike of the human and the literary value of the scholastic writings, loving the glory of this world and intensely interested in his own personality, author of an autobiographical and posing *Letter to Posterity*, devoted above all others to his beloved Cicero, writing immortal sonnets to his earthly Laura in the Italian tongue, yet desiring such lapses from Ciceronian grace to be expunged, insatiable in his search for the manuscripts of the ancients and stirred to wrath by their neglect — he laments that he was born out of his time: "Among the many subjects which interested me, I dwelt especially upon antiquity, for our own age has always repelled me, so that, had it not been for the love of those dear to me, I should have preferred to have been born in any other period than our own. In order to forget my own time I have constantly striven to place myself in spirit in other ages, and consequently I delighted in history." [2] In reality his hearkening to the call of the new and his retention of the old were intensely of his own age. He turned from Aristotle to Plato, remarking, on hearing the former's authority taken, "Sometimes I asked, with a smile, how Aristotle could have known that, for it was not proven by the light of reason, nor could it be tested by experiment." [3] He preferred rational to supernatural explanations of events, yet religiously he was faithful to the medieval world; the Fathers he read, yet it was Augustine the man rather than the thinker whom he admired. His Latins he interpreted allegorically, yet was a careful scholar as to texts. The monastic life he approved of — as giving tranquillity to the scholar. A curious blend of the old and the new, he sums up his attitude. "There is a certain justification for my way of life. It may be only glory that we seek here, but I persuade myself that, so long as we remain here, that is right. Another glory awaits us in heaven and he who reaches there will not wish even to think of earthly fame. So this is the natural order, that among mortals the care of things mortal should come first; to the transitory will then succeed the eternal; from the first to the second is the natural progression."[4] Let us leave him climbing Mount Ventoux for the view — strange aberration, in medieval eyes! — and reading Augustine on sin and concupiscence at the top.

Even beyond Cicero there beckoned another world, a world of cities like Florence, where the widest human interests, in science and philosophy, were made to revolve about man the citizen. Petrarch and his friend Boccaccio yearned for the Greek tongue, and patiently endured the barbarities of a Greek-speaking rogue whom they set up as professor and put to work on a plodding translation of Homer. It was not till the third generation of humanists that any could really read Greek. Glorious was the day when a learned Byzantine, Chrysoloras, accepted a chair at Florence. Bruni gives us the spirit of the age:

I was then studying Civil Law, but . . . I burned with love of academic studies, and had spent no little pains on dialectic and rhetoric. At the coming of Chrysoloras, I was torn in mind, deeming it shameful to desert the law, and yet a crime to lose such a chance of studying Greek literature; and often with youthful impulse I would say to myself, "Thou, when it is permitted thee to gaze on Homer, Plato and Demosthenes, and the other poets, philosophers, and orators, of whom such glorious things are spread abroad, and speak with them and be instructed in their admirable teaching, wilt thou desert and rob thyself? Wilt thou neglect this opportunity so divinely offered? For seven hundred years, no one in Italy has possessed Greek letters; and yet we confess that all knowledge is derived from them. . . . There are doctors of civil law everywhere; and the chance of learning will not fail thee. But if this one and only doctor of Greek letters disappears, no one can be found to teach thee." Overcome at length by these reasons, I gave myself to Chrysoloras, with such zeal to learn, that what through the wakeful day I gathered, I followed after in night, even when asleep.[5]

Petrarch and Bruni represent the first enthusiasm; succeeding scholars grew alike more critical and more influential. The demand for learning seemed insatiable. The answer was the production of books printed on paper from movable type, in place of the old and imperfectly copied parchment manuscripts. Forty-five copyists working for two years under Cosimo de Medici produced only two hundred volumes; by 1500 there were in Europe at least nine million books, of thirty thousand titles, and over a thousand printers. The new printing spread with a rapidity that would have been impossible with the communications of a hundred years earlier. The first surviving specimen was printed in Mainz, on the upper Rhine, before 1447; three years later Gutenberg and Fust had set up there a partnership whence issued the famous forty-two line Bible and the thirty-two line Latin grammar of Donatus, symbolic of sacred and secular learning, the Reformation and humanism. By 1465, the press had reached Italy; by 1470, Paris; London followed in 1480, Stockholm two years later, Constantinople in 1487, Lisbon in 1490, while Spain characteristically lagged behind till 1499. Thus by 1500 all the chief countries of Europe were provided with the means for the rapid multiplication of books. The consequences for intellectual life were momentous. The number of those who could share the best knowledge increased a thousandfold; it became worth while to learn to read, and to write for a wide circle of readers. A library could now contain a wide variety of secular works, instead of the few expensive writings of the fathers and doctors. Prices sank to an eighth of the former cost, and, judged by our standards, were low indeed. Ideas could now be sure of a wide hearing; and though the Church soon attempted to control the new force by her censorship, the printing-press had made it impossible ever to extirpate a living idea.

Above all, the circle of the educated, formerly confined largely to the clergy, broadened immeasurably; that rapid spread of knowledge and beliefs we call a period of enlightenment was made possible. It is difficult to see how the great movements of the next century, the permeation of the humanistic attitude, the spread of the Reformation, the rise of national literatures to consolidate the national state, could have occurred without the printed page. Ducal collectors in Italy might be ashamed to own a printed book, but all Europe learned from them. Universities, too, sprang up in every land as strongholds of the new learning, nine in Germany, seven in Spain; and for the first time schools appeared in the towns, as training places for other than the clergy, like Deventer in Holland and Saint Paul's in London. Princes and merchants vied with each other as patrons, from Alfonso of Naples, whose emblem was an open book and who reverently received a bone of Livy from Venice, to the magnificent Lorenzo, the banker and boss of Florence, patron of all the arts and letters, connoisseur and dilettante, who danced through life singing, "Quant' é bella giovanezza!"

Lefèvre d'Étaples brought the new learning to France in 1492, Colet was leader in England, Reuchlin in Germany. These Northerners shared less of the pagan exuberance of the Italians, and were all more interested in combining their new life with the Christian tradition. Biblical critics and reformers of ecclesiastical abuses, they were intent on making of Christianity a purer and simpler gospel for this world. While the Popes were reveling in beauty and putting the earnest Christian Savonarola to death, d'Étaples was discovering the message of Jesus and the Protestantism of Paul. Greatest of all these apostles of Enlightenment, Dutch Erasmus was editing the Bible, undermining by subtle thrust the medieval ideal and system, and preparing the way for the revolt from the Church that was to break his heart.

The Heritage of Rome and Greece

What did these eager scholars find in the literature of Rome and Greece that so admirably expressed the sentiments they felt rising all about them? They found the arid field of textual criticism, the tools of the grammarian, the thin white light of the scholar's passion; they found the periods of Cicero and the rules of Quintillian. These things doomed Europe to centuries of schooling in the polished and studied but meager literature of Rome, to a formal and barren preoccupation with the bones of language, with style engraved on mediocre thought, to the sodden horrors of imitation Horace and veneer Virgil; if they did not stifle scientific thought, they at least guaranteed that no schoolboy should hear of it. In countless ways the world has paid dearly for the revival of learning. Yet this was not what they were seeking, and it was not the true gold they found. They discovered a great authority for their break with the medieval spirit, and out of the conflict of authorities eventually arose freedom. They discovered the beauty of form, that men about them were prodigally pouring forth, and in Plato its justification. The Platonism of the Renaissance, if it lacked the full-bodied life of the Greek poet and wandered off into the vagaries of Neo-Platonic mysticism, of astrology and magic and strange secret lore, compounded of Arabian and Jewish dreams, had at least regained its joy in beauty. In spiritually minded, disembodied Florence the Platonic Academy lived again as in a vision. There Ficino the translator and the musician sought to reconcile Plato and Moses, Socrates and Christ, and burned his lamp before his master's shrine. There gentle, tolerant, all-sympathetic Pico, "the Earl of Mirandola, and a great Lord in Italy," celebrated Plato's birthday, and sought a universal religion commingled of Platonism, the Jewish Kabbala, and Christianity. There Bembo the Cardinal discoursed of the love that is not of the flesh fleshly, but of the spirit in beauty, and made living again the *Phædrus*, and Socrates' wise priestess, Diotima, like a figure of Botticelli. Tempered with the sanity of Aristotle, Spenser even pressed Plato into the service of the Virgin Queen, and carried a haunting and romantic beauty into the green fields of England. Plato, too, brought mathematics once more into repute, and thus by devious ways led Europe to take up again the thread of Alexandrian natural science. Full earnestly the age believed with the poet of the myths that "the soul that hath most of worth shall come to birth as a poet, lover, philosopher, musician, or artist."

But most of all the humanist scholars brought from their Cicero and their Greeks the happy, natural, and wholesome enjoyment of the goods of human life in a refined civilization, and the wisdom and sanity of balance, temperance, the golden mean. Harmless pleasures and natural tendencies they here found regarded as the means out of which reason is to order a good life, not a thing of the Devil to be repressed by divine aid or else to be indulged in shame and guilt. With these ancients, living well was an art, a skillful technique, not a moment of ecstatic rapture in a day of despairing self-torture. Their ideal was "excellence," the complete and perfect functioning of all the potentialities of human nature; their maxim, "Be perfect," be healthy and skilled in mind and body, do not miss a single opportunity of well-rounded development in this rich world. And though in their new-found freedom from monkly asceticism and self-discipline most of the worshipers of the free life of Greece yearned romantically for all the joys and pains of human experience at once, and burned for that crowded hour of glorious life that is really so remote from Greek prudence, not all flared up like Gaston de Foix, who lay dead in his beauty at twenty, lord of five victories. The true Aristotle of the *Ethics* was discovered in deed as well as in text, and the magnificent energies of a

Leonardo da Vinci were kept in control by the calm wisdom of an indomitable will. In Spenser's vast allegory of the *Faerie Queene* the moral throughout is Aristotelian moderation.

The Revolt from the Christian Ethic

All this meant, of course, a revolt from the Christian ethic: in place of love, joy in the exercise of man's God-given powers; in place of obedience to the will of God, freedom and responsibility under reason; in place of faith, it became more and more clear, the fearless quest of the intellect. Nowhere is this conception of the worth of human personality in itself so nobly expressed as in Pico's *Oration on the Dignity of Man*, which rivals the famous chorus from *Antigone*.

> Then the Supreme Maker decreed that unto Man, on whom he could bestow naught singular, should belong in common whatsoever had been given to his other creatures. Therefore he took man, made in his own individual image, and having placed him in the center of the world, spake to him thus: "Neither a fixed abode, nor a form in thine own likeness, nor any gift peculiar to thyself alone, have we given thee, O Adam, in order that what abode, what likeness, what gifts thou shalt choose, may be thine to have and to possess. The nature allotted to all other creatures, within laws appointed by ourselves, restrains them. Thou, restrained by no narrow bonds, according to thy own free will, in whose power I have placed thee, shalt define thy nature for thyself. I have set thee midmost the world, that hence thou mightest the more conveniently survey whatsoever is in the world. Nor have we made thee either heavenly or earthly, mortal or immortal, to the end that thou, being, as it were, thy own free maker and moulder, shouldst fashion thyself in what form may like thee best. Thou shalt have power to decline unto the lower or brute creatures. Thou shalt have power to be reborn unto the higher, or divine, according to the sentence of thy intellect." Thus to Man, at his birth, the Father gave seeds of all variety and germs of every form of life.[6]

Upon the monk broke the full fury of the onslaught. From the earliest literature of the Middle Ages his failure to attain his professed purity had, of course, made his backslidings seem only the more brute-like; and now that he too felt the urge of the day and abandoned himself to the frank sensuality of Boccaccio's friars or to the noble cultivation of the humanist, the rapier thrusts of an Erasmus grew only the more bitter. He knew himself that not his attainment, but his very ideal, had been discredited. Keenest and most daring of all the Italians, Lorenzo Valla, puncturer of the forged *Donation of Constantine* on which the Papacy rested its legal claim to temporal sovereignty, and hard-headed critic of the Latin Vulgate Bible, in his work on *The Monastic Life* denies all value to asceticism and "holiness," and in his treatise *On Pleasure* sympathizes with the Epicurean who places the highest good in tranquil pleasure, declares that the prostitute is better than the nun in that she makes men happy while the nun lives in shameful and futile celibacy, and calls it irrational to die for one's country or for any other ideal. Even his Christian only postpones happiness to another life. In the Teutonic lands, where monasticism had never been so popular as in the South, many followed Erasmus' lead in extolling the sanctity and chastity of married love, and placing the life of the true Christian in the world. To them contemplation was idleness and solitude mere selfishness.

The Humanistic Spirit

In the South this revulsion inspired a return at times to an almost pure paganism. Three famous aphorisms attributed to Italians well express this spirit. "You follow infinite objects; I follow the finite," said Cosimo de' Medici; "you place your ladders in the heavens, I on earth, that I may not seek so high or fall so low." "If we are not ourselves pious," said Pope Julius II, "why should we prevent other people from being so?" "Let us enjoy the Papacy," said Medicean Leo X, "now that God has given it to us." [7] Italian art well exemplifies the perfect blending of the Christian and the pagan. God or angel, virgin or boy, Cupid or Saint Sebastian, pierced with his own arrows, Saint John the Baptist or Dionysius — who can tell which was in the minds of the Florentines who painted so exquisitely Madonna and Venus alike? Under the great Renaissance Popes, before the Catholic reformation drove Rome with the North back to the Middle Ages, it almost seemed that the new learning, the new art, and the new love of the pulse of life was to be made Christian and assimilated into an even more magnificent synthesis than the great thirteenth century had achieved. Who does not know the legend of Pope Alexander Borgia, reveling in his marvelous chambers in the Vatican, all sprinkled by Pinturicchio with the blue and rose and gold pageantry of Italian life masquerading as holy saints and antique goddesses, the madonna and saints upon the wall, Isis and Osiris on the ceiling? Here he dwelt tasting of every joy with *La Bella Giulia* and his adored children the Duke of Gandia, the idolized Cesare Borgia, and the fair Lucrezia; here, the story goes, he celebrated many a pagan rite on holy feast-days.

The Italians revolted from the Christian ethic to a sheer delight in the million forms of beauty, and cultivated every natural impulse into its appropriate fine art. With the Venetian colorists they heaped up the sumptuous banquet with strange fruits brought by argosies from the Levant, and dined in shimmering silk and ermine against a background of marble palace and wave-lapped gardens, stilling mind and spirit that every sense might lie the more open to the gorgeous sunset splendor of the Adriatic lagoons. They ceaselessly studied with Leonardo, not the surface, but the soul of things, seeking by every art and every science to lay bare the Mona Lisa smile of life. They were content to rest in the tender form and softened color in which simple, soulful Raphael bathed the commonest objects and figures, basking forever in the clear calm sunshine of a summer's afternoon. Or they deliberately provoked with Michelangelo the stark beauty of the strong man in the throes of passion, stopping, like the bravo-goldsmith Benvenuto Cellini, at no crime or madness that in the supreme moment they might thrill with the ecstasy of struggle and discern the lineaments of terror.

But the Northern peoples found more in life than beauty, however tragic; nor were they ever able to transmute each gesture into a picture. Great, sprawling, multitudinous Rabelais, monk and wise physician, grasping with both hands the overflowing fulness of all life from the gutter to the stars, his crammed belly ever shaking with peals of whole-souled laughter, pouring out an unending stream of filthy vituperation upon all who would rob him of a single morsel, however unappetizing — this soul of the ruder and less graceful North devoured the world with no sense of discrimination, no delicacy of nose or palate, and is saved only by his naïve gusto and hearty enjoyment from the sea of mud in which, boy-like, he delights to play. At last Saint Anthony was revenged! Gargantua, his hero, is saved from the monkly stupidity concealed under logic-chopping, to learn all arts, all languages, all sciences, all sports — every scrap of knowledge that

Rabelais' keen eye had ferreted out. But most characteristic of all is the new abbey of Theleme, built by Gargantua as a reward for the help of a lusty monk. To the last detail it is the Renaissance negation of all that Citeaux or Clairvaux had stood for.

There shall be no wall, no clock summoning to duties, no monks or nuns admitted; none but fair women and handsome men are to be allowed, living together in pleasant companionship. There shall be no compulsion to stay; and in place of the monastic vows, every one may marry, and all should be rich and live at liberty. The abbey itself is to be the dream of a Renaissance despot, a veritable Chambord or Blois, with alabaster fountains, courts, picture-galleries, and libraries stocked with books in every tongue. Over the gates is a long inscription excluding all bigots, hypocrites, dissemblers, attorneys, barristers, usurers, thieves, liars, drunkards, and cannibals, and inviting all noble blades and brisk and handsome people, faithful expounders of the Scriptures, and lovely ladies, stately, proper, fair, and mirthful.

All their life was spent not in laws, statutes, or rules, but according to their own free will and pleasure. They rose out of their beds when they thought good; they did eat, drink, labour, sleep, when they had a mind to it, and were disposed for it. None did awake them, none did offer to constrain them to eat, drink, nor to do any other thing; for so had Gargantua established it. In all their Rule and strictest tie of their order there was but this one clause to be observed, *Do what thou wilt*. Because men that are free, well-born, well-bred, and conversant in honest companions, have naturally an instinct and spur that prompteth them unto virtuous actions, and withdraws them from vice, which is called honor. Those same men, when by base subjection and constraint they are brought under and kept down, turn aside from that noble disposition by which they formerly were inclined to virtue, to shake off and break that bond of servitude wherein they are so tyrannously enslaved; for it is agreeable with the nature of man to long after things forbidden and to desire what is denied us.[8]

The very spirit of the Renaissance revolt is in the passage where we are bidden to flee from

that rabble of squint-minded fellows, dissembling and counterfeit saints, demure lookers, hypocrites, pretended zealots, tough friars, buskin monks, and other such sect of men, who disguise themselves like maskers to deceive the world. ... Fly from these men, abhor and hate them as much as I do, and upon my faith you will find yourself the better for it. And if you desire to be good Pantagruelists, that is, to live in peace, joy, health, making yourselves always merry, never trust those men that always peep out through a little hole.[9]

Akin to the Rabelaisian gusto in life high and low are those canvases painted to adorn the homes of solid Flemish merchants, true revelations of the heart of the bourgeois. Riotous tavern rooms, and drunken and obscene festivals, men caught in the performance of the various bodily functions, mingled with the rollicking dance or the skating party, and the satin refinements of middle-class interiors, with their cards, their singers and players, their wooings — rich, comfort-loving Flanders and staider Holland loved the life they saw about them, even when family pride dictated yards of somber and beruffed merchant dignitaries. Gargantuan, indeed, are those sprawling acres of red and yellow Rubens crammed with nude and corpulent Flemish beauties striving desperately to force their peasant strength to appear voluptuous; compared with the grossest abandonment of Venetian Tintoretto or Veronese, they betray the telltale marks of the *nouveau-riche* aping the grace of wealth well-borne that is bred of long traditions of luxury. But in Holland, in the spotless neatness of a servant in the courtyard or a housewife busied about her tasks, in Vermeer and de Hooch, appears that sense of the dignity of thrift and industry, of Luther's chambermaid serving God more truly than any ascetic nun, that tells us that the Renaissance here in the hard-working North has passed into the more Puritan ethic of middle-class virtue. German humanism, too, always prone to forget the end of the enrichment of life in the harsh and crabbed means, delighting in all the minutiæ of the apparatus, finds in the inexhaustible profusion of Albrecht Dürer its appropriate expression. For it there is little of sensuous beauty; but the rude, stark outlines of life itself, the literal-minded dwelling on the last detail of the imaginative vision, the intense seriousness of the preoccupation with the furniture of practical life, whether in the creased strength of those faces of his merchant friends — "I think the more exact and like a man a picture is the better the work," he said — or in the sharp and angular multiplication of his apocalyptic allegories where flame grows in real pillars and the Lamb has in truth seven eyes and seven horns — this explains why the same forces that gave Italy her painters gave Germany her Luther. Dürer, too, is democratic; not content with serving the high-born despot or merchant prince, as the Italians were, he delighted in spreading himself far and wide in woodcuts, and German engraving joined the German printing-press in bringing the Protestant version of the Bible into every household.

The new appreciation of human life, however, gave the North more than Rabelaisian rioting and German patient seriousness; one can rejoice in the play of light upon the surfaces of things and yet discriminate the shadows, one can accord the appetites their full due and still find in the soul of man, its surge of passion and the wonder, the glory of its infinite longing, the utmost of humanity. Dutch Rembrandt knew well how to see life objectively in its beauty and fullness, and yet, by the inevitable darkness in which light is set, point to the mystery of inward unseen things and unexplored continents of the spirit. There is in him a balance and restraint and a hint that the half is not told, that contrasts alike with the finitude of perfect beauty in the Italians, and the monotonous repetition, all on one level, like the endless but flat ocean, of the Rabelaisian Flemings. In these respects he is of kindred spirit to the great Elizabethan poets and dramatists, just as Holland is of all lands most like England. The canvas of Shakespeare is as broad as that of Rabelais, and infinitely deeper; he need not pour himself out in an endless stream, because his world is peopled with an endless variety of finite figures. With him restraint and reserve betoken a power incalculably greater than Rabelais' seemingly inexhaustible profusion. Before us he sends every sort and condition of man, save, significantly enough, the saint, each moving by inward vitality, characters strong and rich yet living in perfect definiteness; in language, too, his poetry has a wealth of robust life without the bombastic lordliness of most of his contemporaries. Throughout there is the intense love of this mortal flesh; the very essence of the new valuation of life is summed up in *Measure for Measure,* where to the Duke's medieval reflections on the nothingness of this life, Claudio in prison can answer only, "It is a fearful thing to die." It is significant, too, of the humanistic spirit that Shakespeare's characters struggle, not with any limited ideas or philosophies of his own age, but with the universal forces of human nature that transcend all particular intellectual formulation; they live by

THE NATURAL MAN

their pure humanity, oblivious to the abstract problems of the succeeding age, the theological conflicts of the era of Milton or the scientific controversies of that of Voltaire. Humanism had an intensely practical interest in the forces within human nature, and bothered little with man's beliefs about the larger setting of his life; it was far more anthropocentric than the thirteenth century, whose chief concern was God, or the eighteenth, whose problems lay in Nature.

Yet perhaps Shakespeare was too much the artist, too sympathetic with the Italian spirit to express truly every side of English aspiration. There is an infinite yearning after the stars, far sweeter than all possible attainment, that lies deep in the soul of the English and the Germans, the Faust-spirit in man thirsting for endless knowledge and power rather than finite beauty; and to the Elizabethans it was given to clothe this spirit in poetry. This romanticism, so alien to the ancient world and so incomprehensible to the Latin mind, which prefers the clear, unclouded survey of a modest segment of life to the dreaming adventure in the realms that are not as yet, the methodical cultivation of the *rentier* of modest but secure income to the blind and ceaseless struggle after power over men and things, touched every nation in the Renaissance, but it took root and flowered in England most of all. Christopher Marlowe, Cambridge scholar, wild and immoderate, fittingly killed in a tavern brawl, in magnificent and bombastic verses pours out this love of something in life more than life.

> Our souls whose faculties can comprehend the world,
> And measure every wandering planet's course,
> Still climbing after knowledge infinite
> And always moving as the restless spheres — [10]

these souls speak in Marlowe. Tamburlaine the world conqueror, boundless in his ambition for power, Barnabas the Jew insatiable for money, Doctor Faustus, that consummate expression of this aspect of the new life, who sold his soul to the Devil in return for the chance to know everything, do everything, feel everything: these men are filled with an eternal dissatisfaction and an everlasting craving for some great vague thing that when grasped reveals itself as power. Not science, not wisdom, not the inward glory of the understanding mind — for this the

Renaissance cared far less than did the thirteenth century, carelessly appropriating new worlds which it never bothered to see as they were — but that enhancement of personality that comes with power: it is for this that Faustus is groping.

> Philosophy is odious and obscure;
> Both law and physic are for petty wits;
> Divinity is basest of the three ...
> 'Tis magic, magic, that hath ravished me.[11]

'Tis magic, indeed, that ravished the age, the magic that abandons understanding to gain power. The power comes easily, but without understanding it is soon squandered in the petty childishness of Faustus' desires; he has lost his soul for mere voluptuousness. The barbarian North has rarely paused in this yearning for power to question, To what end? It is not too much to see in Francis Bacon, that prophet of the fruits of science who blindly opposed the scientific discoveries of his own day, who knew that knowledge was the power to effect all things possible and fell for lack of common honesty, the very epitome of the Faustus spirit in which the modern world has wasted its boundless gifts of Nature's secrets. Our science has indeed been too often a mere magic, a black magic that brings destruction; we know the secret of the atoms — and invent torpedoes and poison gases. And yet — back of all this Baconian thirst for power that leads to the dull degradation of Manchester and the imperialistic massacres of Amritsar, there is an inner striving for a something beyond that counts these products as mere baubles after all.

The monk was gone, and his striving for a perfection beyond life gave way to a striving for a fullness of life. It is for others to decide whether this was an advance; we can only record, and murmur with Bruno, most Elizabethan of Italians, "Even if the longed-for goal be never reached, even though the violence of the striving consume the soul utterly, yet is it enough that it should burn so nobly." [12]

The Diverging Streams of Humanism

It is thus apparent that we should speak of many different aspects of the new spirit rather than of a single homogeneous humanistic urge. The rising tides of a concern with man's life in this world, which did not so much offer a new answer to the old problem of supernatural salvation as push it more and more into the background, took various forms in various minds. These differences in the incidence of the humanistic spirit, most important of which were the divergencies between the South and the North, were one of the earliest indications of the newer nationalistic forms in which European life was to flow. Rooted in diverse traditions and owing perhaps something to the ancient differences of the Latin and barbarian stocks, they certainly took shape chiefly because of the diverging economic pursuits and natural conditions in Italy and Germany. Superficially Italian humanism was far more of a break with the past; the North seemed to keep more of the older spirit. Yet it was the North that felt the impulse of the forces that were to dominate the new age; the North broke from the Church, and turned to commerce, to industry, and to science, while Italy burnt itself out in glorious extravagance and soon returned to agriculture and the spirit of medieval life.

Life offered to the Italian humanist essentially enjoyment and creation; to the German, labor and self-discipline. For the former, the Christian scheme gave way to a Greek morality, in which life was an art, freed from all sense of obligation. Religious interest gave him little concern, unless we can speak of a religion of beauty. His ideal was the universal man, the completely rounded personality of a Leonardo; he strove to absorb everything, and his culture became syncretistic, retaining all the conflicting elements of the Greeks, the Romans, and the Christians, and reconciling them in a universal symbolism. Zeus, Jupiter, God — all meant the same reality. Such an ideal of necessity remained aristocratic, with little rootage in popular feeling; it produced a cosmopolitan and artistic upper class, which easily gave way before the onslaught of the Counter-Reformation. The German turned rather to a Roman morality; life was a Stoic discipline, a task and a calling. He remained strongly religious, though his obligations became ethical rather than supernatural. He was devoted to education and learning rather than to art and beauty. Democratic rather than aristocratic, he sought his ideal as a member of an ordered society rather than as an independent personality; before his eyes hovered a new society of brotherly work rather than of splendid gods. More literal-minded than the Italian, he could not combine diverse elements and see the universal in the multifarious symbols; there is a vast difference between the imagination of the great Italian painters and Dürer, the Dutch and the Flemings. Hence he was led to break with the past rather than to reinterpret it; he became the heretic of the Reformation, not the modernistic and indifferent Medicean. Indeed, the later divergency between the Catholics and the Protestants is already at hand in the diverse forms which the humanistic urge took in the South and the North. The causes of these differences are obscure; fundamental was the fact that commerce was shifting to the North and creating there a new middle class, while the more developed South had lost its commercial urge and was living on its capital.

The Northern humanists passed by easy stages from the medieval faith to an enlightened and urbane cosmopolitanism. The first of the Germans, Rudolf Agricola, Rudolf von Langen, and Alexander Hegius, Rector of the famous school at Deventer, were pupils of Thomas à Kempis, famous mystic and author of the *Imitation of Christ;* touched by the Italian learning, they abandoned scholasticism and worked for educational reform without criticizing the system of the Church. To them succeeded men like Reuchlin and Erasmus, whose learning had freed them from the medieval world view at the same time that they sought to preserve its institutions through drastic reform and modification. More radical, if less sagacious and prudent, were the younger men like Crotus Rubianus and Ulrich von Hutten, whose rebellion led naturally to the Lutheran revolt.

The Modernity and the Tragedy of Erasmus

To the modern mind it is the second group, above all Erasmus, who stood for those ideals with which it has the most sympathy, ideals which, submerged by the Reformation for two hundred years, finally flowered in the naturalism and humanitarianism of the eighteenth century. Erasmus was surely the incarnation of the ideal humanist, in his faults as well as his virtues. His narrow interests reflect the limitations of the humanistic attitude, and explain its impotence before the deeper forces of the age. Caring naught for the marvelous art of his generation, unconcerned with the new world opening before men's eyes, bitterly hostile to a scientific interest as turning men's minds from the human problems of morality, he typifies the humanism that worshiped Roman Cicero rather than the greater Greeks. Nor does he stand out for any original thought, any great new discovery; the best of the past, not the growing future, was his concern. Even in character and temper of mind he stands rather for tolerance, for conciliation and mediation, than for a forceful and courageous facing of new issues. He remained a witty, urbane, and charming conservative; he had not the strength or the convictions to take his place in the van as a pioneer of the new age. These defects must be remembered when we regret that his spirit could not have prevailed rather than Luther's. Consummate in destroying old prejudices and overthrowing the medieval world, he had nothing to offer in its place save a rather negative liberality of mind; and the world was sorely in need of something to take the place of the old. He lived too soon to see that to science belonged the future; and without the sure support of science and its burning faith, the great qualities of his attitude could not prevail. Not until they were firmly allied with the new scientific spirit could naturalism and humanitarianism such as his spread mightily.

Yet his qualities were great, indeed, and shine all the more by contrast with the turbulent fanaticisms from which he shrank, but whose deep passions he was powerless to illuminate with his own reasonableness. The most civilized man of his age, he had an abiding faith that man was destined to be a rational animal and a shrewd vision that told him he has missed his vocation. He was at home in the Augustan age, in the circle of the polished Cicero or the cultivated Horace; and after converse with these friends he found the ruder society of Rotterdam or London or Basel a subject at times for intellectual amusement, at times for condescending pity, and at times for burning indignation. Too keenly alive to the fruits of human folly to tolerate it with the resignation of a Montaigne, too intensely serious in his moral fervor to accept it as inevitable with Spinoza, he spent his great gifts of irony and satire in the hopeless attempt to make sweetness and light prevail against the superstitions of tradition and the eternal passions. A liberal adrift in a sea of warring fanatics, he found his exposure of the irrational side of medieval life popular because men had outgrown it; but his own remedy of the wisdom of the schools of antiquity, above all his rationalized

Christian ethics, fell on deaf ears. He prided himself on being the Christianizer of the Renaissance and the humanizer of Christianity; he saw in Jesus an enlightened moral teacher and in "the philosophy of Christ" the life of reason warmed by benevolent love. He sought to wean men away from the mysteries of faith and attach their piety to the sureties of a civilized culture. For him the gospel and the Greeks merged into a single undogmatic religion of simple morality. "When I read certain passages of these great men," he wrote of the Greeks, "I can hardly refrain from saying, 'Saint Socrates, pray for me.'" [13] "Their philosophy lies rather in the affections than in syllogisms; it is a life more than a debate, an inspiration rather than a discipline; a transformation rather than a reasoning. What else, pray, is the philosophy of Christ?" [14]

With such ideals he found plenty about him to castigate. When he held up to laughter the follies of the monk, of the scholastic doctors, of ceremonial formalism, he won the plaudits of those who felt these passing features of the medieval world anomalous in the new age; and when he exalted the simple virtues of the home and business, he was expressing what all men felt. But when he held the rod of reason up to the new irrationalism of the Reformers and of the rising military nationalism, he found that men discard old superstitions only to welcome new. They might abandon medievalism, but that made them no readier to follow the philosophy of Christ or the life of reason. Erasmus ended his life, as humanism in the narrower sense died out, rejected alike by the priests of the old and the prophets of the new. Not until Voltaire did another cosmopolitan appear who so filled the European stage and so mightily battled against superstition and cruelty and dogmatism, and when Voltaire took up the pen of Erasmus he had what the humanism of the Renaissance never enjoyed, the mighty ally of science.

The Ideal of the Gentleman

We have tried to gain a sense of the new interests and aspirations that, vague, complex, and indefinite as they are, yet form the confused goal that modern man has set himself. In this time of renewed delight in human life there were gradually formulated two more definite ideals that to this day claim a primary allegiance in our civilization. They are the figure of the gentleman and the picture of the industrious, prosperous commercial society. They are complementary class ideals; the state must be industrious if individuals can hope to flourish as gentlemen. The one is pagan and aristocratic and came from Italy; the other is Protestant and industrial and was made in Germany. Both are still supreme, assailed only by the different aims of the awakening working class.

The gentleman was the composite product of the courtly knight of idealized chivalry and the humanistic, artistic graces of the commercial towns. When the feudal lord left his rural isolation he attached himself to the circle of some powerful prince, who had attracted to his own luxurious company a brilliant court. The fascination of an intense social life and the richer revenues that relieved him of remunerative pillaging and foraying drew him irresistibly to his fellows; he was still the courteous knight, but he had laid down the cross to take up the new beauty of human life. This happened first in Italy because the towns there grew wealthy first, and because the Italian nobility first gave way to strong princes who gained power by what they were rather than by what their ancestors had been. At the courts of the great captains and adventurers who grew rich through fighting commercial wars for the merchants who were too busy to bother governing themselves, of the Visconti and the Sforza who ruled Milan, the Malatesta of Rimini, the Gonzaga of Mantua, the Este of Ferrara, and all the rest, or in the circles of the merchant princes who directly ruled more commercial Venice and Florence, the lesser nobles mingled with the artists sprung from the people and assimilated genius and skill as they imparted the graces of gentility. In Italy gentle birth and wealth and individual attainment lived on equal terms; to shine there required a personal brilliance which almost outweighed all else. Thus was created a new type, the "universal man," the all-sided man, the well-rounded personality, who added to the perfect exercise of every physical power a universal learning and a real proficiency in many differing arts. It was the very antithesis of the specialist, the professional, and yet it meant vastly more than the mere dilettante. In Italy the greatest examples of this "uomo universale" were the artist-scholars, men like Michelangelo or, greatest of all, Leonardo, painters, sculptors, architects, poets, engineers, and thinkers.

Typical is Alberti, marvelously dexterous in physical exercises, perfect in archery and riding, master of arms and of music, painter, Latin stylist, whose health broke down at twenty-four from overstudy of law and who turned for repose to physics, mathematics, the crafts, and building churches and temples. In the North, where agriculture was supreme and feudalism lingered on, the universal man was more apt to be the courtier, primarily a soldier and statesman who added thereto all things else. That chevalier "without fear and without reproach," Bayard, was the model of the French court of the Renaissance patron Francis I, while Sir Philip Sidney, idol of the English people, warrior, poet, and truly noble soul, who gave his flask of water to a common soldier as he lay dying on the field of Zutphen, added a sincerity and a romantic English patriotism. The type lives on in the cultivated gentlemen of England's disappearing governing class, like Lord Balfour, equally agile at tennis and at skeptical and urbane conservatism; but the ideal in its outlines is still the aim of every liberal education.

Baldassare Castiglione, himself a perfect exemplar, reported in *The Book of the Courtier* the conversations in the hall of the Duke of Urbino in which the perfect courtier was defined. Translated into many tongues, this code of etiquette carried the Italian graces into the ruder courts of the North; all Elizabethan England went to school to it. Gentle birth is an advantage, as predisposing to the gentle heart; the leisure of riches is essential. The Courtier must be skilled in arms and manly exercises, with grace rather than mere strength; he must be a poet and a musician and an accomplished linguist. Dignity and proud humility must clothe him, loyalty and true friendship must be his. At his side stands the lady, who has stepped down from her chivalric pedestal to become the true companion of the courtier, his equal in freedom and in education — there appears the long procession of Shakespeare's noble women. What inspiration the knight had found in the service and love of God is to be his in the spiritualized and mystic love that, starting with perfect friendship, aspires to the stars.

The New Ethic of Industry and Thrift

This ideal of individual perfection is of necessity aristocratic and exclusive; it presupposes peasants and craftsmen to make it possible. In Holland and in Germany there grew up the ideal of a society that could support such gods.

This new conception of the dignity of a human society in which the walks of life are intrinsically good, and industry, thrift, and productive labor are elevated into the cardinal virtues, though it was best formulated by Luther, really owes little save in a negative way to the Protestant revolt. It is the natural fruit of the marriage of the medieval craft society interpreted in the spirit of restrained sobriety native to the Germans, and the increasing complexity and wealth of economic life. The heart of the North lay in its daily business, and as that grew in importance it cared less and less for monkish asceticism and the control of a spiritual power. It came more and more to love prosperity and success, and to think of solitude as selfish, contemplation idleness, poverty a punishment, and married and industrial life as truly godly. In so far as there is a causal connection, it was this spirit which at bottom created the indifference and hostility to the Catholic sacramental and financial systems that broke out in open religious and political revolt. The Protestant Reformation, in the hands of Luther and his fellows, was in no sense a moral movement seeking to raise the moral tone of society; indeed, ethically its first results were a distinct degradation and sordidness. It was not till the second generation that the fierce passion of Calvin for holiness kindled the consuming flames of Puritanism. The humanists like Erasmus, the true reformers of Christian life and apostles of simple gospel virtue, were swept aside by quite different forces. It mattered little whether the Catholic system were well or ill administered; the important thing was that it was useless and costly.

The significance of Luther's ideas we shall examine later; it is enough to point out here that his religious beliefs were a medieval reaction back to the literal details of the Christian drama, above all to a sense of the overwhelming need of salvation, tempered by his own intense experience that the all-important personal salvation from the wrath of God comes in a direct and mystical relation between God and man without the intermediary of any external church or priest or sacrament whatsoever. When once faith in the forgiving love of God in Christ has freed man from all fear of the wrath to come, he is already saved; he need do nothing more nor concern himself in the slightest with any part of the apparatus of penance and monkly austerity and ascetic denial for the sake of winning his way to some future salvation. Thus at one stroke the whole necessity for regarding the Christian way of life developed by the saints and the monasteries, as in any way essential for the attainment of either present peace of mind or future bliss, is swept away. This does not mean that the nerve of morality is cut; it means only that its whole entanglement with supernatural beliefs and magic practices, the fear of Hell and the taking of the sacraments, has gone by the board, and that in its place the way is left open for a thoroughly naturalistic ideal here in this world. Thus the Protestants who believed that salvation was an entirely unmoral and purely religious thing, in no wise concerned with the ethical perfecting of man's character — in other words, that it was the result of faith and not of good works — found the old ascetic, dualistic ideal of Christianity gone, and the place left open for whatsoever human life they deemed most fit. Protestants were, indeed, as free to give themselves to the new ideal of a dignified and worthy human life in a natural setting as if they had lost all belief in a God or a hereafter. Religion became a special thing apart, not a spirit filling the whole of life, a matter, it soon came naturally enough to be for many, for Sunday observance only, while the week-day was given over to seeking success and prosperity.

But this last is the decay of Protestantism, and no more its essence than cynical formalism is truly Catholicism. It is sometimes a problem, for those who can conceive of virtue only as enforced by the policeman, how it was that Lutherans and Calvinists so often led lives of such singular and exalted purity when they were convinced that this conduct made not one whit of difference, and that they were saved or damned by a pure act of faith over which they even had no control, since faith itself came from God and not man. The answer is that these men really believed in God, believed that morality was supreme in the universe; and they served God's goodness, not for any selfish end of escaping Hell or gaining Heaven, but for pure love of his nature. Where the Catholics acted basely in fear or hope, they had only to glorify God and enjoy Him forever. They believed with Luther in "the Liberty of a Christian Man"; their ethics was based on the profound psychological insight that the noblest life must spring from "confidence instead of fear, liberty instead of bondage, gratitude instead of the desire for reward, love for others instead of thought of self." [15]

For Luther, the life of such a man filled with the sense of a living God will be supremely disinterested. "Whoever turns good works to his own advantage does no good work. If you ask a chaste man why he is chaste, he should say, not on account of Heaven or Hell, and not on account of honor and disgrace, but solely because it would seem good to me and please me well even though it were not commanded. What is it to serve God and do his will? Nothing else than to show mercy to our neighbor. For it is our neighbor who needs our service, God in Heaven needs it not." [16] The man who has faith in God cannot help doing good, for Christian living is the necessary fruit of salvation, not its means. "Where works and love do not appear, there faith is not." Faith, if it be true faith and not mere lip-service, is an impulse to imitate its object, to be like Christ; and it is a mighty force. "O, faith is a living, busy, active, mighty thing. It is impossible that it should not always be doing good. It asks not whether good works should be done, but before one asks it does them, and is always doing them." [17]

Luther thus sets man free from any theological or supernatural moral system; for him ethics becomes, not the sugar-coated pill, but the real test of religion. If a man walks uprightly in love and mercy, that is a sign, and the only sign, that he is saved, that he has a proper faith in God. With such a faith his life will naturally and freely flower in moral virtue. Naturally such complete freedom left to the believer is dangerous, for, being released from the need of obeying any moral law, he can give any content to his life without fear of Hell. Hence while Luther confidently refused to abridge this Christian freedom, Calvin and his followers timidly searched the letter of the Scriptures for prescriptions as to man's duties, and converted the free and natural ideal of the German into Puritan theocracy. Hence, also, the ease with which the Protestant turned to what attracted him most, preoccupation with material welfare. And thus, in spite of the fact that the Reformation was in many respects religiously a renewed intensification of medieval beliefs, it left the way open morally to a thoroughly worldly social ideal of labor and commercial gain. There was every reason for the middle class to welcome Protestantism, and for the growing commercial world of the North to feel at home in it.

Luther himself put this content into the life his free Christian should lead. Since no special religious practices are necessary, all callings, even the most secular and humble, are equally sacred, and God can be best served in the ties of family and business, by doing the daily task faithfully and joyfully with trust in God and devotion to his will.

What you do in your house is worth as much as if you did it up in heaven for our Lord God. For what we do in our calling here on earth in accordance with his word and command he counts as if it were done in heaven for him. It looks like a great thing when a monk renounces everything and goes into a cloister, carries on a life of asceticism, fasts, watches, and prays.... On the other hand, it looks like a small thing when a maid cooks and cleans and does other housework. But because God's command is there, even such a small work must be praised as a service of God far surpassing the holiness and asceticism of all the monks and nuns. For here there is no command of God. But there God's command is fulfilled, that one should honor father and mother and help in the care of the home.[18] Thus it is impossible that he should take his ease in this life, and not work for the good of his neighbors, since he must needs speak, act and converse among men.... It is the part of a Christian to take care of his own body for the very purpose that by its soundness and well-being he may be enabled to labor, and to acquire and preserve property, for the aid of those who are in want.... Here is the truly Christian life, here is faith really working by love, when a man applies himself with joy and love to the works of that freest servitude in which he serves others voluntarily for naught, himself abundantly satisfied in the fulness and riches of his own faith.[19]

There is here a mixture of the medieval ideal of service and the new ideal of work and property-seeking. Since the very core of Luther's teaching was the liberation of man's spirit from religious fears to live what life God in his goodness should prompt him to, sublime confidence in God's love and complete trust in human nature perfected by faith, it was only to be expected that his followers should increasingly devote themselves to the economic activities that seemed to them good. Thus industry and thrift and saving and hard labor for well-earned gain flourished on Protestant soil, and the God-fearing business man took his place with the beauty-loving artist and the resplendent courtier as types of the modern preoccupation with the natural man in his natural setting, and Saint Bernard was left in his cell to thunder and adore alone and Saint Francis in his Umbrian fields to sing unheard.

REFERENCES

1. J. A. Symonds, *Wine, Women, and Song.*
2. *Letter to Posterity*, quoted in Robinson and Rolfe, *Petrarch*, 64.
3. *Ibid.*, 39.
4. *Secretum*, in same, 452.
5. Bruni, *History of his Own Times in Italy*, quoted in H. O. Taylor, *Thought and Expression in the Sixteenth Century*, I, 36.
6. Pico, quoted in J. A. Symonds, *The Revival of Learning*, 35.
7. *Ibid.*, 12, 13.
8. Rabelais, Urquhart and Motteux tr., II, 165.
9. *Ibid.*, 310.
10. Marlowe, *Tamburlaine.*
11. Marlowe, *Doctor Faustus.*
12. Giordano Bruno, *Degl' Eroici Furori.*
13. Erasmus, *Convivium Religiosum*, quoted in Preserved Smith, *Erasmus*, 34.
14. Erasmus, *Paraclesis*, quoted in P. Smith, 53, 54.
15. A. C. McGiffert, *Protestant Thought before Kant*, 39.
16. Luther, quoted in McGiffert, *Protestant Thought before Kant*, 35.
17. *Ibid.*, 39.
18. *Ibid.*, 33.
19. Luther, *Christian Liberty*, Wace and Buchheim, *Luther's Primary Works*, 279.

SELECTED READING LISTS

General Works on the Renaissance Period: B. Groethuysen, "Renaissance," *En. Soc. Sciences.* Preserved Smith, *Age of the Reformation*, chs. 1, 10–14; W. T. Waugh, *H. of Europe from 1338 to 1494;* E. M. Hulme, *Renaissance and Reformation;* excellent social material. J. Huizinga, *Waning of the M.A.;* A. C. Flick, *Decline of the Med. Church;* H. S. Lucas, *The Ren. and the Ref.* J. Burckhardt, *Civilization of the Renaissance in Italy*, classic; J. A. Symonds, *The Renaissance in Italy*, suggestive but biased; R. A. Taylor, *Aspects of the Italian Ren.* a poet's interpretation; H. O. Taylor, *Thought and Expression in the 16th Century*, a useful compilation. *Cam. Modern Hist.*, I, *The Renaissance;* Lavisse et Rambaud, t. IV. J. W. Thompson, etc., *The Civilization of the Renaissance.* Suggestive interpretations in J. H. Robinson, *The New History*, pp. 116–18, 154–60; Karl Brandi, *Das Werden der Renaissance;* W. Dilthey, *Auffassung u. Analyse des Menschen im 15. u. 16. Jahrhunderte*, in *Ges. Schriften*, II.

Economic Influences: C. J. H. Hayes, *Pol. and Cultural H. of Europe*, I; Heaton, Gras, Nussbaum; F. A. Ogg and W. R. Sharp, *Econ. Devel. of Europe;* Day; J. W. Thompson, *Econ. and Soc. H. of Europe in the Later M.A.* W. R. Shepherd, "The Expansion of Europe," in *Pol. Science Qu.*, 1919; W. C. Abbott, *The Expansion of Europe;* J. E. Gillespie, *Influence of Oversea Expansion on England.* L. B. Packard, *The Commercial Revolution, 1400–1776.* R. Ehrenberg, *Capital and Finance in the Age of the Renaissance;* W. Sombart, *Modern Capitalism.*

The Discovery of the Humanities: L. Loomis, *Medieval Humanism;* J. E. Sandys, *History of Classical Scholarship*, II, best description; Voigt, *Die Wiederbelebung des classischen Altertums;* L. Geiger, *Renaissance u. Humanismus in Italien u. Deutschland.* Robinson and Rolfe, *Petrarch, the First Modern Scholar and Man of Letters;* P. Nolhac, *Petrarch et l' Humanisme.* M. Whitcomb, *Literary Source Book of the Italian Renaissance.*

Printing: T. F. Carter, *The Invention of Printing;* J. C. Oswald, *H. of Printing;* G. H. Putnam, *Books and their Makers during the M.A.;* De Vinne, *The In-*

vention of Printing; Wattenbach, *Das Schriftwesen im Mit.*, standard. D. Hunter, *Paper Making through 18 cents.*; H. A. Maddox, *Paper; its Hist., Sources, and Manufacture.*

Humanism — The Spirit of the Classics: Cicero, Virgil, Horace, Livy. Histories of Latin literature by J. M. McKail, M. Dimsdale; Cyril Bailey, *The Mind of Rome, The Legacy of Rome.* Plato's dialogues, esp. *Protagoras, Republic,* and *Socratic dialogues*; Aristotle, *Ethics, Politics, Poetics;* studies of Plato by W. Pater, F. J. E. Woodbridge, Paul Shorey, E. Barker; of Aristotle by T. Davidson, E. Barker, J. A. Stewart. Histories of Greek literature by Gilbert Murray, A. and M. Croiset. R. W. Livingstone, *Legacy of Greece;* G. L. Dickinson, *Greek View of Life;* C. D. Burns, *Greek Ideals;* M. Croiset, *Hellenic Civilization;* W. Jaeger, *Paideia.* For Renaissance Platonism: Bembo, *Gli Asolani;* Spenser, *Faerie Queene, Four Hymns, Epithalamium.*

────── **Italian Humanism:** In addition to general works, E. Gebhart, *Les Origines de la Renaissance en Italie;* P. Monnier, *Le Quattrocento.* Boccaccio, *Decameron;* Bandello, *Novelle;* Ariosto, Tasso. B. Castiglione, *Book of the Courtier; Life of Benvenuto Cellini;* histories of Italian Literature, by R. Garnett, F. de Sanctis, J. A. Symonds, B. Wiese and E. Percopo.

────── **Northern Humanism:** Karl Pearson, *Ethic of Free Thought,* ch. 8, "Humanism in Germany"; P. S. Allen, *Age of Erasmus;* P. Monroe, *History of Education,* ch. VI; M. Creighton, *History of the Papacy,* VI, vi, 1, 2; *Martin Luther and the Reformation,* by C. Beard, ch. III; T. M. Lindsay, *History of the Reformation,* I, 42–78. On Erasmus, lives by Preserved Smith and J. L. Mangan. Erasmus, *Praise of Folly; Letters,* ed. Nichols, P. S. Allen; *Colloquies,* tr. N. Bailey; *Letters of Obscure Men,* ed. G. F. Stokes. J. A. Symonds, *Wine, Woman and Song* (medieval student songs); Marguerite of Navarre, *Heptameron.* Rabelais, Urquhart and Motteux tr. E. Gebhart, *Rabelais.* Montaigne, *Essays.* Marot, Du Bellay, Ronsard, Villon. Histories of French Literature, by G. Lanson (best), Nitze and Dargan, H. C. Wright, G. Saintsbury, E. Dowden; A. A. Tilley, *The Literature of the French Renaissance.* Hans Sachs, Till Eulenspiegel, Faustbuch. Histories of German Literature, by C. Thomas, F. Vogt u. M. Koch. Elizabethan literature is limitless; see especially Sidney, Spenser, Marlowe, and Shakespeare.

Art: E. Faure, *Renaissance Art;* Helen Gardner, *Art through the Ages;* S. Reinach, *Apollo;* W. J. Anderson, *Architecture of the Ren. in Italy;* F. J. Mather, Jr., *H. of Italian Painting;* K. Woermann, *Ges. der Kunst.* G. Vasari, *Lives of the Most Eminent Painters, Sculptors, and Architects.* W. Pater, *The Renaissance.*

CHAPTER VII

THE RELIGIOUS REACTION — THE REVOLT FROM THE MEDIEVAL CHURCH

The Compromise of the Reformation

THESE new interests in man's natural life and his surroundings, and the marvelous new world into which men were ushered by the great discoverers, could not fail to have an enormous influence on the all-permeating religious organization which in the Middle Ages claimed to inspire and order men's every act. But, in so far as we can disentangle the millions of threads binding great tendencies to each other, we can say that the Renaissance, as we have used that word, was not primarily the cause of the great revolt against the medieval Church that shortly followed it in time. That was rather at bottom an independent expression of many of the same tendencies that produced the Renaissance, above all of the great fundamental economic growth of European society and its rising middle class. In different form we may find at work the same individualism, the same capitalism, the same nationalism, and both movements ended in pretty much the same sort of Puritanism that intellectually reaffirmed the medieval beliefs. To neither Renaissance nor Reformation does the modern mind owe directly the intellectual world in which it now lives; that was for a later scientific movement in the seventeenth and eighteenth centuries to bring to pass. But a large part of its ideals and a majority of its institutional formulations do hearken back to that earlier period. The expanding world had broken the bonds of every one of the old forms of life. Men were not ready to give up the old, however, and in divers ways sought to effect some compromise, some remodeling of the old fragments. Such a compromise that could not but be outgrown in turn was the Reformation. Thoroughly medieval in belief, it was of the modern age in its ideals and its practices, and it contained within itself the seeds both of dissolution and rebirth.

It is not for us here to trace the myriad tendencies that converged to produce the Reformation, or to seek to determine how far its spread was due to repugnance to a formalistic and sacramental system, how far to a revolt against the alien monarch at Rome, and how far to the desire of princes and merchants of the towns for the rich plunder of the Church. It is of course true that the Age of the Reformation was not a particularly religious age, and that its anti-clericalism was inspired by a multitude of motives with which intensity of faith and elevation of morals had little to do. But it cast up great religious and moral leaders, and the effect of their success in breaking the universal power of the Church of Rome was to direct the forces which had initially supported them for divers reasons good, bad, and indifferent, into a swelling stream of faith and purity. If the Age of the Reformation was not religiously minded, the succeeding age of the Puritans and the Counter-Reformation was. In the world of Shakespeare and Spenser, religion hardly counts; in that of Milton, it is everything. But already the leaders of thought had turned from the religious to the scientific field, preparing the way for the more thoroughgoing break of the eighteenth century.

We shall attempt to assay the various intellectual changes which the great reformers within and without the Catholic Church accomplished, and judge their part in the making of the modern mind. These men were not moderns, and they did not face modern problems. They were intensely medieval, and they sought, in the face of the growing changes about them, to solve medieval problems in a new way. Naturally we of to-day, who no longer have their problems, find their greatest influence in the various accessory ideas which gathered around their central purpose. But the Renaissance, too, if less medieval, was just as far from being modern in its interests, if by modern we mean the scientific and industrial world in which most of us live.

Though the religious changes of the Reformation may have been caused largely by other factors, they are none the less central. Had not Luther offered men a way of salvation outside the medieval Church, they could never have broken with Rome for political reasons or despoiled the monasteries for greed. Whether rationalizations or not, the new religious beliefs were the justification of all else. Religiously, the Reformation represented three things: first, a simplification of the body of Christian belief and an emphasis upon the doctrine of salvation and its means as the essentials; secondly, an individualistic emphasis upon salvation as a direct and immediate relation between the soul and God,

THE REVOLT FROM THE MEDIEVAL CHURCH 145

on religion as inner and intensely personal; and thirdly, the consequent dropping away of the sacramental system of the medieval Church and its attendant hierarchy of priests. It is obvious that while these changes powerfully affected the Church as the mechanism of salvation, they left untouched the main body of the Christian drama of the destiny of man. They left untouched the cardinal doctrine of the corruption and depravity of man's nature, and of God's wrath and store of eternal punishment; they left untouched man's intense need of salvation, the whole supernatural scheme of redemption through Christ's sacrifice, and the traditional conception of Christ's work as redemptive, that is, mystical or magical, and quite independent of the perfection of his moral character or his teachings. In all this, Protestantism was at one with the medieval Church and absolutely opposed to the humanistic spirit of the Renaissance, whose cardinal doctrine, as we have seen, was the dignity and worth of the natural man. Thus both the Protestant reformers and the Catholics in reaffirming their traditional doctrines at the Council of Trent, both Reformation and Counter-Reformation, were a medieval reaction against the growing naturalism and humanism that was increasingly to mark the modern age.

The Spirit of Reform in the Middle Ages

In these things Luther instituted nothing new. From the thirteenth century and earlier there had existed these same tendencies within the Church toward simplification, individualism, and salvation without external sacraments. The three main groups who in their several ways were thus undermining the authority of the Church were the mystics, the Augustinian Catholic reformers, and the humanists. The break came with Luther because non-religious and social conditions were ready for his revolt.

Mysticism, always present within the Church from Paul himself, grew stronger in the fourteenth and fifteenth centuries as a natural reaction to the rationalism of the scholastics and the increasing mechanical formalism of the ecclesiastical system. The great German mystics, Master Eckhart, Tauler, Suso, and the author of the *Theologia Germanica* that so powerfully influenced Luther, emphasized personal salvation to the exclusion of everything else. This they sought to effect by a direct union with the Divine Being, which was brought about by meditation and prayer without the intermediary of any priest or sacrament. While they did not deny the traditional doctrines, they relegated them to the background as unimportant, and hence proved a disintegrating force. In the words of the *Theologia Germanica*, "Now mark what may help or further us towards union with God. Behold, neither exercises, nor words, nor works, nor any creature, nor creature's work, can do this. In this wise, therefore, must we renounce and forsake all things, that we must not imagine or suppose that any words, works, or exercises, any skill, or cunning, or any created thing can help or serve us thereto. Therefore we must suffer these things to be what they are, and enter into the union with God." [1] In the fourteenth century a simple and devout piety of this sort was widespread in Germany.

From the thirteenth-century Albigensians against whom Dominic preached and Innocent III crusaded, there had been within the Church reformers who from a mixture of piety and of patriotism attacked the Papacy. They quite uniformly took as their authority Saint Augustine, who, we have seen, combined the Catholic faith in an organized Church with an intensely personal preoccupation with grace as a power coming directly from God to give man's higher nature the victory over his lower. Chief of these Augustinians were the national leaders, John Wyclif of England in the fourteenth century and John Hus of Bohemia in the beginning of the fifteenth. Following Augustine, they regarded the true Church as the totality of those God had picked for salvation, and not identical with the Roman Church. On this theory, membership in the visible Church and participation in its sacraments had nothing to do with salvation, and the whole Catholic system was rendered unnecessary. Naturally this cost Hus his life. Wyclif's bitter denunciation of the Pope as the Antichrist, and of the sins of the clergy, and his appeal to the Bible as an ultimate authority — he first translated it into English — paved the way for revolt.

The Northern humanists, though they absolutely opposed the notion of the depravity of the natural man, for different reasons advocated the same three changes. They too sought to simplify Christianity by ridding it of all its elaborate theology and sacramental rites, though what they wished to emphasize was not a mystical salvation, but the ethical religion of the Gospels. They

THE REVOLT FROM THE MEDIEVAL CHURCH

too emphasized religion as essentially a personal thing, though they interpreted it as primarily a life of love, sympathy, and forbearance. And they too ridiculed and attacked the whole sacramental and priestly scheme, not only in its corruptions, but also in its essence. By their scholarly work in Biblical editing and criticism they tried to bring the authority of the Scriptures to bear against what they regarded as the medieval corruption of Christianity. Above all, they pointed out the discrepancies between Biblical Christianity and the traditional system, though they interpreted the Gospel as a very different thing from the Protestants' views.

Lefèvre d'Étaples, the great French humanist, discovered the Gospels underneath the mass of commentary, and also the essentially Protestant writings of Paul. But the chief influence was that of Erasmus. This humane, kindly, and timid apostle of reason was a master of witty irony and subtle innuendo. His ridicule and delicate gibes at all the medieval accretions upon the moral, humanitarian, and undogmatic "Philosophy of Christ" were more effective than any direct, bludgeoning attack. But he desired to reform the Church into a rational aid to the natural moral life that would absorb all the new learning and science into a well-rounded culture, and when he saw Luther revolting and returning to supernatural medievalism he was crushed.

While I was fighting against these monsters [the enemies of learning] a fairly equal battle, lo! suddenly Luther arose and threw the apple of discord into the world.... I brought it about that humanism, which among the Italians and especially among the Romans savored of nothing but pure paganism, began nobly to celebrate Christ.... I always avoided the character of a dogmatist.... The world was put into a deeper slumber by ceremonies than it could have been by mandrake; monks, or rather, pseudo-monks, reigned in the consciences of men, for they had bound them on purpose in inextricable knots.[2]

Erasmus, in terms of our present-day controversies, was a modernist boring from within, not a Fundamentalist like Luther.

The Religious Revolt

These three groups prepared the way for the specific religious changes which the Protestant revolt made popular. In describing the significant ideas of Protestantism, it is important to remember that there soon came to be two general types, united in opposing the medieval Church and on the fundamental changes they introduced, but differing enough in doctrine to cause very considerable divergencies in the broader ideas and ideals they have left as a heritage for us. The one form was that instituted by Luther himself, soon rationalized and made scholastic and more catholic by Melanchthon, which was confined to Germany and the Scandinavian lands; the other was initiated by Zwingli, a contemporary of Luther in Switzerland, systematically formulated by Calvin, and carried from his Geneva to South Germany, Holland, France, Scotland, and England. The difference between the Lutheran and the Reformed faith is due in part to the difference between the characters of their respective founders, and in part to the fact that the original force and vitality of the revolt remained in Lutheranism whereas Calvin belonged to the second generation of more systematic and institutional theologians. Luther was not a humanist, and was not touched by the intellectual and rationalizing influences of his day. He was a man of intense personal religious experience, and around the practical religious life his interests centered. Calvin was a humanist reformer and a lawyer; he sought to build a rationally consistent system upon the authority of the Scriptures. Where Luther was personal and mystical, Calvin was systematic and rational; where Lutheranism flowered in individual piety and a spontaneous moral life, Calvinism was corporate, and sought by theocratic control of the State to regulate human life to the last detail. Lutheranism was aristocratic, conservative socially, fostered the growing nationalism by its insistence on the supremacy of the State, and tended to keep all of the old to which it did not object; Calvinism was democratic — though indirectly — radical, in the sense that it opposed kings and princes in the name of God, and rejected all for which it could not find a Scriptural authorization.

The Gospel of Luther

Luther's whole system was dominated by his deep sense of sin and inner struggle, and the spiritual rest and peace he attained when he found in Christ's gospel the message of God's mercy and forgiving love for all who err. This made him see the corruption and condemnation of the natural man as the central fact in human experience, and release from God's wrath as his supreme need. When once man believes in the gospel message of a God of loving kindness, he is already saved and at peace. There need be no further worry over the pains of Hell, no long transformation of his moral nature by means of the magical power of a priest's sacraments. The means of salvation, in this sense of reinstatement in God's favor, is faith alone, faith that God is the loving Father seeking the lost sheep and welcoming the prodigal. Man can no more buy his heavenly Father's favor by acts of charity and the performance of rites and the payment of money to priests than he could win his earthly father's love by such patently self-interested means. Luther's own deep conviction that such saving faith must come freely from God Himself, in his infinite love seeking his wayward children, made him certain that even faith was not in the power of man apart from God's favor. He thus with Augustine believed in predestination, that God Himself in his wisdom selected those to whom He would reveal his nature and give peace. Because only in Jesus did he find this message of a loving God, he insisted that apart from Christ there could be no faith. This meant that the whole attempt of Thomas to find God by natural reason, the whole of scholasticism, went by the board for Luther, although Melanchthon succeeded in bringing it back later.

As we have already seen, Luther believed that the faith-brought freedom from the fear of punishment released man from all further self-seeking and made the Christian life the spontaneous serving of man, born of utter confidence in God's love. Thus in effect, for the Christian, human life and human ideals spring from a profound trust in man's impulses; and for those Lutherans who preserved this part of their founder's teachings there was really almost complete agreement with the humanists. The outcome of a scheme of salvation built on a medieval need was a thoroughly modern way of life, and free scope was left for man's devotion to economic activities.

Since salvation was thus the fruit of the Gospel, the purpose of the Church for Luther became primarily missionary, to spread the gospel or evangel. Where the Gospel is to be found, there is the Church. The Gospel must be preached to awaken the all-necessary faith. But for priests and magical sacraments there is no need. Some are set apart to preach, but their calling is no more sacred than that of the humble cobbler. If by a priest we mean one who has special access to the divine favor, all believers are alike priests. "We are not only kings and the freest of all men, but also priests forever, a dignity far higher than kingship, because by that priesthood we are worthy to appear before God, to pray for others, and to teach one another mutually the things which are of God." [3] Though he believed that the Gospel alone was really necessary, Luther retained as aids those signs of God's forgiving love, baptism, and the symbol of the Lord's Supper. Through them too might come faith, for God's love was there calling to us.

This Gospel, this Word of God, Luther found in the Bible; it alone gave the Scriptures their real worth. The basis of Luther's faith was not the authority of the Bible; it was his own experience, which he there found confirmed; but naturally he was forced to turn more and more to that authority in disputes with others. However, he never regarded it as infallible, and constantly used the Gospel as the criterion of what in it was and what was not true. Above all, the Gospel of John and the Epistles of Paul have value; but James is only a straw epistle, and the Book of Revelation is altogether worthless. Though overshadowed somewhat in later controversy, this right of free and individual interpretation of the Bible was never lost among the Lutherans, for whom saving faith has never meant mere orthodoxy. Belief, like the moral life, is a fruit of faith, not its essence.

The Calvinistic System

For Calvin and the Reformed Protestants, the central experience was not Luther's gospel of God's love, but the keen sense of God's dominating will and power. With cruel logic Calvin insisted on the utter corruption and impotence of man in the face of God's omnipotence. God is the supreme Sovereign to whom man owes absolute obedience. Hence man needs a knowledge of God's commands, and a power to execute them. Since God is all-powerful, salvation is wholly in his hands; whom He will save He will, whom He will damn is predestined to the eternal flames. The former enhance his mercy, the latter his justice, both alike his glory. For this sole end was man created, that he should do God's will; his chief end, regardless of personal aims, is to glorify

God and enjoy Him forever. In all this our age, of course, sees cruelty, savagery, and bitter immorality; but it misses the sublime selflessness of an utter devotion to something outside one's self, supreme devotion to that great Will which is in itself the standard of Right. And the mark of Calvinism is deep. Not only is it a glorification of absolute monarchy, which came quite naturally in the age of Renaissance despots, but even more it is a spiritual expression of that absolute abandonment to the will of the nation, to patriotism. We may shudder at those who rejoiced to be damned for the greater glory of God, but most of us feel that to lay down our lives and our consciences for the glory of our country is indeed the supreme joy. The parallel is complete, and the influence of Calvinism in promoting such nationalism has been great.

Calvin believed that God ordained men, not only to salvation, but also to holiness, and hence followed his whole conception of the Christian life. Since holiness is a sign that man has been elected for salvation by God, those who shared Calvin's faith naturally sought with intense fervor to live a godly life. Thus the Reformed as well as the Lutheran faith, though it took salvation entirely out of man's power, and made good conduct of no avail whatsoever, really proved an enormous stimulus to the moral life. In the fierce joy of fatalism men believed that God had called them to do his bidding, and with a dignity that could sink to spiritual pride they stood up against the kings of the earth and haughtily refused obeisance. Thus, though Calvin himself was a proud aristocrat, his followers journeyed, through theocracy, to a conception of civil liberty and even democracy; though the path be devious, it was no accident that the Puritans fought autocracy in Scotland, England, and Massachusetts.

For Calvin the Christian life was one of rigorous subjection to God's prescriptions. God's commands the godly man will obey, not because they are good in themselves, but simply because He has commanded them. Calvin had no faith whatsoever in Luther's freedom of the Christian, in his trust in the spontaneous goodness of the child of God. Christian liberty was for him the freedom from the commands of men, from Catholic rites; freedom from all that should prevent him from obeying God to the letter. The Christian must be held in strict subjection to the letter of God's law. "Everything pertaining to the perfect rule of a good life the Lord has so comprehended in his law that there remains nothing for man to add to that summary." [4] Hence for him the office of the Church was not, as with Luther, to proclaim the Gospel to all, but to train its members in holiness and godliness. It was to be exclusive and aristocratic, and under the guidance, both doctrinal and moral, of the ministers of the Word, those whose superior wisdom enabled them to search out God's recorded will. But with all their power the Calvinist ministers were not a priesthood; they ruled men because of their superior godliness and knowledge, not because of any magic power of grace in their hands. Hence the Reformed preachers became a class of men really distinguished in themselves, as the Catholic hierarchy on the whole never had been.

The Bible became, not the mere vehicle of the Gospel, as for Luther, but the supreme and infallible authority in all things. Faith was sound doctrine; godliness, obedience to the commands of Scripture. The Catholic Church had no hold on men, not because it was corrupt, but because it interpreted the Bible wrongly. And from the old and the New Testaments Calvin sought to draw a plan of life correct to the last detail and obligatory upon every man. In his Genevan theocracy he instituted a regulatory spiritual power that went farther in its prying into every man's mind and acts than the medieval Church at its very height had ever done, and claimed to order State and society, science and education, law, commerce, and industry according to the supernatural standpoint of revelation. Naturally this meant that the Church should be supreme in all things, calling on the civil government to enforce its prescriptions; and whereas Luther had entrusted to the State the power of deciding what was in accordance with the Gospel, and stamping out divergencies, Calvin reaffirmed the medieval supremacy of the Church. But since he had broken from the universal organization, and his churches were constituted on a national basis, the effect was the same as with Luther, to strengthen immeasurably the power of the national State so long as it obeyed the ministers of the Word. And since the content of the godliness he found in the Scriptures came to favor the virtues of the industrious life, his authority aided Luther's freedom in fostering the rising capitalism and appealing to the middle class.

In summary, then, Lutheranism stood for a loving and forgiv-

THE REVOLT FROM THE MEDIEVAL CHURCH 153

ing God, a Christian life of peace and spontaneity, lived in this world for the service of men, a missionary Church, and a State supreme in matters of faith. Calvinism stood for a mighty sovereign God, a Christian life of holiness in obedience to his law and for his service, a Church for the regulation of men's lives supreme over the State. Both agreed in offering a way of salvation outside the Catholic Church, in freeing men from formal sacraments, in making a priesthood unnecessary, in finding supreme authority in the Bible; and less directly in exalting the capitalistic, industrial, and commercial tendencies of the age, as well as individualism and the supremacy of the national State. Paradoxically enough, however, Luther's refusal to carry his religious democracy into politics ended in promoting political tyranny, while Calvin's supreme emphasis on the power of God and submission to his will resulted in enhancing the human power of the individual against all earthly authority.

The Catholic Reformation

While these changes were taking place in the religious life of northern Europe, the Catholic Church itself was undergoing a great reformation that brought it into line with many of the same tendencies that found expression in Protestantism. This movement within the medieval Church was only in part a Counter-Reformation, and owed more to the natural growth of the forces that had produced Protestantism than it did to the stimulus of that revolt itself. Scholastic philosophy, as we have seen, had been a consolidating and to some extent a naturalistic movement; mysticism and humanism were both potent in redirecting Catholic energies. The reforming movements, particularly the great councils of the fifteenth century at which an attempt was made to transform the Papacy into a constitutional government, though they had failed to overthrow the papal monarchy, had introduced a new leaven. For a time it almost seemed that the Roman Curia, or Papal Court, permeated as it was with the new spirit of Renaissance humanism, would effect religious changes much more thoroughgoing in their break from the Middle Ages than Luther's.

But many factors kept this from occurring. The Renaissance in Italy was too strong and too exclusively interested in this world to be satisfied with the Protestant compromise. When it was not positively atheistical, it betrayed little or no interest at all in religion; moreover, it was essentially aristocratic, and quite preferred the masses to be kept in submission by the system which most of the leaders of the Church regarded cynically if not skeptically. The Papacy, too, had its seat in Italy, and the money drawn from the rest of Europe flowed into Italian coffers. But perhaps most important of all the social reasons was the increasing political ascendancy of Spain. That land, whose long crusades against the Moors had just ended in a national unification and a fierce fanatical zeal for Catholicism, had bent the Church to the furthering of absolute monarchy; and when Charles V inherited his universal empire he found it politically expedient to utilize the Papacy in strengthening all his dominions, though he personally desired conciliatory reforms. From Spain there spread through his realms a deep and genuine religious revival, quite analogous, though somewhat more medieval in character, to the revival that Protestantism brought. The Italian Popes, who might have preferred a Church humanized and brought into harmony with the spirit of the Renaissance, after much temporizing were swept into the current. Thenceforth the realms that for reasons largely political and nationalistic remained in the Roman Church, enjoyed a reaction to a narrower and more fanatical medievalism whose spirit was as much opposed to the free life of the Renaissance as was that of Protestantism. That new faith in the natural life of man with which Protestantism was gradually forced to compromise was sternly repressed, to break out again, this time with the firm basis of the new science to support it, in the anti-clericalism of the eighteenth-century Age of Enlightenment. The instruments of this reaction were typically medieval: the great Council of Trent; a new appeal to the traditional doctrine; a new monastic order, the Company of Jesus; and a new coercion of mind and body, the infamous Spanish and the more humane Roman Inquisitions, and the Index of prohibited books. By all these means of pressure Latin and southern central Europe, first chiefly by coercion and later by a genuine religious revival, were held for the Catholic Church.

The Catholic reformation, which dates from the pontificate of Paul III in 1534, is really the Catholic counterpart, not of the age of the great Protestant reformers, but of the second stage of

Protestantism, the age of Puritanism. Both movements are strikingly analogous. The Council of Trent authoritatively formulated and affirmed the whole medieval system of doctrine, thus narrowing and making more inflexible the intellectual life of the Church, and bringing it into line with the rigid Protestant creeds. But the very fact that the Church at last had a dogmatic body of theology — there had been wide latitude during the Middle Ages — turned Catholics from theological speculation, and has allowed a far greater liberalism within her fold than until recently has been possible within any single Protestant sect. Thenceforth her intellectual controversies were largely ecclesiastical, over the relative power of the Pope and the bishops. Secondly, in both Catholicism and Protestantism there was a marked growth of Puritanism in moral attitude. Thirdly, the Catholic Church, relying largely on the support of individual countries for nationalistic reasons, lent itself to the rising spirit of nationalism almost as readily as did Protestantism. Finally, in both divisions of Christendom there was a marked interest in education, both for training the clergy and for general instruction. In all these respects the Catholic Church showed the influence of the tendencies that produced the Protestant revolt.

The Moral Revolt

So far we have been considering the significant religious changes wrought by the Reformation. But though these were primary, they brought in their train moral changes even more significant for to-day, because they have outlived the particular problems out of which they grew, and still shape our own aims. The Reformation was a moral as well as a religious revolt. It rejected the medieval dualism with its attendant asceticism and other-worldliness, and it rejected the formalism and externalism of the Church's regulation of the moral life. In these things it was powerfully influenced by the whole humanistic emphasis upon the value of life in this world. The fundamental aim of some of the Italian and most of the Northern humanists was an attack upon the monastic ideal, its solitude, its ascetic discipline, and its celibacy, not only as unnecessary to religious salvation, but even more as inimical to the best type of human life. For it they wished to substitute the simple Gospel humanitarianism of purity of heart and love for one's fellows. Erasmus' long battle was fought primarily for what he called the simple and natural "philosophy of Christ," found alike in the Sermon on the Mount and in the best ethical teaching of Plato and the Stoics. Neither external rites and ceremonies nor monastic striving for purity are necessary to the pious Christian, but inner righteousness flowering in good deeds.

The true way to worship the saints [he writes in the *Handbook of the Christian Knight*] is to imitate their virtues, and they care more for this than for a hundred candles.[5] Truly the yoke of Christ would be sweet and his burden light, if petty human institutions added nothing to what he himself imposed. He commanded us nothing save love one for another, and there is nothing so bitter that charity does not soften and sweeten it. Everything according to nature is easily borne, and nothing accords better with the nature of man than the philosophy of Christ, of which almost the sole end is to give back to fallen nature its innocence and integrity.... Would that men were content to let Christ rule by the laws of the gospel and that they would no longer seek to strengthen their obscurant tyranny by human decrees![6]

Once the machinery of salvation was out of the way, Luther shared this moral ideal. For him the life of the Christian freed from concern about the fate of his soul was to be spent in disinterested love and service of his fellow man — a conception which dignified the commonest calling. But the immediate effect of his teachings seems rather to have lowered the general moral life; he said that when the devil of the Papacy had been driven out, seven other devils took its place, until at Wittenberg a man was considered quite a saint who could say that he had not broken the first Commandment, but only the other nine. Latimer, too, thought that the English Reformation had been followed by a wave of wickedness. Conventional standards had been broken up, and in the controversies and wars that followed dogma was emphasized at the expense of character. In Germany and England the clergy had sunk to a low estate, ignorant, from the humblest classes, and often convicted of serious crime. It is evident that Calvin's distrust of "Christian liberty" and the strict regulation that marked the Reformed churches was called forth by a genuine need.

The Puritan Life

But to the religious revolt succeeded a moral reformation. In Protestant lands this sprang largely from the Calvinistic bodies, and from the middle of the sixteenth century purifying parties increased in power; in Catholicism it dates from the revival of the Council of Trent. The moral ideals of both groups were similar; they can be grouped under the single head of Puritanism. This Puritan way of life, which became so potent during the next century, is a genuinely new ideal in European history, and it still figures prominently as the most popular of standards to this day. It is in many ways a reaction to and a rejection of the naturalism and humanism of the Renaissance, which for a century it quite submerged; but it is not a mere hearkening back to the Middle Ages, for it rejects just as firmly the monkish ideal of asceticism. Its power has been due in large part to the admirable manner in which it harmonized and elevated the aims and purposes of a commercial and industrial society: it is the ideal of the great middle class.

To the Renaissance ideal of the universal man, who in wild abandon cultivated all his powers to the very utmost, the Puritan opposed the ideal of a rationally ordered life devoted to a serious end. His aim was high, to serve God to the best of his abilities in his calling; and to fulfill his service he needed a firm sense of responsibility and a strict discipline that would let no energy go to waste. Instead of prodigally wasting his powers upon a million pursuits, he preferred to concentrate them all on the task to which he felt himself called. Like the soldier, his sense of duty demanded the utmost from him and imposed a high-minded rejection of what interfered with that duty. He was no amateur, no dilettante, but a professional, in the strictest sense. He was really the stern warrior or austere ruler of antiquity, controlling his life by an indomitable will, a veritable Cato reborn. Where the universal man had emphasized the Greek cultivation of all the natural faculties, the Puritan emphasized the other half of the injunction, control by the reason. Neither was quite Greek, but the one strayed no farther than the other; and both were magnificent ideals.

Needless to say, in portraying the Puritan we are not thinking of that man of straw who is the butt of Mr. Mencken's gibes, nor yet the modern product of a decayed New England conscience.

Let us turn to the ideal at its best, as found in Milton and in the wonderful portrait of Colonel Hutchinson, one of the judges of Charles I. Colonel Hutchinson was highly cultured; he was fond of hawking, dancing, and fencing; he loved painting, sculpture, and all liberal arts, especially music, playing masterly on the viol. "He was as kind a father," says his wife, "as dear a brother, as good a master, as faithful a friend as the world had." The lawless loves of the Renaissance he disdained. He loved to converse with wise and virtuous women, but neither in youth nor in riper years did he descend to any impurity. His aim was to attain self-command, to be master of himself, his thought, his speech, his acts. His bearing was marked with a certain gravity and reflectiveness. His life was orderly, sparing of diet and self-indulgence; he rose early, "he never was at any time idle, and hated to see any one else so." Convinced as he was that all men were equal in the sight of God, he transcended the aristocratic class distinctions of the Renaissance. "He had a loving and sweet courtesy to the poorest, and would often employ many spare hours with the commonest soldiers and poorest laborers. He never disdained the meanest nor flattered the greatest." [7]

But Milton is after all the great Puritan. Cultured, loving the arts, a skilled musician, a learned scholar in Latin, Greek, and Hebrew, versed in the literature of France, Italy, and England, he took his pleasures unreproved, as the wealth of *L'Allegro* and *Il Penseroso* reveals. Yet his life was overshadowed by an intense moral concentration. "If ever God instilled an intense love of moral beauty into the mind of any man," he said, "he has instilled it into mine." [8] *Comus* closes, "Love Virtue, she alone is free." Withal he had a certain reservedness of temper, a contempt for "the false estimates of the vulgar," a proud retirement from the meaner, coarser life about him. He "loved all that were godly, much misliking the wicked and profane." [9]

But the Puritan had his darker side. He lacked saving humor, even when possessed of wit. His sense of the seriousness of life robbed him of much spontaneous gayety, his disdain of the unimportant knew no sense of proportion. He tended to shrink from a surplice or a mince-pie at Christmas as he shrank from impurity or untruth. "When I was but a child of nine or ten years old," tells John Bunyan, "these things did so distress my soul, that then in the midst of my merry sports and childish vanities, amidst my vain companions, I was often much cast down and afflicted in my mind therewith; yet could I not let go my sins"; [10] which were a love of hockey and dancing on the village green. Most serious of all, he sought, like Calvin at Geneva, to regulate all men's lives by his own light, with the Bible as the literal rule-book; Calvinist and Catholic alike became intolerant of the ungodly and sought to discipline them from without. Discipline tended to lapse from a self-imposed concentration to a prying interference with others. The education for which he had so high a regard became a repression of man's natural desires. "Parents, remember children are cursed creatures," [11] admonished Bunyan. Art seemed less and less important, and needed control. Calvin had said, "It would be a ridiculous and inept imitation of the papists to fancy that we render God more worthy service in ornamenting our temples and in employing organs and toys of that sort. While the people are thus distracted by external things the worship of God is profaned." [12] And the reforming Popes hated the Greek statues their predecessors had brought to the Vatican as "those idols of the heathen," filled their galleries with fig-leaves, and carefully painted breeches upon all the nude figures in Michelangelo's Last Judgment. The very emphasis on literal truthfulness at all times, which was one of the chief glories of the Puritans, and powerfully aided the scientific temper of mind, made them dislike all symbolism and disapprove of poetry and romance. More and more the Puritan tended to become the professional and nothing else, and in such a Spartan discipline most of the amenities of life were lost.

The Puritan Spirit and Industrialism

Naturally this temper lent itself admirably to the ideals of the middle class.

The moral discipline enforced by Puritanism had a considerable reaction on industry. The Christian life was regarded as essentially an ordered life. The passions were to be under rational control. Puritanism cut men off from wasteful expenditure and worldly pleasure. Forms of indulgence which dissipated both wealth and energy were sternly denounced and repressed. Time and talents were not to be wasted. On the contrary, the Christian's first duty was to make the most of his powers and possessions in whatever might be his calling. Idleness was a sure sign that one's standing in grace was doubtful. No one should be unemployed; even the man of leisure should find some occupation which would be of service to the common weal. Puritan pressure in these directions certainly tended to develop the spirit of enterprise and industry characteristic of modern capitalism. Both by inculcating frugality and by strengthening home ties, Puritanism encouraged thrift and the accumulation of capital. Moreover, by insisting on a careful use of time and on self-control, it helped to form those regular habits on which the conduct of modern industry depends. The business virtues, viz., honesty, punctuality, and steady application to work, were reinforced by the ethic of Puritanism. Once again, the emphasis on personal responsibility which was characteristic of the movement served to make men bring an independent judgment to bear on their business problems, and so increased the power of individual initiative. After 1662 [when the English Puritans were driven from the Church and government] the influence of Puritanism was thrown still more clearly on the side of economic freedom. For the Puritans, having lost power, naturally distrusted state control, while they were in any case convinced opponents of state absolutism. Their first concern was [now] toleration, and they became the champions of the movement for limiting state interference in every direction.[13]

Thus the ultimate outcome of the Reformation morally was a type of ideal, whether the Puritanism of England or the Jansenism of Port-Royal in France, that bent men's energies to industry, and served the middle class. Lutheranism with its emphasis on the sacredness of the calling, and even more Calvinism, stimulated those qualities necessary for worldly success, advocated the stern performance of the daily task to the exclusion of all else, and looked upon prosperity as a mark of God's favor. The great English Nonconformist divine, Richard Baxter, illustrates Puritanism as going even farther. "You may labor in that manner as tendeth most to your success and lawful gain," he said, "for you are bound to improve all your talents.... If God show you a way in which you may lawfully get more than in another way, if you refuse this and choose the less gainful way, you cross one of the ends of your calling, and you refuse to be God's steward." [14]

This characteristic alliance of the spirit of Puritanism with that of the commercial classes lies deeper in the heart of the Northerners than the religious doctrines of Protestantism. It

[13] From Hastings' *Encyclopedia*. Reprinted by permission of the publishers, Charles Scribner's Sons.

THE REVOLT FROM THE MEDIEVAL CHURCH 161

was already present in the German humanists, marking them off most clearly from the Italians, and it became even stronger in the later rationalists who outgrew the rigidity of Calvinism. Thus Wimpfeling, one of the earliest and most conservative of the Germans, laid down *Laws for the Young* in his *Adolescentia* which especially emphasized frugality and bade them seek honest work and avoid idleness; while the intensely practical Benjamin Franklin preached many a sermon on thrift and industry from the text, "Seest thou a man diligent in his business? He shall stand before kings!" [15] But the Puritans went farthest in consecrating business to God. In works like Baxter's *Christian Directory*, the best handbook of Puritan moral theology, and Steele's *Religious Tradesman*, it is clear how the Puritan insistence both on unremitting diligence and toil and on the sin of enjoying riches through wasteful and thriftless consumption combined to enjoin the amassing of wealth as a sacred duty. Work and saving together built up modern capitalism. Even the endless pursuit of money that rests not to make it serve the good life, one of the most lasting heritages of Puritanism in our present age, is directly prescribed. "Though the rich have no outward want to urge them, they have as great a necessity to obey God.... God had strictly commanded work to all." [16] "Next to the saving of his soul the tradesman's care and business is to serve God in his calling, and to drive it as far as it will go," wrote Steele.[17] No wonder that the Puritan attitude has ever been dear to the middle class. "Be wholly taken up in diligent business of your lawful callings when you are not exercised in the more immediate service of God," [18] has to this day been the middle-class ideal.

When the older Calvinism waned, the eighteenth century beheld religious revivals that called men back to this same spirit. It was the Wesleyan north of England that effected the Industrial Revolution; and in Germany Zinzendorf, founder of the Moravians and leader of the pietistic German Puritanism, wrote: "Man works not only to live, but man lives that he may work, and if man has no work he either suffers or dies." [19]

The Political Revolt

The political revolt, which, as truly as the religious or the moral, characterized the Reformation changes from the medieval

Church, had the same effect. We have seen how the chief political struggle of the Middle Ages was waged between a religious and a lay control of society, the contest between the Papacy and the temporal monarchs. Though the Empire was vanquished by the Popes, who reigned supreme in the thirteenth century, the fight went on, and the imperial claims were taken up by the kings of France and England. Boniface VIII, the last of the great medieval Popes, in vain hurled his bulls *Clericis laicos*, forbidding any taxation of the clergy, and *Unam sanctam*, asserting universal papal monarchy, at the English Church. The English Government gained a large measure of control over the Church and almost complete freedom from papal interference. The French king sent his lawyers to kidnap Boniface, and the Papacy was brought to Avignon for the entire fourteenth century, completely subservient to France. The important movement that produced the great Councils of Constance and Basel in the next century, with the double aim of substituting constitutional for absolute government in the Church, and establishing the right of the national civil government to order the Church in its realm, failed, and the Papacy emerged stronger than ever; but this very failure, convincing men that reform was impossible, led on to open revolt. In all the Protestant lands a national church was set up, under the control of the Government. One of the chief reasons for the failure of the Protestant Huguenots in France was the fact that the Gallican or French Church had already become largely a national institution under the royal control. This secular dominance increased when the Pragmatic Sanction of Bourges, which the Gallican Church had exacted at the Council of Basel, and which gave the French bishops in council the supreme power, was succeeded by the Concordat of Bologna in 1516, which put the appointive and taxing powers into the king's hands. Thereafter the Gallican Church, under the king, enjoyed till the Revolution a very large measure of autonomy. The one great power that remained faithful to the Papacy, Charles V's empire of Spain and his German realms, rather controlled it for its purposes than adhered to any cosmopolitan ideal. Everywhere the sovereign State had broken away from the united Christendom of the thirteenth century.

This meant that everywhere the spiritual power of religion was made to serve the ends of the rising absolute monarchs; and the ends of those monarchs, who commenced to claim that their rule was as much by divine right as the Church's, were, as we shall see, in the main identical with those of the capitalistic middle classes. Thus the outcome of the political revolt against the universal monarchy of the medieval Church was a change from the religious ordering of social life to the social and economic ordering of religious life. Those places where the Church still exercised a theocratic rule over the State, Calvinistic Geneva and Scotland and the English Commonwealth, but prove the rule: for there the Calvinistic merchants and tradesmen ruled directly, not by deputy.

To this nationalism and secularism the Papacy replied with Ultramontanism; that is, a reaffirmation of the supremacy of the Pope "beyond the mountains" and independent of individual governments. The Council of Trent, just because the issue was so bitter between the Roman Curia and the bishops, made no statement on their respective powers; but the outcome was to strengthen the Papacy. The Thomists favored it, and in the Jesuits it found a willing and potent servant. But the exigencies of the political situation made all claims for the Papacy seem claims for Spain, and there was little hope for the reëstablishment, even in Catholic lands, of the dream of Innocent III and Dante. Not until the nineteenth century, with new influences at work, did Ultramontanism, in a more genuinely cosmopolitan sense, come into its own, resulting in the new dogma of Papal Infallibility promulgated by Pius IX, and in the growth of clerical parties in the Catholic countries.

The Reformation and the Renaissance

We are now in a position to appraise the general significance of the Protestant and Catholic Reformations for the building of the modern mind. A comparison with the work of the Renaissance is inevitable, and here every possible view has been held, from seeing a complete identity of aim in both to a complete opposition. It has been our contention that both movements, humanism and the Protestant revolt, were essentially the outcome of the same fundamental causes, primarily the growth of the economic basis of European society; and that despite the pronounced antipathy of the leaders for each other, the indirect results, when the smoke of battle had settled, were not dissimilar. Neither Renaissance nor Reformation was the movement that produced the really great revolution from the medieval to the modern world; that was effected by the gradual development of science, and science, though indirectly stimulated by both, was at best an almost accidental by-product in each case. The Reformation, to be sure, was intellectually a return to the cardinal tenets of the medieval world-view, and morally a reaction against the willful naturalism of the Renaissance; but this distinction, important as it seemed at the time, is really not particularly significant; both alike rejected the medieval asceticism and other-worldliness. In one sense the humanism of the Renaissance can be considered also a medieval reaction, for it departed from the growing interest in the world of nature that sprang from the scientific thirteenth century, and through its loss of concern in God became really much more anthropocentric than the great scholastics and their successors. If the Reformation by centering the intellectual interests in theological questions delayed for two hundred years the growth and popular spread of science, it must not be forgotten that the emphasis of humanism on the classics prevented anything like a general scientific education until the middle of the nineteenth century. At best science had to make its way in men's minds against the more or less open disdain of the apostles of both great movements. It is difficult to say whether Protestantism or Catholicism proved the more responsive to the scientific and naturalistic spirit. If in Catholic France the eighteenth-century Enlightenment burst forth in more radical form than in any Protestant country, it owed much to the ideas of Protestant England. To-day there is little to choose between, on this score.

The Renaissance and the Reformation, if we emphasize not those points on which they have left little permanent effect, but those that have influenced the world to the present, show striking similarities. Both sprang from pretty much the same causes, the growth of society and the town class. Both thought they were returning to antiquity, to the golden age of Rome and of Christianity. Both were revolts against medieval scholasticism. Neither was primarily intellectual or scientific. Both were individualistic reactions from the corporate world of the Middle Ages, and from its other-worldliness. The Renaissance saw the cultural, the Reformation the ethical, values of wealth, prosperity, industry, and domestic life. Neither made a complete break with authority, the one retaining the Bible, the other the ancients; neither rejected superstition — astrology and alchemy delighted all the souls of the sixteenth century — nor accepted a rationalistic view. Neither, on the whole, cared for tolerance: if Calvin burned Servetus and the Puritans persecuted the ungodly without cease, the great Renaissance burnt its Savonarolas and its Hussites and its Lollards, and even Erasmus, kindly soul, wished the Anabaptists and all other social radicals stamped out.

Perhaps the most vital difference between the two movements lay in the aristocratic spirit of the Renaissance and the more or less implicit democracy of the Reformation. The humanist sought to educate the classes; the reformer, to convert the masses. Hence, while humanism left the masses an easy prey to the Catholic reaction, the Protestant revolt at least started all men thinking on their beliefs, and was the initial step in breaking down for them the medieval synthesis. Whereas the education that the Catholic reformation instituted was primarily for the upper classes, in all Protestant lands save possibly England literacy and a certain rudimentary schooling became the property of most men. One other difference deserves mention. The Reformation was overwhelmingly an appeal to nationalistic sentiment; the reformers used the vernacular, and the various translations of the Bible became the foundation of national literatures. While humanism indirectly stimulated nationalism and national literatures enormously, many individual humanists, like Erasmus, were pacifists who relied on a cosmopolitan upper-class Latin culture.

The Outcome of the Reformation

What, then, were the effects, indirect but powerful, of the Reformation in bringing the modern world to pass out of the medieval world? Most significant of all, the unity and completeness of the great medieval synthesis was broken. No longer was the Christian system one organic whole. Certain elements had been selected as important and used to criticize the others, and when this process has once begun, no amount of compromise can preserve the remnants intact. Theologians might thunder and state churches persecute, but all was of no avail: the example of the reformers was bound to prove more potent than their efforts to stem the tide. Luther had shown that there could be a way of salvation outside the medieval Church, and had appealed to a rational interpretation of scriptural authority to support him. A breach had been made in the closed universe of medieval belief, and the long fight for liberty, that is, for the right of the individual intelligence to pursue its ends untrammeled by any fixed limits, had been started. If this liberty is now enjoyed more fully in the religious field than anywhere else, it is at least in part due to the fact that the fight began there, reluctant as its protagonists have usually been to accord it to others. When once selection and rejection starts, authority in the intellectual field is doomed.

In the second place, medieval scholasticism, in Protestantism and Catholicism alike, was pushed into the background. However it might linger on in Jesuit theologians like Suarez or Protestants like Melanchthon, it no longer passed current at its old value. Trent had settled the chief questions for the Catholics, the Protestants had substituted Augustine for Aristotle. Medieval science was discredited, and just because the reformers scorned all science the way was left open for a new science to assert its claims to the field.

Thirdly, the individualism of Protestantism was bound to result finally in the transference of the seat of intellectual authority to the experience and reason of the individual. It is true that the much-vaunted Protestant right of private judgment in matters of religion and conscience, of individual interpretation of scriptural authority, meant little at first unless backed up by force. Protestants and Catholics alike of the Reformation era detested reason. "He who is gifted with the heavenly knowledge of faith," said the Catechism of the Council of Trent, "is free from an inquisitive curiosity; for when God commands us to believe, he does not propose to have us search into his divine judgments, nor to inquire their reasons and causes, but demands an immutable faith.... Faith, therefore, excludes not only all doubt, but even the desire of subjecting its truth to demonstration." [20] Thus far had the Church come from the searching intellect of Saint Thomas! Luther thundered against reason, calling her "that silly little fool, that Devil's bride, Dame

THE REVOLT FROM THE MEDIEVAL CHURCH 167

Reason, God's worst enemy"; and said, "We know that reason is the Devil's harlot, and can do nothing but slander and harm all that God says and does. If, outside of Christ, you wish by your own thoughts to know your relation to God, you will break your neck. Thunder strikes him who examines. It is Satan's wisdom to tell what God is, and by doing so he will draw you into the abyss. Therefore keep to revelation and do not try to understand." [21] Calvin abhorred the free inquiry of the humanists as the supreme heresy of free thought.

And all alike called in the civil government to stamp out dissenting beliefs. The Catholics set up their "Holy Office" of the Inquisition, steadfast in their traditional certainty that they possessed the only saving truth. Luther, to be sure, in his early period, before he gained power, demanded tolerance, declaring that "Heresy can never be prevented by force," and that "Faith is free. What could a heresy trial do? No more than make people agree by mouth or in writing; it could not compel the heart." He even at first allowed the Anabaptists to believe what they liked, "be it gospel or lies"; and he never went so far as his followers.[22] But the Lutherans put them to death, and Melanchthon presided over a genuine inquisition in Saxony that murdered its hundreds. Bucer, Zwingli, Calvin, all alike demanded that heretics be executed, and the Scots' Confession of 1560 decreed, "We utterly abhor the blasphemy of those that affirm that men who live according to equity and justice shall be saved, what religion so ever they have professed." [23] Even the humanists, like Erasmus, granted no toleration to the masses, and Sir Thomas More could advocate tolerance for all save social radicals in his *Utopia* and burn heretics in his actual life. In the midst of such an orgy of fanatical hatred the voice of a Montaigne, sagely observing that no belief was worth burning your neighbor for, was a voice whispering in the wilderness. Toleration could not come until men trusted the reason of the individual; it is significant that the first influential pleas came from Bayle and Locke, the popularizers respectively of French and English rationalism. And such trust was possible only when the warfare of competing sects had compelled it.

Yet for all this, toleration and the recognition of the authority of the individual reason and conscience did spring from the Reformation. In spite of all this riot of bloodshed, multitudes were willing to die for what they thought to be true; and the new groups, when in the minority, gradually built up a theory of toleration. The Anabaptists, the Unitarians, the gentle and doughty Quakers, never tasting power, were its steadfast apostles. Huguenots in France, Catholics in Protestant lands like England, even the fanatical Puritans themselves when the Restoration deposed them from power, waxed eloquent on the rights of conscience, and gradually, from prudential reasons, governments hearkened to them. In Holland, which had tasted most bitterly the fruit of persecution, toleration was most completely established, and Holland during the seventeenth century became the refuge of sturdy individualists like the Pilgrims, the "atheist" Spinoza, and the rationalist Descartes, and naturally waxed glorious in her thinkers. And finally Baptists in Rhode Island and Catholics in Maryland actually practiced wide toleration when they themselves were in power. For Luther and even more the Calvinists, in themselves appealing to an interpretation of Biblical authority by human reason, had let loose a stream of rationalism that could not fail to swell, ever increased by the popular education they needed to support their position. It is highly important to point out here that what the Reformation largely accomplished in Protestant lands, the Cartesian faith in reason, springing from that other great liberating force, the scientific temper of mind, brought about in France. It was Cartesian rationalism that, more than any other single factor, kept France from sinking into the intellectual stagnation that has marked Catholic countries since the Counter-Reformation, and cast her lot in rather with the inquiring and questioning Protestants.

Finally, the Reformation, while adding nothing to the content of education, contributed greatly to its spread. The humanist movement had narrowed education from the broad if superficial scope it had possessed during the height of the Middle Ages, to the thorough study of Latin and Greek, and in such a meager curriculum Europe has been schooled till the last generation. Save in the upper-class Jesuit schools, which soon became the best in the world and held their preëminence well into the eighteenth century, nothing was heard of the rising sciences. Such has been our heritage from the great liberating Renaissance! But this education, such as it was, was popularized by the Re-

THE REVOLT FROM THE MEDIEVAL CHURCH

formation. After the first unsettled conditions had subsided, an effort was made in all Protestant lands save England to educate the masses, at least to give them the indispensable means of reading the Bible. Luther's voice was raised mightily for popular education, and from his followers date not only most of Germany's great upper and middle class gymnasia, but even more the village schools that have made her learning. The Calvinists, with their insistence on theological training and the study of the Bible, were naturally the most zealous for widespread education; Geneva and Scotland had the best systems of all, and the Puritans even penetrated England and her colonies. Universities were founded in Protestant Germany in great numbers, though they soon fell into an even narrower scholasticism than the old, and remained aloof from the vivifying touch of science; nine new institutions sprang up in Spain. The University of Paris sank into a lethargy, but Francis I founded the Collège de France to shelter the new humanism and — wonder of wonders! — science. Oxford and Cambridge fell low indeed, until Puritan influences revived them. But the foremost universities were the ambitious new one at Geneva, from which reformed learning flowed all over Europe, and, greatest of all, Leyden in Holland, which for two centuries, thanks to the combination of Calvinism and toleration, clearly led all Europe in learning and in fostering the new science.

REFERENCES

1. *Theologia Germanica*, Winkworth ed., ch. 27.
2. Erasmus, *Letter to Maldonato*, quoted in P. Smith, *Erasmus*, 358.
3. Luther, *Christian Liberty*, Wace and Buchheim ed., 268.
4. Calvin, *Institute of the Christian Religion*, Bk. IV, ch. X, par. 7.
5. Erasmus, *Handbook of the Christian Knight*, quoted in P. Smith, *Erasmus*, 57.
6. Erasmus, *Greek Testament*, Note to Matthew, XI, 30, quoted in P. Smith, *Age of the Reformation*, 58.
7. Mrs. Hutchinson, quoted in J. R. Green, *Short History of the English People*, ch. VIII, sec. 1.
8. *Ibid.*
9. *Ibid.*
10. Bunyan, quoted in same.
11. Bunyan, quoted in article "Puritanism" in Hastings' *Encyclopedia of Religion and Ethics*.
12. Calvin, quoted in P. Smith, *Age of the Reformation*, 690.
13. H. G. Wood, article "Puritanism" in Hastings' *Encyclopedia*.
14. Richard Baxter, *Christian Directory*, I, ch. X, tit. I, Dis. 9, par. 24.
15. Proverbs, ch. 22, v. 29.
16. Baxter, *Christian Directory*, 376.
17. Richard Steele, *The Religious Tradesman*, quoted in R. H. Tawney, "Re-

ligious Thought on Social and Economic Questions in the Sixteenth and Seventeenth Centuries," in *Journal of Political Economy*, 1923.
18. Baxter, *op. cit.*, 336.
19. Zinzendorf, Plitt ed., I, 428.
20. *Catechism of the Council of Trent*, quoted in P. Smith, *Age of the Reformation*, 625.
21. Luther, quoted in same, 625.
22. *Ibid.*, 643.
23. *Scots' Confession of 1560*, quoted in same, 646.

SELECTED READING LISTS

General Interpretations: Preserved Smith, *Age of the Reformation*, most recent and best survey, emphasizing social forces; ch. XIV gives full account of the various interpretations. E. C. Hulme, *Renaissance and Reformation*. T. M. Lindsay, *History of the Reformation*, religious emphasis. *Cambridge Modern History*, vol. II, *Reformation*, III, *Wars of Religion;* Lavisse et Rambaud, t. IV, V. Church histories of W. Moeller, P. Schaff (Protestant); J. Alzog, J. Hergenröther (Catholic). A. C. Flick, *Decline of the Med. Church*, II, Pt. iv; H. S. Lucas, *The Ren. and the Ref.*; J. W. Thompson, *Econ. and Soc. H. of Europe in the Later M.A.*; A. Hyma, *The Christian Renaissance*. Interpretations by Charles Beard, *The Reformation of the 16th century;* E. Troeltsch, *Protestantisches Christenthum u. Kirche der Neuzeit, Die Bedeutung d. Protestantismus für die Entstehung der modernen Welt* (liberal Protestant); Karl Pearson, *Ethic of Free Thought*, c. 9; Santayana, *Reason in Religion;* C. Guignebert, *Christianity, Past and Present* (rationalists). Gibbon's famous estimate is in c. 54 of the *Decline and Fall*. See also Preserved Smith, *Erasmus*, and W. Dilthey, *Weltanschauung u. Analyse des Menschen seit Ren. u. Ref., Ges. Schriften*, II.

New Religious Ideals: A. C. McGiffert, *Protestant Thought before Kant*, lucid survey; J. A. Dorner, *Ges. d. protestantischen Theologie*, standard German work. P. Schaff, *Creeds of Christendom*, III, contains the Reformation formulations. Luther, *Primary Works*, ed. H. Wace and C. A. Buchheim. Lives of Luther by A. C. McGiffert, Preserved Smith, A. Lipsky; J. Köstlin, J. McKinnon, fuller. H. Boehmer, *Luther and the Reformation*. Zwingli, *Selected Works*, ed. S. M. Jackson; life by S. M. Jackson. Calvin, *Institute of the Christian Religion*, ed. B. B. Warfield; lives by G. E. Harkness, W. W. Walker.

The Catholic Reformation: P. Smith, E. H. Hulme; M. C. D'Arcy, *Catholicism*. P. Imbart de la Tour, *Les Origines de la Réforme*, survey of the Church at the time of the Reformation. Lord Acton, *Lectures on Modern History*, pp. 108 ff. L. von Pastor, *H. of the Popes*, standard. A. W. Ward, *The Counter-Reformation;* G. Droysen, *Ges. d. Gegenreformation*. On Jesuits: H. Boehmer, *Die Jesuiten*, Fr. tr. by Monod, concise and unbiased; J. McCabe, *A Candid Hist. of the Jesuits*, hostile but accurate. *Autobiography* of Ignatius Loyola, ed. F. X. O'Conor; T. A. Hughes, *Loyola and the Educational System of the Jesuits;* life by H. D. Sedgwick. E. D. Salmon, *Imperial Spain*. H. C. Lea, *H. of the Inquisition in Spain*, a crushing arraignment; Catholic defenses by E. Vacandard, A. L. Maycock.

The Moral Revolution and Puritanism: J. S. Schapiro, *Social Reform and the Reformation;* E. Troeltsch, *The Soc. Teachings of the Christian Churches*, c. 3. See J. R. Green, *Short Hist. of the English People*, c. 8, for defense of Puritanism; Milton is the best representative. Criticisms from the standpoint of psychology in H. L. Mencken, *Book of Prefaces, Prejudices, 2nd Series;* H. E. Barnes, *Twilight of Christianity*. E. H. Byington, *The Puritans in England and New England;* S. S. Flynn, *Influence of Puritanism on the Pol. and Religious Thought of the English*. Brooks Adams, *The Emancipation of Massa-*

chusetts. H. W. Schneider, *The Puritan Mind;* Perry Miller, *The New England Mind.* J. Haroutunian, *From Piety to Morals.*

Protestantism and Middle Class Ideals: Max Weber, *The Protestant Ethic and the Spirit of Capitalism;* criticism in H. M. Robertson, *Aspects of the Rise of Economic Individualism.* R. H. Tawney, *Religion and the Rise of Capitalism.* O. A. Marti, *The Econ. Causes of the Reformation in England.* M. Beer, *Social Struggles and Socialist Forerunners.* G. G. Coulton, *Art and the Reformation.* Thomas More, *Utopia;* Montaigne, *Essays*, Bk. II, c. 19; Milton, *Areopagitica.*

Toleration: Lord Acton, *History of Freedom;* J. B. Bury, *H. of the Freedom of Thought;* J. M. Robertson, *Short Hist. of Free Thought;* W. E. H. Lecky, *History of Rationalism in Europe;* W. R. Jordan, *Development of Religious Toleration in England.*

The Reformation and Education: P. Monroe, *History of Education*, ch. VII; F. P. Graves, *History of Education during the Middle Ages and the Transition to Modern Times.* F. Paulsen, *Ges. des gelehrten Unterrichts in Deutschland.* T. Elyot, *Boke named the Governour;* R. Ascham, *The Scholemaster;* F. Bacon, *Advancement of Learning*, Bk. II. C. Borgeaud, *Histoire de l'Université de Genève.*

CHAPTER VIII

THE REVOLT FROM FEUDALISM AND A UNIFIED CHRISTENDOM

THE growing forces of European social life burst the bonds of the medieval spiritual power, and created not only new national churches, but also new sects within each nation, in whose mutual rivalry there was finally offered to rationalism and science a firm foothold. In the economic and political life of Christendom these same tendencies worked an even more profound change, and here too new conditions found expression in new theories and ideals. Out of this redirection of social energies that marked the period of the Commercial Revolution, there emerged political conceptions that have dominated thought and action almost to the present day, and ideals of international relations that have not since changed appreciably.

We can summarize the political revolution that in those days came to pass, as the replacement of the medieval ideal of a united Christendom loosely bound together, serving God and man under the guidance of the spiritual power of the Church, by the ideal of a group of independent, irresponsible, absolutely sovereign territorial states, the avowed sanction of whose acts is power. If we compare merely the ideals which found expression in the better thought of the Middle Ages and of most of the modern period, it is indisputable that this change involved a great loss. "For King and Country," "For the glory of France," "My country, right or wrong" — such a chauvinistic and commercial patriotism, above which men rose only in the Age of Reason and, in aspiration, to-day, contrasts ill with the noble medieval conception of a united Christendom. It is only in the last few generations that even the greatest souls have beheld the vision of an internationalism in which the richness of variety and the development of many kinds of excellence might go hand in hand with a unity of nations in humanitarian enterprise. But if we compare the actual attainments, it is to the sober critic fairly clear that the modern national State, with all its vices, is at least no worse in practice than the private warfare of feudalism. Indeed, it may be contended that the era of competitive patriotisms and Machiavellian policy was a real and for its time a necessary advance over the manorial and town economy of the Middle Ages. A national unit of economic life means the production of a greater number of values at a less cost, a more intricate division of labor, and consequently a richer and fuller intellectual life and more varied activities. If these things be good, we can perhaps say with the banker Cosimo de' Medici, "You place your ladders in the heavens; I on earth, that I may not seek so high or fall so low." [1]

The Rise of National Cultures and Sentiment

This fundamental change really contains three component parts. First, under the demands of commerce, the social energies of an increasingly important class were concentrated on the State rather than the local town, and the scale of economic operations was correspondingly enlarged and deepened. Secondly, this very concentration caused the limits of society to narrow from world-empire to the national or territorial State. Thirdly, as a resultant of both these tendencies, the authority clearly shifted from the Church to the civil government, a result largely expressed in the Protestant revolt. But before we analyze these movements and the ideas under which they fought, we must first examine the great sweeping change that came over the minds of the people, the growth of nationalism and patriotism in the modern sense. The three changes produced by the Commercial Revolution benefited and interested directly only a very small class; rightly or wrongly, the vast majority cared little about them. But with the close of the Middle Ages there grew up a great wave of popular sentiment in the peoples of Europe that transformed the old feudal loyalty to an individual lord into a broader and more comprehensive loyalty to country and countrymen. In the West of Europe there appeared for the first time what might definitely be called "National States," domains whose inhabitants were held together by a more or less vague but intensely real feeling of solidarity with their own kind and enmity to all others. This nationalistic or patriotic sentiment is such a commonplace to-day that we can hardly realize that it is not rooted in human nature, but first appeared at a fairly definite era in European history. It explains how the middle class was able to gain popular support for the social and political changes they advocated; without it, it is doubtful if all their economic power would have availed them in a society still overwhelmingly agricultural. By joining to their own economic interests this sentiment of patriotic pride — the middle class were naturally the keenest in their patriotic loyalty — they greatly reinforced the movement toward national sovereignty, and began the alliance so characteristic of all modern history, the intelligent commercial classes both sharing and using for their own ends the powerful but blind force of nationalism. The first step in this tale was the concentration of commercial interest and patriotism upon the king or monarch, and it succeeded triumphantly in defeating the feudal landlords.

It is easy to see the fostering and impelling hand of the middle class in the birth of modern nationalism, but it is also easy to overlook the other forces which served to help it along. Though it is impossible to separate clearly the different tendencies making for the same end, it is plain that, while economic interests dictated the particular form which the nationalistic States took, they were working with forces that would have demanded some expression in any case. There are the beginnings of a national patriotism in the Italian and the German peoples, even though they did not achieve unity and power till the nineteenth century. Before turning to the specific forms that the aspirations of the rising new classes took, let us sketch in this background of popular sentiment.

War seems ever the father of patriotism — which may be a virtue of war, and may be the bar sinister of patriotism. War had contributed to the formation of the three strong national States in Europe in 1500, and had unified the loyalty of their peoples. In the Hundred Years' War between the English and the French, concluded in 1453, Saxon-Celts and Norman conquerors had been welded together on one side of the Channel, while on the other the different States of France had come to feel a common bond. In Spain the various Christian monarchs had been fighting together a long fierce crusade against the Moors, and the very year that marked the expulsion of the last Mohammedans from Cordova marked the beginning of a vastly more important conquest in the New World. The union of all Spain under the one monarch Charles V was the symbol of the triumph of Spanish nationalism over the older particularism. Elsewhere smaller States, like Scotland and Switzerland, had developed the same sense in struggling against their more powerful neighbors. These wars had been conducted on a much larger scale than the earlier operations of the Middle Ages; those, in which men could stop over the week-end, and all go home for the harvest, were scarcely wars in the civilized sense at all. By their close, the various racial stocks that had since the Dark Ages dwelt side by side had in the lands of Western Europe been united into truly national peoples.

Moreover, both English and French patriotism were enormously strengthened by the long civil wars between rival factions of the feudal barons. The Barons' Wars in thirteenth-century England had already flowered in the strengthened monarchy of the Edwards, and the Wars of the Roses between Lancaster and York had exhausted the baronial class, exterminated the older houses, and turned men to Edward IV, who represented both the demand for peace and order and the spirit of trade and commerce. Under the Tudors this had its effect in a rising tide of strong government in the interests of the middle classes, and in the glorification of the Virgin Queen as the symbol of a united, prosperous England. With power and expansion came the creation of English literature by the Elizabethan poets and dramatists. France too had her civil wars, following the expulsion of the English in the fifteenth century, and again in the religious struggles of the next; and the triumph of the patriots over both factions, in the person of the first Bourbon, Henry IV, was the signal for the creation of a great French literature in the seventeenth century.

This rise of truly national cultures is, all in all, the chief element in the formation of the nationalistic sentiment. The thirteenth century had seen the growth of a large lay public interested in literature and learning, and the invention of printing had enabled these men to enjoy the luxury of books. Protestantism brought with it the translation of the Bible into the vernacular, and its wide reading and even worship throughout the Northern peoples; it brought also schools and literacy. In all Protestant lands the native Bible became the foundation of their literatures. These forces had two results. On the one hand, they tended to obliterate the medieval differences between the language of one town and the next, and to prevent the rapid change that is continually taking place in an unwritten and purely spoken tongue; language, which earlier had varied from manor to manor and almost forced recourse to Latin for all communication, and which had changed more in fifty years before than in four hundred years since the invention of printing, now became uniform and standardized over wide areas and stable for generations. On the other hand, the Latin culture of Christendom was disrupted, for the men of one nation now had an adequate vehicle to express their thoughts and emotions; they were acquiring a literature common to themselves and unintelligible to their neighbors.

The humanistic revival strengthened national cultures in several ways. In despising the colloquial and simple Latin of the Middle Ages, easy to learn and speak, and substituting for it an involved and difficult Ciceronian style, quite alien, in fact, to the spoken vulgar Latin of the Roman Empire, it made Latin the property of the learned few and destroyed the possibility of a general language for all Christendom. It is significant that the Italians, among whom humanism was most popular, wonderful as was their achievement in art, never created a first-rate Renaissance literature, while the French, the Spanish, and the English were bursting into song. The early pleas of Dante and his noble example were disregarded, and Petrarch despised his Italian sonnets, which alone of his writings live to-day. Secondly, the reverence for the city-republics of antiquity and for great Rome brought with it a revival of the civic patriotism of the ancient world and its glorification of the State; and many a man like Machiavelli found his patriotic aspirations strengthened by the perusal of the stirring pages of Livy and Virgil.

For examples of this patriotic support of a strong government we have but to turn to Machiavelli in Italy or Shakespeare in England. Machiavelli is the supreme exemplar of the doctrine, "My country, right or wrong"; or, rather, he went farther, for he believed that what strengthened his country could not be wrong. Chancellor of the Republic of Florence, his vision was broad enough to include all Italy, and he searched for years for the strong and ruthless man who would liberate her from the barbarians who treated the Italian States as the pawns in their greater games.

At the present time, in order to discover the virtue of an Italian spirit, it was necessary that Italy should be reduced to the extremity she is now in, that she should be more enslaved than the Hebrews, more oppressed than the Persians, more scattered than the Athenians; without head, without order, beaten, despoiled, torn, overrun; and to have endured every kind of desolation.... Italy, left as without life, waits for him who shall yet heal her wounds and put an end to the ravaging and plundering of Lombardy, to the swindling and taxing of the Kingdom and of Tuscany, and cleanse those sores that for long have festered. It is seen how she entreats God to send someone who shall deliver her from these wrongs and barbarous insolencies.... This opportunity, therefore, ought not to be allowed to pass for letting Italy at last see her liberator appear. Nor can one express the love with which he would be received in all those provinces which have suffered so much from these foreign scourings, with what thirst for revenge, with what stubborn faith, with what devotion, with what tears. What door would be closed to him? Who would refuse obedience to him? What envy would hinder him? What Italian would refuse him homage?[2]

Shakespeare expresses to the full that love of England in the intense, almost physical sense, that breathes through the whole of Elizabethan literature. If Machiavelli longs for an Italy yet unborn, he glories in the noblest pride and the tenderest sentiment for an England already great.

> This royal throne of kings, this sceptered isle,
> This earth of majesty, this seat of Mars,
> This other Eden, demi-paradise,
> This fortress built by Nature for herself
> Against infection and the hand of war,
> This happy breed of men, this little world,
> This precious stone set in the silver sea,
> Which serves it in the office of a wall
> Or as a moat defensive to a house,
> Against the envy of less happier lands,
> This blessed plot, this earth, this realm, this England.[3]

Shakespeare's historical dramas reveal the deep impression made by the Wars of the Roses on the minds of the subjects of the Tudors. The heritage from the struggles of York and Lancaster had been a profound dread of civil war, of baronial turbulence, of disputed succession, from which the Crown seemed the one security, the center and the safeguard of national life. The poet's ideal England is an England grouped round such a king as his beloved hero, Henry V, a born ruler of men, with a loyal people about him and his enemies at his feet. In the power of the monarch he saw the safeguard against feudal interference with the peace and the foreign might of Spain alike.

The Emergence of Centralized National States

Against this background of national self-love and hatred of all foes, within or abroad, who would disturb the growth of the nation's power, there was worked out a change in institutions and in thought which out of the medieval mixture of theocracy and confusion created the modern State. This transformation took place through a long series of struggles, and the parties often seemed to be working at cross-purposes; yet throughout it is possible to discern the increasing force of trade and commerce supporting now this side, now that, in the political field, and ever gaining a surer control over its own destinies. The battle was fought first between the Papacy on the one hand and the feudal nobility on the other, and the national monarch; then, having used him to break their other foes, the middle class, aided by the Protestant sects, demanded and gained from him first fixed rights and then direct control, maintaining the while the irresponsible sovereignty that he had won. The course of this struggle, therefore, called forth political theories and conceptions which, first, should exalt the monarch as against the divinely supported Papacy; secondly, should set him over against the heritage of feudal custom and power; and thirdly, when his work was done and the power lodged in a national government, should take over that power for the middle class. Just as the formulation of the scientific world view takes us beyond Cartesianism to Isaac Newton, so the formulation of the political position won by the Dutch and English takes us to John Locke, and these two great figures stand as the source of the eighteenth-century synthesis, and the fountain-head of the thought of the Enlightenment.

It has been pointed out how even in theory the Middle Ages recognized no such thing as irresponsible power or sovereignty; in the modern and legal sense of the term, there was no State, and no sovereign power. The lord of any domain was bound hand and foot by the obligations of custom and the contractual nature of his feudal obligations to those below him, while even the Emperor was constrained to govern in accordance with the laws of the Church. Theoretically, the Papacy was not an irresponsible power, but set on earth to administer the divine laws; in practice, however, since the Pope was vicegerent of God on earth, he did, with Innocent III or Boniface VIII, lay claim to the supreme power. The only State in the Middle Ages was the Church, and the Pope was not only the absolute monarch over his own spiritual realm, but he claimed and to a large extent exercised that supreme and universal jurisdiction which the lawyers of Rome had claimed for the *imperium* of the sovereign. He was supreme dispenser of law, fountain of all honor, including the regal, sole legitimate earthly source of power, founder of all religious orders, granter of university degrees, supreme judge and divider among nations, guardian of international right, and avenger of Christian blood; the civil or temporal authority was, in the eyes of the papal canonists, merely the police department of the Church. Since the Protestant revolt, these powers have all been transferred to the national State, and the theory of omnipotence, which the Pope held on the plea that any action might come under his cognizance if it concerned morality, has been taken over by the national State on the theory that any action, if it involves money or contract, must be a matter for the courts.

The Birth of Modern Political Theory

The process by which this theoretical power was transferred from the Pope to the national monarch, and from the national monarch to the people, was paralleled by the actual transference of real power from the clergy and manorial lords to the king governing in the interests of the middle class, and from the king to more direct representatives of that class. It was effected by means of ideas and conceptions and types of thinking which seem as obsolete to all but lawyers to-day — for they are still the basis of our legal systems and our written constitutions — as do the theological terms in which the Middle Ages and the era of the Reformation formulated their philosophic problems. Yet underneath both alien forms of thought there beat a living reality, and if we are to understand aright the legal basis of present-day beliefs about government — rights and laws and jurisdiction and sovereignty and all the rest — we must seek to grasp why men formulated their political ideals in the terms in which they did, and what have been the consequences of that formulation outlasting its original purpose. Though it has not yet permeated legal and political practice, there was effected, at the close of the eighteenth century, a revolution in political thinking fully as important as the substitution of mechanical for final causes in natural science. To-day men are pretty well agreed that the test of any political institution or form of government must be public policy, the practical service of some accepted social end. From the Middle Ages down to the beginning of the last century, it was not so. During those centuries men, generalizing from the particular rights of lords and vassals, from customary rights and expressly agreed upon obligations, saw the foundation of all political institutions and the test of their desirability rather as a matter of rights, of legal obligations, whether those rights and that law were of divine or purely human origin. Human welfare and even religion were conceived as things to be decided ultimately by law and legal rights, not as in the modern world, by their utility and promotion of the general welfare. From the struggles of the Papacy and the Empire down to the writing of modern constitutions, men who desired a change in government were not willing to rest their arguments on the claim that it would be desirable and useful, but insisted that it was their *right*, that they had some law, time-honored, like Magna Charta, natural, or divine, upon their side; while the upholders of the established order insisted in opposition that theirs was the right and law. To this day, instead of arguing its social desirability, men will be found opposing the minimum wage on the ground that it infringes the constitutional right of freedom of contract, while others support it as founded in the rights of life, liberty, and the pursuit of happiness. How these notions of right and law were bent to effect changes that seemed useful as public policy we shall now examine.

The feudal nobility had in the fourteenth and fifteenth centuries steadily declined in power, and the theory of mutual obligations as the foundation of social life decayed. In the Wars of the Roses in England, in the religious wars in France, in the religious and Thirty Years' Wars in Germany, rival factions cut each other's throats and engaged in the process of exterminating their order. The rise of capitalism as applied to agriculture, and the decline of serfdom and its replacement by some scheme of tenantry or hired laborers, altered fundamentally the basis of economic power. The expansion of commerce to a national scale created a demand from the middle class for the abolition of private warfare and petty restrictions on trading, and strong national military support in opening up the new trade routes East and West — that is, a demand for the order, uniformity, and power of a strong centralized State, untrammeled by any obligations to the Monarch of Christendom. This demand required strengthening of the king's position against the Papacy on the one hand and against his subjects on the other. It was met by two theories that naturally merged. Against the claim of the Pope to be the sole divine source of power there was developed the theory of the divine right of kings, and against the barons there was developed the theory of the absolute sovereignty of the territorial monarch.

The Theory of Absolute Monarchy

The divine right of kings began as an attempt to emancipate the civil or lay government from the control of the pope and clergy; it was an answer to the claim of the latter to a divine right in temporal things. In an age when men believed all power came from God, it was the claim that secular government was as divinely ordained as ecclesiastical, and hence free to order its life in its own way. Such a claim had been voiced by the Imperialists in the Middle Ages, perhaps nowhere so clearly as in Dante; and when they failed to make it good against the Papacy, it was taken up by the French lawyers and applied to their king. Both Emperor and King of France hold their power direct from God, and hence have a divine right to freedom from papal interference. Wyclif carried the doctrine into England, upholding the divine right of the king to disendow the Church. The struggles over the succession popularized the indefeasible right of heredity, and when England broke with the Pope, and the might of Spain supported papal plots to murder Elizabeth, the divine right of the monarch of necessity coalesced with the right of national sovereignty and independence. Under James I, the heretic who ruled by hereditary right alone, the theory was carefully formulated, as against clerical pretensions both in Rome and in the Presbyterian theocracy of Scotland; and under the Restoration its end was secured in the freedom of the State from Puritan and Catholic ecclesiastical control alike. The accession of Henry IV in France after the Catholics and Huguenots had fought each other to obtain control of the government, and his policy of secular control and toleration, was justified and made possible only by the theory of divine right. Expounded by Barclay, this was developed against papal interference on the one hand and the Huguenot feudal nobility on the other; it flowered under Louis XIV. And the whole influence of Lutheranism was in favor of absolute monarchy as ordained by God. "The princes of this world are gods," wrote Luther, "the common people are Satan." "It is in no wise proper for any one who would be a Christian to set himself up against his government, whether it act justly or unjustly." [4]

So long as any religious body made serious pretensions to a right of interference in civil government, it was necessary for that government to claim that its power too came by a direct grant from God; arguments from reason or expediency would have been of no avail. But there were those whose emancipated minds rejected such a meeting of fire with fire; and at the same time they saw that centralized monarchy was demanded, not for any right of the monarch, but for the good of the nation. Moreover, in the struggles of religious groups on the one hand and traders on the other against a too despotic absolutism, they perhaps foresaw the day when the same forces that were now needing above all things centralized power would require it back again of the kings to whom they had entrusted it. For all these reasons there appeared, in the midst of these struggles, clear thinkers who advocated absolute monarchy and national sovereignty, but did it on rational, not religious, grounds. Machiavelli in Italy, Bodin in France, Hobbes in England, are the three outstanding figures in this stage of political development; and their significance lies in the fact that they develop conceptions in support of despotism that were later of use in combating it, and also that they firmly established the sovereignty of the national State.

Machiavelli was most important as the formulator of the new international statecraft, and in this connection we shall return to him. Here let us point out how Machiavelli's Italian patriotism and his hatred of the selfish machinations of the Papacy in Italy, aided by the Italian emancipation from all religious concern, led him to advocate an art of government whose sole end should be the power, expansion, and material prosperity of the State — the very ideal under which commercial Venice had prospered for centuries and which the commercial states of modern times were to follow out to the letter. The unity and greatness of Italy, human health, power, and wisdom — these were what he sought. Security of person and, above all, property is what men most desire; and though for these they will sacrifice anything, if security is there they will prefer a republic to a monarchy because it gives a greater chance of material gain to more people. To attain this, the state must above all be strong and efficient. Although he himself preferred a republic, or a constitutional monarchy like France, in his search for unity and order he was driven to tyranny as a means to that end, and devoted his life to the examination of the arts by which either republic or despot might wax strong. He was, in fact, the true type of revolutionary idealist pursuing an exclusive goal, and caring more for the ends he regarded as supremely important than for any gain to human character through waiting on the task of educating the public mind to want what he wanted. Such a man is bound to become impatient of average stupidity, contemptuous of all rules, legal, moral, or customary, which delay the accomplishment of his ends. In his own age religious fanatics like Cromwell and the Puritans in England, or the Jesuits, in ours reactionary dictators like Mussolini or communist fanatics, have all practiced his arts.

The middle class was only too willing to follow his precepts. In them he saw the chief support of the state. The baseness of human nature was open to him; "men are ungrateful, fickle, deceitful, cowardly, and avaricious," [5] and for their own good must be ruled partly by an appeal to greed, but mainly by fear. A strong government must respect established institutions and customs, govern well, and leave the property of men alone; it must make itself feared, but never hated. The power of the feudal nobles must be crushed; possessing castles and subjects of their own, they are fatal to all social order. Religion, especially a national religion, is a valuable aid to strong government; but Christianity he hated, theoretically because it is the negation of the patriotic, military virtues of Rome, making men weak and submissive to the strong men who disturb peace and order, practically because the Papacy had prevented the union and peace of Italy. Thus, on a thoroughly rational basis he did all he could to teach rulers to build up a strong, prosperous unified State and banish feudalism and theocracy in favor of the commercial expansion of the middle classes.

Machiavelli lived in the turmoils of Italian diplomacy, where no elaborate theory was necessary to justify "reasons of state." Both Bodin and Hobbes lived in the midst of wars of religious principles, and to build up a strong State they required a theory at least as respectable as the divine sanction appealed to by all parties. Against the disintegrating and turbulent tendencies of religious factions, which in French politics corresponded to the papal intrigues in Italy or the Wars of the Roses in England, Bodin supported the power of the monarch. He was a leader in that party of *Politiques* who contended for the State against both Catholics and Protestants, and triumphed in the establishment of the Bourbon dynasty under Henry IV in 1589. His work on *The State* in 1576 is at once the first scientific treatment of politics in modern times and a strong argument for the supremacy of the monarch; completely breaking with medieval notions, it clearly expounds the doctrine of the absolute sovereignty of the State. A State he defines as "an aggregation of families and their common possessions, ruled by a sovereign power and by reason." [6] This sovereign power, which is absolutely essential if there is to be a State at all, is "supreme power over citizens and subjects, unrestrained by the laws." [7] It is indivisible and inalienable, and its characteristic function is the making of all laws, which are commands generally binding on all subjects. As the source of all law, even of custom, since it rests with him to enforce it or not, the sovereign is free from all restraint, *legibus solutus*. To divine law alone must he give obedience, but it is his to determine what this is: his only obligation is to God. To him belongs the right to declare war and peace, to appoint magistrates, to exercise jurisdiction on appeal, to impose taxes. Here in clear-cut fashion is the theory of what the Renaissance despots were actually doing, modifying and codifying the mass of custom, enforcing peace and order over Church and barons alike. The best form of government for exercising this sovereign power, Bodin insists, is monarchy, in which the subjects are secure in their rights of person and property, while the monarch, respecting the laws of God and nature, in all matters outside of these receives willing obedience to the laws he himself establishes. Under just such a monarchy the Bourbons built up a strong and prosperous State in the seventeenth century, and brought it to ruin by their wars and waste.

Hobbes lived in England in the midst of similar struggles between religious parties, and he developed the same theory of absolute monarchy as Bodin. But in England the commercial classes were far stronger, and felt able to take over and control the maintenance of law and order themselves; they had developed in elaborate form, as we shall see, a theory of popular as opposed to monarchical power. Consequently Hobbes was led to found his theory upon the same popular basis as the Protestant contenders, but to draw opposed conclusions. And here we come upon a concept destined to play a most important part in political thinking, the idea of a social contract.

The social contract had its roots in both Roman and medieval thought. The theory of the Roman Empire as codified in the great *Corpus Juris Civilis* had been that all power and all right of law-making resided in the Roman people, but that by a famous *Lex Regia* these had been surrendered to the Emperor — a natural interpretation of the course of Roman history. "All the rights and all the powers of the Roman people have been transferred to the Emperor. To him alone is it granted to make the laws and to interpret them." [8] When Roman law was revived in the Middle Ages, this theory was seized upon, first by the Emperor and then by all princes, as a weapon against the supremacy of the Church. It fitted naturally into medieval political ideas, in which all relations between governor and governed were mutual obligations; that is, tacit or actual contracts between parties. Thus arose the theory of the social contract, that all civil authority, resting originally in the people, has been conferred by them on the ruler, in order that he may perform certain necessary functions. It is obviously double-edged: it may be used either to assert the omnipotence of the ruler, as being endowed with all authority, or the fundamental sovereignty of the people, as the ultimate source of that authority. The first interpretation was used by the princes against the church, the second by the opponents of civil despotism in the churches and middle class. The whole political struggle up to the French Revolution was fought over this theory.

Hobbes employed it to establish a strong, despotic State, considering that only an appeal to reason — the method of the new Cartesian science in which he was absorbed — could be valid. His theory of human nature was similar to Machiavelli's. The state of nature — another important concept — that is, what human life would be like if there were no common superior to prevent it, is "solitary, poor, nasty, brutish, and short." [9] The basis of all human action is "a perpetual and restless desire for power after power," [10] the power to gratify one's appetites; and hence all men are actuated by motives of competition, fear, and love of glory. Without some superior power to restrain them, men would perish in perpetual strife. *"Homo homini lupus,"* man is a wolf to his fellow man, and *"bellum omnium contra omnes,"* the war of every man against every man — this would be the state of nature if it were possible for such a thing to exist. There would be no standard of right and wrong, of justice and injustice, no private property. The closest approach to such an actual state of nature is to be found among the American Indians, in times of civil war — as in England — and between sovereign states, "having their weapons pointing and their eyes fixed on one another"; [11] and even in civilized life man's actions betray his fears. "When taking a journey he arms himself and seeks to go well accompanied; when going to sleep he locks his doors; when even in his house he locks his chests; consider what opinion he has of his fellow subjects, when he rides armed; of his fellow citizens, when he locks his doors; and of his children and servants, when he locks his chests." [12]

This being the natural state of man, his reason prescribes that he should seek peace and observe it, and, that this may be possible, that he should agree with his fellows to refrain from exercising his unrestricted impulses. Social existence among men is conceivable only on these terms. This agreement involves the setting up of a common power that can at the same time restrain and protect every individual, and for the establishment of this common power it is essential that a single will be constituted. "A commonwealth is said to be instituted when a multitude of men do agree and covenant, every one, with every one, that to whatsoever man, or assembly of men, shall be given by the major part, the right to present the person of them all, that is to say, to be their representative; every one, as well he that voted for it, as he that voted against it, shall authorize all the actions and judgments, of that man, or assembly of men, in the same manner, as if they were his own, to the end, to live peaceably amongst themselves, and be protected against other men." [13] Each individual pledges himself to every other, "I authorize and give up my right of governing myself, to this man, or to this assembly of men, on this condition, that thou give up thy right to him, and authorize all his actions in like manner." [14] In this formulation, all civil power rests on the original consent of the governed. Individual men agree to create a sovereign, and to submit to the decision of the majority as to who that sovereign shall be. Since peace and defense is the end of the contract, obedience to the sovereign must be rendered until he proves impotent to enforce them, when the contract is dissolved and a new one made. It matters not who the sovereign power is, but only that he be powerful; hence Hobbes could support Charles I or Cromwell equally well.

This sovereign requires unquestioning obedience from his subjects; he has made no contract himself, and cannot be held to any account, from within or abroad. He possesses unlimited power and discretion as to the ways and means of enforcing peace and security, power over the expression of opinion, over property, over the courts, over war and peace, over magistrates. As to other sovereign commonwealths, he is absolutely free to do what he can; toward them he is in the state of nature, the war of all. As to his subjects, he is the author of all civil law, and the sole interpreter of all custom, natural law, and divine law. For them, the sovereign's formal judgment *is* the law of God and the law of nature. Naturally the sovereign has complete power in religion; without his headship and command, there can be no real church. Thus the ground is cut away from both Protestant dissenters and the Pope, who is no sovereign in Hobbes' sense.

It is to be noted that while Hobbes himself approves absolute monarchy, as likely to be the strongest government, there is nothing in his theory that cannot be taken as applying to Parliament or any other representative body. This has actually been done by a distinguished school of nineteenth-century British jurists; it illustrates how incidental, in all this Renaissance despotism, was the actual monarch, and how fundamental was the demand for a national government strong within and irresponsible without, a government that could guarantee commercial prosperity.

THE EMERGENCE OF MIDDLE-CLASS CONSTITUTIONALISM

But already the seeds of individual liberty were at work in the world. However willing the middle class might be to support absolutism as opposed to the anarchy of civil war, when it ceased to serve their commercial life and touched pocket and conscience, it must be restrained. We have seen how Machiavelli counsels judicious murders, but never the taking of property; "men more readily forget the death of a father than the loss of a patrimony." [15] Even Bodin introduces inconsistencies into his theory by denying his absolute sovereign right over his subject's property. "Without just cause the sovereign cannot seize or grant away the property of another." [16] This is the point on which absolute monarchy broke down: it was not Machiavellian enough; that is to say, it was stupid, as it always is, and not wise enough, as representative assemblies sometimes are, to know it.

While this is indisputably the background of the struggle for popular rights, it is as indubitable that, largely, perhaps, because the middle class made up their active membership, political liberty owes its force and its theories to the struggle of religious organisms to live. The first assault on the absolute monarch came from religious sects demanding toleration; and freedom of conscience, appealed to by minorities, naturally coalesced with the rights of property. These bodies cared little for toleration if they were in power; but when deposed and persecuted they waxed eloquent against despotism. Though most of the arguments on this side, in the nature of the case, come from Protestant dissenting sects, when Catholics were the under dog they loved liberty as fervently as any Calvinist; and, ironically enough, two of the greatest defenses of popular sovereignty were written by the Spanish Jesuits Mariana and Suarez.

To the days of nineteenth-century Prussia, Lutheranism remained true to its monarchical principles, and no subversive doctrine came from its ranks; but the Reformed Church and Calvinism proved the stronghold of constitutionalism and the rights of conscience and property. In this respect the English Reformation remained Lutheran till about 1580, and then grew more and more Calvinistic. Not only did the democratic church government of Presbyterians and Congregationalists prove an admirable training in self-government; the Calvinists in Geneva, Scotland, Holland, England, America, and France, had to defend themselves against established power. They were usually in a minority, and never, outside Geneva and New England, completely in control. Calvin himself favored an aristocratic theocracy, but in established monarchies he advocated constitutionalism, and resistance to the king, not by private men, but by elected magistrates entrusted with the guardianship of the people's rights. His followers were driven to defend their communions against royal power, and in so doing developed the contract theory into an anti-monarchist weapon, in which, in the struggles in France and England, they were joined by the Catholics. This theory was made the foundation of the Dutch and the British governments, and, rationalized by John Locke, became the starting-point of political thought in the next century.

These anti-monarchists all derived sovereign power from the people by some form of the social contract, and held the king responsible to them for his deeds. If he waxes tyrannical, or prevents the exercise of men's religion, or in any way contravenes the law of God as revealed in Bible or conscience, he may be resisted, passively by private citizens, and actively by cities and magistrates. If he is obdurate, he may be deposed and foreign aid justly called in. In France such doctrine was maintained by the Huguenots Beza, du Plessi-Mornay's *Vindiciæ contra Tyrannos*, and the Catholics La Boëtie, Louis d'Orleans, and Boucher; in Scotland by John Knox and George Buchanan; in Holland by Althusius and Grotius; and in England by Milton, Harrington, and Cromwell. Outside of France they did not stop at words: in 1581 the States-General of Holland deposed Philip II of Spain; in 1560 the Scotch Parliament rebelled against Mary Stuart and in 1566 deposed her; in England Parliament rebelled in 1642 and beheaded Charles in 1649. For its part the Catholic Church had embodied in the very principles of the Counter-Reformation the responsibility of sovereigns in religious matters, and quite generally revived the theory of the deposing power of the Pope and even the duty of tyrannicide; every Catholic king who turned heretic became *ipso facto* a tyrant. Nor must it be forgotten, by those who derive popular liberties from some inner essence of Protestantism, that while the Huguenots raised an aristocratic protest against absolutism, the French Catholics of the Ligue and the Spanish Jesuits were much more democratic and, indeed, Jacobin; and that in Latin lands to-day the chief bulwark for individual liberty against the anti-clerical and uniform sovereign state is the Catholic Church.

In Holland first and in England a century later these movements actually triumphed; and it is by Dutch and English pens that the most powerful arguments for constitutionalism and individual rights were written. These two lands were, with Scotland, the strongholds of Calvinism; they were also most completely dominated by the middle class. Conscience and commerce worked hand in hand to break down the absolutism that they had a century before advocated against their earlier enemies, the nobles and the Church. They now retained the irresponsible national sovereignty of that doctrine, but coupled it with a shift of power within the nation.

Holland was to the seventeenth century what the England of the Revolution of 1689 was to the eighteenth century, a working model of free institutions and the center of light for the rest of Europe. The success of the Dutch revolt against Spain gave a leverage in practice to the ideas men were struggling for in the other lands. There it was proved that a government could be both strong and stable, and at the same time be controlled by the middle class and practice toleration on a large scale. In the light of such practice Althusius and Grotius codified constitutionalism, and served as a model to seventeenth-century England in both commercial and political practice.

Althusius combines the royalist theory of irresponsible national sovereignty with the anti-monarchist theory of its residence in the people. Professor of law in Herborn, Holland, and for many years burgomaster of the neighboring Imperial city of Emden, he was a zealous Calvinist who wrote in 1603 a scientific work on *Politics;* generalizing from the constitution of the Holy Roman Empire and adapting its ideas to the recent course of events in Holland. He agreed with Bodin that there must be in every state one indivisible sovereign power, which he defines as the supreme and super-eminent power of doing what pertains to the spiritual and bodily welfare of the whole people. But this power can only reside in the whole nation which never dies, and to which princes and magistrates must be responsible. It arises from an actual or tacit agreement, not between individuals, but between all the lesser groups within the State, towns, cities, provinces, who support it both from necessity and from natural social feeling. Such a State is "a general public association in which a number of cities and provinces, combining their possessions and their activities, contract to establish, maintain, and defend a sovereign power." [17] The sovereign power, thus founded, enters into another agreement with a ruler to execute its ends; but the people retain, not only all rights not expressly surrendered, but also all rights of general equity and justice, for whose enforcement the government was established. Rulers govern as representatives of the people, and so soon as they infringe the limits of the natural rights imposed on them — so soon as they cease to serve the welfare of the community — they cease to possess any right to obedience. To determine when this point has been reached, every State should have overseers — the various orders and estates in provinces and cities — to appoint the ruler, to support him in the exercise of his rightful powers, to protect the rights of the people, and to depose a ruler who infringes them. In default of this action, the people have the right to depose rulers themselves. The ruler is the executive agent of the people, who undertakes to govern in accordance with the fundamental laws. Every form of government will normally possess these three parts — the sovereign people, the overseer, and the executive; it will be a mixed government. The aim of all government is the welfare of the whole people, spiritual and secular, and hence it must supervise religion, morals, and education, and foster commercial prosperity by regulating trade, coinage, property, and internal peace.

Here in commercial Holland we have for the first time put forth the ideal of a constitutional monarchy, governing for the sake of securing the spiritual welfare and material prosperity — the very type achieved by England in 1689 and rationalized by John Locke, justified in popular sovereignty, the social contract, and natural rights. And we have the beginnings of the conception of federalism, destined to such fruitful development in Holland and America. We shall refrain from examining any of the numerous English representatives of these views who wrote during the Civil Wars on the side of the Puritans, having already sufficiently prepared the way for the doctrine of John Locke, who transmitted them to the eighteenth century.

The Theory of Mercantilism — Paternalistic Nationalism in Economics

We have seen how the middle class, supported by nationalistic sentiment and the desire of religious bodies to maintain their existence, first created the absolutistic national State out of the medieval hierarchical order, and then limited that State where it sought to attack property and conscience. These new national governments, when once established, were made the vehicles of the regulation of economic life. Here as in politics the movement was away from the small unit, the guild and town, and toward intensified competition along national lines. The older guild regulation modified by municipal control and directed toward the medieval ideal of social service was taken over by the national government, and directed toward increasing the commercial prosperity of the nation — at least of its middle class. These two changes, in the regulating unit and in its aim, gave rise to the economic doctrine and ideal known as mercantilism, which might perhaps be better called economic nationalism — the employment of economic regulation to build up a Great Power, and the building-up of such a power to increase the gain of the commercial class.

Since the great increase in money — that is, in gold and silver bullion — was both the immediate cause and the most obvious aspect of the increased prosperity that was the Commercial Revolution, and since the strength of the new national governments was dependent upon their financial resources, it was natural that the possession of a treasure of gold and silver should have been looked upon as the first requisite of a strong government, the sinews alike of war and peace. Nations like Spain which had a great store of bullion in their own domains or colonies, and in which gentlemen adventurers who fought for gold were more prevalent than traders who worked for it, adopted a "bullionist" policy; that is, they passed stringent and universal laws against the export of specie and intended to encourage its import, which, in fact, while they did not stop the flow of coin, did hamper trade. Nations like France and England, which had no mines and in which the middle class was much stronger, endeavored to secure the same amassing of treasure by means of regulating not money, but trade. By prohibiting the export of raw materials and offering bounties on that of manufactured goods, by a rigid reduction of imports to the minimum, it was hoped to receive more money than was paid, and thus create "a favorable balance of trade." Statesmen like Colbert under Louis XIV and Cromwell, as well as theorists like Bodin and Montchrétien, Serra and Mun, set this accumulation of "national wealth" as the aim that would justify every expedient, and the whole power of the nation was turned toward developing the profits of favored merchants. One industry was fostered, another discouraged, charters were granted and monopolies established, colonies were estates to be exploited for the benefit of the home merchants, and the world was parceled out among privileged companies, which watched over the lives and fortunes of their patriotic and prosperous members.

This general exaltation of foreign above domestic trade and its end of "bringing money into the country," in so far as it was successful, while it filled the coffers of merchants and enabled the king to tax them unwisely for his own good, created a sharp rise in prices that brought general distress, for wages were at the same time carefully regulated too. The other half of the mercantilist doctrine, that manufactures rather than agriculture were the true source of national wealth, was not quite so harmful. Men like Colbert took immense pains to establish new infant industries by bounties and privileges of every sort, by direct education and propaganda, by building canals and roads. Governments ceased to prohibit all interest, and confined "usury" to interest above the legally fixed rate. Even more important, the nation took over the supervision of the methods and the quality of goods that had been previously carried on by the guilds; in 1787 the regulations for French manufactures filled eight volumes in quarto. If all this regulation prevented improvement and perpetuated antiquated methods, it must not be forgotten that it was the only means of breaking the power of the monopolistic and still more selfishly conservative guilds; and it did prevent the flood of shoddy goods already flowing from free England. That it failed does not mean that merchants and manufacturers had ceased to desire the interference of the State to foster their own interests, but that the centralized State simply proved itself incompetent to supervise the details of business with wisdom or honesty. The last century has made clear that *laisser-faire* and free trade were merely a more practicable second-best, to be discarded for tariffs and monopoly wherever profitable.

Thomas Mun, whose *England's Treasure by Foreign Trade* published in 1664 remained the economic classic until Adam Smith, clearly states the ideal of the new economic nationalism. It is nation against nation. "The ordinary means to increase our wealth and treasure is by foreign trade, wherein we must ever observe this rule — to sell more to strangers yearly than we consume of theirs in value. For that part of our stock which is not returned to us in wares must necessarily be brought home in treasure."[18] Foreign trade is the chief source of wealth; since in domestic trade the gain of one is the loss of another, and if the others are foreigners, it does not matter. Thus the medieval notion that trade can never produce new value is retained, and merely applied to nationalistic competition. Mun vigorously opposes the narrower bullionist and Spanish theory that money should not be exported; he was a director of the East India Company, which in 1664 obtained the right to unlimited export of bullion. "Money begets trade, and trade increaseth money. We must first enlarge our trade by bringing in more foreign wares, which, being sent out again, will in due time bring far greater treasure than was originally sent out."[19] He concludes in a hymn to the merchant that sums up the ideal of the middle class. "Foreign trade is the great revenue of the King, the honor of the kingdom, the noble profession of the merchant, the school of our arts, the supply of our wants, the employment of our poor, the improvement of our lands, the nursery of our mariners, the walls of the kingdom, the means of our treasure, the sinews of our wars, the terror of our enemies."[20]

Irresponsible National Sovereignty

Our concern to the present has been primarily with the new national State as contrasted with the older feudal order, as the instrument for the aggrandizement of the commercial classes at the expense of nobles and clergy. It remains to point out the consequences of this irresponsible sovereignty in the relations between states, and the substitution of modern statesmanship for medieval Christendom. States became on a national scale the supreme example of the individualism of the age; they pursued their own development and their commercial and territorial expansion quite regardless of competing states, and lived up to the worst side of the Italian ideal of the universal man, imitating a Malatesta or a Cesare Borgia rather than a Leonardo or a Lorenzo. In the Middle Ages, the ideal of Empire and Church had been peace; now war was looked upon, not only as inevitable, but as glorious and divinely ordained. For the first time since Rome had imposed her peace over the civilized world there was no recognized universal code of law; the Protestant revolt replaced canon by cannon law. For the first time nations were everywhere regarded as living in a complete state of nature, with no authority, no judge, no common standard over them. Only the cosmopolitan humanist Erasmus was left to declaim against war and assert that he agreed with the pacifism of Cicero that the most unjust peace was preferable to the justest war. Two men stand out as the theorists of the new international relations, Machiavelli, product of the spirit of boundless expansion and utterly non-moral human power of the Italian Renaissance, and Grotius, offspring of the Reformation that demanded complete individual freedom to obey what it pleased men to call the divine law.

Machiavelli, supreme patriot, worshiper of power and efficiency above all things, laid down the principle that was to be abhorred in public and practiced in private to this day by statesmen and diplomats, that the State is an end in itself and owes allegiance to no law other than that of its own best interests. "When the entire safety of our country is at stake, no consideration of what is just or unjust, merciful or cruel, praiseworthy or shameful, must intervene. On the contrary, every other consideration being set aside, that course alone must be taken which preserves the existence of the country and maintains its independence."[21] "Let the prince, then, look to the maintenance of the State; the means will always be deemed honorable and will receive general approbation."[22] "I believe that when there is fear for the life of the State, both monarchs and republics, to preserve it, will break faith and display ingratitude."[23] *Salus populi suprema lex* — this is to be the maxim of the new order, and that safety is to be commercial prosperity. Every war will be righteous and justified, on both sides, for the power of the State is the supreme right. Machiavelli's heroes are Ferdinand of Aragon, "a prince who always preaches good faith but never practices it," and Cesare Borgia, "who did every thing that can be done by a prudent and able man; so that no better precepts can be offered to a new prince than those suggested by the example of his actions" [24] — the Borgia whose perfect master-strokes were to slay under pretext of conference all the captains who had rebelled against him, and to murder his lieutenant as scapegoat. Machiavelli reproached Baglioni, tyrant of Perugia, for not having slain Pope Julius II when the latter had ventured into his power to depose him; Baglioni, who did not shrink from incest and the murder of near relatives, having once decided on his policy, should have known how to be strong and "splendidly wicked." Thus must the State act ever.

Machiavelli points to the necessity of not merely defending but expanding the power of the State. "All human affairs are in motion, and it is impossible to stand still; they must progress or decline; and where reason does not lead, necessity often drives." [25] Hence monarchies and republics alike must conquer their neighbors; this is the superiority of Rome over the Greek city-states. Not nationalism, though this makes it easier, but conquest, is the goal; "no province was ever united or happy save by becoming subject in its entirety to a single commonwealth or a single prince, as has happened in France and Spain" [26] — two conquering powers he especially admired. The policy of conquest is to follow that of Rome: Increase the population of the city, acquire allies rather than subjects, establish colonies, turn all booty into the treasury, keep the State rich and the individual poor, and above all maintain a well-trained army. For the sole source of the State's right is power, and its sole vice is weakness; hence a national militia and universal conscription — quite unknown in those days of mercenary armies — are essential. "Reason of state" is supreme, conquest and the balance of power are the aims of all diplomacy.

Machiavelli was merely elevating into general principles the common practice of all the Italian States of his day; his precepts had been anticipated by the princes and despots, and perfidy, reason of state, and efficiency had marked the commercial oligarchy of Venice for centuries. But in absolutely freeing himself from all superior codes or laws whatsoever, he seems definitely to have followed the example of the Papacy he so much hated. The Papacy was sovereign as no other State; the Pope, though theoretically bound by the natural law, could dispense with violations of it, like bigamy, and could "interpret" any oath. Moreover, the Council of Constance had decreed in its dealings with Hus that faith was not to be kept with heretics; Machiavelli read State for Church and enemy for heretic, and founded the modern religion of the State. His principles were adopted by the rising national states almost to the letter, but nowhere so thoroughly carried out as in the Society of Jesus, that supreme example of the absorption of the individual by the social organism. In that body, whose ends were recognized as holy, the individual was to become "like a corpse" in the hands of the General.

The Restraining Force of International Law

If Machiavelli laid down the maxims that sovereign states were to follow, and have followed when convenient to this day, Grotius, in his *Rights of War and Peace* (1625), founded the legal theory on which they were to justify their acts and the international ideal that was to be their highest aspiration. Grotius, a Dutch jurist and statesman who saw with his own eyes the consequences of Machiavelli's precepts when applied in the struggle of Holland against Spain and the later Thirty Years' War in Germany, attempted to set some bounds on the unlimited predominance of "reasons of state." He did not try to stop, but only to regulate the competition of sovereign states; his ideal, and that of Europe since, has been "civilized warfare." His contention, like that of Dante, is that all human life is essentially a society, and that certain laws, of which the keeping of pledges is the most important, are therefore as immutable as human nature. The rise of Protestantism and the disavowal of what had hitherto been the universal code, Roman law as preserved and enforced by the Papacy, left, in the absence of any recognized superior, like the medieval Pope, two alternatives: either Machiavelli and an endless and truceless struggle for existence between sovereign nations, or the formulation of some code of honor and good form, some rules for the game. On the whole, even statesmen were not willing to follow Machiavelli all the time, and therefore Grotius was welcomed when he furnished the basis for a code of honor that might or might not be lived up to.

Grotius turned where Alexander had turned when he was confronted with the same problem of ruling a mass of Oriental peoples, and where the Roman lawyers turned, when Rome's sway had been extended over many alien nations — to the law of nature. Confronted by a mass of conflicting customs, it seems easy for the human mind to seek some fundamental principles of justice and fair dealing that shall lie behind and beyond all positive commands and all custom — some standard by which to judge and criticize such things. In an anthropomorphic view of the universe — and until modern science all views were such — these fundamental principles are easily read into the very structure and reason of the world, as divine or natural laws; were they founded in merely human conceptions of what is fair and just, they would seem to lack permanence and universal binding power. The Greeks had reached such a notion in contrasting nature with man's various laws; and in Stoicism this conception of nature as a great rational process, the soul of order and right, was spread through all the Roman rulers. Roman conquest had presented a similar problem: what law is to be applied to the new subjects and foreigners, since the Roman *jus civile* is only for Roman citizens? Roman jurists developed a *jus gentium*, or law of the people of all nations, which was codified by men impregnated with the Stoic ideal of a law of nature; and thus the law of nature and the law of nations were fused as that law which natural reason has established among all men. When Roman law was reintroduced in the twelfth century, this conception of a system of rights and justice quite independent of any human promulgation or agreement was seized upon as the most effective means of criticizing all institutions; anti-Papalists employed it in favor of the Empire, constitutionalists in the Church employed it against monarchy and for a church council. We have already mentioned it in connection with the various attempts to find the rational basis of authority, in Hobbes and Althusius alike. A powerful support to this legal and moral principle came when the new science discovered the harmony and immutable laws of nature in the physical sense; since Nature was through and through rational, it seemed easy to believe that she was the foundation of moral as well as mathematical laws. Only Spinoza's clear vision made the distinction between descriptive and normative law.

This natural law became the basis of all natural rights and universal obligations, and lent itself to the purposes of restraining sovereign nations. Grotius starts, with Aristotle and the Scholastics, by assuming that man is by nature social; both natural appetite and rational foresight draw men to their fellows, and demand the conduct of a social existence. This social life is made possible by certain conditions, without which it could not exist; and natural morality consists in the observance of these conditions. What makes social life, as led by reasonable beings, impossible, is wrong. Natural law, then, originates in principles which are contained in human nature and its demands, and is therefore as universal, as immutable, and as inescapable as human nature itself. Though God, the author of nature, has willed it with all his works, it is independent of his decree; he could no more make what by virtue of reason is wrong right than he could make two and two equal other than four. Man's reason can find what is right by studying the conditions of social life, just as he can find what is true by studying mathematics. The test of rightness in human conduct is rational conformity to the needs of social existence.

As between individuals, these principles form the foundation of all civil government, which owes its power of being obeyed to their recognition. Grotius' originality lay in applying them to the relations between nations as well, treating sovereign powers as individuals in a larger social whole. In this society of nations — such an idea would have been unthinkable in medieval Christendom — just because it is a society, there are certain mutual obligations which cannot be disregarded if that society is to endure. Such principles, embodied in the practice of the best nations, form the *jus gentium* or law of nations. Grotius tried to retain the distinction between the law of nature, what reason prescribed as essential, and the law of nations, actually observed customs; but the variation in custom and the difficulty of arriving at what was essential, practically forced them, as it had in Roman law, to coalesce. Thus international law, as it emerged from Grotius' hands, was not merely a statement of an ideal of national conduct, not merely a description of how nations treated each other, not merely a scientifically ascertainable setting forth of what was necessary if European society was to endure, but a fusion of all three. What Grotius was attempting was to see whether there were not certain common duties generally felt as binding, if not always practiced, and to give to this ideal all the power he could of foundation in custom and reason.

It is easy to see why international law, which has retained the same confusion to this day, has so often covered what are truly the principles of Machiavelli. It leaves the interpretation of what constitutes the usage of the "better nations" to individual publicists, and the criterion of what is necessary to preserve the society of Europe is left to the patriotic statesman. At best it keeps before rulers' minds the notion that states do form a society, and that they do owe some kind of vague obligation to each other not to violate too outrageously established usage; and in the face of Machiavelli this was probably a gain. In a famous pamphlet *The Fight in Dame Europa's School* the suggestion is made that international law is like a code of schoolboy honor: it does not destroy selfishness or quarreling or cheating, and it often cloaks the bully and forces the inoffensive to fight, but it does give something in common. Moreover, the theory of the equality of all sovereign powers, so essential in theory and so disregarded in practice, has emphasized that very national irresponsibility it was designed to check; every small territorial state is encouraged to make as outrageous claims as its larger neighbors. Before our eyes the new states of Europe are following the precedent of the "better nations," glorying in their independence.

Yet for all that, the authority of Grotius did have an influence. Nations may wage war in accordance with natural law, but they must not forget that even between enemies there is the common bond of humanity, if only a common hatred. Since war is fought with peace in mind, it must be carried on fairly and humanely enough to make peace possible. No State is so self-sufficient that it can be indifferent to an ordered intercourse with other states, or to the opinion of humanity at large. On the whole set of principles with which Grotius and the other political theorists were operating, it seems to us obvious that, having dissolved the old society of Christendom under the sovereignty of the Pope and his canon law, the European states should have

THE REVOLT FROM FEUDALISM

entered into a new social contract with each other to set up some sovereign power and some binding law over them. Such proposals, like the Grand Design of Sully and Henry IV and the Project of the Abbé de Saint-Pierre, were indeed made; but the middle class found national freedom in a state of nature too profitable to favor any such thing, and the forces of patriotism already called into being would have prevented it in any case.

Thus was set the keystone upon the arch of theory supporting the new political institutions that had grown out of the dissolving feudalism and ecclesiastical empire of the Middle Ages. The ground was prepared for an increasing assumption of direct control by the middle class, and for the mighty commercial rivalries of the next century. Service to man, mutual obligations, universal peace — these are forgotten, and in their place are wranglings about rights, a wild rush for prosperity and wealth, and wars and rumors of wars. But in the midst of these strange fruits there is growing the flower of toleration and compromise; and a new force, science, has entered the world.

REFERENCES

1. J. A. Symonds, *Revival of Learning*, 12.
2. Machiavelli, *Prince*, ch. 26.
3. Shakespeare, *King Richard II*, Act II, Scene 1.
4. Luther, quoted in P. Smith, *Age of the Reformation*, 594.
5. Machiavelli, *Prince*, ch. 17.
6. J. Bodin, *De Republica*, Lib. I, cap. 1.
7. *Ibid.*, Lib. I, cap. 8.
8. Justinian's *Codex*, I, 17.
9. Hobbes, *Leviathan*, ch. 13.
10. *Ibid.*, ch. 11.
11. *Ibid.*, ch. 13.
12. *Ibid.*, ch. 13.
13. *Ibid.*, ch. 18.
14. *Ibid.*, ch. 17.
15. Machiavelli, *Prince*, ch. 17.
16. J. Bodin, *De Republica* (Frankfort, 1641), 162.
17. Althusius, *Politica*, ch. II, Sec. II.
18. Thomas Mun, *England's Treasure by Foreign Trade*.
19. *Ibid.*
20. *Ibid.*
21. Machiavelli, *Discorsi*, III, 41.
22. Machiavelli, *Prince*, ch. 18.
23. Machiavelli, *Discorsi*, I, 59.
24. Machiavelli, quoted in P. Smith, *Age of the Reformation*, 590.
25. Machiavelli, *Discorsi*, I, 6.
26. *Ibid.*, I, 12.

SELECTED READING LISTS

Economic Growth: In addition to the works cited under Chapter VI: A. F. Pollard, *Factors in Mod. Hist.*; Max Weber, *Gen. Econ. Hist.*; H. Sée, *Modern Capitalism;* J. A. Hobson, *Evolution of Modern Capitalism;* G. N. Clark, *The 17th Century;* F. L. Nussbaum, *Absolutism, Mercantilism, and Classicism.* W. J. Ashley, *Econ. Organization of England;* E. Lipson, *Econ. Hist. of England;* A. P. Usher, *Industrial H. of England;* W. Cunningham, *Growth of English Industry and Commerce;* G. Unwin, *Ind. Organization in the 16th and 17th cents.;* R. H. Gretton, *The English Middle Class.*

Nationalism: J. H. Rose, *Nationality in Mod. Hist.*; C. J. H. Hayes, *Essays in Nationalism, Hist. Evol. of Modern Nationalism.* Hulme, c. 3; Pollard, chs. 1, 3; Acton, c. 9. Machiavelli, *The Prince, Florentine History, Discourses on Livy;* P. Villari, *Life and Times of Machiavelli.* J. R. Green, *England,* c. 7. Historical plays of Shakespeare.

Political Theory: G. H. Sabine, *H. of Pol. Theory;* J. N. Figgis, *Theory of the Divine Right of Kings, Studies in Pol. Thought from Gerson to Grotius;* J. W. Allen, *H. of Pol. Thought in the 16th c.*; O. Gierke, *Natural Law and the Theory of Society, 1500–1800.* F. J. C. Hearnshaw, *Soc. and Pol. Ideas of some Great Thinkers of the Ren. and Ref., of the 16th and 17th cents.* **Theories of the Reformers:** Sabine, c. 18; Allen, Pt. I; Hearnshaw, *Ren. and Ref.,* chs. 7, 8; Troeltsch, c. 3. L. H. Waring, *Pol. Theories of Luther;* H. Baron, *Calvins Staatsanschauung; A Defense of Liberty against Tyrants,* ed. Laski; H. L. Osgood, "Political Ideas of the Puritans," in *Pol. Sci. Qu.,* 1891; H. D. Foster, "Pol. Theories of the Calvinists," in *Am. Hist. Rev.,* 1916; C. E. Merriam, *American Pol. Theories.* **Secular Theories:** Machiavelli, Sabine, c. 17; Figgis, *Gerson to Grotius,* c. 3; Hearnshaw, c. 4; H. J. Laski, *Machiavelli and the Present Time,* in *The Dangers of Obedience.* Bodin, *De la République,* Knolles tr.; Allen, III, c. 8; Sabine, c. 20; Hearnshaw, *16th and 17th c.,* c. 2. Hobbes, *Leviathan, De Cive, Phil. Rudiments; The Phil. of Hobbes,* ed. F. J. E. Woodbridge. Accounts by J. Laird, Leo Strauss; Leslie Stephen, C. Robertson, F. Tönnies. Althusius, *Politica,* ed. Friedrich; Hearnshaw, *16th and 17th cents.,* chs. 4, 7; O. Gierke, *Johannes Althusius.* W. Graham, *English Pol. Phil. from Hobbes to Maine;* G. P. Gooch, *Pol. Thought from Bacon to Halifax, English Democratic Ideas in the 17th cent.* (with H. J. Laski); H. J. Laski, *Rise of Liberalism; ibid.* in *Enc. Soc. Sciences,* I. W. Haller, *Tracts on Liberty in the Puritan Rev.*

Economic Theory: E. Heckscher, *Mercantilism; ibid.* in *En. Soc. Sci.* J. W. Horrocks, *H. of Mercantilism.* G. Schmoller, *The Mercantile System.* C. W. Cole, *French Mercantilist Doctrines, Colbert.* T. Mun, *England's Treasure by Foreign Trade, A Discourse of Trade.*

International Law: Grotius, *On the Law of War and Peace;* Sabine, c. 21. G. G. Butler and S. Maccoby, *Dev. of Int. Law;* T. E. Holland, *Studies in Int. Law;* E. Nys, *Les origines du droit international;* A. Franck, *Réformateurs et Publicistes de l'Europe, 17ᵉ siècle.*

CHAPTER IX

THE NEW INTERESTS OF THE MODERN AGE — THE WORLD OF NATURE

THE Renaissance brought with it a reaction against asceticism and other-worldliness, and turned men's minds to human life as it may be lived on this planet; the Reformation added a religious consecration to all labor in the Lord's vineyard. Here and there during this period there appeared men who with the humanists and the reformers turned away from the wisdom of the Middle Ages to a more humble kind of learning, so it seemed; but these rare figures were fascinated, not by the soul of man and its infinite possibilities, but by the great world in which man's life is lived. In their investigations Western Europe took up once again the long road of scientific discovery where the Alexandrian Greeks had left it a thousand years before. They were few indeed, at first, and they had to make their way against the general contempt if not the open disapproval of both humanists and reformers; but more and more thinkers in lonely tower or solitary study set themselves to search out the ways of Nature, and after long, patient, and hard endeavors they managed, by the end of the seventeenth century, to bring scientific knowledge to bear on the minds of the educated class. It was not humanism, and it was not the Reformation, that was destined to work the greatest revolution in the beliefs of men, however triumphant they seemed for centuries; it was science. Science was to build a new world to take the place of that broken at the Renaissance; science applied to the production of goods by power was to transform medieval society into the great sprawling chaotic civilization in which we live. And though science as a serious factor in either men's beliefs or actions did not make its appearance until the eighteenth century — it was not till the last generation that it really reached the masses of men, and broke down the compromise with the medieval world which had marked modern history — its rebirth in the minds of the few, and the great new ideas on which it is based, entered the world in the humanistic sixteenth century.

Two statements of ideals will serve to contrast the old spirit and the new. The first is from a sermon of John Tauler, mystic and evangelist of Strassburg, who in the fourteenth century shared much of the social interest that was to flower in the Reformation.

Children, ye shall not seek after great science. Simply enter into your own inward principle and learn to know what you yourselves are, spiritually and naturally, and do not dive into the secret things of God, asking questions about the efflux and reflux of the Aught into the Naught or the essence of the soul's spark, for Christ has said: "It is not for you to know the times or the seasons which the Father has put into his own power." Dear children, the Holy Ghost will not teach us all things in the sense that we shall be given to know whether there shall be a good harvest or vintage, whether bread will be dear or cheap, whether the present war will come to an end soon. No, dear children; but he will teach us all things which we can need for a perfect life, and for a knowledge of the hidden truth of God, of the bondage of nature, of the deceitfulness of the world, and of the cunning of evil spirits. As Saint Augustine says, "He is a miserable man who knows all things, and does not know God; and he is happy who knows God, even though he know nothing else. But he who knows God and all else beside, is not made more blessed thereby; for he is blessed through God alone." [1]

The second statement is from the *New Atlantis* of Francis Bacon, in which an English ship, making one of those Elizabethan voyages of high daring to the South Seas, comes upon a Utopian island realm whose chief institution is a great establishment devoted to scientific research. The ruler takes the travelers through this place, saying:

God bless thee, my son; I will give thee the greatest jewel I have. For I will impart unto thee, for the love of God and men, a relation of the true state of Salomon's House ... The end of our foundation is the knowledge of causes, and secret motions of things; and the enlarging of the bounds of human empire, to the effecting of all things possible.[2]

With Tauler we are in the Middle Ages; Bacon is the prophet of the new era.

Medieval Interest in Nature

It must not be supposed that this supreme interest in nature was a new thing in the sixteenth century. Much of the novelty which seems to hang about the rebirth of a scientific interest at that time is due to the disrepute in which the humanistic revival had placed the growing medieval interest in natural objects and events for their own sake, apart from man. In reality, from the first dawn of intellectual interests in the twelfth-century renaissance, the learning bred of the expanding economic life had turned to the scene of man's endeavors. Two main sources of this interest in objective knowledge can be traced in the Middle Ages, the increasing trade that sought ever more distant lands for spices, gold, and fine luxury ware, and the influence of Hellenistic science that came with Aristotle from the Arabs.

The Expansion of Europe

With the rise of commerce and the towns Europeans established trade-routes that were regularly traveled to the East. The Crusades, in reality the first of those imperialistic ventures that Europe has sent out to despoil and appropriate the earth, soon came to be as much commercial as religious enterprises; the canny Italians, too urban already for the unsophisticated faith of the Northern peoples, waxed rich alike from transporting Crusaders and from trading with the wealthy enemy. By the thirteenth century regular connection was kept up with the Moslem realms in the Levant, with India, with farthest Russia, and with China. While the Oriental parts of these caravan routes were for the most part not in the hands of Europeans, many from the West did manage to penetrate thither. Franciscan friars in some numbers had sought to evangelize the Mongol Empire, and merchants and adventurers like Venetian Marco Polo had awakened a romantic interest in far-away Japan. When the Portuguese and Spaniards, impelled by a desire to share in the trade of the Italian ports, turned southward around Africa and westward to India directly, they were but following impulses inevitable in that day. Columbus' voyage would have been made very soon, in any case; it was only his discovery of a new continent on the path to India that was accidental, and even that had been known to the far-venturing Norse. The discovery and robbery of a new world struck the popular imagination because men were already prepared for an interest in such things. Nevertheless, the effect in widening the mental horizon was large; in the East was realm after realm of numerous and cultured peoples whose civilization was far superior to that of Europe — in material affairs the Europeans were forced to admit it — and in the West untold continents; and all these parts were obviously entirely outside the field of medieval Christendom and the Church. The Church had condemned the opinion that human beings lived at the antipodes; they could not have descended from Adam, nor have been saved by Christ: and the Church was found to be wrong. Even the proud Roman Empire that had seemed to men for a millennium to embrace the entire *orbis terrarum*, now shrank to a provincial Mediterranean lake.

We are just beginning to realize how important a rôle was played in the changes that followed so swiftly after 1500 by this rapid enlargement of the horizon of Europe through its swift discovery of the rest of the world. Directly, of course, the new importance of commercial relations with the Orient and the empires built up by the conquistadores in America were the outstanding factors in the great Commercial Revolution from which we date modern times. Thus the expansion of Europe was perhaps the fundamental factor that led to the triumph of town civilization and the trading and manufacturing townsmen; and without this development of commerce on a national and indeed world-wide scale, men would not have so soon found their old beliefs and institutions grown hopelessly inadequate. It is probable that this economic effect of the spread of European influence was really the most significant for men's changing ideas. But it is also true that in countless ways the expansion of Europe forced a direct intellectual reaction upon the mind of Christendom. Throughout history it has always been contact with other civilizations and customs that has produced the breakdown of a crystallized set of institutions and views and given men a more cosmopolitan and enlightened outlook. The renaissance of the twelfth century had already for the Western peoples meant primarily contact with the Moslem world and the ancient culture it had preserved; now with a whole new hemisphere opening before them, to say nothing of the ancient lands of the East, Europeans were bound to lose their naïve provincialism.

To be sure, neither the Renaissance nor the Reformation was profoundly affected by this widened horizon. They were the product of earlier forces coming to maturity, and both were backward-looking, the final flower, indeed, of the Middle Ages rather than the first fruits of the new era. Neither an Erasmus nor a Luther was concerned with the New World. It was not till the Enlightenment of the late seventeenth and eighteenth centuries that Europeans finally realized the magnitude of their world; science and a world-wide cosmopolitanism together ushered in our era. Nor has Europe even to-day thrown off the provincialism that sees in its customs and beliefs, its religious and moral ideals, something naturally superior to those of other civilizations. Doubtless the fact that America was so largely a savage and undeveloped continent confirmed the Europeans in their native sense of superiority. But even before the great Eastern cultures the Westerners gazed in the childlike wonder of the earlier barbarians before Rome or Alexandria, and could hardly rise above the primitive impulse to plunder. The surprise is that the Europeans, who had learned so eagerly from the Moslems and were so anxiously pursuing Greek and Roman wisdom, should have remained so long uninfluenced by their new discoveries. Not so much in direct stimulus as in the heightened imagination, the willingness to admit almost any unheard-of thing, the sense that Christendom was after all but a small part of the earth's surface, were the first intellectual results of the widened European world felt. Naturally enough, it was the men ahead of their time, like Montaigne the naturalistic sceptic, who first realized the significance of the new lands and customs. More and Bacon put their Utopias in the new world, and men began to idealize the noble red man. But Spanish adventurers and English pirates saw only new scope for wealth and power, devoted Jesuits only new converts to the true God. Europe had to wait for her Hobbes and Lockes and Voltaires and the scientific spirit of the eighteenth century before she could take much more than an adolescent interest in the wonders of the earth.

But the glamour of so much new experience, the travelers' tales of wonders and marvels, the gorgeous romances like Camoëns' Lusiads, with which Portugal, first of explorers, celebrated her Indian empire, joined with the new flood of wealth pouring into the towns of Italy and Spain and Holland to push aside as increasingly irrelevant the concerns and problems of the Middle Ages. Here was a world to conquer, here were whole kingdoms of man lying open for the asking. Great was man, marvelous the possibilities of human life.

The Discovery of Arabian Science

In the midst of this enlarging geographical world the men of the Middle Ages turned to the scientific knowledge they found in the learned libraries and universities of the Arabs. Just as the West was awakening in the early Middle Ages, the seat of Moslem culture shifted from the Eastern Caliphate, whence it was driven by fanatical reformers, to Moorish Spain. From Spain came the first knowledge of the great writings of Aristotle; but the Moslems had also salvaged from the ancient world something in which Aristotle for all his genius was totally deficient, mathematical and mechanical science. The greatness of the Arabs seems to have lain in their ability to assimilate the best in the intellectual heritage of the peoples with whom they came in contact, rather than in any striking originality. They took the mathematical and medical knowledge of the Hellenistic world, which the Romans had disdained and Christianity cast aside, and patiently set to work on that long process of slow development and practical adaptation which the Greeks at their best had rather scorned. They gained from India the indispensable "Arabic" notation and the algebraic form of thought without which the moderns could never have built upon the Greeks; and in Spain in the tenth century they created a civilization in which science had ceased to be mere lore and had been applied to the arts and crafts of the practical life. All in all, they stood in the Middle Ages for the type of scientific thought and scientific industrial life which we have come to associate with modern Germany. Unlike the Greeks, they did not disdain the laboratory and patient experimentation; and in medicine, mechanics, and indeed all the arts, they seem naturally to have bent science to the immediate service of human life, instead of preserving it as an end in itself. From them Europe easily inherited what we like to call the "Baconian" spirit of "enlarging the bounds of human empire" over nature.

Moreover, the Arabians were strongly impregnated with the Neo-Platonic philosophy that had been reigning in the Hellenistic lands they first conquered, and even when they fell under the spell of "the philosopher" Aristotle they gave his doctrines a strongly Platonic tinge. Now Plato, and even more those who claimed his name, while possessing little of the systematic and biological interest of the Aristotelian school, did emphasize —

taking it over, perhaps, from the Pythagoreans, that strange group who combined a keen knowledge of the power of numbers with a mystical reverence and worship for them — what is most important for natural science, mathematics; and whereas the Christian tradition absorbed Neo-Platonic mysticism and disregarded its mathematical science, the Arabians had an equal love for both. Hence when the universities arose in Christendom they found in Spain Alexandrian science not only preserved, but considerably developed as well.

The twelfth century saw the major assimilation of this science, chiefly in the two places where Moslem and Christian culture touched, Saracen and Greek Sicily and Moorish Spain — often through the medium of Jewish scholars. As early as 1060 Constantine the African was translating Hippocrates and Galen, and building up a medical school at Salerno near Naples. Scholars eagerly followed the Spanish armies in search of texts; after its capture by the Christians Toledo became a great center of study. Adelard of Bath journeyed to Spain and Sicily, translating mathematical and scientific works; Euclid was turned from the Arabic by 1100. Gerard of Cremona (1114–87) spent years at Toledo, translating some ninety-two Arabic works, including Ptolemy's *Almagest* and Avicenna's medical *Canon*. At Chartres, most renowned school of the twelfth century, this new material was used and taught by Thierry of Chartres (†1155), William of Conches (†1145), and many another. The first to be translated from the Greek were Euclid and Ptolemy, in Sicily in the 1160's. The standard mathematical compendium of the Middle Ages, by Leonardo Pisano, educated in Barbary, introduced the Arabic improvements into Europe. Men like Grosseteste, the light of Oxford, scoured Spain and Europe for works on mathematical and experimental science. His eagerness for books when the Crusaders took Constantinople in 1204 and sent a new flood of Greek manuscripts to Western scholars is pathetic.

Natural Science in the High Middle Ages

From the early twelfth century there thus existed a continuous tradition of natural science, overshadowed during the brief period of Thomistic domination, 1250–1300, but coming to the fore again in the next generation. The basic idea of an experimentally-grounded science of the mathematical structure of nature was associated with optics in the Arabic Neoplatonism of Alhazen and the Jewish Avencebrol. The divine light is the medium of all natural causation and the form of all bodies; hence every natural process is subject to the geometrical laws of optics. Witelo at Padua wrote in 1270 a *Perspective* based on Alhazen; Dietrich of Freiberg treated optics and gave the correct geometrical explanation of the rainbow. The outstanding experimentalist of the century, Pierre de Maricourt, called by his pupil Roger Bacon "the master of experiments," devised many machines and wrote a work on the magnet in 1269. He believed that a mathematical science of nature must be corrected and extended by "the work of the hands."

By the middle of the thirteenth century this Greco-Arabic natural science was firmly established at Oxford, which under Grosseteste became the leading school of mathematical physics, in opposition to the qualitative science of Aristotle. Grosseteste held there is one universal science of nature, optics, the mathematical principles of which are the key to all knowledge of the world. He sought to explain natural phenomena by geometrical lines, figures, and angles; for nature acts always in the mathematically shortest and best way possible.

The works of his apt pupil Roger Bacon (1214–92), though in the main quite representative of the mass of partly sifted traditional lore common to this whole group, are ever and again shot through with what seem to be strangely prophetic insights. Endowed with an insatiable appetite for Greek letters and Hellenistic science, he combined much the same interests as his later namesake Francis Bacon, a distaste for abstract and theoretical science and a yearning for that applied knowledge that is power over nature. He shared also many of the latter's faults, an undue sense of importance and originality, a tendency to ignore and minimize his fellow-scientists, and an ability to deal in glittering generalities hardly supported by his own attainments. He was always complaining, finding excuses why he was not ready to make good his pretentious promises. He invented nothing formerly attributed to him, but wrote about inventions, like those of the compass, the lens, and gunpowder, already long known. Yet amid many fantastic ideas he held that mathematics is "the alphabet of all philosophy," and that the book of nature is written in the language of geometry — a truth that never dawned on the Elizabethan lawyer. An "Experimental Science" must come after we have worked out our optics and our physics, to make their conclusions vivid and concrete and apply them. This is a separate science, not a universal procedure; Bacon has no hint of any clear experimental method.

Experimental Science has one great prerogative in respect to all other sciences, that it investigates their conclusions by experience. For the principles of the other sciences may be known by experience, but the conclusions are drawn from these principles by way of argument. If they require particular and complete knowledge of those conclusions, the aid of this science must be called in. It is true that mathematics possesses useful experience with regard to its own problems of figure and number, which apply to all the sciences and experience itself, for no science can be known without mathematics. But if we wish to have complete and thoroughly verified knowledge, we must proceed by the methods of experimental science.[4]

Further prerogatives of such a science are that it delivers truths within other sciences not discoverable in any other way, new facts to be deductively explained. And it opens up an unexcelled knowledge of past, present, and future, and can perform wonderful works, in machines and inventions. All this sounds at times close to Galileo or Descartes. But it is deceptive; for Bacon then goes on to give a mathematical interpretation of the dimensions of Noah's ark!

The coming of Aristotle introduced a body of materials too impressive to be ignored. Thereafter for centuries the Aristotelian physical writings, however far men might eventually depart from them, were taken as the starting-point for all natural science; and the Aristotelian theory of science, however men might interpret it, remained dominant till the time of Newton. From the beginning of the fourteenth century, however, there set in a persistent and searching reconstruction of the Aristotelian tradition, which when directed to the *Physics* led by gradual stages to the mechanical and mathematical problems of the Galilean age, and when directed to the *Logic* led to the precise formulation of the method and structure of science acclaimed by all the seventeenth-century pioneers.

The Oxford school were the leaders in this intellectual revolt. The chief pathfinder of this *via moderna*, William of Ockham, left his pupils in control not only in Oxford, but in Paris itself, the former stronghold of the Thomists. This new modernism stood for a sceptical empiricism that completely demolished in the fourteenth century the great systems so carefully erected a hundred years before. Gone were all the necessities of reason, all metaphysical entities and distinctions. Nothing could be accounted real in nature that was not an observed fact or relation between facts. Experience was the only test of physical truth. At the same time the Ockhamites built on this basis a positive science of physics that laid the foundations for the astronomy and dynamics of the seventeenth century. A series of great masters at Paris made notable discoveries in the treatment of motion and falling bodies. John Buridan developed the notion of inertia, and considered gravitation as uniformly accelerated motion. Albert of Saxony tried to formulate more precisely the laws of falling bodies and of mass. Nicholas of Oresme took three momentous steps. He invented the idea of analytic geometry; he discovered the formula for uniformly accelerated motion; and he argued cogently for the rotation of the earth, a widely known hypothesis. Thus by 1375 the genius of Descartes, of Galileo, and of Copernicus had been anticipated; natural science had advanced as far as the scientists of 1575. A further rapid development was held back by the shift in intellectual interest to the concerns of literary humanism, that is, by the need of assimilating a new set of values. But the essential ideas of mathematical physics were found by the fourteenth-century Ockhamites two hundred years before technological and commercial experience had progressed far enough to support a steady growth.

The Anti-Scientific Bias of Humanism

For natural science humanism was an almost unmitigated curse. Had it not centered the energies of the best intellects on the essentially non-scientific wisdom of the civic-minded and narrowly ethical Romans, these vigorous scientific interests might have produced a Galileo long before the seventeenth century. A genuinely scientific education might have developed out of the liberal arts, and the world been spared five hundred years of weary wrestling with the bare bones of a Latin and Greek whose true spirit it has rarely understood. Science is hardly the only wisdom; but most of the genuine wisdom and real enlightenment men have achieved in the modern age has come, not through the grammarian's pedantry they have forced on each generation of schoolboys, but through the natural science they have consistently ignored.

From Petrarch down humanists have turned in disdain from nature to man. Petrarch scorns the interest in the popular bestiaries and books of travel. "Even if all these things were true, they help in no way toward a happy life, for what does it advantage us to be familiar with the nature of animals, birds, fishes, and reptiles, while we are ignorant of the nature of the race of man to which we belong, and do not know or care whence we come or whither we go?" [6] Even the great Erasmus showed no concern for the momentous discoveries of his day, for he not only did not care for natural science, he actively disliked it. One of the most trenchant passages in the *Praise of Folly* holds up to ridicule the "natural philosophers" and mathematicians.

The Attack on the Barrenness and Irrelevance of Scholasticism

Nevertheless, humanism aided powerfully the current which in the fifteenth and sixteenth centuries set in against scholasticism, and has succeeded in giving the word the connotations it now bears. Throughout the West, men came to feel a dissatisfaction with a science that seemed quite irrelevant to the immediate interests of a complex urban life, be they in the world of man or the world of nature. Against the Thomistic system and its more nominalistic opponents it was urged not only that such science was fruitless and impractical — both Aristotle and Thomas would have claimed this as its glory — but also that it was poor, meager, and barren even in the realm of truth. This charge was better founded, for since its method eschews experimentation and depends for its premises or starting-points upon authority or common observation, both of which are not only usually erroneous, but even more often scanty and insufficient, the medieval intellect had soon built as large an edifice as it could hope to with the materials at hand, and had commenced those fine drawn distinctions which have given its debased form so evil a name. Francis Bacon well characterized the inevitable fruits of such preoccupation with mere forms of knowledge.

"For the wit and mind of man, if it work upon matter, which is the contemplation of the creatures of God, worketh according to the stuff, and is limited thereby; but if it work upon itself, as the spider worketh his web, then it is endless, and brings forth indeed cobwebs of learning, admirable for the fineness of thread and work, but of no substance or profit." [7] Moreover, the learning of the schools had abandoned its true goal, the glory of God, and become but a means of increasing man's power over his fellow man, enhancing his reputation and his purse by victory in disputation.

To all of these dangers even Roger Bacon, in the thirteenth century, had been awake. Aristotelian science was itself the outgrowth of argument for the sake of convincing an opponent; its logic was the method of getting him to admit a general principle, and then showing that his conclusions therefrom were wrong. Such logic is admirable for expounding and developing an authoritative body of principles, like the law, or a theology rooted in revelation: hence its popularity amongst the schoolmen. But it could teach little that was not already known. "There are two modes in which we acquire knowledge," said Roger Bacon, "argument and experience. Argument shuts up the question, and makes us shut it up too; but it gives no proof, nor does it remove doubt and cause the mind to rest in the conscious possession of truth, unless the truth is discovered by way of experience." [8]

Peter Ramus, French scientist and humanist of the sixteenth century, who defended the thesis that everything taught by Aristotle was wrong, gives a vivid picture of the abuse of a science of argument.

> Never amidst the clamors of the college where I passed so many days, months, years, did I ever hear a single word about the applications of logic. I had faith then (the scholar ought to have faith, according to Aristotle) that it was not necessary to trouble myself about what logic is and what its purpose is, but that it concerned itself solely with creating a motive for our clamors and our disputes. I therefore disputed and clamored with all my might. If I were defending in class a thesis according to the categories, I believed it my duty never to yield to my opponent, were he one hundred times right, but to seek some very subtle distinction, in order to obscure the whole issue. On the other hand, were I disputant, all my care and efforts tended not to enlighten my opponent, but to beat him by some argument, good or bad: even so had I

been taught and directed. The categories of Aristotle were like a ball that we give children to play with, and that it was necessary to get back by our clamors when we had lost it. If, on the other hand, we should get it, we should not through any outcry allow it to be recovered. I was then persuaded that all dialectic reduced itself to disputing with loud and vigorous cries.[9]

Rabelais, in describing Gargantua's education, shows how the humanistic spirit reinforced this disgust. A great Doctor of Theology, Master Tubal Holofernes, succeeds in making his pupil stupider and stupider by forcing him to spend five years on the alphabet until he can recite it backwards, then keeping him for thirteen years, six months, and two weeks on the worst of the medieval textbooks, until he knows them backward, too, and following that with sixteen years on the crude Late Roman compilers whose work had been all that was available for the early barbarians.

But Francis Bacon, in his *Advancement of Learning* (1605), offered the most detailed criticism of medieval science. In its end of enhancing the power of man over man and in its method of disputation alike it is "contentious learning." In its rigorous forms the Aristotelian method aims at demonstration, in its milder forms at persuasion; it carries its candle of the refutation of objections into every corner instead of setting up the one great light of the investigation of truth. "The method of discovery and proof according to which the most general principles are first established, and then intermediate axioms are tried and proved by them, is the parent of error and the curse of all science."[10] What was needed was a method for discovering new truth, not for teaching and proving what was already known — not possession but growth of knowledge. Descartes in 1637 summed it all up by saying, "In respect to logic the syllogisms and the greater part of the other teaching served better in explaining to others those things that one knows (or like the art of Lully, in enabling one to speak without judgment of those things of which one is ignorant) than learning what is new."[11]

The Revival of Alexandrian Mathematical Science

Such dissatisfaction with the aims and the fruits of medieval science was shared by all men; and even during the height of the humanistic preoccupation with literary and ethical interests.

there were many seeking natural knowledge as well as moral wisdom. The actual development of natural science had been proceeding steadily if slowly. There were two major scientific schools during the later Middle Ages, the Ockhamites with their strongholds at Paris and Oxford, and the Averroistic Aristotelians in close contact with the great medical school of Padua. The original work of the Ockhamites belongs to the fourteenth century, that of the Paduans to the fifteenth and sixteenth. The former was done in dynamics, the theory of motion, and the logic of continuity; the latter, in methodology and the further elaboration of dynamics. Both advanced primarily by a constructive criticism of the natural philosophy of Aristotle. From 1400 on the Paduans knew and taught all the Ockhamite innovations. The issues involved were thereafter at the center of attention in northern Italy; and the subsequent development of this critical activity is primarily the work of Italians. Cajetan of Thiene (†1465), the most radical scientifically of the Paduans, initiated a great controversy in which all the arguments for a mathematical as against a qualitative physics were examined. From the time of Paul of Venice (†1429) to Cremonini (†1631) a rigorous Aristotelian physics and a nascent Galilean physics were in definite and conscious opposition at Padua, and this critical conflict contributed greatly to the working out of the latter.

About 1500 there was a revival of interest in the dynamics of the Masters of Paris at the Sorbonne, which led to the printing of their works. It is a fit measure of the scientific ignorance of the humanists that Erasmus and Luis Vives, students there at the time, satirized the "silly discussions" of uniformly accelerated motion, falling bodies, and infinitesimals. But the Paris scholars persisted, until finally in 1545 Domenico de Soto united Albert and Oresme to arrive at the exact law of falling bodies.

Meanwhile Leonardo da Vinci, reading the recently-printed Masters of Paris and the Padua physicists, was opposing the essentials of a mathematical method and of dynamics to the Aristotelians. Throughout the sixteenth century a strong minority current of radical scientists in Italy was working at the theory of projectiles and ballistics. Tartaglia, Cardano, Scaliger and Baldi developed these ideas in successive stages of criticism, until finally in 1585 Benedetti formulated the main principles of Galilean dynamics. The science of dynamics as it reached Galileo was thus the result of the careful reconstruction of the Aristotelian physics in the light of the mathematical interpretation of nature. Indeed, the more fully the record of late medieval and Renaissance thought is studied, the clearer it becomes that the most daring departures from Aristotelian science were carried on within the Aristotelian framework, and by means of a critical reflection on the Aristotelian doctrines — however various the sources of the ideas that fertilized that criticism.

The chief of these newly-discovered ideas were the methods of the Greek mathematicians. Indeed, the one contribution the Humanists can fairly claim to have made to the rise of modern science was to send men to the study of the ancient sources of Alexandrian science. The appeal to Hellenistic mathematics and mechanics introduced Archimedes and Hero, as well as Apollonius, Pappus, and Diophantus. The methods of mathematical analysis and synthesis of Archimedes, of whom Tartaglia published the first Latin edition in 1543, were the one factor which neither the fourteenth-century Ockhamites nor the fifteenth-century Paduans possessed. They carried the day for the quantitative side of the Paduan discussion.

Several practical questions of technology combined to support this interest in a mathematical treatment of natural problems. The extended navigation of the preceding century had called for more exact tables of the stars; the measurement involved turned men to the mathematical astronomy of Ptolemy and finally drove out the Aristotelian non-quantitative treatment. And the new problems of fortification and artillery led to the demand for a practical science of mechanics. When in his *New Science* in 1537 Tartaglia applied mathematical techniques to ballistics, there was an immense flood of works treating this very pressing problem. The stimulus of Archimedes in particular sent men to work upon "practical geometries" and useful "new sciences." What they sought and found in the ancients were primarily effective techniques and fruitful ways of procedure and discovery. It was the artisans and craftsmen who sustained this interest in mathematics, which in turning to technical problems found itself more and more involved in questions hitherto reserved for "natural philosophy." Galileo's *Two New Sciences* therefore opens most appropriately among the workmen in the Arsenal of Venice. It was such craftsmen who gradually raised mathematics to the dominant position it came to hold in the seventeenth century, and Galileo himself was the greatest of all the "practical geometers."

The Direct Appeal to Nature

The natural science of early modern times was thus hardly a complete break with the past, but rather a continuous development from the most critical teachings of the later Middle Ages, stimulated by technical demands and inspired by fresh contact with the achievements of Alexandrian thought. Above all, the independent observation of nature played at first but little part, especially in the mathematical sciences of astronomy and physics. Copernicus found his epoch-making discovery, not by observing the stars — he was far inferior in instruments and patience to the Arabians — but by reading Cicero, who suggested that Hiketas had held the earth turns on its axis daily. From Aristarchus he got the notion that the earth not only rotates but also revolves about the sun. Only after these suggestions did he set to work to elaborate his system, and even then without much reference to fresh observation. Even Galileo owed his formulation of dynamics to no experimental discovery. He tells that he rarely resorted to experiment except to convince his Aristotelian opponents, who demanded the evidence of the senses; and all his life he retained the very considerable error that g, the acceleration of gravity, is fifteen feet per second. He worked out his dynamics rather by applying the mathematical methods of Archimedes to the diagrams of the Paris Ockhamites.

In the Renaissance, as always, men turned to the careful observation of nature only after every other idea and authority had failed. What the revival of ancient learning did for science was to bring a wealth of conflicting suggestions into men's ken, and force them to appeal to reason to decide; just as the Reformation by its warring interpretations of the Bible similarly forced a religious rationalism. With so many newly-found doctrines in the field, bitterly fighting each other, it is no wonder that among the enlightened, like Montaigne, one outcome of the whole period was the growth of scepticism. What after all did men know? Very little as yet. But others of sterner fiber could not be satisfied with such a denial of the mind. Here is Copernicus who says that the earth revolves, and Ptolemy who says it doesn't. Let us catalogue the stars with Tycho, and peer through Galileo's telescope. Here is Aristotle teaching one sort of physics, and Archimedes a totally different sort. Let us with Galileo drop balls from towers and roll them down inclines. In the most practical fields this recourse to nature occurred first. The great artist engineers, Leonardo and Michelangelo and Raphael and Dürer, were forced to study anatomy, mathematical perspective, and mechanics to paint and build aright. It is significant that Stevinus was a military engineer, and that Descartes served as such in the Dutch army. From surgeons came the first genuine knowledge of a purely experimental nature: Vesalius abandoned the practice of conducting operations from Galen, and turned to the dissection of human bodies, Harvey discovered the circulation of the blood, Gilbert described the magnet. Palissy the potter suggested the cause of fossils in looking for his clays.

Nor must we overlook the stimulus that came from the use of increasingly accurate tools and instruments in the more complex economic life of trade and manufactures. When Europeans borrowed from the East the compass and the sextant, so necessary to developing commerce, and began to use astronomical tables to find their way at sea; when gunpowder demanded improved fortifications and new devices, and when the craftsman came to adopt more and more mechanical aids, there grew up a new body of experience and knowledge about nature quite independent of the traditional lore. Above all, men learned the necessity of exact measurement and refined calculations, and acquired mechanical habits of thought that proved their utility in daily life.

The New Method

For those who forsook the authority of the ancients, the chief problem seemed to be an authoritative and infallible method. Science to-day can rest on its achievements without too great a concern about its methods or their theoretical certainty. It was not so when science meant a break with everything that men had reverenced as true. The search for a method that would give certain knowledge was the paramount scientific problem of the sixteenth century. Ironically enough, the very discovery of Copernicus that the earth moved increased the distrust of the senses and experience, and sent men to mathematics as the only unshakable knowledge. If men's eyes lied here, where could they be trusted? This helps to explain why the mathematical method had already worked itself out to completeness in Newton when experimental science had hardly been born. In the sixteenth century Ramus spent years elaborating a new method, and Bruno was able to support himself by lecturing to large crowds in every town on his wanderings on a new method of finding truth.

Every scientific innovator attacked the problem of method; most of them have left detached precepts that betray where the new interest lies. The Spanish scientific and social reformer Vives called experiment the only road to truth; but it was not by mere blind experiment that the new knowledge was to come. Leonardo knew far better when he said, "Nature is full of infinite reasons, which were never in experience." [12] This strange genius, ever questioning, never completing, has left behind many a notebook of jottings which, though characteristically he never published any of them, show him anticipating Galileo by a hundred years. The painter's love of the surface of things kept him true to experience, but the artist thinker's insight saw behind to where science alone can penetrate, mathematics. "Whoever appeals to authority applies not his intellect but his memory." [13] "They say that that knowledge is mechanical which issues from experience, and that is scientific which is born and ends in the mind. But, as it seems to me, those sciences are vain and full of errors which are not born of experience, mother of all certitude, and which do not terminate in observation, that is, whose origin or middle or end does not come through one of the five senses." [14] "But I will make experiment before I proceed, because my intention is first to set forth the facts and then demonstrate by reason why such experience is constrained to work in such fashion. And this is the true rule to be followed by the investigators of natural phenomena; while nature begins from causes and ends in experience, we must follow a contrary procedure, that is, begin from experience and with that discover the causes." [15] But though knowledge must begin and end in experience, its method must be rigidly mathematical. "No human investigation can call itself true science unless it proceeds through mathematical demonstrations." [16] "He who scorns the certainty of mathematics will not be able to silence sophistical theories which end only in a war of words"; [17] and "where there is clamor there is not true knowledge, because truth has a single ending; and when that is made known the contest is ended forever." [18]

Here are almost all the elements for the new method. But not till Galileo were they seriously and convincingly applied, and even in his works precepts on method are more or less by the way, as well as somewhat unclear. The aim of scientific investigation, he says, is "not the true and inner essence of substances, but a knowledge of some of their qualities." [19] This is in opposition to Thomistic science, which sought "essences" — that is, purposes. Experiment and the senses must be the starting point; "It is impossible that a sense experience should be in conflict with truth." [20] And yet, there was Copernicus; in spite of all sense evidence to the contrary, the world does move. We cannot stop with mere observed facts, but must go behind them to their causes. "Sense must be accompanied by reason," which in the last analysis must harmonize and test experience. "Against appearances, in which all agree, we make headway with reason, either to confirm the reality of that experience or to discover its fallacy." [21] His actual practice was what he called a combination of the analytical and synthetic methods — *metodo risolitivo* and *metodo compositivo*. Select a single instance, like that of the ball rolling down the incline, analyze it completely to find the simple mathematical principle exemplified in it — the law of acceleration — deduce the consequences mathematically, and test by further experiment. Completed scientific knowledge will thus have passed both the test of accord with facts and of deduction from fundamental mathematical laws of nature. This has, indeed, been the method of physics to the present day, and to Galileo primarily belongs the honor of its formulation.

But in Galileo it was buried in the midst of the record of his discoveries and his quick-tempered polemical broadsides. At the same time Francis Bacon writing in England his *Novum Organum*, the new logic or tool, was sketching his version of the new method. His patient collection of instances without much plan and without the use of mathematics was not destined to be used by the great seventeenth-century physicists; but looking beyond them and their narrower interests, he foresaw the vaster realms where mathematics has as yet had little scope, and such collecting is the only source of knowledge. In natural history and in biology — in Darwin's formulation of his famous theory — Bacon's method has been most literally followed.

This early faith in method is shared by Bacon and Descartes. Bacon says, "The cause and root of nearly all evils in the sciences is this — that while we falsely extol and admire the powers of the human mind we neglect to seek for its true helps. Neither the naked hand nor the understanding left to itself can effect much. It is by instruments and helps that the work is done, which are as much wanted for the understanding as for the hand." [22] His contemporary Descartes went farther, as well he might, for it was he who formulated, generalized, and popularized Galileo's ideas. "The power of forming a good judgment and of distinguishing the true from the false — common sense or reason — is by nature equal in all men. The diversity of our opinions does not proceed from some men being more rational than others, but solely from the fact that our thoughts pass through diverse channels. For to be possessed of good mental powers is not sufficient; the principal matter is to apply them well" [23] — in a word, Method is the whole secret of success in science, that method which is "a more powerful instrument of knowledge than any other that has been bequeathed to us by human agency, as being the source of all others." [24]

Francis Bacon, writing at the end of this whole formative period of disgust with the old learning and search for a new method, can well summarize the great intellectual change. His attack on "contentious learning" we have already seen; he is just as disdainful of the Greek authorities cited by the humanistic scientists — "delicate learning" is his name for humanism, which is ostentatious without giving power, leans "rather towards copie than weight," and is a study of words and not matter. The famed Greeks "assuredly have that which is characteristic of boys; they are prompt to prattle but cannot generate; for their wisdom abounds in words but is barren of works." [25] "From all these systems of the Greeks, and their ramifications through particular sciences, there can hardly after the lapse of so many years be adduced a single experiment which tends to relieve and benefit the condition of man, and which can with truth be referred to the speculations and theories of philosophy." [26] They knew neither the true aim nor the true way of the only real science; they had the baneful conceit "that the dignity of the human mind is impaired with long and close intercourse with experiments and particulars, subject to sense and bound in matter." [27] They disdained the laboratory. In truth, the old age of the world, which is to-day, is to be accounted the true antiquity, which by its experience deserves to have authority. From all such learning, contentious or delicate, in fact, men were turning to a method that should give them knowledge both certain and useful.

The Baconian Spirit

For that is the greatest note sounded by all these eager seekers — useful knowledge. No longer the glory of God, but the enlarging of the bounds of human empire over nature — that is the new goal of science. With the Platonic alchemists and astrologers and magicians, the world was still the great symbol of its Maker, still a work to be admired for the love of God; but already their main purpose was magic, Power! Pico della Mirandola, feverishly looking for the secret books of the ancient dim seers, calls magic "the practical part of natural science, the noblest part, the absolute consummation of natural philosophy." [28] It gathers Nature's powers which God has scattered through the world and comes to Nature's aid. Paracelsus, strange mixture of wise physician and seeker after the hidden forces in things; Cardano, celebrated physician, scientific apologist for dreams, palmistry, ghosts, portents, astrology — what was this all but the striving to control Nature and bend her to man's will, to produce effects without a knowledge of their natural causes, which is of the essence of magic, as the thirst for magic power is the father of genuine science? Before experience had been appealed to, who could say that Nature might not indeed operate by hidden virtues and affinities? Is the one any more rational than the other, in the last analysis? As Bacon said of this "fantastic learning," its ends are noble if its means are crude and full of vanity.

224 THE NEW WORLD OF THE RENAISSANCE

In this search for power over Nature, this Faust-like spirit of the new science, occurs at last the marriage of the knowledge of the world and the service of man. It was science becoming more humanized, less divine; it was science serving, not them that built the cathedrals to carry them to God, but the rising commercial and industrial classes. All the early scientific thinkers shared this gospel of bending Nature to man's will; but one has made it peculiarly his own by his ringing enthusiasm and iteration, and it is this we mean when we speak of the "Baconian spirit." "Now the true and lawful goal of the sciences is none other than this: that human life be endowed with new discoveries and powers." [29] Not power over men, but power over Nature; and that power is the fruit of knowledge. Nature to be commanded must be obeyed; not by the anticipation of Nature in some magic dream, but by the study and interpretation of Nature will there rise the kingdom of man. Such investigation is "laborious to search, ignoble to meditate, harsh to deliver, illiberal to practice, infinite in number, and minute in subtlety." [30] But none the less it is the noblest jewel in man's possession, for of a truth the knowledge of the causes and secret motions of things has proved to bring the enlarging of the bounds of human empire, to the effecting of all things possible.

That this practical goal of science was shared not merely by the inspired prophet but by the real investigators of physics, needs only a closing quotation from the great formulator of the new world view, Descartes. "It is possible to attain knowledge which is very useful in life, and instead of that speculative philosophy which is taught in the Schools, we may find a practical philosophy by means of which, knowing the force and the action of fire, water, air, the stars, heavens, and all other bodies that environ us, as distinctly as we know the different crafts of our artisans, we can in the same way employ them in all those uses to which they are adapted, and thus render ourselves the masters and possessors of nature." [31]

REFERENCES

1. *Tauler's Sermons*, ed. H. R. Allinson, 324–26, 354.
2. Francis Bacon, *New Atlantis*, World's Classics ed., 265.
3. Albert the Great, *De causis et proprietatibus elementorum et planetarum*, quoted in Lynn Thorndike, *History of Magic and Experimental Science*, II, 535.

4. Roger Bacon, *Opus Majus*, ed. Bridges, II, 172, 173.
5. Dante, *Paradiso*, Canto II, v. 95.
6. Petrarch, *Opera* (1581), 1038, quoted in Robinson and Rolfe, *Petrarch*, 41, 42.
7. Francis Bacon, *Advancement of Learning*, II, 6.
8. Roger Bacon, *Opus Majus*, ed. Bridges, II, 167.
9. F. P. Graves, *Peter Ramus*, 21, 22.
10. Francis Bacon, *Novum Organum*, Bk. I, Aphorism 69.
11. Descartes, *Discourse on Method*, Part II.
12. Leonardo, *Frammenti letterari e filosofici*, ed. E. Solmi, 112.
13. Quoted from Sedgwick and Tyler, *Short History of Science*, 235.
14. Leonardo, *Frammenti*, 94, 95.
15. *Ibid.*, 85–88.
16. *Ibid.*
17. *Ibid.*
18. *Ibid.*, 93–95.
19. Galileo, *Opere*, Edizione nazionale, V, 187.
20. *Ibid.*, XVIII, 247.
21. *Ibid.*, I, 279.
22. Francis Bacon, *Novum Organum*, Bk. I, Aphorism 2.
23. Descartes, *Discourse on Method*, Part I.
24. Descartes, *Rules for the Direction of the Mind*, Rule 4.
25. Bacon, *Novum Organum*, Bk. I, Aphorism 71.
26. *Ibid.* I, 73.
27. *Ibid.*, I, 83.
28. Pico.
29. Bacon, *Novum Organum*, I, 81.
30. *Ibid.*, I, 83.
31. Descartes, *Discourse on Method*, Part 6.

SELECTED READING LISTS

See page 249.

CHAPTER X

THE NEW SCENE OF HUMAN LIFE

THE COPERNICAN REVOLUTION

OUT of all this increased interest in nature and science, this preoccupation with investigation and mathematics and method, the fifteenth and early sixteenth centuries saw take shape a veritable new universe — that is, a very small number of enlightened minds saw it. Two great revolutions in thought had occurred, and the course of intellectual history since that time is primarily the record of the gradual penetration into the beliefs of men of the significant consequences of those revolutions. The eighteenth century became the period of the "Enlightenment" because these consequences were spreading so rapidly amongst the middle classes; in the late nineteenth century science can almost be said to have struck the popular imagination, and there are few literate men alive in the West to-day who, even when they preserve habits of thought that descend from an earlier period, do not harbor side by side with these old ideas a belief in the new world of nature.

These two revolutions broke the bonds of the medieval world, of the neatly ordered hierarchy of beings all leading up to one supreme power, and made that bandbox affair forever impossible for the emancipated mind. Slowly but surely the various compromises that men effected to ease for themselves the shock of the plunge into the strange new universe have broken down, until to-day few who think are unaware of the far-reaching significance of the Copernican and Cartesian revolutions. The former seemed at first merely to overthrow the authority of Ptolemy; in reality it swept man out of his proud position as the central figure and end of the universe, and made him a tiny speck on a third-rate planet revolving about a tenth-rate sun drifting in an endless cosmic ocean. The absolute insignificance of man before the mighty and relentless will of Calvin's stern deity seems pomp and glory indeed compared with the place to which he has been relegated by modern astronomy.

But following swiftly upon this discovery came the even more momentous Cartesian revolution, which made Aristotle's fate far worse than Ptolemy's: while the latter had been refuted in his own field, the former was swept aside with all his works as quite irrelevant and unimportant. Purposes gave way to mathematics, human will and foresight to immutable and inflexible mechanical order. Throughout the whole vast windy stretches of infinity, in stone and plant and animal, nowhere in this universe was there another being like man, nowhere a being who felt and suffered, loved and feared and hoped, who thought and knew. Man was alone, quite alone, in a vast and complex cosmic machine. Gone were the angelic hosts, gone the devils and their pranks, gone the daily miracles of supernatural intervention, gone even was man's imploring cry of prayer. Somewhere, perhaps, in the distant regions whither the eye of man could not penetrate, somewhere beyond the possibility of attainment by human senses, there dwelt the Great Power that had made all this, a Power inflexible and unalterable by human wishes, yet perhaps a Power whose infinite wisdom had comprehended even lowly man in his great cosmic schemes. The minds of men remained for two centuries firm in this faith; to give up, in spite of all the absence of any evidence of sense, this deep-felt hope that man was still cared for, that his good had a place in the heart of almighty power, that he was not alone, was more than the soul could bear. Of all that medieval world, one thing alone was left for those who entered whole-heartedly into this great cold universe — the faith in a Creator in whose image man was made, in a wise and loving Father who had built all this vast machinery for the good of man. Why he had wasted all this power on puny man was not for man to inquire; if his world lay open to the inquiring intellect, the meaning of his ways was past finding out. This last fond remnant of the Christian epic it was left for the nineteenth century, not indeed to refute, for faith can never be disproved, but to make, for many at least, irrelevant and unimportant. For them, man too became a mere part of this vast machine; its finest flower, perhaps — perhaps a cosmic accident and mistake. To that eternal cry of the soul, "Why?" the answer came, *Ignoramus* — nay, *Ignorabimus*.

The Simplicity and Uniformity of Nature

Copernicus set out, as a mathematician, to discover "a more rational system" of the courses of the heavenly bodies, which would explain their apparent irregularities of velocity in terms of a series of uniform motions. In the fifteenth century a school of astronomers at Nuremberg, chief of whom were Peurbach and Regiomontanus, had compared and elaborated the different sets of Arabian and Spanish observation tables and theories of the heavens. The discrepancies between Aristotle's crude physical crystal spheres and Ptolemy's purely mathematical scheme became evident, and in order to harmonize theory with the very considerable body of quite accurate data recently collected, it was necessary to complicate Ptolemy's system still further by the addition of more and more separate and unrelated circular motions of the heavenly bodies.

Conflicting authorities and extreme complexity of theory — this was the situation which Copernicus found when he went to Italy to study the best ancient astronomers in the universities of Bologna and Padua. The confusion and intricacy of the Ptolemaic scheme as elaborated by the Nuremberg school repelled him, for he shared a strong faith in the mathematical simplicity and harmony of the cosmos. By this he meant the dependence, in a single related system, of a multitude of phenomena on a few geometrical axioms. The wisdom of Nature, he says, attains her end elsewhere by the simplest ways, without circumlocutions, and by means of a harmonious interaction between all the elements involved. She seeks to bind many effects to one single cause, rather than to increase the number of causes.

I made every effort to read anew all the books of philosophers I could obtain, in order to ascertain if there were not some one of them of the opinion that other motions of the heavenly bodies existed than are assumed by those who teach mathematical sciences in the schools. So I found first in Cicero that Hiketas of Syracuse believed the earth moved. Afterwards I found also in Plutarch that others were likewise of this opinion.... Starting thence I began to reflect on the mobility of the earth.... I began to think of a motion of the earth, and although the idea seemed absurd, still as others before me had been permitted to assume certain circles in order to explain the motions of the stars, I believed it would readily be permitted me to try whether in the assumption of some motion of the earth better explanations of the revolutions of the heavenly spheres might not be found. And thus I have, assuming the motions which I in the following work attribute to the earth, after long and careful investigation, finally found that when the motions of the other planets are referred to the circulation of the earth and are computed for the revolution of each star, not only do the phenomena necessarily follow therefrom, but the order and magnitude of the stars and all their orbs and the heaven itself are so connected that in no part can anything be transposed without confusion to the rest and to the whole universe.[1]

Every one of the great pioneer scientists who effected the two cardinal intellectual revolutions shared this serene confidence in the mathematical simplicity of nature. To them it was not only a useful principle of method, it was the fundamental fact about the universe. It led to their triumphs, and at times to errors that only observation could expose. Isaac Newton stood in the great tradition from which he came when he formulated it in the classic words, "Nature does nothing in vain, and more is in vain when less will serve; for Nature is pleased with simplicity, and affects not the pomp of superfluous causes."[2] Whether justified as a cosmic principle or not — and there are of course many who would see in it a craving of the merely human mind — this faith was clearly fundamental in bringing an ordered universe out of the complex and heterogeneous medieval world.

Granted such a principle, the arguments of Copernicus were conclusive. Despite all the evidence of the senses and of common observation to the contrary, he stuck to his rational conviction: mathematical analysis must take the place of vulgar experience. Copernicus appealed to the geometer: he would understand the mathematical superiority and the "greater rationality" of the new system, despite mechanical difficulties that seemed at first almost insuperable. The fact that the fixed stars must be an enormous distance from the earth not to betray any apparent change of position, a fact that led Brahe to reject the revolution of the earth, that greatly troubled Galileo, and that was answered experimentally only when in 1838 Bessel did actually observe such a parallax, he thought it preferable to admit in the interest of the greater simplicity of his scheme.

Simplicity, however, led Copernicus astray. He did not seriously question that the universe was finite, enclosed in the old Ptolemaic sphere of the fixed stars. He also retained the notion that the planets move uniformly in orbits that are circular, or compounded of Ptolemaic epicycles. His reason was the good medieval Platonic one that any departure from such uniform circular motion "must arise either from irregularity in the moving power, whether this be within the body or foreign to it, or from some inequality of the body in revolution.... Both of which things the intellect shrinks from with horror, it being unworthy to hold such a view about bodies which are constituted in the most perfect order."[3]

Because of the precautions of his editor, who published in 1543 his work *De Revolutionibus Orbium Celestium* as he himself lay on his deathbed, this theory was presented to the world, not as a reasoned statement of fact about the real nature of the universe, but as an altogether hypothetical attempt at mathematical calculation. As such the astronomical world received it, and it was soon taught side by side with the older system. Though Luther thought the notion foolish, since Holy Writ said that Joshua caused the sun to stand still, and Melanchthon considered it so godless that it should be suppressed, and Francis Bacon called Copernicus "a man who thinks nothing of introducing fictions of any kind into nature, providing his calculations turn out well,"[4] in neither Protestant nor Catholic lands was any official step taken. What had Copernicus accomplished? He had greatly extended the boundaries of the universe, but he had not broken them; he had reduced Ptolemy's seventy-nine circles to thirty-four; he had introduced the novel notion that motion is relative to the observer; he had made the earth move round the sun rather than the sun move round the earth. These were all important ideas, but none was really revolutionary except in a negative sense. The startling thought contained in his work was that the old authorities had been found in error, and that even observation and common sense were fallible; only reason operating by mathematical calculation could be trusted. What was obviously necessary was for men to amass a wealth of accurate observation for reason to work upon.

The Appeal to the Observation of Nature

This labor was performed by Tycho Brahe, a Dane who constructed a great observatory and gathered for years data as accurate as the absence of the telescope would permit. His most brilliant assistant, Kepler, using his observations, drew from them epoch-making conclusions. Kepler learned from Brahe to discipline his Neo-Platonic passion for simplicity and harmony by rigorous mathematics and the closest observation of facts. He spent his life searching for the relations obtaining between the various numerical quantities occurring in the solar system — the "Harmony of the World." The accurate records of Tycho had revealed the impossibility of calculating the orbits of the planets by Copernicus' combination of circular movements; so he tried combination after combination of new circles, calculating the results of each and comparing them with the records. One geometrical scheme coincided with an error of but 8', and he was tempted to rest there. But his conviction of the necessity of verification by fact made him take a momentous step. "Since the divine goodness has given to us in Tycho Brahe a most careful observer, from whose observations the error of 8' is shown in this calculation, ... it is right that we should with gratitude recognize and make use of this gift of God. ... For if I could have treated 8' of longitude as negligible I should have already corrected sufficiently the hypothesis ... But as they could not be neglected, these 8' alone have led the way toward the complete reformation of astronomy, and have been made the subject matter of a great part of this work."[5] It had at last been forced upon men that calculation must be verified by observation!

He tried next, not a circle, but an oval, attempting to fit the data from Mars into an egg-shaped orbit. Then he turned to the simplest known oval curve, the ellipse, and the success of his attempt confirmed his faith in what he called "the simplicity and ordered regularity of Nature." He had discovered at last the true shape of the planet's orbit, an ellipse with the sun in one focus. Elated at this discovery, he sought next the law of the variation of the rate of motion of the planet, for, he argued, as the earth is the abode of measuring creatures, it is reasonable to expect that the measurements of the solar system will bear some simple relation to the dimensions of the earth. He was rewarded by his second law, that equal areas of the ellipse are swept out in equal times. Having now solved Mars' orbit, he was convinced that he had found the laws of all planets, since the harmony of nature demanded that all "have similar habits." A third law expressed the mathematical relation between the times of revolution of the planets and their distance from the sun.

What was the significance of Kepler's work? He had shown the success of the method of seeking simple mathematical relations, and the necessity of verifying them by calculation and observation. He had shown that the heavens follow universal and regular laws. And he had shown that they were not different from those of the earth, and that their movements were not perfect — not circular, and not at a uniform speed. The importance of this last discovery can only be realized when we compare it with the Aristotelian doctrine that the heavens were perfect and invariable, admitting of no change, quite unlike the mutable earth — were formed, indeed, of a different substance entirely, "quintessence," the fifth element. The old idea of a hierarchy of being, qualitatively different, approaching perfection as it receded from the center of the earth, so well expressed in Dante, had given way to uniform mathematical law. No longer were high, sublime, and ideal forces operating in one realm, and lower and material forces on earth. The democracy of individual facts equal in rank had superseded the Aristotelian feudal system of an ordered gradation of unequal rank. And the significance of this change lies in the fact that all things, including the remote and sublime, are to be described and explained in terms of homely familiar events and forces. In other words, the possibility and the necessity of experiment was established. It remained only for Galileo to drive these momentous notions home by actual observation through the telescope.

Galileo had already worked out most of his ballistics and dynamics and was a famous professor of mathematics at Padua when his attention was turned to astronomical observation. In 1604 a new star appeared, which he proved mathematically must be in the region of the fixed stars, thus confirming a similar observation of Tycho in 1572, and proving that changes did take place in the heavens as on earth. A Dutch spectacle-maker had just made, in 1608, the first practical telescope, and Galileo, hearing the news, devised one for himself and trained it on the heavens the next year. In his *Sidereal Messenger*, published in 1610, he gave the world the remarkable fruits of his observation. He saw the mountains of the moon, and calculated their height. He discovered four of Jupiter's satellites revolving about that planet as the moon revolves about the earth. He found that Venus passes through phases like the moon, and therefore must be a dark body resembling the earth in receiving its illumination from the sun. He proved by calculation that the dark spots or "blemishes" on the sun must be very close to its surface, and that their course was exactly what it would be if the sun rotated on its axis in about a month.

The significance of these discoveries was twofold: in the first place, they furnished experimental confirmation of the Copernican theory, and took it definitely out of the realm of mathematics into that of physical existence; in the second, they broke down conclusively the Aristotelian distinction between the earth and the heavens, and substituted for the old gradation of more and more perfect beings the notion of the uniformity of nature. Naturally they aroused a storm of opposition from those scientists who reverenced the authority of Aristotle. To preserve the smoothness and perfect sphericity of the moon one suggested that the apparent valleys were really filled by an invisible crystalline substance: to which Galileo retorted that this suggestion was so excellent that he could maintain the moon had mountains of this crystal ten times higher than those he had observed. The principal scientists would not even look through his telescope at Jupiter's moons.

As I wished to show the satellites of Jupiter to the Professors in Florence, they would see neither them nor the telescope. These people believe there is no truth to seek in nature, but only in the comparison of texts.[6]

One opponent wrote:

There are seven windows given to animals in the domicile of the head, through which the air is admitted to the tabernacle of the body, ... two nostrils, two eyes, two ears, and a mouth. So in the heavens, as in a macrocosmus, there are two favorable stars, two unpropitious, two luminaries, and Mercury undecided and indifferent. From this and many other similarities in nature, such as the seven metals, etc., we gather that the number of planets is necessarily seven. Moreover, these satellites of Jupiter are invisible to the naked eye, and therefore can exercise no influence on the earth, and therefore would be useless, and therefore do not exist... Now, if we increase the number of the planets, this whole and beautiful system falls to the ground.[7]

To all such arguments Galileo replied in the modern spirit:

I can listen only with the greatest repugnance when the quality of unchangeability is held up as something preëminent and complete in contrast to variability. I hold the earth for most distinguished exactly on account of the transformations which take place upon it.[8]

Here was the modern science of manipulation and experiment challenging the ancient science of the contemplation of immutable perfection.

The opposition of Galileo's scientific opponents to his new ideas and to the biting sarcasm which this very peppery-tempered gentleman launched unceasingly at them, led them to seek to enlist the Catholic Church on their side. Reluctantly, for many of the cardinals, including Barberini, who later became Pope Urban VIII, had a high esteem for the man and interest if not full belief in his notions, the Church was drawn to support the Aristotelians, and declare the Copernican theory in contradiction with the authority of Scripture. The real point at issue, it is obvious, was not the movement of the earth, but the glory of the heavens; not Copernicus against Ptolemy, but Galileo against Aristotle. Galileo, who was a sincere Catholic, though his religious beliefs seem to have had little influence over his scientific speculations, was led to decry Scripture as an authority in science, quoting Cardinal Baronius' maxim "That the intention of the Holy Ghost is to teach us not how the heavens go, but how to go to heaven." "Methinks," he wrote, "that in the discussion of natural problems we ought not to begin at the authority of places of Scripture; but at sensible experiments and necessary demonstrations." [9] The Inquisition reported "That the doctrine that the sun was the center of the world and immovable was false and absurd, formally heretical and contrary to Scripture, whereas the doctrine that the earth was not the center of the world but moved, and has further a daily motion, was philosophically false and absurd and theologically at least erroneous." [10] Galileo was accordingly summoned and admonished to abandon the said opinion; and the *De Revolutionibus* was now in 1616 put upon the Index "until it should be corrected." These necessary corrections were officially published in 1620, and embraced only a few alterations to make the Copernican principles appear as mere mathematical hypotheses, convenient for calculation. Thereafter Pope Urban was very friendly to Galileo and granted him many favors.

In 1632 appeared, with the Church's *imprimatur*, his greatest and most influential astronomical treatise, the *Dialogue on the Two Chief Systems of the World*. In thinly veiled dialogue form Galileo marshaled with consummate skill all the arguments in favor of the Copernican view. The chief merit of his scheme is shown to be its marvelous simplicity and harmony in comparison with the confused and complex Ptolemaic scheme. Pope Urban was persuaded by the enraged Aristotelians that Simplicio, the scholastic who is the butt of the whole dialogue, was intended for himself; and, bitterly wounded in his vanity by this supposed insult, he ordered Galileo to appear before the Inquisition. Though he was never formally imprisoned, he was threatened with torture; and, forced to "abjure, curse, and detest the aforesaid errors," he was banished to a country estate in 1633. His *Dialogue* and Kepler were placed on the Index, from which, with Copernicus, they were not withdrawn till 1835.

The Cartesian Revolution

Thus was the Copernican revolution consummated by Galileo; but even more significant was the Cartesian revolution which created a new physics. The mechanical view of Nature crowned generations of steady advance by the mathematicians. With Archimedes and their other new Alexandrian allies they finally won complete victory. In the intoxication of their triumph they were led to abandon the Aristotelian view of Nature as a hierarchy of different types of objects each striving to fulfill its purpose of attaining perfection in its own way, and to substitute for it the sublime faith that Nature is a great harmonious and mathematically ordered machine. Confident in that faith, they proved by actual experiment to their skeptical opponents that such was indeed the case. As Galileo says, "Ignorance has been the best teacher I have ever had, since in order to be able to demonstrate to my opponents the truths of my conclusions, I have been forced to prove them by a variety of experiments, though to satisfy myself alone I have never felt it necessary to make many." [11] This last clause well illustrates how modern science was born of a *faith* in the mathematical interpretation of Nature, held long before it had been empirically verified.

In the fragments of Leonardo this faith burns strong. He is convinced that every power of Nature gives rise to effects of a definite kind, unfolding themselves in a definite order. Necessity is "the eternal bond and rule of Nature," for "Nature is constrained by the reason of her law, which lives infused in her." [12] The essence of these powers — the goal of the Aristotelians —

may be beyond human investigation, but their effects can be learned. "The definition of the whatness — the quiddity — of the elements is not in the power of man, but many of their effects are known." [13] Nature's laws display themselves in the invariable way in which each effect follows its cause.

Nature's laws are both regular and simple, every one of her acts occurring *per la via brevissima*, by the shortest way. This eternal necessity of law is fundamentally mathematical; hence by mathematics alone we can penetrate to them, and by reason of this mathematical constitution of the world, our mathematical knowledge can be applied to experience. Because of this rational order, we can find in a single experiment its mathematical law, and infer therefrom many other truths which experience will then verify. "Proportions are found not only in numbers and measures, but also in sounds, weights, times and places, and in every force.... There is no certitude where some one of the mathematical sciences can not be applied." [14] Mathematics unlocks the true secrets of Nature; "the bird is a machine working through mathematical laws." [15] The whole economy of the world is physical, quantitative, mathematical.

The contrast between this view and the whole Thomistic-Aristotelian science is striking. For the latter, the object of investigation had been the different purposes of objects, the substances or essence of things, their whatness, their qualitative distinctions. Of uniformities, of exactly measured relations between *events*, of the *how* of things, there had been not a trace. With Leonardo all the objects of scholastic research are gone, and we are in the world of the modern scientist.

In Kepler this faith in the simplicity, harmony, and mathematical order of the universe is thoroughly Pythagorean in its mysticism. His first book, the *Mystery of the Universe*, sought the definite mathematical relations in the world that were the revelation of the Divine Spirit. The universe is the image of the Trinity: the central sun is the Father, the surrounding sphere the Son, and the geometrical relations between them and the spheres of the planets constitute the Holy Spirit. His "great discovery" was that the five regular bodies postulated by Pythagoras and Plato might be inscribed in the actual spheres in which the planets moved, and that there was thus a correspondence between the fundamental geometrical forms and the distribution of the planets in space. All his later search for the simple relations of their orbits was done in the faith that "the world participates in quantity," and that "where matter is, there is geometry also." [16] As he checked his theories by accurate observation, his religious interest faded. "Formerly," he said, "I believed that the force which moves the planets was really a soul. In my treatise on Mars I showed that there are no such things, and concluded that it must be corporeal force." [17] His early *Mystery of the Universe* had given way to a *Celestial Physics*, but it remained none the less a *Harmony of the World*.

The Foundation of Dynamics

It was left for Galileo to translate this faith into an exact mathematical procedure. His fundamental principle of method he recorded when he wrote: "To be placed on the title-page of my collected works: Here it will be perceived from innumerable examples what is the use of mathematics for judgment in the natural sciences, and how impossible it is to philosophize correctly without the guidance of Geometry, as the wise maxim of Plato has it." [18] Mathematics best expresses the natural structure of things. "Philosophy is written in that great book which ever lies before our eyes; but we cannot understand it if we do not first learn the language and characters in which it is written. This language is mathematics, and the characters are triangles, circles, and other geometrical figures." [19] And he cites Scripture: "God hath made all things in number, weight, and measure." [20] But he uses the familiar Platonic figure to point, not to a mathematical vision of the world, but to a fruitful method. A verbal definition of the essence of gravitation brings no new knowledge; a mathematical formulation of the measurable relations of falling bodies does. Whatever can be said of Nature in mathematical discourse is truly said, and of the structure it grasps God himself could have no clearer knowledge.

Galileo was preëminently the investigator rather than the speculative system-builder: he worked out "two new sciences," not "the mathematical principles of natural philosophy." By training and temperament he belongs with Tartaglia and the practical geometers; his science is the culmination of the critical tradition of Italian Aristotelianism. On the larger questions he took its fundamental positions for granted. All this appears in his greatest work, the *Mathematical Demonstrations of Two New Branches of Science,* in which he reveals himself as the follower, not of Pythagoras, but of Archimedes. Proudly he summarizes his achievements.

> My purpose is to set forth a very new science dealing with a very ancient subject. There is, in nature, perhaps nothing older than motion, concerning which the books written by philosophers are neither few nor small; nevertheless I have discovered by experiment some properties of it which are worth knowing and which have not hitherto been either observed or demonstrated. Some superficial observations have been made, as, for instance, that the free motion of a heavy falling body is continuously accelerated; but to just what extent this acceleration occurs has not yet been announced; for so far as I know, no one has yet pointed out that the distances traversed during equal intervals of time, by a body falling from rest, stand to one another in the same ratio as the odd numbers beginning with unity.
>
> It has been observed that missiles and projectiles describe a curved path of some sort; however no one has pointed out the fact that this path is a parabola. But this and other facts, not few in number or less worth knowing, I have succeeded in proving; and what I consider more important, there have been opened up to this vast and most excellent science, of which my work is merely the beginning, ways and means by which other minds more acute than mine will explore its remote corners. ... The theorems set forth in this brief discussion will, when they come into the hands of other investigators, continually lead to wonderful new knowledge. It is conceivable that in such a manner a worthy treatment may be gradually extended to all the realms of nature.[21]

That Galileo had set forth the outlines of dynamics is remarkable enough; but for human beliefs his work had an even greater significance. He had turned men from the science of perfections, ranks, and purposes to the conception of a universal law in nature, which has indeed flourished until it seems now the fundamental fact of our universe. There are no differences of rank in numbers, he pointed out, no fixed purposes to be worked out there. Three is not the perfect number for legs, nor is the sphere the ideal form from which to construct walls. To seek purposes in the processes of nature either restricts us to a narrow round of stereotyped happenings, as in the Aristotelian science which could not see beyond the narrow limits of what men observe about them, or, as in the Platonism that sees everything as the result of the divine will, it explains nothing, just because it could equally well explain anything else. God could as easily have made the sun move around the earth as not; therefore to look for the cause of astronomical motions in God's purpose is meaningless. We may not presume to know the ends of the Almighty; it is enough for us to investigate the precise way in which they are accomplished, and utilize our knowledge to bend events to our own human purposes.

Two momentous changes had occurred. The world was perceived to be a mechanical order, and simultaneously it became amenable to human control. "Nature," says Galileo, "is inexorable and immutable, and never passes the bounds of the laws assigned her, as one that nothing careth, whether her abstruse reasons and methods of operating be or be not exposed to the capacity of men." [22] And a modern writer sums up the transformation of nature:

When the rigid clamp of fixed ends was taken off from nature, observation and imagination were emancipated, and experimental control for scientific and practical purposes enormously stimulated. Because natural processes were no longer restricted to a fixed number of immovable ends or results, anything might conceivably happen. It was only a question of what elements could be brought into juxtaposition so that they would work upon one another. Immediately, mechanics ceased to be a separate science and became an organ for attacking nature. The mechanics of the lever, wheel, pulley and inclined plane told accurately what happens when things in space are used to move one another during definite periods of time. The whole of nature became a scene of pushes and pulls, of cogs and levers, of motions of parts or elements to which the formulæ of movements produced by well-known machines were directly applicable.[23]

The Mechanical Interpretation of Nature

Galileo was a physicist who confined himself to his study of mechanical and astronomical phenomena, and hesitated to generalize his methods and principles. Descartes, his contemporary, brilliant mathematician, formulator of optics, was able to see with startling distinctness the wider significance of these things. He it was who first brought to the learned world a realization of the consequences of the scientific work we have been examining, and sketched out in clear words the full outline of the new universe into which men had been ushered. In 1637 he published his first works, his *Discourse upon Method* and the first fruits of

[23] From *Reconstruction in Philosophy*, by John Dewey. Reprinted by permission of the publishers, Henry Holt & Company.

its application in geometry, optics, and general physics. At his death in 1650 he had spread the fame of the mathematical interpretation of nature through the length and breadth of Europe, given confidence to many a lonely investigator to pursue his work, and raised up a host of disciples in France, Holland, Germany, and England. Germany was bleeding to death in the "religious" struggles of the Thirty Years' War, England was turning all her energies to religious and political controversy, Italy was in the clutches of the Counter-Reformation; but France had at last achieved national unity under a strong absolute monarchy run for and by the middle class, and in Holland political freedom and commercial prosperity had crowned the bitter struggle against Spain. These two lands were the intellectual center of Europe for the whole seventeenth century, until England came to the fore in the last decades. And in Holland and France Cartesianism became almost the official philosophy: for the first time the new science was actually popular among the educated classes. Men like Fontenelle wrote dainty little expositions of it to adorn my lady's dressing table. The ground was prepared for Newton, who may almost be called the greatest of the Cartesians, to effect his great synthesis, and for the public to receive with awe and reverence his harmonious world-machine.

The vision that was Descartes' was well expressed in the epitaph written by his closest friend Chanut: "In his winter furlough comparing the mysteries of nature with the laws of mathematics he dared hope that the secrets of both could be unlocked with the same key." [24] The reference is to the incident that determined the course of his whole life. After the best education that France afforded, disgusted with all that had been taught him save mathematics, he had turned to "the great book of the world," and sought knowledge in courts and armies and experience with men, convinced that he "might meet with much more truth in the reasonings that each man makes on the matters that specially concern him, and the issue of which would very soon punish him if he made a wrong judgment, than in the case of those made by a man of letters in his study touching speculations which lead to no result." [25] The diversity he found in men's beliefs taught him to distrust custom and listen only to reason. One day, confined to his room by the cold, he resolved to discard all his beliefs that could not pass the test of reason. He had been speculating much on mathematical problems, and now there came to him the vision that here, in combining the best in geometrical analysis and algebra, lay the source of all true science. "As I considered the matter carefully it gradually came to light that all those matters only are referred to mathematics in which order and measurement are investigated, and that it makes no difference whether it be in numbers, figures, stars, sounds or any other object that the question of measurement arises. I saw consequently that there must be some general science to explain that element as a whole which gives rise to problems about order and measurement, restricted as these are to no special subject matter. This, I perceived, was called universal mathematics." [26] "Such a science should contain the primary rudiments of human reason, and its province ought to extend to the eliciting of true results in every subject. To speak freely, I am convinced that it is a more powerful instrument of knowledge than any other that has been bequeathed to us by human agency, as being the source of all others." [27]

That night Descartes seems to have had an intense vision in which the Angel of Truth appeared and bade him trust his new science; it would indeed give him all knowledge. He rose on fire to carry out his analysis in geometry, and soon had perfected the branch we now call analytical geometry. This meant nothing less than the complete correspondence between algebra and the realm of space — that is, the real world. By algebra man could hope to discover the secrets of the universe; this was the key to the great cipher of nature, this the new method men had been seeking.

To Descartes thenceforth space or extension became the fundamental reality in the world, motion the source of all change, and mathematics the only relation between its parts. It is significant that this Cartesian faith, so similar to that of the pioneers in astronomy and physics, lacked any trace of the mystic Platonism that had marked all of them. He had made of nature a machine and nothing but a machine; purposes and spiritual significance had alike been banished. Descartes himself worked out the principles of optics in detail; but his significance lies rather in his general conception. He had reached the notion of seeking an explanation of all things in the world in purely mechanical terms. Intoxicated by his vision and his success, he boasted, "Give me extension and motion, and I will construct the universe." The whole working-out of mechanical physics in the next two centuries is but the development of this idea. All energy is reduced to kinetic energy, the energy of motion; all qualitative differences in the world to quantitative differences of the size, shape, and speed of motion of particles of matter. Living beings form no exception; life becomes a mere matter of chemical and physical changes, all animals are mere automata, even the body of man is a purely physical machine. The world of the Middle Ages has been explicitly and entirely rejected for the world of modern physics. Descartes in his enthusiasm suggested mechanical explanations too simple and too little checked up by observation; but Newton, in actually working out in detail the *Mathematical Principles of Natural Philosophy*, set the keystone in the arch of Cartesianism.

The Infinite Worlds

Thus was accomplished the revolution from the medieval to the modern universe. It still remained for men to effect an emotional readjustment, to realize the full significance of this change in the place of man in his world. Two great thinkers, the one inspired by Copernicus, the other by Descartes, stand out as the earliest representatives of this readjustment. Giordano Bruno in the sixteenth century really *felt* the infinity of the universe, Benedict Spinoza in the seventeenth really assimilated the reign of mechanical law. Each made a religion of the new science.

Bruno, a Dominican friar who fled the cloister and wandered up and down Europe lecturing and disputing in the universities of Rome, France, England, Germany, Geneva, to fall at last a victim to the Inquisition and die in flames in Rome, the great martyr of the new science, was a man whose soul was set on fire by the Copernican discoveries. To him the great achievement of the new astronomy was its principle of the relativity of all place and motion. If the sun is the center and not the earth, as Copernicus taught, where then is the real center of the universe? In his boyhood his native mountain of Cicada seemed the center of the world, and far-off Vesuvius on the outer rim. When he climbed Vesuvius, Cicada faded into insignificance. Which was the center? Can there be any real center? If not the earth, why the sun? A candle flame grows smaller as we recede; why may not suns do likewise? Why, indeed, may not all the stars be themselves suns, and each new sun appear to itself the center of the universe? Where, then, are its limits? Has it limits? Is it not rather infinite, an infinity of worlds like our solar system? There must be hundreds of thousands of suns, and about them planets rolling, each one, perhaps, inhabited, by beings possibly better, possibly worse, than ourselves. Throughout, nature must be the same, everywhere worlds, everywhere the center, everywhere and nowhere. The narrow bonds of the Ptolemaic world, which even Copernicus had not really broken, fly asunder for Bruno as he launches his soul into infinite space.

But what, then, are the consequences for man? In such a world, what becomes of the central episode of Christianity? No longer is man the only child of God; perhaps he is lost in the infinity of worlds. "Man is no more than an ant in the presence of the infinite. And a star is no more than a man." How can man be the central figure in such a world? How, indeed, can there be any drama enacted on a boundless stage? Perhaps the epic of redemption is being repeated over and over again for the sake of God's other children. Perhaps He is at this moment redeeming with His life the dwellers on some star yonder in the night. Perhaps there is no redemption, perhaps it is all a meaningless whirl of rolling suns.

From such a nightmare the soul of Bruno shrank. No, God cannot be found anywhere in the boundless universe just because He must be everywhere; as it is the same life that in me beckons with my finger, beats with my heart, thinks with my brain, so God must be the single life and soul of this infinite universe; "Nature is God in things." The power, the life that animates the whole must be that which lives in each of the parts. And so Bruno passed from Platonism to a mystic pantheism, feeling the pulse of God in every natural force, seeing and adoring his glory in the vast profusion of that universe that can be but his body. Losing God from the world, he found Him again in the rhythmic life of the universe, in the falling waters and the ripening grain and in the circling of sun on sun.

Up and down Europe Bruno wandered, on fire with his vision, the "Excubitor," he called himself, the awakener of sleeping minds.

Lo! here is one who has swept the air, pierced the heavens, sped by the stars and passed beyond the bounds of the world, who has annihilated the fantastic spheres with which foolish mathematicians and vulgar philosophers had closed us in. The key of his diligent curiosity has opened to the view of every sense and every power of reason such closets of truth as can be opened by us. He has stripped nature of her robe and veil. He has given eyes to the mole, vision to the blind.... No longer is our reason imprisoned within the confines of imaginary heavens.... We know that there is but one heaven, one immense ether, where magnificent fires maintain their proper distances by reason of that eternal life in which they have part. These flaming bodies are the ambassadors which announce the excellence of God's glory and majesty.[28]

The Reign of Law

Bruno lived after the Copernican but before the Cartesian revolution, when men could still find even an infinite universe pulsating with life. Spinoza too knew that the universe is without limit, but he knew also that that universe displays not life but the reign of inexorable mechanical law. Spinoza was a learned Jew of Amsterdam who lived an uneventful life amidst these startling intellectual changes. Outwardly he was but a poor lens-grinder, supporting himself by his labors and indulging much in study; but beneath this monotonous exterior there burned an inward glory, the calm clear light of the mind that looked upon the very face of God. For Spinoza the end of knowledge was just what it had been for Aquinas, the contemplation of that truth which is the origin of all truth. But though the problems he solved for himself were the highest problems of the scholastic wisdom, the solutions were those of one who had grasped and thoroughly understood the significance of the seventeenth-century mathematical world. His intensely religious nature sought that to which he might wholly abandon himself, and in the religion of science he found what for him was God. Not even Calvin had a keener sense of the glory and joy of absolute devotion and selfless resignation to the power and order of the universe.

The Cartesian world had exempted two things from its all-embracing mechanical sweep, God the creator, and the soul of man. For Spinoza the latter was as much a part of immutable order as anything else, and God was nothing other than that order itself. "By God we mean a being supremely perfect and

THE NEW SCENE OF HUMAN LIFE 245

absolutely infinite"; [29] then so far as man's mind can penetrate his being, he must be the great order of the universe, the order of mathematical law. From this being flow laws and events, facts and objects, as the properties of a triangle flow from its nature.

Others think that God is a free cause, because he can, as they think, bring it about, that those things which we have said follow from his nature — that is, which are in his power, should not come to pass, or should not be produced by him. But this is the same as if they said, that God could bring it about, that it should not follow from the nature of a triangle, that its three interior angles should be equal to two right angles; or that from a given cause no effect should follow, which is absurd.[30] God never can decree, nor ever could have decreed, anything but what is; God did not exist before his decrees, and would not exist without them.[31]

This, indeed, is but carrying out the logical consequences of the new science. But Spinoza cannot stop here. What becomes of the God in whose image man was made? Away with such petty human imaginings!

Moreover, I will show ... that neither intellect nor will appertain to God's nature.... If intellect and will appertain to the eternal essence of God, we must take these words in some significations quite different from those they usually bear. For an intellect and a will which would constitute the essence of God would perforce be as far apart as the poles from the human intellect and will, in fact, would have nothing in common with them but the name; there would be about as much correspondence between the two as there is between the Dog, the heavenly constellation, and the dog, an animal that barks.[32]

Gone is the wise and loving Father, to whom man can appeal in prayer; irretrievably gone is the great Friend behind the world who cares.

The scene of human life is an infinite immutable order.

Nothing comes to pass in nature in contravention to her universal laws, nay, everything agrees with them and follows from them, for whatsoever comes to pass, comes to pass by the will and eternal decree of God; that is, whatever comes to pass comes to pass according to laws and rules which involve eternal necessity and truth; nature, therefore, always observes laws and rules which involve eternal necessity and truth, although they may not all be known to us, and therefore she keeps a fixed and immutable order.[33]

Gone is every vestige of purpose and final cause.

All such opinions spring from the notion commonly entertained, that all things in nature act as men themselves act, namely, with an end in view. It is accepted as certain that God himself directs all things to a definite goal. ... Men do all things for an end, namely, for that which is useful to them, and which they seek. Thus it comes to pass that they only look for a knowledge of the final causes of events, and when these are learned they are content, as having no cause for further doubt. If they cannot learn such causes from external sources, they are compelled to turn to considering themselves, and reflecting what end would have induced them personally to bring about the given event, and thus they necessarily judge other natures by their own. Further, as they find in themselves and outside themselves many means which assist them not a little in their search for what is useful, for instance, eyes for seeing, teeth for chewing, herbs and animals for yielding food, the sun for giving light, the sea for breeding fish, etc., they come to look on the whole of nature as a means for obtaining such conveniences. Now as they are aware, that they found these conveniences and did not make them, they think they have cause for believing, that some other being has made them for their use. As they look upon things as means, they cannot believe them to be self-created; but judging from the means which they are accustomed to prepare for themselves, they are bound to believe in some ruler or rulers of the universe endowed with human freedom, who have arranged and adapted everything for human use. ... In their endeavor to show that nature does nothing in vain, i.e., nothing which is useless to man, they only seem to have demonstrated that nature, the gods, and men are all mad together. Consider, I pray you, the result: among the many helps of nature they were bound to find some hindrances, such as storms, earthquakes, diseases, etc.; so they declared that such things happen because the gods are angry at some wrong done them by men, or at some fault committed in their worship. Experience day by day protested and showed by infinite examples, that good and evil fortunes fall to the lot of pious and impious alike; still they would not abandon their inveterate prejudice, for it was more easy for them to class such contradictions among other unknown things of whose use they were ignorant, and thus to retain their actual and inborn condition of ignorance, than to destroy the whole fabric of their reasoning and start afresh. They therefore laid down as an axiom, that God's judgments far transcend human understanding. Such a doctrine might well have sufficed to conceal the truth from the human race for all eternity, if mathematics had not furnished another standard of verity in considering solely the essence and properties of figures without regard to their final causes. ...

There is no need to show at length, that nature has no particular goal in view, and that final causes are mere human figments. ... That which is really a cause this doctrine considers as an effect and *vice versa:* it makes that which is by nature first to be last, and that which is highest and most perfect to be most imperfect.[34]

This was the first great revolution which Spinoza saw in the

THE NEW SCENE OF HUMAN LIFE

new science; its second consists in placing man and his life at the very core of the great machine.

> Most writers on the emotions and on human conduct seem to be treating rather of matters outside nature than of natural phenomena following nature's general laws. They appear to conceive man to be situated in nature as a kingdom within a kingdom: for they believe that he disturbs rather than follows nature's order, that he has absolute control over his actions, and that he is determined solely by himself.... Nothing comes to pass in nature, which can be set down to a flaw therein; for nature is always the same, and everywhere one and the same in her efficacy and power of action; that is, nature's laws and ordinances, whereby all things come to pass and change from one form to another, are everywhere and always the same; so that there should be one and the same method of understanding the nature of all things whatsoever, namely, through nature's universal laws and rules. Thus the passions of hatred, anger, envy, and so on, considered in themselves, follow from this same necessity and efficacy of nature; they answer to certain definite causes, through which they are understood, and possess certain properties as worthy of being known as the properties of anything else, whereof the contemplation in itself affords us delight. I shall, therefore, treat of the nature and strength of the emotions according to the same method as I employed heretofore in my investigations concerning God and the mind. I shall consider human actions and desires in exactly the same manner as though I were concerned with lines, planes, and solids.[35]

And so he wrote his great work, *Ethics demonstrated in the Geometrical Manner*.

We cannot touch on the further doctrine of this mighty intellect; indeed, he was a hundred years ahead of his time in seeing so clearly as he did what the Cartesian revolution had really done to man and his world. And by the time men came to understand what he really meant, and their epithets of "hideous atheist" had given way to warm approval, science was already effecting a further revolution which, if it altered nothing of what we have quoted above, did transform his further conclusions.

Let us take leave of these two titanic revolutions in men's beliefs with the calm closing hymn to science, in which Spinoza anticipated the real religion of the next age.

> I have thus completed all I wished to set forth touching the mind's power over the emotions and the mind's freedom. Whence it appears, how potent is the wise man, and how much he surpasses the ignorant man, who is driven only by his lusts. For the ignorant man is not only distracted in various ways by external causes without ever gaining the true acquiescence of his spirit, but moreover lives, as it were unwitting

of himself, and of God, and of things, and as soon as he ceases to suffer, ceases also to be.

Whereas the wise man, in so far as he is regarded as such, is scarcely at all disturbed in spirit, but, being conscious of himself, and of God, and of things, by a certain eternal necessity, never ceases to be, but always possesses true acquiescence of spirit.

If the way which I have pointed out as leading to this result seems exceedingly hard, it may nevertheless be discovered. Needs must it be hard, since it is so seldom found. How would it be possible, if salvation were ready to our hand, and could without great labor be found, that it should be by almost all men neglected? But all things excellent are as difficult as they are rare.[36]

REFERENCES

1. Copernicus, *De Revolutionibus, Letter to Pope Paul III*.
2. Newton, *Principia*, Bk. III.
3. Copernicus, *De Revolutionibus*, quoted in A. Berry, *Short History of Astronomy*, 101.
4. Francis Bacon, quoted in Sedgwick and Tyler, *History of Science*, 203.
5. Kepler, *Commentary on the Motions of Mars*, Part II, ch. 19.
6. Galileo, quoted in Sedgwick and Tyler, 222.
7. J. J. Fahie, *Galileo*.
8. Galileo, *Dialogue on the Two Chief Systems of the World*, quoted in Sedgwick and Tyler, 225.
9. Galileo, *Letter to the Grand Duchess Christine*.
10. Quoted in Berry, *History of Astronomy*, 159.
11. Quoted in J. J. Fahie, *The Scientific Works of Galileo*, in C. Singer, *Studies in the History and Method of Science*, II, 251.
12. Leonardo, *Frammenti*, ed. Solmi, 97.
13. *Ibid.*, 113.
14. *Ibid.*
15. *Ibid.*
16. Kepler, quoted in H. Höffding, *History of Modern Philosophy*, 170.
17. Kepler, *Opera*, I, 176.
18. Galileo, ed. naz., VIII, 613.
19. *Ibid.*, IV, 171.
20. Quoted in *ibid.*, IV, 52.
21. Galileo, *Two New Branches of Science*, ed. Crewe and De Salvio.
22. Galileo, *Letter to the Grand Duchess Christine*.
23. John Dewey, *Reconstruction in Philosophy*, 68.
24. J. P. Mahaffy, *Descartes*, 27, quoted.
25. Descartes, Haldane and Ross ed., I, 86.
26. *Ibid.*, 13.
27. *Ibid.*, 11.
28. Bruno, quoted in E. Singer, *Modern Thinkers and Present Problems*, 13.
29. Spinoza, Elwes tr., Letter 2, II, 277.
30. *Ibid.*, 60.
31. *Ibid.*, 72.
32. *Ibid.*, 60, 61.
33. *Ibid.*, I, 83.
34. *Ibid.*, II, 75–77.
35. *Ibid.*, II, 128–29.
36. *Ibid.*, 270.

THE NEW SCENE OF HUMAN LIFE

SELECTED READING LISTS

General Accounts of the Rise of Modern Science: A. N. Whitehead, *The First Physical Synthesis,* in F. S. Marvin, *Science and Civilization;* F. S. Marvin, *The Living Past,* ch. VII, VIII; F. M. Stawell and F. S. Marvin, *Making of the Western Mind.* A. E. Shipley, *The Revival of Science in the Seventeenth Century;* Oliver Lodge, *Pioneers of Science.* A. D. White, *History of the Warfare of Science with Theology in Christendom* (classic). For the intellectual significance of the new science, see the histories of philosophy by H. Höffding and W. Windelband; esp. J. Dewey, *Reconstruction in Philosophy,* ch. II, III. E. A. Burtt, *The Metaphysical Foundations of Modern Physical Science,* by far the most illuminating treatment; also A. N. Whitehead, *Science and the Modern World,* chs. I, II, III.

Histories of Science and the Sciences: General: W. C. D. Dampier-Whetham, *H. of Science;* Preserved Smith, *H. of Modern Culture,* I; A. Wolf, *H. of Science, Technology, and Philosophy in the 16th and 17th cents.;* W. T. Sedgwick and H. W. Tyler, *Short H. of Science;* F. Dannemann, *Die Naturwissenschaften in ihrer Entwicklung.* Histories of mathematics by W. W. R. Ball, F. Cajori, V. Sanford; classic is M. Cantor's *Ges. der Mathematik.* A. Berry, *Short H. of Astronomy;* J. Mädler, *Ges. der Himmelskunde,* J. L. E. Dreyer, *H. of Planetary Systems;* P. Duhem, *Le Système du Monde.* Histories of physics by F. Cajori, E. Gerland, F. Rosenberger; E. Mach, *Science of Mechanics;* P. Duhem, *L'Évolution des Théories Physiques.*

Medieval and Alexandrian Origins: T. L. Heath, *Archimedes, Apollonius of Perga.* Archimedes, *Works,* ed. Heath. Lynn Thorndike, *H. of Magic and Experimental Science, Science and Thought in the 15th cent.* C. H. Haskins, *Studies in the H. of Med. Science;* C. Singer, *Studies in the H. and Method of Science; From Magic to Science.* P. Duhem, *Système du Monde.* Randall, *Development of Scientific Method in the School of Padua,* in *Jour. of the Hist. of Ideas,* 1940. P. Duhem, *Études sur Léonard de Vinci.*

The Pioneers: J. E. Gillespie, *H. of Geographical Discovery;* Keltie and Howarth, *H. of Geography.* *Three Copernican Treatises,* ed. E. Rosen; Copernicus, *De Revolutionibus Orbium Celestium,* Germ. tr.; Kepler, *Opera Omnia;* see Burtt, Höffding, Dreyer. Dreyer, *Tycho Brahe.* Leonardo da Vinci, *Notebooks,* tr. E. McCurdy; *Des Manuscrits,* ed. C. Ravaisson-Molien; *Frammenti,* ed. E. Solmi; E. McCurdy, *The Mind of Leonardo.* Galileo, *Opere,* Nat. Ed.; *Dialogues concerning Two New Sciences,* ed. Crewe and De Salvio; *Two Greatest Systems of the World,* tr. Saulsbury; J. J. Fahie, *Galileo, His Life and Work;* L. Olschki, *Galilei u. seine Zeit;* Burtt; F. Wieser, *Galilei als Philosoph;* P. Natorp, in *Phil. Monatsh.,* 1882. D. Stimson, *The Gradual Acceptance of the Copernican Theory of the Universe.* A. P. Usher, *H. of Mechanical Inventions;* R. N. Merton, *Science, Technology, and Society in England in the 17th cent.;* G. N. Clark, *Science and Invention in the Age of Newton.*

The Philosophers of the New Science: Descartes: *Oeuvres,* ed. Adam et Tannery; *Philosophical Works,* ed. Haldane and Ross; *Selections,* ed. Eaton; *Rules for the Direction of the Mind, Discourse on Method, Principles of Phil.,* I; *Traité du Monde, de l'Homme.* Studies by A. B. Gibson, J. P. Mahaffy; E. Gilson; G. Milhaud, O. Hamelin. N. K. Smith, *Studies in the Cartesian Phil.;* F. Bouillier, *H. de la Phil. Cartésienne.* **Francis Bacon:** *Works,* ed. Ellis, Spedding and Heath; ed. J. M. Robertson; *Novum Organum, Advancement of Learning, New Atlantis.* Studies by J. Nichol, C. D. Broad; John Dewey, *Reconstruction in Phil.,* c. 1. **G. Bruno:** *Dialoghi Metafisici,* ed. Croce; Germ. tr. by Kuhlenbeck. Lives by J. L. McIntyre, W. Boulting, G. Gentile, L. Kuhlenbeck; E. Singer, *Modern Thinkers,* c. I. **Spinoza:** *Opera,* ed. Gebhardt, ed. Van Vloten and Land; tr. Elwes; *Selections,* ed. J. Wild; *Political Phil.,* ed. A. G. A. Balz. *Ethics,* tr. W. H. White; *Tractatus Politicus, Tractatus Theol.-Politicus.* Studies by R. McKeon, F. Pollock, H. A. Wolfson, R. A. Duff.

BOOK III
THE ORDER OF NATURE — THE DEVELOPMENT OF THOUGHT IN THE SEVENTEENTH AND EIGHTEENTH CENTURIES

CHAPTER XI
THE NEWTONIAN WORLD-MACHINE

In the front of an old edition of the works of Rousseau there is an engraving which beautifully illustrates the intellectual spirit of the eighteenth century. Rousseau is seated at his writing-table, facing a pleasant pastoral landscape of green fields, sheep, and graceful willows — that rationally ordered Nature which he and his contemporaries accorded so respectful an admiration. On his desk are two volumes, which, in the absence of any other books, seem designed to sum up the learning of the age — the *Principia Mathematica* of Isaac Newton, and the *Essay concerning Human Understanding* of John Locke.

In truth Newton and Locke were the two luminaries of that brilliant Augustan age in which, under William III and Queen Anne, England assumed for a period of some forty years, from 1680 to 1720, the undisputed intellectual leadership of the world, only to lose it again or at least to share it with first France and then Germany. Theirs are beyond doubt the outstanding names in that epoch which, succeeding to the discoveries and the liberations of the Renaissance and the Reformation, and preceding the rapid change and varied currents of the nineteenth century, made so heroic an attempt to order the world on the basis of the new "Physico-Mathematicall Experimental Learning." The significance of these two men, in spite of their own outstanding achievements, lies not so much in what they themselves did, as in what they stood for to that age, and in the very fact that they became to an increasing multitude the symbols for certain great ideas. Under their standards the new science for the first time actually entered into every field of human interest, and captured the mind of every educated man. Under such banners was actually effected that outstanding revolution in beliefs and habits of thought which we sometimes mistakenly associate with the Renaissance — that complete break with the spirit of the Middle Ages that prepared the way for the further growth of the next century. The age that hailed them as acknowledged masters, that introduced the spirit of the Renaissance into religion, that placed man squarely in the midst of the new ordered world, that erected a science of man and of social relations, that formulated a complete and rounded philosophical view admirably framed for the middle class which the Industrial and the French Revolutions were so soon to bring into direct control, and which disseminated these ideas among the whole membership of this class — such an age is fittingly styled the "Age of Enlightenment and Reason." It laid the foundations for our present-day beliefs in every field, and it led on naturally to the two great ideas which the nineteenth century has added to the achievements of its predecessor, evolution and relativity.

In one sense both Newton and Locke were the systematizers of the ideas we have already traced in their formative stage. Newton stands at the end of that row of scientific geniuses who effected the Copernican and the Cartesian revolutions: he finally drew up in complete mathematical form the mechanical view of nature, that first great physical synthesis on which succeeding science has rested, and which has endured unchanged until a present-day revolution bids fair to modify it. Locke stands as apologist and heir of the great seventeenth-century struggles for constitutional liberties and rights and toleration. It is to this expression in systematic form of ideas which had become common property by 1700 that the two owed their immense popularity in the new century. But in another sense both Locke and Newton stand at the threshold of a new era, Newton as the prophet of the science of nature, and Locke as the prophet of the science of human nature. From their inspiration flow the great achievements of the Age of Enlightenment; in their light men went on to transform their beliefs and their society into what we know to-day.

Possessed of a successful scientific method, a combination of mathematics and experiment, and of a guarantee of truth, that "reason" which was both an individual and a universal authority, men set about the task of discovering a natural order that should be both simple and all-embracing. In the words of Fontenelle, the popularizer of Cartesianism, "The geometric spirit is not so bound up with geometry that it cannot be disentangled and carried into other fields. A work of morals, of politics, of criticism, perhaps even of eloquence, will be the finer, other things being equal, if it is written by the hand of a geometer." [1]

THE NEWTONIAN WORLD-MACHINE

Isaac Newton effected so successful a synthesis of the mathematical principles of nature that he stamped the mathematical ideal of science, and the identification of the natural with the rational, upon the entire field of thought. Under the inspiration of Locke, the attempt was made to discover and formulate a science of human nature and human society, and to criticize existing religious and social traditions in the light of what seemed rational and reasonable. The two leading ideas of the eighteenth century, Nature and Reason, as outstanding then as Evolution in the last generation, derived their meaning from the natural sciences, and, carried over to man, led to the attempt to discover a social physics. Man and his institutions were included in the order of nature and the scope of the recognized scientific method, and in all things the newly invented social sciences were assimilated to the physical sciences. There grew up the idea of a simple and all-embracing social order in which free play should be left to the activities of every man. It is this great eighteenth-century synthesis in its most important ramifications that we shall now examine, starting with the rational order of the world, as expressed in the Newtonian system of nature, scientific method, and scientific ideals, and proceeding to trace its applications in religion, and in the comprehensive science of human nature that embraced a rational science of the mind, of society, of business, of government, of ethics, and of international relations.

The Success of the Mathematical Interpretation of Nature

The outstanding fact that colors every other belief in this age of the Newtonian world is the overwhelming success of the mathematical interpretation of nature. We have seen how Galileo found that he could explain and predict motion by applying the language of mathematics to the book of Nature, and how Descartes generalized from his method and its success a universal principle of scientific investigation and a sweeping picture of the universe as a great machine; how both thinkers arrived at the conception of uniform natural laws that are essentially mechanical in nature. But Descartes' cosmic picture was a sketch which neither the progress of mathematics nor of physical observation enabled him to fill in by the time of his early death. To his disciples he left a system of the world worked out as a provisional hypothesis, which he had not had time to verify by those careful experiments that he increasingly recognized as necessary to determine just what actual phenomena, of the many possible ones that could be deduced from the mechanical principle, really took place. Not to the strict Cartesians, who accepted as final this sketch and did not bother to verify it by the master's method, but to the more original minds who shared Galileo's emphasis on experiment and refrained for a generation from attempting a general hypothesis, were due the discoveries that made Newton's work possible. Especially successful were the triumphs of mathematics in the fields of fluids and gases. Torricelli, Galileo's pupil, in 1643 invented the barometer and weighed the atmosphere, and Pascal confirmed his measurements four years later by his famous experiment of carrying a barometer up a mountain and observing the diminishing atmospheric pressure. To Pascal, too, is due the formulation of the laws of pressure in liquids, while Robert Boyle, who had studied under Galileo, discovered the law of pressure in gases. It is significant that within twenty years these facts had been used in machines for raising water, and that by the end of the century Newcomen's steam engine had begun the application of steam power to industry. To light, too, mathematics was astoundingly applied, and the science of optics, originated by Kepler and Descartes, was systematically developed by the Dutch Huygens and by Newton, who gave it its classic formulation; in 1695, Roemer actually measured the speed of light.

In all this work, mathematics and experimentation were successful allies. The spirit of the new science is exemplified in the foundation of the Royal Society in London in 1662 "for the promoting of Physico-Mathematicall Experimental Learning." This institution for that scientific coöperation so urgently demanded by Descartes, was largely inspired by Bacon's vision of a great scientific establishment; but it wisely followed the mathematical methods of Galileo rather than the purely experimental searching of the Elizabethan. Science rested on experiment, but its main object, for another century at least, was to connect the observed processes of nature with mathematical law. The leading member of the Royal Society, Robert Boyle, shares with Huygens the distinction of being the greatest investigator between Galileo and Newton; he managed to draw together the threads of alchemy and mathematical physics, and his generalization of Galileo's method of mathematical experimentation strongly influenced Newton. Mayow, another member, in 1674 discovered oxygen, although it was a century before Priestley and Lavoisier were able to fit it into a chemical science.

The Mathematical Synthesis of Newton

All this experimental work, together with much advance in mathematical theory, took place in the single generation after Descartes' death. But the great formulator of seventeenth-century science, the man who realized Descartes' dream, was born in 1642, the very year of Galileo's death. Though he did not publish his immortal work, the *Philosophiæ Naturalis Principia Mathematica*, till 1687, Newton made his chief discoveries when he was but twenty-three years of age. At that time, he tells us, he discovered:

first the binomial theorem, then the method of fluxions [the calculus], and began to think of gravity extending to the orb of the moon, and having found out how to estimate the force with which a globe, revolving within a sphere, presses the surface of the sphere, from Kepler's rule I deduced that the forces which keep the planets in their orb must be reciprocally as the squares of their distances from their centres: and thereby compared the force requisite to keep the moon in her orb with the force of gravity at the surface of the earth, and found them to answer pretty nearly. All this was in the two plague years of 1665 and 1666, for in those days I was in the prime of my age for invention and minded Mathematicks and Philosophy more than at any time since.[2]

The thirty years that had passed since Galileo published his *Dialogue on the Two Systems* had seen an enormous intellectual change. Where Galileo was still arguing with the past, Newton ignores old discussions, and, looking wholly to the future, calmly enunciates definitions, principles, and proofs that have ever since formed the basis of natural science. Galileo represents the assault; after a single generation comes the victory. Newton himself made two outstanding discoveries: he found the mathematical method that would describe mechanical motion, and he applied it universally. At last what Descartes had dreamed was true: men had arrived at a complete mechanical interpretation of the world in exact, mathematical, deductive terms. In thus placing the keystone in the arch of seventeenth-century science, Newton properly stamped his name upon the picture of the universe that was to last unchanged in its outlines till Darwin; he had completed the sketch of the Newtonian world that was to remain through the eighteenth century as the fundamental scientific verity.

That Newton invented the calculus is perhaps an accident; Leibniz, building on Descartes' analytic geometry, arrived at it independently, while several other mathematicians, like Pascal, seemed almost on the verge of it. Be that as it may, it was inevitable that after the Frenchman had brought algebra and geometry together, men should advance and apply algebra also to motion. Descartes had shown how to find the equation that would represent any curve, and thus conveniently and accurately measure it and enable calculated prediction to be applied to all figures; but the science of mechanics, and with it any measurement of the processes of change in the world, demands a formula for the law of the growth or falling-off of a curve, that is, the direction of its movement at any point. Such a method of measuring movement and continuous growth Newton discovered; he had arrived at the most potent instrument yet found for bringing the world into subjection to man. Since any regular motion, be it of a falling body, an electric current, or the cooling of a molten mass, can be represented by a curve, he had forged the tool by which to attack, not only the figures, but the processes of nature — the last link in the mathematical interpretation of the world. By its means a Lagrange in the eighteenth or a Clerk-Maxwell in the nineteenth century could bring all measurable phenomena into the unified world of mathematics, and calculate, predict, and control light, heat, magnetism, and electricity.

Newton himself used it to formulate the general laws governing every body in the solar system. Kepler had arrived at the law of planetary motion by induction from observed facts, Galileo had similarly discovered the laws of falling bodies upon the earth. Newton united both in one comprehensive set of principles, by calculating that the deflection of the moon from a straight path, that is, her fall towards the earth, exactly corresponded with the observed force of terrestrial gravitation; and he further showed that on his hypothesis Kepler's law of planetary motion followed mathematically from the law of gravitation. The significance of this lay in the proof that the physical laws which hold good on the surface of the earth are valid throughout the solar system. What Galileo divined, what Descartes believed but could not prove, was both confirmed and made more comprehensive. This meant, on the one hand, that the secrets of the whole world could be investigated by man's experiments on this planet; and on the other, that the world was one huge, related, and uniform machine, the fundamental principles of whose action were known. One law could describe the whirling planet and the falling grass blade; one law could explain the action of every body in the universe. Newton expressed this fundamental principle in a famous rule:

We are to admit no more causes of natural things than such as are both true and sufficient to explain their appearances. Therefore, to the same natural effects we must, as far as possible, assign the same causes. The qualities of bodies that cannot be diminished or increased, and are found to belong to all bodies within the reach of our experiments, are to be esteemed the universal qualities of all bodies whatsoever. For since the qualities of bodies are only known to us by experiments, we are to hold for universal all such as universally agree with experiments.... We are certainly not to relinquish the evidence of experiments for the sake of dreams and vain fictions of our own; nor are we to recede from the analogy of Nature, which uses to be simple, and always consonant with itself.... We must, in consequence of this rule, universally allow, that all bodies whatsoever are endowed with a principle of mutual gravitation.[3]

Using this principle and his new mathematical tool, Newton proceeded "to subject the phenomena of nature to the laws of mathematics."[4] "I am induced by many reasons to suspect," he says, "that all the phenomena of nature may depend upon certain forces by which the particles of bodies, by some causes hitherto unknown, are either mutually impelled towards each other, and cohere in regular figures, or are repelled and recede from each other."[5] Every event in nature is to be explained by the same kind of reasoning from mechanical principles: the whole program of science is "from the phenomena of motions to investigate the forces of nature, and then from these forces to demonstrate the other phenomena."[6] The world is a vast perpetual motion machine, and every event in it can be deduced mathematically from the fundamental principles of its mechanical action; the discovery of these mathematical relations is the goal of science. The universe is one great harmonious order; not, as for Thomas and the Middle Ages, an ascending hierarchy of purposes, but a uniform mathematical system.

The universal order, symbolized henceforth by the law of gravitation, takes on a clear and positive meaning. This order is accessible to the mind, it is not preëstablished mysteriously, it is the most evident of all facts. From this it follows that the sole reality that can be accessible to our means of knowledge, matter, nature, appears to us as a tissue of properties, precisely ordered, and of which the connection can be expressed in terms of mathematics.[7]

Newton's great mathematical system of the world struck the imagination of the educated class of his time, and spread with amazing swiftness, completing what Descartes had begun. Prior to 1789 some eighteen editions of the difficult and technical *Principia* were called for; British universities were teaching it by the end of the seventeenth century, and Newton was accorded a royal funeral when he died in 1727. In 1734, Bernoulli won the prize of the French Academy of Sciences with a Newtonian memoir; in 1740 the last prize was granted to an upholder of Descartes' physics. Voltaire was struck by Newtonianism during his visit to England in 1726-1728, and popularized him in France in his *English Letters*, in 1734, and his *Elements of the Newtonian Philosophy* in 1738; thenceforth Newton reigned in France as in England. From the presses there poured forth an immense stream of popular accounts for those unable or unwilling to peruse the classic work. His conclusions and his picture of the world were accepted on authority. By 1789 there had appeared about the *Principia* forty books in English, seventeen in French, three in German, eleven in Latin, one in Portuguese, and one in Italian, many of them, like those of Desaguliers, Benjamin Martin, Ferguson's *Lectures for Ladies and Gentlemen*, and Count Alogrotti's *Le Newtonianisme pour les Dames*, running through edition after edition. Newton's name became a symbol which called up the picture of the scientific machine-universe, the last word in science, one of those uncriticized preconceptions which largely determined the social and political and religious as well as the strictly scientific thinking of the age. Newton *was* science, and science was the eighteenth-century ideal.

The Method of Newtonian Science

Hence the method of the new physical science became all important, for men proceeded to apply it in every field of investigation. Just as the success of biology under Darwin led to the importation of the biological method into all the social sciences, and the more recent success of psychology has led to the wider application of its methods, so the social sciences, which, in the absence of any sure method of their own, always borrow from the striking science of the day, were in the Age of Enlightenment almost completely under the domination of the physico-mathematical method. Hence a closer examination of that method is of the utmost importance. Though experiment entered as one of its parts, and became in science increasingly prominent as the century advanced, what was thus borrowed was for the most part overwhelmingly deductive and mathematical: typical is Spinoza, whom we have seen attempting, in his *Ethics*, to deal with men's passions and motives as if they were part of a geometrical system. The new science had not yet led men to give up the medieval Thomistic and Aristotelian ideal of a body of knowledge that could be deductive, universal, and infallible, one great logical system; it had only, as in Descartes and Spinoza, changed its type from the syllogistic logic of Aristotle to the geometrical propositions of Euclid. Such a science must be founded, like geometry, upon a small number of definitely true axioms, from which every law of nature will follow deductively; and it is characteristic of the eighteenth-century scientific ideal that, however much it might turn to experience to suggest these axioms, and to formulate the specific laws governing phenomena, no law was regarded as conclusively established until it could be fitted into such a great universal deductive system. Newton, by proving mathematically that Kepler's inductive law of planetary motion must result from the general principle of gravitation, had given an immense impetus to this ideal. Under the spell of the triumphant mathematical physics men waxed optimistic, and believed that such an infallible and complete science would soon exhaust all experimentation and be able to dispense with every appeal to experience. The world of facts seemed simpler then, and men had not yet learned that experimental research raises more problems than it solves, so it was easy to hope for a speedy return to a non-experimental procedure. With Descartes all save those actually making experimental discoveries in physics believed, throughout the century, that the surest foundation of truth was not any appeal to the fallible testimony of sense experience, so often proved wrong, but rather the clear and distinct intuition of geometrical axioms. We *know* intuitively, with absolute certainty, that the whole is equal to the sum of its parts, and that a straight line is the shortest distance between two points: similarly it was hoped that such intuitive axioms could be discovered in mechanics, in morals, in politics, and in religion. Even Locke, who in some respects stood for a different conception of science, hoped for such a deductive system of religion and of ethics. Rationalism of the geometrical type was the popular intellectual method of the Age of Reason.

We shall trace the influence of this scientific method upon the newly invented social sciences, and observe its influence in every field. Typical of the popular social ideals of the century are Rousseau, who started with such fundamental axioms as that all men are created free and equal, and deduced therefrom a revolutionary system of politics; and the physiocratic economists, who started from the axioms of private property and individual liberty and deduced a geometrical science of business. Such conceptions were overwhelmingly successful in providing a leverage for overthrowing the old ideas and ushering in a régime that provided free scope to the rising middle class; but throughout the nineteenth century they proved incapable of building a new social order, and have worked to this day untold harm and mischief, in their cavalier disregard of the actual facts of human society.

The Rise of the Experimental Method

The social sciences remained conservatively deductive; the physical sciences grew increasingly experimental, paving the way for the borrowing of their newer inductive methods in the next century. Galileo had insisted upon experimental analysis of natural events as the basis and the final verification of all mechanical law; even Descartes, more responsible for this rationalism than any other one man, was keenly aware of the necessity of the appeal to experiment in these two places, though he hoped that a completed science would be deductive. Newton himself, inspired by both the mathematical Descartes and the experimental Boyle, effected a harmonious reconciliation of the two elements. His method was, by analysis of observed facts, to arrive at some fundamental principle, then to deduce the mathematical consequences of this principle, and finally by observation and experiment to prove that what follows logically from the principle is in agreement with experience. Indeed, Newton is remarkable for the caution with which he insists that the faith in the mathematical interpretation of nature must be at every step guided and checked by experiment. As against the bold world-picture of Descartes, he insists that such speculative hypotheses have no place in exact science; sound principles must be deduced from the phenomena themselves. "Whatever is not deduced from the phenomena is to be called an hypothesis; and hypotheses, whether metaphysical or physical, whether of occult qualities or mechanical, have no place in experimental philosophy. In this philosophy particular propositions are inferred from the phenomena, and afterwards rendered general by induction." [8] In his fourth rule of philosophizing, he makes it clear that although science is composed of laws stating the mathematical behavior of nature solely, and is thus the exact mathematical formulation of the processes of the natural world, the ultimate test of this formulation must remain agreement with observed fact. "In experimental philosophy we are to look upon propositions collected by general induction from phenomena as accurately or very nearly true, notwithstanding any contrary hypotheses that may be imagined, till such time as other phenomena occur, by which they may either be made more accurate, or liable to exceptions." [9] Thus in Newton himself there is clearly recognized the increasing importance of experimental verification; though most of the applications of his method to realms other than physics tended to overlook this caution.

But the eighteenth century saw also the rise of new scientific investigations in fields that were now for the first time broader than those simplified aspects of nature with which physics deals. Men turned to the amassing of a vast body of concrete descriptive facts about the things in the world, which they were content for the most part to gather and classify; these remained as the indispensable prerequisite for the great hypotheses characteristic of science in the first half of the nineteenth century, hypotheses which only the last generation has brought into the general physico-mathematical system. As Diderot wrote in the initial volume of the *Encyclopédie* in 1775, "Men's minds seem caught in a general movement towards natural history, anatomy, chemistry, and experimental physics."[10] What was loosely called "natural history" became very popular. Men who made pretensions at scientific learning, like Voltaire, and the various "enlightened rulers" of the day, collected their cabinets of specimens of plants, birds, fossils, rocks, and the like. Naturalists like Buffon, whose great *Natural History* was the mid-eighteenth-century counterpart of our Wells' *Outline of History;* Lamarck, Curator of the Paris *Jardin des Plantes;* Cuvier, head of the "School of Facts," and Saint-Hilaire, his colleagues; and Linnæus, the great systematizer of botany, were all indefatigable in collecting and classifying specimens. Geologists like Werner and Hutton and William Smith mapped the rocks and laid the foundations for the epoch-making theories of Lyell in the next age. Here, too, belong the real foundations of experimental chemistry. Cavendish in 1766 reported the discovery of hydrogen, and in 1784 the synthetic production of water; Rutherford in 1772 isolated nitrogen; Priestley in 1774 discovered oxygen; and Lavoisier, by his unremitting use of the delicate balance, founded the science of quantitative chemistry, weighing accurately oxygen and carbonic acid. The ground was cleared for Dalton in the beginning of the next century to place the atomic theory upon a definite and mathematical basis, and usher in modern chemical investigation.

Careful observation of nature and accurate experimentation had at last become as respectable as mathematical physics. "The only good science," wrote Buffon in vindicating such investigation, "is the knowledge of facts, and mathematical truths are only truths of definition, and completely arbitrary, quite unlike physical truths."[11] Hume marks this turning from the spirit of the seventeenth to that of the nineteenth century, when he insists that the contrary of every matter of fact remains possible, and that no amount of deductive reasoning from first principles can decide in advance what course nature actually follows. Only by experimental reasoning can matters of fact be determined; only by experience can man ever learn that fire burns and water is wet, and to such facts all the mathematics in the world helps no whit. Indeed, reason itself is built up from experience. Even a physicist like Holbach has come to feel by 1770 that "the faculty we have of gaining experiences, of remembering them, of calling to mind their effects, constitutes what we designate by the word *reason*. Without experience there can be no reason."[12]

The foremost theoretical exponent of the experimental method in the Age of Reason was Diderot, the editor of the great French *Encyclopédie* that, appearing between 1751 and 1777, was the outstanding work that popularized all the new scientific ideas. His *Thoughts on the Interpretation of Nature*, in 1754, deserves to rank with Bacon's *Novum Organum* and Descartes' *Discourse on Method* as a classic of scientific method.

We have three principal means: the observation of nature, reflection, and experiment. Observation gathers facts, reflection combines them, and experiment verifies the result of the combination.... We have distinguished two kinds of science, experimental and rational. The one has its eyes bandaged, proceeds feeling its way, seizes everything that falls into its hands, and at last finds precious things and seeks to form from them a torch; but its supposed torch up to the present has served it less than the cautious advance of its rival, and that is as it should be. Experiment infinitely multiplies its movements; it is always in action; it sets about seeking phenomena all the while that reason looks for analogies. Experimental science knows neither what will come nor what will not come of its work, but it never ceases working. On the other hand rational science weighs possibilities, pronounces judgment, and stops short. It boldly says, "Light can not be decomposed." Experimental science hears and remains silent for whole centuries, then suddenly displays the prism and says, "Light has been decomposed."[13]

Diderot rather underemphasized the importance of mathematics even in experimental investigation.

We are on the point of a great revolution in the sciences. Judging by the inclination that the best minds seem to have for morals, for belles-lettres, for natural history and for experimental physics, I almost dare to predict that before a hundred years are over there will not be three great mathematicians in Europe; that science will stop short where it will have been left by the Bernoullis, the Eulers, the Maupertuis, the Clairauts, the Fontaines, and the D'Alemberts. It will have erected the pillars of Hercules; men will go no further; their works will last through the centuries to come like the pyramids of Egypt, whose bulks, inscribed with hieroglyphics, awaken in us an awful idea of the power and the resources of the men who built them.[14]

Diderot it was who rescued Francis Bacon from the oblivion to which his scorn of mathematics had relegated him for a century, and created the myth that it was he who had really founded modern scientific method. Bacon's vogue dates from the days of this new interest in experimental investigation. Diderot was himself a convinced Baconian, intensely interested in the practical application of scientific knowledge to the physical welfare of man. Perhaps the chief new note in his *Encyclopédie* is the way in which he brushed aside the traditional intellectual interests and placed the emphasis upon the mechanical arts and crafts. Fascinated by industrial processes, he spent days in the workshops of the craftsmen drawing sketches of every conceivable type of practical technique for the eleven volumes of plates that made such an impression upon his subscribers. His was the spirit of the new industrial revolution just appearing across the Channel.

From this experimental side of the scientific method there sprang a new ideal of science, differing from the reigning mathematical rationalism. Though it did not, save in a few rare and outstanding cases like Hume, capture the imaginations of those who were working out the new social sciences, it was destined, ere the century was out, to effect a new revolution there also and usher in the nineteenth-century spirit and methods in the science of man. This new ideal of science received in the eighteenth century the name of *empiricism*, was adapted by Kant toward the close of the age as *phenomenalism*, and was worshiped in the next century under Comte's term of *positivism*. Of course these three tendencies differed markedly among themselves, but they agreed in a certain fundamental opposition to the rational mathematical ideal we have described as on the whole dominant throughout the eighteenth century, endeavoring to effect a more or less harmonious adjustment with its acknowledgedly successful methods and results.

The Problem of Knowledge and the New Ideal of Science

Here we reach one of the most perplexing and difficult paradoxes in the history of thought. The conceptions and methods which the special scientific investigators were employing to win vast new continents of facts and laws, whatever their ultimate and theoretical foundation, have indisputably been supremely successful in enabling men to manipulate and control their physical environment. Yet these very methods practically forced reflective men to raise the question of what this new scientific knowledge was really knowledge of, and what its actual relation was to the world it purported to describe. That this knowledge was useful and important and almost indefinitely extensible in degree, has remained incontestable, and men have never allowed these anxieties and perplexities about the nature and foundation of science to deter them from its vigorous prosecution, convinced as they are forced to be that it must possess some very real validity. But the very age that has seen so impressive a growth in scientific knowledge has also been profoundly troubled by the thought that it seems very difficult to understand how in any intelligible sense such a science is possible of attainment by the human mind. This paradox may be somewhat explained if we realize that scientists were attempting to discover a *kind* of knowledge which their very methods made it impossible for them to arrive at: by modern scientific methods of investigation they were trying to reach an absolute system of truth quite independent of any limitations of the mental powers of the essentially imperfect and biological creature that man seems to be. In a word, they were trying to arrive at that complete and perfect understanding and explanation of the universe that only a God could possess, by the methods possible for a being who is not a God but a rational animal. Their ideal was still a *system of revelation*, though they had abandoned the *method* of revelation. They found knowledge, and valid knowledge, to be sure; but it gradually and painfully dawned upon them that the knowledge they could find and have been finding is a different sort of knowledge from that which they thought they were finding. Just what sort of knowledge it is, men are even to-day by no means agreed; but they have been forced to admit that it is neither absolute nor independent of the biologically adaptive nature of the human animal. It has taken over two centuries for an altered scientific method to force an altered conception of the ideal of scientific knowledge, and the end is not yet. But if we are to understand the confusions and vague gropings of men during that period we must try the difficult task of tracing the changes in that ideal of science. Only one thing remained certain, that men really were discovering important and useful knowledge, and that their methods were successful; why they were and what they found is hardly to-day cleared up.

The trouble initially came to light because Galileo and more systematically Descartes, whose methods revealed to them a world of matter in motion governed by mathematical laws, could find no place in that world for the kind of thing that the soul and mind of man seemed to be. Back of them was the long tradition of the Greeks and the Christians, that within the human body there resides a definite entity and thing which observes passively what is going on in the world, as a spectator might sit and gaze upon a motion picture screen, and that knowledge is essentially this securing of a picture of what the world is like. This passive observation constitutes *experience*, and looking upon it the mind perceives the objects and the processes of nature. The goal of science was the attempt, in terms of purpose, to understand why they are as they are; that is, to discover their uses in the economy of nature.

So long as science thus in its content remained Aristotelian, and things were supposed to be just what their picture seemed to the mind to be, no difficulties arose; water was a fluid, wet, formless, of a certain temperature, which did a great many things obviously useful not only for man but also for the other objects it touched. But Galileo revealed a new universe: water now seemed to be nothing but a number of particles of matter whose motion followed definite laws, and whose uses were irrelevant to scientific investigation. If the qualities of wetness and coolness and the like, and the uses of water, were no longer properties of water itself, they must somehow reside, not in the water, but in the mind that perceived the water. Descartes led the way in shoving off these qualities, so inconvenient for the mathematical physicist, into a separate and totally distinct kind of thing, the mind, which he erected into a second type of substance that served as a ready dumping-ground for everything in experience which physics did not read in mechanical nature. Because he was interested in investigating the mathematical properties of nature, and because he believed that in the last analysis knowledge of that nature depended, not upon experience, but upon axioms of geometry and mechanics which the mind intuitively perceived to be true, he was not particularly worried by the fact that this procedure made the world that science described a totally different thing from the picture of experience which the mind actually saw, with all its qualities and uses and purposes. He was concerned with proving that these axioms and the system derived therefrom did really contain the plan on which the world was built; and he tried, unsuccessfully, to show that a wise and good God had created man's mind in such a way that what it intuitively felt to be true could be relied upon in actual experience. His successors, notably Spinoza, abandoned the attempt to *prove* this correspondence, and boldly *assumed* that the order of men's scientific ideas was, in the nature of things, the same as the order of objects in the world. But the chasm between the observing mind, one kind of substance, and the world described by science, a quite different kind, became increasingly apparent. The picture that the mind perceives in experience and the real world that physics depicts seemed totally different; how, then, could the mind be certain that its physics was a genuine knowledge of the world in which man was really living? If the mind perceives only a picture that bears no resemblance to what science persuades it to believe is true, how can it be sure of that science? The bold assertion that the two do correspond seemed a slender foundation upon which to build.

The second generation of Cartesians was too convinced of the necessity of a constant appeal to experience in experiment, and had seen too many ideas that intuitively appealed as certain fall before the test of fact, to stomach such a mere assertion. For them the all-important theoretical problem was how to bridge the chasm between the picture spread before the mind, and the knowledge of physics. John Locke, both a good Cartesian and a confirmed experimentalist, wrote his famous *Essay concerning Human Understanding* about this cardinal problem of the origin, extent, and certainty of science. He waged a brilliant polemic against the Cartesian notion that its origin lay in mathematical axioms, easily showing that such axioms, in the real world, were non-existent, and that first principles must come from the observation of the facts of experience. But because Descartes had relegated all such facts to the mind, taking them out of the world of nature, Locke was led into the momentous step of asserting that experience was essentially *mental*, not physical; that its picture was *in* the mind itself. This naturally created an insoluble problem. How can the mind get outside of itself to a physical and mathematical real world when it is forever shut up inside its own walls? How can we get from sensations to physics? Too honest to claim a solution when there was none, Locke became hopelessly confused in the impossible attempt to reconcile his conception of the method of knowledge as starting inside the mind with his Cartesian ideal of an independent and certain mathematical physics that described nature. His provisional conclusion was that such a science was unattainable, and that man could at best arrive at probable knowledge, a modest light sufficient to guide men's footsteps in conduct.

Thus the eighteenth century was launched upon its career of developing a science which, however practical and useful, seemed, when critically examined, to crumble away into a mere creation of the imagination, which might or might not bear some relation to the world apart from man's mind. The attempts made to bridge the chasm have shown that, if we start with Locke's assumptions, we are bound to end up with Kant, that whatever certainty our science may have, it does not give us any light upon the basic structure of the world; in other words, that the mind of man cannot know reality as it exists, if indeed there be any such world at all apart from man's mind. The only possible method of such science cuts us off from all hope of ever attaining its supposed object, though we may stumble upon valuable light in the attempt. It was not until nineteenth-century biology gave men a quite different conception of the mind and of experience and of knowledge that the difficulty seemed to lessen. If we regard man as a biological creature actively adjusting himself to an environment, and experience not as a picture in the mind but such a process of adjustment, and knowledge, not as a copy of a real world, but as a definite relation between an intelligent organism and its environment, then the problem is transformed, and, set in new terms, seems possible of solution.

It is not necessary here to recount the struggles by which men tried to extricate themselves from their predicament. Suffice it to say that they came gradually to feel that the Cartesian object of science, a knowledge of the real world as it actually is, was impossible and misdirected; that science must confine itself

THE NEWTONIAN WORLD-MACHINE

to what can actually be verified by experience, and that this means that if experience is a moving picture in the mind, then science is a description of that picture, an ordering of mental elements, and their succession in time; that we can never hope to prove mathematically that these elements must succeed each other as they do, but have to rest content with discovering the order in which they do it; in a word, that the fact that we can formulate a mathematical physics of these elements is a happy accident. This program is sometimes known as *phenomenalism*, which emphasizes the belief that objects and events are "appearances" or pictures, not real things; sometimes as *empiricism*, which stresses the origins of knowledge in such an experience; sometimes as *positivism*, which claims that the object of science must be only what we can positively know, the relations between observed phenomena; sometimes as *agnosticism*, which declares that all further knowledge of an independent reality must remain unknown to man.

This scientific ideal has been accepted to the present day by the vast majority of scientific men; but gradually they have come to lose interest in the kind of world Descartes thought his science was describing, and to rest content with a world that is discoverable in experience and a science that does formulate the laws of that experience, seeing there the only reality that need concern an investigator. Hence the upshot has been that, while at first men thought they were changing the *object* of their science, abandoning a real world for a picture world, they now realize that they were rather changing its *nature*, from a mathematically necessary deductive system that would explain the reasons for things, to a mathematically formulated but experimentally derived description of events as they occur in the life of an intelligent animal. In the seventeenth century, science was rational, deducing events from axioms; in the eighteenth, it was empirical, describing the succession of pictures that presented themselves in experience; in the nineteenth, it became experimental, manipulating a biological environment.

The Empiricists' Attack on Tradition

Although this changed conception of the nature of science did not really penetrate into all fields until the days of Hume and Kant, toward the end of the Age of Enlightenment, and even then the popular social sciences conservatively lagged behind with the older method, it did produce certain highly important results. The empiricists who, following Locke, took Europe by storm, were essentially critics: standing face to face with a traditional body of beliefs in which they profoundly disbelieved, particularly in religion, morals, and politics, they used their method to brush aside traditions and clear the ground for newer and better ideas. They were all active reformers; they sought to remove the dead weight of the past by discovering the natural history of the origin and growth in the mind of the ideas connected with objectionable and outworn beliefs and customs. They tried to show up the irrational origin of things which they hated. But when they came to build up new beliefs, they for the most part were forced to have recourse to the rationalistic method again. It took the keen mind of a Hume to make clear that a method that could destroy traditional irrationalities was equally sharp against "natural" and "rational" substitutes. It remained for the nineteenth century to attempt the only possible constructive method, careful and patient experimentation and the verification of hypotheses. But in the Age of Reason "empiricism" was employed by a Voltaire to destroy revealed religion and absolute monarchy and Christian asceticism, and by the same Voltaire "reason" was used to erect a "rational" theology and "natural" rights and a "natural" moral law. This seems a contradiction; and, though it is now easy to see why the eighteenth century universally fell into it, a contradiction it was.

Other consequences of this empiricism were less valuable. Psychology was divorced from biology, and became a barren and fruitless study of mental states and their analysis and integration. Since all knowledge seemed essentially man-made or mind-made rather than real, confidence in the possibility of any principles of morality or religion was weakened. Belief was emphasized, rather than truth, and the good and the true became merely the satisfaction of the needs of man's nature. Problem after problem was approached from the standpoint of a passive psychology rather than of an active, experimental biology.

Though Locke symbolizes this empirical attitude struggling with the older scientific ideal, the Scotchman Hume is undoubtedly, in both its beneficial and its harmful aspects, the greatest apostle of empiricism. He combines a remarkable perception of the nature and method of modern scientific inquiry with the contemporary notion of disillusioned rationalism, in his case half serious and half sceptical, that its object is not the real world but a picture world inside men's heads. At times, indeed, he seems to abandon as meaningless the eighteenth-century distinction between real world and picture world, and to feel that the world that man can experience is real enough for all human purposes. To him, no knowledge for which some antecedent sense impression was not discoverable could claim any validity. The consequences of a ruthless application of this sword can be imagined. Theology, rational morality, Cartesian science, crumbled beneath his touch; and when he was through, he uncompromisingly concluded, "When we run over libraries, persuaded of these principles, what havoc must we make? If we take in our hand any volume; of divinity or school metaphysics, for instance; let us ask, *Does it contain any abstract reasoning concerning quantity or number?* No. *Does it contain any experimental reasoning concerning matter of fact and existence?* No. Commit it then to the flames: for it can contain nothing but sophistry and illusion." [15] But what in these fields appeared purely destructive was in science a potent means of purification. By the same tests, force, energy, causal necessity and all rationalistic explanation of what has to be and of why things are as they are and do as they do, go by the board, and scientists are left only to describe the relations of actual experience. Man can explain nothing, he can only observe and depict.

The Scientific Ideals of the Age of Reason

But while empiricism worked itself out to such conclusions, it must not be supposed that it seriously disturbed the imposing edifice of the Newtonian world-machine, even if it did cast doubts upon the existence of that machine apart from human experience. So long as man lived, he lived in such a mechanical world; it really mattered little what the world was to God. Nor did the changing conception of the location of the object of science affect its main outlines. If the world of science was a human world, it still contained whirling planets and unchanging if not unchangeable laws of gravitation and motion. Throughout the eighteenth century all thinkers believed that the scene of human life was set in a great, fixed, geometrical and mechanical order of nature, a mighty machine eternally pursuing the same unchanging round of cyclical processes. And the dominating ideals by which they swore and by which they tested all human conceptions were Nature and Reason.

Nature meant, not the world of inanimate objects apart from man, as the term is perhaps most commonly used to-day, but the whole rational order of things, of which man was the most important part.

Man always deceives himself when he abandons experience to follow imaginary systems. He is the work of Nature. He exists in Nature. He is submitted to her laws. He cannot deliver himself from them. It is in vain his mind would spring forward beyond the visible world: an imperious necessity ever compels his return — for a being formed by Nature, who is circumscribed by her laws, there exists nothing beyond the great whole of which he forms a part, of which he experiences the influence. The beings his imagination pictures as above Nature, or distinguished from her, are always chimeras formed after that which he has already seen, but of which it is utterly impossible he should ever form any correct idea, either as to the place they occupy, or their manner of acting — for him there is not, there can be nothing, out of that nature which includes all beings.... The universe, that vast assemblage of everything that exists, presents only matter and motion: the whole offers to our contemplation nothing but an immense, an uninterrupted succession of causes and effects.... Nature, therefore, in its most extended signification, is the great whole that results from the assemblage of matter, under its various combinations, with that contrariety of motions, which the universe offers to our view.[16]

Men saw in the world no more chaos, no more confusion, but an essentially rational and harmonious machine.

This was an intoxicating discovery. It was inevitable that men should be struck by the contrast with human society and institutions: in comparison with the simplicity and order of the laws of gravitation, man's laws were anything but harmonious and orderly. If Nature is so much more perfect than human arts, it must be, so men thought, the handiwork of a much more perfect being than man; it must be the harmonious masterpiece of God. Natural laws were regarded as real laws or commands, decrees of the Almighty, literally obeyed without a single act of rebellion. Says Nature to the scientist, in Voltaire, "My poor son, shall I tell you the truth? I have been given a name that does not suit me at all. I am called Nature, and I am really Art"[17] — the art of God. One of Newton's chief disciples sums it up thus:

> Natural science is subservient to purposes of a higher kind, and is chiefly to be valued as it lays a sure foundation for Natural Religion and Moral Philosophy; by leading us, in a satisfactory manner, to the knowledge of the Author and Governor of the universe.... To study Nature is to study into His workmanship; every new discovery opens up to us a new part of his scheme.... Our views of Nature, however imperfect, serve to represent to us, in the most sensible manner, that mighty power which prevails throughout, acting with a force and efficacy that appears to suffer no diminution from the greatest distances of space or intervals of time; and that wisdom which we see equally displayed in the exquisite structure and just motions of the greatest and the subtilest parts. These, with perfect goodness, by which they are evidently directed, constitute the supreme object of the speculations of a philosopher; who, while he contemplates and admires so excellent a system, cannot but be himself excited and animated to correspond with the general harmony of Nature.[18]

With distinguished scientists, from Newton down, voicing such worship of the perfection of Nature, it is but natural to expect popular thinkers like Alexander Pope in his *Essay on Man* to express this new religion:

> All are but parts of one stupendous whole,
> Whose body Nature is, and God the soul; ..
> All Nature is but Art, unknown to thee;
> All chance, direction, which thou canst not see;
> All discord, harmony not understood;
> All partial evil, universal good:
> And, spite of pride, in erring reason's spite,
> One truth is clear, whatever is, is right.[19]

For the eighteenth century, Newton had actually proved this; and Newton was the greatest mind of the ages. Pope sang:

> Nature and Nature's laws lay hid in night:
> God said, *Let* Newton *be!* and all was Light.[20]

One great difference marks off this Newtonian world from the world of modern science: in such a machine, time counted for nothing. Processes rolled on their way in cyclical fashion, completing themselves, like the orbits of the planets, in recurrent definite intervals; but there was no real change. The world had always been such an order, and always would be; of growth, of development, of evolution, the greatest single new conception introduced by the last century, there was not the slightest idea. For a few radical thinkers, like Holbach, the universe itself was eternal; but from Newton down the vast majority looked upon it as a machine that had been created at a definite point in time. Men could form no conception of how it could have *grown* to be what it was, and they therefore had no difficulty in imagining it to have sprung full-blown from the hand of God 4004 years B.C., as the tradition had it. The very idea of a machine, of a watch, to which it was constantly compared, implied a builder, a watchmaker; and once granted this, he could have made it just as it is at any time. The whole form of Newtonian science practically forced men, as a necessary scientific hypothesis, to believe in an external Creator, just as the very form of nineteenth-century evolutionary science has made that idea all but impossible, and substituted for it the notion of God as immanent, as a soul or spirit dwelling within the universe and developing it through long ages.

Nature was through and through orderly and rational; hence what was natural was easily identified with what was rational, and conversely, whatever, particularly in human society, seemed to an intelligent man reasonable, was regarded as natural, as somehow rooted in the very nature of things. So Nature and the Natural easily became the ideal of man and of human society, and were interpreted as Reason and the Reasonable. The great object of human endeavor was to discover what in every field was natural and reasonable, and to brush aside the accretions of irrational tradition that Reason and Nature might the more easily be free to display its harmonious order. In religion, the Christian tradition was for the first time seriously criticized in the light of this ideal, and the conception of a Natural or Rational Religion was the dominating idea. In social life, particularly in politics and in business, such notions lent powerful support to the demands of the middle class for freedom from absolute monarchy and mercantilistic restrictions on trade and industry, and formed the banners under which throughout the century business men fought the old régime. Never in human history, perhaps, have scientific conceptions had such a powerful reaction upon the actual life and ideals of men. Whatever differences the reformers may have had in their aims, all agreed in seeking to find a natural and rational order in human affairs and in desiring the existing confusion to be swept aside.

Starting from such premises, the Natural and Rational took on various shades of meaning. Since scientific laws were general and uniform, the Natural in human affairs was first of all the universal, those customs and ideals which could be detected everywhere as the core underlying apparent surface divergencies. It became immensely popular to go to the recently discovered and as yet but half-understood Oriental societies, Persia and especially China, to discern what laws and institutions were common to them and to the West. "Persian" and "Chinese letters" were issued in great profusion, with the aim of criticizing European civilization in the light of such world-wide principles. Thus men were naturally led to an ideal of Cosmopolitanism: they became in truth citizens of the world, and regarded particular national ideas as but "patriotic prejudices" unworthy of the scientist.

This easily passed over into an identification of the Natural with the original and primitive; what existed before man interfered with rational ways of doing things. Most popular writers read this back into the past, and actually believed that in some remote Golden Age men had had a natural religion that commended itself as inherently reasonable, which succeeding ages of scheming priests and monarchs had for their own advantage corrupted into superstition. They believed in an original State of Nature, in which human society had been well-ordered and perfect, until usurpers gained control and introduced silly regulations and foolish schemes that served only to spoil everything. More profound thinkers did not attempt to posit that such a state of nature had ever actually existed; they thought rather that it was something in the present underlying the accretions which man had added. For both classes the implication was that to perfect social arrangements one had only to abolish man-made institutions and allow Nature to function by herself — *laisser-faire* and liberty in all things was its practical import. Such an idea was particularly influential because it was precisely the kind of liberty that the middle class was demanding for itself. Thus the natural was in theory what God had intended the world of man to be, and in practice it was what seemed reasonable to the commercial classes, complete freedom from governmental interference.

This emphasis on the Natural as the original merged into interest in the savage: primitive life among the forests of America or in the South Sea islands was idealized. The Noble Red Man came into his own as the very type of what a free existence should be. Many were the volumes glorifying his rational society, free from all the conventions that hemmed in Europeans, perhaps the most famous being Diderot's *Voyage of Bougainville*, narrating the experiences of that famous French explorer of the Pacific. He found a simple idyllic people — in Diderot's pages — who had no notion of the moral taboos, especially as regards sex, that were the bane of French life. That polished and cultivated age took great delight in reading interminable traveler's romances and dreaming of modifying the society of Paris or London until it resembled the life they thought the Noble Red Man lived.

Again, the Natural was the reasonable and the socially useful, and all that seemed to have no apparent value was unnatural and to be destroyed. It was the ideal, that which men wanted to realize themselves; and it easily passed over into the divine. Nature was God's model for man; nay, it was the very face of God himself.

"O thou," cries this Nature to man, "who, following the impulse I have given you, during your whole existence, incessantly tend towards happiness, do not strive to resist my sovereign law. Labor to your own felicity; partake without fear of the banquet which is spread before you, with the most hearty welcome; you will find the means legibly written on your own heart.... Dare, then, to affranchise yourself from the trammels of superstition, my self-conceited, pragmatic rival, who mistakes my rights; denounce those empty theories, which are usurpers of my privileges; return under the dominion of my laws, which, however severe, are mild in comparison with those of bigotry. It is in my empire alone that true liberty reigns. Tyranny is unknown to its soil, slavery is forever banished from its votaries; equity unceasingly watches over the rights of all my subjects, maintains them in the possession of their just claims; benevolence, grafted upon humanity, connects them by amicable bonds; truth enlightens them; never can imposture blind them with his obscuring mists. Return, then, my child, to thy fostering mother's arms! Deserter, trace back thy wandering steps to Nature! She will console thee for thine evils; she will drive from thy heart those appalling fears which overwhelm thee ... Return to Nature, to humanity, to thyself! ... Enjoy thyself, and cause others also to enjoy those comforts, which I have placed with a liberal hand for all the children of the earth, who all equally emanate from my bosom.... These pleasures are freely permitted thee, if thou indulgest them with moderation, with that discretion which I myself have fixed. Be happy, then, O man!" [21]

The eighteenth century raised its voice as one man in a pæan of praise to Nature.

O Nature, sovereign of all beings! and ye, her adorable daughters, Virtue, Reason, and Truth! remain forever our revered protectors! it is to you that belong the praises of the human race; to you appertains the homage of the earth. Show us then, O Nature! that which man ought to do, in order to obtain the happiness which thou makest him desire. Virtue! animate him with thy beneficent fire. Reason! conduct his uncertain steps through the paths of life. Truth! let thy torch illumine his intellect, dissipate the darkness of his road. Unite, O assisting deities! your powers, in order to submit the hearts of mankind to your dominion. Banish error from our mind; wickedness from our hearts; confusion from our footsteps; cause knowledge to extend its salubrious reign; goodness to occupy our souls; serenity to occupy our bosoms.[22]

The whole educated world in the eighteenth century was convinced, as never before or since, that the most beneficent and the most divine force in human life, man's supreme achievement and his brightest jewel, is Science. "Without the sciences," wrote Mercier to the Academy of Sciences, "man would rank below the brutes." [23] For the first time in man's long history, it was generally believed that human happiness and human knowledge go hand in hand. Speaking of the early Babylonian astronomers, and seeing there, like his fellows, the rays of the Golden Age, Buffon sounded the spirit of his times: "That early people was very happy, because it was very scientific." [24] And all enlightened men agreed in finding in the pursuit of science the sum of human wisdom: "What enthusiasm is nobler than believing man capable of knowing all the forces and discovering by his labors all the secrets of nature!" [25] The eighteenth century was preëminently the age of faith in science.

REFERENCES

1. Fontenelle, *Œuvres Complètes* (1818), *Préface sur l'utilité des mathématiques et de la physique*, I, 34.
2. Quoted in F. S. Marvin, *Living Past*, 179.
3. Isaac Newton, *Mathematical Principles of Natural Philosophy*, Bk. III.
4. *Ibid.*, Author's Preface.
5. *Ibid.*
6. *Ibid.*

280 SEVENTEENTH AND EIGHTEENTH CENTURIES

7. Léon Bloch, *La Philosophie de Newton*, 555.
8. Newton, *Principles*, Motte tr. (1803), II, 314.
9. *Ibid.*, Bk. III, 4th Rule of Reasoning in Philosophy.
10. Diderot, *Encyclopédie*, art. "Encyclopédie."
11. Buffon, quoted in L. Ducros, *Les Encyclopédistes*, 326.
12. Holbach, *Système de la Nature* (1770), I, 142.
13. Diderot, *Pensées sur l'Interprétation de la Nature*, 15, 23.
14. *Ibid.*, 4.
15. David Hume, *Enquiry concerning Human Understanding*, Pt. III, sec. 12.
16. Holbach, *Système de la Nature*, ch. I.
17. Voltaire, *Dictionnaire philosophique*, art. "Nature."
18. Colin Maclaurin, *An Account of Sir Isaac Newton's Philosophical Discoveries*, 3, 4, 95.
19. Alexander Pope, *Essay on Man*.
20. Pope, *Works*, Cambridge ed., 135.
21. Holbach, *Système de la Nature*, ch. 14.
22. *Ibid.*
23. Quoted in L. Ducros, *Les Encyclopédistes*, 315.
24. Buffon, *Époques de la Nature*, VII.
25. Buffon, quoted in L. Ducros, *Les Encyclopédistes*, 316.

SELECTED READING LISTS

The Advance of Mechanical Science: Dampier-Whetham, *H. of Science*; P. Smith, *H. of Modern Culture*, vols. I, II; A. Wolf, *H. of Science, Technology, and Phil. in the 18th cent.*; Sedgwick and Tyler, *Short H. of Science*; Dannemann; Burtt, *Met. Foundations of Mod. Physical Science*, best interpretation of significance: Whitehead, *Science and the Modern World*. *Cam. Mod. Hist.*, V, c. 23; VIII, c. 1; Lavisse et Rambaud, VI, c. 10; VII, c. 15; by Tannery. *H. des Sciences en France*, in G. Hanotaux, *H. de la Nat. Française*, XIV. See histories of the sciences listed under Ch. X, esp. Berry, Cantor, Mach, Gerland; H. Crew, *Rise of Modern Physics*; F. Rosenberger, *Ges. der Physik*. M. Ornstein, *Role of the Scientific Societies in the 17th cent*. G. N. Clark, *The Seventeenth Century*; *Science and Invention in the Age of Newton*. Robert Boyle, *Works*, ed. Birch; Life by F. Masson. Huygens, *Oeuvres*. Isaac Newton, *Principia Mathematica*, ed. Cajori; *Opticks*. Lives by D. Brewster, L. T. More, S. Brodetsky; studies by L. Bloch, F. Rosenberger; see Burtt.

The Rise of Experimental Science: In addition to the above, E. Gerland and F. Traumüller, *Ges. der physikalischen Experimentierkunst*; L. Hogben, *Science for the Citizen*. Histories of chemistry by E. Thorpe, J. M. Stillman, A. Ladenburg; of geology by K. A. von Zittel, H. A. Woodward; of biology by E. Nordenskiöld, W. A. Locy, L. C. Miall, H. F. Osborne; of medicine by F. H. Garrison, V. Robinson. W. Harvey, *On the Movement of the Heart and the Blood*; W. Gilbert, *On the Magnet*; Boyle's writings. The empirical theory of science: J. Glanvill, *Scepsis Scientifica*; J. Locke, *Essay conc. Human Understanding*; G. Berkeley, *De Motu*, *Siris*; D. Hume, *Enquiry concerning the Human Understanding*; Diderot, *Thoughts on the Interpretation of Nature*.

Nature and Reason: Carl Becker, *The Heavenly City of the 18th century Philosophers*; *The Declaration of Independence*, c. 2; W. Marvin, *H. of Eur. Phil.*, c. 23; Höffding, I, 212–35; brief accounts of the influence of the Newtonian ideal. R. B. Mowat, *The Age of Reason*; K. Martin, *French Liberal Thought in the 18th cent.*; D. Mornet, *French Thought in the 18th cent.*; L. Ducros, *Les Encyclopédistes*; E. Cassirer, *Das Zeitalter der Aufklärung*. L. Lévy-Bruhl, *H. of Mod. Phil. in France*; P. Damiron, *H. de la Phil. au 18e s.*; F. A. Lange, *H. of Materialism*; J. Fabre, *Les Pères de la Révolution*; E. Faguet, *Le 18e siècle*; H. Hettner, *Litteraturges. des 18. Jahrh.*; E. Lavisse, *H. de France*, VIII, pt. ii, bk. iii, c. 3; IX, pt. i, bk. iv; VII, pt. ii, bk. vii. Leslie Stephen, *H. of English Thought in the 18th cent.*; John Morley, *Voltaire* (defense of the age), *Diderot*, *Rousseau*, *Condorcet*. Colin Maclaurin, *An Account of Sir*

Isaac Newton's Philosophical Discoveries (best popularization); Voltaire, *English Letters*, ed. Lanson; *Éléments de la philosophie de Newton;* art. "Nature" in *Phil. Dictionary;* studies by Morley, G. Brandes, N. L. Torrey; G. Pellissier, *Voltaire Philosophe.* H. Robinson, *Bayle the Sceptic.* Buffon, *Natural History;* Holbach, *System of Nature* (most thoroughgoing statement); D'Alembert, *Preliminary Discourse to the Great Encyclopedia;* J. S. Schapiro, *Condorcet and the Rise of Liberalism in France.* G. E. Lessing, lives by T. W. Rolleston, Erich Schmidt. For influence on literature, Boileau, *L'Art Poétique;* A. Pope, *Essay on Criticism, Essay on Man.*

The Problem of Knowledge and Empiricism: John Dewey, *Reconstruction in Philosophy*, chs. 3, 4, gives the best orientation; see also Burtt and Whitehead. Traditional accounts in the histories of philosophy, of which B. A. G. Fuller, H. Höffding, E. Bréhier, and W. Windelband, *Ges. der Neuren Phil.*, are the best. E. Cassirer, *Das Erkenntnisproblem*, full and comprehensive account. J. G. Hibben, *Age of the Enlightenment.* For the German background, see Leibniz, *Selections*, ed. Latta, Montgomery, Duncan, Langley; studies by J. T. Merz, John Dewey, Bertrand Russell. John Locke, *Essay conc. Human Understanding*, esp. bks. II, IV; *Selections*, ed. S. P. Lamprecht. Studies by F. J. E. Woodbridge, in *Essays in Honor of John Dewey, Studies in the H. of Ideas*, III; by A. Hofstadter, J. G. Clapp, J. Gibson. George Berkeley, esp. *New Theory of Vision, Principles of Human Knowledge, Three Dialogues;* F. J. E. Woodbridge, *Realism of Berkeley*, in *Stud. Hist. Ideas*, I. For developed empiricism, David Hume, esp. *Treatise of Human Nature, Enquiry concerning the Human Understanding; Selections*, ed. Hendel. Studies by John Laird, C. W. Hendel; S. P. Lamprecht, in *Stud. Hist. Ideas*, II; Thomas Huxley. Condillac, *Traité des Sensations, Essai sur les Origines des Connaissances Humaines.* Helvétius, *De l'Esprit, De l'Homme.*

CHAPTER XII
THE RELIGION OF REASON
The Spread of the Humanistic Spirit

This deification of reason and its identification with Nature first secured a strong foothold in religious ideas. We have seen that the Protestant revolt from the Catholic monarchy was really an increased emphasis upon certain of the medieval ideas, and that the succeeding age of Puritanical reformation, in Protestantism and Catholicism alike, was a reaffirmation of the necessity of doctrinal orthodoxy and an external law of faith and practice. The attempts of the humanists, like Erasmus, to promulgate a rational and ethical faith, proved abortive, and instead of feeling the influence of the humanistic notions of the moral and intellectual dignity of man, and the rationalism of the new science, religion was for two centuries buried under an even narrower and more barren scholasticism. By the end of the great scientific seventeenth century, however, these two influences had grown so strong as to make an impression upon minds weary of bitter theological controversy, and increasingly skeptical of authority in every field. Especially those enamoured of the new science and methods of investigation found it impossible, with their leader Newton, to keep that spirit in an isolated compartment, and were bound with him to carry it into the field of religion as well. At last the humanism of the Renaissance, supported by the methods of scientific reasoning, was able to make a breach in the Christian tradition; and for the first time there appeared religious ideas forming a definite break with the Middle Ages.

From humanism, religion was permeated by a rejection of the traditional notion of the impotence and depravity of human nature, and the Renaissance emphasis on man's moral and intellectual worth; from the new science, by a spirit of subjecting all beliefs and practices to the tests of reasonableness and utility in this life. The religious tradition was vigorously criticized from the standpoint of human standards of right and reasonableness. Here is the religious system, with its hoary antiquity. Judged by the standard of the simplicity, order, rationality, and usefulness of the system of Nature, What is it worth? What in it is reasonable? What earthly good does it contain? The whole spirit of such a religious ideal, and its disintegrating effect upon the traditional beliefs, is admirably illustrated by the remark of one of the characters in an early work of Diderot. To a speaker who maintains the importance of keeping the people in bondage to certain prejudices, he retorts: "What prejudices? If a man once admits the existence of a God, the reality of moral good and evil, the immortality of the soul, future rewards and punishments, what need has he of prejudices? Supposing him initiated in all the mysteries of transubstantiation, consubstantiation, the Trinity, hypostatical union, predestination, incarnation, and the rest, *will he be any the better citizen?*" [1] Such is the test — good citizenship, social utility; and all that can pass this test is the religion of reason. All that cannot is relegated to the other field of revealed or supernatural religion.

Such a program was just as much a break with the spirit of Protestantism as with that of Catholicism. That it eventually made its home in Protestantism rather than in the Catholic fold was not because the former was in principle more tolerant of divergent views, but because the divisions amongst the Protestants made toleration a necessity. As Voltaire put it, "Were there but one religion in England, its despotism would be fearful; were there but two, they would cut each other's throats; but there are thirty, and they live in peace and happiness." [2] The power of the medieval Church had been broken, and a century of religious warfare had forced a mutual forbearance. Hence when the modern spirit appeared in religion, it found a refuge amongst the many sects of Protestantism, each of which violently hated it, yet could not well resort to the extirpation favored by the Catholics. Because Reformed Calvinism insisted more on a rational interpretation of the Scriptures, because there new sects multiplied most rapidly, and because Calvinism itself was the most medieval of all the Protestant systems, religious rationalism first gained a foothold within its ranks, in seventeenth-century Holland. The theological wars in England, terminating in the Toleration Act of 1689, which made all dissent from Anglicanism legal save Catholicism and Unitarianism; and the very fact that the Anglican communion was the result of a compromise holding together men of a great variety of opinions, transferred the seat of the new religion of reason to that country, whence, throughout the next century, it spread in great streams to France and Germany.

The Growth of Religious Rationalism

This new rationalistic spirit appeared first in the sixteenth century among the Socinians. These radicals were the followers of two Italian humanists who fled to Poland and there established a group called the Polish Brethren, which flourished for a century until exterminated by the Catholic revival in 1661. The Socini, uncle and nephew, were not interested in the medieval reaction of Protestantism, but were typical humanists, seeking, like Valla or Erasmus, an ethical religion purified of irrational mysteries. They laid the supreme emphasis upon the power and ability of human nature to lead a moral life without supernatural aid — the typical view of the humanists. Hence they were naturally led to reject most of the traditional theology built upon the assumption, shared by Catholics, Lutherans, and Calvinists alike, that human nature was evil and needed a divine miracle to transform it. They denied the doctrine of original sin: man is not a fallen creature. They denied man's moral bondage, his unconditional predestination, his need of any magical redemption or transformation of nature, and hence they found no use in the theory of Christ's atonement for man's sins or, indeed, for any divine nature in Christ at all. This Unitarianism became the most notorious of their doctrines, though with them as with all Unitarians it has never been the central belief, but only a corollary following from the cardinal insistence on the dignity of human nature. The necessity, not only of the system of ecclesiastical sacraments, but also of the Protestant "faith," went by the board.

These humanizing and rationalizing Socinians were not thoroughgoing: they retained many supernatural doctrines taught in the Scriptures, and they placed a great emphasis, like all the Protestants, upon the literal authority of the Bible, holding to everything proclaimed by the prophet and man Jesus. But they insisted upon a thoroughly rational interpretation of this authority: whatever God has revealed there cannot be contrary to human reason. This principle, and their cardinal faith in human ability and human reason, made them genuine forerunners of later more radical rationalism. Where the Reformation created an essentially medieval system with modern elements, they held to a modern system that retained some medieval elements.

Driven from Poland in 1661, many fled to the seat of toleration, Holland, and carried on their work in that land. Here they found rationalism already present in a mild form in the Arminian reaction against strict Calvinism, and destined to greater development under the influence of the French skepticism of Montaigne, Charron, Descartes, and Bayle. The Arminians of the early seventeenth century were not so radical as the Socinians, and they stood for only a minor modification of the strict doctrine, but they did represent the same humanistic and scientific tendencies at work. Arminius could not stomach the total depravity of human nature, nor the injustice of condemning men to hell or heaven without any regard to human merit. He still believed in the necessity of the supernatural aid of grace, but he believed that such aid was given only to men who really strove to deserve it. Accepting Calvin's premises, he was unwilling to follow them to the logical conclusion, and tried to effect a compromise. The importance of Arminianism, aside from its foreshadowing of further developments, lay in its acceptance by most Anglicans, and by the later eighteenth-century Methodist revival.

It was in England that the religion of reason was first consistently worked out. Already, in 1624, Lord Herbert of Cherbury had sought certain universal Christian principles that could be agreed upon by all men regardless of their specific theological differences; and this attempt was increasingly popular as controversy went on. By the end of the century most intelligent religious leaders were divided into two camps. Both agreed that the core of religion was a set of doctrines that could be established by the unaided natural reason: both orthodox and radicals accepted as fundamental the religion of nature or reason. The orthodox insisted also upon the importance of revelation besides; they were supernatural rationalists, who made the distinction between what could and what could not be rationally established, and accepted both elements of the tradition. The radicals, who were known as Deists, differed from them in rejecting revelation entirely, and insisting on the sufficiency of natural and rational religion. For a generation the controversy was over the question of whether revelation was or was not necessary, in addition to this natural religion; then more thoroughgoing critics came to question even the premises of rational religion, and by the middle of the century there was developed a complete skepticism which, carried into France, eventuated in widespread atheism.

This religion of reason was really implied in the widespread Cartesianism of the preceding century. Descartes himself was of too exclusively scientific a turn of mind to take much interest in religious questions, and he was rather provoked at the popularity of his single theological work, the *Meditations*, which he had written largely to secure a certain foundation for his scientific axioms. But when Cartesianism captured the minds of all Frenchmen, its exponents split into two schools: those who were primarily interested in natural science, and those who were chiefly interested, like Malebranche and Bossuet and Fénelon, in establishing tottering religious ideas upon the firm Cartesian foundation of the method of reason. Malebranche particularly attempted to prove by reason the truth of the religious tradition. Now it was inevitable that such an attempt should lead to a minimizing of all those elements that could not be so established; and Pascal, who almost alone of first-rate French thinkers felt the insufficiency of the purely rational method in religious matters, rightly pointed out that a rational proof of religion in general cannot be a proof of any particular religious revelation, and that Malebranche's attempt might just as easily have established Mohammedanism or Judaism; — might better have done so, in fact, since they contained fewer "mysteries" than orthodox Christianity. But this did not deter minds, in France or England, who were captivated by the new scientific method; and as they built up a religion of reason particular differences inevitably dropped away. In England every one, from Newton and Locke down, was convinced of the possibility and desirability of such a natural theology, however they might disagree on whether further revelation were needful.

The Religion of Reason, or Natural Religion

The three outstanding leaders of the more conservative supernatural rationalists were, aside from Newton himself, John Tillotson, Archbishop of Canterbury, Locke, and Samuel Clarke, foremost theologian and after Locke's death most famous philosopher in England. All of these men were convinced Newtonians, believing in the methods of scientific rationalism and in the world-machine that was their outcome. All of them agreed that religion is not an instinctive need and activity of the human soul, but essentially a science like physics, that is, a system of rational propositions given from without and to be tested as any other propositions are tested, by the evidence of the human reason. Its only method of arriving at the truths that must be believed is the same kind of reason that one employs in accepting a law of physics, a political principle, or a financial investment. Its value and purpose is similarly quite definite: it is solely to provide a divine sanction for a satisfactory human morality, a powerful motive for the doing of good. All that is useless for this very specific purpose is unimportant. Such a sanction and such a motive is provided by natural religion, consisting of a few propositions that appeal to the reason of every man. These propositions are three: there is an omnipotent God, he demands virtuous living on the part of man in obedience to his will, and there is a future life in which he will reward the virtuous and punish the wicked. Man, employing his faculty of drawing conclusions from given premises, will thus see the advantages of living a righteous life, and will rationally order his life to attain a reward in heaven.

This simple creed remained throughout the century as the content of rational religion. Paley, writing toward the end, went so far as to define virtue as "the doing good to mankind in obedience to the will of God and for the sake of future rewards." [3] Voltaire stated it definitely: "I understand by natural religion the principles of morality common to the human race." [4] It contained nothing else. This creed was accepted, by orthodox and radicals together, as the essential content of the religious tradition of Christianity. It seemed to them so obviously true that until pressed by more thoroughgoing critics they hardly bothered to try to prove its validity, concentrating their energies rather on debating whether it alone was a sufficient incentive to morality. The orthodox said no, the Deists yes. On natural religion itself there was singular unanimity; from Herbert of Cherbury in 1624 to Paley in 1798, its purpose and its content remained unaltered. Conservative Locke wrote: "In all things of this kind, there is little need or use of revelation, God having furnished us with natural and surer means to arrive at a knowledge of them. For whatsoever truth we come to a clearer discovery of from the knowledge and contemplation of our own ideas, will always be certainer to us than those which are conveyed to us by traditional revelation." [5] In such a spirit Locke examined the New Testament, and there found set forth only two conditions of salvation: the belief that Jesus is the Messiah, and a righteous life. "These two, faith and repentance, that is, believing Jesus to be the Messiah, and a good life, are the indispensable conditions of the new covenant to be performed by all those who would obtain eternal life." [6] Matthew Tindal, in the book *Christianity as Old as the Creation*, which remained the best statement of the radical position and earned the title of "the Deists' Bible," expresses precisely the same idea of natural religion. True religion consists "in a constant disposition of mind to do all the good we can, and thereby render ourselves acceptable to God in answering the end of our creation." [7] The only difference between morality and religion is that the former is "acting according to the reason of things considered in themselves," while the latter is "acting according to the same reason of things considered as the will of God." [8]

The Place of Revelation

To this natural religion the supernatural rationalists added revelation as a supplement, directed to the same end, teaching the same things, what every man knows, more clearly and effectively, and adding a few truths and a few duties. Locke laid down the principles on which revelation was to be accepted. Religious truths fall into three classes.

By what has been before said of reason we may be able to make some guess at the distinction of things into those that are according to, above, and contrary to reason. According to reason are such propositions whose truths we can discover by examining and tracing those ideas we have from sensation and reflection; and by natural deduction find to be true or probable. Above reason are such propositions whose truth or probability we cannot by reason derive from those principles. Contrary to reason are such propositions as are inconsistent with, or irreconcilable to our clear and distinct ideas. Thus the existence of one God is according to reason; the existence of more than one God contrary to reason; the resurrection of the dead above reason.[9]

The first group constitute natural religion; the second, superstition; the third, revelation. Locke's disciple John Toland, in his *Christianity not Mysterious*, further pointed out that the first and last formed really but one class: reasonable truths may be discovered by us for ourselves, or may be made known to us by the testimony of others, and this testimony may be given by revelation. All that is contradictory of what experience teaches, however, must be discarded.

Such thinkers with such methods had two things to prove in order to support revelation: first, they must show that revelation was not inconsistent with natural religion — that is, that it was both rational in itself and in accordance with natural morality; and secondly, that there were positive grounds for believing in the specific Christian revelation, which amounted to two kinds of evidence, prophecy and miracles. Tillotson's arguments are typical. Natural religion is not enough; men need a stronger motive for morality. Revelation does not alter natural religion, but simply makes it clearer and more effective. "Natural religion is the foundation of all revealed religion, and revelation is designed simply to establish its duties." [10] The latter does not impart any new faculty of truth or any new test; it gives an additional motive for acting on what we know to be true. Why do we accept it? First, because it is in complete harmony with natural religion and human nature; secondly, because it was foretold in the Old Testament by prophecies, and confirmed in the New by miracles. Both are visible signs to prove the divine mission of the worker, a sort of stamp of genuineness, like "sterling" or "twenty-four carat."

Now there are two things must concur [says Tillotson] to give the mind of man full satisfaction that any religion is from God. First, if the person that declares this religion gives testimony of his divine authority, that is, that he is sent and commissioned by God for that purpose. And secondly, if the religion which he declares contain nothing in it that is plainly repugnant to the nature of God.... For though a doctrine be never so reasonable in itself, this is no certain argument that it is from God if no testimony from heaven be given to it; because it may be the result and issue of human reason and discourse; and though a doctrine be attested by miracles, yet the matter of it may be so unreasonable and absurd, so unworthy of God and so contrary to the natural notions which man has of him, that no miracles can be sufficient to give confirmation to it; and therefore in some cases the Scripture forbids men to hearken to a prophet though he work a miracle.[11]

Locke's position is identical.

> For since no evidence of our faculties by which we receive such revelations can exceed, if equal, the certainty of our intuitive knowledge, we can never receive for a truth anything that is directly contrary to our clear and distinct knowledge.... There can be no evidence that any traditional religion is of divine origin, ... so clear and so certain as that of the principles of reason ....[12] Divine revelation receives testimony from no other miracles but such as are wrought to witness his mission from God who delivers the revelation. All other miracles that are done in the world, how many or great soever, revelation is not concerned in.[13]

In his *Reasonableness of Christianity* he contended that the Christian revelation passes such tests — that is, in its Anglican form. It was necessary because men, in spite of the fact that reason could have led them to it, had widely lost the knowledge of natural religion. As Clarke succinctly put it:

> There was plainly wanting a divine revelation to recover mankind out of their universal corruption and degeneracy, and without such a revelation it was not possible that the world should ever be effectually reformed. For if the gross and stupid ignorance, the innumerable prejudices and vain opinions, ... which the generality of mankind continually labor under, make it undeniably too difficult a work for men of all capacities to discover every one for himself, by the bare light of reason, all the particular branches of their duty, ... there was plainly a necessity of some particular revelation, to discover in what manner, and with what kind of external service, God might acceptably be worshipped.... There was a necessity of some particular revelation, to give men full assurance of the truth of those great motives of religion, the rewards and punishments of a future state, which, notwithstanding the strongest arguments of reason, men could not yet forbear doubting of.[14]

To such a pass had the Newtonian world brought the great Christian tradition, with all its passionate feeling and yearning for God. It had become merely a philosophical system appealing to the cool and deliberate reason of the man of common sense, and the inner experience of the presence of the divine, the immediate vision of God's living reality, was condemned as unwholesome "enthusiasm" — the worst sin during the Age of Reason. It is no wonder that mystics heard again the voice of God within the heart, and that the same century saw the great revivals of medieval faith that became Pietism in Germany and Wesleyan Evangelicalism in England. But such things were not for the intelligent man, or the middle class; they spread among the lower classes.

The Deistic Attack on Revelation

With revelation appealing to such arguments, it is easy to see that those not encumbered by the necessity of maintaining their own position as priests or bishops should see little cause for retaining it. On every hand there sprang up Deists who clung only to what Arthur Bury in 1690 called *The Naked Gospel*. Their contention was simple: God has not added anything to the duties required by natural religion. Their arguments were twofold: the God who created the Newtonian world-machine and acts always by universal laws, would not do such a thing, and besides neither prophecy nor miracles furnish any adequate ground for believing in the Christian revelation. Herbert of Cherbury maintained that God's perfection demands a way of salvation open to all men. Particular revelations are necessarily partial and preferential, and the universal God possesses no such character. What is necessary must have been implanted by him in man's natural reason, and be equally accessible in all ages and places. Tindal's *Christianity as Old as the Creation* gave this argument most elaborately. Natural religion has always existed as a perfect thing, and therefore revelation can add nothing to it. God asks only the good of man, human perfection and happiness, secured by universal benevolence. "To imagine God can command anything inconsistent with this universal benevolence is highly to dishonor him; 'tis to destroy his impartial goodness, and make his power and wisdom degenerate into cruelty and craft." "Duties neither need nor can receive any stronger proof than what they have already from the evidence of right reason." [15] Miracles and prophecy, and all particular religious rites and beliefs, are mere superstition.

Not content with this general position, the Deists waged a vigorous attack on all that distinguished Christianity from natural religion — an attack calm and moderate in England and Germany, but exceedingly bitter and impassioned in the France of corrupt Catholic prelates, of Cardinals Dubois and d'Orléans and de Rohan. Tindal and Morgan delighted in pointing out the irrational absurdities and the cruel inhumanities and futilities of much of historical Christianity; Chubb declared that Jesus was a Deist, and in typical humanist fashion opposed the "religion of Jesus" to Christianity. The French went farther; Diderot exploded — in private, to be sure:

The Christian religion is to my mind the most absurd and atrocious in its dogmas; the most unintelligible, the most metaphysical, the most intertwisted and obscure, and consequently the most subject to divisions, sects, schisms, and heresies; the most mischievous for the public tranquillity, the most dangerous to sovereigns by its hierarchic order, its persecutions, its discipline; the most flat, the most dreary, the most Gothic, and the most gloomy in its ceremonies; the most puerile and unsociable in its morality, considered not in what is common to it with universal morality, but in what is peculiarly its own, and constitutes it evangelical, apostolic, and Christian morality, which is the most intolerant of all. Lutheranism, freed from some absurdities, is preferable to Catholicism, Protestantism (Calvinism) to Lutheranism, Socinianism to Protestantism, Deism, with temples and ceremonies, to Socinianism.[16]

Voltaire thought Jesus of Nazareth entirely too noble a character to insult by calling a Christian, and wrote:

Every man of sense, every good man, ought to hold the Christian sect in horror. The great name of Deist, which is not sufficiently revered, is the only name one ought to take. The only gospel one ought to read is the great book of Nature, written by the hand of God and sealed with his seal. The only religion that ought to be professed is the religion of worshipping God and being a good man. It is as impossible that this pure and eternal religion should produce evil as it is that the Christian fanaticism should not produce it.[17]

THE CRITIQUE OF PROPHECY AND MIRACLES

The chief support of revelation, prophecy and miracles, were devastatingly criticized. Anthony Collins, who had already written a *Discourse of Free-Thinking*, in another work maintained both that the only proof of the divine origin of the Christian revelation is the prophecy in the Old Testament, and that a careful examination of this prophecy, taken in a literal and not a highly figurative sense, makes it quite impossible to believe that Jesus ever fulfilled a single one. The last stand of the supernatural rationalists was hence made upon miracles; and Woolston, and above all the great philosopher Hume, so demolished their value that to this day apologists have had their greatest difficulties, not in proving Christianity by miracles, but in explaining how such impossible ideas ever crept into the record. Woolston, scurrilous in language but acute in criticism, claimed that the miracles recorded in the New Testament were in most cases foolish, trivial, contradictory, absurd, unworthy of a divinely commissioned teacher, and characteristic only of a sorcerer and wizard. Even if true, they offer not a jot of evidence as to the moral and spiritual value of Jesus' teachings. Since miracles have been most often performed under diabolical influence, they have in themselves absolutely no value in establishing the divine mission of their worker.

It remained for Hume to administer the *coup de grace*. In his famous *Essay on Miracles*, in 1748, he proved so conclusively that intelligent men have rarely questioned it since, that a miracle, in the sense of a supernatural event as a sign of the divinity of its worker, cannot possibly be established. Even could it be shown that the events recorded did actually take place, that they were supernatural, and that they suffice to establish a religion, it is impossible to demonstrate. No such event can contain any evidential value.

> No testimony is sufficient to establish a miracle, unless the testimony be of such a kind, that its falsehood would be more miraculous, than the fact, which it endeavors to establish. . . . A miracle can never be proved, so as to be the foundation of a system of religion. . . . Suppose all the historians who treat of England should agree [that Queen Elizabeth died, and after being buried a month returned to her throne and governed England again]. I should not doubt of her pretended death, and of those other public circumstances that followed it: I should only assert it to have been pretended, and that it neither was, nor possibly could be real. . . . I would still reply, that the knavery and folly of men are such common phenomena, that I should rather believe the most extraordinary events to arise from their concurrence, than admit of so signal a violation of the laws of nature. But should this miracle be ascribed to any new system of religion; men, in all ages, have been so much imposed on by ridiculous stories of that kind, that this very circumstance would be a full proof of a cheat, and sufficient, with all men of sense, not only to make them reject the fact, but even reject it without farther examination. . . . As the violations of truth are more common in the testimony concerning religious miracles, than in that concerning any other matter of fact; . . . this must make us form a general resolution, never to lend any attention to it, with whatever specious pretence it may be covered.[18]

In other words, for one who accepts Newtonian physics, unless he assumes that he has so complete a knowledge of the workings of nature as to be able to exclude every natural cause — a thing obviously impossible — it is impossible to prove that any given event was supernaturally produced. Whatever its cause, it is far easier to believe it effected by some natural factor. Hume's argument has never been refuted, and since it was fully understood no man has ever attempted to establish revelation upon any such purely external grounds.

The Rationalistic Attack on Deism

The supernatural rationalists were refuted, and Deism, the pure religion of nature, was alone left with an argument to stand upon. That it too soon crumbled, and that religion has since been forced to rely, not upon any rational proof, but upon some kind of faith or mystic intuition, was due to the fact that before the Deists had well concluded their attack upon revelation, a more thoroughgoing rationalism had launched its arrows against natural religion itself. This second stage of the rationalistic religious debate in the eighteenth century was thus no longer over the question of whether a reasonable man should believe in revelation in addition to natural religion: it was whether such a man should or should not believe in natural religion itself. For the first time serious attention was forced upon the arguments in support of the cardinal tenets of natural religion.

The Arguments of Natural Theology

To understand the attacks made on natural religion by these complete skeptics, it is necessary to examine first the reasons given, by both supernatural rationalists and by Deists, for believing in its tenets. To the mind familiar with the modern conception of the world, that contains as a fundamental factor the notion of evolution and development, it is difficult to feel the force of these eighteenth-century arguments. To realize their cogency, it must be remembered that that whole age had no conception of the universe as a growing organism, but thought of it rather, following Newton, as a machine, in which time could cause no changes of structure. In such a Newtonian science the arguments of the advocates of natural religion were not only not absurd, but were genuine scientific hypotheses. They were not the arguments that would have appealed to preceding ages, nor do they appeal to the nineteenth century with its changed science; they were possible only in the Newtonian world, and there they seemed almost forced on men's minds.

These arguments can be reduced to two: that from the necessity of a first cause, and that from design. Though both can be found in Thomas Aquinas, they did not mean for him the same thing as they did for the eighteenth century, nor did they have the same cogency. We can find both well stated, as implied in mathematical physics, by Newton himself. Such a harmonious and orderly machine as he had discovered the world to be, taken in conjunction with the fact that it seemed always, from its first beginnings, to have existed in its present form, appeared to him to demand an intelligent Creator to construct it. The very conception of the world as a machine or a complex watch implies a machinist or watch-maker to build it and to plan its intricate harmony and order. Watches and machines, in our experience, do not just happen; they are made, and they are intelligently made, to fulfill a definite purpose. So if the universe is conceived on such an analogy, it must be a product of *art:* that is, it must have had a first cause, and it must have had an intelligent designer. Thus argued Newton, so cogently, it seemed, that Voltaire could say, "I have never seen a single Newtonian who was not a theist, in the most rigorous sense of the word." [19] God was the great watchmaker, entirely apart from his created world, its quite external architect. Newton himself thought that certain disturbances in the movement of the planets and comets required periodic adjustments on the part of the Creator; that is, the watch-universe had to be sent to the jeweler for repairs! This idea did not meet with much favor, and later the French mathematicians Laplace and Lagrange proved that these irregularities are periodical and equalize one another. On the whole, the Deists refused to follow Newton here, and would brook no divine interference with the order of nature once it was established. The function of God became for them simply that of starting the machine in the first place; since then, God has not needed to concern himself with the operation of his perfect creation, and his sole value intellectually, aside from giving a scientific explanation of the origin of things, was to guarantee that the world was operated upon a moral basis, that it was permeated by a moral order that would punish in hell the unrighteous and reward the righteous.

Newton's arguments were most systematically developed in France, where the skeptical attack was more popular than in England, even though its greatest single representative was the

Scotchman Hume. We find the two arguments for God's existence well stated by Voltaire, who was remarkable for his tenacity in Deism to the end of his long life, in 1778, by which time most French thinkers had advanced beyond it to skepticism and atheism. He emphasizes the argument from design. "When I see a watch whose hands mark the hours, I conclude that an intelligent being has arranged the springs of this machine so that its hands will mark the hours. Thus, when I see the springs of the human body, I conclude that an intelligent being has arranged these organs to be received and nourished for nine months in the womb; that the eyes are given to see, the hands to grasp, etc." [20] The harmonious adaption of the eye was an especially cogent argument, receiving its classic expression in the later *Natural Theology* of the Englishman Paley. By its side we may put the statement of the nineteenth-century German investigator of optics, Helmholtz, that had he been the Creator he would have been ashamed to have produced so faulty and inefficient an instrument for seeing. But such knowledge was not available for the eighteenth century.

The second argument, that from the necessity of a final cause, Voltaire gives as follows:

I exist, hence something exists. If something exists, then something must have existed from all eternity; for whatever is, either exists through itself, or has received its being from something else. If through itself, it exists of necessity, it has always existed of necessity, it is God; if it has received its being from something else, and that something from a third, that from which the last has received its being must of necessity be God.... Intelligence is not essential to matter, for a rock or grain do not think. Whence then have the particles of matter which think and feel received sensation and thought? it cannot be from themselves, since they think in spite of themselves; it cannot be from matter in general, since thought and sensation do not belong to the essence of matter: hence they must have received these gifts from the hands of a Supreme Being, intelligent, infinite, and the original cause of all beings.[21]

Voltaire recognizes difficulties in such reasoning, but he concludes, "In the opinion that there is a God, there are difficulties; but in the contrary opinion there are absurdities," [22] a statement that can well stand for the thought prevalent amongst most of the intelligent scientists of his day. It is noteworthy that Thomas Huxley, later the great popularizer of evolution, held precisely this view before the publication in 1859 of Darwin's epoch-making book.

So much for the existence of God; the rational theologians had more trouble with their other tenets of a future life and of a moral order in the world. On the whole, immortality seemed to them probable, as necessary for moral reasons: Voltaire says: "Without wanting to deceive men, it can be said we have as much reason to believe in as to deny the immortality of the being that thinks." [23] But it was clear that the Newtonian world here gave them no support; they were merely retaining an attractive traditional belief that could not be disproved, and the most they could say was that since the world was rationally ordered, it must be so ordered as to meet the needs of reasonable beings. With the question of the moral governance of the world, the age-old problem of evil, they did no better than their predecessors; here, too, they could only have faith that a rational order must be a moral order. Some, like Leibniz, took pages to prove that this is the best of all possible worlds, a belief sometimes called optimistic, but which strikes many as being the height of pessimism: if it is, God help the human race! Pope's ringing "Whatever is, is right," sounded even to the eighteenth century suspiciously like whistling to keep up one's courage. Others, like Voltaire, were too keenly aware of the injustices wreaked by nature and man upon man not to be revolted by such a faith; Voltaire's most famous tale, *Candide*, is one long ridicule of Leibniz' position. It was inevitable that since God came more and more to be identified with the mathematical order of nature, he should lose any moral quality whatsoever, once the consequences of this were consistently worked out. Spinoza, a century before, had done so, and arrived at precisely this conclusion, that nature has nothing to do with human standards of right and wrong; and it was probably just because the Deists realized that their logic would lead them here that they so hated and shunned Spinoza. Voltaire, who had a much deeper moral sense than most of the Deists, hesitated, and often seems to agree with the author of the *Ethics;* "It would be as absurd to say of God that he is just or unjust as to say, 'God is blue or square.'" [24] At best, "Moral evil is just as impossible to explain by materialism as by God." [25] But for the most part the Deists closed their eyes to such disagreeable logic, and tried their utmost to worship harmony and order as supremely good.

Skepticism and Atheism

Such were the arguments of the upholders of natural religion in favor of their creed. Obviously when the attack had once shifted to a questioning of this reasoning, it was not difficult to sweep it away by the same methods that the Deists had employed against revelation. This was done by two groups: the convinced skeptics and materialists, and the traditionalists who thought that by showing the inconsistencies of natural religion they could convince men that it was as shaky as revelation. This these latter did; but they did not find men adopting their corollary, that therefore both revelation and natural religion must be accepted on faith.

Two men especially in England tried to defend Christianity by questioning natural religion, William Law and Bishop Butler. Law wrote *The Case of Reason, or Natural Religion fairly stated*, as an answer to the "Deists' Bible" of Tindal. He was a famous mystic, and he declared that religion need not submit itself to any test of reason or morality. Its sole proof was that from prophecy and miracles. "It seems, therefore, to be too great and needless a concession which some learned divines make in this matter, when they grant that we must first examine the doctrines revealed by miracles, and see whether they contain in them anything absurd or unworthy of God, before we can receive the miracles as divine.... Miracles in such a state as this are the last resort; they determine for themselves and cannot be tried by anything further." [26] "A course of plain undeniable miracles attesting the truth of a revelation is the highest and utmost evidence of its coming from God, and not to be tried by our judgements about the reasonableness or necessity of its doctrines." [27] This is, of course, a complete denial that reason can establish any religious truth whatsoever; for those adopting such a position, the choice was clear: choose between abandoning religion or abandoning reason. The mystic Law took the latter course; the eighteenth-century rationalists naturally abandoned religion. The same choice had been unequivocally offered the French by the scholarly skeptic Pierre Bayle, at the end of the previous century. To the scientists and philosophers he said:

Do not try to understand mysteries; if you could understand them they would be mysteries no longer. Do not even try to lessen their apparent absurdity. Your reason here is utterly powerless; and who knows but that absurdity may be an essential ingredient of mystery? Believe as Christians; but as philosophers, abstain.

To the rationalizing theologians he said:

You are quite right in demanding that we should believe; but make this demand in the name of authority only, and do not be so imprudent as to try to justify your belief in the eyes of reason. God has willed it so, God has done so; therefore it is good and true, wisely done and wisely permitted. Do not venture any further. If you enter into detailed reasons for all this, you will never see the end of it, and, after a thousand disputes, you will be compelled to fall back upon your original reason, authority. In this matter, the best use to make of reason is not to reason. Moreover, if you do consent to discuss the point, you will be beaten.[28]

Bishops might prefer to abandon reason, but more and more men chose rather the other horn of the dilemma.

The other great apology for religion which really led to skepticism was the famous *Analogy of Religion, Natural and Revealed*, of Bishop Butler. He claimed that the much acclaimed natural religion was really just as irrational as the specific Christian revelation, and just as much a matter of faith. The religious tradition, in other words, was all of one piece, and had to be accepted or rejected as a unit; no halfway compromise was possible. In particular Butler pointed out that the actual course of nature, the handiwork of God and his divinely established moral order, is much more incomprehensible to the human reason than the so-called injustices of the Scriptures. "Upon supposition that God exercises a moral government over the world, the analogy of His natural government suggests and makes it credible that His moral government must be a scheme quite beyond our comprehension, and this affords a general answer against all objections against the justice and goodness of it."[29] Never, probably, was such a double-edged sword employed to defend the Christian faith. It seems not to have occurred to the good Bishop that if natural religion were, rationally considered, on no firmer a foundation than revelation, there might be men willing to reject them both.

Henry Dodwell, in 1742, published a work called *Christianity not founded on Argument*, the first turning of such reasoning to a definitely skeptical purpose. But the three great and conclusive summaries of all that could be said against natural religion, books which made it quite impossible for an intelligent mind any longer to attempt the apology for even rational religion by the customary arguments of the century, were written by Hume, by the Frenchman Holbach, and by the German Kant. Hume, in religious matters at least, was a typical skeptic: he refused to draw any positive conclusions from his destructive critique. Holbach was a convinced materialist and a good deal of a pantheist; while Kant, summing up the rationalistic attack on rational theology, also laid the foundations for the various attempts of the nineteenth century to establish religion upon feeling and intuition and some special religious sense — attempts which, however successful in themselves, at least have avoided the keen edge of the rationalistic sword.

We have already seen Hume's powerful criticism of the argument from miracles in support of revelation. His equally telling attack on natural religion is to be found in his *Essay on Providence and a Future State*, in 1748, and in his *Dialogues concerning Natural Religion*, written in 1751, but not published till after his death in 1779. Hume, it will be remembered, was the most consistent of the empiricists; that is, he eschewed all rationalistic argument from axiomatic principles, and brought to bear the test of experience upon every belief. His method was to ask how much of traditional religious beliefs could be actually derived from facts observable in nature; and his verdict was, very little. He pointed out that there is no justification for observing that the present world is imperfect, and from it assuming a perfect Creator who will yet produce a perfect world. We have no reason for concluding from a life in which rewards and punishments do not accord with human deserts, that there is another in which they do.

That the divinity may possibly be endowed with attributes which we have never seen exerted; may be governed by principles of action, which we cannot discover to be satisfied: all this will freely be allowed. But still this is mere possibility and hypothesis. We never can have reason to infer any attributes, or any principles of action in him, but so far as we know them to have been exerted and satisfied. "Are there any marks of a distributive justice in the world?" If you answer in the affirmative, I answer that, since justice here exerts itself, it is satisfied. If you reply in the negative, I conclude, that you have then no reason to ascribe justice, in our sense of it, to the gods. If you hold a medium between affirmation and negation, by saying, that the justice of the gods, at present, exerts itself in part, but not in its full extent: I answer, that you have no reason to give it any particular extent, but only so far as you see it at present exert itself.[30]

Having thus disposed of the rational basis for faith in the moral governance of the world, Hume went on, in his *Dialogues*, to show that there could not even be any argument for the existence of an all-wise and all-good Creator. There is no necessity of the universe having had a first cause. It is as easy to conceive of it as self-existent and eternal as to assume an external cause with those qualities. There is no analogy between an object in the world, like a watch, and the entire world; we have seen watches made, but not worlds. Order may be as natural as chaos, and hence harmony and universal law need no further reason for their existence, other than that we find them to obtain. From a finite world as effect we could assume at the most only a finite cause. If the universe did indeed have an author, he may have been an incompetent workman, or he may have long since died after completing his work, or he may have been a male and a female god, or a great number of gods. He may have been entirely good, or entirely evil, or both, or neither — probably the last.

Hume suggested doubts: he questioned the tenets of natural religion. Holbach categorically denied God, freedom, and immortality. In his repetitious *System of Nature* (1770), and especially in his keen and vigorous *Common Sense* (1772), an immensely popular work, he delivered what is probably the most telling attack ever directed against Christianity as a system of propositions offered for rational belief. Holbach was primarily a physicist who believed that the Newtonian science offered a complete explanation of the universe, requiring no further addition whatsoever. Thus he completely pulverized the argument from a First Cause:

We cannot go beyond this aphorism, *Matter acts because it exists, and exists to act.* If it be inquired how, or why matter exists? We answer, we know not; but reasoning by analogy of what we do not know, by what we do, we should be of opinion, it exists necessarily, or because it contains within itself a sufficient reason for its existence. In supposing it to be created or produced, by a being distinguished from it, or less known than itself, which it may be for anything we know to the contrary, we must still admit that this being is necessary, and includes a sufficient reason for his own existence. We have not then removed any of the difficulty, we have not thrown a clearer light on the subject, we have not advanced a single step; we have simply laid aside a being, of which we know some few of the properties, but of which we are still extremely ignorant, to have recourse to a power of which it is utterly impossible we can, as long as we are men, form any distinct idea; of which, notwithstanding it may be a truth, we cannot by any means we possess, demonstrate the existence.[31]

Thoroughgoing materialism seemed to him much more rational.

Is it not more natural and more intelligible to derive everything which exists from the bosom of matter, whose existence is demonstrated by every one of our senses, whose effects we each instant experience, which we see acting, moving, communicating motion and generating ceaselessly, than to attribute the formation of things to an unknown force, to a spiritual being which cannot develop from its nature what it is not itself, and which, by the spiritual essence attributed to it is incapable of doing anything and of setting anything in motion?[32]

On the argument from design Holbach was just as severe.

The worshippers of a God find especially in the order in the universe an invincible proof of the existence of an intelligent and wise being who governs it. But this order is only a sequence of necessary motions produced by causes and circumstances which are now favorable and now harmful to us: we approve the first and complain of the second.... To be surprised at seeing a certain order reigning in the world is to be surprised that the same causes produce constantly the same effects. To be shocked at seeing disorder, is to forget that when causes are altered or impeded in their action the effects can no longer be the same. To be astonished at the sight of an order in nature, is to be astonished that something can exist; it is to be surprised at one's own existence. What is order for one being is disorder for another. All beings that work evil find that everything is in order when they can with impunity disorder everything; they find on the contrary that everything is in disorder when they are hindered in the exercise of their evil tendencies.[33]

In a word, order and purpose is a man-made distinction that has no meaning in the world apart from man.

It will no doubt be argued, that as nature contains and produces intelligent beings, either she must be herself intelligent, or else she must be governed by an intelligent cause. We reply, intelligence is a faculty peculiar to living organisms; that is to say, to beings constituted and combined after a determinate manner; from whence results certain modes of action, which are designated under various names; according to the different effects which these beings produce: wine has not the properties called *wit* and *courage;* nevertheless, it is sometimes seen, that it communicates those qualities to men who are supposed to be in themselves entirely devoid of them. It cannot be said nature is intelligent after the manner of any of the beings she contains; but she can produce intelligent beings by assembling matter suitable to form the particular organization, from whose peculiar modes of action will result the faculty called intelligence. . . . In short, experience proves beyond a doubt that matter, which is regarded as inert and dead, assumes sensible action — intelligence — life — when it is combined after particular modes.[34]

Finally, as to the moral governance of the world and the righteousness of the power at work in the universe, Holbach says:

More than two thousand years ago the wise Epicurus said: "Either God wants to prevent evil, and cannot do it; or he can do it and does not want to; or he neither wishes to nor can do it, or he wishes to and can do it. If he has the desire without the power, he is impotent; if he can and has not the desire, he has a malice which we cannot attribute to him; if he has neither the power nor the desire, he is both impotent and evil, and consequently is not God; if he has the desire and the power, whence then comes evil, or why does he not prevent it?" For more than two thousand years the best minds have been waiting for a rational solution of these difficulties, and our doctors teach us that they will be removed only in a future life.[35]

It is perhaps worth remarking that Holbach combined with his atheism and materialism a singularly noble moral ideal of benevolence, justice, and humanity. To such men the discarding of traditional religion meant a liberation from superstition and the possibility of a genuinely enlightened and universal morality.

With Holbach, who represented in a frank way what most intelligent Frenchmen had by 1770 come to believe, we have arrived at a complete and thoroughgoing atheism and materialism. The course of our discussion has made it clear that the Age of Reason, starting with the religious assumptions natural in Newtonian science, was bound to develop just such a complete denial of every one of the tenets of traditional Christianity. A hundred years earlier Spinoza, saturated with Cartesian science, had laid down a similar and on the whole more profound system; but men had not in his day really assimilated the principles of the new science nor understood to what their logical working-out would lead. Hence it is no wonder that in Holbach's day Spinoza was discovered and came to exercise an all-powerful influence over many of the best intellects, especially in Germany. Most men, of course, were unwilling to follow Spinoza and Holbach to the bitter end; save in France, where the social policies of the Catholic Church and its alliance with the old régime and its abuses drove every intelligent man into fierce opposition, not only to the Catholic ecclesiastical system, but also to everything connected with it, to religion itself, and led Voltaire to hope to see "the last king throttled in the bowels of the last Jesuit," men still longed for a religious world-view, and tried to effect some kind of compromise with Newtonian science. But in France at least it seemed that for an intelligent man religion was absolutely dead. In 1798 a Deist started to address the Institute on his religious beliefs; there was a cry of anger from the assembled intellectuals, and one exclaimed, "I swear there is no God and I demand that his name be not pronounced in this place!" [36] The poor Deist had to retire, while the Institute debated whether God's name ought to be pronounced within its enlightened walls.

Everywhere it was recognized that religion had no rational basis whatever, and that the only way of escaping atheism and materialism lay in attacking the competency of reason and rational experience to reveal final truth. A revival of the personal religion of Paul and Augustine, finding its sanction, not in reason, but in the inner religious experience, had already assumed large dimensions in Germany, where it was known as Pietism, and in England, where it was known as Evangelicalism or Wesleyanism; and had in the latter country triumphed among the people in Methodism and the low church movement within the Anglican fold. This revival deliberately turned its back upon science and reason and clung to faith; and hence it had little influence upon the intellectual class. The latter group was first reached by the German philosopher Kant, who attempted to prove conclusively that reason and science were valid only within a certain field, and that outside this field faith — Kant called it "practical reason" — could still establish the tenets of natural religion, God, freedom, and immortality. Kant's arguments seemed epoch-making; more than any one intellectual factor they saved the day for religious belief, and made possible the religious revival of the first half of the nineteenth century. The new source of religious truth acclaimed by Kant lies beyond our immediate subject here; we shall return to it in considering nineteenth-century thought. Here we have only to note that Kant seemed to have disproved forever the possibility of a purely rational religion.

His demolition of rational theology was contained in his *Critique of Pure Reason*, published in 1781. He announces his program:

> There are only three possible ways of proving the existence of God by the speculative reason.... The first is the argument from design, the second the argument from a first cause, the third the ontological argument. There are no more, and there can be no more. I shall show that the reason can accomplish as little in the one way as in the other, and that it spreads its wings in vain in the effort to rise above the world of sense by the mere power of speculation.[37] I assert then that all the attempts at a mere speculative use of the reason in the field of theology are entirely fruitless and in their very nature null and void.[38]

His actual arguments do not differ greatly from those we have already seen employed by Hume and Holbach; but the inclusive system in which they were embedded seemed to make them even more irrefutable. While Deism and natural religion lingered on in some minds — Paley wrote in England in 1798, Robespierre was a convinced Deist during the Revolution, and German rational theologians taught into the nineteenth century — to the vast majority of intelligent minds interested in religion it seemed that the primary task, in view of the abandonment of a rational basis of the religious life, was to effect a reconstruction on some non-rational or superrational principle. But a consideration of these attempts we must postpone until the next book.

Thus the working-out of the principles of Nature and Reason, the cardinal ideals of the age that worshiped the Newtonian world-machine, when applied to the great Christian tradition, seemed wholly destructive, and the attempt to build a new scientific religion upon them completely failed. Multitudes, of course, were quite untouched by these lines of thought, just as they were quite impervious to the new scientific knowledge; but the thinking middle-class, to whom the future belonged, accepted them unreservedly, on the whole. When the reconstruction of the Christian tradition and its adaptation to the new intellectual world was undertaken, it was with the clear understanding that the eighteenth century had made the foundation of religion upon the principles of scientific reason henceforth impossible.

REFERENCES

1. Quoted in John Morley, *Diderot*, 72.
2. Voltaire, *Lettres Philosophiques*, Lettre 6.
3. William Paley, *Moral and Political Philosophy*, Bk. I, ch. 7.
4. Voltaire, *Éléments de la Philosophie de Newton*, ch. 6.
5. Locke, *Essay on Human Understanding*, Book IV, ch. 18, sec. 4.
6. Locke, *Reasonableness of Christianity*, 1696 ed., 202.
7. Matthew Tindal, *Christianity as Old as the Creation*, 18.
8. *Ibid.*, 272.
9. Locke, *Essay*, Bk. IV, ch. 17, sec. 23.
10. John Tillotson, *Works* (ed. 1857), II, 333.
11. Tillotson, *The Miracles Wrought in Confirmation of Christianity*, *Works*, III, 493.
12. Locke, *Essay*, Bk. IV, ch. 18, sec. 10.
13. Locke, *Discourse of Miracles*.
14. Samuel Clarke, *Boyle Lectures*, 1705, *A Discourse concerning the Unchangeable Obligations of Natural Religion, and the Truth and Certainty of the Christian Revelation*.
15. Tindal, *Christianity as Old as the Creation*, 63, 342 ff.
16. Diderot, *Letter to Damilaville*, 1766, in *Œuvres*, ed. Assézat et Tourneux, XIX, 477.
17. Voltaire, *Bolingbroke*.
18. Hume, *Enquiry concerning Human Understanding*, sec. 10.
19. Voltaire, *Éléments de la Philosophie de Newton*, ch. 1.
20. Voltaire, *Traité de Métaphysique*, ch. II.
21. *Ibid.*
22. *Ibid.*
23. Voltaire, *Homélie sur l'athéisme*.
24. Voltaire, *Traité de la Métaphysique*, ch. II.
25. *Ibid.*
26. William Law, *The Case of Reason*, 109.
27. *Ibid.*, 110.
28. Pierre Bayle, quoted in Lévy-Bruhl, *History of Modern Philosophy in France*, ch. IV.
29. Bishop Joseph Butler, *Analogy of Religion*, Pt. I, ch. 7.
30. Hume, *Enquiry concerning Human Understanding, Providence and a Future State*.
31. Holbach, *Système de la Nature*, ch. IV.
32. Holbach, *Le Bon-Sens*, sec. 22.
33. *Ibid.*, sec. 44.
34. Holbach, *Système de la Nature*, ch. V.
35. Holbach, *Le Bon-Sens*, sec. 57.
36. F. Picavet, *Les Idéologues*, 218.
37. Kant, *Kritik der reinen Vernunft*, *Werke*, Phil. Bibl. ed., I, 510.
38. *Ibid.*, 543.

SELECTED READING LISTS

General Works: A. C. McGiffert, *Protestant Thought before Kant*, chap. X (illuminating survey); *Rise of Modern Religious Ideas*, Part I. Leslie Stephen, *History of English Thought in the Eighteenth Century*. G. V. Lechler, *Ges. des englischen Deismus*; J. Tulloch, *Rational Theology in England in the*

Seventeenth Century; J. Leland, *A View of the Principal Deistical Writers* (by a hostile contemporary); O. Pfleiderer, *Ges. der Religionsphilosophie.* H. Höffding; Hettner, *Litteraturges. des* 18. *Jahrh.* J. M. Robertson, *Short History of Free Thought;* A. W. Benn, *History of English Rationalism in the Nineteenth Century;* Lecky, *Rationalism in Europe.* J. Texte, *Rousseau et les Origines du cosmopolitanisme littéraire.* K. R. Hagenbach, *German Rationalism;* W. Oncken, *Das Zeitalter Friedrichs des Grossen;* E. Cassirer, *Das Zeitalter der Aufklärung.* H. M. Morais, *Deism in 18th Cent. America;* G. A. Koch, *Republican Religion.* Foster, *Genetic History of New England Theology;* Cooke, *Unitarianism in America.* See also works of Faguet, Damiron, Morley, cited in preceding chapter.

Rise of Deism: Lord Herbert of Cherbury, *De Religione Gentilium, De Veritate.* R. Cudworth, *Intellectual System of the Universe;* J. Tillotson, *Works;* John Locke, *Reasonableness of Christianity, Essay,* Bk. IV; Samuel Clarke, *Discourse concerning the Unalterable Obligations of Natural Religion,* etc. (best example of rational supernaturalism); W. Wollaston, *Religion of Nature Delineated;* Anthony Collins, *Discourse of Free Thinking;* M. Tindal, *Christianity as Old as the Creation* (the "Deist's Bible"); J. Toland, *Christianity not Mysterious;* W. Paley, *Natural Theology.* Voltaire, *English Letters, Elements of Newton's Philosophy, Treatise on Metaphysics; Philosophical Dictionary.* Diderot, *Philosophical Thoughts,* Jourdain ed. Rousseau, *Émile,* Bk. IV, *Confession of Faith of a Savoyard Vicar.* Reimarus, *Wolfenbüttel Fragments,* ed. by Lessing; Lessing, *Eine Duplik, Das Testament Johannis, Nathan der Weise, Die Erziehung des Menschengeschlechts.*

The Attack on Natural Religion: William Law, *The Case of Reason;* Joseph Butler, *The Analogy of Religion;* conservative appeals to faith; E. K. Mossner, *Bishop Butler and the Age of Reason.* Henry Dodwell, *Christianity not founded on Argument.* David Hume, *Essay on Miracles, Of Providence and a Future State; Dialogues on Natural Religion; A Natural History of Religion.* Diderot, *Promenade of a Sceptic;* Holbach, *System of Nature, Common Sense* (issued as Jean Meslier, *Superstition in all Ages*). Immanuel Kant, *Critique of Pure Reason,* Müller ed., pp. 595–670; *Religion innerhalb der Grenzen der blossen Vernunft.*

CHAPTER XIII

THE SCIENCE OF MAN — THE SCIENCES OF HUMAN NATURE AND OF BUSINESS

THE CREATION OF THE SOCIAL SCIENCES

HAVING observed the operation of these conceptions of Newtonian science in their essentially destructive effects upon the religious tradition, let us turn to their working-out in the sciences of human nature and human society, where they indeed proved as incompatible with traditional beliefs, but did further succeed in building up a positive body of principles. Here we are in that field which is the chief glory of the eighteenth century. Natural science had been virtually outlined, in the form it was to retain for almost two hundred years, in the preceding age; and eighteenth-century religious ideas mark simply a stage in the course of religious thought, the next age attempting reconstruction on entirely different principles. It is in the building up of a science of man, perhaps even more in the very vision of the possibilities and necessity of such a science, that the eighteenth century can rest its soundest claim to important achievement. In this field it laid the foundations of most of the beliefs accepted up to the present generation by all save a comparatively small number of thinkers, who have in turn modified these conceptions of the Age of Reason in accordance with further developments in biological and psychological science. Its motto can stand, in the words of Buffon, "Man must take his place in the class of animals."[1]

We may hope to gain at least two things in studying this science of man. In the first place, we can understand how the whole conception of human and social sciences, under the influence of the success of the natural sciences, came to occupy the important place it has ever since held in the minds of thoughtful men. This is the permanent achievement of the eighteenth century. In the second place, we can reach an understanding of why the particular methods and principles and content of these new sciences assumed the form that they did; and the importance of this lies in the fact that in this field the issue between eighteenth-century and present-day human science is still extremely live and vital. On the whole, those in positions of authority still hold to the political and moral and economic principles worked out in the eighteenth century, under the reign of strictly Newtonian conceptions and methods, and in response to the strictly eighteenth-century social needs of an overwhelmingly agricultural and commercial society. But to-day we no longer live in the Newtonian world nor in an agricultural and commercial society: we have discovered biology and psychology, and we have felt the full effects of the Industrial Revolution. Our fundamental scientific conceptions and our social needs have both been profoundly altered, and there is good reason for believing that principles developed in the eighteenth century and highly efficacious under those conditions are no longer adequate to meet our modern problems. At present the newer social ideas are pitted against the older principles. Notions that were profoundly radical and even revolutionary then have been adopted by apologists for both the bad and the good in the present established social order; and in order to understand present controversies and their meaning it seems exceedingly important to examine the origin and the value in their own day of the older conceptions. This investigation will occupy the remaining chapters of Book III.

The eighteenth-century thinkers, combining at last the two strains of the humanistic emphasis upon the dignity and worth of man's life upon this earth, and of the scientific emphasis upon universal law and a harmonious causal order in every part of nature, created a science of human nature in the individual and in society. Carrying on their work as they did profoundly influenced by the reigning Newtonian ideal of science and of scientific method, they could hardly have failed to produce a science that resembled, as closely as their new subject-matter would let them — indeed, probably far too closely — the ideal and the method of mathematical physics. They went so far as to claim to have discovered a veritable mental and social physics. Practically, these new sciences exerted a deep influence upon the transformation of the old society into an order more closely approaching the ideals of the triumphant commercial middle classes; their greatest intrinsic value seems clearly to have been their fitness for this destructive work. Theoretically and constructively, their effect has not been so happy. Inadequate and even false ideas can tear down what is clearly no longer useful; they cannot build up a substitute. It has taken most men a century to recognize this fact.

The Deductive, Mechanical Method

It has already been remarked that the methods employed in erecting the new science of man lagged somewhat behind the most advanced scientific methods of the day. Whereas the latter were becoming increasingly experimental, the former remained, up until the great social revolutions of the end of the century, predominantly mathematical and deductive. It was hoped that, just as in physics, an analysis of a few simple cases would reveal fundamental axiomatic principles from which a whole science of human society could be developed deductively. It was exactly such a science that was used by Locke to justify the English Whig revolution of 1689, by French thinkers to justify a revolution in France, by political economists to justify the demands of the commercial classes for freedom from governmental interference, and that formed the basis of the political and economic principles incorporated in the American constitution, in the French constitutions of the revolutionary era, and in the British reforms of 1820 to 1867. Following the example of physics, men sought first to analyze the nature of the individual human being, and then to apply the principles there discovered to the problems of economic, moral, and political life. Hence the new science of man included two branches. There was first the fundamental investigation of human nature, which was represented by a long series of works upon the knowledge and the motives of the individual man: Locke's *Enquiry concerning Human Understanding* (1690), which remained the point of departure, Berkeley's *Principles of Human Knowledge* (1710), Hume's *Treatise of Human Nature* (1739), and his *Inquiries concerning the Human Understanding* (1749) and *concerning the Principles of Morals* (1751), Hartley's *Observations on Man* (1749), Condillac's *Essay on the Origin of Human Knowledge* (1746) and his *Treatise of Sensations* (1754), Helvetius' *On the Mind* (1758) and *On Man* (1772), and Bentham's *Principles of Morals and Legislation* (1780). Secondly, there was a host of works applying these principles to the particular social sciences.

With the single exception of the works of Montesquieu, the method employed in all these books was essentially deductive and "geometrical," or, more properly speaking, mechanical. The actual attempt to derive some quantitative principle was not made except by Bentham, who developed what he called a "calculus of pleasures and pains"; but the spirit was none the less that of the reigning natural science. Voltaire well expresses this ideal of method in speaking of Locke: "There was perhaps never a mind wiser and more methodical, or a logician more exact than Locke; and yet he was not a great mathematician. He could never submit to the fatigue of calculation nor to the dryness of mathematical truths, which at first present no sensations to the mind; and no one has proved better than he that one can have the geometrical spirit without the aid of geometry." [2] This means that he analyzed human nature into what seemed to him its component elements, just as Galileo had analyzed the nature of motion, and that from these elements he sought to build up by reasoning an adequate conception of the society demanded by such a being. In this endeavor he was followed by all the thinkers above mentioned. Superficially it seemed that this school had succeeded in arriving at a mechanistic psychology, and from it deriving principles that could serve as the axioms of the social sciences. Actually, the gulf between psychology, and politics and economics, was pretty wide, and for the most part it looks suspiciously as though thinkers had arrived at certain social axioms, like the equality of all men, that seemed obvious and reasonable, and had sought to find some basis for them in a further analysis of human nature. In other words, these axioms, in every case principles that seemed to be demanded by the interests of the middle class, were primary, and the science of human nature upon which they were ostensibly founded seems to have been developed largely as an apologetic for them.

THE SCIENCE OF HUMAN NATURE

The seventeenth-century father of this type of psychological analysis was the materialist and social philosopher Thomas Hobbes. To him first occurred in modern times the notion that man is an integral part of the natural order, not only his body — Descartes and the physiologists of his school had developed this side — but his entire mental and conscious life as well. He first maintained that it is possible to hope for a science of human nature in the rigorous sense of a human physics. Its source is to be observation and analysis of the processes of thought within one's own mind — introspection. "Whosoever looketh into himself and considereth what he doth when he does think, opine, reason, hope, fear, etc., and upon what grounds; he shall thereby read and know, what are the thoughts and passions of all other men, upon the like occasions." [3] The laws derived from such an analysis are to be employed in depicting the society that will satisfy the needs of such a being — an absolute monarchy, as we have seen.

"Concerning the thoughts of man, I will consider them first singly, and afterwards in trayne, or dependence upon one another. ... The original of them all is what we call sense; (For there is no conception in a man's mind, which hath not at first, totally or by parts, been begotten upon the organs of sense.) The rest are derived from that original." [4] Hobbes and his successors were led to this rather remarkable step of finding in sensation the fundamental element of mental life largely because they were good Cartesian scientists: they were certain that matter in motion was the only reality in the world outside man's mind, and that this reality could only affect man through physical contact with his sense-organs. Hence in building up a psychological atomism of compounds formed from simple atomistic components, they naturally hit upon sensations as these elements. We now know that sensations are neither simple, nor elements, nor primary, and prefer to build up from elements that are biological, like reflex-arcs, rather than from those that are the product of a combined logical and physical analysis into sensation-qualities; Hobbes' materialism was mechanical, whereas ours is biological. But Hobbes illustrates how his type of psychological atomism was natural within the Newtonian world.

As all knowledge derives from sensations, it is necessary to formulate the laws by which these units are combined to form adequate pictures and trains of reasoning. A sensation, lingering on by the mechanical law of inertia, becomes an image in the "imagination" or memory. "Imagination is nothing but decaying sense." [5] Such images follow each other in the mind in the order in which they were originally impressed upon the senses.

"We have no transition from one imagination to another, whereof we never had the like before in our senses." [6] When the first of a train of such images arises, the others originally associated with it follow by force of cohesion; thus the image of an apple will call up that of the tree, etc. This principle later received the name of "association by contiguity." But

this trayne of thoughts, or mental discourse, is of two sorts. The first is unguided, without design, and inconstant ... in which case the thoughts are said to wander, and seem impertinent one to another, as in a dream. ... The second is more constant, as being regulated by some desire and design. ... From desire ariseth the thought of some means we have seen produce the like of that which we aim at; and from the thought of that, the thought of means to that means; and so continually, until we come to some beginning within our own power.[7]

Such a regulated chain of images is intelligent thought. Speech is the attaching of names as signs to these images, and reasoning is the addition or subtracting of names.

By this it appears that reason is not, as sense and memory, born with us; nor gotten by experience only, as prudence is; but attained by industry; first in apt imposing of names, and secondly in getting a good and orderly method in proceeding from the elements, which are names, to assertions made by connection of one of them to another, ... till we come to a knowledge of all the consequences of names appertaining to the subject in hand; and that is it, men call science. ... Science is the knowledge of consequences, and dependence of one fact upon another: by which, out of that we can presently do, we know how to do something else when we will, or the like, another time.[8]

Thus Hobbes, in his *Leviathan*, in 1651, had already sketched the main outlines of the science of human nature which was to remain unquestioned for over two centuries. Its fundamental principle was sensationalism, that all knowledge and all mental life starts from the reception of sensations from without; its laws were those of the association of these elements into various more complex groups. Throughout, the analogy with Newtonian physics was complete. Locke was the man who primarily popularized and developed the sensationalism, Hartley he who most elaborately formulated the laws of association. In a famous figure Locke compared the mind to a *tabula rasa*, a completely blank tablet.

Let us then suppose the mind to be, as we say, white paper, void of

all characters, without any ideas: — how comes it to be furnished?...
To this I answer, in one word, from EXPERIENCE. In that all our knowledge is founded; and from that it ultimately derives itself. Our observation employed either about external sensible objects, or about the internal operations of our minds perceived and reflected on by ourselves, is that which supplies our understandings with all the *materials* of thinking. These two are the fountains of knowledge, from whence all the ideas we have, or can naturally have, do spring.[9]

It was such a conception that Locke stood for to the eighteenth century; and many were the attempts made to develop explicitly the laws by which these sensations were combined to form the adult mind, the memory, thought, personality, character, and sentiments of the mature man. To these processes of combination Locke himself gave the name of "reflection," proclaiming that sensation and reflection are the only originals from whence all our ideas take their beginnings. Hume and Hartley and Condillac attempted to analyze more critically the process of reflection, that is, the laws of the association of ideas. Hume writes:

It is evident that there is a principle of connection between the different thoughts or ideas of the mind, and that, in their appearance to the memory or imagination, they introduce each other with a certain degree of method and regularity.... Though it be too obvious to escape observation, that different ideas are connected together; I do not find that any philosopher has attempted to enumerate or class all the principles of association; a subject, however, that seems worthy of curiosity. To me, there appear to be only three principles of connection among ideas, namely, *Resemblance, Contiguity* in time or place, and *Cause* or *Effect*.[10]

Further analysis practically reduced them to the single principle of contiguity or "custom."

David Hartley, however, stands as the real founder of the associationist psychology; its most extended development is to be found in James Mill's later *Analysis of the Human Mind* (1829). Hartley believed that his principle of association would do for human nature as much as Newton's gravitation had done for astronomy. He sought to describe "the influence of association over our opinions and affections, and its use in explaining those things in an accurate and precise way, which are commonly referred to the power of habit and custom, in a general and indeterminate one."[11] His method is of course mathematical.

The proper method of philosophizing seems to be, to discover and establish the general laws of action, affecting the subject under consideration, from certain select, well-defined, and well-attested phenomena, and then to explain and predict the other phenomena by these laws. This is the method of analysis and synthesis recommended and followed by Sir Isaac Newton.[12]

He laid down the propositions:

Sensations, by being often repeated, leave certain vestiges, types, or images, of themselves, which may be called, Simple Ideas of Sensation.[13] Sensory vibrations, by being often repeated, beget, in the medullary substance of the brain, a disposition to diminutive vibrations.[14] Any sensations, A, B, C, etc., by being associated with one another a sufficient number of times, get such a power over the corresponding ideas, a, b, c, etc., that any one of the sensations A, when impressed alone, shall be able to excite in the mind b, c, etc., the ideas of the rest. Simple ideas will run into complex ones, by means of association.[15]

The further details of Hartley's system we can here pass over; what does interest us is the way in which he gets from his science of human nature to the principles of morals and politics.

It is of the utmost consequence to morality and religion, that the affections and passions should be analyzed into their simple compounding parts, by reversing the steps of the associations which concur to form them. For thus we learn how to cherish and improve good ones, check and root out such as are mischievous and immoral, and how to suit our manner of life, in some tolerable measure, to our intellectual and religious wants. And as this holds, in respect of persons of all ages, so it is particularly true, and worthy of consideration, in respect of children and youth. If beings of the same nature, but whose affections and passions are, at present, in different proportions to each other, be exposed for an indefinite time to the same impressions and associations, all their particular differences will, at last, be overruled, and they will become perfectly similar, or even equal. They may also be made perfectly similar, in a finite time, by a proper adjustment of the impressions and associations.[16]

The Omnipotence of Environment

Here we have the connecting link: since all that men are comes from experience, all present differences and inequalities must be due to differences in environment, and men must *at birth* be exactly equal. Such was the corollary that men drew from Locke's sensationalism, the necessary foundation for the democratic faith that men are born equal and that education alone is needed to perfect human life and to bring into being the ideal democratic society. No wonder that the men of the eighteenth century were intensely hopeful of the future: all that is bad is due to a faulty education and a faulty social environment. Once change these, and there is no limit to the possibilities of human nature. Fourier was only expressing the universal optimism in an extreme form when he looked forward to seeing, with the proper changes in social organization, a French nation of thirty million scientists as great as Newton and thirty million poets as great as Shakespeare! Since so much was hoped from a change in environment, and since this hope seemed firmly grounded in the new science of human nature, it is easy to see why that science should have provided so powerful an incentive, on the one hand, to social reform and revolution, and on the other why the middle class, desiring certain definite changes, should have appealed to it as a convincing support.

All thinkers drew such corollaries from Locke and Hartley, to some extent, but the French naturally went further than the English, since French conditions were more unfavorable for the middle class. Hence it is easy to see why the French first developed the democratic ideas of human equality. The connection between Locke and the democratic faith — a connection Locke himself totally failed to notice — becomes most explicit in the writings of Helvetius. Helvetius was one of the group gathered about Diderot who hoped that a wise king, by instituting the proper reforms in his dominions, especially in education, could bring about a millennium of sagacious and noble citizens. Above all he wanted to prove that the reformer can reform, that he can get at men from outside and remake them into his own image. Locke's science of human nature seemed to offer a basis for this hope. Hence he held to an absolute sensationalism, maintaining that all men's ideas and beliefs come from the senses alone. Locke's further fountain of "reflection" seemed to him to introduce some inaccessible factor within the mind of each man; so he, with his contemporaries, sought to explain this reflection as but the development of sensation. Judgment itself is but a physical sensation, he thought, a perception of the agreement or disagreement of our ideas. Since the statesman's task is easiest if he can assume that men act always intelligently, from motives of predictable and controllable self-interest, Helvetius, with his century, assumed that self-interest is the only human motive. The task of the statesman is then simple: he has only to provide the proper rewards and punishments by law, and he can get men to do anything he deems good.

This faith in legislative reform Helvetius expressed in numerous aphorisms. "The vices of a people are rooted in its laws; there one must dig if he would unearth the roots of its vices." "'Tis the good law-maker who makes the good citizen." "'Tis only by good laws that you can make virtuous men." [17] This side of his gospel was widely popularized, in a form we shall examine in due time, by his disciple the English legislative reformer Jeremy Bentham; its dependence on Locke's principles is obvious. But Helvetius went even further. His faith in education led him to maintain the equality and similarity of all men at birth, and to disregard entirely any hereditary causes of individual differences.

Two opinions to-day divide scientists on this subject. One group says, The mind is the effect of a certain kind of temperament and internal organization; but no one has yet been able by any observations to determine the kind of organ, temperament, or nurture that produces the mind. This vague assertion, destitute of proofs, is reduced to this statement, The mind is the effect of an unknown cause or an occult quality, to which I give the name of temperament or organization. Quintillian, Locke, and I myself, say, The inequality of minds is the effect of a known cause, and this cause is the difference of education.[18]

Who can be sure that differences of education do not produce the differences we find between minds; that men are not like those trees of the same species whose seed, indestructible and absolutely the same, never being sown in exactly the same soil, nor exposed to precisely the same winds, or the same sun, or the same rain, must necessarily in developing assume an infinity of different forms? [19]

For Helvetius this seemed a creed of golden promise.

If I could demonstrate that man is indeed but the product of his education, I should undoubtedly have revealed a great truth to the nations. They would then know that they hold within their own hands the instrument of their greatness and their happiness, and that to be happy and powerful is only a matter of perfecting the science of education.[20]

My general conclusion is then that genius is common, and the circumstances fitted to develop it very rare. If we can compare the profane with the sacred, we can say that in this matter many are called and few are chosen.... Thus the whole art of education consists in placing young people in a set of circumstances fit to develop in them the germs of intelligence and virtue.... I feel how strongly the existing opinion that genius and virtue are pure gifts of nature is opposed to the progress of science and education, and favors laziness and neglect.[21]

Helvetius' claims were so extreme that they were probably quite erroneous; a century of popular education and "reform" has left us somewhat disillusioned. Yet his emphasis was needed, and was most valuable; and it is still far preferable to the contrary gospel that some cynical minds have drawn from our present-day intelligence tests, if we take it as a working hypothesis rather than as a statement of absolute fact. Helvetius and his contemporaries developed the doctrine of the equality of men as a support for the reforming benevolent despot: he concludes: "These principles, adopted by an enlightened and benevolent prince, could become the germ of a new legislation, more suited to the happiness of men." [22] He dedicated his second work to Catherine II of Russia, who toyed with such ideas and called Diderot to St. Petersburg to institute the new order. But they obviously lent themselves as readily to the democratic faith, when supported by the further conviction of civil and moral equality; and they formed, with the ideas of Rousseau, the basis of those ringing statements in the later revolutionary documents. Jefferson was under their influence when he wrote into the American Declaration of Independence the statement: "We hold these truths to be self-evident, That all men are *created* equal"; and so were the authors of the French Declaration of the Rights of Man: "All men are *born* free and equal."

THE SCIENCE OF SOCIETY

Such were the consequences drawn directly from the new science of human nature initiated by Hobbes and Locke. All men are at birth equal. They build up their knowledge and beliefs from sense-experience, a process entirely dependent upon the environment in which they live. They act always from the single motive, what they assume to be to their own interest. In the particular fields of human activity, like business, government, and morals, these principles are to be supplemented by further axioms peculiar to them, and with these as a basis it is possible to build up complete and deductive social sciences, on the model of physics. To this task a host of thinkers set themselves, always profoundly influenced by the desire to criticize existing institutions in the light of the demands of the middle class for freedom and control, always starting from a quite inadequate knowledge of the complexity of human society, always convinced that a few simple truths could be discovered and from them a complete science developed, always arriving at a social theory able to break down traditional beliefs but incapable of substituting a more comprehensive system. They all had the all-important *idea* of a social science, but they none of them possessed the method nor the facts which we have learned are essential to such an undertaking. Hence the social sciences that grew up in the eighteenth century, admirable critical instruments as they were, developed into complete and stereotyped systems, as woefully inadequate to deal with the new problems of the industrial age as the earlier sketch of Cartesian physics had proved to be in describing the actual complexities of nature. They have since had to be entirely revised in the light of improved biological and psychological knowledge, while their forms, which originally gave the commercial middle class what they wanted, have been largely retained by those classes to justify their continued dominance of modern society. They are a cardinal example of notions and ideals that, developed to suit a particular situation, and lingering on when that situation has altered, have become obstacles to further progress.

To these generalizations there exists one outstanding exception. Better perhaps than any other eighteenth-century political thinker, the works of Montesquieu have stood the test of time, and they have done so largely because he alone saw farther than the typical eighteenth-century ideal and method of a social physics. He almost alone was so struck by the conception of a unified science of human society, and by the enormous amount of investigation necessary before such a science could hope to take form, that he spent more time in amassing facts than in formulating some systematic scheme in support of one or another program of action. He alone realized that human societies are exceedingly complex, and that what suits one set of conditions will by no means satisfy another. He alone was impressed by the necessity of scholarly historical investigation to suggest real principles; others went to the past to select instances confirming their own preconceptions, when they bothered to go at all. In consequence, his concrete suggestions were specific and limited in scope, like his advocacy of a system of governmental checks and balances, or his disapproval of slavery; and his great work, *The Spirit of the Laws*, stood not so much for any definite political creed — though he was on the whole a moderate constitutionalist — as for an inexhaustible mine of information and suggestions that practical legislators could consider. Hence, although the great clarion call of revolt in France was sounded by Rousseau, when the deputies of the different estates had journeyed to Versailles and the pressing problem was what immediate measures to take, it was to Montesquieu that men of all parties turned for practical help and knowledge.

Montesquieu was a lawyer with the temperament, not of a physicist, but of a naturalist like Linnæus or Buffon. He loved the rich variegation of human institutions, and delighted to add new specimens to his collection; he hated uniformity and universality — a rank heresy in his day. He early set about the preparation of material for a great work on human society, a task to which he devoted his life. After twenty years of accumulating facts, he made a selection which he published in 1748. *The Spirit of the Laws* is in no sense systematic, nor would it have been had he postponed it a hundred years. It is a mine of information, organized about a method of inquiry, a critical interpretation of customs and laws. Montesquieu had visited every land of Europe, and had read all he could find of past institutions; he was particularly fascinated by Rome, which seemed to offer a complete specimen of the rise and fall of a society. Out of such materials he made six hundred fascinating and intelligent chapters.

It is Montesquieu's conception of a science of society, and his method, that are here significant; we shall return later to some of his specific suggestions. "I first examined men," he writes, "and I believed that in their infinite diversity of laws and customs they were not conducted solely by their caprice and fancy." [23] Underlying all particular laws, he sought the reason of laws, the universal laws governing positive legislation. Where Helvetius and Bentham started with men's desires, their self-interest, he preferred to seek rather, in a scientific and objective spirit, the natural conditions of man's well-being. What makes them here desire one thing, and there another? here find satisfaction in one institution, and there in another? He did not discover the answer himself: the geographical conditions, particularly climate, which he especially emphasized, were all too simple. But he did lay the foundations for an exceedingly fruitful nineteenth-century investigation of comparative jurisprudence, morals, and sociology. Nor, though he sought always the natural causes for varying institutions and ideals, did he assume a purely theoretical attitude; he did not believe in a rigorous determinism. "A region is monarchist, not a man; a zone is republican, not a man."[24] But "bad lawgivers are those who favor the vices of their climate, and good ones are those who oppose them."[25] If the physical causes produce evil, then moral causes are to be directed against them. Such social control, however, can operate only within limits, and any attempt at reform must first determine those limits, that is, the particular needs of any group that must in some way be satisfied. By birth, training, and temperament a moderate, who could sympathize with the appeal of every program while recognizing its inadequacy, he naturally found much to admire in the British Constitution; just such a slow growth, developed by the genius of the English race, he regarded as the only possible type of governmental progress. But he did not wish to import it into France; there he inclined on the whole to favor a development of the medieval "Gothic government" which answered the needs of the French people. His book remained a landmark to which disillusioned radicals returned again and again; and its value lay, not in any originality of analysis, nor of observation, but in its temper of mind, its attitude, its method, its fundamental idea of a social science rather than in the carrying out of that idea, from which he somewhat shrank. He is distinguished, like the James Bryce of later date, not by any acute solutions for problems, but by a kind of inspired common sense that contrasts pleasantly with the doctrinaire spirit of most of his contemporaries.

Political Economy

But his immediate successors did not develop the social sciences along such lines: they were more ambitious and less disinterested. We shall examine their systems of business, of politics, and of moral ideals; and we shall start with business, although actually the science of political economy was the last to receive formulation, because it expresses best the demands and the ideals of the new commercial class whose assumption of power was the underlying cause of most of the social changes of the century.

We have seen how the rise of a money economy, with its attendant expansion of capitalism and commerce and manufactures, broke down the medieval economic ideals, and resulted, in the seventeenth century, in the popularity of the economic theory of mercantilism. This substituted national regulation of trade for the earlier control by the city guilds. Merchants and craftsmen still demanded governmental protection and aid against unscrupulous competitors at home and against merchants of other nations. By the middle of the eighteenth century the merchant and manufacturing class had so increased in power that it felt strong enough to stand by itself, and the regulation imposed by the government, in the restrictions it placed both on commerce through tariffs and navigation acts and on the processes of manufacture, grew increasingly irksome. Hence from the middle classes in the economically developed nations like France and England and Holland there came a growing demand for freedom from interference, together with strong protection of the rights of property and contract, so essential to business life. This dual demand for protection in fundamentals and freedom in all else is the controlling principle in the development of the science of political economy. Ostensibly a disinterested attempt at a social physics of wealth, it was really a systematic rationalization of the demands for greater freedom to make money, which borrowed what it needed from the new natural and human sciences.

Two stages are to be distinguished in the development of the ideas of this group, collectively known as the "classic economic liberals." The first deals essentially with the problems confronting men in trade and agriculture; it originated in France with the Physiocrats, and was then adapted with great originality by Adam Smith to the English situation. The industrial revolution had not advanced, even in England, sufficiently to color men's conceptions, and political economy to the end of the century was essentially commercial, offering a creed of promise to the merchant class and through them to the whole nation. The very title of Adam Smith's work, *The Wealth of Nations* (1776), indicates this spirit. But when the mushroom growth of the factory system and the mill towns had created their horrible conditions, manufacturers applied the same principles to the carrying-on of industry, and during this period, political economy laid off its earlier rosy hues and became the "dismal science," essentially a justification for the supremacy of profit-seeking and for the continuance of poverty. The turning-point is marked by Malthus' gloomy predictions about the growth of population, and by the "iron laws" of Ricardo. However satisfactory political economy had been in dealing with commercial problems, in the face of industrial conditions it had no remedy or hope to offer, and the very fact that it had developed as a strict science seemed now to make its dreary conclusions inevitable. This is the clearest example of the inadequacy of eighteenth-century social science and its methods and assumptions. Yet the ideas formulated by these "liberals" have remained with little change to the present day, stifling most attempts to develop something better.

Social Physics and Laisser-Faire

The Physiocrats, of whom Dr. Quesnay and Dupont de Nemours were the chief theoretical and Turgot the chief practical exponents, looking upon the contrast between the confusion of human society and the harmonious order of nature, believed it possible to arrive at a natural science of the production of wealth. Discover nature's rational laws, they said, and abandon all of man's foolish interference. Their very name indicates that they shared the Newtonian belief in the "rule of nature."

All social facts are linked together in the bonds of eternal, immutable, ineluctable, and inevitable laws, which individuals and governments would obey if they were once made known to them.[26]

The task of economic science is to discover and proclaim these laws.

These laws are the rules of justice, of morality, of conduct, useful to all and to each. Neither men nor governments *make* them nor can *make* them. They recognize them as conforming to the supreme reason which governs the universe; they declare them; they present them to the obedience of good men, even to the conscience of the wicked.... These laws are irrevocable, they pertain to the essence of men and things; they are the expression of the will of God; and the more one reflects, the more one reveres them.[27] The sovereign authority is not instituted to *make laws;* for *laws are completely made* by the hand of him who created *rights* and *duties.*[28]

What are these necessary laws of human society? They are simple; they are axiomatic; they are three: Property, Security, and Liberty.

The social laws established by the Supreme Being prescribe only the preservation of the right of property, and of that liberty which is inseparable from it. The ordinances of sovereigns which we call positive laws, can be only *acts declaratory of these essential laws of the social order.* If the ordinances of sovereigns were contradictory to the laws of the social order, if they prohibited the respect of property, if they commanded men to burn crops, if they prescribed the sacrifice of little children, they would not be *laws*, they would be insane acts obligatory upon no one. Thus there is a natural judge, a court of final appeal, for the ordinances of sovereigns themselves, and this judge is the evidence of their conformity or their opposition to the natural laws of the social order.[29]

The middle class could hardly have used stronger language to say to the king, Hands Off!

For the Physiocrats the function of government was to be very simple: it was to secure and enforce the two natural rights of property and liberty, and little else. Above all, it should refrain from interfering in business, which should be left exclusively to business men. It should trust their enlightened self-interest; they are the best judges of how to make money, not stupid officials. It should abolish all mercantilistic restrictions on manufacturing, and, above all, all tariffs. Indeed, said Quesnay, "The most useful work any legislative body can do is to abolish useless laws." [30] Hands off! *Laissez-faire!* This motto should be followed to the utmost. Nature — expressing herself through business competition — should be left to her natural harmonious functioning. The State should become, in a famous phrase, merely a "passive policeman," and should interfere only when called by the business man. Still, it should be a policeman; and so fearful were the Physiocrats of attacks upon their right of property that they demanded a strong absolute monarch, combining executive and legislative powers in his single person. Lest he wax tyrannical, and appropriate too much property, laws should be interpreted by an independent body of magistrates, who should judge all positive laws by their conformity to the natural order, physiocratic textbooks in hand. Lest even these be corrupted, they should be in turn restrained by an educated public opinion—educated primarily in political economy.

Hence the Physiocrats wanted the government, when not protecting private property, to promote universal education, and they had no objection to its building public works, good roads and canals — they were useful to business.

Adam Smith and Commerce

Were this ideal realized, and were men granted complete economic freedom to follow their own interests, the Physiocrats believed the hand of God that keeps the planets in their courses could not fail to bring prosperity to men. This faith was shared by Adam Smith. Since France was primarily an agricultural nation, the Physiocrats naturally exalted that calling, making it the source of all wealth; and they decried all indirect taxation, demanding a single tax on land. But England, though largely agricultural, had a much stronger commercial class, and Adam Smith's theories differed from those of his masters chiefly in emphasizing commerce. He was, moreover, less mechanically deductive and more of an observer than the Frenchmen; though his followers soon purified political economy of these disturbing traits. He shared their optimistic faith in a divine natural order, in enlightened self-interest, in the function of government, in the natural rights of property and liberty, in free-trade, in the abolition of mercantilism, in economic freedom, free competition, and *laisser-faire*. He laid much more emphasis on trade, believing that labor and not land was the source of wealth; and he preferred a tax on incomes to a tax on land. He was aware of the industrial revolution, and hoped for a great increase of production from the division of labor; though in industry he remained the theorist of the domestic rather than the factory system.

Adam Smith himself seems to have sympathized more with the farmers and the workingmen than with traders and manufacturers. Of the latter, important as they are, he cannot help being suspicious. "Their interest is never exactly the same with that of the public," [31] they having "generally an interest to deceive and even to oppress the public, and who accordingly have, on many occasions, both deceived and oppressed them." [32] High wages are admirable.

The liberal reward of labor, therefore, as it is the effect of increasing wealth, so it is the cause of increasing population. To complain of it is to lament over the necessary effect and cause of the greatest public prosperity.... What improves the circumstances of the greater part can never be regarded as an inconveniency to the whole. No society can surely be flourishing and happy, of which the far greater part of the members are poor and miserable. It is but equity, besides, that they who feed, clothe, and lodge the whole body of the people, should have such a share of the produce of their own labor as to be themselves tolerably well fed, clothed, and lodged.[33]

High profits, however, are in a different pass.

Our merchants and master-manufacturers complain much of the bad effects of high wages in raising the price, and thereby lessening the sale of their goods, both at home and abroad. They say nothing concerning the bad effects of high profits. They are silent with regard to the pernicious effects of their own gains. They complain only of those of other people.[34]

He clearly sees the economic power of the masters.

It is not difficult to foresee which of the two parties must, on all ordinary occasions, have the advantage in the dispute, and force the other into a compliance with their terms. The masters, being fewer in number, can combine much more easily; and the law, besides, authorizes, or at least does not prohibit their combinations, while it prohibits those of the workmen.... In all such disputes the masters can hold out much longer.... The workmen, accordingly, very seldom derive any advantage from their combinations, which, partly from the interposition of the civil magistrate, partly from the superior steadiness of the masters, partly from the necessity which the greater part of the workmen are under of submitting for the sake of present subsistence, generally end in nothing, but the punishment or ruin of the ringleaders.[35]

The masters control Parliament:

Whenever the legislature attempts to regulate the differences between masters and their workmen, its counsellors are always the masters. When the regulation, therefore, is in favor of the workmen, it is always just and equitable; but it is sometimes otherwise when in favor of the masters.[36]

Such misplaced sympathies were indicative of a backward look; they were not shared by the economists of triumphant industry. Adam Smith's views on workmen were conveniently forgotten, and he came to stand primarily for *laisser-faire* and free trade.

All systems either of preference or restraint being thus completely taken away, the obvious and simple system of natural liberty establishes itself of its own accord. Every man, as long as he does not violate the laws of justice, is left perfectly free to pursue his own interest his own way, and to bring both his industry and capital into competition with those of any other man, or order of men. The sovereign is completely discharged from a duty, in the attempting to perform which he must always be exposed to innumerable delusions, and for the proper performance of which no human wisdom or knowledge could ever be sufficient; the duty of superintending the industry of private people, and of directing it towards the employments most suitable to the interest of the society. According to the system of natural liberty the sovereign has only three duties to attend to; three duties of great importance, indeed, but plain and intelligible to common understandings: first, the duty of protecting the society from the violence and invasion of other independent societies; secondly, the duty of protecting, as far as possible, every member of the society from the injustice and oppression of every other member of it, or the duty of establishing an exact administration of justice; and, thirdly, the duty of erecting and maintaining certain public works and certain public institutions which it can never be for the interest of any individual, or small number of individuals, to erect and maintain.[37]

THE DISMAL SCIENCE OF THE FACTORY SYSTEM

This ideal of complete *laisser-faire* struck the popular imagination; trade was increasing, and the horrible example of mercantilism in provoking the American Revolution was apparent. With the exception of the Corn Laws, a tariff on grain retained by the landlords till 1846, England speedily adopted Smith's program; and the Corn Laws only kept his ideas before the public mind. Applied to commerce, the effect was undoubtedly beneficial; but in the factories of the industrial revolution the tale was otherwise. It is needless to repeat the long and bitter wail of woe that rose from the children and young girls in whom enterprising mill-owners found a gold mine; nor is it necessary to grow sick over the nauseating justification of such conditions, with which the middle class consoled itself. A single example of such a description of children of eight years toiling sixteen hours a day will suffice.

They seem to be always cheerful and alert; taking pleasure in the light play of their muscles, enjoying the mobility natural to their age. The scene of industry, so far from exciting sad emotions in my mind, was always exhilarating. It was delightful to observe the nimbleness with which they pieced broken ends, and to see them at leisure, after a few seconds' exercise of their tiny fingers, to amuse themselves in any attitude they chose, till the stretch and winding on were once more completed. The work of these lively elves seemed to resemble a sport, in which habit gave them a pleasing dexterity. As to exhaustion by the day's work, they evinced no trace of it on emerging from the mill in the evening; for they immediately began to skip about any neighboring playground, and to commence their little games with the same alacrity as boys issuing from a school.[38]

The science of business, having become a science of industry, set about discovering the inevitable laws that made poverty and disease and the living hell of the early industrial régime a part of God's natural order. The creators of this "dismal science" were T. R. Malthus, a benevolent clergyman, and David Ricardo, a wealthy banker and reforming member of Parliament. Malthus found the reason and the justification of it all in the laws of population. Believing in original sin, he revolted from the optimistic hopes of Locke and Helvetius, and wrote his *Essay on the Principle of Population* in 1798, largely out of his own head; then he gathered confirming facts for a second edition. He laid down the axioms that population, if unrestrained by natural causes, doubles every twenty-five years, increasing in geometrical progression, while the available food-supply increases only arithmetically. The surplus has in the past been kept down by God's wisdom in providing epidemics, wars, panics, and such "natural" checks; if man is wise, he will by abstaining from marriage restrict the population and prevent the necessity of such pestilences. But he is not, and hence any improvement in his lot will but bring more children into the world and only intensify the distress. Population hovers always at the verge of the food-supply; it can never permit the removal of poverty. Above all, no legislation, no charity, private or public, can hope to alleviate man's miserable lot.

I see no way by which man can escape from the weight of this law which pervades all animated nature. No fancied equality, no agrarian regulations, in their utmost extent, could remove the pressure of it even for a single century. And it appears, therefore, to be decisive against the possible existence of a society, all the members of which should live in ease, happiness, and comparative leisure.... Famine seems to be the last, the most dreadful resource of nature. The power of population is so superior to the power in the earth to produce subsistence for man, that premature death must in some shape or other visit the human race. The vices of mankind are active and able ministers of depopulation. They are the precursors in the great army of destruction; and often finish the dreadful work themselves. But should they fail in this war of extermination, sickly seasons, epidemics, pestilence, and plague, advance in terrific array, and sweep off their thousands and ten thousands. Should success be still incomplete, gigantic, inevitable famine stalks in the rear, and with one mighty blow levels the population with the food of the world.[39]

To remove the wants of the lower classes of society is indeed an arduous task. The truth is, that the pressure of distress on this part of a community is an evil so deeply seated, that no human ingenuity can reach it. Were I to propose a palliative; and palliatives are all that the nature of the case will admit; it should be, the total abolition of all the present [forms of public charity and relief]. To prevent the recurrence of misery, is, alas! beyond the power of man. In the vain endeavor to obtain what in the nature of things is impossible, we now sacrifice not only possible but certain benefits.[40]

This naturally consoled mill-owners with uneasy consciences, and inspired kind-hearted women to write popular tales of political economy for children. It remained for David Ricardo, in 1817, to apply Malthus' ideas to the science of Adam Smith. Ricardo was a successful banker, and his sympathies lay with the commercial class in its struggle after the Napoleonic Wars with the landed interests who controlled the English Parliament. He was a reformer, within the narrow limits in which he believed reform possible, even a radical; he honestly believed that the state of England in his day, with its misery and its conflicts of economic classes, represented the inevitable and permanent working out of the unchangeable natural laws governing human society. In the main he retained Smith's faith in *laisser-faire* and free competition, and he shared his intense conviction of the necessity of the natural order; but he was too clear-sighted and logical in the face of the existing situation to see it in any rosy hue. In his hands the natural order grew rather diabolical than divine. But where he regretfully sketched in the shadows he saw about him, the middle class saw in his picture only the scientific justification for things as they were. His doctrines, in reality only the first tentative thinking through of the problems of distribution on the basis of an over-simplified and far from adequate knowledge of human nature and of social organization, soon hardened into a party and class platform, and became the accepted dogma of the middle-class faith.

Ricardo saw three groups in the community, landowners, capitalists, and wage-earners, between whom nature had ordained an inevitable antagonism of interest; harmonious coöperation could not but remain an idle dream. It is significant to note that Karl Marx took his point of departure from the class conflict theory of the financier Ricardo. For the latter, the natural laws of wages, profit, and rent made it inevitable that through no merit or fault of his own the landlord would continue to wax rich while the capitalist and worker saw profits and wages steadily decline. In his Iron Law of wages the nineteenth-century science of business for the business man found a fitting keystone.

The natural price of labor is that price which is necessary to enable the laborers one with another to subsist and to perpetuate their race without either increase or diminution.[41]

If population increases, real wages must go down below the subsistence level, and men will starve.

In the natural advance of society the wages of labor will have a tendency to fall, as far as they are regulated by supply and demand; for the supply of laborers will continue to increase at the same rate, whilst the demand for them will increase at a slower rate.... The condition of the laborer will generally decline, and that of the landlord will always be improved.... It is a truth which admits not a doubt, that the comforts and the well-being of the poor cannot be permanently secured without some regard on their part or some effort on the part of the legislature to regulate the increase of their numbers, and to render less frequent among them early and improvident marriages.... There is no means of improving the lot of the worker except by limiting the number of his children. His destiny is in his own hands. Every suggestion which does not tend to the reduction in number of the working people is useless, to say the least of it. All legislative interference must be pernicious.[42]

There is a fixed amount of goods, a definite "wages fund," to be divided among the workers. If one gets more than his share, the rest will suffer. Hence all attempts at raising wages, by legislation or by collective bargaining, must inevitably fail: real wages cannot rise above what is necessary to support the workers. One recourse is left: to raise the subsistence standard of living. But this means in turn a lowering of profits, as there is only a definite amount to divide between masters and workers. "A rise of wages would invariably lower profits."[43] The antagonism, not only between workers and employers, but between more favored and less favored workers, is absolute. Of a truth this is an Iron Law!

It is not for us to examine here into the truth of these doctrines. It is of course now generally agreed that what validity the laws of Malthus and Ricardo do possess does not make necessary the hopeless interpretation they gave to them. The important fact is that their contemporaries implicitly believed them; that they employed their arguments to repel any attempt at changing conditions; that they were sincerely convinced that the terrible problems presented by the Industrial Revolution were really insoluble, and that all meddling by individuals or by governments would only make things worse. Upon the natural order alone was laid the whole burden of effecting an adjustment; man could hope to do nothing. In practice this meant the deprecation of charity and state-relief, an inalterable opposition to factory legislation, which was only forced through Parliament by vengeful landlords against the opposition of every "liberal" manufacturer and merchant, and strict laws against labor unions and strikes of any sort. Thus had the science of man, so promising in the eighteenth century, become the chief weapon in the hands of conservatism.

We can well close our survey of this particular branch of eighteenth century social science with a quotation from Herbert Spencer, in many ways a son of the Age of Reason, despite his advocacy of evolution in the middle of the next century. Spencer, too, believed in the order of nature, in the unalterable laws of human society, and in economic "freedom," *laisser-faire*, and "liberalism."

The poverty of the incapable, the distresses that come upon the imprudent, the starvation of the idle, and those shoulderings aside of the weak by the strong, which leave so many "in shallows and in miseries," are the decrees of a large, far-seeing benevolence. It seems hard that an unskillfulness, which with all his efforts he cannot overcome, should entail hunger upon the artisan. It seems hard that a laborer incapacitated by sickness from competing with his stronger fellows, should have to bear the resulting privations. It seems hard that widows and orphans should be left to struggle for life or death. Nevertheless, when regarded not separately, but in connection with the interests of universal humanity, these harsh fatalities are seen to be full of the highest beneficence — the same beneficence which brings to early graves the children of diseased parents, and singles out the low-spirited, the intemperate, and the debilitated as the victims of an epidemic.

There are many very amiable people — people over whom in so far as their feelings are concerned we may fitly rejoice — who have not the nerve to look this matter fairly in the face. Disabled as they are by their sympathies with present suffering, from duly regarding ultimate consequences, they pursue a course which is very injudicious, and in the end even cruel. We do not consider it true kindness in a mother to gratify her child with sweetmeats that are certain to make it ill. We should think it a very foolish sort of benevolence which led a surgeon to let his patient's disease progress to a fatal issue, rather than inflict pain by an operation. Similarly, we must call those spurious philanthropists, who, to prevent present misery, would entail greater misery upon future generations. All defenders of a poor-law must, however, be classed amongst such. That rigorous necessity which, when allowed to act on them, becomes so sharp a spur to the lazy, and so strong a bridle to the random, these paupers' friends would repeal, because of the wailings it here and there produces. Blind to the fact, that under the natural order of things society is constantly excreting its unhealthy, imbecile, slow, vacillating, faithless members, these unthinking, though well-meaning, men advocate an interference which not only stops the purifying process, but even increases the vitiation — absolutely encourages the multiplication of the reckless and incompetent by offering them an unfailing provision, and *dis*courages the multiplication of the competent and provident by heightening the prospective difficulty of maintaining a family. And thus, in their eagerness to prevent the really salutary sufferings that surround us, these sigh-wise and groan-foolish people bequeath to posterity a continually increasing curse.[44]

REFERENCES

1. Buffon, Opening of *Histoire Naturelle*.
2. Voltaire, *Lettres Philosophiques*, sur M. Locke.
3. Hobbes, *Leviathan*, Introduction.
4. *Ibid.*, Part I, ch. I.
5. *Ibid.*, Part I, ch. II.
6. *Ibid.*, Part I, ch. III.
7. *Ibid.*, Part I, ch. III.
8. *Ibid.*, Part I, ch. V.
9. Locke, *Essay*, Bk. II, ch. 1.
10. Hume, *Enquiry concerning Human Understanding*, **sec. 3.**
11. David Hartley, *Observations on Man*. ch. I.
12. *Ibid.*
13. *Ibid.*, sec. II, prop. viii.
14. *Ibid.*, prop. ix.
15. *Ibid.*, prop. x, xii.
16. *Ibid.*, prop. xiv.
17. Helvetius, *De l'Esprit*, III, ch. 22.
18. Helvetius, *De l'Homme*, sec. II, ch. 1.
19. Helvetius, *De l'Esprit*, III, ch. 1.
20. Helvetius, *De l'Homme*, sec. II, ch. 2.
21. Helvetius, *De l'Esprit*, III, ch. 30.
22. Helvetius, Conclusion to *De l'Homme*.
23. Montesquieu, *Spirit of the Laws*, Author's **Preface.**
24. Helvetius, *De l'Esprit*, III, ch. 22.
25. *Ibid.*
26. Gide and Rist, *History of Economic Doctrines*, 2.

27. Dupont de Nemours, *Maximes du Docteur Quesnay.*
28. Dupont de Nemours, *Origines et Progrès d'une Science nouvelle.*
29. *Ibid.*
30. Gide and Rist, *History of Economic Doctrines,* 33.
31. Adam Smith, *Wealth of Nations,* Bk. I, ch. 2.
32. *Ibid.*
33. *Ibid.,* Bk. I, ch. 5.
34. *Ibid.,* Bk. I, ch. 9.
35. *Ibid.,* Bk. I, ch. 8.
36. *Ibid.,* Bk. I, ch. 10, Pt. 2.
37. *Ibid.,* Bk. IV, ch. 9.
38. Dr. Andrew Ure, *Philosophy of Manufactures,* 301.
39. T. R. Malthus, *Principles of Population,* 1798 ed., chs. I, VII.
40. *Ibid.,* ch. V.
41. D. Ricardo, *Principles of Political Economy,* ch. V, sec. 35.
42. *Ibid.,* ch. V.
43. *Ibid.,* ch. VI.
44. Herbert Spencer, *Social Statics,* ed. 1850, ch. 25.

SELECTED READING LISTS

The Economic Background: In addition to the works cited under Chs. VI and VIII: P. J. Mantoux, *The Industrial Revolution in the 18th cent.*; F. C. Dietz, *The Ind. Rev.*; M. and C. H. B. Quennell, *Rise of Industrialism*; L. C. A. Knowles, *The Ind. and Com. Revs. in G. Britain, Econ. Dev. in the 19th c.*; J. L. and B. Hammond, *Rise of Modern Industry, The Town Labourer, The Village Labourer;* W. Bowden, *Ind. Soc. in England in the 18th c.*; H. Sée, *Econ. and Soc. Conditions in France during the 18th c.*; *La vie économique de la France, 1815–48.* L. Mumford, *The Culture of Cities;* G. D. H. Cole, *The Common People, 1748–1938;* F. Engels, *Condition of the Working Class in England in 1844.*

Psychology: Histories of psychology by M. Dessoir, O. Klemm, J. M. Baldwin, G. S. Brett; Gardner Murphy, W. B. Pillsbury. H. C. Warren, *History of Association Psychology;* G. S. Bower, *David Hartley and James Mill;* D. F. Markus, *Die Associationtheorien im 18. Jahrh.* Thomas Hobbes, *Leviathan, De Corpore; The Philosophy of Hobbes,* ed. F. J. E. Woodbridge; see bib., Bk. II, ch. 8. Locke, *Essay;* David Hartley, *Observations on Man;* Hume; Condillac, *Traité des Sensations, Logique;* Helvetius, *De l'Esprit, De l'Homme;* A. Keim, *Helvétius.* James Mill, *Analysis of the Human Mind* (most elaborate); Huxley, *On the Hypothesis that Animals are Automata,* in *Method and Results.*

Montesquieu and the Science of Society: *The Spirit of the Laws.* Condorcet, *Commentary and Review of M.'s Spirit of the Laws,* tr. Duane; A. Sorel, *Montesquieu;* treated in Bluntschli, Faguet, Franck.

Political Economy: C. Gide and C. Rist, *History of Economic Doctrines* (best); also histories of economics by L. H. Haney, J. K. Ingram, E. Ginzberg, *House of Adam Smith.* J. Bonar, *Philosophy and Political Economy* (good). H. Higgs, *The Physiocrats;* G. Weulersse, *Le Mouvement Physiocratique en France de 1756 à 1770.* Critical interpretations by W. C. Mitchell, in R. G. Tugwell, *The Trend of Economics;* T. Veblen, *The Preconceptions of Economic Science,* in *The Place of Science in Modern Civilization;* O. F. Boucke, *Development of Economics,* esp. ch. II on method; W. Hasbach, *Allgemeine Philosophische Grundlagen der von F. Quesnay u. A. Smith begründeten Politische Oekonomie. Les Physiocrates,* ed. Daire, esp. Dupont de Nemours, *Origines et Progrès d'une Science Nouvelle.* Adam Smith, *Wealth of Nations,* ed. Cannan, Seligman; F. W. Hirst, *Adam Smith.* T. R. Malthus, *Principles of Population;* D. Ricardo, *Principles of Political Economy and Taxation;* Nassau Senior, *Political Economy.* Herbert Spencer, *Social Statics,* 1850 ed.; *Man vs. the State.*

CHAPTER XIV

THE SCIENCE OF MAN — THE SCIENCE OF GOVERNMENT

THE DECLINE OF ABSOLUTE MONARCHY

OUR consideration of political economy took us well into the nineteenth century; we must now turn back to the closing decades of the seventeenth to investigate the development of the science of government, which likewise drew its assumptions from the fundamental science of human nature. Our preliminary account of that branch that dealt particularly with business has given us an insight into the basic demands of the middle class, which dug the channels that all thought dealing with human society was bound to follow: it has displayed the real creed and ideals of the business man. On turning to government and the attempt to build up a social physics in that field, we find ourselves in the presence of ideas in large measure determined by these economic demands. The whole structure of government had lost, by the eighteenth century, whatever of religious significance it had possessed during the Middle Ages, and had become frankly and openly a means to a further purely social end, a form of machinery for the proper ordering of the real business of life. Hence though the economic aims only became explicit somewhat later, they were really the determining factors in the whole development of eighteenth-century political science, and a proper understanding of those aims is essential to an understanding of that development.

Taking Western Europe as a whole, until the end of the century the reigning type of political ideal was still the absolute monarchy whose rise in the Renaissance period we have already traced. Such absolutism, however, had ceased to be supported as of divine origin; the necessity for such a defense against ecclesiastical control had disappeared with the acknowledged supremacy of the national state. Its theoretical basis had now become thoroughly "scientific" rather than religious: the purely secular foundation of Machiavelli, systematized by Hobbes, had in the Newtonian world won the day, and the typical ideal of the "benevolent despot" governing in accordance with the laws of political economy and for the material prosperity of the nation, was but the rationalization of Renaissance absolutism. It seemed, almost everywhere on the continent, that the future belonged to such a political system; and certainly, to men primarily interested in economic and social reform, it was but natural that the efforts of intelligent monarchs like Frederick the Great of Prussia, Charles III of Spain, Catherine II of Russia, or Joseph II of Austria, the leading "enlightened despots" of the age, should appeal more strongly than the conservative, corrupt, stupid, and hidebound oligarchy that controlled the British Constitution. As one of the great motives for constitutional and limited monarchy, the desire of minority religious sects for toleration, faded into the background before the growing religious indifference and the general tendency to religious toleration, it seemed to the vast majority of men that the other, the desire for economic freedom, could best be satisfied under an intelligent and "philosophic" monarch, unhampered in his reforming zeal by traditional privileges and rights.

Venice and Genoa still retained their decaying constitutional republics; otherwise only in Switzerland, in commercial Holland, and in Great Britain, did ideals of self-government by the middle class possess much power. In England especially men's allegiance was still given to the constitutionalism won at such great cost in the preceding century; but though England became a center of inspiration throughout the century for other Europeans in political matters, it was the fruits of the English Constitution in civil and economic liberty and in toleration that they admired, and not the actual machinery of that constitution. Voltaire, for example, who more than any one else popularized these English achievements, seems to have had no conception whatever that they were based on a long historical development of self-government; he wondered at Parliament, and admired the restraints it placed upon a stupid and evil prince, but he never understood it, and always thought it at best a very clumsy arrangement for securing rights and liberties which could be much more efficiently attained at the hands of an enlightened and powerful despot like Frederick.

What finally drove the French to look kindly upon English constitutionalism, and to develop far more radical ideas of a really democratic government, was primarily the fact that however despotic the Bourbons might be, in the eighteenth century they were obviously not enlightened. This practical breakdown of absolutism, coupled with the example of successful constitutionalism freed from the English defects in the American Republic, finally led many Frenchmen to reject the whole ideal of absolutism; though under Napoleon they were quite willing to give it one more trial. The exigency of events, when the Revolution was once under way, forced the party of republicanism and democracy into temporary power, and did much to prepare the ground for its popularity in the nineteenth century.

Eighteenth-century political science, then, contained four chief tendencies. There was first the notion of a scientific and enlightened despotism, which carried the day, except in England, until the very eve of the French Revolution. Secondly, there was the rationalization of Dutch and English achievements in the preceding century, which flourished in England and America as constitutionalism based on natural rights, and gradually won influential adherents in France. Thirdly, there was Democracy based on natural rights, expounded by Rousseau, tried during the Revolution, and adapted to American conditions by Jefferson and Jackson. Fourthly, there was the development of a new rational method of approaching all political and social problems, which in the nineteenth century became allied with democracy, and which received from Bentham and his school the name of Utilitarianism. How these four tendencies were systematized and brought into the form of a genuine political science, on the model of Newtonian physics, we shall now attempt to explain.

The Theory of Absolutism Founded on Reason

No rational defense of absolute monarchy, rooted in the science of human nature and systematically developed, was worked out in the eighteenth century, comparable to the masterpiece of Hobbes. Tradition and inertia probably account for the widespread popularity of the ideal as much as the actual arguments advanced. Voltaire, the group of "Encyclopedists" gathered around Diderot, and the Physiocratic school of practical economic statesmen, had after all only a secondary interest in political problems, and seem naturally to have turned to the monarchs whose ears they could catch, as the most obvious instruments for effecting their desired reforms. They all admired the fruits of constitutionalism in England, but thought that a Catherine or a Frederick was the best means of achieving them. They agreed in advocating civil liberty, jury trial, toleration, freedom of speech and of the press, commercial liberty and *laisser-faire*, and above all absolute respect for and defense of the right of private property against both the envy of the masses and the arbitrary confiscation and regulation of the monarch. They were all intellectual aristocrats, with little or no faith in the common people; on the one hand they despised the decaying hereditary and landowning nobility, on the other they had no idea of any natural equality of talents or any actual control of government by propertyless men. Voltaire's position is typical:

Divide the human race into twenty parts, and there will be nineteen composed of those who work with their hands, and who will never know that there was a Locke in the world; in the twentieth part remaining, how few men are there who can read? and among those who can, there will be twenty who read romances, to one who studies science. The number of those who can think is excessively small.[1]

Voltaire had no idea of letting the notions of the Enlightenment get out of the hands of this small minority of intelligent bourgeois:

Philosophize among yourselves as much as you please. I fancy I hear the dilettanti giving for their own pleasure a refined music; but take good care not to perform the concert before the ignorant, the brutal and the vulgar; they might break your instruments over your heads. Let a philosopher be a disciple of Spinoza if he likes, but let the statesman be a theist.[2]

Diderot is even more explicit. Recommending an advisory council to inform the absolute monarch of the needs of the middle class, he says:

It is property that makes the citizen; every man who has possessions in the State is interested in the State, and whatever be the rank that particular conventions may assign to him, it is always as a proprietor; it is by reason of his possessions that he ought to speak, and that he acquires the right of having himself represented.[3]

Though these advocates of absolutism believed fervently in liberty, it was in that liberty that consists in obedience to natural law, particularly the economic laws of property, security, and *laisser-faire*. The monarch should enforce such natural rights, and above all should refrain from what they called "despotism"; that is, capricious and unpredictable imposition of his own whims and tyranny. He must be strong enough to give security to property and person, but he must be law-abiding, and refrain from arbitrary interference. It was not the absolutism, but the caprices of the mistress-ridden Bourbons, to which they objected.

Liberty [says Holbach, the best theorist of this group], is the power of taking the measures necessary to secure one's well-being.... Liberty does not consist, as some imagine, in a supposed equality between fellow-citizens: this chimera, adored in democratic states, is totally incompatible with our nature, which makes us unequal in our faculties of body and mind.... True liberty consists in conforming to the laws which remedy the natural inequality of men, that is, which protect equally the rich and the poor, the great and the small, sovereigns and subjects.... In a word, to be free is to obey only laws.[4]

The sovereign should protect the property of rich and poor alike!

These men all hated tyranny, the religious authority of the Church, war and military government, and above all the whole system of taxation and governmental extravagance. Their enlightened monarch would alter all such iniquities. He would govern his State just as God governed the Newtonian world, by setting down certain uniform laws for the advantage of all and then confining his energies to the rigid enforcement of these natural laws of human society. Indeed, there is a complete parallel between their political and their religious beliefs. Whereas the God of Calvin was an absolute despot whose very will was the source of all law — conceived, of course, on the model of the Renaissance despots — their God and their monarch alike were rulers who consistently observed the natural order of reason. With the Physiocrats they believed that the king should be primarily a scientist who searched out the natural laws of social well-being, and, manual of political economy in hand, enforced them. Holbach summarizes the precepts of statesmanship when he says: "Politics ought to be the art of regulating the passions of man, of directing them to the welfare of society, of directing them into a general current of happiness, of making them flow gently to the general benefit of all." [5] Just as God has instituted a moral law and enforced it by the judicious administration of rewards and punishments in a future life, which rational self-interest can nicely calculate, so the king should aim to establish a similar natural order upon earth. He should be the expert administrator, determining what is best for people, and by the proper legislation, instituted once and for all, leading them to do it.

There is much food for thought, for those to-day who, disgusted with the failures of a century of "democratic government," look kindly upon the rule of such an uncontrolled expert, in the fact that this ideal, however appealing on paper, was actually tried out during the eighteenth century and found miserably wanting. It failed for several reasons. Hereditary monarchy furnished no guarantee that the monarch would be enlightened and expert; not only the Bourbons, but even the heirs of the real philosopher kings, proved utterly incompetent. Moreover, even a king like Joseph II found it quite impossible to govern rationally and introduce reforms without enlisting the active coöperation of his subjects. When he attempted to force reforms on the people of the Austrian Netherlands, he provoked an open revolt; and yet a few years later, when the French armies triumphantly "liberated" Flanders, these and far more radical changes were enthusiastically adopted by the Flemish. There is that in human nature that rejects all such "liberty" handed down from above, and prefers hesitating and tentative advances conducted by themselves to any amount of benevolent despotism. It is this fundamental fact that proved the ultimate undoing of the whole system of rational and scientific politics administered by an expert, and gave the future rather to the self-government that was being slowly developed in England. Hence let us turn to the theories of those who were elaborating the science of constitutional and representative government, where we left them, with Althusius, in a previous chapter.

The Theory of Modern Constitutionalism

The name of John Locke, so preëminent in the science of human nature, stands also at the head of this group of eighteenth-century constitutionalists in government. Historically, Locke possesses in political science a double significance: on the one hand he summed up the ideas that had been worked out in the seventeenth-century struggles, and formulated them into a system that furnished the official apology for the English Revolution of 1689; on the other, this apology became the starting-point of eighteenth-century theorizing, and received in America and in France an elaboration that would have much surprised and perturbed Locke himself. Now an apologist is bound by definite limitations. He cannot be in any sense original, or his whole argument will fail of the universal acceptance he desires. He must operate with the concepts and the ideas commonly employed, and though he can draw certain new conclusions from them, even here he must not arrive at any propositions which have not been long before the public. Hence neither Locke's justification of the English revolution, nor the Americans' justification of theirs, was in any save an indirect sense new and original. They were rather a systematic manipulation of the notions already agreed upon, to prove certain definite contentions. Only in France, where there had been no antecedent seventeenth-century speculation on natural rights and constitutionalism, did political science grow more free and assume startlingly new forms.

Hence we find all these thinkers discussing the law of nature, natural rights, the state of nature, the social contract, and the right of revolution. These concepts had come down from an almost immemorial antiquity, and had furnished the lines on which the controversies of the late medieval and early modern political movements had in theory been fought out. What distinguishes the different thinkers is the particular interpretation and content they give to each of these concepts; and here we must be careful lest we assume that two men, like Locke and Rousseau, for example, when they use the same words, really mean the same thing. Each new political system involves in reality a reinterpretation of these traditional ideas; and these interpretations are on the whole determined by the practical exigencies of the situations they are designed to meet. All these theorists, of course, agreed on the fundamental principles of Newtonian natural science, and on the general outlines of the science of human nature. When they used the adjective "natural," they could not help thinking of the harmonious and rational order of divinely ordained laws which Newton had popularized. They employed the deductive method, and they identified the natural with the rational. They started with axioms that seemed "natural" and rational to them — that is, what they took to be reasonable, and socially useful to the middle class, seemed to them necessarily written into God's system of natural laws for the universe. In this way, they appeared to be enlisting the creator of the world behind their own particular political demands. Not until Bentham and the Utilitarians do we find men who are willing to acknowledge that what is socially useful can stand on its own feet, without the additional support of roots in the natural and divine order.

The Whig Apologetic of John Locke

Locke, like his predecessors, started in his *Treatise on Civil Government* (1689), with the "state of nature" that is, with an analysis of human nature as it would be without civil government; and thus sought to determine the natural needs of man that led to the institution of such government and prescribed the forms it must take if it were to answer those needs. In other words, Locke is following the accepted scientific methods of analysis and deduction. His picture of human nature, and consequently his conception of "the state of nature," since he is not trying, like Hobbes, to justify absolutism, forms a complete contrast with the latter's "war of all against all." His motives and his analysis resemble rather those of Grotius and Althusius; for him the state of nature was something that might actually have existed in the past, and does exist in the present in certain relations: it is pre-political, but not, like Hobbes', pre-social. It is the relation which exists between all men who have no common political superior; and Locke believed that a fairly harmonious life might well be possible in such conditions.

To understand political power aright, and derive it from its original, we must consider what estate all men are naturally in, and that is, a state of perfect freedom to order their actions, and dispose of their persons and possessions as they think fit, within the bounds of the law of nature, without asking leave or depending upon the will of any other man. A state also of equality, wherein all the power and jurisdiction is reciprocal, no one having more than another, there being nothing more evident than that creatures of the same species and rank, promiscuously born to all the same advantages of Nature, and the use of the same faculties, should also be equal one amongst another.[6]

But though this be a state of liberty, yet it is not a state of license.... The state of Nature has a law of Nature to govern it, which obliges every one, and reason, which is that law, teaches all mankind who will but consult it, that being all equal and independent, no one ought to harm another in his life, health, liberty or possessions.... And that all men may be restrained from invading other's rights, and from doing hurt to one another, and the law of Nature be observed, which willeth the peace and preservation of all mankind, the execution of the law of Nature is in that state put into every man's hands, whereby every one has a right to punish the transgressors of that law to such a degree as may hinder its violation.[7]

The content of this law of Nature is the familiar list of rights demanded by the middle class. "Man ... hath by Nature a power to preserve his property — that is, his life, liberty, and estate, against the injuries and attempts of other men."[8] Property Locke considers the most fundamental natural right of all; whatever man has mixed his labor with becomes his private possession.

This state of nature differs from civil society in one and only one factor: in the former there is not, and in the latter there is, a common organ for the interpretation and execution of the law of Nature. Such a state actually exists between independent and sovereign nations, and also in circumstances such as a Swiss and a Frenchman meeting in the forests of America. Now it is obvious that if men actually did live in such a state, great confusion would result from each individual's exercising his natural right of punishing infringements upon his other natural rights. Hence it naturally occurs to men to combine together to institute some common authority to interpret the law of nature and to secure each in his rights. This combination and agreement is the "Social Contract."

Men being by nature all free, equal, and independent, no one can be put out of this estate and subjected to the political power of another without his own consent, which is done by agreeing with other men, to join and unite into a community for their comfortable, safe, and peaceable living, one amongst another, in a secure enjoyment of their properties, and a greater security against any that are not of it.... When any number of men have so consented to make one community or government, they are thereby presently incorporated, and make one body politic, wherein the majority have a right to act and include the rest.[9]

Thus the social contract involves the submission of the individual's right to protect his property to the determination of the majority. This single right he gives up to obtain security for his others. In this matter alone he agrees to abide by the decision of the majority; he also agrees to contribute his force, when necessary, to carry out the decisions of the political authority to which he submits. Locke inclines to believe, disagreeing with Hobbes and with later thinkers, that this contract was an historical event that actually took place; he had in mind just such contracts founding the American colonies, and the institution of the reign of William III in England. So far as the individual is concerned, however, by his mere remaining in a community or holding property there he gives a tacit assent to its terms. Like all the eighteenth-century theorists, Locke cared little about how governments had actually been instituted, but was interested intensely in the question whether there was any justification of their being what they were. Such a justification he believed his theory offered. But it defined carefully the proper functions of all governmental authority; and provided a test whereby to judge when that government had exceeded its due purpose.

The great and chief end, therefore, of men uniting into commonwealths, and putting themselves under government, is the preservation of their property; to which, in the state of Nature, there are many things wanting. First, there wants an established, settled, known law, received and allowed by common consent to be the standard of right and wrong, and the common measure to decide all controversies between them.... Secondly, there wants a known and indifferent judge, with authority to determine all differences according to the established law.... Thirdly, there often wants power to back and support the sentence when right, and to give it due execution.... Hence the power of the society or legislative constituted by them can never be supposed to extend farther than the common good, but is obliged to secure every one's property by providing against those three defects above mentioned that made the state of Nature so unsafe and so uneasy. And so, whoever has the legislative or supreme power of any commonwealth, is bound to govern by established standing laws, promulgated and known to the people; ... and all this is to be directed to no other end but the peace, safety, and public good of the people.[10]

Civil authority can rightly extend no farther than the securing of men's natural rights.

This leads directly to Locke's main thesis: that under certain conditions when government has infringed upon and failed to secure these rights, a revolution is naturally and rationally justified. Any government can be no more than the delegate of the community, which remains the ultimate seat of all civil power.

The community perpetually retains a supreme power of saving themselves from the attempts and designs of anybody, even of their legislators, whenever they shall be so foolish or so wicked as to lay and carry on designs against the liberties and properties of the subject.[11]

Wherever law ends, tyranny begins, if the law be transgressed to another's harm; and whosoever in authority exceeds the power given him by the law, and makes use of the force he has under his command to compass that upon the subject which the law allows not, ceases in that to be a magistrate, and acting without authority may be opposed, as any other man who by force invades the right of another.[12] Whensoever, therefore, the legislative shall transgress this fundamental rule of society, and either by ambition, fear, folly, or corruption, endeavor to grasp themselves, or put into the hands of any other, an absolute power over the lives, liberties, and estates of the people; by this breach of trust they forfeit the power the people had put into their hands for quite contrary ends, and it devolves to the people, who have a right to resume their original liberty, and by the establishment of a new legislative (such as they shall think fit), provide for their own safety and security, which is the end for which they are in society.[13]

Locke is not explicit upon the way in which this dissolving of a tyrannical government is to take place. He is far more concerned with justifying the Whig revolution of 1689 than with paving the way for new revolutions against the control of the propertied classes. He can only say that "the people" possesses this right "to appeal to Heaven," and he seems confident that they will resist government only under extreme provocation.

It is obvious that Locke, like all the eighteenth-century theorists, is primarily concerned with setting limits to the power of any government over men's lives and property; government must observe the natural laws guaranteeing freedom and security. In this he is rationalizing the long struggle of the English people, led by the middle class, against the Stuarts. He differs from the absolutists in France, not in the aim of government, but in fearing the infringements of the monarch more than those of the poorer classes. Hence his arguments for the British constitution emphasize the checks it puts upon governmental power rather than the authority an enlightened monarch might have to institute reforms; and this well illustrates the differing needs of the middle class in England and on the continent, — traditional regulation and ecclesiastical privilege had lasted longer there. He insists on the advantage of separating the legislative power, which must inhere in the representatives of the people, from the executive. If the latter also make the laws, "they may exempt themselves from obedience to the laws they make and suit the law, both in its making and its execution, to their own private wish, and thereby come to have a distinct interest from the rest of the community." Hence the two powers are distinct "in all moderated monarchies and well-framed governments." [14] The absolutists hoped to achieve the same end by separating the monarch and the judicial power.

This device for curbing governments was elaborated by Montesquieu, who shared the fear both of a tyrannical despot and of the mob, into a complicated scheme for preventing a government from doing almost anything, lest it should do something bad. In his most famous chapter, an analysis of the English constitution, he indeed misread the course that constitutional development was to take, to the almost absolute power of Parliament; but he laid down the theory of the separation of powers and of checks and balances that was written into our own constitution. There are in every state three powers, executive, legislative, and judicial; and the difficult task of devising a government that shall guarantee men's rights consists in placing these three powers in different hands, and playing them off against each other by checks of the one upon the others and balances between the three. Only in the English constitution is the executive opposed to both the legislative and the judicial branch. The king, the Lords, the Commons, and the independent courts with citizen juries, each have sufficient power to prevent the others from infringing upon the liberties of the people.

The Theory of the American Constitution

These principles of Locke, and the devices of Montesquieu, were especially popular amongst the American colonists. In the artificial institution of their forms of government, by charter or compact, they had excellent examples of social contracts; their governments had, on the whole, confined themselves to what Locke considered the proper sphere of civil authority; and above all they were fully accustomed, under pioneer conditions, to a very large amount of actual liberty and freedom from interference. Hence such a government obviously seemed to them natural, rational, and divinely ordained; and when the tightening of the mercantilistic restrictions on their economic freedom that followed the expulsion of the French brought them face to face with a government that did seem bent on infringing upon their natural and traditional rights, all the varying forces making for nationalistic divergency between America and the mother-country were brought to a head under the active leadership of the commercial interests who suffered most by the Tory policies. Arguments which had justified one revolution by Englishmen could well support another; and the "patriots" of the Revolutionary era naturally drew upon the accepted views of Locke to justify their successive steps against a meddlesome English government. When Jefferson set to work to draft the Declaration of Independence, he had only to write down the ideas that were shared by all thinking persons.

I turned to neither book nor pamphlet while writing it [he states]. I did not consider it as any part of my charge to invent new ideas altogether and to offer no sentiment which had ever been expressed before.... Not to find out new principles, or new arguments, never before thought of, not merely to say things which had never been said before; but to place before mankind the common sense of the subject, in terms so plain and firm as to command their assent.... It was intended to be an expression of the American mind.... All its authority rests then on the harmonizing sentiments of the day, whether expressed in conversation, in letters, printed essays, or the elementary books of public right, as Aristotle, Cicero, Locke, Sidney, etc.[15]

Thus this document was a new appeal to the right of revolution so valiantly defended by Locke, in the terms of Locke's argument.

The Revolutionary Fathers were well agreed on the purpose of government: as John Hancock put it, "Security to the persons and properties of the governed is so obviously the design and end of civil government, that to attempt a logical proof of it, would be like burning tapers at noonday to assist the sun in enlightening the world." [16] Their efforts, practical and theoretical, were toward curbing a government that had gone further than this, and hence their central motive was the fear of what any such authority might do. Naturally they favored the decentralization and the weakness of the executive that succeeded the Treaty of 1783. But ideas suited to justify a revolt do not always build up a government strong enough to secure liberty and property; and upon the Revolutionary epoch there followed a reaction to principles approaching those of the French advocates of "strong" government. Jefferson, author of the Declaration, was conveniently absent when the far-seeing lawyers and business men and men of great possessions drew up the Constitution. These latter feared the tyranny of a ruler far less than the tyranny of a mob; their primary concern was to guarantee the rights of individual property owners against the majority of the people. Hamilton, Madison, and John Adams stand out as the spokesmen for the rights of the commercial and propertied classes; and it was such men who wrote and secured the adoption of the Constitution. They had the difficult task of devising an instrument of government that would set popular checks against too strong a civil power, and at the same time be strong enough to protect individual rights against the people. In such an endeavor they succeeded remarkably well. They were assisted by the lack of any democratic franchise in the individual states. Franklin, for example, believed that "as to those who have no landed property the allowing them to vote for legislators is an impropriety"; [17] and Hamilton thought that those who possessed no property could not rightly be regarded as having any will of their own. In no one of the new state constitutions was the vote granted to as much as half the adult male population. Office-holders were required to possess a considerable property in land: in Massachusetts the governor had to possess a freehold valued at £1000, in Maryland at £5000, and in South Carolina at £10,000. Moreover, in every State but New York and Rhode Island there were further religious qualifications for holding office. Not even in the Revolutionary era, much less in the Constitution, were ideas we should recognize as democratic widely advocated or put into practice. Nearly all the Fathers believed in what they called a "natural aristocracy"; the problem was to insure that it should rule.

In the Constitutional Convention the concern for guaranties against too much democracy, especially when it assailed propertied interests, was the dominant note. Gerry asserted that "the evils we experience flow from the excess of democracy," and confessed that "he had been too republican heretofore; he was still, however, republican, but had been taught by experience the danger of the leveling spirit." [18] Randolph said that the source of dissatisfaction among landed and commercial interests was commonly recognized to lie "in the turbulence and follies of democracy." [19] But the outstanding expression of the conservative social theory that lay back of the Constitution is to be found in *The Federalist*, its official apology, and in the writings of John Adams.

The Federalist accepts the fundamentals of Locke's position, though it emphasizes the need of the unruly passions of men for restraint as necessitating civil government, thus sharing much of Hobbes' fear of uncontrolled human nature. Its whole aim is to conciliate men still fearing a strong government, by pointing out the numerous checks and balances in the Constitution that would prevent the Federal Government from infringing upon men's natural liberties; and at the same time to convince them of the necessity of forming " a more perfect union" that would prevent both popular tyranny and "anarchy," each alike dangerous to property rights. The Constitution is so drawn up as to insure that the Government will be able to do nothing but secure such rights, and at the same time have enough power to perform this narrow duty. The necessity of a strong executive to curb the legislature and preserve law and order is vigorously argued. Above all, an omnipotent legislature must be guarded against; for, as Jefferson said of the Virginia body, "173 despots would surely be as oppressive as one." [20] By the system of two houses, by the Presidential veto, by the reserved powers of the States, and by the independence of the Supreme Court, popular passions in Congress will be impotent to attack natural rights; while long terms for the President and the Senate, and the indirect election of the latter body, will insure delay and careful consideration of radical measures. By such means *The Federalist* hoped to guarantee property rights; and it is significant that it argues strongly against any inclusion of a bill of personal and civil liberties, as both unnecessary and dangerous. The Bill of Rights was of course only added to the Constitution when forced by the demands of reluctant States, as an inducement to ratification.

In the aristocratic theories of John Adams, leader of the essentially landed and commercial Federalist Party, this fear of popular interference is even stronger.

> We may appeal to every page of history we have hitherto turned over, for proofs irrefragable, that the people, when they have been unchecked, have been as unjust, tyrannical, brutal, barbarous and cruel as any king or senate possessed of uncontrollable power. The majority has eternally and without one exception usurped over the rights of the

minority.... All projects of government, formed upon a supposition of continual vigilance, sagacity, virtue, and firmness of the people, when possessed of the exercise of the supreme power, are cheats and delusions.[21]

Not such a mob should rule, but rather the "natural aristocracy of the wise, the rich, and the good." Adams abhors the idea of human equality; every society contains such an aristocracy of well-born gentlemen, sharply set off from the mass of "simple men, the laborers, husbandmen, mechanics, and merchants in general, who pursue their occupations and industry without any knowledge in liberal arts or sciences, or in anything but their own trades or pursuits." [22] The distinguishing marks of this aristocracy are that it is "educated, well-born, and wealthy." Naturally Adams condemned rotation in office, and advocated life tenure and even a hereditary monarch. "A hereditary first magistrate at once would perhaps be preferable to elections by legislative representatives." [23] Adams clearly had no objection to the British system for America. Yet he accepted the Constitution as embodying his most important contentions. He was delighted by its many checks and balances, which he thought sufficient to guarantee individual rights against all possible encroachments. His fundamental aim was throughout the same as that of Locke and Montesquieu, to protect the free action of the wealthy middle class against absolute monarchy and democracy alike. In 1825 he wrote: "The fundamental principle of my political creed is, that despotism, or unlimited sovereignty, or absolute power, is the same in a majority of a popular assembly, an aristocratical council, an oligarchical junto, and a single emperor." [24] In other words, he was simply a rather conservative representative of that whole political theory, so appealing to the middle class in the eighteenth century because it promised economic freedom coupled with security of property, which we have called constitutionalism based on natural rights.

Democracy on the Basis of Natural Rights — Rousseau

But Locke's premises could also be made the basis of a much more radical democratic theory, a theory destined to conquer in the nineteenth century. Democracy, as we know it to-day, is not an English product; it originated in France, was adopted in America by the more popular party of Jefferson and Jackson, and only became influential in England toward the end of the nineteenth century after a long struggle by the working-class and many threats of revolution. We must now turn to its systematization by Rousseau, and its development in America. Rousseau is one of the strangest figures that has ever attained to wide popular influence. Living in the Age of Reason, he was not of it; all his life he felt rather than thought. Like his contemporaries, he cared little for facts; but he also failed to share the general faith in logic and reasoning. He never saw things as they are, in the ordinary sense; his every book, his life itself, as reported in his *Confessions*, became inevitably a romance. Uneducated, he wrote what has been one of the most influential books ever written on education, the *Émile;* hating men and society, he swept men off their feet as few others have done, and became the lion of society; almost incapable of fulfilling any social duties whatsoever, he wrote the most powerful work ever penned upon the supreme duty of political obligation, the *Social Contract;* hating progress and advance through the application of reason, he contributed probably more than any of his contemporaries to the progress of society.

Yet the very sensitivity of Rousseau's nature and the strength of his feelings made him peculiarly aware of the force and the significance of ideas which to the rest of his time remained rather abstract. Having established a reputation as a social thinker, by a paradoxical work denying the possibility of moral progress, he set to work at the age of forty to make a serious study of the theories of his predecessors. Just because he was not bound by the interests and the logic of his age, he was able to perceive very clearly certain great principles to which his contemporaries were blind; and after ten years he published, in 1762, his two chief contributions to the science of society, the *Émile*, dealing with education, and the *Social Contract*, dealing with government. These were masterpieces of propaganda rather than systematic investigations; they accepted the concepts and the ideas common to eighteenth-century political and social science, but they in large measure cut loose from the historical antecedents of those ideas, and from the science of human nature upon which they were ostensibly founded. Whatever is original in Rousseau — and his influence was far too great to make that very extensive — is due to his expression of the *feelings* of his time, and his blending of those feelings with the accepted ideas. If his conception of human nature, founded in large part upon his own abnormally sensitive and emotional temperament, is woefully inadequate, still its shortcomings lay in an overemphasis on precisely those aspects of human nature which the Age of Reason disregarded; and the combination of Enlightenment ideas with Rousseau's sentiments was admirably fitted to secure wide acceptance. Thus, where others demonstrated the Religion of Nature, Rousseau actually believed it; where others assumed liberty and equality, he really believed in putting them into practice. Hence in spite of all that is despicable and pathological in his character, we cannot escape the conviction, any more than his contemporaries could, that at bottom there was something sterling there, something that attracted warm admirers and gained him a patient indulgence for all his foibles; he was sincere, he rang true. Into the atmosphere of more or less hypocritical rationalization of both traditional beliefs and new demands, of unreality and artificiality, of cynicism and intellectual insincerity, he brought something, something new, something needed, something powerful and strong, that served as a flaming banner of genuine revolt.

Rousseau's problem was simple. Man is good; he felt it in others, and he knew it in himself. Yet men are bad, and society is evil; this his pride and his inability to adjust himself to others told him. Why? What can be done about it? He felt he knew. Men are at bottom fundamentally good, that is, potentially they might have been good. They can still become far better than they are. Why, then, do they not realize their true capacities? Their education is all wrong, their whole social environment is all wrong. Give them a new education and a new environment, and they will naturally flower into something admirable and lovely. Men must be made by art what they are naturally in germ; intelligence must seize upon their natural instincts and develop them aright. This is Rousseau's simple message; and he spent the rest of his life trying to popularize the eighteenth-century ideas as means of effecting such a development. And it was because he offered a scheme for attaining in the individual through education, and in the state through a proper ordering of government, the liberty that the middle class so much desired, that he became the standard-bearer of his generation.

The *Social Contract* takes as its fundamental problem the attainment of this liberty through political government. But Rousseau meant by "liberty" something different from preceding theorists, something far closer to what the middle class really desired. By temperament and by his irresponsible life he was not prepared to define liberty, with the absolutists and Montesquieu, as obedience to perfect law; he insisted as well, with Helvetius and his followers, that it should also take account of men's actual desires. Yet it took little reflection to realize that such an absolute liberty to do whatever one wanted was impossible in society. Hence his famous definition of liberty as obedience to law, but to law that the individual freely accepts for himself. In this way he hoped to combine the two elements essential to any ordered society, the freedom to do what one wants, and the law that will produce social well-being. "The mere impulse of appetite is slavery, while *obedience to a law which we prescribe to ourselves* is liberty." [25] In developing the ideal of a government in which such a law is supreme, he naturally turned to the republican traditions and theories of his native city-state of Geneva, of which he was always proud to boast himself a citizen.

In the state of nature — a conception which Rousseau did not regard as in any necessary sense a historical reality, but which his imagination could not refrain from idealizing and romancing about — man is free, there is no law, no conditions for social well-being. A society that combines both must rest on the principle of the social contract; that is, all men must at least tacitly consent to the rule of the majority; and having once assented, they must be bound by the will of that majority when it commands things that are really best for all the members. Rousseau is led to make an important distinction between what he calls the "will of all," what any actual democratic vote decides, and the "general will," which is not really an expressed will at all, but is defined wholly as an ideal, as what is really best for every member of the society. By definition, the general will aims always at the social well-being; if it does not, it is simply not the general will. The will of all, on the other hand, is the record of what the majority actually desires. The problem of government, then, is to determine and bring about the conditions under which the general will and the will of all will coincide, that is, under which the majority will actually want the precise measures which form the content of what it really wants, what is best for it. It is at this point that Rousseau's assumption, his democratic faith, enters. He thinks that under certain very definite conditions a majority vote will actually coincide with what is really best for a people.

When in the popular assembly a law is proposed, what the people is asked is not exactly whether it approves or rejects the proposal, but whether it is in conformity with the general will, which is their will. Each man, in giving his vote, states his opinion upon that point; and the general will is found by counting votes. When therefore the opinion that is contrary to my own prevails, this proves neither more nor less than that I was mistaken, and that what I thought to be the general will was not so. If my particular opinion had carried the day, I should have achieved the opposite of what was my will; and it is in that case that I should not have been free. This presupposes, indeed, that all the qualities of the general will still reside in the majority; when they cease to do so, whatever side a man may take, liberty is no longer possible.[26]

In other words, in an actual democratic vote, the majority can be trusted to know what is really best for it.

What guaranty has Rousseau that it will? When will men actually know what is best for them? Obviously only when they are educated and wise. Hence it is no accident that from Rousseau down all democratic theorizers have insisted on the cardinal importance of education. Without an intelligent citizenry, majority rule, and with it all hope of combining liberty with law, becomes quite impossible. Rousseau thought that such a happy condition could only obtain in a city-state of intelligent voters, like Geneva.

How many conditions that are difficult to unite does such a government presuppose! First, a very small state where the people can be readily got together and where each citizen can with ease know all the rest; secondly, great simplicity of manners, to prevent business from multiplying and raising thorny problems; next, a large measure of equality in rank and fortune, without which equality of rights and authority cannot long subsist; lastly, little or no luxury — for luxury either comes of riches or makes them necessary.[27]

It is indisputable that democratic government has succeeded in just the measure in which, in colonial America, in Switzerland, in Norway, in New Zealand, it has actually realized these conditions. Men will freely choose what is best for them only when they are wise, and they have been wise only in such a state.

Not only Rousseau's followers, but in many passages he himself, were not always true to this important principle. It seemed all too easy to assume that any election could really determine what all men would want if they knew enough. Hence all actual governments have followed Rousseau in claiming a wisdom they may or may not possess, and in exercising despotic powers to force a minority to give way. The sovereign power, which strictly belongs only to the ideal general will, is naturally claimed by any majority, with baneful results. If it really knows better than the individual what is good for him, it can force him against his actual desires to do what it assumes he really would want to do if he were wise enough. "It follows that the general will is always right and tends to the public advantage; but it does not follow that the deliberations of the people are always equally correct. Our will is always for our own good, but we do not always see what that is." [28] Hence if any man or any group can convince itself that it sees better than the majority, it will be easy for it to use Rousseau's arguments in support of a benevolent tyranny. The exploits of Robespierre and Napoleon illustrate what this doctrine can lead to. Whoever can successfully claim to know the general will, can tyrannize over the man who disagrees; "This means nothing less than that he will be forced to be free." [29]

Thus Rousseau's deification of the majority in practice has led to the abandonment of any conception of natural rights for the individual which cannot be infringed; it is the very antithesis of the theory of Locke, admirably expressed in John Adams, that the majority is as much to be feared as any monarch. It gives supreme power to a popular government to do what it wishes, where the English theory had tried to prevent government from doing much. The nineteenth century has seen the attempt at combining these two incompatible ideals, and in the face of conditions obviously demanding some kind of action, Locke and Adams have had to give way before Rousseau. We have agreed, with the Genevan, that "Each man alienates by the social compact, only such part of his powers, goods, and liberty as it is important for the community to control; but it must also be granted that the Sovereign [the majority] is sole judge of what is important." [30] Thus it is Rousseau's theory, as developed in the French Revolution, that has furnished the basis of the modern collectivistic state.

But these seeds of future socialism were not apparent to most of Rousseau's contemporaries. They saw rather that he made the People sovereign, and that government was but an executive officer set up to execute the popular will. Where Locke's natural rights justified constitutional restrictions on government, Rousseau's popular sovereignty supported an actual revolution that would establish the rule of the majority. From the latter came the clarion call to revolt:

> The institution of government is not a contract, but a law; the depositaries of the executive power are not the people's masters, but its officers; it can set them up and pull them down when it likes; for them there is no question of contract, but of obedience; in taking charge of the functions the state imposes on them they are doing no more than fulfilling their duty as citizens; without having the remotest right to argue about the conditions.[31]

Jeffersonian Democracy

In France this theory was used to justify the pretensions of the middle class against the traditional government; in America it was seized as a weapon against the commercial and landed Federalist Party by the popular leaders. By Jefferson it was developed to support the small planter against the large planter and the merchant, and triumphed in 1800; with Jackson it was thoroughly assimilated to American pioneering conditions. Whereas in France liberty, equality, and self-government were theories, in America they were largely facts, indigenous and of the soil. The farmer-pioneer was in the great majority; he had always lived almost free from any governmental interference, and he had been forced to develop the shrewd ability of the jack-of-all-trades to meet any practical problem in his remote life. Hence liberty and equality seemed to him the obvious, customary, and natural condition of man, and democratic theory axiomatic. Jefferson merely well expressed what most Americans who were not, like the plantation owners of the South and the city merchants, raised above their fellows by large properties, actually wanted, believed in, and possessed.

Jefferson's ideal was the simple, frugal, agricultural community of the colonies. He hated cities and industry, and thought that they were quite incompatible with a healthy and intelligent society.

Those who labor on the earth are the chosen people of God, if ever he had a chosen people, whose breasts he has made his peculiar deposit for substantial and genuine virtue. It is the focus in which he keeps alive that sacred fire, which otherwise might escape from the face of the earth. Corruption of morals in the mass of the cultivators is a phenomenon of which no age nor nation has furnished an example. Dependence begets subservience and venality, suffocates the germ of virtue, and prepares fit tools for the designs of ambition.... When the Americans get piled upon one another in large cities, as in Europe, they will become corrupt as in Europe.[32]

Though Jefferson was familiar with France, it was the French example rather than French theory that attracted him; his own democratic ideas he had developed from Locke before he ever heard of Rousseau. He adapted Locke to suit these American conditions, as Rousseau had adapted him to suit France. He believed firmly in natural rights, and that in the social contract we do not give them up, but only provide for their better enforcement. He accepted, far more than the Federalists, very narrow limits on the function of civil authority. But he emphasized the sovereignty of the people, and claimed that the active consent of the governed is absolutely essential. He went so far as to welcome insurrections like Shays' Rebellion, and feared lest the Americans should lose the habit of rising against their government. "God forbid," he said, "that we should ever be twenty years without such a rebellion."[33] He believed that each generation should live under a constitution of its own making, and having calculated that in eighteen years and eight months half of those over twenty-one will have passed away, he wanted a revision of the Constitution, a new social contract, at least every nineteen years. He even questioned whether man might not get along better without any government at all, in the original state of nature.

Though he wrote equality into the Declaration of Independence, he did not actually believe that men are equal in talents. There is a natural aristocracy, not, like Adams', founded on birth and wealth, but rather made up of those in every rank who are naturally superior to their fellows. "That form of government is the best which provides the most effectively for a pure selection of these natural *aristoi* into the offices of government." [34] A democracy will naturally elect the good and wise, the cultured plantation owners like Jefferson himself. Above all, the people are to be trusted. Average men can select rulers who will administer in accord with the interests of society, — provided the society conforms to the conditions that Rousseau had also prescribed. Indeed, it was this trust in the wisdom of the people that almost alone set him off from the Federalists like Adams. "We both love the people, but you love them as infants whom you are afraid to trust without nurses, and I as adults whom I freely leave to self-government." [35] Such faith, coupled with the insistence that the government confine itself rigidly to the functions of preserving men's natural rights, is the essence of Jeffersonian democracy. In actual practice, this worked out, in the hands of the Republican party that in 1800 drove the Federalists out of power, in a strong distrust of a firm, centralized government. "Jeffersonian Democracy simply meant the possession of the Federal government by the agrarian masses led by an aristocracy of slave-holding planters, and the theoretical repudiation of the right to use the government for the benefit of any capitalistic group, fiscal, banking, or manufacturing." [36]

JACKSONIAN DEMOCRACY

By 1824 conditions had changed. There was a large pioneer class in the new West that no longer believed even in "natural aristocracy," and in the cities a laboring class had grown up. Hence the Jacksonian Democracy that was swept into power in 1828 was more inclined to insist on equality, while just as firm for men's natural rights. Where Jefferson's followers had elected the best men to the legislatures and left them to govern as they saw fit, Jackson's had come to distrust such men and fear their favors to special interests. These aristocratic though popularly chosen bodies had especially served the planters in the South and the merchants in the North, no matter how great their benevolent devotion to the sturdy farmer. The plain people of the West and of the cities now sought to curb this legislative aristocracy through a strong executive. Jackson was elected as the tribune of the people against the patrician legislators, and the blows he so doughtily dealt at the moneyed and

[36] From *Jeffersonian Democracy*, by Charles Beard. Copyright, 1915, by The Macmillan Co. Reprinted by permission.

slave interests were inspired by a sense of his public trust. The governors of the States also received a large accretion of power. Popular suspicion seemed now to be directed, not so much against a tyrannical executive, as against "encroaching aristocracy." Together with this increased responsibility of the executive went the abandonment of the old theory that the people's representatives were to legislate as they thought best. The electoral college lost its meaning; legislators came to bind themselves to their constituents; their terms were shortened, and property qualifications, aimed to secure cultured gentlemen, were abandoned. Rotation in office, on the theory (largely true in the pioneer West) that one man is as good as another for any position, and that too long tenure of office makes one unresponsive to popular needs, took the place of permanent appointments. By 1830 in all the States property restrictions on the franchise had given way to manhood suffrage. Everything tended toward a democracy in which one strong, responsible head should be chosen by all the people and held accountable to them for his acts. Thus American conditions produced an ideal remarkably similar to the effects of Rousseau's theory in France, and Jackson reigned almost as truly as Robespierre or Napoleon.

The Utilitarian Method

These three important strains of political thought had all this in common: they were designed to sweep away traditional institutions and establish new conditions in which the middle class would be both secure in its property rights and free to make money as it desired. Absolutism trusted an enlightened scientific monarch, constitutionalism trusted legally guaranteed rights, democracy trusted the people. None of the three, powerfully influenced as they were by the science of human nature, was systematically developed from it in a truly scientific spirit; the basic axioms were all independent intuitive principles which reflected immediate demands, rather than conclusions from an investigation of man. A fourth group of thinkers, though in practical program they agreed with the constitutionalists, arrived at their conclusions by methods far more scientific; and these methods form so significant a contrast and so well express the spirit of the next age that they are worth close scrutiny.

All three of the preceding tendencies treated government from the legal point of view. They looked for natural rights which belonged to man either through legal custom or through divine legislation. In practice, of course, all the theories of natural rights were really seeking to get a firm leverage in nature or in God for the privileges which they thought it socially desirable to secure to individuals. They were enlisting the whole weight of the much-revered natural and divine order against the existing social disorder and in favor of changes that seemed to them useful. But all confused the rights which it seems useful for societies to grant their members with rights which those members received directly from God. In the instance of the political economists we have seen how this led to a rigid and static conception of the social order, and passed rapidly, as conditions changed, from an instrument of reform to an instrument of reaction. The Utilitarians alone felt that human society, like every other institution and belief, could afford to rest squarely upon a rational basis, without bringing in either Nature or God to give it firmer support. To them the question of whether any scheme of society was natural or divine was unimportant; what counted was whether it were reasonable and socially useful. They claimed that the human reason was in itself sufficiently cogent to criticize time-honored and ridiculous traditions in politics as in religion, and that outside help was worse than useless. Hence the criticism which they directed both against the old and against the popular defenses of the new was thoroughly in accord with the principles of eighteenth-century science, and while it may not have proved as powerful an agent of propaganda, did prove much more flexible and adaptable to changing social conditions.

We can trace this spirit in Locke himself, and its development in Helvetius. But it is in Jeremy Bentham that it received its fullest and classic expression. Bentham received the training of a lawyer, but his mind revolted at the mass of confused and irrational traditional beliefs which then made up the body of the English law. He had no respect whatever for the past or for what claimed to be of hoary antiquity. In typical eighteenth-century fashion he thought all law should be tested by its service of the needs of to-day, and what cannot pass that test should be summarily discarded, no matter how time-honored, or how great the reputations of its apologists. Find out what men desire and need, and frame laws to secure that: these were the principles of his program of legal and constitutional reform. All the apparatus of natural rights, states of nature, social contracts, and historical investigation in general, simply drop away: Bentham is intelligent enough to realize just what all the theorists of his age were actually doing, and frank enough to announce it openly.

Bentham accepted and tried to make more exact the science of human nature. Analyzing the springs of human action, he concluded, with his age, that men act from two motives, the desire to secure pleasure and to avoid pain. "It is for them alone to point out what we ought to do, as well as to determine what we shall do." [37] Thus every man strives to attain happiness, that state in which he experiences the greatest number of pleasures and least number of pains. It is for morality to calculate what general principles of action will bring him to such a state; and Bentham devoted many acute pages to the attempt to work out such an exact calculus of pleasures and pains. It is for the science of legislation to determine, in a similar manner, what will bring the greatest happiness to the greatest number, and to enact it into law. "An action may be said to be conformable to the principle of utility when the tendency it has to augment the happiness of the community is greater than any which it has to diminish it." [38] What is the interest and happiness of the community? "The community is a fictitious body, composed of the individual persons who are considered as constituting as it were its members. The interest of the community then is what? — the sum of the interests of the several members who compose it." [39] The problem of the social reformer is no longer to seek what is natural or divine in society; it is to investigate what measures will really give the greatest pleasure to the greatest number. "The happiness of the individuals of whom a community is composed, that is their pleasures and their security, is the end and the sole end which the legislator ought to have in view: the sole standard, in conformity to which each individual ought, as far as depends upon the legislator, to be made to fashion his behavior." [40]

Bentham thus reaches the logical conclusion from the common eighteenth-century premises. It was agreed that in his universe God was just such a legislator, enacting laws for the universal happiness of all mankind. Hitherto men had sought to find those laws of God in Nature. Now with Bentham they sought rather to imitate God, and enact similar laws for human society. What God did for nature and man alike, the lawgiver should do for society.

On the whole, although our conception of human nature and human needs has grown much more complex than Bentham's, his method has now won almost universal acceptance. It is scientific, in that it is a program for investigation, and it can adapt itself flexibly to any condition. Whether modern theorists advocate private property or community of goods, whether they seek complete democracy or some form of aristocracy, it is to Bentham's principle of the greatest good of the greatest number that they appeal. Only when they can find no such basis for their projects do they to-day fall back upon natural or traditional rights.

Bentham himself was the spokesman for the English middle class, and it seemed to him that what they demanded was best for society. Absolutism, mercantilism, governmental interference in general, were not useful; a constitutional government enforcing security and justice, individual liberty, especially free economic competition, civil liberties, and the right of property, was. Hence he joined the constitutionalists of the natural rights school in denouncing what they denounced and in advocating what they advocated; but he supported their demands for different reasons, and he criticized their arguments as vigorously as he did those of the traditionalists.

With a view of causing an increase to take place in the mass of national wealth, ... the general rule is, that nothing ought to be done or attempted by government. The motto, or watchword of government on these occasions, ought to be — *Be Quiet.* For this quietism there are two main reasons: — 1. Generally speaking, any interference for this purpose on the part of government is *needless.* ... There is no one who knows what is for your interest, so well as yourself — no one who is disposed with so much ardor and constancy to pursue it. 2. Generally speaking, it is moreover likely to be pernicious, viz. by being unconducive, or even obstructive, with reference to the attainment of the end in view. It is, moreover, universally and constantly pernicious in another way, by the restraint or constraint imposed on the free agency of the individual. Pain is the general concomitant of the sense of such restraint, wherever it is experienced.... With few exceptions, and those not very considerable ones, the attainment of the maximum enjoyment will be most effectually secured by leaving each individual to pursue his own maximum of enjoyment, in proportion as he is in possession of the means.... The art, therefore, is reduced within small compass: *security* and *freedom* are all that industry requires. The request which agriculture, manufacturers, and commerce present to governments, is modest and reasonable as that which Diogenes made to Alexander: "Stand out of my sunshine." We have no need of favor — we require only a secure and open path.[41]

Thus Bentham criticized the old. The new theories he attacked by the same method. In any contract theory he has no interest whatever. Not contract, but utility, is the test of an institution. Men obey laws for one reason: "The probable mischiefs of obedience are less than the probable mischiefs of disobedience." [42] The concept of legal right has a meaning, and so has the concept of moral right, but a natural right, like a natural law, is meaningless and confused. Commenting on the French Declaration of the Rights of Man, he says:

How stands the truth of things? That there are no such things as natural rights — no such things as rights anterior to the establishment of government, — no such things as natural rights opposed to, in contradistinction to, legal: that the expression is merely figurative; that when used, in the moment you attempt to give it a literal meaning, it leads to error, and to that sort of error that leads to mischief — to the extremity of mischief.... *Natural rights* is simply nonsense: natural and imprescriptable rights, rhetorical nonsense, — nonsense upon stilts. What is the language of reason and plain sense upon this same subject? That in proportion as it is *right* or *proper*, i.e., advantageous to the society in question, that this or that right should be established and maintained, in that same proportion it is *wrong* that it should be abrogated: but as there is no *right*, which ought not to be maintained so long as it is on the whole advantageous to society, so there is no right which, when the abolition of it is advantageous to society, should not be abolished. To know whether it would be more for the advantage of society that this or that right should be maintained or abolished, the time at which the question about maintaining or abolishing is proposed, must be given, and the circumstances under which it is proposed to maintain or abolish it; the right itself must be specifically described, not jumbled with an undistinguishable heap of others, under any such vague general terms as property, liberty, and the like.[43]

Individuals should be allowed the freedom which is socially useful, and no more; they should enjoy the security which is advantageous, and no more. Thus by a very different path Bentham reaches the same conclusion as Rousseau, that the sovereign power has an absolute right to determine just what privileges it shall retain for itself, and what it shall accord its individual members; this power is limited only by the resistance which they will make when they calculate that the evils following resistance will be less than those of submission. "The supreme governor's authority, though not infinite, must unavoidably, I think, unless where limited by express convention, be allowed to be indefinite." [44] In the last analysis, it is in the power of the majority to determine what is useful to them, and what is not, and though they may be mistaken, they will on the whole have their way. When any form of government becomes so harmful that the ills of a revolution are counterbalanced by the advantages of a change, then a revolution will be justified.

Bentham himself, and his greatest follower J. S. Mill, made powerful pleas for individual liberty on the basis of its social utility; but the very principle they used has in many cases since been turned against them in a changed situation. Thus Utilitarianism, like Rousseau's Democracy, though originally individualistic, contained within it the seeds of collectivism. It is significant, too, that both theories, founded on popular intelligence, gave powerful incentives to the movement for popular education. Thus on the one hand natural rights, and on the other the method of a genuine social science, originally employed to effect the social changes demanded by the middle class in the eighteenth century, were bent in the nineteenth to the service of the ends of a transformed society.

REFERENCES

1. Voltaire, *Lettres Philosophiques*, sur M. Locke.
2. Voltaire, quoted in Lévy-Bruhl, *Modern Philosophy in France*, 196.
3. Diderot, *Encyclopédie*, art. "Répresentants."
4. Holbach, *Système Social*, II, 3.
5. Holbach, *Système de la Nature*, ch. 8.
6. Locke, *II Treatise on Civil Government*, ch. II.
7. *Ibid.*
8. *Ibid.*, ch. VII.
9. *Ibid.*, ch. VIII.
10. *Ibid.*, ch. IX.
11. *Ibid.*, ch. XIII, sec. 149.
12. *Ibid.*, ch. XVIII, sec. 202.
13. *Ibid.*, ch. X, sec. 222.
14. *Ibid.*, ch. XII, sec. 143; ch. XIV, sec. 159.
15. Thomas Jefferson, *Writings*, ed. 1869, VII, 407.
16. Niles, *Principles and Acts of the Revolution in America*. 13.
17. John Adams, *Works*, ed. C. F. Adams, 1856, IV. 221.

18. *The Madison Papers*, II, 753.
19. *Ibid.*, 758.
20. Cited in C. E. Merriam, *History of American Political Theories*, 110.
21. John Adams, *A Defence of the Constitutions of Government of the United States of America. Works*, VI, 10, 166.
22. *Ibid.*, 185.
23. *Ibid.*, 122.
24. *Works*, X, 174.
25. Rousseau, *Social Contract*, Bk. I, ch. 8.
26. *Ibid.*, Bk. IV, ch. 2.
27. *Ibid.*, Bk. III, ch. 4.
28. *Ibid.*, Bk. II, ch. 3.
29. *Ibid.*, Bk. I, ch. 7.
30. *Ibid.*, Bk. II, ch. 4.
31. *Ibid.*, Bk. III, ch. 18.
32. Jefferson, *Works*, Washington ed., VIII, 405.
33. Jefferson, *Works*, Ford ed., IV.
34. Jefferson, Washington ed., IX, 425.
35. Jefferson, Ford ed., X, 23.
36. Charles Beard, *Jeffersonian Democracy*, 467.
37. Jeremy Bentham, *Principles of Morals and Legislation*, ch. I, sec. 1.
38. *Ibid.*, ch. I, sec. 6.
39. *Ibid.*, ch. I, sec. 4.
40. *Ibid.*, ch. III, sec. 1.
41. Bentham, *Manual of Political Economy*, ch. I.
42. Cited in W. A. Dunning, *History of Political Theories*, III, 216.
43. Bentham, *Anarchical Fallacies*, Article II.
44. Bentham, *Fragment on Government*, ch. IV, sec. 23.

SELECTED READING LISTS

General: See Ch. VIII, esp. Sabine, Dunning. D. Ritchie, *Natural Rights*; O. Gierke, C. Becker, L. Stephen. H. J. Laski, *Pol. Thought from Locke to Bentham, Rise of Liberalism*. Selections in Bayet et Albert, *Les écrivains politiques, 18ᵉ s.*

The Theory of Absolutism: Voltaire, *English Letters*; Pellissier, *V. Philosophe*, c. 4. The Physiocrats, qu. in Bayet et Albert; Holbach, *Système Social, Système of Nature*. Helvétius, *De l'Esprit*, Bk. II. K. Martin, *French Liberal Thought*; Hearnshaw, *Age of Reason. Enlightened Despots*, by G. Brunn, by L. Gershoy.

The Theory of Constitutionalism: W. H. Hamilton, "Constitutionalism," in *En. Soc. Sciences*. Locke, *Two Essays on Civil Government*; S. P. Lamprecht, *Moral and Pol. Phil. of J. Locke*; P. Larkin, *Property in the 18th c.* Montesquieu, *Spirit of the Laws*, Bk. XI. C. E. Merriam, *American Pol. Theories*; C. Becker, *Declaration of Independence*; C. Beard, *Econ. Int. of the Const. The Federalist*; John Adams, *Thoughts on Government, Defense of the Constitutions of Government of the U.S., Discourses on Davila.*

Democracy on a Natural Rights Basis: Laski, "Democracy," *En. Soc. Sciences*. Rousseau, *Social Contract*, ed. G. D. H. Cole, ed. Dreyfus-Brissac. Studies by C. Hendel, Höffding, Faguet, E. H. Wright. Bosanquet, *Phil. Theory of the State*. Paine, *Rights of Man*. Jefferson, *Notes on Virginia; Selections*, ed. John Dewey; life by F. W. Hirst. Beard, *Jeffersonian Democracy*. Crane Brinton, *The Jacobins*; A. Aulard, *H. Pol. de la Rév. Française*.

The Utilitarian Approach: Helvétius, *De l'Esprit*; studies by M. Grossman, A. Keim. Bentham, *Anarchical Fallacies* (criticism of natural rights), *Fragment on Government, Manual of Pol. Econ., Int. to the Principles of Morals and Legislation*; James Mill, *Essays on Government*. E. Halévy, *Growth of Phil. Radicalism*; Leslie Stephen, *English Utilitarians*; W. L. Davidson, *Pol. Thought from Bentham to J. S. Mill.*

CHAPTER XV

THE MORALITY OF REASONABLENESS — HUMANITARIANISM

THUS the Newtonian world of orderly and harmonious law worked itself out in religion, in the new science of man, in political economy, and in government. It remains to consider the great, outstanding ideas and principles which, because they colored the whole of men's lives, we can regard as the fundamental moral notions and ideals of the Age of Enlightenment. Though the nineteenth century, following the methods and the inspiration of its predecessor, achieved in most fields a far deeper insight into the causes of things, it is doubtful whether its accomplishments in laying down noble and generous ideals for the human race to follow went beyond the humanitarianism of the eighteenth century. Indeed, many to-day feel that the great leaders of the Enlightenment marked the furthest advance that men have yet made in the realm of moral progress; and it is indisputable that in many respects even our professions fall considerably short of those principles to which many then gave allegiance. In actual practice, he is bold who will hazard a judgment on the respective attainments of any two periods; at most, we can say that if we no longer inflict some of the terrible things upon our fellow men which the conscience of the eighteenth century regarded with equanimity, we have in our turn grown accustomed to other cruelties and wrongs which that age would have rather shrunk from approving. At any rate, many of the greatest achievements which the last century made in bringing about more humane and just conditions among men, were but the realization of the hopes which filled the souls of the eighteenth-century apostles of Reason and Nature.

THE RATIONAL SCIENCE OF MORALITY

It will be remembered that one of the three great tenets of the Religion of Reason was the belief that the Order of Nature contained an order of natural moral law as well, to be discovered and followed like any other of the rational principles of the Newtonian world-machine. This meant that the principles of right and wrong, of justice and injustice, were for the eighteenth century incorporated into the scheme of reason and science, and that it was universally admitted that the science of ethics was as independent of any theological or supernatural foundation as any other branch of human knowledge. God had indeed commanded them, as he had commanded the law of gravitation; but the content of his commands, like the content of all other laws of nature, was to be discovered by the rational and experimental methods of Newtonian science. Bolder spirits felt with Montesquieu, "Were there no God at all, freed as we should be from the yoke of religion, we should not be freed from that of equity."[1] The methods applicable to the science of man, of politics, of economics, and of society in general, were to embrace in their scope morals as well. Such a program had been proclaimed in the seventeenth century, by men like Hobbes and Spinoza, and Locke cherished the hope that a deductive system of morals comparable to mathematics might be developed; but it remained for the Age of Reason to accept the suggestion wholeheartedly and try to carry it out.

With the principles of the different schools of thinkers who set themselves this problem, we are not particularly concerned; for while they differed in their varying foundations, they pretty much agreed on the practical precepts and virtues which they offered to action. In divers ways they sought to apply to the moral traditions of the West the same standard of rationality and naturalness which were commonly employed in every field, with the result that they were left with a morality of reasonableness that, discarding whatever seemed irrational or unnatural in the Christian ethic, emphasized those elements that seemed sound and useful for the ordering of the good life. The main principles of Christian morality, however they were founded, were retained; they seemed so obviously reasonable and natural that they were not subjected to any thoroughgoing criticism. Deists and atheists and orthodox alike accepted without question all of the gospel ethic that was not bound up with the Oriental and medieval asceticism which appeared incompatible with a rational existence in the world. In this all thinkers were in general agreement with the earlier humanists like Valla or Erasmus, who had decried dualistic austerities and proclaimed the "philosophy of Christ." This philosophy, designed to enable men to live most conveniently with their fellows, they assumed to be universally valid, and inherent in the very order of Nature.

The development of such a naturalistic ethics was of course powerfully influenced by the reigning scientific ideals. In seeking the "natural order of morals" men sought what was universal, uniform, original, primitive, uncorrupted by tradition, and socially useful. They assumed that human nature is always and everywhere the same, and that rules useful in France will be equally useful in Persia, China, the forests of America, or the South Sea islands. A favorite method of destroying customs they disliked was to put their criticism in the mouth of some wise Chinaman or some Noble Red Man; literature was full of Persian and Chinese and Indian letters attempting to bring these universal moral truths to bear upon European provincialism. In England, in France, and in Germany men set to work to analyze human nature, and to make their results the basis of a rationalization and a simplification of the traditional Christian customs and beliefs.

A few examples will illustrate the general method and results. Samuel Clarke, supernatural rationalist and disciple of Newton, sought in the Order of Nature the eternal fitness of things.

> The same necessary and eternal different Relations, that different Things bear to one another, and the same consequent Fitness or Unfitness of the Application of different things or different Relations one to another, with regard to which, the Will of God always and necessarily does determine itself, to choose to act only what is agreeable to Justice, Equity, Goodness, and Truth, in order to the Welfare of the whole Universe, ought likewise constantly to determine the Wills of all subordinate rational Beings.... These eternal and necessary differences of things make it fit and reasonable for Creatures so to act; they cause it to be their Duty so to do, even separate from the consideration of these Rules being the positive Will of God, and also antecedent to any respect of any particular private and personal Advantage or Disadvantage, Reward or Punishment, either present or future, annexed either by natural consequence or by positive appointment to the practising or neglecting of those Rules.... He that refuses to deal with all men equitably, is guilty of the very same unreasonableness and contradiction in one Case, as he that in another Case should affirm one Number or Quantity to be equal to another, and yet That other at the same time not to be equal to the first.... In a word; All wilful wickedness and perversion of Right, is the very same Insolence and Absurdity in Moral

Matters, as it would be in Natural Things for a man to pretend to alter the certain Proportions of Numbers, to take away the Demonstrable Relations and Properties of Mathematical Figures.[2]

Clarke lays down three such axiomatic eternal rules of Righteousness:

First, in respect of God, that we keep up constantly in our Minds, the highest possible Honor, Esteem, and Veneration for him.... Secondly, in respect of our Fellow-Creatures, that in particular we so deal with every man, as in like Circumstances we could reasonably expect he should deal with Us, and that in general we endeavor, by an universal Benevolence, to promote the welfare and happiness of all Men. The former Branch of this Rule is Equity, the latter is Love.... Thirdly, with respect to ourselves, that every Man preserve his own Being, as long as he is able, and take care to keep himself at all times in such temper and disposition both of Body and Mind, as may best fit and enable him to perform his Duty in all other Instances.[3]

With Clarke morality is an affair just like mathematics; with Bishop Butler it is more like mechanics, demanding an initial analysis of human nature before general principles are apparent. Such an analysis reveals, that

Mankind has various instincts and principles of action, as brute creatures have; some leading most directly and immediately to the good of the community, and some most directly to private good. Man has several which brutes have not; particularly reflection or conscience, an approbation of some principles or actions, and disapprobation of others.... Self-love and benevolence, virtue and interest, are not to be opposed, but only to be distinguished from each other.... The goodness or badness of actions does not arise from hence, that the epithet, interested or disinterested, may be applied to them, but from their being what the state of the case requires, or the contrary.... There are as real indications in human nature, that we were made for society and to do good to our fellow-creatures, as that we were intended to take care of our own life and health and private good.... Men follow and obey their nature in both these capacities and respects to a certain degree, but not entirely.... It is manifest, that nothing can be of consequence to mankind or any creature, but happiness. We can therefore owe no man anything, but only to further and promote his happiness, according to our abilities. And therefore a disposition and endeavor to do good to all with whom we have to do, in the degree and manner which the different relations we stand in to them require, is a discharge of all the obligations we are under to them.... From hence it is manifest that the common virtues, and the common vices of mankind, may be traced up to benevolence, or the want of it. And this entitles the precept, *Thou shalt love thy neighbor as thyself*, to the preëminence given to it.[4]

Benevolence, justice, the Golden Rule — whatever the starting point, all these moralists end here. One school sought its origin in a particular moral sense, an innate source of the knowledge of right and wrong, which prescribes the proper balance of self-love and benevolence, and insures the identity of private and public interest; Lord Shaftesbury, a famous Deist, and Hutcheson, held to this view. Another school, following Hobbes, took self-interest as the whole motive of human nature, and found in the sentiment of sympathy, which causes us to rejoice and weep with others, the bridge which connects our self-interest with benevolence in general. Mankind approves that which is useful to its interests, and the individual is led by sympathy to admire whatever is thus useful to all.

In all determinations of morality, this circumstance of public utility is ever principally in view; and wherever disputes arise, either in philosophy or common life, concerning the bounds of duty, the question cannot, by any means, be decided with greater certainty, than by ascertaining, on any side, the true interests of mankind. ... It appears, also, that, in our general approbation of characters and morals, the useful tendency of the social virtues moves us not by any regards to self-interest, but has an influence much more universal and extensive. It appears that a tendency to public good, and to the promoting of peace, harmony, and order in society, does always, by affecting the benevolent principles of our frame, engage us on the side of the social virtues. And it appears, as an additional confirmation, that these principles of humanity and sympathy enter so deeply into all our sentiments, and have so powerful an influence, as may enable them to excite the strongest censure and applause.[5]

Of this view the philosopher Hume and the economist Adam Smith were the chief exponents. Finally a third school, starting with the same analysis of human motives into complete self-interest, sought to make Utility, individual and social, the sole criterion of the goodness of any act. Under Helvetius in France and the systematic Bentham in England this Utilitarianism won the day, and marveled at the natural order that made each man's seeking his own best interests work together to produce the happiness of a whole society. But no matter what the theoretical foundation, all men agreed that Benevolence was the highest virtue, and Utility and Happiness the sole criterion of morality.

Possessed of such a standard, the French wits especially launched their biting shafts of satire against all those institutions which were of no discoverable social value. Is monasticism useful? No! Then away with it! Is asceticism of any social value? Are any of the traditional tabus on the enjoyment to the full of the rich gifts that nature has spread before man, reasonable? Away with them all! Let every man seek as many pleasures and as much happiness as he can, without depriving his fellows of their share, and down with all those who would say him nay! Men like Diderot and Holbach and Rousseau, convinced as they were that Nature and everything natural were fundamentally good and divine, questioned every limit that had been set up, and saw no virtue even in the traditional demands for chastity between the sexes. Whatever relations gave pleasure to all concerned could not but be good. The celibacy of the clergy seemed especially ridiculous. To a priest who, wandered into the South Seas, objected to the offer of a chief to bestow on him his daughter, the reply is made, by Diderot, "I do not know what the thing you call religion is, but I cannot help thinking ill of it, since it prevents you from enjoying an innocent pleasure, to which nature, our sovereign mistress, invites us all."[6] Rousseau in ringing words deified all the natural tendencies:

God makes all things good; man meddles with them, and they become evil.... As soon as we become conscious of our sensations we tend to seek or shun the things that cause them, at first because they are pleasant or unpleasant, then because they suit us or not, and at last because of judgments formed by means of the ideas of happiness and goodness which reason gives us. These tendencies gain strength and permanence with the growth of reason, but hindered by our habits they are more or less warped by our prejudices. Before this change they are what I call Nature within us. Everything should therefore be brought into harmony with these natural tendencies.[7]

Only those pleasures that produced harm to society could be rejected.

The Humanitarian Ideal

Out of this attitude of faith in nature and in what reason approved grew the great ideals of the Age of Enlightenment, humanitarianism, toleration, pacifism, cosmopolitanism. All men have equal rights to happiness and liberty, no man has the right to deprive any other man of the exercise of his rights. The scope of that society whose good is to be the final test of every institution, is as broad as the human race. In calculating the pleasures by which happiness is to be measured, each man should count for one and only one. The whole temper of the times led writers to think in terms of Man and of Mankind, and to ignore any specific differences between individual men. In order to prove that they were as good as those in the seats of power, the middle classes were naturally led — in theory — to affirm the equal rights of all. Hence the Age of Reason became the great age of humanitarianism. Along with Nature and Reason it took as its watchword Humanity — made, so Condorcet said, "of compassion for all the ills that afflict the human race, of horror for everything that, in public institutions, in the acts of governments, and in private actions, adds new griefs to the inevitable griefs of nature." [8]

This generous sentiment was by no means confined to those who accepted this naturalistic ethics. It was shared by rationalists and by sincere Christians alike; the one point upon which all could agree was the equal worth and dignity of every human being. Human slavery and the horrors of the negro slave trade awoke the indignation and wrath alike of Quakers, Wesleyan evangelicals, conservatives like Montesquieu and Samuel Johnson, and radicals like Voltaire and his followers. It was the combined forces of Christian love and rationalism that finally stamped out these iniquities. A similar humanitarian spirit sought to awake Europe from its provincial condescension to the great Oriental civilizations. The Abbé Raynal, a French *philosophe*, in his *Histoire des deux Indes*, and James Mill, disciple of Bentham, in his *History of British India*, stirred up public opinion against the brutalities of the rule of the English East India Company; and Burke's terrific indictment of the empire of Warren Hastings in India enlisted the greatest orators and statesmen of the time in favor of that oppressed people. Burke declared himself stupefied by "the desperate boldness of a few young men, who having obtained a power of which they saw neither the purpose nor the limits, tossed about, subverted, and tore to pieces, as it were, in the gambols of a boyish unluckiness and malice, the most established rights and the most ancient and revered institutions of ages and nations." [9] And Condorcet, statesman and follower of Rousseau, believed all nations capable of reaching the enlightenment of the French. "Will all nations some day approach the state of civilization now attained by the most enlightened peoples, the freest and most unprejudiced, like the French and the Anglo-Americans? Will the immense distance which separates these peoples from the slavery of nations groaning under kings, from the barbarism of the African tribes, from the ignorance of savages, little by little vanish? Are there on the globe countries whose inhabitants nature has condemned never to enjoy liberty, never to exercise their reason?" No! "Peoples will learn that they cannot become conquerors without losing their own liberty.... The time will come when the sun will shine only upon freemen, recognizing no other master than reason; when tyrants and slaves, priests and their stupid or hypocritical tools will exist only in history and on the stage." [10]

The Age of Reason, too, saw the first beginnings of a humane and intelligent treatment of the insane and the criminal. It was the French materialistic physicians who, seeing the causes of mental disturbances in purely physical factors, did away with the tortures to which the demented were commonly subjected; Pinel proclaimed that the insane were neither criminals nor possessed by the devil, but really sick men, and by his cure of George III in 1789 did much to insure a better treatment of the abnormal. It was Beccaria, under the influence of similar ideas, who sought to substitute rational penalties for crime for the reigning barbarous vengeance; while John Howard the Quaker, who became the father of English penology, showed that the "teachings of Christ" could be as humane as those of materialism.

The Argument for Toleration

The leaders of the Enlightenment were also the great advocates of toleration. We have seen the social and religious forces that made for the practical acceptance of the notion that even error should be permitted to exist unattacked save by reason; the late seventeenth century saw the classic formulation of the apology for this saving doctrine. Protestant dissenters had indeed earlier argued for it. The first great statement was written by Roger Williams, to whom belongs the honor of having actually put it into practice in Rhode Island when he was in power. In his *Bloudy Tenent of Persecution for Cause of Conscience* (1644), Williams argues that the State is a purely secular

HUMANITARIANISM

power and should have no jurisdiction over any religious belief or body. "The Church is like unto a corporation, society, or company of East India or Turkie merchants, or any other societie or companie in London, which may wholly break up and dissolve into pieces and nothing, and yet the peace of the citie not be in the least measure impaired or disturbed." [11] The true Church is spiritual in nature, and, as such, has no need of the support of the civil magistrate to maintain its proper position. It should use, not worldly weapons, but "the breastplate of righteousness, the helmet of salvation, and the sword of the spirit." [12] Over the relations between man and God it has no jurisdiction. Williams cited the dire results of departing from this doctrine of the separation of Church and State. Milton accepted the same position; his *Areopagitica* (1644) is one of the classic defenses of freedom of conscience and speech. Censorship will conduce "to the discouragement of all learning and the stop of truth, not only by disexercising and blunting our abilities in what we know already, but by hindering and cropping the discovery that might be yet further made, both in religious and civil wisdom." [13] "Give me the liberty to know, to utter, and to argue freely according to conscience, above all other liberties," [14] he concludes.

Though minority sects might adopt this position, and though works like Jeremy Taylor's *Liberty of Prophesying* (1646) might support it, it was not until the influence of the faith in unaided reason was felt that toleration as a principle rather than as a mere expedient secured wide adherence. Newtonian rationalism produced the two great works, the French Pierre Bayle's *Philosophical Commentary on the Text "Compel them to come in"* (1686), and Locke's apology for the English Toleration Act of 1689 in his *Letters concerning Toleration*. Bayle recognizes no other test of truth than reason. "The supreme tribunal which is the court of last resort from which there is no further appeal is reason speaking by the axioms of the light of nature." [15] Reason clearly teaches that to force any man to believe what his reason tells him is false, is absolutely irrational and immoral. Even if it were a right principle to suppress error by force, no truth is certain enough to justify us in applying the theory. "Everything that an enlightened conscience permits us to do to advance the truth, a mistaken conscience permits us for what we believe to be the truth." [16]   There simply is no truth sure enough to justify persecution; Bayle has abandoned the idea of an absolute revealed truth, for the scientific conception of truth as something to be gradually discovered.   One man cannot be the judge of the reason of another; between a man and his conscience there can be no other judge but God.   Even a belief that seems to us wrong must be tolerated, because it may possibly be right. Moreover, to this sceptical argument Bayle adds a moral one. No amount of force can alter a man's beliefs; it can only make him a hypocrite.   To compel such hypocrisy is wrong; and if any man claims to have from God the right to do so, that is in itself enough to refute his claim.

Who has constituted Parliaments the sovereign judges of the liberty of my conscience?   To wish to force the conscience is surely a crime against the rights of God. . . .   It is a self-evident proposition that any man who does anything which his conscience tells him is evil, or who does not do what his conscience tells him he must, is committing a sin. . . . There is no error in religion, of whatever nature, which is a sin when it is involuntary. . . . We have an inalienable right to profess those doctrines which we believe conformable to the pure truth.[17]

Only when a doctrine is fraught with danger to the public order is there any justification in repressing it; and the chief danger of any religion is that it will be intolerant.   The State should tolerate everything but intolerance.   For this reason, and because they owe allegiance to a foreign sovereign, Bayle excludes Catholics from the benefit of toleration.   No man who does not owe absolute allegiance to his civil government can be permitted to live under it; "such is a Roman Catholic under a Protestant sovereign, since he can, without violating his religion, disregard the oath of fidelity which he has sworn to his master." [18]   When Popes were absolving men of such oaths, Bayle had a real point.

Locke's apology was founded upon these moral reasons rather than upon the more scientific arguments drawn from the difficulty of discovering an absolute truth.   For him the purpose of government is purely secular, to enforce men's rights; it has nothing to do with saving men's souls.   A Church is merely "a free and voluntary society." [19]   If God is offended by false beliefs, that is his affair; Locke agreed with the maxim of the Emperor Tiberius, "If the Gods are insulted, let them see to it themselves."   Civil government can only use force, and force cannot alter an opinion. "It is absurd that things should be enjoined by laws which are not in men's power to perform. And to believe this or that to be true does not depend upon our will." [20] Moreover, once concede the right to enforce uniformity, and you have given it to false religions as well as the true one. One religion alone would be right, and all other countries would be wrong; "and that which heightens the absurdity, and very ill suits the notion of a deity, men would owe their eternal happiness or their eternal misery to the places of their nativity.... What is true and good in England will be true and good at Rome, too, in China, or Geneva." [21] Toleration is the principle which gives to the true faith the best chance of prevailing.

Locke agrees with Bayle in excluding Catholics from toleration, for the same reason, "because they teach that faith is not to be kept with heretics, that kings excommunicated forfeit their crowns and kingdoms," [22] and because they obey a foreign Prince, the Pope. They are politically dangerous. He also excepts atheists. "Those are not to be tolerated who deny the being of God. Promises, covenants and oaths, which are the bonds of human society, can have no hold upon an atheist. The taking away of God, though but even in thought, dissolves all. Besides also, those that by their atheism undermine and destroy all religion, can have no pretence of religion to challenge the privilege of a Toleration." [23] In other words, the Enlightenment was willing to tolerate religious dissent, but not political; and to this day governments have drawn the line at this point. Catholics were not relieved of their political disabilities in England until 1829, atheists not till 1888.

In greater or less degree these principles of toleration were proclaimed by all the thinkers of the eighteenth century. Voltaire, for example, though ready to lend his powerful help to any victim of persecution, even the Jesuits, did not advocate as extensive a toleration as Bayle or Locke; he would confine public offices and dignities to those who belonged to the state religion, being convinced that religion was necessary to keep the people in restraint. Full religious liberty was first accorded in any European State in Prussia under Voltaire's friend Frederick II. By the time of the French Revolution, which indeed introduced a great wave of political intolerance on both sides, there were some who were willing to draw no line whatever. Mirabeau protested against the very words:

> The most unlimited liberty of religion is in my eyes a right so sacred that to express it by the word "toleration" seems to me itself a kind of tyranny, since the authority which tolerates might also not tolerate.[24]

Thomas Paine's *Rights of Man* made the same protest:

> Toleration is not the opposite of Intolerance, but is the counterfeit of it. Both are despotisms. The one assumes itself the right of withholding liberty of conscience, and the other of granting it. Were a bill brought into any Parliament, entitled "An Act to tolerate or grant liberty to the Almighty to receive the worship of a Jew or a Turk," or "to prohibit the Almighty from receiving it," all men would startle and call it blasphemy. There would be an uproar. The presumption of toleration in religious matters would then present itself unmasked.[25]

But few were willing to go so far; and one cannot escape the conviction that the leaders of the eighteenth century developed principles of religious toleration more because of their indifference to religion than because of their faith in toleration itself. From that day to this such principles have caused endless embarrassment to those who are not prepared to follow them whither they logically lead.

Cosmopolitanism and Pacifism

The same rational ethics of utility that led to humanitarianism and to toleration developed also a deep opposition to both war and to "patriotic prejudices" in general. Not only did war seem obviously harmful and bad, as waged by dynastic and commercial rivals; but the whole spirit of considering human nature, humanity, and mankind as a whole, and disregarding any special differences between different groups or individuals, was utterly opposed to nationalistic sentiment. In consequence, the scientific culture of the eighteenth century marks the closest approach in modern times to the universal and cosmopolitan spirit that marked the Roman Empire and, in a different way, the Middle Ages. The scientific temper had caused the Renaissance patriotisms rather to fade away, while the economic forces of the commercial class, in proclaiming a universal free trade rather than the mercantilistic economic nationalism, seem to have required primarily freedom from governmental restrictions in place of the earlier governmental support. The rebirth of nationalism during the French revolutionary wars, and the growth of new economic interests with the Industrial Revolution, made the history of the nineteenth century a quite different story. But the great figures of the Age of Reason looked upon these manifestations of nationalism as fundamentally irrational and unnatural, and as most harmful to human welfare. Even conservatives like Samuel Johnson, in other things a convinced Tory, openly proclaimed that "patriotism is the last refuge of a scoundrel"; while Lessing, the great leader of the Enlightenment in Germany, could express the heartfelt wish, "that there were men in every country who had advanced beyond the prejudices of the populace, and knew exactly when patriotism ceased to be a virtue." [26]

In place of the ideal of patriotism, they advocated cosmopolitanism, an ideal of universal scope, differing from more modern internationalism in recognizing no intermediate loyalties between the individual and humanity as a whole. To such men it seemed natural and obvious that the thinker should be, not a citizen of any particular country, but rather the citizen of the world. We may choose two outstanding representatives of this particular point of view, Voltaire and Goethe. Voltaire, though his thought was primarily directed to the reform of conditions in France, in his sympathies and his influence was primarily a European, even a world, figure. He saw no differences between men and countries other than those of reason and humanity. "It is a maxim adopted by all publicists, that every man is free to choose his own country." [27] To those who sought service under the enlightened king of Prussia, he wrote: "If you have anything to complain of in your own country, you would do well in accepting another." [28] Voltaire himself but preached what he practiced, taking service under Frederick and ending his days in Switzerland. "Under a good king, one has a country; under a bad one, one has none." [29] Most men who think they love their country really love the goods which it affords them; it is a matter of their economic interest primarily.

But his chief quarrel with patriotism is for the humanitarian reason that it seems to require hatred of the rest of the human race. To love one's country, in the common estimation, means to hate all foreign lands.

It is sad that often, to be a good patriot, one is the enemy of the rest of mankind. Ancient Cato, that good citizen, used to say in speaking before the Senate, "Such is my opinion, and let Carthage be destroyed." To be a good patriot is to wish one's country enriched by commerce, and powerful in arms. It is clear that one land cannot gain save at the expense of another, and that it cannot conquer without making others miserable. Such is the condition of the human race, that to wish the greatness of one's own country is to wish ill to its neighbors. He who should wish that his country should never wax greater, nor smaller, richer, nor poorer, would be a citizen of the universe.[30]

Hence against the follies of the patriot Voltaire waged an unceasing war of ridicule. Every one remembers the satire in the first chapters of *Candide*, where the hero is beguiled into the army of the King of the Bulgarians during his war with the Abarians.

Nothing was so fine, so smart, so brilliant, so well-ordered as the two armies. The trumpets, the fifes, the hautboys, the drums, the cannon, made such a harmony as never was heard in hell. The cannons began by mowing down about six thousand men on each side; then the musketry removed from this best of worlds about nine or ten thousand rogues who infested its surface. The bayonet was also the sufficient reason of the death of some thousands of men. The total might have amounted to thirty thousand souls. Candide, trembling like a philosopher, hid as best he could during this heroic butchery. Finally, while the two kings were having *Te Deums* sung, each in his own camp, ... he passed among the heaps of dead and living, and reached a neighboring village; it was in ashes; it was an Abarian village which the Bulgarians had burnt according to the laws of public right. There old men, covered with blows, were watching their wives die with their throats cut while they held their babes to their bleeding breasts; there disembowelled girls, after having satisfied the natural needs of some hero, were breathing their last sighs; others half burnt were crying for death. Brains were scattered on the ground side by side with severed legs and arms. Candide fled as fast as he could to another village; it belonged to the Bulgarians, and the Abarian heroes had treated it in the same way. Candide, walking over palpitating limbs, or through ruins, finally got outside the theatre of war.[31]

In his own way Goethe too lifted himself above all prejudices of country or military glory.

The poet will love as man and citizen his native land, but the country of his poetic powers and his poetic work is the good, the noble, and the beautiful, which is bound to no particular province and to no particular land, and which he seizes and works upon wherever he finds it. In this he is like the eagle, who flies with free glance over every land, and to whom it makes no difference whether the hare, on which he descends, dwells in Prussia or in Saxony. What does it mean, then, to love one's country, and what does it mean to be a patriot? If a poet is busy all his life fighting evil prejudices, removing narrow views, enlightening the mind of his people, purifying their taste and ennobling their opinions and thoughts, how could he do better or be more patriotic?[32]

National hatreds are peculiar things. You will always find them strongest and most vigorous among the lowest stages of culture. But there is a stage where they entirely vanish, and where one stands in a certain measure above all nations, and feels the happiness or the woe of a neighboring people as though it were his own. This stage of culture suited my nature, and I was firmly rooted in it before I had reached my sixtieth year.[33]

Hence it was that Goethe could stand unmoved on the battlefield of Jena, pondering the force and the ability of the conqueror Napoleon, while his countrymen were feverishly seeking means to drive out the foreign invader.

This cosmopolitan spirit waxed so strong that as late as 1805, just a year before Jena galvanized him into an ardent nationalism, the same Fichte who inspired later so many a German breast, answered his question:

What is the fatherland of the truly educated Christian European? In general it is Europe, in particular it is in every age that country in Europe that stands at the peak of civilization. Every country that dangerously errs will surely fall in time, and thenceforth cease to stand at the peak of civilization. But just because it falls and must fall, there rise others, and among these preëminently one, and it now stands at the peak at which its predecessor stood. The earthborn, who see their fatherland in the clod, the river, the hill, remain citizens of the sunken state; they keep what they desired and what makes them happy. But the sunlike spirit will be irresistibly attracted and turn to where is Light and Right. And in this cosmopolitanism we can rest completely unperturbed by the actions and fates of states, for ourselves and our posterity, to the end of time.[34]

Perhaps just because men everywhere looked forward to the dying out of national distinctions and the establishment of universal relationships between individual men, the Age of Reason, so kindly and so humanitarian in all things else, effected no real change in the theory of international relations that had been worked out during the Renaissance period. It seems probable that had not cosmopolitanism been their goal, they would have introduced into international law the same destructive and purifying concepts that they employed in every other field; but as it was, while jurists systematized and clarified the body of public right, if anything they strengthened the notion of absolutely irresponsible national sovereignty. Moreover, all those political theories that made either for a strong centralized government or, like Rousseau, emphasized above everything the sovereignty of the people, whatever their value in shifting the basis of power within the nation, served but to intensify the clash between nations. Constitutionalists, absolutists, democrats, and utilitarians united in seeing the highest authority in the national State; and the last group especially, who with the Rousseauians divided men's allegiance at the end of the century, developed into the most outspoken advocates of the irresponsible State. It was a utilitarian, John Austin, who early in the nineteenth century emphasized the absolute power of Parliament to determine whatsoever acts it might wish, against internal minorities and external states.

Hence the schemes for some European society of nations remained paper affairs which no one bothered to attempt to put into practice. Such schemes were prepared, at the assembling of the Congress of Utrecht at the close of the War of the Spanish Succession, by the Abbé Saint-Pierre, and during the Revolutionary Wars, by the German philosopher Kant. They had no practical result whatever. Saint-Pierre hoped to revive Henri IV's "Project for Perpetual Peace" by a union of the monarchs of Europe, with a congress or senate of royal delegates and a common army, both to repel external foes and to "render prompt and adequate assistance to rulers and chief magistrates against seditious persons and rebels." [35] But all the forces of constitutionalism and democracy were against such a league of rulers, which might well have preserved peace at the expense of what men held of higher worth. Kant's essay *On Perpetual Peace* (1795) saw clearly that any effective society of nations must be based rather on popular government; it laid down the conditions that since wars are largely caused by monarchs, all members must have popular governments, that international law must be backed by a federation of free states, that ownership in foreign lands must not be permitted, and that no state may violently interfere with the constitution and internal administration of another. But no government was prepared to accept any one of these prerequisites; and when the international league of the Holy Alliance actually emerged from the Congress of Vienna, it was founded upon conservative principles that made it impossible for it to withstand the rising tides of nationalism and democracy. The highest reaches of the vision of the eighteenth-century thinkers were for, not a league of nations, but rather a single European or world government ruling over equal subjects. It was Napoleon, with his dream of universal empire, who in this as in so many things served as the best embodiment of eighteenth-century ideals, who came closest to an actual realization of such a *pax Gallica* or better *pax philosophica Napoleonica*. And the combined forces of nationalism and the Industrial Revolution made a repetition of his attempt impossible.

The Idea of Progress

It was rather from the spread of reason and science among individual men that the great apostles of the Enlightenment hoped to bring about the ideal society of mankind. And from this spread they hoped for a veritable millennium. From the beginning of the century onward there rose one increasing pæan to progress through education. Locke, Helvetius, and Bentham laid the foundations for this generous dream; all men, of whatever school, save only those who clung like Malthus to the Christian doctrine of original sin, believed with all their ardent natures in the perfectibility of the human race. At last mankind held in its own hands the key to its destiny: it could make the future almost what it would. By destroying the foolish errors of the past and returning to a rational cultivation of nature, there were scarcely any limits to human welfare that might not be transcended.

It is difficult for us to realize how recent a thing is this faith in human progress. The ancient world seems to have had no conception of it; Greeks and Romans looked back rather to a Golden Age from which man had degenerated. The Middle Ages, of course, could brook no such thought. The Renaissance, which actually accomplished so much, could not imagine that man could ever rise again to the level of glorious antiquity; its thoughts were all on the past. Only with the growth of science in the seventeenth century could men dare to cherish such an over-weening ambition. To Fontenelle, whose long life stretched from the days of Descartes to those of the Encyclopedia, belongs the chief credit for instilling the eighteenth-century faith in progress. He was a popularizer of Cartesian science, and it was from science and reason that he hoped that Europe would not only equal but far surpass antiquity. All men, he proclaimed, are of the same stuff; we are like Plato and Homer, and we have a vastly richer store of accumulated experience than they. Men reverence age for its wisdom and experience; it is we moderns who really represent the age of the world, and the ancients who lived in its youth. A scientist to-day knows ten times as much as a scientist living under Augustus. So long as men continue to accumulate knowledge, progress will be as inevitable as the growth of a tree; nor is there any reason to look for its cessation.

This opinion may strike us as almost platitudinous, but to Fontenelle's contemporaries it seemed the rankest of heresies. He found himself involved in a furious battle, and all France took sides in the conflict between the Ancients and the Moderns; a paler reflection of the controversy in England has been immortalized in Swift's *Battle of the Books*. But of the ultimate outcome there could be no question; all the scientists, from Descartes down, despised the ancients and carried the day for the faith in progress. By the middle of the next century it was clearly recognized that only in literature could the ancient world hope to hold its own; and with the rejection of the classic taste by the rising romantic school, the ancients even here fought a losing battle.

It remained for Condorcet to sum up the hopes and the confidence of the whole age. Mathematician, statesman, educator, Revolutionist, Condorcet's life stands as the symbol of the very soul of the French Revolution. His liberal views in the Convention did not accord with what were deemed the practical necessities of French policy, and he was forced to flee for his life, to lie hidden in the back room of an eating-house, and finally to take his own life that he might escape the guillotine. Yet though he himself was consumed by the forces he so ardently advocated, though, trembling at every sound, he lived constantly in fear of the death that finally overtook him, he was capable of utterly forgetting his own fate in the wondrous new vision of progress for the whole human race through the great Revolution. While in hiding for his life he spent his time composing the most sublimely confident book that has ever been written, the *History of the Progress of the Human Spirit*. He is the fitting symbol of France herself, willing to pour forth her best blood on the battlefields of Europe that through her glorious sacrifice future generations might know liberty. Looking back upon the past, he finds there, in the increasingly rapid growth of knowledge and enlightenment, the platform from which to launch the soul of man into the triumphs of the future. No longer, with Condorcet, is the watchword, Back to Nature! but rather, Onward to the Ideal!

> The result of my work will be to show, by reasoning and by facts, that there is no limit set to the perfecting of the powers of man; that human perfectibility is in reality indefinite; that the progress of this perfectibility, henceforth independent of any power that might wish to stop it, has no other limit than the duration of the globe upon which nature has placed us. Doubtless this progress can proceed at a pace more or less rapid, but it will never go backward; at least, so long as the earth occupies the same place in the system of the universe, and as the general laws of this system do not produce upon the globe a general destruction, or changes which will no longer permit the human race to preserve itself, to employ the same powers, and to find the same resources.[36]

The principles of the Revolution, that is, of eighteenth-century faith in reason, will spread over the entire earth; liberty and equality, a real economic and social and intellectual equality, will be continually strengthened; peace will reign on earth; "War will come to be considered the greatest of pestilences and the greatest of crimes." [37] Nay, more; a better organization of knowledge, and an intelligent improvement in the quality of the human organism itself, will lead not only to the disappearance of disease and an indefinite prolongation of human life, but to the actual attainment of the perfect conditions of human well-being.

In the midst of his personal evils he ends upon a note of sublime hope:

> What a picture of the human race, freed from its chains, removed from the empire of chance as from that of the enemies of its progress, and advancing with a firm and sure step on the pathway of truth, of virtue and of happiness, is presented to the philosopher to console him

for the errors, the crimes, and the injustices with which the earth is still soiled and of which he is often the victim! It is in contemplating this vision that he receives the reward of his efforts for the progress of reason, for the defense of liberty. He dares then to link them to the eternal chain of human destiny; it is there that he finds the true recompense of virtue, the pleasure of having created a lasting good, which fate cannot destroy by any dread compensation, bringing back prejudice and slavery. This contemplation is for him an asylum whither the memory of his persecutors cannot pursue him; where, living in thought with man established in his rights as in the dignity of his nature, he forgets him whom avarice, fear, or envy torment and corrupt; it is there that he truly exists with his fellows, in a paradise which his reason has created, and which his love for humanity enriches with the purest of joys.[38]

We can close our consideration of the eighteenth century with two expressions of what its achievements meant to those who lived in it. The first is drawn from a history of philosophy written in 1796 by J. G. Buhle.

We are now approaching the most recent period of the history of philosophy, which is the most remarkable and brilliant period of philosophy as well as of the sciences and of the arts and of the civilization of humanity in general. The seed which had been planted in the immediately preceding centuries began to bloom in the eighteenth. Of no century can it be said with so much truth as of the eighteenth that it utilized the achievements of its predecessors to bring humanity to a greater physical, intellectual, and moral perfection. It has reached a height which, considering the limitations of human nature and the course of our past experience, we should be surprised to see the genius of future generations maintain.[39]

In the steeple knob of the church of Saint Margaret at Gotha, in Germany, there was recently discovered this message, placed there in 1784 for posterity to read.

Our age occupies the happiest period of the eighteenth century. Emperors, kings, and princes humanely descend from their dreaded heights, despise pomp and splendor, become the fathers, friends, and confidents of their people. Religion rends its priestly garb and appears in its divine essence. Enlightenment makes great strides. Thousands of our brothers and sisters, who formerly lived in sanctified inactivity, are given back to the state. Sectarian hatred and persecution for conscience' sake are vanishing. Love of man and freedom of thought are gaining the supremacy. The arts and sciences are flourishing, and our gaze is penetrating deeply into the workshop of nature. Handicraftsmen as well as artists are reaching perfection, useful knowledge is growing among all classes. Here you have a faithful description of our times.

HUMANITARIANISM

Do not haughtily look down upon us if you are higher and see farther than we; recognize rather from the picture which we have drawn how bravely and energetically we labored to raise you to the position which you now hold and to support you in it. Do the same for your descendants and be happy.[40]

REFERENCES

1. Montesquieu, *Lettres Persanes*.
2. Samuel Clarke, *Discourse on Natural Religion*.
3. *Ibid.*
4. Bishop Butler, *Sermons*, Preface to Sermon I, II.
5. Hume, *Enquiry concerning the Principles of Morals*, sec. 2, Pt. II; sec. 5, Pt. II.
6. Diderot, *Supplément au voyage de Bougainville*, sec. 3.
7. Rousseau, *Émile*, Book I.
8. Quoted in L. Ducros, *Les Encyclopédistes*, 368.
9. Burke, quoted in F. S. Marvin, *Western Races and the World*, 134.
10. Condorcet, *Progrès de l'Esprit Humain*, 10ᵉ Epoque.
11. Roger Williams, *The Bloudy Tenent of Persecution for Cause of Conscience*, ch. VI.
12. *Ibid.*, ch. XLV.
13. Milton, *Areopagitica*.
14. *Ibid.*
15. Bayle, *Commentaire philosophique sur les paroles de Jésus-Christ*, Œuvres, II, 367.
16. *Ibid.*, 422.
17. Bayle, *Critique Générale*, Œuvres, II, 76, 77; *Commentaire philosophique*, II, 422; *Supplément au commentaire philosophique*, II, 504; *Nouvelles lettres critiques*, II, 227.
18. *Supplément au commentaire philosophique*, II, 540.
19. Locke, *Letter on Toleration*.
20. *Ibid.*
21. *Ibid.*
22. *Ibid.*
23. *Ibid.*
24. Mirabeau, quoted in J. B. Bury, *History of Freedom of Thought*, 111.
25. Thomas Paine, *Rights of Man*.
26. G. E. Lessing, quoted in T. Ziegler, *Die Geistigen Strömungen des 19. J. in Deutschland*.
27. Voltaire, *Dictionnaire Philosophique*, art. "Philosophe."
28. Voltaire, *Lettre à Maupertuis*, 21 July, 1740.
29. Voltaire, *Dict. Phil.*, art. "Patrie."
30. *Ibid.*
31. Voltaire, *Candide*, ch. III.
32. Goethe, *Conversations with Eckermann*, March, 1832.
33. *Ibid.*, March 14, 1830.
34. J. G. Fichte, *Die Grundzüge des gegenwärtigen Zeitalters*.
35. Abbé de Saint-Pierre, *Articles of the Fundamental Treaty for Preserving the Peace of Europe* (1713).
36. Condorcet, *Progrès de l'Esprit Humain*, Époque I.
37. *Ibid.*, Époque X.
38. *Ibid.*
39. G. B. Buhle, quoted in F. Paulsen, *System of Ethics*, 147.
40. Hettner, *Litteratur des 18. Jahrhunderts*, III, 2, 170.

SELECTED READING LISTS

General: J. B. Bury, *History of the Freedom of Thought;* J. M. Robertson, *Short History of Free Thought;* W. E. H. Lecky, *Rationalism in Europe;* L. Ducros, *Les Encyclopédistes.*

The Science of Ethics: L. Stephen, *English Thought in the Eighteenth Century;* histories of ethics by F. Paulsen, W. Wundt, J. Martineau, F. Jodl. Selections in L. A. Selby-Bigge, *British Moralists.* Thomas Hobbes; John Locke; R. Cudworth, *Intellectual System of the Universe;* S. Clarke, *Discourse on the Obligations of Natural Religion;* Lord Shaftesbury, *Characteristics,* ed. J. M. Robertson; F. Hutcheson, *Inquiry into the Ideas of Beauty and Virtue;* Hume, *Treatise,* Bk. III, *Enquiry concerning the Principles of Morals;* Joseph Butler, *Sermons upon Human Nature;* Adam Smith, *Theory of the Moral Sentiments.* William Paley, *Principles of Morals and Political Philosophy;* Jeremy Bentham, *Principles of Morals and Legislation.* Helvetius, *De l'Esprit;* Diderot, *Supplement to Voyage of Bougainville;* Holbach, *System of Nature;* Rousseau, *Émile;* Volney, *La Loi Naturelle.* For humanitarianism, Raynal, *Histoire des Deux Indes;* C. Beccaria, *Crimes and Punishment.*

Toleration: E. W. Nelson and others, *Persecution and Liberty;* W. E. Garrison, *Intolerance;* D. S. Muzzey, in *Essays in Intellectual Hist. dedicated to J. H. Robinson;* H. W. Van Loon, *Tolerance;* A. A. Seaton, *Theory of Toleration under the Later Stuarts;* T. V. Smith, *Creative Sceptics;* H. M. Kallen, ed., *Freedom in the Modern World.* Milton, *Areopagitica,* Hales ed.; Roger Williams, *The Bloudy Tenent of Persecution for Cause of Conscience;* Jeremy Taylor, *Liberty of Prophesying.* The classic defenses: John Locke, *Letters concerning Toleration;* P. Bayle, *Philosophical Commentary on the Text,* "Compel them to enter in," in *Oeuvres,* II. Thomas Paine, *Age of Reason, Rights of Man.* Lessing, *Nathan the Wise.*

Pacifism and Cosmopolitanism: Voltaire, *Candide,* etc., *Phil. Dict.,* art. "Patrie." Abbé Saint-Pierre, *Project for Perpetual Peace* (app. to Duggan, *League of Nations);* Immanuel Kant, *On Perpetual Peace.* Goethe, esp. in *Conversations with Eckermann.*

Progress: J. B. Bury, *The Idea of Progress;* W. D. Wallis, *Culture and Progress;* F. J. Teggart, ed., *The Idea of Progress, a Collection of Readings;* R. Flint, *History of the Philosophy of History;* J. Delvaille, *Histoire de l'Idée de Progrès jusqu'à la fin du 18e siècle.* Swift, *Battle of the Books;* Condorcet, *History of the Progress of the Human Spirit;* Herder, *Ideas for the History of Humanity.*

BOOK IV
THE GROWING WORLD — THOUGHT AND ASPIRATION IN THE LAST HUNDRED YEARS

CHAPTER XVI

THE ROMANTIC PROTEST AGAINST THE AGE OF REASON

The Social Basis of Intellectual Complexity and Change, and the Demand for its Organization

It is possible to find in the eighteenth century a fairly definite, coherent, and systematically organized body of beliefs and ideals, to which the great majority of the intellectual classes gave assent. The history of thought in that age is largely the history of the spread to all fields of human interest of the method and aims of Newtonian science. This is not to deny that the culture of those times, like that of any other period in the ever-changing web of Western history, was still heavy with the persisting past, and already big with the future. The curious have not unnaturally found the seeds of all our surprising later growths already budding between the trim and ordered alleys of the Enlightenment gardens. The wise have rightly pointed out that the heavenly city the eighteenth-century philosophers worshiped, and even their adored reason itself, link them far more closely to the great classic tradition of ages past than to the manifold irrationalisms of the present and the earthly purgatory to which we soberly look forward. Yet we can discern a characteristic pattern of Enlightenment thought and aspiration, which is emerging the more distinctly as so much we had taken for an enduring legacy recedes into the background, made impossible for us by what we must do to meet our own problems.

In the restless inquiry and searching that have marked men's intellectual pursuits since those days, it is hard to find any such clear picture. Not only did men in the aftermath of the middle-class revolutions fail to reach a measure of agreement on fundamentals; even within particular fields it is not easy to trace any simple line of development. In many ways the last century seems analogous to those transitional generations that transformed the world and the mind of the Middle Ages into the world and the mind of the Enlightenment; though naturally enough, since we are convinced the issues we are facing today are the most momentous ever confronting the human race, the period that generated them now strikes us as far more revolutionary. In this year of grace 1940 intelligent men are prophesying the imminent disappearance in Europe of anything remotely resembling the kind of civilization and culture we have known for over two centuries. Even the longer perspectives of recent years have spread the conviction that the Age of Liberalism and the Age of Capitalism are about over. If by "liberalism" we mean the gospel of the French Revolution and the classic economists, and by "capitalism" the economic arrangements of the late nineteenth century consecrated in our economic theory, this seems a safe assumption, even for our own land. But despite our passionate programs for to-day's crisis, we are as yet in no position to say with confidence what form or forms the organization of industrial society will eventually assume. Still less can we predict the nature of the new intellectual synthesis, if indeed we can expect ever again, save for brief periods of crisis, to arrive at any such unified body of knowledge and belief as both the thirteenth and the eighteenth centuries exemplify.

Hence in the last hundred years it is exceedingly difficult to separate the important tendencies from the passing currents of reaction, revolt, and compromise. Another decade, in clarifying the tendencies destined to be accepted by the future, may well bring a quite new perspective on what has been important in the nineteenth century. But we can at least hope to analyze those movements of thought and action which have generated our present intellectual issues, and to examine the major problems faced and dealt with by the nineteenth century that led men to hammer out the ideas they left for our uses. Our picture of the maze of conflicting tendencies and cross-currents at work in the nineteenth century can hardly hope to achieve the unity we discern in those periods whose outcome we already know. Yet the course of events is rapidly producing a unification in terms of the problems that have eventuated and the intellectual instruments put at our disposal. The choices we must make and the allegiances forced upon us have already thrown into relief much of the pattern of nineteenth-century thought and values. Where formerly a large element of personal preference and sympathy entered into any selection of what was important, today the issues have grown so pressing that they have brought to a common focus those ideas that are of enduring significance, and set them off from the mere surface eddies.

Back of the multiplicity and diversity of nineteenth-century tendencies lies the ever-accelerated rate at which the economic forces of social change have been proceeding. The triumphant middle class has itself split into a number of sections; the great body of industrial workers that emerged has been subdivided in a myriad of ways. Instead of a few simple classes among which an urban population was developing, for several generations we have had a society broken up into a great number of special groups, each with its own interests and ideals, and each conflicting with the others on important points. Nationalism too has entered in to cut across all such economic lines and create new divisions among men, and new groupings.

This splintering of Western society into a welter of ill-coordinated groups has provoked its own reaction, already far advanced in Europe. It is plain that the system of irresponsible sovereign states, with boundaries inherited from a simpler economy, is wholly incompatible with the demands and the promise of modern technology. It is equally plain that the unrestrained flow and expansion of trade and economic power, which alone made that system endurable, has broken down and cannot be restored. In the momentous events of to-day we are doubtless witnessing the first crude attempts to organize industrial society in terms of several great regional aggregates, with a kind of direction and unified control so far acceptable only as a war economy. The attendant struggles and brutalities are strikingly reminiscent of the age of religious wars in which the sovereign national state and the main features of early modern capitalism took form. They are the symptoms of an equally drastic revolution, the death-rattle of an old order, and the birth-pangs of a new. In the all-important problem of enlisting coöperative support for this reconstruction of industrial society, hard-pressed Europeans have resorted to a variety of great unifying social faiths, the like of which, with the need, had disappeared from our world since the Middle Ages. In those lands still euphemistically called liberal and capitalistic, the very complexity and conflicts of group ideas and interests —

their critics call it confusion, anarchy, and chaos — have also made clear the necessity for greater organization and integration. Even in America, hitherto preserved by its rich continental resources and its relative isolation from any very insistent pressure to bring more social efficiency into its industrial system, it should to-day be apparent that the choice has become, not whether we shall organize our economic life and aspirations, but what kind of socialized control and what kind of unifying faith we shall resort to, in order to live with modern technology, and with those peoples who have taken its demands more seriously. For us there still seems at least more choice than proved possible in Europe.

Nor did science and philosophy remain uninfluenced by the same nineteenth-century movement toward a splitting-up into a number of divergent tendencies and ideals. The various sciences that used to be embraced in the one comprehensive "natural philosophy" have gone their separate ways to goals that seem quite diverse; while instead of certain common principles and attitudes universally accepted in philosophy, the attempt to get some general view of the world and some clear distinction between the things that are worth while and those that are not worth while for a good life, has become more and more a group and even an individual task. In the generations immediately past we encounter conflicting and contrasting philosophies, rather than a widespread philosophy expressing the views and aspirations of a whole age, or even of an entire group. By the side of all the new ideas and ideals brought into the world since the days of Newton and Locke, there have remained all the old ones as well; and this has led to innumerable attempts at effecting some kind of compromise between the many diverse strands that go to make up the content of the modern mind.

As a counterpart to the desperate search for economic and political organization, the demand has been raised for some new intellectual synthesis that can draw together the various partial views of our competing groups and narrow specialists, and integrate them in terms of a common and shared set of social ideals and values. Unfortunately the unifying social faiths that have already appeared abroad to meet this widely felt need give little evidence that the kind of new synthesis likely to prove popular and effective could ever satisfy a mind accustomed to the free and inquiring spirit of the recent past. They have notoriously been negative and intolerant, exclusive rather than inclusive, and bitterly directed against each other. They leave out so much that men have profoundly cherished, above all they set so little store by the scientific inquiry which is the very nerve of the industrialism they were created to serve, that though they be understandable as desperate resorts in times of acute crisis, it seems incredible that they can long endure in their present form. Like those other fanatic and narrowly intolerant Reformation theologies that unified men against the institutions of the decaying medieval world, they belong rather to the past that is being abandoned than to the new culture of an industrial society for which they are unwittingly preparing the ground. And like them also, our own secular theologies will doubtless be expanded, reinterpreted and enriched as the pressure grows less acute. The present appeal of such dogmatic and intolerant social creeds is but added evidence of the terrific pressure that makes men sacrifice all their other hard-won values to the need for social organization.

Yet it seems unlikely that even America can avoid a more unified social faith than was necessary in the laxer days of untrammeled economic expansion. The recent eager exploration of the American tradition and historic American ideals, crowning several decades of searching social self-criticism, gives hope that the synthesis we shall forge can preserve more of continuity with the core at least of the great values of our past than has seemed possible elsewhere. With our fortunate advantages there is the chance worth fighting for that out of American efforts at industrial organization we can build a synthesis that is comprehensive rather than exclusive, that is not narrowly chauvinistic and nationalistic, and that will focus its faith upon the critical methods of science and intelligence rather than upon empty slogans and hatred for other groups. American thinkers have already laid down the outlines of such a humane and enlightened faith. Whether their present formulations can ever prove widely popular enough, and by what measures that political education can be made effective, it is as yet too soon to speculate. But in the measure that the present analysis of the thought of the last hundred years involves a selective choice of what has been important, it is concern with the problem of achieving such a goal that has furnished the criterion.

The one generalization about the period that will pass unchallenged is that every field of interest and knowledge has been undergoing a rapid growth and expansion. The one conception that all sorts and conditions of thinkers have accepted is that, whatever else the world may be, it is no static and finished thing, but is itself, as a whole and in each of its parts, in process of change and growth. This deep sense of the importance of time, of historical change, extending from stars and atoms to human society, beliefs, and ideals, is the common intellectual climate of recent times. As to what our world, cosmic and human, may be growing into, and whether this growth may properly be termed a progress or not, there is general disagreement. But few would doubt the basic character of temporal change itself. Hence if we are justified in viewing the eighteenth-century world in terms of the essentially timeless Order of Nature, we are right in distinguishing the universe in which men have lived ever since as a Growing World, in which time and temporal processes are of fundamental importance.

The recent shift of intellectual temper that sets our own generation off from the nineteenth century has only emphasized more strongly the fact of growth and evolution. The eternal verities that managed somehow to escape the onslaught of historians and evolutionists up to a generation ago have now all received dates in some epoch or some historical culture. It is rather our notion of the very nature of growth and evolution that has been profoundly transformed. The Divine Providence of the nineteenth-century evolutionists, which guaranteed an easy and automatic progress down the ringing grooves of change, and made of that progress a freedom broadening down from precedent to precedent, has gone to join the heavenly city of the eighteenth century. Growth, we now know, is anything but easy and automatic; it involves sweat and toil and blood and tears, conflict and struggle and bitter travail, and above all the most sustained kind of human effort. And the organization of the conditions of freedom is an even more perplexing task. Whatever kind of progress we still hope for to-day we regard not as the gift of God or evolution, but as the responsibility of human intelligence and planning. We have far less confidence than our fathers that the results of what we do will be good; but we are far more convinced that whatever is done we shall have to do ourselves. Our human world is growing more rapidly than ever; but that very fact we now take as a challenge to direct, guide, and organize that growth. This new conception of temporal change accords well with our basic social need of organizing society around the instruments of technology. For several generations the Growing World seemed an exhilarating liberation, a promise of new enterprises and new freedoms. To-day it has become at bottom a problem of politics, of getting men to do things together in new ways.

In one sense there has been an indubitable progress during the whole period. Scientific knowledge has been piling up at an increasing rate. Every year we have learned how to do more things than we could do before, especially with the natural forces and materials our world so richly offers to our skills. But our very science itself has been transformed, like everything else in our culture, from a free growth into a problem of social organization. In the nineteenth century science was still an ever-broadening vision of Truth. To-day, in our theories as in our practice, it has become more ultimately a human instrument, to be perfected and used for human purposes. And the strategy of those purposes is the basic problem of these times.

Reaction Against the Age of Reason

The initial steps in the transformation of the eighteenth-century world into that in which men live to-day were marked by a strong current of reaction against the scientific methods and ideals of the Age of Reason. Toward the close of the century there developed in Europe a number of tendencies representing in part a reaction against the ideas of the Newtonian world, in part a recrudescence of forces that had remained present in Western civilization since the Renaissance. These tendencies, loosely grouped together as romanticism, emphasized the emotional rather than the rational side of human nature, a richly diversified development of individuals and groups rather than a mathematical uniformity, and, most significant of all, the genesis and growth of things rather than their mechanical ordering. The first half of the next century was marked by conflicting conceptions, the struggle of the old society against the revolutionary ideals, the middle class notions against the rising forces of an industrial civilization, of romanticism against the steady advance of scientific knowledge. Out of these cross-currents there gradually was effected a fusion between the eighteenth-century ideals and the newer tendencies, an intellectual atmosphere favorable to the acceptance of the great nineteenth-century idea of Evolution. Supported by the rapid economic and social changes, and confirmed by the vast new body of experimental science, this idea of growth and development was broadened to include and color all man's interests; while at the same time scientific investigation pushed on until it could claim to have sketched out the broad outlines of a wholly naturalistic explanation of the entire realm of human experience. The resulting changes and readjustments in philosophic, religious, and social thought and ideals, diverse and often conflicting as they were, have probably exceeded in importance and extent those necessary to transform the world of Saint Thomas and Dante into the universe of Newton and Locke. To these changes we must now address ourselves.

It was inevitable that the Age of Reason should provoke men to a reaction. A comparison of the eighteenth- with the thirteenth-century synthesis cannot fail to-day to reveal that, however great the scientific formulation of the former, and however wide its extent and scope, it was a far less adequate vehicle for the expression of all the manifold tendencies and interests of human nature. Not only does the point of view of Dante seem far closer to the experience of the average man, and far easier for him to grasp and assimilate — science and a scientific temper of mind are at best rare and difficult things, to be acquired by much labor and exertion, and perhaps above the attainment of a considerable body of men — but an exclusive emphasis on reason and intelligence certainly fails to take account of much that is both eternal and valuable in human experience. It was no accident that the scientific age of the Enlightenment produced little that can rank with the world's greatest art and poetry. The palaces and gardens of Versailles, the artificial fêtes of Watteau, the heroic couplets of Pope, the sparkling comedy of Molière, and the wit of Voltaire — these were the natural fruits of the Newtonian world, and great as they are

PROTEST AGAINST THE AGE OF REASON 397

they include but a small part of the experiences that have been expressed in the highest works of art. In spite of its many and just claims, the Age of Reason to-day is in disrepute; and it is in disrepute, not because its beliefs were not true, not because they were not sound, but because the ideal of life it offered men was thin and flat and meager. Man may be a rational animal, but his animality is more deeply rooted than his rationality; he cannot live by truth alone. In the nineteenth century most men were either not rational enough, or too rational, to accept the rationalism of the Enlightenment. They either went backwards, for example, to a frank supernaturalism founded on faith, or they went on to a naturalism that could see the greatness and the values of the religious traditions without falling into the pit of too naïve a literal-mindedness. To-day to both orthodox and "emancipated" alike the thin-bodied austerity of Unitarianism seems to make but a modest appeal.

Nothing so well illustrates the new spirit as the reception accorded by Goethe and his Strassburg friends in 1770 to that consummate expression of the Age of the Enlightenment, Holbach's *System of Nature*. It is romanticism standing face to face with Newtonian science, and finding it not so much wrong as irrelevant.

We had neither impulse nor tendency to be illumined and advanced in a philosophical manner: on religious subjects we thought we had sufficiently enlightened ourselves, and therefore the violent contest of the French philosophers with the priesthood was tolerably indifferent to us. Prohibited books, condemned to the flames, which then made a great noise, produced no effect upon us. I mention as an instance, to serve for all, the *Système de la Nature*, which we took in hand out of curiosity. We did not understand how such a book could be dangerous. It appeared to us so dark, so Cimmerian, so death-like, that we found it a trouble to endure its presence, and shuddered at it as at a spectre. The author fancies he gives his book a peculiar recommendation, when he declares in his preface, that as a decrepit old man, just sinking into the grave, he wishes to announce the truth to his contemporaries and to posterity.

We laughed at him; for we thought that we had observed, that by old people nothing in the world that is lovable and good is, in fact, appreciated. "Old churches have dark windows: to know how cherries and berries taste, we must ask children and sparrows." These were our gibes and maxims; and thus that book, as the very quintessence of senility, appeared to us as unsavory, nay, absurd. "All was to be of necessity," so said the book, " and therefore there was no God." But might not there be a God by necessity too? asked we. We indeed confessed, at the same time, that we could not withdraw ourselves from the necessities of day and night, the seasons, the influence of climate, physical and animal condition: we nevertheless felt within us something that appeared like perfect freedom of will, and again something which endeavored to counterbalance this freedom.

The hope of becoming more and more rational, of making ourselves more and more independent of external things, nay, of ourselves, we could not give up. The word freedom sounds so beautiful, that we cannot do without it, even though it should designate an error.

Not one of us had read the book through, for we found ourselves deceived in the expectations with which we had opened it. A system of nature was announced; and therefore we hoped to learn really something of nature — our idol. Physics and chemistry, descriptions of heaven and earth, natural history and anatomy, with much else, had now for years, and up to the last day, constantly directed us to the great, adorned world; and we would willingly have heard both particulars and generals about suns and stars, planets and moons, mountains, valleys, rivers and seas, with all that live and move in them. That, in the course of this, much must occur which would appear to the common man as injurious, to the clergy as dangerous, and to the state as inadmissible, we had no doubt; and we hoped that the little book had not unworthily stood the fiery ordeal. But how hollow and empty did we feel in this melancholy, atheistical half-night, in which earth vanished with all its images, heaven with all its stars. There was to be a matter in motion from all eternity; and by this motion, right and left and in every direction, without anything further, it was to produce the infinite phenomena of existence. Even all this we should have allowed to pass, if our author, out of his moved matter, had really built up the world before our eyes. But he seemed to know as little about nature as we did; for, having set up some general ideas, he quits them at once, for the sake of changing that which appears as higher than nature, or as a higher nature within nature, into material, heavy nature, which is moved, indeed, but without direction or form — and thus he fancies he has gained a great deal.

If, after all, this book had done us some harm, it was this — that we took a hearty dislike to all philosophy, and especially metaphysics, and remained in that dislike; while, on the other hand, we threw ourselves into living knowledge, experience, action, and poetizing, with all the more liveliness and passion.[1]

It is idle to debate the question whether the movement of romanticism was a step "backward" or "forward." That it was to be expected, is clear; that it meant the overshadowing of some things of priceless importance is also as clear as that it brought into the world a new and needed emphasis upon sides of man's variegated personality that in theory at least had been neglected. It may perhaps be said of the eighteenth century ideal of a life from which all that is not rational and useful is excluded, what Rousseau said of pure democracy, that it is fit only for a society of gods; and men are not gods, nor would they wish to be. If we to-day find that science has pursued its path unmindful of whether its sacred fires purify or destroy the good life, and that men's strivings after better things are rarely illumined by the light of exact knowledge, much of that divorce must be attributed to romanticism. If we moderns can fairly claim that our aspirations rest on a sounder basis than did those of Thomas and Dante, and that we have tempered science with saving wisdom better than did the Age of Enlightenment, that too must be attributed to the more or less happy union we have managed to effect between Reason and Romanticism. For better or worse, the nineteenth and the twentieth centuries are blest with a rich heritage from the romantic revolt; nor does it seem that that heritage can ever permanently disappear from human experience.

Emphasis on the Less Rational Side of Human Nature

Fundamentally, that tendency or attitude to which we have given the name of Romanticism was a reaction against a too narrow construing of human experience in terms of reason alone. It was an emphasis on the less rational side of human nature, on everything that differentiates man from the coldly calculating thinking machine; and correspondingly a revolt against viewing the world as nothing but a vast mechanical order. It was the voicing of the conviction that life is broader than intelligence, and that the world is more than what physics can find in it. It was the appeal from science alone to the whole breadth and expanse of man's experience; its creed, if so formless a persuasion can be said to have a creed, has been admirably summed up by him who is perhaps the foremost living romanticist, Bergson: "We cannot sacrifice experience to the requirements of any system."[2] Experience, in its infinite richness and color and warmth and complexity, is something greater than any intelligible formulation of it; it is primary, and all science, all art, all religion, is but a selection from a whole that must inevitably slip through whatever human net is set to catch it. In this sense, even our science, in breaking from the narrow and fixed forms of eighteenth-century mechanics and mathematics, and becoming frankly inquiring and experimental, has felt the romantic influence; while our knowledge of nature and human nature has been vastly heightened and deepened, and under its spur has almost added a whole new dimension. The virtues of the romantic attitude are its open-mindedness, its receptivity to whatever of truth and whatever of value any experience may reveal; as William James put it, although the past has uniformly taught us that all crows are black, still we should continue to look for the white crow. Its besetting vice is that it may lead men to disregard all standards of truth and value, to refuse to make any of the distinctions that are essential to an ordered life; like the drunken man, who accepts all things as of equal worth, the romanticist often fails to criticize his experience, and in the mere joy of living remains oblivious to the greater joys of living well.

Goethe, the great poet of romanticism, can serve as the best illustration of its strength and of its weakness. His indefatigable energies drove him into almost every path of life and every field of human endeavor; and in each he accomplished a few perfect bits and much that is of value. Yet aside from a few lyrics which, the crystallization of passing emotions, need no larger setting, he never produced, in poetry, in science, in philosophy, a perfect whole; superb in individual passages as is his *Faust*, it is not a finished work of art. Goethe himself, his mind, his genius, his life, remains far greater than anything he wrote. Though he aspired after the stars, he never really saw them; he never rose far enough above the level of human experience to criticize it, to discern clearly what is and what is not of worth. Hence while he throbs with the very pulse of life, in its infinite fullness, he never reaches the heights from which the Greeks and Dante and Shakespeare saw it as a whole with a definite meaning for man; he never found any other justification for life save life itself.

As Santayana puts it:

Goethe gives us what is most fundamental — the turbid flux of sense, the cry of the heart, the first tentative notions of art and science, which magic or shrewdness might hit upon. ... In fact, the great merit of the romantic attitude is that it puts us back at the beginning of our experience. It disintegrates convention, which is often cumbrous and confused, and restores us to ourselves, to immediate perception and primordial will. That, as it would seem, is the true and inevitable starting-point.... It follows, however, that one who has no philosophy but this has no wisdom; he can say nothing that is worth carrying away; everything in him is attitude and nothing achievement.... Here is profundity, inwardness, honesty, waywardness; here are the most touching accents of nature, and the most various assortment of curious lore and grotesque fancies.... How, indeed, should we draw the sum of an infinite experience that is without conditions to determine it, and without goals in which it terminates? Evidently all a poet of pure experience can do is to represent some snatches of it, more or less prolonged; and the more prolonged the experience represented is the more it will be a collection of snatches, and the less the last part of it will have to do with the beginning.... To be miscellaneous, to be indefinite, to be unfinished, is essential to the romantic life. May we not say that it is essential to all life in its immediacy; and that only in reference to what is not life — to objects, ideals, and unanimities that cannot be experienced but may only be conceived — can life become rational and truly progressive? Herein we see the radical and inalienable excellence of romanticism; its sincerity, freedom, richness, and infinity. Herein, too, we may see its limitations, in that it cannot fix or trust any of its ideals, and blindly believes the universe to be as wayward as itself, so that nature and art are always slipping through its fingers. It is obstinately empirical, and will never learn anything from experience.[3]

The Natural No Longer Equivalent to the Reasonable

From this general attitude of romanticism there follow a number of more definite tendencies. In emphasizing the less rational side of human nature, the early romanticists accepted the eighteenth-century ideal of the Natural, but they gave to it a new interpretation. This is very clear in Rousseau, who is sometimes regarded as the fountainhead of the later movement, but whose importance seems rather to consist in his popular expression of tendencies that had already been germinating for some time. Rousseau went as far as any of the rationalists in deifying the "natural man"; but his conception of what is natural in human nature was derived, not from the Newtonian order of nature, but rather from his own personal experience. For him the natural man is not the rational thinker, judging everything by its usefulness to himself and his fellows, but rather the man of passion and feeling. Intelligence and reason, he believed, are largely the products of social environment, an environment that seizes upon the plastic nature of the child and dis-

---

[3] From *Three Philosophical Poets*, by George Santayana. Reprinted by permission of the publishers, Harvard University Press.

torts it by pressing it into a traditional mould that must remain alien to it. "Everything is good as it comes from the hands of the author of nature; but everything degenerates in the hands of man." [4] "The whole sum of human wisdom consists in servile prejudices; our customs are nothing more than subjection, worry, and restraint. Civilized man is born, lives, and dies in a state of slavery; at his birth, he is sewn up in swaddling clothes, at his death, he is nailed in a coffin; so long as he preserves the human form he is fettered by different institutions." [5] "We must choose between making a man and a citizen; for we cannot make both at once." [6] Yet since man must live with his fellows, he must live his life in accordance with law; but if he is to remain free, if he is to retain in society the good tendencies which are his by nature, he must be governed and directed by the laws of his own nature. The whole aim of education should be thus to preserve the natural man, and ensure that the habits he forms are not the artificial ones of custom and tradition and reason, but rather those in which his nature will flower of itself. Rousseau's elaborate scheme of education, recounted in the *Émile*, is to preserve the child from any formal teaching by other human beings. It is primarily negative, consisting, "not in teaching the principles of virtue or truth, but in guarding the heart against vice and the mind against error." [7] If this endeavor is successful, the real education of the child will come from the free development of his own nature, his own powers, his own natural inclinations. "All instruments have been tried but one, the only one which can succeed — well-regulated liberty." [8] "The only habit which the child should be allowed to form is to contract no habit whatever." [9]

What this means, of course, is that the instinctive judgments, primitive emotions, natural instincts, and first impressions are more trustworthy as a basis for action than all the reflection, the caution, the experience that comes from association with others. "Morality and religion are not matters of reasoned thinking, but of natural feeling. Man's worth depends not on his intelligence, but on his moral nature, which consists essentially of feeling; the good will alone has absolute value." [10] That is to say, the sentiments are the important element in our mental life, and it is not through the development of the intelligence that man becomes perfect, but through the development of feeling; for the ideal man is he that is filled with sympathy for his fellows and is "inspired by religious feeling, gratitude, and reverence." [11]

It is this conception of human nature as essentially feeling that forms the basis for all Rousseau's theories. He feels that the tenets of Deism are true, and therefore while he agrees in the doctrines of his religion with the rationalists, he founds them, not on reasoned demonstrations, but on the religious feelings that he finds natural to the human breast. Similarly, though he uses the machinery of the orthodox political thinking of his day, his fundamental conviction of the equal worth of all individuals is likewise founded upon what he felt in his heart to be true. And in his *Confessions* he sought to lay bare his soul, proclaiming that at last he would show the world a real man — a picture which certainly contains little of the rational.

Even before Rousseau the first efforts of novelists had succeeded in displaying the subordinate part played by reason in the average life. The French romances and the meandering portrayals of the female heart with which Richardson gained great popularity led to a large number of sentimental outpourings, of which Mackenzie's *Man of Feeling*, who floods every page with copious tears at the slightest provocation, is perhaps the most extreme example. On the other hand, writers of clearer vision, like Fielding and Smollett, in portraying "real men," had presented even more cogent reasons for doubting the complete adequacy of the popular psychology that saw the only motive of human nature as rational self-interest.

Tradition Found Truly Natural

Rousseau's emphasis on the original feelings and passions of mankind was revolutionary in intent: he wanted to transform social institutions until they conformed to these needs of human nature. But it is just as easy, if one takes feeling rather than reason as a criterion of truth, to feel that the accustomed and the traditional is natural to man, and that radical proposals for alteration are unnatural and even inhuman. On the whole, since the great French Revolution was so largely the outcome of eighteenth-century rationalism, the romanticists tended to align themselves on the side of the conservative opposition; and since feelings could easily change, romantic poets like Coleridge and Wordsworth passed rapidly from an initial enthusiasm to revulsion and repudiation when their hearts were hardened by the reign of terror and the Napoleonic attacks. Moreover, it is much easier for traditional beliefs in politics or religion to defend themselves by their "instinctive appeal to the human heart" than to elaborate a rational apology; and hence traditionalists in every field found in Rousseau's method, though not in his conclusions, a golden opportunity. That rationalism led consistently to criticism and reform, while romanticism was at the disposal of every sentiment, only reinforces what has been already said as to the lack of any standard in the latter attitude.

The conservative side of romanticism was clearly foreshadowed by a man who himself could hardly be claimed for the movement, Hume. In breaking down by his appeal to experience not only the rational defense of the religious tradition, but just as well the rational method itself in science, he showed with great force that human nature is largely a matter of habit and custom. What seems reasonable and axiomatic is really the effect of education and existent institutions. It was natural that this skepticism as to the power of reason should have led Hume to fall back upon custom and habit as the only foundation of beliefs; the genuine skeptic, who sees no certain truth anywhere, can hardly share the enthusiasm of the doctrinaire revolutionary, who has no experience but only reason to support him. After all, if we can find no secure truth in religion and politics, we had best adhere to the established church and the established government; it at least has the advantage of being established. Hence skeptical souls, from Montaigne to Lord Balfour, have often been convinced Tories and traditionalists; they see no reason for believing that anything else would be better. When to this distrust of reason is added the positive feelings for familiar institutions endeared by long association, it is easy to see how romanticism became the bulwark of beliefs that had seemed to crumble before the onslaughts of rational criticism.

Emphasis on Faith — As a Support to Religion

If the eighteenth century saw the rise of determined opposition to trust in reason, it saw also the positive counterpart of reliance upon faith. Naturally this complete denial of rationalism appeared first in the interests of religion, since it was in religion that reason first revealed its destructive conclusions. As the century wore on, far-sighted religious leaders who understood the complete skepticism and the dogmatic atheism in which the Enlightenment was bound to end, and to whom the religious traditions of mankind were nevertheless important and dear, rejected completely the specious support which rationalism had seemed to offer to the fundamental doctrines of Christianity, and, following the advice of Bayle and Hume alike, turned to the impregnable foundation of faith. In mysticism, in the inner experience of the soul, they sought the surest bulwarks against disbelief and what seemed to them its attendant moral laxity. This movement of "pietism" first appeared on a large scale in Germany, as a reaction, not against the radical rationalism of the Deists and their successors, but against the equally barren and formal orthodox rationalism of seventeenth-century Lutheran scholasticism. Its influence was felt in England by Wesley, who made it the basis of the great evangelical revival against all degrees of rationalism. Finally the appeal to the inner experience was itself rationalized and systematically formulated by Kant, into whose thought the pietistic tradition entered as a powerful factor.

In Germany the theological and political controversies that culminated in the Thirty Years' War had accentuated the tendency to emphasize doctrinal orthodoxy and correct belief at the expense of the religious and moral life. The abstract Protestant scholasticism that had come to be the essential thing in both the Reformed and the Lutheran churches left many with the sense of a great lack. The man who raised the standard of revolt was a Lutheran pastor, Spener, who in a popular book published in 1675, *Pia Desideria,* called men to emphasize the "religion of the heart," a personal religion flowering in a purer moral life, rather than the formal and ecclesiastical religion then prevalent. Spener did not attack any part of the orthodox system, but he did claim that parts of it were much more important than the rest; and he wished to bring into special prominence those which had a direct effect upon the personal religious life, particularly the doctrines of salvation. The value of a belief for him was in its practical bearing. He emphasized the doctrine of regeneration, and insisted that the all-important thing was the transformation of character through vital union with Christ. Only where the life is actually changed, and the spirit of Christ's love controls one's conduct, has a person any right to think that he has been born again and is among the saved. Not some external sacramental system administered by a church, but the inward experience of conversion and faith, is the kernel of the Christian life. Purity, piety, holiness of life — that is, moral character — these are the essentials.

Since our entire Christianity consists in the inner or new man, and its soul is faith, and the effects of faith are the fruits of life, I regard it as of the greatest importance that sermons should be wholly directed to this end. On the one hand they should exhibit God's rich benefits, as they affect the inner man, in such a way that faith is advanced and the inner man forwarded in it. On the other hand they should not merely incite to external acts of virtue and restrain from external acts of vice, as the moral philosophy of the heathen does, but should lay the foundation in the heart. They should show that all is pure hypocrisy, which does not come from the heart, and so accustom the people to cultivate love to God and to their neighbors and to act from it as a motive.[12]

Spener's followers emphasized Biblical study for practical and devotional purposes, depreciation of scholastic theology and its controversies, the feelings and will at the expense of the intellect, love for mystical and devotional literature, the necessity of personal faith and growth in Christian perfection, and the formation of *collegia pietatis* or lay groups for prayer and character-building. They stood for a reaction to some of the medieval tendencies, particularly in the need and means of salvation, and in the turning from the common worldliness of the average Christian to an asceticism fostered by group activity in the world rather than monastic withdrawal from it. But in its emphasis on these groups of laymen, and its hostility to ecclesiasticism, sacramentarianism, sacerdotalism, and in fact all dependence on the organized ministrations of the church, it was as profoundly individualistic and disintegrating in its way as rationalism itself. It substituted a new orthodoxy for the older correctness of doctrine; what it refused to tolerate was the impious life.

Most of the German pietists remained within the Lutheran fold, where they soon became the dominant party and founded a large number of institutions for the care of the poor, of orphans, for the education of the young, and for the promotion of missions to the heathen. But the most thoroughgoing pietists were the

PROTEST AGAINST THE AGE OF REASON

Moravian Brethren, founded by Count Zinzendorf, who formed separate communities exemplifying the pure Christian life, and dispatched earnest and self-sacrificing missionaries to all parts of the world, from Greenland to Ceylon. Many of these Moravian groups settled in the congenial Quaker atmosphere of Pennsylvania, where, as the "Pennsylvania Dutch," they have exerted great influence on the religious life of America.

The same reaction against formal rationalism and moral laxity was led in England by John Wesley. Here, however, the movement was a revolt, not against scholasticism, but rather against Deism, skepticism, and religious indifference within the Church of England. Wesley was converted to the "religion of the heart" by a small group of Moravians in London, in 1738; and for fifty years he and his brother Charles and his friend Whitefield conducted evangelical revivals throughout England and America. In England as in Germany the bulk of the evangelicals remained within the State Church, where they formed the so-called "Low Church" party; but the more thoroughgoing also broke away to found the Methodist Church. Wesley found fertile soil for his message among the growing factory population of the North, which not even the rationalistic humanitarians had thought worth bothering about. It is not too much to say that until the factory legislation that began in the 1830's, the Wesleyan evangelicals were the only men who did much to relieve the suffering and to further the education of the working classes.

In opposition to the humanistic and rationalistic notion of the dignity and worth of human nature, Wesley insisted on the older doctrine of original sin and the Fall. "The fall of man is the very foundation of revealed religion. If this be taken away, the Christian system is subverted, nor will it deserve so honorable an appellation as that of a cunningly devised fable." [13] Hence the divine power of grace, through faith in Jesus Christ, is essential to the leading of a moral and Christian life. The rationalistic theory that revelation merely makes clearer the knowledge of man's duty, seemed utterly inadequate; man needs not only knowledge, but power to act in accordance with it. Hence Wesley emphasized the whole traditional doctrine of Christ's redemption and atonement, and attacked the very conception of natural religion. He who trusts to his own virtue, who lives honestly and uprightly and purely, but does not depend for salvation upon Christ alone, is the most dangerous of men. There is hope for the most abandoned sinner; he may be brought to a sense of his corruption and helplessness, and of his need of divine grace. But the righteous man who prides himself upon his own rectitude and moral strength, is lost. The religious man will not, like the rationalist, do his duty recognizing it as God's will, but will do it as the result of a vivid religious experience and an ever-present consciousness of the divine power and goodness.

Every good gift is from God, and is given to man by the Holy Ghost. By nature there is in us no good thing. And there can be none; but so far as it is wrought in us by that good Spirit. Have we any true knowledge of what is good? This is not the result of our natural understanding. The natural man discerneth not the things of the Spirit of God; so that we can never discern them until God reveals them unto us by His Spirit.[14]

Thus reason is impotent, and the only true knowledge comes by a special spiritual organ, Faith.

Faith is that divine evidence whereby the spiritual man discerneth God and the things of God. It is with respect to the spiritual world what sense is to the natural. It is the spiritual sensation of every soul that is born of God. ... Till you have these internal senses, till the eyes of your understanding are opened, you can have no proper apprehension of divine things, no just idea of them. Nor consequently can you either judge truly or reason justly concerning them; seeing your reason has no ground whereon to stand, no materials to work upon.[15]

Faith and faith alone is sufficient; all rational argument either for or against religious truth falls away.

Thus the whole appeal to faith in the interests of the religious tradition resulted in a new orthodoxy, evangelicalism. It was this orthodoxy, and not the older Calvinism, that was spread in England and America through the great religious revivals of the beginning of the nineteenth century; and it is this evangelical orthodoxy, very different from the medieval doctrine and from the Reformation doctrines alike, that is strong to-day as "Fundamentalism." Its main features are primarily the result of the reaction against the eighteenth-century rationalism. What has been its general effect?

It put an end to the barren rationalism of the eighteenth century; it substituted immediate experience for reasoned demonstration, direct knowledge for indirect, in the religious sphere, and so circumvented the skeptics whom the apologists were impotent to overcome; it brought the feelings once more into repute, and aided the nineteenth century reaction against the narrow intellectualism of the eighteenth; it gave a new meaning and an independent value to religion; it promoted individualism and emancipation from the bondage of ecclesiasticism; and, above all, it vitalized and revived religion throughout the length and breadth of the land. On the other hand, it brought back much of the old system, including many of its most obnoxious features which rationalism had relegated to oblivion, as it was supposed, for ever. It turned its face deliberately toward the past instead of toward the future in its interpretation of man and his need. It sharpened the issue between Christianity and the modern age, and promoted the notion that the faith of the fathers had no message for their children. Becoming identified in the minds of many with Christianity itself, its narrowness and medievalism, its emotionalism and lack of intellectuality, its crass supernaturalism and Biblical literalism, its want of sympathy with art and science and secular culture in general, turned them permanently against religion. In spite of the great work accomplished by evangelicalism, the result in many quarters was disaster.[16]

Faith as a Support to Revolutionary Tendencies

But while the new appeal to faith as against reason found expression in these great popular revivals of doctrines drawn from the older religious tradition, it was just as strongly a radical force as well. The feelings, the passions, and the intuitions of the natural man, when made the ultimate source of all knowledge and aspiration, led as easily to principles and attitudes that were genuinely subversive of the whole established order. If a Spener and a Wesley appealed to intuition and faith to support the old, a Rousseau could with equal facility use them to confirm a burning zeal for a new order. And when the spirit of romanticism had finally captured a large part of the intellectual classes, the orthodox realized with amazement that faith was an even more wild and wayward thing upon which to found an established system than dangerous reason itself. The inner experience of men by no means agreed in leading to the conclusions of Paul or Wesley, but gave birth rather to a host of strange and new religions and philosophies the like of which had never been on land or sea. At the height of the romantic period it almost seemed that every man's intuitions were a law unto himself, and even single individuals, as they ran the gamut of human life from youth to age, poured forth in inexhaustible profusion a kalei-

[16] From *Protestant Thought before Kant*, by A. C. McGiffert. Reprinted by permission of the publishers, Charles Scribner's Sons.

doscopic gallery of new visions of the world and man, lovely and beautiful as the iridescent bubble, and as thin and impermanent. It is not for nothing that the Catholic Church has always preferred rationalism to the uncontrollable experience of the individual, tempered ever with an insistence upon authoritatively given premises; and has elevated her Thomases above her mystics, suspicious of even Augustine himself, the root of all heresies. When the really great apologies for the past were provoked by the French Revolution, Burke and De Maistre rejected alike the rationalism of a Bentham and the intuition of a Rousseau, and turned to the pure authority and appeal of a time-honored tradition.

The possible revolutionary implications of faith had already been made plain in the seventeenth century, when the Quakers George Fox and Barclay disregarded all customs and traditions in response to the clear vision of the "inner light." The Quakers, while remaining true to the Christian tradition — alone of all sects, they claim — in the name of their private experience of the voice of God stood up against kings and prelates as even the Calvinists never did. And both the German pietists and the English evangelicals, while they started as movements within the state churches, flowered in the independent organizations of the Moravian Brothers and the Methodist Church. When feeling and intuition made its appearance in the political and social field as well, it was until the Revolution nearly always on the side of the middle-class revolt against the old régime. For however much romanticists and rationalists might differ, they agreed in one thing: they were convinced individualists. Hence both equally served as the intellectual expression of the aspirations of the individualistic commercial classes. Rousseau and Bentham and Locke had one thing in common: they demanded freedom from governmental restrictions. The romantic attitude came in to reinforce the rationalistic critique of tradition, and to add fire to the clear light of reason; and if the rationalists were not always reasonable, neither were the romanticists always irrational. So long as there was a common inspiration, hatred of the old system, and a common interest, the demands of the middle classes, they could well coöperate.

In every land romanticism at first added fuel to the flames kindled by the rationalists. In France, Rousseau; in Germany, the revolutionary poets of the so-called "Storm and Stress," the Goethe of *Goetz von Berlichingen* (1771), and the Schiller of *The Robbers* (1781), *Fiesco*, and *Kabale und Liebe* (*Plot and Passion*) (1784); in England, the Coleridge of the first part of the *Ode to France*, the Wordsworth of the *French Revolution*, and the more consistently revolutionary Shelley of *Queen Mab*, *Hellas*, and *Prometheus Unbound*, to say nothing of Byron; and in America the later Transcendental individualists Emerson and Thoreau — all sang songs of Promethean revolt under the inspiration of the radical social changes of the end of the century. The poets put into lyrical rhapsodies the emotions they felt for the principles developed by the rational scientists.

The Rational Justification of Faith

While these enthusiasms for faith and imaginative intuition were spreading among the lower classes and among the artists and poets, the educated men of the Enlightenment were rather reluctant to abandon reason: faith was not yet intellectually respectable. Before thinkers could desert the approved scientific method, some means must be found of proving rationally that reason must be supplemented by some further organ of knowledge. Hume indeed had seemed to subvert the rational method entirely; but the men who had seen a vast science of nature and of human nature grow under their eyes, however they might feel that the scientific method was inadequate to answer many important problems, were not prepared to do away with it entirely. What they wanted was some proof, in terms of their thought and interests, like that which Thomas had given in the thirteenth century for his, that reason was valid within limits, and that outside those limits it must halt impotent before faith. Such a convincing argument was finally put forward in 1781 by Immanuel Kant in the most famous and influential philosophical work in modern times, the *Critique of Pure Reason*.

The details of this difficult and confused book are too intricate to recapitulate; suffice it to say that Kant, by an analysis of the nature of knowledge and of the powers of the human mind, sought to prove that science and the methods of mathematical physics and mechanics are quite valid in describing the world of which it is possible for man to have any *rational* experience, but that they are quite incapable of revealing to us what the world is really like when not viewed through the highly selective instrument of the human mind. Science is a true description of *phenomena*, that is, of things as the structure and mechanism of our minds permits us to experience them, but it can justify us in neither affirming nor denying anything about the *real world*, the world as it is in itself, or as it would appear to a perfect mind, freed from all human limitations, like that of God. "We are brought to the conclusion that we never can transcend the limits of possible experience, and therefore never can realize the object with which metaphysic — i.e., rational theology — is primarily concerned." [17] We can know the world only in the peculiar and definite and imperfect way in which it is possible for us to know it, not as it really is.

This, of course, amounts to saying that our science does not and cannot include everything within its scope. But what reason have we for assuming that the world is in reality different from, as well as more extensive than, what the scientific method can describe? Here Kant stands as the spokesman for all the romantic tendencies we have been sketching: we have other experiences, those of conscience and beauty and of the religious impulse, which, while they are not properly speaking scientific or rational experiences at all, and while they cannot be fitted into the scheme of mechanistic physics, nevertheless are too strong and too important to be dismissed as mere illusions. They are quite unintelligible unless we assume that the world is really a somewhat different kind of place from what science can prove it to be; and since we can never *know* scientifically what the universe is really like, we are justified, for practical reasons, to enable us to live as it is inevitable that human beings will live, in assuming that somehow it is an appropriate setting for the complex of reason and feeling which we find human nature to be. We do and must act from a sense of moral obligation, we do and must feel a religious reverence for something in the world greater than ourselves, we do and must respond to a beauty in things that cannot be scientifically explained. Hence, since we can neither prove nor disprove by the methods of science that we must choose the right rather than the wrong, that we are free so to choose, and that the universe is governed somehow by a moral law, and since we are absolutely compelled, being the creatures that we are, to live as though these things were true, we are justified in assuming that they are. Where science can neither prove nor disprove, we are justified in having faith.

Such a rational defense of faith has seemed cogent to multitudes of men; it was enthusiastically accepted by the romanticists who felt already that rational science was inadequate. By claiming that science is limited in scope, however valid within those limits, it opened the door to a host of other methods for arriving at religious, moral, and philosophic beliefs about the place and destiny of man. If you did not believe that truth can be attained by any other than the scientific method, you were an *agnostic;* if you did, nobody at least could prove that you were wrong. Far from thinking that these limits placed on the powers of the mind were discouraging, most men welcomed Kant's "critical philosophy," as it was called, as the open door to the freedom to believe almost anything they sincerely wanted to believe. In the next generation dozens of different proposed roads to reality were offered by enthusiastic poets, philosophers, and theologians. Kant's own road was not so important as the license he seemed to have given men to blaze new trails of their own through the irrational wilderness of faith and intuition. Kant summed up his great contribution to intellectual happiness in the words: "From the critical point of view the doctrine of morality and the doctrine of science may each be true in its own sphere; which could never have been shown had not criticism previously established our unavoidable ignorance of the real world, and limited all that we can *know* scientifically to mere phenomena. I have, therefore, found it necessary to deny *knowledge* of *God, freedom,* and *immortality,* in order to find a place for *faith.*" [18] All the careful tests of truth which generations of scientists had built up went by the board, and men were free to believe anything which the interests of the whole of human nature impelled them to believe. Almost any kind of faith had been made intellectually respectable.

Kant's book stimulated romanticists to a flood of special systems founded on faith. Man, they claimed, is not fundamentally intellectual. Rather human nature is at bottom made up of instincts and feelings; and his instinctive and emotional life should dominate his career and paint for him both his conception of the world and his conception of human life. In other words, the poet or the saint is a truer and better guide on the pathway of life and thought than the scientist. Religion, morals, art, literature, social and political philosophy, and education should recognize this fundamental fact and build upon it. Religion is not a science to be demonstrated, but a matter of the heart, a life to be lived. Morality is not a science, but essentially the good will and the performance of one's duties. Art is not a matter of form and structure, but of rich sentiment and feeling. Society is not a cold-blooded enterprise founded on self-interest, but a vast organism pressing onward to realize dimly seen ideals, in which all are members one of another. The whole universe is not a machine, but a living body, to be interpreted on the analogy of man's life.

Herder, for example, the father of the German romanticists, founded all truth upon the feelings, on faith rather than reason, described as an inner, unanalyzable certainty. Jacobi, perhaps the most popular and influential, though not the soundest, of these thinkers, frankly called intuition the source of ultimate knowledge, and abandoned any attempt to reconcile its certainty with the scientific laws of nature. The immediate certainty of the direct inward vision is far more certain than logical demonstration. He first called this faculty by which spiritual truths are perceived "*Glaube*" or "Faith," but later, to the confusion of many, dubbed it "*Vernunft*" or "Reason," in contradistinction to the scientific reason to which he gave the name "*Verstand*" or "Understanding." He was widely followed in this contrast between "Reason" or Faith, and mere "Understanding"; its reverberations were heard in Coleridge and Carlyle in England, and in Emerson in America. Schleiermacher adapted it with great originality to religion, Schelling to art, and Hegel to the whole of human history and thought. What differentiates these various systems is interesting, but not nearly so important as the fundamental principles and assumptions they held in common. The resulting religious philosophies and apologies were a strange but often beautiful mixture of elements that rationally at least seemed rather incompatible. David Friedrich Strauss, the great nineteenth-century rationalistic theologian, who went perhaps further than even Hume or Holbach had gone in the preceding century in assailing the truth of the Christian tradition, made a rather scornful comment on this sort of medley. "Not everybody can pulverize Christianity and Newtonian science so as to mix them. Most men end up with sausage; the meat is orthodoxy, the fat is Schleiermacher, the spice, Hegel." [19]

Emphasis on the Individual Personality and its Expression

This complete liberty given to the individual to pick his faith where it pleased him meant, of course, that the individual character and personality became the all-important determining factor. As against the eighteenth-century disregard of everything not universal in human nature, the romanticists emphasized individuality and personality above all things. Their whole ideal for man was, not the spread of rational knowledge and science, but rather the fullest development of the unique potentialities of every man. We have seen how Rousseau built his educational program about such an ideal; it was eagerly adapted by the Germans Basedow, Pestalozzi, and Froebel, and introduced to the United States by Horace Mann. By the German poets and thinkers Goethe, Fichte, and Schlegel, by Coleridge and Carlyle in England, by Emerson in America, the whole aim of culture and of life was proclaimed to be the development of the freedom, individuality, and self-expression of the individual. "Be yourself; cultivate your personality; gain the largest possible acquaintance with all the rich heritage of the best that has been thought and said in the past; above all strive for the richest and most varied experiences with your fellow-man; only thus can you develop into a truly noble personality." By some poets and artists this was interpreted as meaning, "If necessary break all the laws of God and man in order to express yourself"; but on the whole this disregard of law and convention and complete trust in the insight and instincts of the individual justified itself in rich and noble and intensely fascinating lives. Though none of the real leaders went so far as to counsel disregard of others, and most saw in devotion and service to the welfare and the similar development of other personalities a most important means of self-development, it is indisputable that the markedly individualistic emphasis of the romanticists provided a powerful stimulus and a respectable justification for the economic individualism that was building the factory system and modern capitalism. A Goethe or an Emerson, in counseling self-reliance, may not have had the remotest idea of producing the self-made business man and "captain of industry" — the phrase comes from the hero-worshiping Carlyle — but the influence has trickled down by devious channels until even to-day our magazines are full of appeals to "Cultivate your personality — make $50,000 a year" — a horrible travesty upon the romantic ideal.

Here again the best example of the richness, the humanity, the strength, and the weakness of the romantic attitude is to be found in Goethe, who managed to include in his titanic output every divergent tendency of the movement. His adaptation of the old Faust legend is one long passionate yearning for the richness and the fullness of life. Into it he wrought his youthful passion and aspiration, and his mature wisdom, the distillation of his own varied experience. Faust, the weary student, has learned the vanity of all sciences; his years of toil have brought him nothing but barren learning. He turns in disgust to magic, in the hope that there, in the Macrocosm, the totality of all wisdom, he may find himself face to face with truth. He does; but he finds also, as the romanticists felt in rejecting eighteenth-century science, that not even perfect science, perfect truth, will suffice; it is life, not the picture of life, for which he yearns. Experience, the totality of human experience and life — that alone will satisfy him. But when he conjures up the Earth-Spirit and sees the monstrous vision of all life spread before him, he cringes; not at one leap, not the whole of life, is given to any mortal to enjoy. Such general experience bursts the bounds of any personality; Faust must content himself with a long and painful acquisition of those experiences which he can assimilate. So he summons Mephistopheles, the spirit of that growth and development which must involve the destruction of the old with the assumption of the new — of experience, in a word, in the only form that it can come to man. The latter confirms Faust in his belief that

> Gray and ashen, my friend, is every science,
> And only the golden tree of life is green.[20]

Faust longs for life, in its pains and joys, its pleasures and sorrows; and that Mephistopheles can give him, growth and development through living. So the two go out into the world to live through the various events that can come to man, festivity, love, crime, remorse, power and wealth, beauty, the glory of the

PROTEST AGAINST THE AGE OF REASON

past and its recreation in the present, artistic activity. Finally, in laboring ruthlessly for what he takes to be the good of others, Faust finds satisfaction; and in that moment his life is done and his lesson learned. But there is, there can be, no real end; growth may be cut down, but it can never stop, for him who is truly saved. In whatever heavens there be Faust will go on using the angels to develop his personality and tasting of the joys and sins of the Celestial City.

> This is wisdom's final word:
> Worthy alone is he of life and freedom
> Who conquers them anew each day.[21]

He who strives, strays, yet in that striving and straying finds his salvation. And the angels, carrying Faust's soul to its new scenes of endeavor, sing:

> Whose ceaseless striving never tires,
> We have the power to save him.[22]

Nature Interpreted in Personal Terms

But the romanticists did not stop with making personality the key to human life; they read its striving and growth into nature also, and behind the screen of mechanistic physics they saw the real world as at bottom a process of realizing ideals. In many ways they sought to interpret the universe in personal terms, feeling that will and aspiration, the deepest things in human experience, must be akin to the fundamental forces of nature. This faith-built doctrine is called idealism; its cardinal tenet is that the experiences of the heart and soul are safer guides, when once we seek to penetrate further than our science can go, than the reason that can find only a mechanistic order. Since faith is such an individual thing, and since what is deepest in the human soul can hardly admit of objective determination, the idealists naturally differed among themselves as to what in the heart of man must be taken as the true key to the riddle of reality in the world. For Kant, the feeling of moral obligation was fundamental, and he saw the world beyond the reach of science as essentially a universal moral order. For his follower Fichte, not duty so much as the ceaseless striving after perfection stirred his soul; and hence for him the world was a great moral struggle of the forces of good against the powers of evil, in which the great

Will of which individual men are but the members sets up obstacles that in overcoming them it may rise to ever higher levels. The poets saw the world as an activity of the creative imagination, the religiously minded saw it as a God calling unto men, the romantic scientists, as a superhuman reason unfolding itself in time and space. For Fichte, who gloried in the good fight, it was a Will that must ride on to victory; for Schopenhauer, who felt the sad futility of human aspiration, never resting, never satisfied, ever seeking that which it lacks, it was a dumb and aimless Will whose uneasy groping can bring only pain and sorrow and sadness. These far-flung imaginative visions of what life can mean to those who live it, will stand as undying monuments to those who conceived them; they can hardly be judged by the standards of rational and literal truth which their creators scornfully rejected. Whatever may be thought of them as literal descriptions of what nature is really like, it will remain true that they are sublime poetic insights into the possibilities of human experience. When Fichte proclaimed that the world, when looked upon as the scene of man's moral duties, does become for him such a place, he was speaking the truth; as he was when he said that the kind of world a man lives in, that is, what seems to him of worth and value, is determined by what kind of a man he is. There is a most important sense in which it is true that the reformer lives in a world of moral struggle, the poet in a world of poetic beauty, and the scientist in a world of scientific truth. The only error of romanticism would consist in believing that these self-made worlds are factually true in a scientific sense; as interpretations of human experience in terms of its significance they are true beyond question.

Romantic idealism, in a word, is poetry, not science, and it is the poets who give its best expression. To them the world is instinct with a spirit that answers to the call of man; nature is no dead machine, but a living force in whom we dwell and move and have our being. In communion with nature they find with Wordsworth the true wisdom, which is still a very human wisdom. Not in science, but in the poet's vision, lies truth.

> One impulse from a vernal wood
> May teach you more of man,
> Of moral evil and of good,
> Than all the sages can.

PROTEST AGAINST THE AGE OF REASON

> Sweet is the lore which Nature brings;
> Our meddling intellect
> Mis-shapes the beauteous forms of things:
> — We murder to dissect.[23]

To one thus open to the universe in every sense, it is truly divine.

> For I have learned
> To look on nature, not as in the hour
> Of thoughtless youth; but hearing oftentimes
> The still, sad music of humanity,
> Nor harsh nor grating, though of ample power
> To chasten and subdue. And I have felt
> A presence that disturbs me with the joy
> Of elevated thoughts; a sense sublime
> Of something far more deeply interfused
> Whose dwelling is the light of setting suns,
> And the round ocean and the living air,
> And the blue sky, and in the mind of man:
> A motion and a spirit, that impels
> All thinking things, all objects of all thought,
> And rolls through all things.[24]

Whatever their differences in interpretation, the romanticists all agreed in feeling behind phenomena some great will or force or super-personal personality to which the name God might not inappropriately be applied, and toward which the religious feelings might be directed. But for them God was a very different being from the God of the eighteenth-century rationalists. For the latter, he was the creator, the watch-maker, absolutely apart from his universe, with whose works man might become familiar but with whom in himself it was impossible to hold any communion. This external deity completely disappeared for the romanticists and idealists: the world was no machine, it was alive, and God was not its creator so much as its soul, its life. Of this universal life of God all things were a part, but man more particularly was its highest expression. This theory of the so-called "immanence" or indwelling of God approaches pantheism, from which it differs chiefly in interpreting the life of the universe through the soul of man rather than through the observed course of nature; and hence it was natural that Spinoza, who had similarly identified God and Nature, should attain wide popularity among the romanticists. The task of reinterpreting his scientific religion, of translating it from Cartesian science into romantic poetry, was accomplished by Herder in his *Dialogues on God* (1787). From this little book flowed an increasing stream of faith in the immanence theory; the universe is divine, and to be open to its every influence, to live in closest harmony with it and develop in response to its development, is to know God and feel one's self a part of his spirit. It was on such a basis that, under the leadership of Schleiermacher, men rehabilitated and transformed the religious faith that the Age of Reason had seemed to make impossible for an intelligent man. In a word, romanticism *is* religion.

The reflection of the pious man is only the immediate consciousness of the general existence of all that is finite in the infinite, of all that is temporal in the eternal and through the eternal. To seek and find this in all that lives and moves, in all becoming and all change, in all doing and suffering, and even in immediate feeling to have and know life itself only as this existence — this is religion. And so religion is life in the endless nature of the whole, in one and all, in God; having and possessing all in God and God in all.... The usual conception of God as a single being outside of the world and behind the world, is not the beginning and end of religion, but only a way of expressing it that is seldom entirely pure and never adequate. [25]

The Romantic Science of the Individual

The more intellectualistic of the romanticists carried their emphasis on individuality not only into the interpretation of human life and of nature as a whole; they tried to develop a new kind of science within the very realm which Kant had left for the undisputed sway of physics. Returning in some ways to the Aristotelian and medieval conceptions of the object of knowledge, they insisted that even science, to be adequate, must try to describe the individual in terms of its relations to the larger wholes of which it is a part, and not merely seek the general laws of the behavior of a multitude of individual things. Hegel, the most rationalistic of all the romanticists, if indeed he can be properly said to belong to that school in any strict sense, made this conception of knowledge exceedingly popular. For him, really to understand and explain any thing or event in the world meant to set it off from every other thing in the universe, and to show its particular place in the great totality of things. Not connection with some preceding cause, but connection with the whole of the great world process, gives true understanding. Philosophy, the highest wisdom, seeks thus to interpret phe-

PROTEST AGAINST THE AGE OF REASON

nomena in terms of their significance, their purpose in the whole, their value in serving the great all-embracing ideal of the universe. To comprehend all there is to know about any object whatever, a watch, for instance, we must really understand the whole of nature, mechanics and time and motion, and the whole of human society and its life throughout history, in which time and time-keeping play so important a part. Nothing exists in and by itself, but only as a part of a total world of interrelated individuals into which it must be set and from which it must be distinguished. This conception is familiar enough from the lines of Tennyson,

> Flower in the crannied wall,
> I pluck you out of the crannies,
> I hold you here, root and all, in my hand,
> Little flower — but *if* I could understand
> What you are, root and all, and all in all,
> I should know what God and man is.[26]

In one form or another this conception of a science of the individual has entered widely into the aim of knowledge, along with the Newtonian science of causal relationships.

Interest in Human History and Tradition

This tendency is closely allied to a still further attitude which, of all romanticism, most powerfully influenced the nineteenth century. If knowledge means fitting things into a larger whole, if nature is alive and growing, if the feelings that attach men to larger groups and to the past are more fundamental than reason, then human history and human traditions take on a new and vital significance. To understand any belief, any ideal, any custom, any institution, we must examine its gradual growth from primitive beginnings to its present form. The character of an individual and the civilization of a nation are the result of a long development; they are to be judged and evaluated only in the light of a thorough knowledge of their past. And if man's life is such a slow growth, the universe to which it is the surest key must also be a process of evolution. Time and history are of fundamental importance. Viewed in such a light, the eighteenth-century science of human nature was utterly transformed. Every one of the conceptions that had sprung from Locke and Newton gave way to a quite different set; the genetic and historical method supplanted the analytical and mechanical, first in human affairs, and then in every branch of natural science, and from being the very model of science mathematics found itself reduced to an almost incomprehensible anomaly. The test of any institution or idea was no longer its reasonableness and its utility, but its origin and its history. From being the useful, the rational became the traditional. *"Die Weltgeschichte ist das Weltgericht,"* sang Schiller: history is the final court of appeal. Hegel, who founded his whole philosophy on this assumption, summed it up in the dogma, "What is rational is real, and what is real is rational," [27] interpreting both as the great cosmic process of universal evolution.

The romantic conception of growth and expansion and development as the fundamental thing in human experience, and therefore in the universe at large, naturally coalesced with the rationalistic conception of progress, as typified by Condorcet in France and Lessing in Germany. Together they led to an emphasis on the ceaseless change of human institutions, on the value of each stage and on the necessity of further alteration. Crude attacks on the old and bitter hostility to the new were both deprecated; history revealed the steady march of mankind toward some far-off divine event. Every nation, every religion, every institution, every group, was essentially the embodiment of some ideal unfolding itself according to its own laws through time. The task of the wise man is to study the past to discover those laws of development, and then play his part in the further unfolding. Philosophies of history, purporting to reveal just such ideals and their laws of growth, were very popular. Herder, in his *Philosophy of History for the Education of Mankind* (1774), and his *Ideas for the History of Man* (1784), set the fashion that was most systematically elaborated by Hegel.

For Hegel, the all-important thing in man is the growth of his spirit, the process of thinking that involves a continual revision and abandonment of the old. Hence the world itself, the whole of existence, is at bottom just such a process of thinking. Not reason, in the sense of some static organ for picturing the world, not logic in the sense of some system of fixed laws, but dialectic, the very process of thinking, is the supreme reality in man and nature. Being, the world, the totality of all things, the absolute — this is in essence a great process of Becoming. To exist means to be always growing, always rejecting some of the old and combining it in new forms. Every institution is the march through time of the Absolute Spirit realizing itself. For the world, as for Goethe's Faust, life is continual striving after some never-attained goal; its meaning and significance lie in the striving itself, and hence, while to cease growing is to die, in reality every stage of the infinite attainment is valuable and good in its own place. For Hegel, as for Leibniz and Pope, whatever is is right; but this only means that everything that exists is a necessary moment in the advance to something further. It is for man to examine every institution, discover the particular ideal it embodies, and carry it forward in accordance with the necessary laws of its growth. To rebel at anything is the height of folly and unwisdom, but to attempt to stop the march of progress and evolution, to find satisfaction in the present stage, is, as in *Faust*, death.

Universal history is the exhibition of Spirit in the process of working out the knowledge of that which it is potentially. And as the germ bears in itself the whole nature of the tree, and the taste and form of its fruits, so do the first traces of Spirit virtually contain the whole of that history.... The history of the world is none other than the progress of the consciousness of Freedom.... The destiny of the spiritual world and *the final cause of the world at large*, we allege to be the *consciousness* of its own freedom on the part of Spirit, and *ipso facto* the *reality* of that freedom.... That the history of the world, with all the changing scenes which its annals present is this process of development and the realization of Spirit — this is the only true *theodicy*, the justification of God in history. Only this insight can reconcile Spirit with the history of the world — viz., that what has happened, and is happening every day, is not only not "without God," but is essentially his Work.[28]

Valuable as was this emphasis on the continuity of tradition, so far as it gave a more adequate knowledge of the forces actually at work in society, it is easy to see how in the hands of conservatives shocked by the spirit of the Enlightenment enforced by revolutionary assemblies it could become a potent instrument of reaction. To this use was it put in Germany by the patriotic "historical school" that, starting from jurisprudence, sought to carry into all social action a new *laisser-faire* — a Hands Off! that was directed to the preservation of old forms and institutions. Law and society cannot be rationally guided; they must grow of themselves. Savigny became the official theorist of this new traditionalist application of the romantic doctrine of development. "All law," he insisted, "comes into being in the manner which prevalent, but not quite exact, idiom designates as the *law of custom;* that is, it is first produced by custom and popular faith, then through jurisprudence; *everywhere, that is, through internal, silently working forces, not through the arbitrariness of a lawgiver.*" [29]

If this is true, each age does not act arbitrarily and in an egoistic independence, but is entirely held to the past by common and indissoluble bonds. Each epoch then ought to admit certain previous elements, which are necessary and at the same time voluntary; necessary in the sense that they do not depend on the will and arbitrariness of the present; voluntary in the sense that they are not imposed by an outside will (such as that of the master in regard to his slaves) but that they are given by the very nature of the nation considered as a whole which subsists and maintains itself in the midst of its successive developments. The nation of to-day is only a member of this perpetual nation. It wills and acts in this body, and with this body, so that it can be said that whatever is imposed by the body is at the same time freely accomplished by the member.[30]

On the whole this romantic faith in traditional growth was a conservative and anti-revolutionary force, especially in Germany; but its fundamental ideas of continuity and change brought with them a point of view that was destined to transform the face of thought. For these were to be the categories of the new evolutionary science; and from romanticism was received the greatest stimulus to a study of man and the world in terms of their genetic development. This is the inestimable debt science owes to irrationalism.

The romantic reaction which began with the invasion of 1794 was the revolt of outraged history. The nation fortified itself against the new ideas by calling up the old, and made the ages of faith and of imagination a defense from the age of reason. Whereas the pagan Renaissance was the artificial resurrection of a world long buried, the romantic Renaissance revived the natural order and restored the broken links from end to end. It inculcated sympathy with what is past, unlovable, indefensible, especially with the age of twilight and scenes favorable to the faculties which the calculators despised. The romantic writers relieved present need with all the abounding treasure of other times, subjecting thereby the will and the conscience of the living to the will and conscience of the dead. Their lasting influence was out of proportion to their immediate performance. They were weak because they wanted strictness and accuracy, and never perceived that the Revolution was itself historic, having roots that could be profitably traced far back in the ages. But they were strong by the recovery of lost knowledge, and by making it possible to understand, to appreciate, and even to admire things which the judgment of rationalism condemned in the mass of worthless and indiscriminate error. They trifled for a time with fancy, but they doubled the horizon of Europe. They admitted India to an equality with Greece, medieval Rome with classical; and the thoughts they set in motion produced Creuzer's *Comparative Mythology* and Bopp's *Conjugations*, Grimm's enthusiasm for the liberty and belief of Odin's worshipers, and Otfried Müller's zeal for the factor of race.[31]

To live is to grow, to assimilate more and more of the riches of the world, to project upon the background of the setting of human life more and more of the infinite possibilities resident in human nature, and in so doing, to become more and more aware of the infinite ties binding all men to each other and to the great forces of the universe of which they are the noblest manifestation — in a word, to live is to bend all one's energies toward the creation of a higher, better, and richer world, to realize God himself in the universe. This was the sum of the wisdom and the aspiration of the romanticists. No wonder that Wordsworth could write,

> Bliss was it in that dawn to be alive,
> But to be young was very heaven![32]

REFERENCES

1. Goethe, *Dichtung und Wahrheit*, Bk. XI, Oxenford tr.
2. Henri Bergson, *Creative Evolution*, ch. I, 39.
3. George Santayana, *Three Philosophical Poets*, 204, 194–99.
4. Rousseau, *Émile*, ch. I.
5. *Ibid.*
6. *Ibid.*
7. *Ibid.*, ch. II.
8. *Ibid.*
9. *Ibid.*, ch. I.
10. Rousseau, quoted in W. M. Marvin, *History of European Philosophy*, 370.
11. *Ibid.*
12. P. J. Spener, *Pia Desideria* (Leipzig, 1841), 101.
13. John Wesley, *Works* (New York, 1827), I, 176.
14. *Ibid.*, VIII, 264.
15. *Ibid.*, 188, 195.
16. A. C. McGiffert, *Protestant Thought before Kant*, 175.
17. Kant, *Critique of Pure Reason*, XIX.
18. *Ibid.*, XXX.
19. D. F. Strauss.
20. Goethe, *Faust*, Part I, Studierzimmer Scene.
21. *Ibid.*, Part II, Act 5.
22. *Ibid.*

---

[31] From *Historical Essays and Studies*, by Lord Acton. Reprinted by permission of the publishers, Macmillan & Co., Ltd., London.

23. Wordsworth, *The Tables Turned*.
24. Wordsworth, *Tintern Abbey*.
25. Schleiermacher, *Reden über die Religion*, Lommatzsch ed., 106, 194.
26. Tennyson, *Flower in the Crannied Wall*.
27. Hegel, *Philosophy of Right*, Introduction.
28. Hegel, *Philosophy of History*, Introduction and Conclusion.
29. Savigny, *Vom Beruf unserer Zeit für Gesetzgebung und Rechtswissenschaft*, quoted in A. W. Small, *Origins of Sociology*, 54.
30. Savigny, *Zeitschrift für geschichtliche Rechtswissenschaft*, 1, quoted in Small, 57.
31. Lord Acton, *Historical Essays and Studies*, 346.
32. Wordsworth, *French Revolution*.

SELECTED READING LISTS

General: W. T. Marvin, *H. of Eur. Phil.*, c. 26; John Dewey, *German Phil. and Politics*; A. C. McGiffert, *Rise of Modern Religious Ideas*; G. Santayana, *Three Phil. Poets*, Goethe; G. H. Mead, *Movements of Thought in the 19th c.*; J. T. Merz, *H. of Eur. Thought in the 19th cent.*; A. W. Benn, *H. of English Rationalism in the 19th cent.*; G. Brandes, *Main Currents of 19th cent. Thought*; histories of philosophy by Höffding, Bréhier, Windelband, etc. H. Heine, *The Romantic School*; T. Ziegler, *Die geistigen u. socialen Strömungen des 19. Jahrh.*; R. Haym, *Die romantische Schule*; W. Dilthey, *Schriften*, IV.

The Religious Reaction: Pietism: A. C. McGiffert, *Prot. Thought before Kant*, IX; histories by A. Ritschl, Hübener, Grünberg, *P. J. Spener*. **England:** Lecky, *H. of England in the 18th cent.*, II; L. Stephen, A. W. Benn; J. M. Robertson, *H. of Freethought in the 19th c.*; Townsend, Workman, and Eayrs, *New H. of Methodism*; John Wesley, *Journal, Works*; G. C. Cell, *Rediscovery of J. Wesley*. See also George Fox, *Journal*. J. H. Newman, *Apologia*; G.G. Atkins, *Life of Newman*; W. G. Peck, *Social Implications of the Oxford Movement*. **France:** Robertson; R. Flint, *Phil. of Hist. in France*; G. Boas, *French Phils. of the Romantic Period*. **Idealism and Religion:** Herder, *God*, ed. Burkhardt; Schleiermacher, *Speeches on Religion, Soliloquies*, ed. Friess; Schelling, *Human Freedom*, ed. Gutmann; Hegel, *Phil. of Religion*; C. C. J. Webb, *Kant's Phil. of Religion*.

Philosophical Idealism: Kant, *Critique of Pure Reason*, tr. Smith; *Theory of Ethics*, ed. Abbott; *Prolegomena. Selections*, ed. T. M. Greene, J. Watson; studies by A. D. Lindsay, N. K. Smith. J. Royce, *Spirit of Modern Phil., Lectures on Mod. Idealism*. Herder, *Ges. der Menschheit, Beförderung der Humanität*; F. J. Jacobi, *Lehre Spinozas, David Hume*; Wilde, Lévy-Bruhl. Fichte, *Vocation of Man, Addresses to the German Nation*; R. Adamson. F. Schlegel, *Phil. of Life, Phil. of History*. Schopenhauer, *World as Will and Idea; Selections*, ed. I. Edman, Parker. Hegel, *Phil. of History; Phenomenology; Phil. of Right; Aesthetics; Selections*, ed. J. Loewenberg. Royce, E. Caird, W. T. Stace; Croce, *What is Living and Dead in Hegel*. See also Nietzsche, Eucken, Bergson.

Literary Expressions: Rousseau, *Émile, Confessions*. B. Croce, *Eur. Literature in the 19th cent*. G. Pellissier, *The Lit. Movement in France during the 19th c.*; Lanson, Nitze and Dargan. Châteaubriand, Hugo, Lamartine, De Musset. Histories of German Literature by C. Thomas, K. Francke, Vogt und Koch, R. M. Meyer. Goethe, esp. *Faust, Goetz von Berlichingen, Werthers Leiden, Wilhelm Meister*, lyrics; lives by Lewes, Brandes, Bielschowsky. Schiller, *Räuber*, lyrics. H. A. Beers, *English Romanticism*; Oliver Elton, *English Literature, 1780–1880*; A. Symons, *Romantic Movement in English Poetry*. Wordsworth, Shelley, Coleridge, esp. *Biographia Literaria, The Friend, Aids to Reflection*; Carlyle, esp. *Sartor Resartus*; Emerson, *Essays, Nature*.

CHAPTER XVII

THE CONFLICT OF SOCIAL IDEALS TO 1848

HAVING traced the growth of the various romantic tendencies of revolt against the scientific methods and ideals of the eighteenth century, we are now in a position to turn to the conflict of social ideals that marked the first half of the next century. It must not be supposed that romanticism ever entirely displaced the spirit of the Age of Reason, or even that it claimed the undivided allegiance of its most devoted adherents. Outside of art and poetry and religion, for which rationalism seemed to have no message at all, the older appeal to reason remained side by side with the newer appeal to faith, sometimes reinforcing it, sometimes contradicting it, more often resulting in some kind of compromise and synthesis. Hence the characteristic of the philosophies that were developed to defend the claims of the different social groups produced by the Revolutionary period is a complexity of method and ideal; only rarely does a thinker remain uninfluenced by the mixture of attitudes.

Three main classes can be discerned. First there were the conservatives, those who opposed the Revolution during its progress and came back triumphantly to power in the years between 1815 and the revolutions of 1830. Secondly, there were the middle-class liberals who had engineered the Revolution, who were in the opposition until 1830 in France and until 1832 in England, and who definitely triumphed in the French Revolution of 1848 and in the repeal of the Corn Laws in England in 1846. Their rapidly increasing strength in all lands was primarily due to the spread of the Industrial Revolution throughout Europe; their assumption of power in any nation was coincident with the growth in that nation of the factory system and capitalism. Thirdly, there appeared a new group, the factory hands and their spokesmen. They become prominent in the second generation of industrialism, play a powerful part in the revolutions of the mid-century, but though increasing rapidly in numbers remain definitely in the opposition. The first half of the century witnesses the struggle between the conservatives and the liberals, with voices of protest from the third group; the second half sees the conflict shift to the battle between the two classes of an industrial civilization. There are, then, three main philosophies to be considered: Conservatism, Individualistic Liberalism, and the theories of Industrial Society.

The Philosophy of Conservatism

Throughout the long eighteenth-century attack upon the old régime, there had been no serious attempt at an intellectual defense of the existing order. Those who upheld it either considered it strong enough to stand by itself without any apology, or else, being in control, resorted to the readiest weapon of the entrenched conservative, force and suppression. But the outbreak of the Revolution at last raised up real opponents of the radical attack, and during the Revolutionary and post-Revolutionary periods a few great men formulated a serious and systematic philosophy of opposition to the eighteenth-century spirit. Stung by their overthrow, they attempted a defense of their ideas that still stands as the ablest exposition of the philosophy of conservatism.

This philosophy was largely apologetic, and its main lines were determined by the nature of the attack to which it was the answer. It was developed to justify the position of the privileged classes under the old régime, the Court, the Church, and the great body of landholders. Its chief representatives were not reactionary; they were willing to accept as just most of the contentions of the middle class, providing they themselves were permitted to remain in the enjoyment of their most important privileges. They were even prepared to champion, within limits, the rights of the industrial workers against the more hated business men and manufacturers. Concerned as they were more with defending themselves than with maintaining the traditional principles, they were willing to incorporate such new changes and ideals as were already accomplished facts. Of blind reaction there can probably be no intellectual defense; but intelligent conservatism, however much it may rely upon prejudice and inertia, is certainly capable of a respectable apology.

This conservatism accepted the more important middle-class ideals. The absolute right of private property, especially in land, it warmly acclaimed, and was as zealous as any business man in defending it against arbitrary governmental confiscation on the one hand and inroads by the masses on the other. The French *émigrés* nobles on their return were wise enough not to attempt to get back the estates that had been divided amongst their former peasants; the mere proposal to give them a compensation from the public treasury was enough in 1830 to precipitate their final downfall. The conservatives, too, gladly accepted the whole program of the economic liberals in commerce and industry; they had no interest in forcing the old guild and governmental regulations upon reluctant business men. Metternich in his most reactionary moments was an ardent upholder of *laisser-faire*, and his economic measures in Austria and Italy unwittingly went far to strengthen the forces that eventually overthrew him. His program was benevolent despotism in the sphere of business. The Tories in England, too, under Robert Peel and Huskisson, effected many *laisser-faire* reforms in the twenties; while in France the doctrines of Adam Smith, popularized by his follower J.-B. Say, gained wide adherence. The one point on which the conservatives drew back was their insistence on the retention of privileges for the agricultural interests; they finally consented to the abolition of the profitable Corn Laws only when betrayed by the commercial members who had crept into the Tory Party. Then in rage and desperation they listened to a few humanitarians like Lord Shaftesbury, and consented to pass factory legislation which they hoped would secure the gratitude of the workingmen and curb the manufacturers.

One other new and popular tendency the conservatives tried to make their own, in France and England, the rising tide of patriotism and nationalism. The recrudescence of this passion during the Revolutionary wars made it plain that it would serve as the strongest possible standard under which to rally a whole nation behind any government. By its means Napoleon I had united all groups in France; and when the cosmopolitan and business administration of Louis Philippe managed to identify profits with peace rather than with patriotism, it was sufficient to bring back his nephew to power for twenty-two years. The Tories kept back Reform for years by hurling the gallant Duke of Wellington into the breach and proclaiming the glories of Waterloo; they went even farther, and developed an enthusiasm for the principle of nationalism in any land where its advocacy would restore the balance of power. Canning used it with great effect against Metternich, and Palmerston's bellicose notes — he was the outstanding conservative in the Liberal Party — aroused the enthusiasm of the nation and held the Austrians in check. In central and eastern Europe, where the Congress of Vienna had applied the principles of legitimacy and compensations rather than nationalism, conservatives still clung to the eighteenth-century upper-class cosmopolitanism, feeling that any group of men had the right to be made the subjects of a good prince. Only when nationalism meant territorial aggrandizement did they espouse it; and then, like Bismarck, they were careful to apply it with discrimination.

Acceptance of the Romantic Protest against Rationalism — The Appeal to Faith

But while the philosophy of conservatism accepted these elements from the theories of the commercial middle class, its main defense was rooted in the romantic protest against rationalism. Faith rather than reason could best rally men to the support of tradition; not the wayward faith of the romanticists, but the authoritative and social faith of religion, the faith in the tried wisdom of the fathers transmitted from generation unto generation through a great tradition. The two greatest theorists of conservatism, Joseph de Maistre in France and Edmund Burke in England, both shrank from the bold and blasphemous enlightenment doctrine that the reason of the individual should presume to examine and criticize the time-honored wisdom of the race. Both appealed rather to the lessons of experience, de Maistre to the experience of the Catholic Church, Burke to that of the British Constitution, and both assailed in no uncertain terms the whole eighteenth-century rationalistic social and human science. Their aim, as de Maistre put it, was "absolutely to kill the whole spirit of the eighteenth century."

Joseph de Maistre was a native of Savoy, the hereditary dominion of the King of Sardinia. He sprang from a family of magistrates, and in his youth he had the opportunity of observing the workings of the old feudal society at perhaps its best. Overwhelmed by the French Revolution, he was driven into exile, served as chief magistrate himself in Sardinia, and then spent fifteen years as Sardinian minister at the court of St.

Petersburg, where he had the opportunity of studying the most conservative government in the world at first hand. The key to de Maistre's thought is the indescribable fascination of power. Before strength, before what exists, no matter what reason or moral principle may say, he simply must bow down and worship. This humility before whatever is, this deep-seated reverence for traditional institutions, he did not, like Hegel, who shared his respect for facts however brutal, seek to understand; it was enough to accord to power unlimited admiration. It was the titanic force of the French Revolution that awoke him to reflection. He simply could not understand it; it was so utterly irrational, so powerful, so fascinating. Nothing could prevail against it, yet its leaders were rascals, foolish, mad. It must be the hand of God, the God of the cruel and ruthless universe, the God of things as they are! Generalizing from the Revolution, de Maistre saw all human history as the operation of great forces quite beyond all human control, playing with men as with puppets. His conception, in fact, was remarkably similar to that of Thomas Hardy in the *Dynasts*.

If de Maistre worshiped power above all things, it was in unity that he sought it, the unity that binds nations together and welds them into one whole. Appalled at the chaos and anarchy of the Revolution, like Hobbes in similar circumstances he felt that only some great cohesive force could bring men together. Human nature is dual: it sees the light, but it is evil and corrupt, and must be compelled to follow it. To attempt to found society on reason is the height of folly; to attempt, with Rousseau and the democrats, to found it on the corrupt wills of the governed, is worse. The problem is to find some force strong enough to check reason and control the evil wills of men. Individualism must be crushed.

Such a force can only be the mystic faith in religion.

If every man thinks out for himself the principles of government, civil anarchy and the destruction of political sovereignty must quickly follow.[1]

Reason divides, only faith can unite.

The Revolution is the revolt of individual reason against universal reason, and consequently it is the most evil thing imaginable. It is the essential enemy of all belief common to many men, which makes it the enemy of the human race.[2]

The whole science of government, in fact, is fundamentally irrational.

Everything in this science which at the outset seems to common sense an evident truth is almost always found, when experience has spoken, to be not only false, but even pernicious. To begin at the beginning, if one had heard nothing of governments, and if men were called upon to deliberate, for example, on hereditary as against elective monarchy, he would be rightly regarded as mad who should vote for the former. The arguments against it come to mind so naturally that it is useless to recall them. Nevertheless history, which is experimental politics, demonstrates that hereditary monarchy is the most stable, most happy, and most natural of governments for man, and that elective monarchy, on the contrary, is the worst kind of government known. In population, in commerce, in prohibitive laws and in a thousand other important subjects, almost always the most plausible theory is contradicted and annulled by experience.[3]

Edmund Burke, the English Whig leader who defended the British Constitution of 1689 first against the attempts of George III and his party to subvert it at home and in the colonies, and then against the equally dangerous democratic doctrine in France, is just as disdainful of untried theory, however rational, and just as reliant upon the wisdom of past experience. He was primarily a utilitarian, a worshiper of the expedient, who was convinced that the mere fact that any custom or institution had grown up over a long period of time established an overwhelming presumption in its favor. The whole business of appealing from tradition to reason and nature was distasteful to him.

One sure symptom of an ill-conducted state is the propensity of the people to theories.[4] The lines of morality are not like ideal lines of mathematics. They are broad and deep as well as long. They admit of exceptions; they demand modifications. These exceptions and modifications are not made by the process of logic, but by the rules of prudence. Prudence is not only first in rank of the virtues political and moral, but she is the director, the regulator, the standard of them all.[5] No rational man ever did govern himself by abstractions and universals.[6]

To reason he opposed prescription, what has worked in the past. The presumption of wisdom is on the side of the past.

Prescription is the most solid of all titles, not only to property, but to what is to secure that property, to government.... The species is wise, and when time is given to it, as a species it almost always acts right.... Truth may be far better than prescription ... but as we have scarcely ever that certainty in the one that we have in the other, I would, unless the truth were evident indeed, hold fast to peace, which has in her company charity, the highest of the virtues.[7]

Any change is apt to shake the all-important security. "We ought to venerate where we are unable presently to comprehend."[8] This reverence for all existing institutions led him to oppose vigorously the attempt to abridge, by new mercantilistic restrictions, the liberty which a policy of "salutary and wise neglect" had allowed to grow up in the colonies, to denounce Warren Hastings and the East India Company for their interference with the age-old society of India; and at the same time to resist every effort at Parliamentary reform. The oligarchical confusion of the British Constitution, its rotten boroughs and its lack of any representation for the growing towns, he thought excellent because it had worked for ages. "Our representation is as nearly perfect as the necessary imperfections of human affairs and of human creatures will suffer it to be. The machine itself is well enough to answer any good purpose, provided the materials were sound."[9] This temper was perfectly exemplified by the Duke of Wellington, who at the very moment that the country was seething with revolution and demanding a Reform Bill in 1830, solemnly announced:

The English Parliament answers all the good purposes of legislation, and this to a greater degree than any legislator has ever answered in any country whatever; it possesses the full and entire confidence of the people.... I will go further. If at the present moment I had imposed upon me the duty of forming a legislature for any country — and particularly for a country like this, in possession of great property of various descriptions — I do not mean to assert that I could form such a legislature as we possess now, for the nature of man is incapable of reaching such excellence at once, but my great endeavor would be to form some description of legislature which would produce the same results.[10]

Against any aims or criticisms of the individual the conservatives opposed the great living body of society. Society is no artificial creation of reason and interest, it is a vast living organism in comparison with which the present moment is as nothing, and the wisdom of any man or group of men of little worth. The nation is a mystic unity in which the individual must sink himself completely, as the soul loses itself in God. Thus de Maistre and Burke sought to fuse the old traditions and the new mystic religion of nationalistic patriotism; thus Napoleon succeeded. What, after all, is my country? Is she a group of discordant little men who have agreed to live together to serve their own selfish interests? Is she founded on an artificial contract, on a man-made and written constitution? A thousand times No! She is My Country! She is something sacred, something living, something one and eternal, the central source of my life, my aspirations. She is greater than any man, than all men now living, than all generations of men: she is an organic whole, one and indivisible, a past, a tradition. "My country is an association on the same soil of the living with the dead and with those yet to be born." [11] Is France the thirty million men living between the Channel and the Pyrenees? No, she is all the Frenchmen who have ever lived and all those who will live in ages to come, welded into one great whole. Shall I then dare to alter their work? Shall I in my pride seek to tear down the edifice which they wrought with tears and blood? It is rather for me humbly and meekly to add my small stone to the great cathedral that has already been building for countless generations, and to spring to its defense against the mad and sacrilegious fools who would overthrow it. My country is everything, I am nothing. My king is her symbol, the nobles are her true knights, the Church is her guide and tutor. Let me then fight and die for king and nobles and Church and country!

This is not rationalism, not humanitarianism, not cosmopolitanism, not the eighteenth century. It is romanticism, it is the true religion of the present age, it is the one unfailing appeal to which conservatives have always been able to resort ever since the Revolution — it is modern Nationalism, the religion of irrational patriotism. De Maistre appealed to Frenchmen to save France and her king; Burke called on Englishmen to defend England and the British Constitution: and thus has every statesman called on his fellows to preserve the great traditions of their native land. Before such an appeal all reason, all criticism, all demand for reform, must shrink away abashed. Society is not to be judged by its serving of any rational interests; it is to be loved, to be worshiped, to be defended at all costs.

Thus wrote Burke:

> Society is indeed a contract ... but the State ought not to be considered as nothing better than a partnership agreement in a trade of pepper and coffee ... to be taken up for a little temporary interest and to be dissolved by the fancy of the parties. ... It is a partnership in all science, a partnership in all art, a partnership in every virtue and in all

perfection. As the ends of such a partnership cannot be obtained in many generations, it becomes a partnership not only between those who are living, but between those who are living, those who are dead, and those who are to be born. Each contract of each particular state is a clause in the great primeval contract of eternal society, linking the lower with the higher natures, connecting the visible and invisible world, according to a fixed compact sanctioned by the inviolable oath which holds all physical and all moral natures each in their appointed place.[12]

Gone is the right of revolution, gone is every right of the individual against such a mystic body of Christ. "The place of every man determines his duty."

In France the traditionalist de Bonald and in Germany a host of idealistic philosophers and jurists worked out elaborate theories of the State as an organism, a personality with a life and development and laws of growth of its own, interference with which would be sacrilegious. Most influential of all was the doctrine of Hegel, laid down in his *Philosophy of Right*. For him the State is the highest manifestation in the world of the great Spirit whose development through time is the purest reality and the supreme ideal. The World-Spirit has revealed itself in the past in the Orient, in Greece, and in Rome, and to-day it has reached its fullest development in the Teutonic nation, in the Prussian constitutional monarchy of the 1820's.

The State is the Divine Idea as it exists on earth.... It is the Idea of Spirit in the external manifestation of human will and its Freedom.[13]

The individual and his private development can only take place through his proper functioning in the existent State.

It is the moral whole, the State, which is that form of reality in which the individual has and enjoys his freedom; but on the condition of his recognizing, believing in, and willing that which is common to the whole. And this must not be understood as if the subjective will of the social unit attained its gratification and enjoyment through that common Will; as if this were a means provided for its benefit; as if the individual, in his relations to other individuals, thus limited his freedom, in order that this universal limitation — the mutual constraint of all — might secure a small space of liberty for each. Rather, we affirm, are Law, Morality, and Government, and they alone, the positive reality and completion of Freedom. Freedom of a low and limited order is mere caprice.[14]

True Freedom, in other words, consists in finding one's station in the existing order and faithfully performing its duties.

The outcome of all such notions is clear; rational criticism of such a living organism, such a mystical embodiment of the Will and Purpose of God on earth, is entirely aside from the point. Accept the State God has given you, live in it, die for it; but do not presume to question its wisdom or alter its forms. Under the teachings of Savigny, an army of lawyers and jurists set to work to find the reason and the justification for the legal forms that have come down from the past, and to explain how any radical alteration in them would be unthinkable. The theory that legal and political institutions are the result of a slow and organic development, and that any great modification in them is contrary to all the experience and authority of the past, has been so well taught in American law schools that time and again it has been written into the decisions of the Supreme Court, to the disgruntlement of social reformers who have been in more of a hurry to change laws than the Spirit or Genius of the Law has seemed to be.

De Maistre and the French conservatives went further than national patriotism; if the mystic religion of the State be valid, then the further unity of the world, devotion to a World-State, is demanded unless nations are to perish in blood. Such a State exists: it is the Catholic Church, and its monarch is the Pope. But the philosophy of Ultramontanism, increasingly powerful in Catholic lands, made no appeal in Protestant Germany or England; they accepted nationalism without its logical crown of a universal religious society.

The Worship of Tradition

The substitution of faith and mysticism for reason, the notion of society as a living organism realizing spiritual and religious ends, led naturally to great emphasis on the conserving of tradition, and the slow and evolutionary development of those features, and only those, that could be discovered in the national genius. Do not break with the past; study it, find its principle of growth, and if you must change things, do it gradually, and do it only in such directions as are consonant with the whole national tradition. Everywhere the past was studied eagerly; new proposals were tested, not by their social utility, as in the Age of Reason, but by their inclusion in the course of national growth since the Middle Ages. And the more the past was studied, the more men marveled at its wisdom, and the less they felt like interfering with it. Hegel, Savigny, and the German jurists in general revered history above all things; Burke and the English Tories swore by it. De Maistre wrote:

> It does not belong to man to change institutions for the better.... All men feel this truth, without being able to explain it. Hence that automatic aversion of all good men for innovations. The word *reform*, in itself and before any investigation, will always be suspect to wisdom, and the experience of all the ages justifies this instinct. We know only too well what has been the fruits of the finest speculations in this field.[15]

But Burke is the true poet of the past.

> Is it in destroying and pulling down that skill is displayed? Your mob can do this as well at least as your assemblies. The shallowest understanding, the rudest hand, is more than equal to that task. Rage and frenzy will pull down more in half an hour than prudence, deliberation, and foresight can build up in a hundred years.... At once to preserve and to reform is quite another thing.... A spirit of innovation is generally the result of a selfish temper, and confined views. People will not look forward to posterity, who never look backward to their ancestors.... By a constitutional policy working after the pattern of nature, we transmit our government and our privileges, in the same manner in which we enjoy and transmit our property and our lives. The institutions of policy, the goods of fortune, the gifts of Providence, are handed down to us, and from us, in the same course and order. Our political system is placed in a just correspondence and symmetry with the order of the world, wherein, by the disposition of a stupendous wisdom, moulding together the great mysterious incorporation of the human race, the whole, at one time, is never old, or middle-aged, or young, but, in a condition of unchangeable constancy, moves on through the varied tenor of perpetual decay, fall, renovation, and progression. Thus, by preserving the method of nature in the conduct of the State, in what we improve, we are never wholly new; in what we retain, we are never wholly obsolete.... A disposition to preserve, and an ability to improve, taken together, would be my standard of a statesman.[16]

> One of the first and most leading principles on which the commonwealth and the laws are consecrated, is lest the temporary possessors and life-renters in it, unmindful of what they have received from their ancestors, or of what is due to their posterity, should act as if they were the entire masters; that they should think it among their rights to cut off the entail, or commit waste on the inheritance, by destroying at their pleasure the whole original fabric of their society; hazarding to leave to those who come after them a ruin instead of a habitation — and teaching these successors as little to respect their contrivances, as they had themselves respected the institutions of their forefathers. By this unprincipled facility of changing the state as often, and as much, and in

as many ways, as there are floating fancies or fashions, the whole chain and continuity of the commonwealth would be broken. No one generation could link with the other. Men would be little better than the flies of a summer.[17]

In Burke's reverence for the past, and for the intricate beauty of the British Constitution, there is discernible a still further argument to which the conservatives successfully appealed. The past, viewed through the eyes that forget its struggles and its turmoils, its cruelties and its filth, is haunted with a romantic beauty that the real world can never know. Men, freed from the exclusive scientific ideal of the Age of Reason, turned back in æsthetic admiration to the Middle Ages, to the Renaissance, to whatever had put on the halo of familiarity, endeared by long association. Kings might be unjust, but they added to the pageantry of life; priests might be superstitious, and faith untrue, but they had built cathedrals and painted pictures of surpassing beauty. The romantic artists reveled in the dramatic color and the pathos of lost causes, and they carried millions with them. From the sensuous barrenness of the Enlightenment and from the present discontents men turned to the Middle Ages. Gothic art brought with it a longing for Gothic customs and Gothic beliefs. In Germany and in France Catholicism was reborn; it owed as much to the medieval revival as to any other factor, and its popular appeal was primarily æsthetic. Châteaubriand knew his public when he made his apology the *Beauties of Christianity*. The Catholic party in the Church of England, the Oxford Movement of Keble, Pusey, and Newman, owed its strength to the tender sentiment of romanticism. The novels of Scott led the way in awakening a childish enthusiasm for the Middle Ages and for the lost cause of the Jacobites. The whole body of romantic literature, outside France, was largely a support for the conservatives; and men who loved stained-glass windows found themselves marshaled under the Ultramontanism of de Maistre.

In fact, the positive ideal of the conservatives became, as it had for Montesquieu a century earlier, a kind of idealized and developed feudalism. There was to be an expert governing class, a tried body of generous knights; Metternich rang the changes upon the advantages of a trained and capable prince assisted by devoted nobles. The functional organization of medieval society was, not without reason, extolled by de Bonald as far superior to the grasping competition of business life. Men should possess the rights necessary to play their part in the organism of society; they should be free to devote themselves self-sacrificingly to their high duties. Above all, the ideal of society as essentially the performance of some great spiritual purpose, the very core of the theory of the romantic idealists, possessed much in common with the medieval aim of the service of God by all estates of man. The conservatives hoped that they might retrieve their past errors and return to the noble mission of their ancestors as the stewards of God's kingdom, the knights of a new social chivalry. And yet — in spite of all their dreams and ideals, in spite of all that is appealing in the philosophy of conservatism as contrasted with the enlightened self-interest theories of the eighteenth century, the conservatives achieved none of their hopes. The typical conservative remained, in the classic picture of Morley, "with his inexhaustible patience of abuses that only torment others; his apologetic words for beliefs that may not be so precisely true as one might wish, and institutions that are not altogether so useful as some might think possible; his cordiality towards progress and improvement in a general way, and his coldness or antipathy to each progressive proposal in particular; his pygmy hope that life will one day become somewhat better, punily shivering by the side of his gigantic conviction that it might well be infinitely worse." [18] Conservatism, like the poor, is always with us; but the conservatives of the Congress of Vienna have departed with all their works.

The Philosophy of Liberalism and Individualism

The conservatives developed what was essentially a new philosophy of society; the liberals and individualists could still rest on the theories of the eighteenth century, all the more appealing now that they represented both a glorious achievement and what seemed to be a lost cause. The heat of the Revolutionary days had worked out a practical program and creed for the enlightened business and professional classes, which only spread the more widely under the repressive measures of the British Tories, the French royalists, and the whole Metternich system of the Holy Alliance. The high tide of the reactionary movement was reached in 1819 and 1820; in England, where the Corn Laws, the Enclosure Acts, and the Poor Relief Laws, all in the interests of the landlords, had reduced the peasantry to starvation and pauperdom, and brought the country nearer to a violent revolution than at any other time in its history, this climax is found in the suspension of habeas-corpus (1817) and the Six Acts (1819). In France the Ultra-Royalists gained control in 1820 after the assassination of the Duc de Berri; while in 1819 Metternich secured the Carlsbad Decrees, and the next year won the Czar from his dalliance with liberalism to a whole-hearted support of the reactionary system, a conversion consummated in the Protocol of Troppau against all revolutionary and reform measures in Europe.

But the Industrial Revolution was on the side of the liberals, and slowly but surely they gained control. The Revolutionary heritage, the faith of Condorcet, expressed the hopes of the business class, and gathered to it most of the ardent idealists and young patriots. For such men, liberty was no glittering generality; it meant a definite opposition to definite oppression, and because it was endangered became the great rallying cry. It stood primarily for economic liberalism, individualism, free competition, and *laisser-faire;* in politics it meant the actual assumption of control by the middle-class. Equality, too, meant a definite removal of specific privileges and inequalities; it meant the equality of opportunity for every man to rise to the top of the business scale. And above all the liberals stood for progress — progress through the advance of scientific knowledge and the growth of industry.

Two new forces and ideals had been added, however, to the eighteenth-century liberalism. The first was nationalism. Especially in central and southern Europe, where all progress of any kind seemed dependent upon breaking the domination of foreign despots, the "Young Italy" and the "Young Germany" movements were primarily patriotic in their appeal for the principles of the French Revolution against the Metternich régime. The liberals had no intention of allowing the conservatives to monopolize this burning issue. The second new idea was the common romantic belief in evolution and progress as rooted in the very course of nature. The stars, men thought, were on their side against the upholders of the established order; and the idea became widespread that any institution which remained static must for that very reason be bad. The French romantic movement, coming later than in any other country, was almost alone largely on the side of the liberals; Victor Hugo raised the banner of literary and political revolt, while under the erstwhile traditionalist Lamennais and Montalembert an abortive attempt was even made in the thirties to align the Catholic Church behind the new doctrine. Perhaps in no book does the deep religious faith of the liberals come out so clearly and powerfully as in the *Words of a Believer* of Lamennais, with his Jeremiah-like curses upon the seven kings who had trampled upon man and God alike. His vision of their sinister plottings ends in their overthrow, where, wandering as ghosts through the fog, they meet and wail:

What avail have been all our plans? Faith and thought have broken the bonds of the people; faith and thought have freed the earth. We wished to divide men, and our oppression united them against us. We shed their blood, and it is on our heads. We sowed corruption, and it took root in us and devoured our bones. We thought we had throttled Liberty, and her breath has dried up the roots of our power. Christ has conquered: cursed be he! And with one voice all answered: Christ has conquered: cursed be he! [19]

Utilitarianism

Three general formulations of this nineteenth-century liberalism are worthy of special note: the English utilitarianism, the new faith in progress and evolution represented by Herbert Spencer, and the liberal nationalism and internationalism of the continental "men of 1848." Utilitarianism is a direct continuance of the eighteenth-century reasonableness. Its patron saint is Jeremy Bentham; under his teachings a whole group of so-called "radicals" gathered, whose leader was John Stuart Mill, greatest of the utilitarians and without much question the outstanding English thinker from 1830 till his death in 1873. His method and approach, and his social ideal, remained those of the master Bentham; but he brought to his gospel of reason and utility a broader background, a knowledge of and a respect for history, and a more temperate wisdom than the great reformer had been able to marshal. He was a confirmed individualist, and a genuine believer in the value of liberty; but like Bentham he had no use for the eighteenth-century natural rights doctrine.

For him, the great argument for individual liberty was its social usefulness; and no more convincing support has ever been penned for the rights of the individual in all things than is contained in his famous book *On Liberty*, published in 1859. Without a trace of romanticism, without a single appeal to sentiment or feeling, he upheld a theory of the purpose and organization of government admirably fitted to express the aspirations of the rising Liberal party, and to strike the business man as common sense.

Government is a problem to be worked like any other question of business. The first step is to define the purposes which governments are required to promote. The next, is to inquire what form of government is best fitted to fulfill these purposes.[20] The first element of good government being the virtue and intelligence of the human beings composing the community, the most important point of excellence which any form of government can possess is to promote the virtue and intelligence of the people themselves. The first question in respect to any political institutions is, how far they tend to foster in the members of the community the various desirable qualities, moral and intellectual.... The government which does this the best, has every likelihood of being the best in all other respects, since it is on these qualities, so far as they exist in the people, that all possibility of goodness in the practical operations of the government depends.[21]

The foundation for the merit which any set of political institutions can possess

consists partly of the degree in which they promote the general mental advancement of the community, including under that phrase advancement in intellect, in virtue, and in practical activity and efficiency; and partly of the degree of perfection with which they organize the moral, intellectual, and active worth already existing, so as to operate with the greatest effect on public affairs. A government is to be judged by its action upon men, and by its action upon things; by what it makes of the citizens, and what it does with them.[22]

Such ends the government can best attain, not by any positive action, but by providing for every man as large a scope as possible for the development of his own powers. Hence the jealous guarding of liberty in thought and action is the most useful task a government can undertake.

The sole end for which mankind are warranted, individually or collectively, in interfering with the liberty of action of any one of their number, is self-protection. The only purpose for which power can be rightfully exercised over any member of a civilized community, against his will, is to prevent harm to others. His own good, either physical or moral, is not a sufficient warrant.... The only part of the conduct of any one, for which he is amenable to society, is that which concerns others. In the part which merely concerns himself, his independence is, of right, absolute. Over himself, over his own body and mind, the individual is sovereign. Here advice, instruction, persuasion, and avoidance by other people if thought necessary by them for their own good, are the only measures by which society can justifiably express its dislike or disapprobation of his conduct.[23]

Mill's *Political Economy*, which for fifty years superseded all other works on the subject, stands as the climax of the individualistic school. Yet his insistence on social utility as the basis of all liberty brought him to sympathize with many forms of economic collectivism; his method was flexible, not absolute. There are natural and immutable laws of production, he believed; but all distribution is man-made. "The laws and conditions of the production of wealth partake of the character of physical truths. There is nothing optional or arbitrary in them.... It is not so with the distribution of wealth. This is a matter of human institution solely. The things once there, mankind, individually or collectively, can do with them as they like." [24] *Laisser-faire* does not necessarily bring true liberty with it; "the restraints of communism would be freedom in comparison with the present condition of the majority of the human race." [25] The social problem, as he saw it, is: "How to unite the greatest individual liberty of action, with a common ownership in the raw material of the globe, and an equal participation of all in the benefits of combined labor." [26] Thus the utilitarian method, in the face of changed conditions, was able to cope with the problems of an industrial society.

One other doctrine of the eighteenth century continued among the liberals of England, cosmopolitanism. The Manchester School of economists, McCulloch, Nassau Senior, and John Stuart Mill, were convinced advocates of free trade and of a world economic system; from them the leaders of the Liberal Party, Richard Cobden, the Quaker John Bright, and Gladstone, developed a hostility to the newer ideals of Nationalism and Imperialism and came to stand for peace, free trade, and the ideal of "little England." To them colonies were but a financial drain, and colonial warfare and rivalry a madness. Before the rebirth of imperialistic adventures in the seventies and eighties, most of Europe had followed England's lead in abolishing protective tariffs and regarding colonies as unnecessary appendages. Cobden's ideas on peace and free trade are singularly modern in their ring.

Our Free Trade agitation and the Peace Movement are one and the same cause.... The efforts of the Peace Societies, however laudable, can never be successful so long as the nations maintain their present system of isolation. The colonial system, with all its dazzling appeals to the passions of the people, can never be got rid of except by the indirect process of Free Trade, which will gradually and imperceptibly loose the bands which unite our Colonies to us by a mistaken notion of self-interest. Yet the colonial policy of Europe has been the chief source of wars for the last hundred and fifty years.[27]

The Worship of Progress

The second of the middle-class liberal philosophies grew naturally out of utilitarianism. As they saw industry growing and liberalism advancing by steady strides, with science building up an imposing edifice, it is easy to understand how the middle class should wax optimistic and actually come to identify material and political progress with the course of nature and the hand of Providence. Even more than the eighteenth, the nineteenth century was a century of hope. No longer was progress something to be effected by human endeavor; strive as men might, it was inevitable. Tennyson, who expressed the faith of his day in popular measures, might doubt immortality and even God; he never doubted progress, till age and sixty years had brought its disillusionments.

Yet I doubt not through the ages one increasing purpose runs,
And the thoughts of men are widened with the process of the suns. ...
Not in vain the distance beacons. Forward, forward let us range,
Let the great world spin forever down the ringing grooves of change.
Thro' the shadow of the globe we sweep into the younger day;
Better fifty years of Europe than a cycle of Cathay. ...
For I dipt into the future, far as human eye could see,
Saw the vision of the world, and all the wonder that would be;
Saw the heavens fill with commerce, argosies of magic sails,
Pilots of the purple twilight, dropping down with costly bales;
Till the war-drum throbb'd no longer, and the battle-flags were furl'd,
In the Parliament of Man, the Federation of the world.[28]

Herbert Spencer went further: he believed that progress was not merely a human phenomenon, but that it was the fundamental law of the whole of nature. The stars in their courses are for him no less certain than that the whole universe must advance from simple forms to complex and organically interrelated individuals. Individualism is the end of creation; nothing on earth can stop its steady advance.

Whether it be in the development of the Earth, in the development of Life upon its surface, in the development of Society, of Government, of Manufactures, of Commerce, of Language, Literature, Science, Art, this same evolution of the simple into the complex, through successive differentiations, holds throughout. From the earliest traceable cosmical changes, down to the latest results of civilization, we shall find that the transformation of the homogeneous into the heterogeneous, is that in which Progress essentially consists.[29] Progress is not an accident but a necessity. What we call evil and immorality must disappear. It is certain that man must become perfect.... The ultimate development of the ideal man is certain — as certain as any conclusion in which we place the most implicit faith; for instance, that all men will die.... Always toward perfection is the mighty movement — towards a complete development and a more unmixed good.[30]

The ideal society which must come about was for Spencer the Utopia of the utilitarians, the economic liberals, the business men.

The duty of the State is to protect, to enforce the law of equal freedom; to maintain men's rights, or, as we commonly express it, to administer justice.... Whenever the State begins to exceed its power of protector, it begins to lose protective power. Not a single supplementary service can it attempt without producing dissent; and in proportion to the amount of dissent so produced by it, the State defeats the end for which it was established.... And as the essential ought not to be sacrificed to the non-essential, the State ought not to do anything but protect.... Consider it then in what light we may — morally or scientifically, with reference to its practicableness, or as a question of political prudence, or even in its bearings upon religious faith — we find this theory, that a government ought to undertake other offices besides that of protector, to be an untenable theory.[31]

The romanticists of the Young Germany and Young Italy Movements, eager alike for liberty and for country, sought more or less successfully to make some adjustment between their dislike of governmental interference in thought and industry, and their love for the developing genius of their nation. The *Limits of the Activity of the State*, published in part by the German reformer Wilhelm von Humboldt in 1792, and completely in 1851, tried to show that while the nation is a growing body, government is only one of the means of aiding its welfare, a means whose sole aim should be to provide security for social development. "The grand, leading principle, towards which every argument unfolded in these pages directly converges, is the absolute and essential importance of human development in its richest diversity." [32] In practical *laisser-faire* he was at one with Mill and Spencer.

Liberal Nationalism and Internationalism

The third of the new middle-class philosophies of the century, liberal nationalism, as opposed to the conservative nationalism of a de Maistre, was naturally strongest in Germany and in Italy, where the Vienna settlement aligned the patriots with the liberals. Taking its rise in the great wave of patriotic feeling that swept over the Germanies after the Prussian defeat at Jena in 1806, it found many a protagonist among the professors and poets, and came to perhaps its most appealing expression in the passionate rhapsodies of the Italian idealist Mazzini. For Fichte, the fiery soul whose moral energies Jena turned against Napoleon, it was the nation, the German people, and not their divided and trampled governments, who embodied on earth the primordial, the divine, the eternal Will. Wherever a society of men reveals in its natural and spiritual life the progressive development of the divine in accordance with some special law, there is a Nation. The individual, through identifying himself with the Nation of which he is a part, can by word or deed incorporate his personality into the Eternal, and thus achieve a lasting immortality. Through patriotism men make themselves a part of God. After raising the German temper to a fever heat by his stirring *Addresses to the German Nation* (1807), Fichte devoted his life to just such self-sacrifice, and on the field of battle attained immortality.

This doctrine agreed with Hegel and Savigny in all but the particular group embodying the divine will. For the liberals, it was the German nation, in practice, the German-speaking peoples, and not any reactionary government. There was much discussion during the struggles against the Metternich system of what constituted the criterion of a nationality. Language, race, geography, and more and more a common culture, a common tradition, a common aspiration toward unity, were all made part of the test of a nationality; the precise mixture was ordered in the interest of the specific nationalistic movement. Perhaps the best formula is that of the South German liberal romantic historian Bluntschli:

> A union of masses of men of different occupations and social strata in a hereditary society of common spirit, feeling and race, bound together especially by language and customs in a common civilization which give them a sense of unity and distinction from all foreigners, quite apart from any governmental bond.[33]

Of vital importance was the question, should nationality and state coincide? Should every national group be politically independent? A few reactionary upholders of the Austrian Crown answered in the negative; the great mass of the German historical theorists, even the conservative Prussians, who hoped to unify Germany under the Prussian monarchy, and the patriotic liberals everywhere, flocked to the banner of national independence. A nationality can become a People, in the full sense, only if it becomes an independent State, proclaimed Savigny and the jurists. The more liberal Bluntschli taught that a state became truly worthy of respect only if it was the organized government of a group already united by the bonds of nationality. Both schools had their eyes on the German situation. The subject nationalities of the Habsburg monarchy seized upon these ideas, and went up and down the land seeking to awaken the different language groups to a sense of their national unity. The past was diligently studied; each group found national heroes greater than Pericles or Cæsar, and national epics surpassing Homer. So long as the governing class of the Austrian empire remained truly cosmopolitan in spirit — so long, for example, as they were willing to utilize Latin as an universal language — there was a cogent argument, from the economic side, for the preservation of that cosmopolitan rule; but the administration itself became imbued with the spirit of German nationalism, sought to stamp out the other languages and movements, and in that moment its doom was sealed. Nationalism was to prove stronger than any possible argument based on mere peace and economic expediency.

It was in Italy that the nationalism of the liberals of 1848 proved strongest. It is enshrined at its best in the writings of the great republican statesman and dreamer, Giuseppe Mazzini, who rose above the squabbles and hatreds of so many of the patriots of his day to the conception of a noble internationalism founded on the full recognition of the principle of nationality.

To one who sees in a Nation something more than an aggregation of individuals born to produce and consume corn, the foundations of its life are, fraternity of faith, consciousness of a common *ideal*, and the association of all faculties to work in harmony and with success towards that ideal. ... The first condition of this life is the solemn declaration, made with the unanimous and free consent of our greatest in wisdom and virtue, that Italy, feeling the times to be ripe, rises with one spontaneous impulse, in the name of the Duty and Right inherent in a people, to constitute itself a Nation of free and equal brothers, and demand that rank which by right belongs to it among the Nations that are already formed. The next condition is the declaration of the body of religious, moral, and political *principles*, in which the Italian people believes at the present day, of the common ideal to which it is striving, of the *Special* mission that distinguishes it from other peoples, and to which it intends to consecrate itself for its own benefit and for the benefit of Humanity. And the final condition is to determine the methods to be employed, and the men to whom the country should delegate the function of developing the national conception of life, and the application of its practical consequences to the manifold branches of social activity. Without these, a *country* may exist, stumbling along from insurrection to insurrection, from revolution to revolution, but there cannot exist a NATION.[34] Our party is faithful to the ideal of our country's Traditions, but ready to harmonize them with the Traditions of Humanity and the inspirations of conscience.[35]

What is true for one Nation is true as between Nations. Nations are the individuals of Humanity. The internal national organization is the instrument with which the Nation accomplishes its mission in the world. Nationalities are sacred, and providentially constituted to represent, within Humanity, the division or distribution of labor for the advantage of the peoples, as the division and distribution of labor within the limits of the state should be organized for the greatest benefit of all the citizens. If they do not look to *that* end, they are useless and fall. If they persist in evil, which is egotism, they perish: nor do they rise again unless they make Atonement and return to Good.[36]

This is nationalism as a liberal and struggling force — the nationalism of a group that has not yet obtained an independent government and sovereign politicians. It is a far cry from Bluntschli and Mazzini to the "*Deutschtum*" of the *Alldeutscher Verband* or the "sacred egoism" of Mussolini. The tragedy of the last half-century is the capture of this noble nationalism of 1848 by the forces of reaction and chauvinism, and the almost complete disappearance of its complement of internationalism.

The New Philosophy of Industrial Society

We have seen the doctrines upon which the conservatives agreed; we have traced the liberal notions which opposed and overthrew them. There is no such unanimity in the tentative and exploring philosophies put forward by the champions of the rising new class, the industrial proletariat. These men, for the most part generous middle-class idealists, agreed in opposing the conservatives; they agreed also in attacking the *laisser-faire* individualism of the liberals. But they differed widely in the positive programs they advocated; the workers themselves had not yet become articulate, and it hardly occurred to their champions to ask them what they wanted. Two main groups can be distinguished, the paternalists and the democrats. The first advocated a benevolent industrial order; the second, some form of "social democracy."

From many quarters there came drastic criticism of the dismal science of the classic political economy. Its callous disregard of human suffering and woe in the face of early factory conditions, the disastrous financial crises and panics which the new industrial system underwent, in 1815, in 1818, and in 1825, and its general minimizing of nationalism and patriotic sentiment, led to a scrutiny of its underlying assumptions. From the standpoint of economic science itself the Swiss Sismondi criticized free competition and exclusive reliance upon the motive of self-interest or unlimited gain, advocating governmental regulation of competition to prevent overproduction and panics, and various forms of social legislation, including the encouragement of unions. The German Friedrich List criticized free trade and *laisser-faire*, demanding instead a national system of political economy that would build up a self-sufficient state, with social legislation for the improvement of working conditions. He became the founder of the modern theory of "neo-mercantilism," with its protection of agriculture and infant industries, and its government subsidies for shipping and commerce. His ideas were ultimately adopted by all the states which were striving to develop an industrial system rivaling England's; they powerfully influenced, first American policy, and later, after 1879, Germany and France.

Even more drastic attacks were made upon the liberals. Fourier tried to overthrow the rationalistic psychology upon which the classic individualists had relied, and to substitute for it a sounder view of the multiplicity of human motives. Instead of an industrial system founded on gain, which could not fail to result in the antagonistic interests and mutual destruction prophesied by Ricardo and born out by the facts, he wished to found industry on the needs of human nature, and saw a means in the formation of productive units of free producers. Proudhon, following the Englishman William Godwin, pushed the logic of the liberals beyond their compromise, and claimed that the reigning *laisser-faire*, in its retention of the right of property, failed above all to secure for men liberty. For him, only the substitution of the rule of reason through voluntary agreement for all forms of compulsion, could hope to better the situation. Religious leaders, like Frederic D. Maurice and Charles Kingsley in England, Lamennais, Ozanam, Buchez, and Le Play in France, Ketteler, Moufang, and Hitze in Germany, and humanitarians like Carlyle and Ruskin, protested in the name of God and humanity at the results of unrestrained individualism. Even Mill, upholder of individual rights, was forced to admit that there was nothing in the nature of things to prevent some form of economic collectivism if conditions failed to suit men.

The one idea of a substitute common to all these critics was the notion of organization — "the organization of labor" came to be the battle-cry of the French workers in 1848. It was generally felt that liberalism and individualism had done a good and useful work in overthrowing the old system, but that it had lamentably failed as the basis of a new one. The need was for some kind of reconstruction and reorganization, in industry, in knowledge, in religion, in every field of human endeavor, some group control and regulation. The philosophy of Auguste Comte, developed in the thirties and forties, tried to lay a scientific foundation for some such reorganization of society. He felt that with the development of a genuine social science it would be possible to rebuild society on a new basis, to bend industry once more, as it had been bent during the Middle Ages, to the service of a spiritual end. "To generalize our scientific concepts, and to systematize the art of social life"; [37] "to reëstablish in society something spiritual that is capable of counterbalancing the influence of the ignoble materialism in which we are at present submerged"; [38] to harmonize knowledge and aspiration, to subordinate science and industry to human purposes, the mind to the heart — this was the aim of his endeavor. His "System of positive philosophy," culminating in a religion of humanity and altruism, became as popular in Europe as the individualistic philosophy of Herbert Spencer himself. But it remained an ideal, and failed to inspire the working class.

Benevolent Industrialism

Amongst the French romanticists and the English Tories there grew up the ideal of a benevolent industrial feudalism, a society run by captains of industry for the benefit of the working classes. In France this aim was upheld by the followers of the Count de Saint-Simon. Looking at the horrible results of uncontrolled industrialism in England, the Saint-Simonians conceived the idea of combining business enterprise and religious idealism, that the industrial revolution might prove a blessing rather than a curse. It seemed to them possible to organize a society under the leadership of industrial experts, creating material goods with a view to the best social conditions for all, taught and guided by a body of scientists devoted to discovering new truth and popularizing the old. They devised elaborate schemes for the proper functioning of the artist, the scientist, and the captain of industry in the new order. Under the Religion of Jesus, "religion should direct society toward the grand goal of the speediest amelioration possible of the lot of the poorest classes." [39] Their slogan was reconstruction, organization, and "Everything for the worker, nothing by the worker." [40]

There is much that is fantastic in the theories of the Saint-Simonians — their combination of religious mysticism and shrewd business enterprise, their meetings in the back rooms of Jewish bankers to found the New Christianity and build railroads and canals, their appeals to Louis XVIII, to the Pope, to the great financiers Lafitte and Baron Rothschild to lead the new Christianity of social service for the worker; but they managed to enlist many of the men who were destined to build up French industry, and it is interesting to speculate what might have been the result if the industrial revolution in France had gone forward under their benevolent auspices. Later, vagaries with regard to free love broke up the school, and the industrial feudalism that was introduced was not quite so benevolent as they had hoped;

but their ideal was very influential under the Second Empire, and served to mitigate some of the worst features of the new régime.

Somewhat less doctrinaire and more fruitful were the doctrines of the English "Tory Socialists," who, from a mixture of humanitarianism and hatred for the liberal business interests, exposed in Parliament the iniquities of the factory system and forced through the first industrial legislation. They hoped to unite the old aristocracy and the working classes against the manufacturers, and carry on the best traditions of the country gentleman régime. Michael Sadler wrote books against Malthus, claiming that with a higher standard of living the birth rate would decrease; he served as chairman of the first Factory Commission in 1831–33, from whose reports can be gleaned most of the harrowing tales of early child labor in the cotton mills. Lord Shaftesbury, greatest of the benevolent Tories, opposed the Reform Bill and the repeal of the Corn Laws, and worked valiantly for factory legislation and improved housing conditions. Disraeli, in the course of his brilliant and checkered career from law clerk and dandy to Prime Minister, Peer, and society novelist, did much to break down the liberalism of the Cobden School, which bitterly opposed, in the name of individual liberty, all factory legislation and all labor unions. His crowning achievement, in the light of history, was his gift to the workers of the franchise in 1867, the political means of working out their own salvation. In this he was aided by the great Liberal John Bright, too much of a Quaker to be a good middle-class individualist, and by the rumblings of an unmistakable popular revolt.

To these apostles of a benevolent industrialism must be added the sincere Christians who shrank from the selfishness of enlightened self-interest. Maurice and Kingsley, the "Christian Socialists," championed the Chartist Movement in 1848, the first great awakening of the British working-class; they helped to popularize, in sermon and novel, the revolt against *laisser-faire*, and lent their prestige to the recently founded Coöperative Movement. From them can be traced such organizations as the Guild of Saint Matthew, a High Church socialist group in the Anglican Church, and much of the present-day tendency toward "social Christianity" in England and America. The French and German Catholics instituted similar societies for more or less drastic curtailment of economic individualism. Lamennais and Lamartine, "Catholic Democrats" in 1848; Ozanam, founder of the charitable society of Saint Vincent de Paul; and Buchez, revolutionary and president of the Constituent Convention in 1848, all united in espousing trade unions under religious auspices, working for factory legislation, and helping the working classes in general. Later churchmen in France and Germany sought to revive the medieval guilds as the industrial units, and merged into the contemporary party amongst the continental clericals of the "Catholic Socialists."

Social Democracy

These various groups, while they all opposed the philosophy of liberalism and individualism, were aristocratic in nature; they proposed to aid and guide the workers, not to trust them to their own devices. Their success was limited by their dislike of democracy. The same period saw the rise of numerous attempts at some sort of social democracy, industry organized and run by the workers as well as for them. Their common principle was the substitution of coöperative group enterprise for individual competition. Their specific proposals ran from the establishment of self-sufficient communities, of which great numbers were founded in Europe and America during the forties, to the guild socialism of Louis Blanc and the state socialism of Karl Marx. Robert Owen, a successful business man who ran model factories with profit-sharing schemes very much like those made famous by Henry Ford, and who like Ford found it paid handsome profits, devoted his energies to the establishment of Owenite communities in Great Britain and America. When these failed, he turned to organizing coöperative societies and labor unions. Fourier and Cabet put forth similar proposals in France, and their followers were for a time successful in America. Proudhon, the keenest critic of liberal economics, more ambitiously proposed to reorganize the whole of society upon the basis of voluntary association; his philosophic anarchism has made him the intellectual father of the French labor movement. None of these schemes of Utopian socialism or "communism," as they were then called, proved successful; but they left behind them a growing murmur of discontent with individualism as administered for and by the middle classes, and specific proposals for profit-sharing, coöperative societies, and trade-unionism. They stand as the first attempts to formulate a working-class philosophy.

Perhaps the best statement of the general ideals of this whole industrial movement that centered about the revolution of 1848 is to be found in the writings of Louis Blanc, the leader of the proletariat in France. His actual attempt in the early days of the revolution to establish "national workshops" proved abortive; the middle class might use him, but it had no intention of putting his ideas into practice. The patriotic flag-waving of Louis Napoleon finished what the musketry and butchery of the middle-class republican General Cavaignac had begun, and put an end to all hope of the reorganization of industry in France. We quote from his *Socialist Catechism* of 1849.

What is socialism? — It is the Gospel in action. How so? — Socialism has as its goal to realize among men the four fundamental maxims of the Gospel: Love one another; Do not unto others what you would not have that they should do unto you; The first amongst ye shall be the servant of the rest; Peace to all men of good will.

What is Liberty? — It is the power given to man to develop his faculties completely, under the empire of justice and the safeguards of the law. What is Equality? — It is, for all men, the *equal* development of their *unequal* faculties, and the *equal* satisfaction of their *unequal* needs. It will only exist truly when each, following the law written in his heart by God himself, shall *produce according to his powers and consume according to his needs*. Does Liberty exist in society to-day? — No! for if the tyranny of individuals has been destroyed, at least in part, with the feudal régime, the tyranny of things remains, and many of our brothers are chained to poverty, which is slavery to ignorance and famine. Is this slavery a necessary consequence of the present organization of society? — Yes; for on the one hand, education being granted only to those who can pay for it, and the greater number being in no condition to pay, ignorance is an absolutely necessary fate for the greater number; and, on the other hand, work being neither sufficiently paid for, nor guaranteed to all, misery is an inevitable fact for the greater number. How does it come that work is not guaranteed? — Because present society has admitted the principle that every man must be left to his own resources; to pursue his own course, and to work out his own destiny. At the threshold of this human lottery, so much the worse for him who has not found in his cradle the winning number! The powers that be have as a maxim, let things go; and since those who *go* very often lack bread and have no means to earn it, *let things go* very often means *let men die*.

What do you understand by individualism? — It is the principle in virtue of which each thinks only of himself, and hurries to the triumph of his own private interest, whether that be at the expense of the interests of others, or even of society as a whole. What is competition? — It is the effort of each to enrich himself by ruining others; among the proletarians who have to earn their bread, it is the effort of each to be employed in preference to the others. How shall we pass from the present social order to the one we desire? — By the intervention of the State. In summary, what society will follow from the principles you have just developed? — It will be a society where through a common, free, and compulsory education, all citizens will be able to raise themselves as high as possible by their intelligence and will; where the domain of industry, and that of agriculture, instead of presenting the spectacle of a battle-field strewn with ruins and with dead, will be made fertile by fraternal associations, bound to one another by ties of solidarity; where the distribution of work and the division of its fruits will be based on the principle which to-day regulates the family: From each man in accordance with his powers, and to each man in accordance with his needs.[41]

With the further growth of the industrial revolution, these three philosophies, of the landholders, of the liberal business men, and of the working class, were developed and modified: the business men came more and more to abandon portions of their liberalism, and to fuse their individualism with the conservative attitude, while the working class carried out their opposition in more constructive programs and ideals. But the rise of these contemporary doctrines must be postponed until we have made a further study of the growth and development of men's general beliefs during the nineteenth century.

REFERENCES

1. J. de Maistre, *Mélanges*, 230.
2. *Ibid.*, 510.
3. De Maistre, *Essai sur le Principe Générateur des Constitutions Politiques*, 223.
4. Edmund Burke.
5. Edmund Burke, *An Appeal from the New to the Old Whigs*.
6. Burke, quoted in H. J. Laski, *Political Thought in England from Locke to Bentham*, 243.
7. *Ibid.*, 244, 245.
8. *Ibid.*
9. *Ibid.*
10. Quoted in May, *Constitutional History of England*, I, 331, 332.
11. De Maistre, *Essai sur le Principe Générateur*.
12. Burke, *Reflections on the Revolution in France*, 105, 106, World's Classics ed.
13. Hegel, *Philosophy of History*, Introduction.
14. *Ibid.*
15. De Maistre, *Essai sur le Principe Générateur*.
16. Burke, *Reflections on the Revolution in France*.
17. *Ibid.*

18. John Morley, quoted in J. H. Robinson, *The New History*, ch. VIII.
19. F. Lamennais, *Paroles d'un Croyant*, sec. 14.
20. J. S. Mill, *Considerations on Representative Government*, Oxford Univ. ed., 145.
21. *Ibid.*, 167, 168.
22. *Ibid.*, 170.
23. *Ibid.*, 15, 115.
24. Mill, *Principles of Political Economy*, Bk. II, ch. I, par. 1.
25. *Ibid.*, p. 210.
26. J. S. Mill, *Autobiography*, Popular ed., 133.
27. R. Cobden, *Letter to Henry Ashworth*, April 12, 1842.
28. Tennyson, *Locksley Hall*.
29. H. Spencer, *Illustrations of Universal Progress*, ch. I.
30. Spencer, quoted in W. R. Inge, *The Idea of Progress*.
31. Spencer, *Social Statics*, 1850 ed., chs. 21, 22.
32. Wilhelm von Humboldt, *Sphere and Duties of Government*.
33. J. K. Bluntschli, *Theory of the State*, Eng. tr., 90.
34. Mazzini, *To the Italians*, in *Essays*, Everyman ed., 235, 236.
35. *Ibid.*, 239.
36. *Ibid.*, 241.
37. Auguste Comte, *A General View of Positivism*, Bridges tr., Introductory remarks.
38. *Ibid.*
39. Saint-Simon, *Le Nouveau Christianisme*.
40. G. Weill, *Saint-Simon et son Œuvre*, 180.
41. Louis Blanc, *Catéchisme des socialistes*.

SELECTED READING LISTS

General: See chs. XIII, XIV. F. S. Marvin, *Century of Hope*. Sabine, Dunning, Laski, Davidson. Hearnshaw, *Revolutionary Era, Age of Reaction and Reconstruction, Victorian Age*. C. E. Vaughan, *Studies in the H. of Pol. Phil.* Crane Brinton, *English Pol. Thought in the 19th cent.* Faguet, *Politiques et Moralistes du 19ᵉ s.*; M. Ferraz, *H. de la Phil. en France au 19ᵉ s.*; Bayet et Albert, *Écrivains Politiques du 19ᵉ s.*, selections.

Conservatism: Burke, *Reflexions on the Revolution in France, Appeal from the New to the Old Whigs*; Sabine, c. 29; E. Barker, *Burke and Bristol*; A. Cobban, *Burke and the Revolt against the 18th cent.*; J. MacCunn, *Pol. Phil. of Burke.* Hugh Cecil, *Conservatism.* J. de Maistre, *Considérations sur la France, Soirées de Saint-Pétersbourg, Principe Générateur des Constitutions*; Morley, *Miscellanies*, II; Laski, *Problem of Sovereignty*, V; Faguet. M. de Bonald, *Législation primitive; Selections*, ed. Montesquiou; Laski, *Authority in the Mod. State*, II; Faguet. **German Idealism:** J. K. Bluntschli, *Ges. d. neueren Staatswissenschaft*, chs. 12, 14, 18; Bosanquet, *Phil. Theory of the State*, chs. 9, 10; John Dewey, *German Phil. and Politics* (critical). Fichte, *Werke*, III, IV; H. C. Engelbrecht, X. Léon. Hegel, *Phil. of History, Phil. of Right*; Sabine, c. 30; Hearnshaw, *Reaction and Reconstruction*, c. 3; G. S. Morris, *Hegel's Phil. of the State*; H. A. Reyburn, *Ethical Theory of Hegel*; H. Heller, *Hegel u.d. nationale Machtstaatsgedanke in Deutschland*; F. Rosenzweig, *Hegel u. der Staat.* Savigny, *System des heutigen römischen Rechts*. See A. W. Small, *Origins of Sociology*.

Liberalism: Sabine, c. 31; Laski; Brinton; J. MacCunn, *Six Radical Thinkers*; L. T. Hobhouse, *Liberalism*; E. Barker, *Pol. Thought from Herbert Spencer to the Present Day*; works on Utilitarianism under ch. XIV. J. Austin, *Lectures on Jurisprudence*; J. S. Mill, *On Liberty, Representative Government, Political Economy, Autobiography*; Richard Cobden, *Speeches, Political Writings*; J. A. Hobson, J. Morley, on Cobden; John Bright, *Speeches*; Trevelyan, *John Bright.* Herbert Spencer, *Social Statics*, ed. 1850; *Progress: its Law and Cause.* W. Donisthorpe, *Individualism.* William Godwin, *Political Justice*; Shelley, *Queen Mab, Mask of Anarchy*; H. N. Brailsford, *Shelley, Godwin, and their Circle.* W. Hazlitt, *Characteristics of the Present*

Age; Emerson, *Essays;* Thoreau, *On Civil Disobedience;* H. M. Kallen, *Freedom in the Modern World.* W. von Humboldt, *Sphere and Duties of Government;* F. Lamennais, *Paroles d'un Croyant,* Victor Hugo, *Hernani, La Légende des Siècles.*
Nationalism: Articles "Nationalism," "Nationality," in *En. Soc. Sciences.* Rose, *Nationality in Mod. Hist.;* C. J. H. Hayes, *Essays on Nationalism, Hist. Evol. of Mod. Nationalism.* Fichte, *Addresses to the German Nation;* H. C. Engelbrecht. Savigny, *System des heutigen römischen Rechts,* I. secs. 7-10; Hegel, *Phil. of History,* Introduction; Bluntschli, *Theory of the State,* Bk. II, chs. 1-6. G. Mazzini, *Essays,* ed. B. King; G. O. Griffith, *Mazzini.* E. Renan, "Qu'est-ce qu'une nation?", in *Discours et Conférences.* J. C. Calhoun, *Disquisition on Government.*
Industrial Society: Gide and Rist, *H. of Econ. Doctrines,* Bk. II; H. E. Barnes, *Social Reform Programs and Movements,* in *Encyc. Americana.* Hearnshaw, *Age of Reason, Rev. Era;* Laski, *Socialist Tradition in the French Rev.* H. Martin, *Christian Reformers of the 19th cent.;* C. E. Raven, *Christian Socialism, 1848–54;* J. L. and B. Hammond, *Age of the Chartists.* Thomas Kirkup, *H. of Socialism;* M. Beer, *H. of British Socialism;* H. W. Laidler, *H. of Socialist Thought;* S. and B. Webb, *History of Trade-Unionism.* Robert Owen, *Autobiography;* G. Wallas, *Francis Place.* Writings of Disraeli, esp. *Sybil;* W. J. Wilkinson, *Tory Democracy;* F. D. Maurice; Charles Kingsley, esp. *Alton Locke;* M. Hovell, *The Chartist Movement.* G. Isambert, *Les idées sociales en France de 1815 à 1848;* L. von Stein, *Ges. der Sozialbewegung in Frankreich;* Boas, Faguet, Ferraz. Saint-Simonians: *Oeuvres Choisies de Saint-Simon,* ed. Lemonnier; *Doctrine de Saint-Simon, Exposition.* A. J. Booth, *Saint-Simon and Saint-Simonism;* G. Weill, *Saint-Simon et son oeuvre, L'École Saint-Simonienne;* Bayet et Albert. Fourier, *Selections,* ed. Gide. Louis Blanc, *Organisation du Travail, Catéchisme Socialiste.* A. Comte, *General View of Positivism, Positive Politics.* P. J. Proudhon, *Système des contradictions économiques, What is Property? Philosophie du Progrès.* Karl Marx, *Communist Manifesto, Poverty of Philosophy, Capital, Gotha Program.* S. Hook, *From Hegel to Marx, Towards the Understanding of Karl Marx;* G. D. H. Cole, *What Marx Really Meant;* S. H. M. Chang, *Marxian Theory of the State;* Laski, *The State in Theory and Practice;* criticism by T. Veblen in *The Place of Science in Modern Civilization,* pp. 405–56.

CHAPTER XVIII

THE WORLD CONCEIVED AS A PROCESS OF GROWTH AND EVOLUTION

The Two Scientific Revolutions

The ideas that have formed the scientific world-view of our generation are the product of two major intellectual revolutions, two significant reorientations in scientific thought. The first, associated with the names of Darwin, Wallace, Huxley, and Haeckel, spread the notion of evolution, of change, growth, and development, from its focus in biological investigation to swift domination of the entire climate of opinion of the age. The second, carried through by the genius of Einstein, Planck, de Broglie, Heisenberg, and Schrödinger, introduced a novel set of fundamental concepts and principles into mathematical physics, and has puzzled our generation with the theory of relativity, quantum and wave mechanics, and the triumphs and mysteries of the structure of the atom. We have now lived for some fourscore years with the evolutionary ideas, long enough to have got over the first shock of bewilderment or enthusiasm. We have explored with some thoroughness their further implications, both their more profound though less spectacular consequences and the limits an initial exuberance overlooked. We are still, however, in the midst of the first impact of the revolution in physical concepts. For all but the specialist, the novelty of half-assimilated paradox as yet obscures a more sober realization of their intellectual bearing.

When new scientific ideas, worked out to meet some specific difficulty, win wide popularity at the hands of speculative generalizers, it is their fate to be taken first as the answers to old problems rather than as stimulating new inquiry. We have seen how the Newtonian Order of Nature provided the whole eighteenth century with a new heavenly city, and how men realized but gradually that when carefully examined it made all heavenly cities irrelevant. In like manner the idea of evolution came as a godsend to Romanticists seeking a new cosmic faith sanctioning their optimistic confidence in human progress. The evolutionary philosophers of the last generation expanded it as a new principle of cosmic explanation, a new primary cause. From Spencer to Bergson, evolution was spread far and wide as the greatest and most seductive of the Romantic faiths. Only recently have we begun to appreciate the real significance of the biological nature and setting of human life, and of taking time and temporal process seriously.

The new concepts of physical theory are suffering the same kind of career. Paradoxical popularizers find them completely demolishing the classical structure of nineteenth-century physics, and even the very notion of causal law; resolving the old controversy between determinism and free-will in favor of the latter; and enthroning strange new gods in our universe of light. Tempted by Gifford lectureships, some of our most eminent physicists have blossomed forth as the most daring speculative theologians of the day. It is too early to say how far these philosophical flights of the physicists will turn out to be justified, or whether professionally trained philosophers are right in construing the newer physical ideas as supporting their respective systems — and which. But it already seems that the most significant outcome of the revolution in physical theory is not these speculative and transitory conclusions about the universe, but rather the changed conception it is bringing of the nature and function of the scientific enterprise itself, and of the rôle of physical theory in the scheme of things.

The effect of the biological revolution of the last century was on the whole naturalistic: that is, it placed man and his enterprises squarely in the setting of a natural environment, and gave them a natural origin and a natural history. In the long run the outcome has been humanistic as well: man has been transformed from a being supernaturally divorced from and elevated above the rest of nature, and wholly dependent on his Creator, into a creature capable of interacting and coöperating with the other forces and resources in his natural environment, and in some measure bending them to his will. The effect of the present physical revolution seems primarily humanistic: it emphasizes the human factor in scientific interpretations, and it points to a world in which human life can be a natural life. Not only has it underlined the genuine intellectual creation involved in scientific theory — a creation that has seemed to many to support some form of philosophical idealism. It has definitely removed from the structure of science those basic assumptions and speculative generalizations of nineteenth-century thought which seemed most clearly to conflict with the demands of human life, and which made the "scientific world-view" of physics an alien world in which man and his interests could find no intelligible place. Nineteenth-century physics, though far richer than Newtonian mechanics, clung to the same fundamental assumption of a closed mechanical and material order; it remained far closer to the crude and simple systems of the seventeenth century than to the tentative, cautious, and experimental science of today. Our electrical world of radiant energy is of a richness and complexity that does not seem so alien to the maze of human experience; the concepts to make it intelligible are not of a totally different order from those applicable to human life. To embrace both in a common scheme no longer involves an obvious distortion of one or the other.

Yet this gain has been mainly negative and liberating rather than positive. Its naturalism was really implied in, and had indeed been already derived from, the working out of the earlier biological revolution. The shift of popular interest from biological to physical concepts in the last two decades is somewhat misleading. It is still doubtful whether the new physical theory, revolutionary as it has been for our notions of nature, will have anything like the impact on man and his position in the world that the biological revolution has already exerted. Its chief lesson may well be the reminder that it was not physics that created the world or human life, but the world that brought forth both physics and physicists.

Nor must it be thought that these successive intellectual revolutions in any sense cancel out their predecessors. In its ideas the scientific enterprise has been cumulative as well as original — a fact abundantly illustrated in the progress of physical theory. The essential insights of the older views have been incorporated and reinterpreted but not discarded with each new advance. The seventeenth-century Order of Nature has been retained and pushed further in every field, even when profoundly modified, first by the historical and biological viewpoints of the nineteenth century, and then by the novel electrical conceptions of to-day. And though the newer physical notions have been forced on investigators by the demands of their enlarged subject-matter rather than borrowed from other disciplines, the effect has been to push them independently to ideas and principles already suggested in the sciences of life. It is this convergence of the concepts of physics and of the biological and social sciences that has made possible the naturalistic philosophies of to-day, so much more adequate than the "naturalisms" of the nineteenth century which, bound by the dogmas of an earlier physics, did scant justice to the facts of human experience.

It is physics and not biology that has for a generation been providing the spectacular new ideas. Yet it is still true that the idea of Evolution, of change, growth, and development, has been the most revolutionary notion in man's thought about himself and his world in the last hundred years. This transformation of the setting of human life did not come about suddenly, overnight, it does not date from the justly epoch-making publication of Darwin's *Origin of Species* in 1859. Rather that event symbolized the new attitude that had in many ways been making its progress in men's thinking since the middle of the preceding century. Darwin's book, in fact, stands to our present-day scientific synthesis much as Newton's *Principia* stood to the earlier mechanical synthesis, as the confident marshaling of evidence and the systematic formulation in strictly scientific terms of a view that had already been for some time gaining acceptance by the best intellects. Both the rationalistic thinkers of the Enlightenment, in their growing emphasis on progress, and the romantic reaction, in its singling out of a process of development in time as the fundamental fact in human experience, had paved the way for a successful biological formulation of Evolution. Only such a state of affairs can explain the almost instantaneous acceptance of Darwin's doctrine when it was put forth in 1859.

Eighteenth-Century Ideas of Progress and Evolution

Already in the full tide of the Age of Reason men had developed a conception of progress as no merely human movement, but as a great process of universal sweep and scope. Buffon, a member of the group of Encyclopedists, had published as early as 1749 his famous *Natural History*, which combined a detailed exposition of what the naturalists had gathered about the species of animals and plants, with a great cosmic epic of the growth of nature from its beginnings in the formation of the earth to its culmination in man. Buffon saw a gradual ascent, with no sharp breaks, from the humblest beginnings to the summit; and though in good eighteenth-century fashion he regarded the whole process as divine, at no point did he have recourse to any supernaturalistic explanations. He wrote, too, in the spirit of the newer experimental science, rather than in that of the reigning mathematical physics; he proceeded at each step by patient investigation and observation. In the narrower field of biological evolution he raised all the questions that have remained unanswered to the present day. What is Nature? he asks. It is not a fixed thing, a static being, but "the system of laws established by the Creator for the existence of things and the succession of beings." [1] It is alive; it is an eternal process. "Time, space, and matter are its means; the universe is its object; motion and life is its goal." [2] The emphasis throughout is on the glory of Man, as the culmination of the whole process of Nature; Man is the revolutionary, changing the surface of the earth, uniting with his fellows to subdue nature and bend her processes to his own purposes. Buffon's bulky work remained for the eighteenth century a monument not unlike H. G. Wells' *Outline of History* to-day.

In Germany the great leader of the *Aufklärung* or Enlightenment, G. E. Lessing, gave powerful expression to much the same idea in the religious field in his *Education of the Human Race*, in 1780. He claimed that in the life of the race revelation occupies the same place as education in the life of the individual; that is, it is progressive and never-ending. The common conception of an original religious revelation from God, since obscured by the ignorance and the scheming of men, is all wrong; in its stead we should look upon the history of religion as a progressive revelation of God's truth, an advance from a primitive animism and superstition to the Christian religion. But even the Old and the New Testaments are but stages in this process of growth; Christianity is but one step in the evolution of the highest spiritual religion. Men by their own efforts receive from God one great truth after another as they are ready for it, and at no period is the revelation final and complete. The whole of human history exemplifies the growth of humanity in knowledge and truth under divine guidance.

Herder generalized this notion of evolution into a theory of the whole of civilization. In his *Philosophy of History* (1774), he says:

> Has there not been progress and development in a higher sense? The growing tree, the struggling man, must pass through various stages always progressing. But the striving is not simply individual and temporal, it is eternal. No one is alone in his age; he builds on what goes before. The past and the present are the bases of the future. This the analysis of nature and of God's works in general shows. Thus it is also with the human race. The Egyptian could not be without the Oriental; the Greek built on both; the Roman rose upon the shoulders of the entire world. Genuine progress, constant development, even if no individual gain anything thereby, this is the purpose of God in history.[3]

In an extensive work published in 1784 he recounted the history of human development from the very beginnings of life. His influence upon the whole romantic school in Germany, especially upon Schelling and Hegel, was very great indeed; they made the notion that civilization has been a slow development from small beginnings a fundamental principle for all educated men. From the revolutionary Condorcet in France and from the more conservative Hegelians in Germany there sprang a long line of historians concerned with tracing the laws and stages of social development and evolution.

The Idea of Growth and Development in Human Society

Many forces combined to popularize this conception. The very changes which in the Revolutionary period succeeded one another so rapidly gave to most men a new sense of the mutability of human affairs, and shook them from their belief that society was a mechanical and timeless kind of thing like the state of the solar system. Moreover, men of all faiths were led to appeal to the past in justification of their present policies: all the new social philosophers, from the traditionalist de Maistre to the radicals Comte and Fourier, felt it necessary to preface their own criticisms of the existing order and their recommendations of change with a philosophy of history explaining how they stood in the direct line of social advance. The whole romantic interest in human life and institutions as essentially the progressive realization of ideals, turned men to a preoccupation with the past as the revelation and the condition of those ideals. The great age of historical investigation began, at first merely in justification of preconceived notions of what was desirable, and then increasingly, under Niebuhr and Ranke, as an objective and scientific research. The technique of historical research and historical criticism was refined and applied to every field of interest, religion, literature, institutions, science, philosophy, laws. From the Hegelian school in Germany and from its follower Victor Cousin in France proceeded an increasing army of trained historians. The eighteenth-century scorn of the Middle Ages as barbarous and "Gothic" gave place to an earnest investigation of the origins and roots of the present in those far-off days. The conservative or "right wing" Hegelians sought to display the continual growth of ideal forces in religion and social life; the radical or "left wing" group, accepting contemporary scientific principles of explanation, undertook a naturalistic and historical critique of origins. Instead, with the eighteenth century, of criticizing traditional ideas in religion and society as irrational and futile, a line of attack that could not reach romanticists who rejected reason and utility as ultimate standards of what was valuable, they adopted the far more deadly weapon of explaining things in terms of their crude beginnings. They thus succeeded in showing that however reasonable and useful they might once have been, mankind had now outgrown them and was bound to advance to something further. Where it was easy to cling on faith to something that appeared merely irrational, and reverence what was not clearly understood, it was far more difficult to retain any veneration for institutions that were neatly "explained" as survivals from primitive animism or barbarism.

Hegel himself and his more orthodox followers had interpreted all institutions, particularly religious doctrines, in terms of their ideal significance, as symbols for spiritual truths about the eternal process of God. The radical theologians David Strauss, Baur, and Feuerbach went farther; for them such doctrines were not literal facts or truths at all, but only symbols. Strauss' famous *Life of Jesus* (1835), a pioneer of the "higher criticism" of the New Testament, denied the very existence of any supernatural events in the career of Jesus; the whole story was merely an imaginative and mythological embodiment of spiritual truths about human experience. Feuerbach denied everything in religion not of naturalistic and human origin; the very conception of God is merely a changing ideal that men set up for themselves in response to the needs of the religious experience. The problem of religious investigation became, not to discover historical evidences of revelation, but rather to explain how supernatural beliefs took their rise and secured wide acceptance.

The same kind of naturalistic critique of origins was applied by Karl Marx to human society. A pupil of Hegel, he interpreted his master's theory of the advance of the world spirit through history by means of thesis, antithesis, and synthesis, in terms of the economic struggle of conflicting social classes. Where Hegel sought to show how history culminated in present-day institutions, Marx tried to prove that the same logic would drive society inevitably to assume new forms through the growth and the assumption of power of the proletariat. His combination of the rationalistic psychology of enlightened self-interest, on which the classic economic liberalism had been founded, and of the Hegelian idea of irresistible development through continual conflict — his famous "economic determinism" or "materialistic interpretation of history" — spread to many historians, and seems at the present day to be at the foundation of most historical investigation.

The Spread of Naturalistic Uniformitarianism

More and more this historical research adopted genuinely scientific principles: that is, it assumed that the laws and relationships observed and experimentally verified to-day have been operating in the same manner at every stage in the past development, and that the past is to be explained by a consistent appeal to such laws and such laws alone. This is the great principle of naturalistic "Uniformitarianism," which asserts the universal and uniform operation of causes and forces observable to-day. This conception, so basic in any scientific study of origins and growth, first gained popularity in the field of human affairs; from there it spread, throughout the nineteenth century, to all the fields of natural science as well. Many and diverse have been the developments in scientific knowledge, but they can all be summed up under two general principles: first, that all complex processes are to be explained as combinations of more elementary processes discriminated as factors in them, and secondly, that causes observable to-day suffice to account for the origins of all present forms of activity. The universal application of the method of analysis into simpler elements and processes, and the idea of a uniformitarian evolution, were the two great dominating concepts of the science of the last century. They were at once the fundamental generalizations that emerged from the mass of detailed investigation, and the basic assumptions on which that investigation had been conducted. The steady pushing of the first of these principles has elaborated the Newtonian world-machine of mechanical motions into a much more complex and subtle structure of electrical processes expressible in the equations for radiation. And the application of the second has at the same time transformed it from something conceived on the analogy of a man-made mechanism, springing fully constructed from the hands of its Creator, into a system of energy that, following its own laws of development, has grown from simpler beginnings to its present complex structure. The character of the fundamental equations and laws has changed, the process of development has revealed new complexities. But these two principles still sum up the kind of explanation the scientist is seeking.

The Method of Mechanistic Analysis Universalized and Broadened

Explaining complex phenomena by isolating simpler elements and processes whose behavior can be mathematically formulated and predicted, came to be known in the nineteenth century as the method of "mechanistic" analysis. Practically, it meant the search for the mechanism involved: by suitable manipulation and combination new ways of acting could be discovered, and the amazing technical triumphs of science achieved. Theoretically, it meant the drive toward formulating the basic natural processes in mathematical terms so general that the various types of observed phenomena could be exhibited as special cases. This search for elements with a uniform type of behavior is as old as the Greek atomists; its aim and method had apparently triumphed with the Newtonians. By the end of the nineteenth century the elementary substance was assumed to be the atom of "matter" with its fixed mass, and the elementary process, the motion formulated in the equations of dynamics. Even phenomena like light that did not seem to possess the two characteristics of matter, inertia and gravitation, were conceived as wave-motions of an "ether" itself considered as a kind of substance. In view of what has since happened to the basic concepts of this closely-knit theory, matter, energy, and ether, it is well to realize that the method of "mechanistic" analysis is not bound up with the limitations of this older materialistic and mechanical view. Nineteenth-century science took the motion of matter as the ultimate process and form of energy. To-day periodic energy has become more basic than "matter"; hence our science is no longer, strictly speaking, "materialistic." And the laws of mechanical motion are not so universal as those of the behavior of a field of radiation, and may indeed be but a special form of that behavior. Hence our science is no longer, like Newton's, "mechanical." But its basic method has remained that of "mechanistic" analysis.

In one important respect this method and type of explanation have been broadened. Having found simpler elements and processes, men have gone on to investigate how they act when combined in a complex system. In the various analytic sciences from physics to psychology, it has proved necessary to consider the way in which processes function, not only in isolation, but also in the relevant context or "field" in which they normally operate. The structure of this field or system of interacting processes has thus assumed increasing importance; in the more mathematical sciences it is this structure which the fundamental equations have come to formulate. To the mechanistic analysis into component processes there has been added the functional analysis into the specific way they act in the total situation. The sciences no longer tend to "reduce" complex wholes to their atomic constituents, assuming that no modification of behavior takes place in the combination, and thus "explaining away" the systematic factor. They endeavor rather to discover its precise pattern. But on the other hand they are as eager as ever to find the elementary mechanisms that function in those structures. In consequence, the older issue, in sciences like biology, for instance, between a "mechanistic interpretation" and its denial has ceased to have much importance. Elements are elements of systems, and neither factor can be neglected.

Scientists to-day are more confident than ever of the validity of their general method, in this broadened form. But their earlier dogmatism as to the specific conclusions and generalizations they had achieved has been swamped under the mass of detailed observations and experiments those theories could not deal with adequately. Scientists are the first to admit that the sum of their knowledge is paltry compared with the domain still to be investigated, that their hypotheses are obviously too crude and inadequate on many crucial points, and that the basic theoretical concepts are at present in a highly unstable state of rapid flux. For all we know, whole new sets of forces as central as radio-activity may be revealed which will fundamentally alter our present scientific ideas. So far as complete "proof" is concerned, it is still possible in all fields to maintain that quite different factors are operating. Multitudes of men who, for one reason or another, do not want to accept the view of the universe being worked out by even the broadened method of mechanistic analysis, remain either sceptical and agnostic about the whole validity of natural science as an explanation of things, or advance against it other theories which seem to them equally well founded on the facts of human experience.

In recording the way in which the method of mechanistic analysis has penetrated every barrier set up to keep it out of privileged fields, we must realize that we are tracing the growth of a scientific faith in a certain method rather than of any final scientific knowledge. The body of believers is still far outnumbered by the masses of the infidels, and within the ranks of investigators themselves there are still heretics, as honest and as sincere as the more orthodox majority. But with the liberalization of that method the number of scientific heretics has been rapidly diminishing.

Basic Generalizations Unifying the Fields of Physics and Chemistry

Three main movements are discernible in the nineteenth-century spread of mechanistic analysis: first, the unification of the fields of physics and chemistry through fundamental generalizations; secondly, the introduction of such analysis into the realm of biology, of living beings; and thirdly, the application of the same viewpoint and method to the study of human nature itself. This is not the place to enter into any detailed consideration of the progress of scientific discovery and theory; that fascinating story has been often told. But since it is beyond question the most important intellectual force in the last hundred years, it is worth while to present even a very inadequate summary of its significance. It was science, the mathematico-physical experimental learning of the seventeenth and eighteenth centuries, that really wrought the changes from the intellectual world of the Middle Ages, changes that neither Renaissance nor Reformation had been able to bring about; and increasingly it has been the growth of scientific knowledge that has caused the steady spread of the naturalistic viewpoint in every field. Science remained unperturbed by the romantic reaction; and science has seen that tide reach its height and roll back, though its waves still beat incessantly upon the citadel of knowledge. What the scientists learned from the romanticists, in a broader and more flexible outlook and method, in a wider conception of the extent of human experience, in a conviction of the fundamental importance of studying origins and development, has served only to intrench more strongly the scientific method and the scientific criterion of truth in the minds of all educated men.

Those sciences, like physics and astronomy and chemistry, in which the Newtonian world had been rooted, witnessed a double movement: on the one hand, they became less confident of mathematical hypotheses unchecked by the most careful experimentation, and engaged in a great coöperative enterprise to bring to light the multitudes of detailed facts about the world; on the other, this very mass of observations led men to the formulation and verification of sweeping generalizations stating in mathematical terms the fundamental relationships between physical phenomena. Physicists, no longer content with the mechanics of gross bodies, carried their analysis further and further. In the kinetic theory of matter they worked out in detail a molecular mechanics that would draw together all the investigations of solids, fluids, and gases, together with the phenomena of heat and sound, and explain all so-called physical properties of bodies in terms of the energy of motion of their component particles. The vast sciences of electricity and magnetism, mere idle curiosities in the previous century, opened up a new world of electro-magnetic energy following laws even more basic than those of mechanics; to explain these phenomena it became necessary to distinguish a further component factor within the atom, the electron. Chemists, bringing order into their science by a verifiable atomic theory set in mathematical terms, discovered the Periodic Law of atomic weights, and were led to the same analysis of the atom into electrons and a nucleus of varying complexity which had been necessary in physics. The two sciences merged in their roots into one, the study of the behavior of the factors within the atom and of the compounds it enters into; and to-day matter and motion together are dissolving into a common form of periodic energy, whose laws when completely formulated promise to include all physical and chemical laws as special instances.

In the achievement of such a mathematical synthesis of all physical phenomena, three main stages may be distinguished. The first was the work of the seventeenth century; Galileo and Newton formulated the universal laws of motion and gravitation. The second sprang chiefly from a study of the steam engine and the other heat-producing machines of the early nineteenth century; it is expressed in the great generalization of the Conservation of Energy. This developed from the determination of the mechanical equivalent of heat, undertaken by Rumford and Davy; but the final enunciation is due mainly to Joule in England and Mayer and Helmholtz in Germany. The latter phrased it:

> The last decades of scientific development have led us to the recognition of a new universal law of all natural phenomena, which, from its extraordinarily extended range, and from the connection which it constitutes between natural phenomena of all kinds, even of the remotest times and the most distant places, is especially fitted to give us an idea of the character of the natural sciences. This law is the Law of the Conservation of Force; it asserts, that the *quantity of force which can be brought into action in the whole of Nature is unchangeable*, and can neither be increased nor diminished.[4]

This law is often called the First Law of Thermodynamics; the second law, formulated by Kelvin, is that of the Dissipation of Energy, that while the total energy in the universe is constant, the sum of useful energy is diminishing by its ultimate conversion into non-useful or dissipated heat: that is, kinetic energy seems to be undergoing a degradation into purely molecular motion. These great generalizations, it should be noted, like the earlier Newtonian principle of the universal scope of the laws of mechanics, while marvelously valuable in uniting the varied phenomena of nature under a few fundamental laws, are assumptions rather than absolutely verified theories, assumptions necessary to science, but assumptions of the scientific faith none the less.

It still remained to bring the phenomena of light, electricity, and magnetism together, and to link them with the foundations of mechanics and of chemistry. As a result of the work of Thomas Young and Fresnel, it was definitely established that light is a form of wave-motion in some medium. Coulomb and Ampère in France, Ohm in Germany, and Faraday and Kelvin in England, discovered and formulated the laws of electrostatics, electro-magnetism, and of galvanic currents; and Faraday suggested, with brilliant intuition, though he did not work his theory out mathematically, that all these facts could be referred to the effects of motion in what he called an electromagnetic field, and that this field possessed much in common with the medium, ether, which the wave theory of light made it necessary to assume.

Thus three great generalizations had been achieved by the middle of the century: Newtonian mechanics, the atomic theory in chemistry, and the kinetic theory of matter, light, electricity, and magnetism.

None of these three principles, however, appeared sufficient to cover the whole field. The law of gravitation embraced cosmical and some molar phenomena, but led to vagueness when applied to molecular actions. The atomic theory led to a complete systematization of chemical compounds, but afforded no clue to the mysteries of chemical affinity. And the kinetic or mechanical theories of light, of electricity, and magnetism, led rather to a new dualism, the division of science into sciences of matter and of the ether. The unification of scientific thought which was gained by any of these three views, was thus only partial. A more general term had to be found under which the different terms could be comprised, which would give a still higher generalization, a more complete unification of knowledge.[5]

This conception was electro-magnetic energy, and its definition and formulation, begun by Clerk Maxwell, Helmholtz, and Hertz, lies at the foundation of all subsequent study of the electron and radio-activity, as well as of the mathematical synthesis of the other three principles.

Maxwell set to work to study the energy of the electro-magnetic field by applying the law of the conservation of energy. Where Faraday had been content with a mechanical analogy for his fruitful conception, Maxwell, a brilliant mathematician, reduced its properties to exact measurement. He succeeded in identifying all the various experimentally ascertained electric and magnetic phenomena, fixing their nature and quantities in conformity with experience, and arriving finally at the conclusion that the velocity of the transmission of electro-magnetic forces must be the same as that of light, light being but a special form of such wave-motion. "We can scarcely avoid the inference that light consists in the transverse undulations of the same medium which is the cause of electric and magnetic phenomena." [6] Hertz verified Maxwell's calculations by detailed experiment, proving the fundamental character of the electro-magnetic field and its energy. The equations expressing these systematic relationships, "Maxwell's equations," have remained the basis of the new mathematical synthesis. Einstein has described their formulation as the most important event in physics since Newton's time. They not only express the radiation of both electro-magnetic and light waves — the two differ only in wave-length — thus bringing both electrical and optical phenomena under the same formulae. They represent the structure of a field of radiation, and enable us to predict the changes in that field. All the newer developments in physical theory converge on the radiation of energy within a field of definite structure as the most fundamental type of process so far discovered in nature; and the field equations express the laws of this basic and universal type of activity.

The Newer Concepts of Physics

At the close of the century physical theory seemed to be reaching a stable and perfected form. Whatever was not matter and its energy of motion — of which heat had been proved an instance — was the energy of motion of the "ether." The various forms of energy were mutually convertible without change of quantity. In this closely-related scheme of matter, energy, and ether, there was a place for every known physical phenomenon.

Then in 1895 Röntgen produced X-rays by bombarding a metal target in a vacuum tube with "cathode rays" or streams of electrons; and the next year Becquerel found the same types of emission and radiation in radio-active substances. The study of the radiation of energy, and of the structure of the atom in terms of the particles and waves it can be made to give off or absorb, took an immense spurt. Now energy had always been regarded as continuous, unlike matter with its atomic structure: bodies could absorb or lose it by smooth and gradual change. But in 1900 Max Planck was led to suggest that energy too must be atomic or granular in character, that in radiation it is transmitted in indivisible units or "quanta." Planck's quantum theory has proved of basic importance in the further study of radiation and of atomic structure. Applied to radiation of the frequency of light, it treats a light ray as a stream of quanta of light-energy, or "photons," rather than as a continuous wave-motion; it takes the different wave-lengths of the spectrum as different degrees of energy in the particular photons for each color. This quantum theory of light is a revival in much subtler form of Newton's corpuscular theory. It has been found to explain certain phenomena which the wave-theory does not; but it fails to explain others, like diffraction, or the bending of light rays around small obstacles, which first established the wave-theory a century ago. In certain relations, light behaves like a shower of photons; in others, like a wave. This situation, in which two mutually inconsistent theories are both needed to deal with the different aspects of light, in which, it has been said, we have to use the wave theory on Mondays, Wednesdays, and Fridays, and the corpuscular theory on Tuesdays, Thursdays, and Saturdays, has been a standing challenge to find a comprehensive and unifying hypothesis. The same problem has developed with the quanta or units of matter: electrons behave not only like particles, but also on occasion like waves. This contradiction led de Broglie and Schrödinger to work out a wave or quantum mechanics, which tries to combine both aspects by treating the matter statistically. In this latest development of the quantum theory, the older classical mechanics of particles or masses appears as a special instance of a more general wave mechanics; and the units or quanta of matter — the electrons — are found to exhibit the same laws as the quanta of energy.

This development of the theory of energy has been intimately connected with the work on the theory of atomic structure. For our knowledge of atoms depends upon the different kinds of charged particles and radiation we can find emanating from them. On the basis of these emissions we try to work out mathematically a mechanism that will act in that precise way. We then employ that structure to suggest new experiments; when they fail to turn out as the theory predicts, we try to reconstruct the equations. Since we thus observe atoms primarily as sources of complex radiation — the lines in that atom's spectrum are a cardinal example — any advance in the knowledge of radiation at once suggests new facts about the atom. The most fruitful model so far devised, that of Bohr, was derived by applying the quantum theory to Rutherford's suggestion of 1911 that the atom consists of a positively charged nucleus with one or more negatively charged electrons revolving about it, like planets about the sun. In Bohr's hypothesis, the revolving electrons could radiate energy only when they jumped to a new orbit, and the number of possible orbits was limited by the quantum unit of energy. The ninety-two elements in the periodic table differed in possessing from one to ninety-two revolving electrons. For over ten years this hypothesis was remarkably successful in explaining the experimental facts. But Bohr's equations and planetary model proved too crude to account for all the observed facts; above all, its view of the electron as a charged particle could not explain why electrons at times behaved like waves. De Broglie, developing wave mechanics by applying the theory of relativity to the quantum theory, furnished Schrödinger with a more adequate mathematical expression for the events going on within the atom; the Schrödinger atom has superseded Bohr's. It is difficult to state its structure in non-mathematical terms, which may well be an advantage, for mechanical "models" are misleading as well as illuminating. In this view the atom is not a system of revolving particles, but a continuous electrical charge fluctuating in density with a complex frequency — a kind of pulsating sphere of electricity. The electrons emitted are treated as little bunches of waves or vibratory energy rather than as particles.

Thus wave mechanics, taking seriously the equivalence of matter and energy already calculated by Einstein, regards the older particles or material points as narrow parcels of waves, systems of waves so interfering with each other that they cancel each other out everywhere except at the position occupied by the material point. Matter and energy are mutually convertible, and in place of the principles maintaining their separate conservation, there is the broader principle of the conservation of matter-energy.

An unexpected consequence of the quantum theory is that the position and the velocity of an individual electron cannot both be determined at the same time, and hence its behavior cannot be precisely calculated. To ascertain its position, we must direct rays upon it, and thus alter its velocity; to ascertain its velocity makes its position indefinite. The accuracy of the two measurements varies inversely, and is limited theoretically as well as practically by the quantum constant. We can no more follow the movement of an individual electron than we could see a colored picture whose dimensions were smaller than the wave length of its color. The impossibility of predicting the behavior of any individual electron was formulated by Heisenberg as the principle of uncertainty or indeterminacy. This principle has been made the starting-point for much dubious speculation about the absence of strict causality and determinism in nature, and has been extended far beyond the atomic field to which it is relevant. But methodologically it means that the physicist can deal only with masses of electrons, and in statistical terms. The equations of quantum physics consequently take the form of probability functions, and state the periodic changes or waves of the probability of certain events. Such statistical rules make prediction and verification possible under all conditions of observation. But they concern an aggregate, not individuals; and they are verified by a series of repeated measurements.

The major phenomenon so far left out of our account of the unification of physical science in terms of the energy of radiation is gravitation. To bring mechanics and radiation together, to unite both gravitation and electricity in a comprehensive "field theory," has been the basic drive of all Einstein's work. In formulating his special theory of relativity in 1905, he set forth a general scheme for the motion of bodies, including those with a velocity approaching that of light, for which classical mechanics breaks down; Newton's laws appear as a special case for the slower velocities. Einstein's "special theory" was limited to events taking place in systems in uniform rectilinear motion, for which the Newtonian law of inertia holds. In 1917 he went on in his general theory of relativity to deal with systems in any kind of motion, and worked out the equations for the gravitational field.

Starting from the negative results of the Michelson-Morley experiment, which attempted to detect changes in the velocity of light due to the earth's absolute motion through the supposed medium of the ether, he laid down two principles: first, the velocity of light is constant, and unaffected by relative motion between the observer and the light's source; secondly and more generally, the laws of physics are not altered by the motion of the system in which the events are occurring; they are the same in all coördinate-systems moving uniformly relative to each other. This principle had been established for mechanics since Galileo; it was now extended to electro-dynamics as well. To be sure, various surprising things would seem to be happening on another system moving with a high velocity with reference to the observer: there would appear to be a contracting of everything in the other system in the direction of its motion, and clocks in it would seem to be running slow. To an observer on the other system, the same things would be apparent in the system of the first observer. But by taking account of the relative motion between the two systems, and applying the proper rules — the Lorentz transformation laws — the familiar physical laws, for example, Maxwell's equations, would be found obtaining in both systems after this translation. That is, the laws of physics would be invariant with respect to the Lorentz transformation. In just the same way the laws of mechanics are found to be the same in the two systems when the apparent motions in the one are suitably translated by the classical transformation rules. A further consequence of the special theory of relativity is that there is no essential distinction between mass and energy. Energy has mass, mass represents energy, the two are convertible, and their equivalence has been precisely calculated.

The general theory of relativity goes on to consider systems in accelerated motion with respect to each other. Such systems are identical in behavior and structure with a gravitational field. Thus the equations for such motion will describe the operation of gravitational forces; they are formulated in the complicated mathematics of the tensor calculus. Gravitation is looked upon, not as an attractive force inherent in masses, but as the property of a field with a definite structure, in which masses tend to move toward the point of least stress. Einstein's problem was to find the coördinate system or type of geometrical "space" which would describe that structure. He worked out a non-Euclidean or "curved" system in which light rays, following the "shortest" path, are bent or deflected when passing near large masses like the sun. It is to be noted that the experimental consequences of the general theory of relativity differ on only a few points from those of classical mechanics, though on these points observation has confirmed it. Its main advantage is the mathematical simplicity and consistency of its fundamental assumptions.

Einstein's equations for the gravitational field are still quite different from Maxwell's equations for the field of electromagnetics. In that sense, gravitation has not yet been integrated mathematically with the electrical theory of matter and energy. Einstein has several times announced a general unified "field theory," based on a new coördinate system, or type of space, from which he hoped to deduce both the electromagnetic and the gravitational equations as special instances. But the task has proved more difficult than he anticipated, and the theory of a comprehensive "field physics" has not yet been constructed. That final unification remains to be accomplished.

The significance of these generalizations is obvious. Modern science began with the attempt to analyze all phenomena into the behavior of certain ultimate components uniting to form various combinations. In the Newtonian world, these elements were masses, and their laws were those of motion. To-day, the elements seem to be rather the waves of energy in an electromagnetic field, and their laws, the laws of the structure and behavior of such a field. The various portions of physical theory are all in a state of rapid flux: quantum theory still holds untold possibilities of further development, the analysis of the structure of the nucleus of the atom is proceeding apace, no atomic model is completely adequate to the facts, the integration of matter and gravitation into a unified field theory belongs to the future. Many inconsistencies are left, between theories, and between theory and experiment. But if the eighteenth-century vision of a universal mathematico-mechanical synthesis was far too crude, and failed to realize the complexity of analysis required to bring all facts within its comprehensive sweep, its fundamental principles of method and attitude, unswervingly maintained, deepened and broadened in recent years, have reaped their reward: our present-day Order of Nature may be far more intricate, but it is also far more comprehensive and far more solidly established than ever before.

It is hardly surprising that this revolution in physical theory and concepts has provoked an immense amount of philosophizing, both about the new pictures of the world suggested, and about the very nature of the scientific enterprise itself. On the one hand, speculative cosmologies have been erected, only to crumble with some new discovery or change in theory. On the other, both philosophers and scientists have undertaken a careful and critical analysis of the function and nature of scientific theory in general, and of the mathematical formulations of physical theory in particular. The older view that Newtonian science was a direct reading of the structure of nature is no longer tenable. Scientific theory and concepts, it is only too apparent, develop and change in time; and he would be hardy to-day who maintained that any of the present ideas express "the way things really are." The primary function of theory and hypothesis, it is now clear, is to organize discoveries already made and suggest new questions to put to nature. Whether and how far the coördinating ideas themselves represent anything to be found in nature is a minor matter, on which our philosophies of science differ. That the equations for probability waves are highly abstract is obvious; and most physicists are now content with a set of mathematical formulae that will predict the events in the field of radiation, and have ceased to look for a mechanical model of the atom that can be pictured in the imagination. This growth of a positivistic and functional attitude toward scientific theory is a major feature of our philosophies of science to-day; they are increasingly concerned with what science does and how it does it, with methods and procedures, rather than with its conclusions of the moment.

Mechanistic Explanations in Biology

While physics and chemistry were thus formulating their generalizations, the same mechanistic principles of explanation were being introduced into the sciences of life. In biology, this has meant the interpretation of all the processes of living organisms in purely chemical terms. The German chemist Liebig was the pioneer in organic chemistry; he and his great pupil Johannes Müller, with the Frenchman Claude Bernard, initiated the study of the chemistry of the living being in its products and its processes. From this it was but a step to the conception and investigation of life as a series of especially complicated chemical reactions. Names are too numerous to mention; to Americans, Jacques Loeb will stand as the symbol of the achievements and the promise of experimental biology. Experiments seem to point to the conclusion that in the lower forms of life at least all the processes of the organism, both in its parts and in its behavior as a whole, are capable of explanation solely in chemical terms. In Loeb's words, "Living organisms are chemical machines consisting chiefly of colloidal material and possessing the peculiarity of preserving and reproducing themselves.... The essential difference between living and non-living matter consists in this: the living cell synthetizes its own complicated specific material from indifferent or non-specific simple compounds of the surrounding medium, while the crystal simply adds the molecules found in its supersaturated solution. This synthetic power of transforming small 'building stones' into the complicated compounds specific for each organism is the 'secret of life' or rather one of the secrets of life."[7] All the actions of any organism, from lowest to highest, hold such biologists, can be analyzed into "chemotropisms"; that is, into chemical reactions of a specific type.

Life in its processes, then, is purely chemical; so it must be in its origins as well. Offspring have been produced in bisexual organisms by means of artificial fertilization of the egg-cell, without the presence of any male spermatazoa; by such means animals as complex as the frog have been developed from the female egg alone. Most biologists regard the actual creation of life from non-living matter as something to be accomplished in the laboratory, so soon as the regulative chemical or enzyme has been isolated and synthetized. "The beginning of life was not a fortuitous event occurring millions of years ago and never again repeated, but one which in its primordial stages keeps on repeating itself all the time and in our generation.... Given the presence of matter and energy forms under the proper conditions, life must come inevitably." [8] "The ultimate aim of the physical sciences is the visualization of all phenomena in terms of groupings and displacements of ultimate particles, and since there is no discontinuity between the matter constituting the living and the non-living world, the goal of biology can be expressed in the same way." [9]

It is true that there are a few dissenting biologists who feel that this confidence is somewhat premature; but since their theories are wholly negative, merely refusing to admit that living processes are completely explicable in chemical terms, and offering only the vaguest suggestions of what else is needed, it is only natural that the great majority refuse to listen to men who deny the possibility of a biological science. Mechanism seems to offer the only program of investigation, while "vitalism," insisting in addition on some "principle of life" as an explanatory factor, can point to no such impressive experimental achievements.

The newer ideas in physics have had as yet only incidental application in biology. The analogies between the electromagnetic field and the self-regulatory systems within which biochemical processes take place have indeed suggested that living beings may be fruitfully treated as complex electrical structures. Already experiments on the electrical states of the organism and its forms of radiation, like brain waves, have confirmed this hope. The future of biophysics seems very bright.

More generally, by emphasizing the systematic character and organic structure of its own field, recent physics has tended to break down the old distinction between the "inorganic" and the organic. And in method also it is joining biology: both are adopting a similar statistical procedure. Present-day naturalistic philosophies accordingly now find it easy to fit living processes into the new world of systems of energy: thus Whitehead, for example, can define biology as the study of the larger and more complicated organisms, physics as that of the smaller and simpler organisms. Just as the experimental biologist analyzes biochemical processes not in isolation but as factors in the complicated medium of a living system or organism, so the physicist has now come to approach his processes as factors in their context of a field of radiation. Looking beyond the purely atomic limits of nineteenth-century mechanical physics and mechanistic biology, neither neglects the "organic" character of the system he is analyzing; but both are seeking with redoubled vigor the elementary processes or mechanisms which control that system. Thus in the face of a broader functional analysis, the need for a "vitalistic" protest in biology is disappearing. The organic properties and activities characteristic of living things are no longer perplexing anomalies with no intelligible place in a purely mechanical nature. They are merely special complications of traits found universally in all systems of natural events.

Mechanistic Analysis in Psychology

The last field into which naturalistic explanation on an experimental basis has entered has been that of human behavior, psychology. Men like Hartley in the eighteenth century had made a crude beginning, but the backwardness of biology had prevented much fruitful work. If biology is now regarded as a very complex branch of chemistry, psychology is coming to be treated by most of the experimentalists as a branch of biology or physiology. Experimental psychology as a natural science was developed by physicians who approached the whole matter from the physiological point of view. Wundt in Germany and William James in America were the pioneers. With James, the problem of a biological psychology became the discovery of the physiological changes in the nervous system which would serve as the mechanism of human behavior and of man's mental life. The American "behaviorists," under the leadership of John B. Watson, have pushed this biological approach in its most radical form. They have made of psychology the study of the physiological reactions of the human organism as a whole. Their science tries to analyze human nature, not, with the eighteenth century, into sensations and ideas, but rather into the biological reactions of the nervous system to specific stimuli.

The whole of mental life, even in its highest reaches of reflective thought, the Behaviorists maintain, can be studied and its laws formulated solely in terms of the physiological structure and activity of the body.

> Psychology, as the behaviorist views it, is a purely objective, experimental branch of natural science which needs consciousness as little as do the sciences of chemistry and physics.... This suggested elimination of states of consciousness as proper objects of investigation in themselves will remove the barrier which exists between psychology and the other sciences. The findings of psychology become the functional correlates of structure and lend themselves to explanation in physico-chemical terms.[10]

To such a science, thought can be accounted for as a series of reactions of the larynx, the organ of speech, which in themselves are dependent on mechanisms in the central nervous system.

> It is not different in essence from tennis-playing, swimming, or any other overt activity, except that it is hidden from ordinary observation and is more complex and at the same time more abbreviated so far as its parts are concerned than even the bravest of us could dream of.[11]

On such a view the human being comes into the world a bundle of prepotent reflexes, ready to be set off by the proper physical stimulus. During the course of a lifetime various stimuli, from without and within, condition these mechanisms and build them into long trains of habits; the entire process is ultimately a physico-chemical modification of the nervous system. Perhaps the most extreme statement of such a chemical explanation of human actions is to be found in Loeb.

> The highest manifestation of ethics, namely, the condition that human beings are willing to sacrifice their lives for an idea is comprehensible neither from the utilitarian standpoint nor from that of the categorical imperative. It might be possible that under the influence of certain ideas chemical changes, for instance, internal secretions within the body, are produced which increase the sensitiveness to certain stimuli to such an unusual degree that such people become slaves to certain stimuli just as the copepods (small crustaceans) become slaves to the light when carbon dioxide is added to the water. Since Pawlow and his pupils have succeeded in causing the secretion of saliva in the dog by means of optic and acoustic signals, it no longer seems strange to us that what the philosopher terms an "idea" is a process which can cause chemical changes in the body.[12]

Experimental psychology has to-day lost most of this brash self-confidence; the negative dogmas of the early Behaviorists have been forgotten. But their biological attitude, method, and viewpoint have won general acceptance, at least in America.

Most scientific psychologists to-day are "behavioristic" in using the methods of experimental science to study publicly observable human behavior. They have gone on from a primary concern with the elementary constituents of activity to the functional problems of their interaction and integration in the complex adjustments of the organism to its environment. Atomic analysis into minute segments of behavior has been unable to get very far without considering the larger patterns in which they coöperate. The same emphasis on the functioning of simpler processes within a complex system or field which we have seen emerging in physics and in biology has expressed itself here in movements like psychoanalysis and Gestalt psychology. The latter group in particular have not been content, like most of the critics of an analytic method in the sciences of life, merely to attack the validity of a purely atomic or reductive analysis into elements. They have brought a mass of experimental evidence to support the view that organisms respond not merely to isolated stimuli but to complex structures or patterns of relation (*Gestalten*) in the field of behavior. Psychology is likewise broadening its methods to include a functional analysis of its field.

Experimental Analysis Applied to the Origin of Present Forms

Upon these principles science attempts to explain the processes of nature observable to-day; long before they had been elaborated into their present forms, the endeavor was made to apply them also to the origin and development of the world and all the objects therein. Here the nineteenth century was doing more than extending the realm of the Newtonian Order of Nature; it was applying its methods to an entirely new field. The impulse came, as we have seen, from the realization of the importance of history in the social sciences; but it only became exact and fruitful when applied by scientists rather than romantic poets. Here, too, the order of advance was from astronomy, in which the mathematical interpretation of nature had begun, to the field of man. Because such a naturalistic explanation of origins was newer, and was carried on at a much more rapid rate, the consequent readjustment of the entire realm of men's beliefs was more difficult and led to more struggle and conflict. Hence it is probably true that the chief intellectual changes of the century were brought about in the endeavor to adjust men's older beliefs to the new idea of a universal development and evolution. First in astronomy, then in geology, then in biology, and lastly in the social sciences, the conception of evolution altered the entire intellectual map of the world. The chief points of friction were at the outset in the adjustment in the field of religion, whose very acclimatization in the static Newtonian world made it all the more difficult to set up a new reconciliation; and then in economics and morals, which are still to-day loath to admit the full consequences of the new scientific beliefs.

The Development of the Solar System

The conception of a scientific theory of origins first reached definiteness in astronomy. Laplace, following directly in Newton's path, published in 1799 his *Treatise on Celestial Mechanics*, an infinitely extended and enriched version of Newton's *Principia*. His ambition was "to offer a complete solution of the great mechanical problem presented by the solar system, and bring theory to coincide so closely with observation that empirical equations should no longer find a place in astronomical tables." [13] But he attacked also another problem that Newton had excluded, the origin and development of the solar system into its present form. Newton had believed that God made the solar system and its laws at a single moment in time; it was a machine, but a machine created by God with a definite purpose in mind. Buffon had already suggested that the sun originally existed alone, and that a comet falling upon it had started a swirl of matter from which the planets developed. Laplace, following the proposal of Kant, made in 1755, advanced the nebular hypothesis. The solar system existed originally as a great nebula, with a central kernel. Cooling caused this gaseous nebula to condense into concentric rings, which themselves formed new nebulæ, from which the planets developed. This theory, while much modified in detail, and while supplemented by an alternative "planetesimal hypothesis" that seems to bear even closer resemblance to what we can observe in the various spiral nebulæ in the heavens, has been accepted by astronomers in general. Its significance lies in its viewing celestial phenomena as essentially processes of development in time rather than as eternal recurrences; and, as the story goes, when Laplace was asked by Napoleon as to where the Creator came in under his view, he drew himself up haughtily and replied, "Sire, I have no need of that hypothesis." The stars, no less than the elements or than life, are the product of a process of growth.

The Development of the Earth

Laplace's hypothesis gave the geologists a basis for their work, to describe the stages in the emergence of the present form of the earth from its original incandescent state. Toward the end of the eighteenth century James Hutton and William Smith made patient, accurate, and detailed studies of fossils and their distribution, and of erosion and other work of water, collecting a mass of data from which a generalization could be drawn. Hutton especially insisted that the present is the key to the past, and that all past changes of the earth's surface are to be explained, not as due to great catastrophes, as was commonly held, but as the result of "causes now in operation." Just as the crust of the earth is being changed to-day by the action of rain, rivers, the sea, chemical decomposition and internal disturbances, so continents have always been altered and the various strata deposited. This doctrine of Uniformitarianism was seized upon by Charles Lyell and made the basis of his *Principles of Geology*, which, published in 1830, impressed upon the scientific mind the conception that the present state of affairs is due to the operation of constant natural causes over immense spaces of time. Upon the opening page of Lyell's book was inscribed this quotation from Playfair: "Amid all the revolutions of the globe, the economy of nature has been uniform and her laws are the only things which have resisted the general movement. The rivers and the rocks, the seas and the continents have been changed in all their parts; but the laws which direct those changes, and the rules to which they are subject, have remained invariably the same."[14] Lyell proceeded to apply this principle to all the phenomena of geology, with the result that he brought order and harmony out of what had before been chaos.

The significance of this work was not only, as Darwin put it, that this principle of Uniformity, the explanation of the past as like the present in its natural forces, "altered the whole tone of one's mind," and made past development of cardinal importance in science; "it was necessary for the supporters of this doctrine to take for granted incalculable periods of time, in order to explain the formation of sedimentary strata by causes now in diurnal action."[15] The Newtonian conception that the world and its furniture sprang into being complete a few thousand years ago at the simple fiat of the Creator became impossible, and in its place was imposed the necessity of believing that untold ages of development have preceded the present. Where Bruno set the world in the midst of an infinity of other worlds, Lyell placed it in well-nigh infinite time. Modern geologists hold that the oldest rocks of the Azoic or Archæozoic Age have endured for anywhere from 500,000,000 to 1,000,000,000 years.

The Development of the Forms of Life

It was but a step to the most revolutionary change of all, the application of the uniformitarian principle to biology and the origin of present forms of life. Already in the eighteenth century men had revived the ancient Greek speculations that the existing species of life are the result of a long process of growth. But the accepted view was that of the Swedish naturalist and classifier Linnæus, that "We reckon as many species as issued in pairs from the hands of the Creator,"[16] and that species have remained absolutely fixed from the period of their creation as described in Genesis, the only change being that of extension in numbers, not of variation in kind. *Nullæ species novæ* was a doctrine well fitted for the Newtonian world. Yet from many sources this theory was being attacked. Naturalists like Buffon, Erasmus Darwin, grandfather of Charles, and Geoffroy Saint-Hilaire, the opponent of Cuvier, an adherent of Linnæus's position; and romantic poets and philosophers like Goethe, Oken, and Schelling, attempted to formulate the evolutionary conception in various ways. Greatest of all was Lamarck, friend of Buffon, and zoölogist at the *Jardin des Plantes* in Paris. Lamarck attempted to develop a theory that would give some causal explanation of the evolution of species, in the absence of which such a theory must remain unintelligible. Refining upon the ideas of Buffon, who had held that the environment acts directly upon animals to produce new forms, he maintained that such changes were the result of an adaptation to a changed environment, transmitted to the offspring.

1. Life by its internal forces tends continually to increase the volume of every body that possesses it, as well as to increase the size of all the parts of the body up to a limit which it brings about. 2. The production of a new organ or part results from a new need or want, which continues to be felt, and from the new movement which this need initiates and causes to continue. 3. The development of organs and their force or power of action are always in direct relation to the employment of these organs. 4. All that has been acquired or altered in the organization of individuals during their life is preserved by generation, and transmitted to new individuals which proceed from those which have undergone these changes.[17]

This was a uniformitarian principle, but Lamarck had no opportunity for extended observation and experiment; and many facts, especially the limited time then allowed to the history of the world — it was supposed to have been created 4004 B.C. — led to a rejection of his views by most naturalists. But when Lyell revolutionized geology, and destroyed all confidence in the Mosaic cosmogony, the notion of organic evolution came to the fore again. Two things remained to be established: first, a detailed investigation of the distribution of living and fossil forms of life that would paint the picture of the succession of species in time; and secondly, a verifiable theory giving some causal explanation of the process. These things were achieved by Alfred Russel Wallace and Charles Darwin, working simultaneously.

For thirty years Darwin painstakingly gathered evidence of all sorts for the fact that species have developed in time. The mass of evidence in his *Origin of Species* (1859), drawn from geographical distribution, from paleontology, from comparative anatomy, from embryology, and from experimental breeding, sufficed to convince the biologists that whatever its explanation, evolution is a fact. Perhaps even more important in gaining acceptance was his causal explanation of the process. He had been much impressed by Malthus's doctrine that the food-supply increases at a much slower rate than the offspring of animals. The bitter struggle for existence which Malthus found in man's economic life Darwin took as the key to the whole of nature; inevitably only the most favored individuals would survive. Since slight variations from the parent are always occurring, "favorable variations would tend to be preserved, and unfavorable ones to be destroyed. The result of this would be the formation of a new species. Here then I had at last got a theory by which to work."[18] Turning to the efforts of the breeders of domesticated animals, he saw the same factors at work, with the exception that in this case the parents were artificially selected by man. Substitute for the breeder the natural struggle for existence, and in natural selection and the consequent survival of those fittest to survive, lies the key to the *cause* of evolution.

Theologians might rage when Darwin applied the same ideas to *The Descent of Man*, in 1871, but biologists and scientists in general had no doubts. Nor from that day to this has a single fact been discovered to shake the conclusions of Darwin that all living beings have evolved from earlier simpler forms; rather the mass of cumulative evidence has grown mountain high, so that no intelligent man can possibly deny to-day the *fact* of organic evolution. Darwin's particular theory of the causal *factors* involved in the process, however, has not seemed so successful. It is obvious that for natural selection to operate certain variations in offspring are necessary. Darwin himself held that the common slight variations between parents and offspring are sufficient grist for the mill of natural selection; but a more detailed knowledge of the mechanism of heredity makes it difficult to believe that such variations could possibly be perpetuated. The theory of de Vries, that inheritable variations must be large and sudden, must be complete jumps or "mutations," which appeals to a few actually observed mutations and the impossibility of slighter ones being preserved, is that at present generally accepted.

But to take chance in large gulps instead of small driblets really gives no more explanation of how and why such changes occur. Some biologists have revived the theory of Lamarck, that the individual adapts himself to his new environment, and that these new characteristics are then inherited; but investigations connected with the name of Weismann, which show that the germ plasm, the seed of the future offspring, seems almost from the formation of the embryo so completely shut off from the rest of the body that it is difficult to imagine how any such functional adaptations could possibly influence it, have led the vast majority of biologists to deny that acquired characteristics can be inherited at all, and throw the whole problem of the origin of the new form back upon chance variation in the germ plasm itself. At present biologists admit that, strictly speaking, we do not know anything about the causes of the origin of new species: the scientific faith holds that they occur because of chemical changes in the germ plasm. Experiment has shown that an environment of different temperature, or treatment with X-rays, can directly alter the genes that determine heredity. This suggests that the X-ray-like "cosmic rays" that fill our atmosphere may be the immediate cause of novelty. But the words of T. H. Morgan still sum up the situation: "The causes of the mutations that give rise to new characters we do not know, although we have no reason for supposing that they are due to other than natural processes." [19]

On one other element in the process of evolution much light has been thrown: the work of the obscure Austrian monk Gregor Mendel has led to the formulation of the laws of normal heredity, and stimulated the search for its mechanism. In the germ plasm itself there have been discovered bodies called chromosomes, made up of strings of bead-like genes. These genes are found in pairs, one from each parent; each pair has a definite function in producing the new organism, so that a change in one specifically alters it. This mechanism of heredity rests upon an atomic basis: the genes that unite to form a given individual are the elements that determine its inherited characters. But here too it is a functional atomism: no single gene determines any particular character of the organism, except negatively, if it be defective; every feature is a product of the interaction of many contributing genes. Furthermore, each cell contains all the genes, and what it will grow into depends not only on them, but also on its cellular environment. But though we have observed plenty of mutations, this precise knowledge of heredity has hardly revealed their causes.

The Effect of the Notion of Development on Scientific Ideals

But in spite of these difficulties, the beliefs of men to-day have become thoroughly permeated with the conception of evolution. The great underlying notions and concepts that meant so much to the eighteenth century, Nature and Reason and Utility, have largely given way to a new set better expressing the ultimate intellectual ideals of the Growing World. Many social factors conspired to popularize the idea of development and its corollaries. The fundamental social fact of the Industrial Revolution, with its continually accelerated change in the technique of applied science, and the revolution in the life of man brought about by the growth of cities and the utilization of new inventions, has brought home to every man the realization that our whole civilization is in process of thoroughgoing reorganization. Ways of life that seemed firmly established a single generation ago now have by the very pressure of circumstance been made almost obsolete, and few are so blind as to escape the significance of this fact of social change for every human institution. Transformations of political, economic, religious, and moral life are now commonplaces; every idea and custom has to be dated if it is to be understood properly. All these elements in modern civilization have driven home the fundamental nature of the idea of Change and Continuous Development, and powerfully reinforced the purely scientific reasons for making it a basic idea. Just as in considering the eighteenth century we were led to trace the effects of the idea of the Newtonian Order of Nature in every field, with the consequent attempts to readjust men's older beliefs to the new scientific ideal, so in sketching the intellectual changes of the past century we shall be forced to regard them all as primarily reactions, in one way or another, to the idea of Evolution.

Perhaps the fundamental emphasis brought by Evolution into men's minds has been upon the detailed causal analysis of the specific processes of change. Instead of seeking to discover the end or purpose of the world-process as a whole, or to discern the ultimate cause or ground of all existent things — the fundamental task of earlier science and philosophy — men have come to examine just what the process is and just what it does in its parts. They have rejected the ultimate goal of both Thomas and Spinoza, the contemplation of a fixed and static structure of Truth, and adopted instead the aim of investigating all the little truths which experimentation can reveal. Not that Truth which is the source of all truths, lifting man's soul above all human experience to the realm of the eternal, whether it be, with Aristotle and Thomas, the ultimate purpose of all things, or whether it be, with Spinoza, the universal mathematical system and structure of the world; but the patient, tireless, and endless search after an infinity of finite truths in our experience — this is the present-day goal of all scientific and philosophical endeavor. Men all agree to-day with Lessing:

> Not the truth which a man possesses or thinks he possesses, but the steadfast task to which he has applied himself of striving after truth, is the true worth of man.... If God held concealed in his right hand all truth, and in his left only the ever eager impulse after truth, and said to me: "Choose!" I should reverently take his left hand and say: "Father, give unto me! The absolute truth is for Thee alone." [20]

The new logic outlaws, flanks, dismisses — what you will — one type of problems and substitutes for it another type. Philosophy forswears inquiry after absolute origins and absolute finalities in order to explore specific values and the specific conditions that generate them.

In the second place, the classic type of logic inevitably set philosophy upon proving that life *must* have certain qualities and values — no matter how experience presents the matter — because of some remote cause and eventual goal. The duty of wholesale justification inevitably accompanies all thinking that makes the meaning of special occurrences depend upon something that once and for all lies behind them. The habit of derogating from present meanings and uses prevents our looking the facts of experience in the face; it prevents serious acknowledgment of the evils they present and serious concern with the goods they promise but do not as yet fulfill.... The displacing of this wholesale type of philosophy will doubtless not arrive by sheer logical disproof, but rather by growing recognition of its futility. Were it a thousand times true that opium produces sleep because of its dormitive energy, yet the inducing of sleep in the tired, and the recovery to waking life of the poisoned, would not be thereby one least step forwarded. And were it a thousand times dialectically demonstrated that life as a whole is regulated by a transcendent principle to a final inclusive goal, none the less truth and error, health and disease, good and evil, hope and fear in the concrete, would remain just what and where they now are. To improve our education, to ameliorate our manners, to advance our politics, we must have recourse to specific conditions of generation.[21]

Secondly, the success of evolution in the biological field brought a new emphasis on the methods and attitude of the biological and psychological sciences, rather than on those of

---

[21] From *The Influence of Darwin on Philosophy*, by John Dewey. Reprinted by permission of the publishers, Henry Holt & Co.

physics and mathematics. Since Darwin the social and human sciences in general, which always turn for methods and viewpoints to the reigning natural science, have followed biology and psychology in politics, economics, and morals, just as in the eighteenth century they took their cue from mathematical physics. Slowly but steadily this new attitude has made its way in the fields which the "geometrical spirit" sought to conquer in the Newtonian world; and the conception of man as an organism reacting to and acting upon a complex environment is now basic. All ideas and institutions are to-day thought of as primarily social products, functioning in social groups and springing from the necessity of effecting some kind of adaptation between human nature and its environment. All the fields of human interest have undergone this general sociologizing and psychologizing tendency; the example of religion and theology will be a sufficient illustration. Whereas the eighteenth century thought of religion and theology as a deductive and demonstrative set of propositions, men now consider religion as primarily a social product, a way of life springing from the social organization of men's religious experiences, and theology as a rationalization of certain fundamental feelings and experiences of human nature. We no longer prove the existence of God, we talk rather of the "meaning of God in human experience"; we no longer demonstrate the future life, we investigate the effect of the belief in immortality upon human conduct.

Thirdly, evolutionary thought has brought a new emphasis on the complexity of organization in beliefs and society, and upon the various shades of differentiation. Not fixed and universal types, but infinitely varied individuals, are now the elements investigated; not "man," but the individual differences between one man and another, as developed in the wholes in which men function. This tendency is closely related to the realities of a complicated industrial system and an infinitely interrelated national and international life. Not universality, with the Age of Reason, not absolute individuality, with some of the romanticists, but individuality within and between social groupings — this is the color of our thought.

Fourthly, evolution has introduced a whole new scale of values. Where for the eighteenth century the ideal was the rational, the natural, even the primitive and unspoiled, for us the desirable is identified rather with the latter end of the process of development, and our terms of praise are "modern," "up-to-date," "advanced," "progressive." Just as much as the Enlightenment we tend to identify what we approve with Nature, but for us it is not the rational order of nature, but the culmination of an evolutionary process, which we take for our leverage in existence. The eighteenth century could think of nothing worse to call a man than an "unnatural enthusiast"; we prefer to dub him an "antiquated and outgrown fossil." That age believed a theory if it were called rational, useful, and natural; we favor it if it is "the most recent development." We had rather be modernists and progressives than sound reasoners. It is perhaps an open question if in our new scale of values we have not lost as much as we have gained.

Fifthly, the idea of evolution, as it has finally come to be understood, has reinforced the humanistic and naturalistic attitude. It has emphasized the part that human beings can and must play in social change, if that change is to eventuate in anything worth while. The earlier idea of the romanticists and of Spencer, that progress is an inevitable thing — a modern substitute for Divine Providence — has given place to the belief that if society is changing, its change must be intelligently guided. With the universalization of mechanistic law, we possess an immensely more potent tool in our science than men have ever had before; and with the conviction that society has not always been as it is to-day, and can well be quite different in the future, there is the promise that we can remould it in the directions in which we desire it to go. The conception of a social science no longer means for us, as it did for the eighteenth century, a static physics of society, a system of laws to be discovered and religiously obeyed. It means to-day a detailed study of the specific causes that produce specific results, and an intensive manipulation of our social heritage to produce what seems to us good.

Finally, the biological and psychological attitude of evolution has with curious irony reinforced the very irrationalism it has sought to combat. If beliefs are primarily means of adaptation to an environment, what becomes of truth, nay, of science itself? It can be only a specific form of biological adaptation, revered because of its successful functioning in maintaining life; truth in any other sense, the absolute truth of the older rationalists, is meaningless in an evolving world. Cannot then any belief that works be true? To many the gate is opened to a new justification of their cherished faiths. Moreover, the analysis of the actual processes of the mind has led to the discovery of all the irrational elements that determine its thought and action, until it seems that amid the play of impulse, habit and emotion, and all those tendencies the Freudians place in the "unconscious," the still small voice of reason is quite drowned out. Are not all our beliefs but more or less concealed rationalizations, the reasons we invent for believing what we really believe because of quite different influence? Can intelligence do more than imagine such plausible justifications? Here is a disquieting question indeed! It has already destroyed the naïve faith of the Enlightenment in the unclouded reason of the average man, the very basis of liberalism and toleration; to many it seems the very suicide of science.

It is indeed a difficult problem; it is the old question of the freedom of the will in modern scientific guise. But however we solve it theoretically, it is evident that we must have faith in our ability to find truth; and if our early confidence has gone, a knowledge of the difficulties in the way must serve to make it easier to overcome them.

We close with a few words from a thinker who, probably more than any other man, has caught the vision of what the scientific method and the idea of evolution really means, John Dewey.

Thought can at least lighten the burden of humanity by emancipating mankind from the errors which thought has itself fostered — the existence of conditions which are real apart from their movement into something new and different, and the existence of ideals, spirit and reason independent of the possibilities of the material and physical. For as long as humanity is committed to this radically false bias, it will walk forward with blinded eyes and bound limbs. And thought can effect, if it will, something more than this negative task. It can make it easier for mankind to take the right steps in action by making it clear that a sympathetic and integral intelligence brought to bear upon the observation and understanding of concrete social events and forces, can form ideals, that is aims, which shall not be either illusions or mere emotional compensations.[22]

---

[22] From *Reconstruction in Philosophy*, by John Dewey. Reprinted by permission of the publishers, Henry Holt & Co.

GROWTH AND EVOLUTION

REFERENCES

1. Buffon, *Histoire Naturelle*, Introduction.
2. *Ibid.*
3. Herder, *Philosophie der Geschichte der Bildung der Menschheit.*
4. Helmholtz, quoted in Sedgwick and Tyler, *History of Science*, 358.
5. J. T. Merz, *History of European Thought in the Nineteenth Century*, II, ch. 6.
6. Maxwell, quoted in Sedgwick and Tyler, 358.
7. Jacques Loeb, *The Organism as a Whole*, 128, 23.
8. Benjamin Moore, *Origin and Nature of Life*, 190, 191.
9. Loeb, *The Organism as a Whole*, 1.
10. John B. Watson, *Behavior*, 27.
11. Watson, *Psychology*, 325.
12. Jacques Loeb, *Mechanistic Conception of Life*, 62.
13. R. S. Ball, *Great Astronomers.*
14. Quoted from Playfair, on title-page of Lyell's *Principles of Geology.*
15. Darwin, *Autobiography.*
16. Linnæus, quoted in H. F. Osborn, *From the Greeks to Darwin*, 129.
17. Lamarck, quoted in Osborn, 166.
18. Darwin, *Autobiography.*
19. T. H. Morgan, *Critique of the Theory of Evolution*, 193.
20. G. E. Lessing, *Duplik*, in *Werke*, ed. Lachmann-Muncker, XIII, 23, 24.
21. John Dewey, *The Influence of Darwin on Philosophy*, 13, 15, 16, 17.
22. John Dewey, *Reconstruction in Philosophy*, 130, 131.

SELECTED READING LISTS

General: See Chapter XI. Dampier-Whetham; D. Dietz, *Story of Science;* B. Ginzburg, *Adventure of Science;* H. G. Garbedian, *Major Mysteries of S.;* H. B. Lemon, *From Galileo to Cosmic Rays;* C. H. Ward, *Exploring the Universe.* A. N. Whitehead, *Science and the Modern World;* Bertrand Russell, *The Scientific Outlook.* L. Hogben, *Science for the Citizen;* B. Bavink, *The Concepts and Problems of Science.* W. Davis, ed., *The Advance of S.* Older surveys: J. T. Merz, *H. of European Thought in the 19th Cent.* (best); general histories of science by Dannemann, Gerland and Traumüller, R. Eisler, and O. Bryk; Lavisse et Rambaud, *Histoire Générale*, excellent arts. by Tannery, X, ch. 20, XI, ch. 25, XII, ch. 17.

Astronomy: Berry, Forbes, Mädler, etc. Harlow Shapley, *Flights from Chaos;* J. Jeans, *Mysterious Universe, Through Time and Space;* H. T. Stetson, *Man and the Stars.*

Analysis and Synthesis in Physics and Chemistry: Older histories of physics by Cajori, Gerland, Rosenberger, Poggendorff; of mechanics, by Mach, Dühring; of chemistry, by Thorpe, Darrow, Ladenburg, and E. von Meyer. O. Lodge, *Pioneers of Science;* W. Ostwald, *Grösse Männer.* E. Thorpe, *Humphry Davy;* Michael Faraday, *Researches*, ed. Everyman; J. Tyndall, *Faraday as a Discoverer;* S. P. Thompson, *M. Faraday.* Lord Kelvin, *Popular Lectures and Addresses;* life by S. P. Thompson. J. Clerk Maxwell, *Treatise on Magnetism and Electricity*, ed. J. J. Thomson; R. T. Glazebrook, *J. C. Maxwell and Modern Physics.* Helmholtz, *Conservation of Energy;* Mach, *Hist. and Root of the Principle of the Cons. of Energy;* M. Planck, *Das Prinzip der Erhaltung der Energie.*

The Revolution in Physical Concepts: A. Einstein and L. Infeld, *The Evolution of Physics;* P. R. Heyl, *Fundamental Concepts of Physics, New Frontiers of Physics;* R. T. Cox, *Time, Space and Atoms.* Max Planck, *The Universe in the Light of Modern Physics, Philosophy of Physics.* C. L. Mantell, *Sparks from the Electrode;* A. S. Eddington, *New Pathways in Science;* R. A. Millikan, *Electrons, Protons, Photons, Neutrons and Cosmic Rays.* W. H. Bragg, *The Nature of Things, The Universe of Light.* Einstein, *Relativity, The World as I See It;* Cunningham, *Relativity and the Electron Theory;* Freundlich,

Foundations of Einstein's Theory of Gravitation; Eddington, *Space, Time, and Gravitation.*

Evolution: Merz, ch. ix. A. Geikie, *Founders of Geology;* K. A. von Zittel, *Hist. of Geology and Paleontology.* Lyell, *Principles of Geology.* C. Singer, *Story of Living Things;* L. C. Miall, *H. of Biology;* W. A. Locy, *Growth of Biology, Biology and its Makers;* E. Nordenskiöld, *H. of Biology.* H. F. Osborn, *From the Greeks to Darwin;* J. W. Judd, *Coming of Evolution.* Darwin, *Life and Letters,* esp. I, ch. xiv, on reception, and II, chs. i, ii, letters and reviews; *Origin of Species, Descent of Man.* Thomas Huxley, *Life and Letters,* by L. Huxley; "American Addresses," in *Darwiniana; Science and Hebrew Tradition, Man's Place in Nature.* Herbert Spencer, *Principles of Biology;* E. Haeckel, *Natural History of Creation* (classic popularizations). A. R. Wallace, *Darwinism* (1889); G. J. Romanes, *Darwinism and After Darwin;* H. de Vries, *The Mutation Theory;* A. Weismann, *The Evolution Theory, The Germ-Plasm.* **On evolution today:** H. H. Newman, ed., *Nature of the World and of Man, Evolution Yesterday and Today;* F. B. Mason, ed., *Creation by Evolution;* W. B. Scott, *Theory of Evolution;* R. S. Lull, *Organic Evolution;* T. H. Morgan, *Critique of the Theory of Evolution* (best criticism), *Scientific Basis of Evolution.* H. S. Jennings, *Biological Basis of Human Nature;* J. A. Thomson, *Darwinism and Human Life;* E. G. Conklin, *Heredity and Environment.* H. G. Wells, J. S. Huxley, and G. F. Wells, *Science of Life.*

Mechanistic Analysis in Biology: Thomas Huxley, *On the Hypothesis that Animals are Automata,* in *Method and Results.* Jacques Loeb, *Mechanistic Conception of Life, The Organism as a Whole* (most thoroughgoing). B. Moore, *Origin and Nature of Life;* F. Le Dantec, *Nature and Origin of Life;* H. F. Osborn, *Nature and Evolution of Life;* J. Needham, *Man a Machine, The Sceptical Biologist* (Neo-mechanism). R. C. Pummett, *Mendelianism;* T. H. Morgan, *Experimental Zoology, Experimental Embryology;* Jennings. **Vitalism:** Hans Driesch, *Theory of Vitalism, Science and Phil. of the Organism;* J. S. Haldane, *Mechanism, Life, and Personality;* Bergson, *Creative Evolution,* ch. I. **Organic Mechanism:** C. Lloyd Morgan, *Emergent Evolution; Life, Mind and Spirit;* L. von Bertalanffy, *Modern Theories of Development;* J. H. Woodger, *Biological Principles;* E. S. Russell, *Interp. of Development and Heredity;* G. R. de Beer, *Intro. to Experimental Embryology, Embryology and Evolution;* W. E. Ritter and E. W. Bailey, *The Organismal Conception of Life.*

Mechanistic Analysis in Psychology: Histories of psychology by Baldwin, Brett, Dessoir, Klemm; G. S. Hall, *Founders of Modern Psychology;* G. Murphy, *Hist. Intro. to Modern Psychology;* E. G. Boring, *Hist. of Experimental Psych.;* W. B. Pillsbury, *H. of Psych.* Cabanis, *Des Rapports du Physique et du Moral de l' Homme* (most elaborate statement of 18th century materialism). Fechner, *Psychophysik;* W. Wundt, *Physiological Psychology, Outlines of Psych.* W. James, *Principles of Psych.;* E. L. Thorndike, *Educational Psych.;* J. B. Watson, *Behavior, Psychology, Lectures on Psych.* R. S. Woodworth, *Dynamic Psych., Contemporary Schools of Psych.;* J. C. Flugel, *A Hundred Years of Psych.;* G. Adams, *Psychology: Science or Superstition?* W. Köhler, *Gestalt Psychology.*

Intellectual Outcome: Huxley, *The Advance of Science in the Last Half-Century* (1889); A. R. Wallace, *The Wonderful Century; The 19th Century, a Review of Progress. Evolution in Modern Thought,* ed. Mod. Lib. F. S. Marvin, *Recent Developments in European Thought.* F. R. Lankester, *Kingdom of Man.* J. Langdon-Davies, *Man and His Universe, Man Comes of Age;* G. Heard, *These Hurrying Years;* H. G. Wells, *William Clissold.* H. Levy, *Universe of Science;* Bertrand Russell, *The Scientific Outlook;* M. Planck, *Where is Science Going?* G. A. Baitsell, ed., *Evolution of Earth and Man;* C. E. M. Joad, *Guide to Modern Thought.* Criticism in John Dewey, *Influence of Darwinism on Philosophy, Reconstruction in Philosophy;* F. J. E. Woodbridge, *The Purpose of History,* "Evolution," in *Nature and Mind;* A. N. Whitehead, *Science and the Modern World, Nature and Life;* M. R. Cohen, *Reason and Nature.*

CHAPTER XIX

THE SCIENCE OF MAN IN THE GROWING WORLD

Of all the consequences that followed from the new evolutionary world of science, what seemed most momentous was the definite inclusion of man within the scope of the cosmic process. Not only was man an integral part of Nature, bound by her laws and subject to her forces; the eighteenth century had already learned that, but the knowledge had seemed to spread human reason throughout the universe rather than place man within a natural setting. Now after Darwin, however, there could be no further blinking of the fact that man was a product as well as a part of nature, that he had climbed to his present estate from lowly origins, and that all his works had been painfully acquired in the struggle against a hostile environment. While men had long recognized that man is a rational animal, they had perhaps not unnaturally emphasized his distinguishing mark of rationality; but now reason was well-nigh forgotten in the new realization of his common animality. Man was an animal species like any other, and he and his interests were the proper field of biology.

The social sciences, which for all their eighteenth-century pretensions to objectivity and precision had remained more rationalizations of contemporary demands than disinterested analyses, felt the full force of this new biological orientation. The revolution in the natural sciences effected by the emergence of the genetic viewpoint was as nothing to the transformations wrought in the human sciences. Indeed, it almost seems that nothing was left of the eighteenth-century science of man save its very conception, and the social sciences commonly date their birth from the coming of the evolutionary attitude. But a closer view reveals that far more of the spirit and method of the Enlightenment was preserved than evolutionists care to admit; while until the present generation the formulators of the new sciences of man were really much more influenced by the historical spirit drunk in from romanticist sources than by the smattering of biological terminology with which they veneered their systems. We have seen how the evolutionary attitude originated first in the social field, as a part of the general romantic reaction to the mechanical ideal of the Enlightenment; and it must be confessed that long after the natural sciences had purified the genetic method of its idealistic and purposive husk, and turned to the experimental observation of the processes of change, theorists of society retained their romantic faith in great deductive systems and simple formulæ based on the slightest of observations.

Hence it can hardly be denied that, though the nineteenth century has seen an immense amount of intellectual energy devoted to the scientific study of man and his society, the results so far attained, as measured by verified and universally accepted knowledge, fall far short of the imposing edifice of physics, chemistry, and biology. The social studies have largely remained the playground of conflicting schools of thinkers, and an original formula still attracts much more attention than a careful investigation of fact. Bitter controversies rage about the basic methods to be employed; since each new theorist feels that he must overthrow the erroneous ideas of his predecessors and start from the ground up, there has been very little of the scientific spirit of coöperative building upon the achievements of previous investigators. Even where, as in psychology or anthropology, a great mass of facts has been painfully accumulated, the very observation of these facts has been so embedded in a host of premature hypotheses that it is doubtful whether they can be disentangled from speculative theory. In a word, the social sciences are just to-day emerging from a stage comparable to that of astronomy and physics in the days of Copernicus and Kepler; and unfortunately no such happy guess as the mathematical interpretation of nature has been hit upon for them.

Certain definite achievements, however, can be recorded. Whereas the science of man in the eighteenth century was almost entirely an apologetic and a practical program, in the evolutionary world it has come to be a relatively impartial analysis. There has been heaped up a mass of detailed investigations of the growth of particular institutions, the indispensable prerequisite to any sound generalizations. Various methods have been explored, their possibilities and their limitations discovered, and their valid claims assimilated. And despite the present confusion, it can be confidently asserted that though the science of man still awaits its Newton, though even its Galileo has not yet appeared, special branches have already won their way to a sound method and fruitful categories. In the memory of the present generation, psychology has eschewed unchecked speculation and has settled down to experimental investigation and inductive generalization; while anthropology has come out of the jungle of evolutionary mythology and has achieved the most critical method of any of the social sciences.

The Search for an Adequate Method

The record of the growth of the sciences of man since the Age of the Enlightenment is primarily the search for an adequate method and valid categories. To the orthodox deductive analysis of Newtonian physics succeeded the historical method of the irrational and conservative Romanticists. For a time each field was divided between its "analytic" and its "historical" school. Then after 1859 came the impulse from biology, with all its Darwinian prestige, reinforcing the evolutionary viewpoint, though not so much changing method as introducing new concepts and new premises. But the early great deductive and speculative systems, which arranged the facts to fit their assumptions, like those of Comte or Spencer, collapsed under the attacks of the investigators they had themselves inspired. Ensued a period of more modest collection and classification of phenomena, with little pretence at formulating laws — a "natural history" of society, to which the more adequate picture of human nature furnished by the new psychology contributed. Gradually men turned from mere classification to experimentation on the one hand, and to the mathematical methods of statistics and correlation on the other. The social sciences seemed almost scientific; critical analysis was at last replacing dogmatism. To a closer scrutiny of these conflicting and vacillating methods we shall now turn.

The Persistence of the Eighteenth-Century Mechanical Ideal

The immense prestige of the deductive method of the Enlightenment, modeled on mechanics, which well suited theorists with few facts to go upon, gave it a dominating position to the present century. The ideal of a social physics, so strong at the beginnings of political economy, has remained entrenched in economics longer than anywhere else; but it is just as deeply rooted in the pioneers of what purported to be an inductive science of society, sociology. Saint-Simon, Fourier, and the other Forty-Eighters in France searched for a Newtonian law of social gravitation, from which all social phenomena could be deduced; Fourier thought that he had found it. Quetelet entitled his epochmaking work on statistics *Physique Sociale*. Auguste Comte had an elaborate scheme of social statics and dynamics, with its laws of social action and reaction. Even such outstanding evolutionists as Herbert Spencer and the American Lester F. Ward, however much they might embroider their pages with biological terms, remained essentially deductive and apriori, starting from certain assumed premises and elaborating therefrom orderly systems.

This is abundantly clear in the case of Spencer, who approached evolution with the prejudices of the eighteenth century for mechanics in science and for *laisser-faire* in society. In his lengthy *Synthetic Philosophy*, appearing between 1860 and 1893, he tried to deduce the laws of every field, from astronomy to sociology and ethics, from the fundamental principle of evolution, defined in mechanical terms as "an integration of matter and concomitant dissipation of motion; during which the matter passes from an indefinite, incoherent homogeneity to a definite, coherent heterogeneity; and during which the retained motion undergoes a parallel transformation." [1] In other words, Spencer sought to force all the facts into a single harmonious cosmic evolutionary process, in which everything should develop from a simple and undifferentiated state to a highly individualized organic condition. In good eighteenth-century fashion he tried to prove that the whole weight of the universe lies behind the individualistic theory of society. Thus, important as was his prestige in introducing the general idea of development into the study of social institutions, it also carried over the deductive method and the model of physics into the concepts of evolution. It took a generation to free the social sciences from this heavy burden of misleading technique and dogmatic assumption, and long before he concluded his monumental task the pages of his work had grown yellow and antiquated.

In both law and economics deduction has remained to this day the orthodox method. The jurisprudence of Bentham, systematized and simplified by John Austin, gave rise in England and America to the analytical school of legal theory, in which the function of the court is seen as the purely deductive application of authoritative premises found in statute or constitution. Although modified or abandoned by leading jurists to-day, this technique is still in control of most of the courts; it has made exceedingly difficult the adaptation of legal principles to the unprecedented conditions of industrial civilization. Political economy, which in Adam Smith's hands was fairly close to the facts of commercial life, became increasingly abstract and deductive as it was made the dogmatic creed of the Liberals. In the Manchester school it seemed to lose all sight of economic facts in its endeavor to approximate the rigor of mathematics. John Stuart Mill, the great figure of the mid-century, in general an advocate of scientific induction, put the weight of his magisterial authority behind deduction as the only possible method for the social sciences. In the face of the humanitarian and working-class protests at the unreality and cruelty of the classical doctrines, orthodox economists turned only the more blindly to the mechanical ideal of the Newtonian world. The seventies saw a vigorous defense, in England, France, and Austria, of the abstract point of view, which, in the name of "pure economic theory," seized upon the antiquated and abandoned pleasure-pain psychology of a century before for its premises, and showered upon them all the resources of dialectics and mathematics. The mazes of the resulting marginal utility economics have only in the last decade seemed to the younger economists purified of all contact with the world of actual social processes; the revolt to a more realistic view is still led by a minority.

The Historical Method of the Romanticists

Thus in countless ways the social sciences have retained their eighteenth-century legacy. But from Germany and romanticism there spread the second great stream of influence. Born of Hegelian idealism and the traditionalist reaction to the scientific views of the Enlightenment, the historical school turned to the record of the past, and sought to trace the slow and inevitable development of human society and institutions from immemorial antiquity. The newly awakened interest in history led to an indefatigable poring over of musty documents in the fervent faith that somehow the exact determination of the long course of growth through which all things human have passed would of itself give a complete understanding of man and his society to-day. The romantic parentage of this historical method betrays itself in the ease with which history was itself deified and made into a sacred force with which mortal hands must not meddle; for the course of human events was held to be guided by some vague but purposive power, to interfere with whose designs were sacrilege. It was the prevalence of this teleological view of history that made it easy to assimilate the new evolutionary philosophy when it pressed in from biology; Darwin seemed only to have furnished an exact scientific confirmation of the presence of this cosmic power. History was strangely looked upon, not as a record of the effects of the interplay of complex forces, but as itself a force which produced things, and evolution, to the historical school, was objectified as both the preordained plan and the Great Cause which realized its hidden purposes.

In fact, the historical method, as applied to social institutions, means the abandonment of science, in the sense of experimentally verified causal principles, and the reliance instead for explanation upon a chronological survey of successive facts. It holds that to understand what the present is and how it came about, it is only necessary to know what has preceded it in time. To take an analogy from astronomy, it is as though men were to rest content with the careful record of the positions of the planets, and to feel no need of going on to celestial mechanics. It is not to be denied that a knowledge of historical development is of cardinal importance as enormously enlarging the range of observed phenomena, as suggesting the forces at work in society, and as giving a sense of the relativity of present forms and the omnipresence of change. But the historical method in the social sciences claimed more: it purported to give of itself a science of man. This overenthusiastic claim was perhaps but natural in the intoxication of the widened horizon; but just as biology has left the past to paleontology and itself turned more and more to experimentation, so the social sciences must not forget the present, the only field for genuine scientific investigation, in their wonder at the past. Social paleontology can never take the place of an analysis of contemporary forces; indeed, only as we understand the present in its own terms can we hope to find the true key to the interpretation of past forces. Neither history nor evolution is itself a causal explanation; both are rather phenomena themselves to be explained.

The historical school marked, indeed, one great achievement; it perfected the critical methods for determining objectively just what the past had been. Scientific historical investigation arose first in Germany; Niebuhr and Ranke in political history, Baur and the Tübingen school in sacred history, A. F. Wolf in classical philology, laid the foundations for critical history. Men found the instruments for reading aright the past. In their delight at this discovery, the other social studies devoted themselves whole-heartedly to history. The science of society became the history of society; each branch saw itself swallowed up by its own past. Philosophy became the history of philosophy, jurisprudence the history of law, anthropology the history of social institutions, economics the history of economic institutions, politics, the study of constitutional development, ethics, the growth and development of human customs, theology, the history of religion. The promising utilitarian attitude of the eighteenth century was forgotten in the ridicule of its lack of historical sense.

Innumerable were the masses of detailed investigations eagerly undertaken to trace the development of particular institutions. Studies of the evolution of religion, of moral customs and beliefs, of marriage and the family, of social groups, of economic forms, and indeed of everything remotely connected with man's life, poured from the press in great profusion, to the enrichment of men's knowledge of the past and to the confusion of their ideas. Men sought everywhere simple and inevitable lines of development, with the result that they usually falsified, fully as much as had the earlier romanticists, the actual complexity and diversity of the past.

Moreover, the tendency grew to look to the origins of a belief or custom for its value to the present; and men thought that when they had displayed a course of development through centuries they had explained both the causes of that development and its present utility. For example, the historical method applied to the study of religion too often meant that men turned away from a fruitful investigation of human nature in its present environment, to a preoccupation with "primitive religion," and looked for the true explanation of religious phenomena in the practices and beliefs of savage tribes. This is much like studying the oak tree, not in the forest giant, but in the acorn; and it becomes all the more confusing when it is remembered that such "primitive" tribes are themselves not the ancestors of our present civilizations, but the most rudimentary organizations existing to-day in out-of-the-way corners of the world. The genetic method bade men study the oak tree, not even in the acorn from which it grew, which is obviously impossible, but in some other seed which we are not even sure resembles that acorn in essential characteristics. And it is evident that no amount of study, even of the original acorn, will determine the present shade or timber value of the oak. Thus the historical attitude has bade fair to obscure the fruitful eighteenth-century attitude of investigating institutions primarily in connection with their relevance to human nature to-day and the needs they must now meet.

The Evolutionary and Biological Methods

The establishment of biological evolution only reinforced this historical attitude, which, while retaining its romantic spirit, now dubbed itself the "evolutionary method," and borrowed prestige without enlightenment. Without the slightest regard for the mechanisms of change in biology, every history blossomed out into an "evolution." Sociologists and anthropologists, following Spencer, conceived elaborate schemes of the stages of social development, and with fine display of scientific erudition accumulated customs and ideas gathered from widely divergent times and places to substantiate their speculative theories. This hodge-podge of deduction and preconception they dignified as the "comparative method"; by its means it was easy to prove any theory whatsoever.

In fact, anthropology, sociology, and the social sciences in general have had in the last generation to retrace their steps painfully and found themselves anew upon psychology and an analysis of present conditions. Most of the contemporary literature in these fields is still concerned with pointing out the dangers of assuming any simple, single, and uniform line of more or less automatic development, and with emphasizing the manifold causal strains and influences that have entered in to transform ancient institutions into the present forms that, while bearing the same names, are patently much altered in structure and function. Thus the science of man, already struggling with its traditional deductive method, was still further confused by the historical attitude of romanticism.

But Darwin did far more than merely reinforce the romantic strain in the science of man; in forcing biology into the limelight and giving it almost the prestige for the last half of the nineteenth century that mechanics had held during the eighteenth, he added a third biological strain to the two that already held the field. Biology was now the reigning science, hence to biology the social sciences now went for new concepts and analogies. In the conception of the social organism they found one that offered endless possibilities for elaboration. Society is not the product of a mechanical contract, as the Enlightenment had fondly believed; it is a genuine living organism, a unity of harmoniously functioning cells. This idea was already familiar from the romanticists, who had insisted that the State was far more than the sum of its members; indeed, the organism analogy, though it only came into its own with the rise of biology, like the idea of simple development owes most of its content to the idealistic impulse of Fichte, Schelling, and Hegel.

A good example of the early fusion of idealistic and biological concepts is the political theory of Bluntschli, the German nationalist. The State is "by no means a lifeless instrument, a dead machine, but is a living, and therefore organic being.... It does not stand on the same level as the lower organisms of plants and beasts, but is of a higher kind.... When we call the State an organism, therefore, we are not thinking of the activity of natural beings in seeking, appropriating, and assimilating nourishment, and in reproducing their kind." The analogy consists in the three points:

(a) Every organism is a union of corporeal, material elements and vital, psychic forces — in short, of body and soul. (b) Although an organic being is and remains a whole, it is, nevertheless, in its parts endowed with members, which are animated by special impulses and capacities, in order to satisfy in various ways the changing life-needs of the whole. (c) The organism has a development from within outwards and an external growth.[2]

Bluntschli was so enamoured of his figure that he went on to attribute sex to his social organism, the State being male and the Church female.

Auguste Comte, in his *Positive Philosophy* (1830–1842), was the earliest thinker to maintain that the science of society must found itself explicitly upon biology. He saw a definite development through which every science had to pass, culminating, in the "positive stage," in a unified science of society with definitely formulated laws of growth. As the highest science, sociology must seek its foundation in its immediate predecessor, biology. The laws of sociology are the counterparts of those of biology. But to Herbert Spencer is primarily due the introduction of the biological ideal into the science of man. He carried out in great detail the organism analogy, a speculation that was pushed to even more absurd lengths by later sociologists like Lilienfeld, Schäffle, and Worms, for whom it was no mere analogy but the literal truth. Far more important was his insistence on the notion of social adaptation to environment; that is, the categories of the mechanism of biological evolution. With the publication of Darwin's theory, men vied with each other to interpret the development of social groups in terms of the struggle for existence, natural selection, and the survival of the fittest. These social Darwinists, among whom the most important were Bagehot in his *Physics and Politics*, and the Austrians Gumplowicz and Ratzenhofer, saw the conflict of racial, national, and social groups in purely biological terms, with war as the primary instrument of social evolution. For Bagehot, the struggle for existence amongst men takes place between groups, rather than individuals; but group competition is all the fiercer for this cooperation.

Whatever may be said against the principle of "natural selection" in other departments, there is no doubt of its predominance in early human history. The strongest killed out the weakest, as they could. ... In every particular state of the world, those nations which are strongest tend to prevail over the others; and in certain marked peculiarities the strongest tend to be the best. ... The best institutions have a natural military advantage over bad institutions.[3]

Gumplowicz, surveying the racial struggles of the Austrian scene, saw in group struggle the key to the origin of civilization.

Out of frictions and struggles, out of separations and unions of opposing elements, finally come forth as new adaptation products the higher socio-psychical phenomena, the higher cultural forms, the new civilizations, the new state and national unities ... and this merely through social action and reaction, entirely independent of the initiative and will of individuals, contrary to their ideas and wishes and social striving.[4]

Groups, both racial and economic, have inevitably conflicting interests, and in the ensuing and unending conflicts the strongest will dominate the weaker. Everywhere such conquest leads to the subjection by an economically powerful minority of the economically weak majority; this subjection both creates and is maintained by the state and political institutions.

Such "social Darwinism" found many adherents. The philosopher Nietzsche gave it an idealistic turn; biologists like Galton and Karl Pearson applied it to the conflicts of racial stocks, deducing a practical program of national eugenics. Before 1914 it formed one of the mainstays of the "scientific" defense of war and militarism; latterly it has been used to bolster the various prejudices of Nordic supremacy, anti-Semitism, and nationalistic intolerance. Biological methods lent themselves as easily as mechanical to the special interests of various classes.

Darwinian biology contributed one further important strain to the science of man: it founded the classical or comparative anthropology of Tylor, Lang, Frazer, and Morgan. It set men to collecting specimens of primitive cultures and institutions, by the proper ordering of which great speculative systems of social development could be created. It was upon such heterogeneous material and hasty generalizations that the science of sociology was erected, with its absurdly simple social laws and its facile explanations.

In spite of the revolutionary emphasis on the biological nature of man, the methods and concepts borrowed by the social sciences from biology after 1859 thus introduced as much confusion as clarification into the science of man. The organic analogy drew men's attention from a fruitful study of actual society; the natural selectionists obscured the significant ways in which social evolution differs from organic; and the comparative method led to the distortion and falsification of facts. So much valuable effort had to be expended in criticizing these erroneous half-truths that the progress of the social sciences in the last generation has been largely the careful disproof of the great theories inspired by Darwinian evolution.

The Influence of Psychology and Experimentalism

Still another set of confusing ideas, however, has been introduced from psychology, which to-day has almost obscured the prestige of the biological methods. In the *cul-de-sac* to which the historical and evolutionary methods seemed to lead, men turned eagerly to the new science of human nature slowly emerging at the end of the century, and sought once more to found the social sciences upon psychology. Obviously such an approach is far more fruitful of genuine scientific results; but unfortunately it was just the most hypothetical conclusions of the infant science that were seized upon as axioms. In economics, which felt the impulse first of all, the psychological school indeed turned back to the old ideas of the Enlightenment, and reached grotesque conclusions. In sociology, the old tale of biology was repeated: now this, now that factor was isolated and made an all-explaining principle, into which facts were fitted at will. Sympathy was the great key, as in Sutherland and Giddings; or imitation was deified, as in the school of Tarde and Le Bon. With the discovery of the irrational basis of human action, each of the great "instincts" could support a system. One school concentrated on the "instinct of the herd"; the Freudians spread sex over all life; still others, desiring a fuller palette, followed McDougall in composing lists of the elementary impulses from which society is built up. In each case the method was the same; the principle was first formulated on the basis of a few observations and then the search was started for further facts to make out a case against all rivals.

Thus the net result of a century of investigation, classification, and theorizing was that though the detailed knowledge of human societies had enormously increased, and though a host of new conceptions had been pressed into service, the discovery of any verified and established scientific laws in the social field was little nearer than it had been a hundred years before. If one sought a rigorous science of society, the eighteenth-century deductive method was still available; though to be sure the premises had multiplied into a swarm of conflicting principles. If one wearied of the fruitless task of adding system to speculative system, one could retire to history, and trace the stages in the development of the past. Even here it was almost impossible to avoid selecting one's facts by the touchstone of some preconceived theory. What the system builders had erected, the critics tore down; in economics, in anthropology, in sociology, in political science, in every field the best minds were coming to feel that all theories were contradicted by more adequate knowledge, that the sciences so carefully erected and so confidently proclaimed in the seventies and eighties were but shams and impostures, and that every classification of the multitude of social facts was about as good, and as fruitless, as every other. One thing, and only one, seemed definitely won: men must find the facts, and let the theories suffer. Such was the general status of the social sciences at the beginning of the present century. From the presses there still poured new systems; but the abler men were modestly and often blindly studying minor segments of history or society.

Out of this methodological *impasse* men are just now struggling to emerge. They are seeking a sounder and more critical psychology, convinced that the science of human nature must be basic. They are critical of all one-sided and facile explanations, and demand a survey of all the facts. They are grasping at the possibility that statistics, first formulated by Quetelet in 1835, seems to offer an exact measurement of social forces, and pathetically they are trying correlation after correlation in the hope of stumbling upon something significant. Above all, they are seeking to become as experimental as possible; and where they still see hope in biology, it is the careful laboratory methods of the experimentalists that now attract them. By a criticism of past theories, to discover their germs of truth, by a patient analysis of existing institutions and their functioning, by the statistical testing of their tentative conclusions, and by the unremitting insistence on investigation and experimentation, they are hoping that at last some general principles worthy of the name of a science may come to light.

While the progress of the social sciences in the growing world seems thus somewhat disappointing, in the light of their high hopes and higher pretensions, the special branches have slowly if somewhat fitfully blocked out their fields, laid firm foundations, and acquired both a critical sense and a promising technique. This process has gone farthest in the fields which are most limited in subject-matter and least exposed to the play of prejudice, above all which offer most scope for detailed investigation; psychology and anthropology have become genuinely scientific while economics, political science, and preëminently the general science of society, sociology, are still struggling to free themselves from preconceptions and group prejudices. In turning to a brief survey of the individual sciences, we can best note the measure of advance over the pioneer efforts of the Age of Reason.

The Development of Psychology

We have already traced the spread of the mechanistic method of natural science to the field of human behavior, culminating in the behavioristic psychology of Watson and his followers. But this tendency has been neither steady nor unopposed, and in view of the widespread popularity of a new romantic psychology at the present day it is perhaps premature to maintain that the science of man has yet been embraced within the scheme of universal mechanism. During most of the century, two different attitudes held the psychological field. There was on the one hand the old eighteenth-century association school of Hartley and James Mill, which followed the Newtonian mechanical method but took as its elements the unique data of "sensations," reached by an analysis of the individual consciousness. This empirical school was dominant in England, where its alliance with the utilitarian philosophy and the psychological assumptions of the economists and liberals made it almost a party platform. Its natural corollaries were hedonism, that the sole motive of human action is the desire for pleasure and the avoidance of pain, and rationalism, that men act always consciously and rationally to attain these ends. It formed the background of English individualism almost to the World War, and was written into all political, economic, and social theory. Opposing it stood the psychology of the romanticists, dominant in Germany and widespread in France. This school rejected the idea that man's mind can be explained in mechanical terms, but retained the method of introspection. The romanticist found hidden springs of reality when he gazed within his own soul; it hurt him to subject this flow of life to definite analysis — he preferred to feel, to trust his intuitions. Amongst the more logical French introspection revealed all the traditional elements: soul, will, freedom, reason. When Auguste Comte came to classify the sciences, he felt so convinced of the metaphysical nature of this psychology that he found no place for such a science in his scheme. The impulse to a fresh analysis came from neither of these rather barren schools, but from biology and physiology.

In his *Principles of Psychology*, published in 1855, Herbert Spencer made the first attempt at a thoroughgoing biological view of human nature. Though he could not free himself from the older ideas, he did envisage mind not as a substance set within the mortal frame, but as "an adjustment of internal to external conditions," a form of human adaptation to a biological environment. Slowly with the development of neurology came a more detailed physiological analysis of human action. At first men retained the older notion of purely psychic elements, which they endeavored to correlate with the newly discovered neural processes; the orthodox view was "psycho-physical parallelism," the doctrine that there were two realms, one mental and one physical, between which there was a close correlation but no causal relation. A nervous impulse was associated with a mental one, but men's actions would be the same without the running accompaniment of consciousness. This view freed the physiologist to perfect his mechanical analysis, while the psychologist could introspectively trace the correlated mental structure built up of sensations, volitions, and emotions. The chief work of such a structural psychology was to associate the various conscious discriminations of color, sound, taste, etc., with their physiological stimuli. On such a basis Weber and Fechner did much experimental work, and in 1879 Wundt founded the first psychological laboratory in Leipzig.

This experimental psychology was systematized by William James in his great *Principles of Psychology* in 1890. Though he still considered consciousness as something different and distinct from the body, he regarded it not as a fixed structure but as a flowing functional adaptation to the environment; and he consistently sought a physiological basis for all its activities. Most of the investigation that has since been done was inspired by his chapters on instinct, habit, the emotions, the will, and the self. But to the functional experimentalist the presence of this intangible and indescribable entity became increasingly useless, and James later came to question seriously the value of retaining the concept of consciousness or mind at all — a suggestion that has met with growing favor. With James must be placed as a pioneer G. Stanley Hall, who fruitfully applied the genetic method with much the same results. An added impetus to a purely biological psychology came from the study of animal behavior, where introspection and its resulting mental structure are obviously not applicable. Following carefully controlled and statistical methods, James McKeen Cattell and Edward Lee Thorndike were able to approach human behavior in the same way, with the result that Watson took the inevitable step of discarding consciousness entirely and relying upon a completely objective laboratory study of human behavior.

The Problem of the Elements of Human Behavior

The behavioristic school saw as its fundamental problem the discovery of the simple physiological mechanisms out of which is integrated the behavior of the human organism as a whole, and the analysis of the details of the synthesizing process of habit formation. By a careful analysis of the reactions of human infants, Watson has determined the behavior patterns with which man starts life, and has explored the way in which these simple reflex actions are built up into more complicated forms. Basing his work upon the conception of the "conditioned reflex" investigated by Pavlov in Russia — a response acquired by associating a new stimulus with the one accustomed — he has shown how quickly the native reflexes and random movements are built up into learned reactions. Habit upon habit is formed by the conditioning environment, which, operating upon the given physiological patterns, thus literally moulds the integrated behavior of the adult.

While all agreed that these elements of behavior are physiological in nature, and that they are largely only dimly conscious to the individual, controversy has waxed furious over the question whether they are fixed in some simple inherited pattern at birth, so that the basic human traits can fairly be considered constant and unalterable, or whether they are chiefly habits formed by the environment out of a relatively plastic human nature of almost limitless possibilities. Thorndike in his *Original Nature of Man* and especially McDougall in his *Social Psychology* took the former view, and built up an imposing scheme of original tendencies or instincts. from the combination of which behavior atoms mature conduct arises.

Any man possesses at the very start of his life [said Thorndike] numerous well-defined tendencies to future behavior. Between the situations which he will meet and the responses which he will make to them, pre-formed bonds exist. It is already determined by the constitution of the two germs, that under certain circumstances he will see and hear and feel and act in certain ways.... The behavior of man in the family, in business, in the state, in religion, and in every other affair of life is rooted in his unlearned, original equipment of instincts and capacities.[5]

For McDougall these instincts were powerful forces resident in man, impelling him to action, the driving springs without which he would be limp and passive.

We may, then, define an instinct as an inherited or innate psychophysical disposition which determines its possessor to perceive, and to pay attention to, objects of a certain class, to experience an emotional excitement of a particular quality upon perceiving such an object, and to act in regard to it in a particular manner, or, at least, to experience an impulse to such action.[6]

He found some eleven major instincts in man, chief of which are the instinct of flight, of repulsion, of curiosity, of pugnacity, of self-abasement, of self-assertion, and the parental instinct. This is, it must be observed, a logical and teleological classification, in which the instincts are defined in terms of the purposes they serve. Many were the social theories founded upon it.

A decade of careful criticism of this simple atomic conception of human nature has led to the general agreement that it is more fruitful to seek definite and specific reactions that can be experimentally isolated, and that in complex human behavior these reflexes are overlaid by habit after habit conditioned by the environment. Such a view does not give the facile "explanations" of action that come from reading it in terms of a few dominant instincts; but the suspicion has arisen that to attribute the cause, for example, of men's congregating in large cities to a "gregarious instinct" is much like the scholastic dormitive powers of opium, a labeling and not an explanation. In pointing out that the elements of behavior are exceedingly numerous and complex, it destroys a simple atomism, but it opens the way for a closer analysis of individual histories and for a genetic treatment of habit formation that will both predict and control.

The practical consequences of this shift from the vague and animistic "instinct" to the precise "conditioned reflex" as the basic unit are to place a more adequate emphasis on the determining factor of the environment, minimized by the McDougall school, and hence to read human nature as a function of the cultural situation into which it is born rather than as a fixed entity inevitably flowering into the given society. It is no accident that the earlier theory of a fixed and simple human nature has been seized upon everywhere by conservatives opposed to social change, while the critics of that theory, like John Dewey, are hopeful of social amelioration through education and institutional reform. This is especially apparent in the problem of how far individual and group differences, which experiment has revealed and measured and which seem definitely to have overthrown the eighteenth-century theory of the equality of man, so basic in traditional social theory, are hereditary and unalterable, and how far they are environmental products and hence subject to control. Conservatives welcome the former view, seeing the existent order as pretty much biologically necessary, while progressives hope to push back the limits of fixed native endowment as far as possible. This tendency is reflected in the conflict between the biological and the cultural determinists in anthropology, politics, and sociology. But obviously the controversy between the inherited and the acquired can only be solved along the lines of Watson's experiments, with a much fuller knowledge of facts than we now possess.

The Problem of the Functioning of the Integrated Personality

But this attempt at a new atomic conception of human nature, like that of the eighteenth century except that biological processes have replaced passive sensations as the elements, has other problems to face than those of the nature of its elements. How are these fundamental units built up into their complex human manifestations? Is the process simply an additive one, in which the original units are clearly discernible, or does so much modification and assimilation take place that the value of the whole analytical treatment can be doubted? There has lately grown up a feeling of dissatisfaction with the results of this elucidation of behavior atoms, this "muscle-twitch psychology." The most important psychological phenomena are complex and involve a total situation. Can such situations be reproduced under laboratory conditions? The analysis into behavior-segments gets along famously up to the decorticated rat, but with human actions, conditioned by the individual's entire past experience, it has not proved so fruitful. Can human psychology disregard the response of the whole person to a situation?

The Gestalt school of Wertheimer, Koffka and Köhler maintains that response is always to a set of related stimuli, and exhibits non-additive and transposable patterns subject to "wholeness laws" like those of the structure of an electrical field. Others have also tried to apply "organismic" concepts.

Being interested primarily in human conduct [writes J. R. Kantor], we are therefore required to investigate the actions of human individuals as distinct humanistic occurrences of very particular types. In effect this means that we must take account of the numerous human conditions and institutions which give rise to psychological phenomena and which condition their occurrence. Only by taking into consideration the intimate nuances and refinements of human interactions with things and persons can we hope to describe adequately human behavior and avoid worthless artifacts. We deem it to be the essence of valid scientific method thus to study any given fact as it actually transpires and not to reduce it to something else, not even to a simplified part of itself.[7]

Organismic psychology is based upon the premises that we must never admit anything into our scientific thinking but that which can be actually observed. Nor must we assume for our convenience that the part is the whole. . . . Basing our investigations upon this platform we consider the subject-matter of psychology to be the concrete reactions which an organism makes to its stimuli surroundings. Naturally all the varieties of surroundings are considered; so that organismic psychology considers as part of its subject-matter not only the simple behavior to natural stimuli but also the complex adaptations to social and human institutions. . . . The causes of the organism's reactions are not brain or mental conditions, but the needs of the organism as dictated by the surrounding objects and events. . . . For such a view the explanatory features of the science consist for the most part in the detailed study of the reactional biographies of individuals throughout their various contacts with their actual surroundings.[8]

As yet the elements of behavior are probably too little understood to make such an attempt other than vague, but with a genetic understanding of the more complex forms of habit forma-

[8] From *Principles of Psychology*, by J. R. Kantor. Reprinted by permission of the publishers, Alfred A. Knopf, Inc.

tion it is inevitable that the higher organizations of behavior will come to be more and more central. The task will be infinite, as it involves the whole social setting; but only when it is accomplished will the science of human nature be able to furnish a fruitful basis for the other social sciences.

Psycho-analysis

It was precisely this attempt to deal with personality as a whole, especially in a practical way on its pathological side, that led to the development by psychiatrists of the theory of psycho-analysis. Out of their clinical experience they have erected a whole system of psychology that has little sympathy with the scientific mechanical analysis we have just traced, and arrogates to itself the title of "the new psychology." As formulated by Freud and his followers, psycho-analysis is a mixture of important experimental discoveries, of fruitful new concepts for attacking the behavior of integrated personalities, and of a general speculative background that can only be called romantic and fantastic in the extreme, made to serve an astonishingly successful therapeutic method. Its core is the principle that the great majority of human reactions are produced by impulses or motives that are below the level of consciousness, and that the precise nature of these impulses in any individual must be explained in terms of his past experience. In particular, most of the pathological disturbances of behavior are due to the unsuspected persistence of emotional drives or complexes occasioned by events or desires that were unpleasant or socially disapproved and hence repressed. It is in bringing to light the emotional consequences of such repression of fundamental impulses that psycho-analysis has most enlarged our knowledge of human nature: a lack of adjustment between the various tendencies in an individual may cause all sorts of disturbances when the cause has been long forgotten, if it was ever known. In cataloguing the emotional drives resulting from typical repressions, such as the Œdipus complex, the inferiority complex, etc., the Freudians have furnished a new set of behavior elements that offer control as well as understanding. They have added new facts to the contention of those who would understand behavior in terms of the building up of habits and associations in the individual's experience, and out of their clinical records have illuminated the process of such formations. So far these behavior elements have been more fruitful in the social sciences than the more rudimentary conditioned reflexes of the behaviorists.

But these ideas have been projected against a conception of mind and a set of theories that, logically inconsistent, necessarily hypothetical and unverifiable, often deliberately involved and fantastic, and in conflict with much that is definitely established, is a recrudescence of the older psychology of the romanticists. The faults of the instinct theory are multiplied; not content with recording the presence of types of behavior that are "unreflective, non-discriminative, immediate and uncontrolled in operation, ineradicable, and affective," [9] the Freudians go on to explain this as the expression of an assumed "unconscious," thought of now as a definite realm, now as a mysterious and insistent source of psychic energy. In Freud himself this energy or libido is overwhelmingly sexual, though the limits of sex are so broadened as to rob the term of most of its meaning; in others, like Jung, it forces its way through the three channels of the sex instinct, the ego instinct, and the herd instinct. This energy is vaguely thought of as demanding a fixed quantitative expression, failing which it increases, constantly fed from the inherent energy of the instinct or complex, until it bursts through the obstacle or cuts a new channel. It can be drawn off in another direction by "sublimation." In addition to this mystical foundation, Freud's theory contains such sweeping, dogmatic, and wholly hypothetical elements as to have provoked dissent from most of his own followers; and his readiness to apply it in fields like anthropology where he was patently ignorant has not heightened his prestige among the scientifically minded. But it indisputably contains elements of truth that, interpreted in more objective and experimental terms, will do much to clarify the integration of human personality. The mutual assimilation of the behavioristic and the Freudian genetic attitudes is already proceeding apace.

The Contemporary View of Human Nature

If we ask on just what points the modern experimental science of human nature has modified the views of its eighteenth-century predecessor, we find basic changes of revolutionary importance for the social sciences. First, the picture of man as a purely logical machine, who first thinks of some end which he desires, and then calculates the means by which that end can be attained, has given way to the infinitely more complex creature of impulse and passion and emotional preference who occasionally directs his irrational desires to some intelligent end. Reason is but the umpire among often unruly and conflicting impulses.

The function of consciousness does not seem to be so much creative as selective and inhibitive. I cannot voluntarily create a wish to do something in my mind. I can only eliminate those wishes (or their expression in conduct) that seem to me inexpedient. Energy must then be directed unconsciously rather than consciously. Since instincts are the great directors of energy, it follows that unconscious instinct motivations must control most of the human organism's mental energy, and that the most important of these will be the permanently unconscious motivations. These will regulate the dominant streams of energy of the man's life.[10]

It is such a man who must take his place in any modern economic or political theory.

Secondly, though just what their limits are is still uncertain, it is clear that human behavior is largely determined by forces and energies which demand certain definite normal outlets, failing which they will give rise to disastrous conflicts and outbursts. Human nature, plastic as it is, cannot be distorted too far or changed too suddenly without danger. Rousseau's insight was sounder than Helvetius'. The environment must be so made as to give adequate scope to the more important impulses; asceticism, of either medieval or Puritan variety, can succeed only when directed to ends of extraordinary intensity.

Thirdly, men are individuals. They are not alike at birth, but differ widely in their capacities and aptitudes; and each man's character is a personal and unique synthesis, embodying distinctive traits. Social institutions must recognize that they are dealing with men, not man.

Finally, men live and develop in groups, and what they are is largely a product of the traditions and customs of the group. The group is the conditioning environment of all human action, without which all that is characteristically human would be lost. As Dewey puts it, "Anything which may properly be called mind or intelligence is not an original possession, but is a consequence

[10] From *Problems in Dynamic Psychology*, by John T. McCurdy. Copyright, 1922, by the Macmillan Company. Reprinted by permission.

of the manifestation of instincts under the conditions supplied by associated life in the family, the school, the market-place and the forum." [11] Society comes first in point of time, and moulds individuals more or less successfully in its own image.

Dewey summarizes the consequences of the new science of man for all the social studies:

> It transfers attention from vague generalities regarding social consciousness and social mind to the specific processes of interaction which take place among human beings, and to the details of group behavior. It emphasizes the importance of knowledge of the primary activities of human nature, and of the modifications and reorganizations they undergo in association with the activities of others. It radically simplifies the whole problem by making it clear that social institutions and arrangements, including the whole apparatus of tradition and transmission, represent simply the acquired transformations of original human endowments.[12]

The Schools of Sociology

On the basis of such a science of man the various sciences of society have been gradually reconstructed. The most ambitious and universal of all, sociology, which claims to be "the science of human behavior in both its contemporary and its genetic aspects," [13] with the best of intentions has been successively the prey of all the social currents of the century — the historical method, the evolutionary method, the waves of biology and the winds of psychology. In the hands of its great pioneers, Comte, Spencer, and L. F. Ward, it has been well called "at once a philosophy and a faith — a cosmogony, a theology, and a religion." [14] After passing through these preliminary speculative phases, in which some method, some conception, some great principle was regarded as all important and fundamental, it has settled down to "approach knowledge of human experience as a whole through investigation of group aspects of the phenomena," [15] and to "account for the origin, growth, structure, and activities of society by the operation of physical, vital, and psychical causes, working together in a process of evolution." [16] Though sociologists are still divided by their adherence to various cherished principles of explanation, for the last few decades their most important work has unquestionably been in the detailed investigation of institutions and their functioning; the newer psychology has hardly as yet developed a genuine social science. There has been a marked falling off of system building, and a tendency toward the intensive cultivation of specialized fields. Sociology is still hesitant about its method. The physical and biological terminology and concepts have largely given way to psychological ones, and there is a growing demand for the development of specifically social categories, especially among the anthropological sociologists. More and more reliance is placed on the statistical technique, fed by the social survey.

In our introductory survey we have traced the main methodological developments in sociology; here it will suffice to point out the various explanatory principles that recent students have emphasized. There has been a strong tendency to investigate the effects upon society of its physical environment, especially topography, cultural contacts, climate, food, and natural resources. A whole new science of anthropogeography has revealed the fundamental limits to social activity imposed by these factors. Secondly, there has been the emphasis on specific biological forces at work; the earlier vague biological analogies have given way to the analysis of the social implications of actual biological processes, the organismic and the social Darwinist schools to eugenics, the effect of group selection, the racial factors in social development. Thirdly, all the psychological tendencies have had their sociological counterparts. The main influences of psychological concepts have been, first, to investigate the social bearings of the individual instincts and habits; secondly, to emphasize the moulding of the individual traits by the social heritage; and thirdly, to analyze the functioning of integrated groups. In the fourth place, the cultural determinists have emphasized the importance of the historical perpetuation and transmission of social institutions, especially economic. Each of these four sets of factors obviously enters into the determining causes of social forms, but as yet there has been no satisfactory synthesis with a critical adjustment of all the principles of explanation. Sociology, in fact, can hardly accomplish its object of founding a universal synthetic science of society until these preliminary investigations have been advanced far beyond the stage in which they now find themselves.

The Achievement of a Critical Method in Anthropology

In the much narrower field of anthropology, the early history of mankind — "the whole history of man as fired and pervaded by the idea of evolution" [17] — after the play of speculation had had its day, there has been worked out the most impressive and precise methodology of all the social scientists, and the most reliable conclusions. Anthropology was created in the evolutionary faith by Herbert Spencer and E. B. Tylor, who generalized from a few observations simple and rigid schemes of institutional development which unrolled automatically by themselves, following the same order in all parts of the world. Everywhere society had to traverse the same rigid stages, from a primitive communism and promiscuity to the "higher" forms of present-day European civilization. Facts were cavalierly fitted into these formulæ, and little attention was paid to the means whereby the changes were effected: they came "by evolution." Among these dogmatic evolutionists were Lewis H. Morgan, who found his scheme in the Iroquois Indians — unfortunately a unique group — and J. G. Frazer, whose *Golden Bough* so delightfully purveys third-hand misinformation.

After such a start, anthropology entered a period of the destruction of its cherished theories by cold facts. The idea of a fixed unilinear development had to give way before closer investigation. The "comparative method" was utterly discredited. There was no simple pattern of stages, and social change took place in part as the result of changed environment, chiefly through the diffusion of institutions through cultural contacts. It could be either gradual or cataclysmic, backward or forward, progress or decay. The only road to an understanding of social development lay through patient and intensive exploration of restricted local cultures in their historical and geographical setting.

After the rigid evolutionary formulæ had been disposed of, the cultural diffusionists proceeded to erect a new dogmatism. Every social change comes from without; original inventions are few. Similar customs necessarily imply historic contact, though the seven seas separate the tribes. Under Graebner, W. H. R. Rivers, G. Elliot Smith, and W. J. Perry, fantastic migrations of culture were spread around the world on flimsy evidence of similarities. It was quite forgotten that there are only a limited number of ways of responding to man's environment, and that such adjustments may well arise spontaneously in more than one place.

The emergence of a more critical historical school is the achievement of a single American, Franz Boas. From physics and mathematics he brought exact technique and unremitting zeal for investigation. Concrete observation of each primitive culture in relation to its physical and cultural environment replaced sweeping generalizations, either evolutionary or diffusionist. Under his teachings a number of critical observers have collected facts on all the phases of primitive life, and given objective pictures of the functioning of savage societies. Thus anthropology, because the data for the refutation of a-priori systems were easily available, was able to emerge from the speculative stage to a due humility sooner than any other social science. A. L. Kroeber confesses the honest ignorance with which the anthropologist, remembering the disastrous past, is exceedingly critical of any pretension at generalized laws of human development.

The processes of civilizational activity are almost unknown to us. The self-sufficient factors that govern their workings are unresolved. ... The historian as yet can do little but picture. He traces and he connects what seems far removed; he balances; he integrates; but he does not really explain, nor does he transmute phenomena into something else. His method is not science.... What we all are able to do is to realize this gap, to be impressed by its abyss with reverence and humility, and to go our paths on its respective sides without self-deluding attempts to bridge the eternal chasm, or empty boasts that its span is achieved.[18]

Slowly and tentatively anthropology is trying to build anew a social synthesis by means of a critical social method. This realization, indeed, that the social sciences, while borrowing much from biology and psychology, can find an adequate technique in no other science, but must work out method, tools, and concepts from the concrete subject-matter of society itself is the most important contribution so far made by anthropology, and places it in the van of the science of society. As against geographical, biological, and psychological determinists, it maintains that the forces at work in society are social and irreducible.

The cultural facts, even in their subjective aspect, are not merged in psychological facts. They must not, indeed, contravene psychological principles, but the same applies to all other principles of the universe.... But the principles of psychology are as incapable of accounting for the phenomena of culture as is gravitation to account for architectural styles. Over and above the interpretations given by psychology, there is an irreducible residuum of huge magnitude that calls for special treatment and by its very existence vindicates the *raison d'être* of ethnology.[19]

The Creation of a Realistic, Genetic, and Experimental Economics

In the science of economics, much the same development has taken place. The traditional method — in this case the mechanical deductive, not the evolutionary — with its sweeping assumptions and intrenched prejudices, is crumbling before the assault of facts; and most economists are, like the anthropologists, spending their time on detailed and specific investigations of society until a more adequate technique can lead to a new synthesis. We have seen how the Ricardian deductive analysis of the process of distribution, entangled with extraneous political and social interests, has remained the orthodox economic science to this day, despite the vigorous onslaught of social radicals of all schools and creeds. Pure economic theory of this type became more and more rarefied as the world from which it had first been generalized disappeared; but its exponents hardly troubled themselves with such new phenomena as corporation control of industry and centralized credit systems. They felt society already economically mature; all that remained was to analyze logically the presuppositions of the price-system. System after system repeated the main outlines of this "pecuniary logic," daringly modifying some minor point. When such theorists felt uneasily that their science should have some firmer basis in human nature, they turned to the antiquated hedonistic psychology of the eighteenth century — they knew of no other — and developed it dialectically with mathematical precision. Jevons in England, Menger in Austria, Walras in France, and John Bates Clark in America, explored the theory of value and the determinants of price, and rang the changes on marginal utility.

Utility analysis from these four sources impressed most economists as radically different from Ricardo's type of theory, because Ricardo had explained value mainly by cost of production, taking utility for granted. After due deliberation, lasting some twenty years, the economists became excited and began a lively controversy on the relative merits of cost analysis and utility analysis. Zealous spirits took sides, as if the issue were of the either-or variety. But more cautious men, like Alfred Marshall, the most conspicuous of later English theorists, refused to subsume cost under utility or utility under cost, and held that both factors in conjunction determine values. Such men were dubbed eclectics for their caution.[20]

But it was a tempest in a teapot: the issue made no real difference in the crystallized system, which had become explicitly "the science that treats phenomena from the standpoint of price." [21]

In Germany alone did economics refuse to follow this abstract form. Utterly alien to the strong bureaucratic tradition, out of harmony with the popular historical, romantic, and social spirit, classical economics in spite of its prestige could not become acclimated in Germany. For a century earnest students attempted to substitute the British cosmopolitanism and atomic individualism for the German particularism and collectivism, but oil and water would not mix. The second of the great nineteenth-century social attitudes, romantic evolution, found its way into economics with the rise of the Historical School in the 1840's. As in the other social sciences, the appeal to historical fact succeeded logical systems. The German critics of English political economy finally felt it necessary to discard the whole structure of abstract theory, and devote over a generation to the collection of historical materials, before making a fresh start at generalization. In 1843 Wilhelm Roscher issued the manifesto of the new method.

Our aim is an exhibit of that which, in economic respects, peoples have thought, willed, and felt, what they have attempted and accomplished, why they have attempted and accomplished it. Such an exhibit is possible only in closest alliance with the other sciences of collective life, especially with legal, constitutional, and cultural history.... The philosopher is after a system of ideas or judgments, as abstract as possible, utterly denuded of all the accidents of time and space. The historian wants a delineation of human developments and relationships, represented as faithfully to actual life as possible. The former has explained a fact when he has defined it, and when no idea appears in his definition which had not been already discussed in earlier parts of the system. The latter is presumed to have explained a fact when he has pictured the people by whom and upon whom the action came to pass....

One sees that this method aims to accomplish for political economy what the Savigny-Eichhorn method did for jurisprudence. It is far from the school of Ricardo, though it does not oppose that school directly, and even thankfully appropriates its results.[22]

Roscher was followed by Hildebrand and Knies, the latter of whom saw economic history as in itself the only material for economic science.

Like economic conditions themselves, so also the theory of political economy, whatever be its form and structure at a given time, whatever be the arguments and results which it urges, is an outcome of historical development. These conditions and this theory are in vital articulation with the entire organism of a human and historical epoch. They grow out of the peculiarities of the time, the place, the nationality.... They cannot exhibit the "universal laws of political economy" in any other way than as a historical explication and a progressive manifestation of the truth.... Neither in their totality nor in their formulation may they be regarded as something final.[23]

On such a basis Gustav von Schmoller, in his *Grundriss der allgemeinen Volkswirtschaftslehre* (1900), made the historical position dominant among German economists, and carried its method, in Thorold Rogers, Cunningham, and Ashley, to England itself. From a relativistic and genetic point of view, he dealt with the facts and processes of economic evolution in relation to all the major departments of social life. For him there is complexity, change, and growth everywhere; a logical system is impossible. From Schmoller's followers there came a flood of detailed investigations; and far from supporting laisser-faire in the interests of the business man, they instituted a vigorous and successful campaign for state intervention in the interests of national welfare. The leaders in this "State" or "Professorial Socialism" of the seventies and eighties were Schmoller himself, Adolf Wagner, and A. E. F. Schäffle. Thus the historical attitude has resulted both in thorough surveys of the actual organization and functioning of human nature engaged in the satisfaction of all its needs, and in comprehensive programs for its more effective reorganization.

Abstract theory has reached a mathematical perfection in the pecuniary logic of a Davenport, Moore, or Hotelling; and at London Robbins and Hayek have revived a neo-classicism. But many economists have preferred to investigate the actual functioning of economic institutions. Thorstein Veblen's satirical criticism of existing practices, by a suggestive analysis of institutionalized habits, has turned men like Wesley Mitchell and Walton Hamilton to the newer behavioristic social psychology to clarify economic action. These American "institutionalists," with the Webbs and Hobson in England, and Sombart in Germany, claim that quantitative investigation of the evolution and operation of economic institutions must precede any attempt at generalization. For them, economics is the exact study of changing economic behavior. By combining statistical methods with an understanding of men's plastic social habits, they hope to forge tools adequate to the complex social regulation and organization now demanded by our economic life. In our crises of depression and war economy, the need for workable techniques has obscured concern with the formal theory of rapidly changing institutions. The present mood is — investigate and experiment. Experiment in any event we must.

Investigation in Jurisprudence and Political Science

The tale is the same in law and political science. Jurisprudence too has had its mechanical, abstract, analytical school, still powerful in the courts; its evolutionary, historical school of Savigny and the Germans, Henry Sumner Maine and Maitland; its various philosophical schools, each magnifying some one principle and technique; and is to-day becoming sociological, that is, interested in investigating the social effects of legal forms and processes.

Sociological jurists look to the working of the law rather than to its abstract content; they regard law as a social institution involving both finding by experience and conscious making — an institution which may be improved by conscious human effort; they lay stress upon the social ends which law subserves rather than upon sanctions; they look on legal precepts and doctrines and institutions functionally and regard the form of legal precepts as a means only.[24]

Political science, even more than economics the servant of group interests and ideals, has found it especially difficult to become descriptive and critical because of the religious sanctity which nineteenth-century nationalism has thrown about the state. Whether regarded as the guarantee of individual rights, with the Benthamites and Liberals, or as the highest expression of the Absolute, with the Idealists, or as the divinely ordained power for man's governance, with the Traditionalists, the state has shrunk from sacrilegious analysis. Political scientists at first tried to content themselves with the definition of political terms, the classification of political institutions, and the logical elucidation of written constitutions. When such a systematic and deductive treatment had exhausted its possibilities, they turned to the historical method, at first with a romantic and idealistic veneration, then from the standpoint of biological evolution, and traced the stages of political and constitutional development. On the basis of the factual knowledge revealed by such studies, and of the sense of the relativity and constant change in political forms, men sought in the analysis of the actual functioning of political institutions an insight into the causal factors at work. The structure and operation of democratic government, especially party machinery, attracted eager investigators like Wilson, Bryce, Ostrogorski, and Michels. This led to the placing of political institutions in their broader social setting, as one of the means of social control; and politics found itself joining psychology, economics, and sociology. Particular political expedients have been statistically surveyed and analyzed, both genetically and functionally. The cloak of sanctity has been stripped from the state, which is now seen to be but the umpire among conflicting social groups, often the pawn of some dominant economic interest. In the laying bare of the facts of political control, the formation of public opinion, the genesis of legislation, the technique of party government, political scientists have ceased to care for logical systems. Their primary concern is the investigation of functioning and the devising of improved machinery for democratic government. Statistical surveys have taken the place of deductive analyses.

As a result, most of the eighteenth-century doctrines have crumbled, for the scientist if not for the politician and statesman. Natural law and natural rights, having served their historical purpose of bringing about an industrial society, have disappeared; in the face of the centralized and reasonably efficient action demanded by modern society, the separation of powers and checks and balances have in fact and theory gone into the discard. National sovereignty, so important a theory in creating the liberal state, has been attacked mercilessly; in place of omnipotence observers have found in democratic governments only a limited power of enforcement in conflict with many strong group interests. Indeed, political theory now insists on group action as fundamental, and has abandoned atomic individualism. The modern state deals, not with individuals, but with groups; its control is exercised by and for specific groups. L. Duguit, H. J. Laski, and G. D. H. Cole, following Gierke and Maitland, have emphasized the fact of political "pluralism."

The wide-spread breakdown of democratic government in practice under the stress of just such group tensions has provoked a reaction. Communist and Fascist groups that have captured the state have no sympathy with pluralism, and even democratic theorists like Laski himself now desire to strengthen authority to prevent such a capture. Discussions of sovereignty have given way to analyses of political power and its techniques, from the psychological power of symbols and propaganda to the naked power of military force. Political science has left the tolerant age of Locke to return to Hobbes. Belated interest has been aroused in the social theories of the mathematical economist V. Pareto, and his predecessor G. Mosca, whose harsh Machiavellian "realism," so in accord with the present temper, analyzed the nature and operation of the "élite groups" who always control the state. Though with the revolutions of 1918 party government seemed to have conquered the earth, the pressure of events has since reinforced all the older criticisms of the democratic dogmas. Psychology has revealed the wide variation in individual abilities, and the ease with which group opinion can stifle individuality and originality. The difficulty of expert administration and of vigorous action in a democracy, and the facility with which party machines can govern in the interest of privileged economic groups, have impressed all observers. Even to its advocates, democratic control seems to-day rather a *pis aller* than a creed of promise.

Yet the faults of the democratic ideal seem primarily its failure to achieve social control over powerful groups in a rapidly changing economic structure. Hence the dominant note, in America at least, is the demand for more democracy, democracy in industrial as well as in political life, without which the latter remains a mere veneer for economic exploitation. What is needed is genuine education — the old democratic cry — and the invention of political machinery able to reorganize an industrial society. Above all, we need to know how to enlist the cooperative support of men in applying the social knowledge we already possess.

THE SCIENCE OF MAN

The Need for Popularizing the Social Sciences

More education — that is the insistent need of the science of man to-day. Systems have run their course, sound methods have gradually been found after many trials, and valid techniques have built themselves on an unparalleled knowledge of the facts of social life. But the social sciences, not being able to show any such impressive results as the imposing pile of mechanical inventions, have earned neither the wide dissemination nor the prestige of the natural sciences. The task of giving to all men their already established results, and above all a sense of their problems and their critical techniques, remains the greatest single objective of the science of man in the twentieth century. If what is already known by experts were actually incorporated into our social life, many of our pressing maladjustments could be at once alleviated. But far more important, with a sympathetic acceptance of their goal, the understanding of man and the bettering of his life, passionate prejudices and antediluvian ideas could be swept away, and the atmosphere created in which genuine advance in knowledge is possible. It is from experimentation that the science of man can hope to learn most; and in society, experimentation is only possible and successful if it can enlist widespread sympathy and understanding. Most important of all the achievements of the social sciences is the creation, in the minds of the few, of the experimental attitude and the critical technique when face to face with man in his group life; and before much more can be done, this attitude and this technique must be spread abroad. If man is ever to solve the social problems which his science, creating the growing industrial world, has brought upon him, he must place himself and his institutions squarely in the world of nature and subject them also to the play of scientific intelligence.

We have a long way to go before we shall be able to realize the dream of Auguste Comte and Lester F. Ward in making social science the basis and acceptable guide of practical statesmanship. In addition to the necessary improvements in social science, we have a much more difficult problem ahead in converting the mass of the population to the belief that we must rely for guidance upon scientifically ascertained fact instead of animism and rhetoric. . . . In spite of the fact that human conduct is the most complicated of terrestrial problems and, properly guided, calls for the collaboration of a greater number and variety of experts than any other human perplexity, this is, along with religion, the one field which we reserve for the sovereign authority of the herd as expressed by the clergyman and the illiterate "man in the street." In short, it will avail little to go ahead with the very salutary process of improving the scientific level of the social sciences, unless we are able to parallel this development with the securing of a better connection between the social sciences on the one hand, and public opinion and practical statesmanship in business and politics, on the other.[25]

REFERENCES

1. H. Spencer, *First Principles*, 407.
2. J. K. Bluntschli, *General Theory of the State*, I, 18, 19.
3. Walter Bagehot, *Physics and Politics*, 24, 43, 215–16.
4. L. Gumplowicz, *Soziologie und Politik*, 94.
5. E. L. Thorndike, *Original Nature of Man*, 1, 2.
6. Wm. McDougall, *Introduction to Social Psychology*, 29.
7. J. R. Kantor, *Principles of Psychology*, I, p. xvii.
8. *Ibid.*, 30.
9. John T. McCurdy, *Problems in Dynamic Psychology*, 258.
10. *Ibid.*, 264.
11. John Dewey, "The Need for Social Psychology," in the *Psychological Review* (1917), 270, 271.
12. *Ibid.*
13. H. E. Barnes, *The New History and the Social Studies*, 331.
14. F. H. Hankins, in H. E. Barnes, *The History and Prospects of the Social Sciences*, 256.
15. A. W. Small, art. "Sociology" in *Encyclopedia Americana* (1919 ed.), XXV, 208.
16. F. H. Giddings, *Principles of Sociology*, 1.
17. R. R. Marett, *Anthropology*, 7.
18. A. L. Kroeber, in *American Anthropologist*, XIX, 212, 213.
19. R. H. Lowie, *Culture and Ethnology*, 25, 26.
20. Wesley C. Mitchell, in R. G. Tugwell, *The Trend of Economics*, 15.
21. *Ibid.*, 16.
22. Wilhelm Roscher, *Grundriss zu Vorlesungen über die Staa'swirtschaft nach geschichtlicher Methode.*
23. Karl Knies, *Politische Oekonomie vom geschichtlichen Standpunkte*, 23.
24. Roscoe Pound, *Jurisprudence*, in H. E. Barnes, *The History and Prospects of the Social Sciences*, 458.
25. H. E. Barnes, *The New History and the Social Studies*, 592, 594.

SELECTED READING LISTS

General: The *Encyclopedia of the Social Sciences* is now basic; see esp. the historical introduction, vol. I. H. E. Barnes, ed., *Hist. and Prospects of the Social Sciences* (excellent surveys); *The New History and the Social Studies* (much hist. and critical material); W. F. Ogburn and A. A. Goldenweiser, eds., *The Social Sciences and their Interrelations;* E. C. Hayes, ed., *Recent Developments in the Social Sciences;* H. W. Odum, ed., *American Masters of Social Science.* A. J. Todd, *Theories of Social Progress.*
Psychology: See Chapter XVIII. James, *Princ. of Psych.*; G. S. Hall, *Adolescence, Youth;* J. M. Baldwin, *Mental Development in the Child and the Race, The Individual and Society.* — **Instinct Problem:** W. McDougall, *Introduction to Social Psychology;* Thorndike, *Original Nature of Man;* criticism in R. S. Woodworth, *Dynamic Psychology;* L. L. Bernard, *Instinct.* J. B. Watson, *Behavior, Psych. from the Behavioristic Standpoint, Lectures on Psych.* — **Social Psychology:** F. B. Karpf, *American Social Psychology;* K. Young, in *Hist. and Prospects of the Social Sciences.* J. M. Baldwin;

C. H. Cooley, *Human Nature and the Social Order, Social Organization;* John Dewey, *Human Nature and Conduct, Freedom and Culture;* F. H. Allport, *Social Psych.* — **Gestalt Psychology:** Wertheimer; W. Köhler, *The Mentality of Apes, Gestalt Psychology;* K. Koffka, *Growth of the Mind.* J. R. Kantor, *Principles of Psych.* — **Psychoanalysis:** Freud, *General Introduction to Psychoanalysis; Selections,* ed. Modern Lib.; F. Wittels, *Freud and His Time.* Jung, *Psych. of the Unconscious, Psych. Types.* W. Healy, ed., *The Structure and Meaning of Psychoanalysis;* W. A. White, *Outlines of Psychiatry.* W. L. Northridge, *Modern Theories of the Unconscious;* J. T. McCurdy, *Problems of Dynamic Psych.* — R. S. Woodworth, *Contemporary Schools of Psychology;* G. Adams, *Psychology: Science or Superstition?*

Sociology: H. E. Barnes and H. Becker, *Hist. of Sociological Thought;* Barnes, *Sociology and Political Theory;* Merz, IV, ch. x; F. H. Hankins, in *H. and Prospects of the Soc. Sciences.* L. L. Bernard, ed., *The Fields and Methods of Sociology;* P. A. Sorokin, *Contemp. Sociological Theories;* F. N. House, *The Range of Social Theory;* G. A. Lundberg, *Social Research.* V. Pareto, *The Mind and Society.* A. W. Small, *Origins of Sociology, General Sociology,* Pts. I and II; *Adam Smith and Modern Sociology* (much information); E. S. Bogardus, *History of Social Thought;* J. P. Lichtenberger, *Development of Social Theory;* L. M. Bristol, *Social Adaptation* (best survey). F. Müller-Lyer, *History of Social Development;* P. Barth, *Die Phil. der Geschichte als Soziologie;* L. Stein, *Die soziale Frage im Lichte der Philosophie;* P. Jacobs, *German Sociology.* — **Biological tendencies:** F. W. Coker, *Organismic Theories of the State;* R. Mackintosh, *From Comte to Benjamin Kidd;* A. A. Tenney, *Social Populations and Democracy;* A. Keller, *Societal Evolution;* S. J. Holmes, *Trend of the Race.* — **Psychological tendencies:** M. M. Davis, *Psychological Interpretations of Society* (esp. Tarde); G. Wallas, *Human Nature and Politics, Great Society;* A. G. A. Balz, *Basis of Social Theory;* W. A. Brown, *Psych. and the Sciences.* — **Geographical Emphasis:** F. Ratzel, *Anthropogeographie* (E. Semple tr. as *Influences of Geographic Environment*); J. Brunhes, *Human Geography.* — **Biological Emphasis:** Auguste Comte, *Principles of Positive Philosophy,* Martineau tr.; M. Defaunay, *La Sociologie Positiviste.* Herbert Spencer, *The Study of Sociology, Principles of Sociology;* Lester F. Ward, *Dynamic Sociology, Outlines of Sociology, Pure Sociology, Applied Sociology;* F. H. Giddings, *Principles of Sociology.* — **Organic Theory:** H. Spencer; J. K. Bluntschli, *General Theory of the State;* A. Schäffle, *Bau u. Leben des socialen Körpers;* R. Worms, *Organisme et Société.* — **Social Darwinism:** W. Bagehot, *Physics and Politics;* L. Gumplowicz, *Der Rassenkampf, Outlines of Sociology;* G. Ratzenhofer, *Wesen u. Zweck der Politik;* F. Oppenheimer, *The State;* L. F. Ward. Criticism in J. Novicow, *Les Luttes entre les Sociétés Humaines;* G. Nasmyth, *Social Progress and the Darwinian Theory.* — **Racial Determinism:** E. A. de Gobineau, *Essay on the Inequality of the Human Races;* Madison Grant, *Passing of the Great Race.* Criticism by F. Boas, *Mind of Primitive Man;* F. H. Hankins, *Racial Basis of Civilization;* A. L. Kroeber, *Anthropology.* **Psychological Emphasis:** F. H. Giddings; G. Tarde, *Laws of Imitation;* G. Le Bon, *The Crowd;* W. McDougall, *Intro. to Social Psychology;* Graham Wallas, *Our Social Heritage;* C. H. Cooley, *Human Nature and the Social Order, Social Organization;* John Dewey, *Human Nature and Conduct, Freedom and Culture;* W. F. Ogburn, *Social Change.*

Anthropology: A. A. Goldenweiser, *Cultural Anthropology,* in Barnes, *History and Prospects of the Social Sciences;* A. C. Haddon, *History of Anthropology.* — **Evolution Dogmatists:** H. Spencer, *Principles of Sociology;* E. B. Tylor, *Primitive Culture, Anthropology;* L. H. Morgan, *Ancient Society.* W. Wundt, *Elements of Folk Psychology;* J. G. Frazer, *Golden Bough;* E. Durkheim, *Elementary Forms of the Religious Life.* — **Diffusionists:** F. Gräbner, *Methode der Ethnologie;* W. H. R. Rivers, *Psychology and Politics; Social Organization;* G. Elliot Smith, *Migrations of Early Culture;* W. J. Perry, *Children of the Sun.* — **Critical School:** F. Boas, *Mind of Primitive Man;* A. L. Kroeber, *Anthropology;* A. A. Goldenweiser, *Early Civilization;* R. H. Lowie, *Culture and Ethnology, Primitive Society, Primitive Religion;* C. Wissler, *Man and Culture;* G. G. McCurdy, *Human Origins;* P. Radin, *Primitive Religions.*

History: H. E. Barnes, *History of Historical Writing;* "History, its Rise and Development," in *Encyclopedia Americana; The New History and the Social Studies; History and Social Intelligence.* J. H. Robinson, *The New History;* J. T. Shotwell, "History," in *Encyclopedia Britannica, Intro. to the Hist. of History.* H. Berr, "History," in *En. Soc. Sci.* G. P. Gooch, *Hist. and Historians in the 19th Cent.;* E. Fueter, *Ges. der neueren Historiographie;* K. Lamprecht, *What is History?*

Economics: Histories of economic theory by Gide and Rist, L. H. Haney, J. K. Ingram; A. Dubois, R. Gonnard, J. Roubaud; G. Cohn, A. Damaschke, H. Eisenhart, J. Kautz, A. Oncken. P. T. Homan, ed., *Contemporary Economic Thought.* T. Surányi-Unger, *Economics in the Twentieth Century.* For critical interpretation, see T. Veblen, *Place of Science in Modern Civilization;* R. G. Tugwell, *Trend of Economics;* O. F. Boucke, *Development of Economics.* — **Classical School:** D. Ricardo, T. Malthus, N. Senior, J. R. McCulloch, J. B. Say, F. Bastiat. — **Neo-Mercantilists:** Sismondi, *New Principles of Political Economy;* F. List, *National System of Political Economy.* — **Historical School:** A. W. Small, *Origins of Sociology.* W. Roscher, *Grundriss zu Vorlesungen; System der Volkswirtschaft;* K. Knies, *Die P. Oekonomie vom Standpunkte der geschichtlichen Methode;* G. von Schmoller, *Ges. der allgemeinen Volkswirtschaftslehre;* A. Wagner, *Grundlegung.* — **Psychological School:** W. S. Jevons, *The Theory of Political Economy;* C. Menger, *Grundsätze der Volkswirtschaftslehre;* J. B. Clark, *Distribution of Wealth.* H. L. Moore, *Laws of Wages, Economic Cycles;* F. Fetter, *Principles of Economics.* A. Marshall, *Principles of Economics;* F. W. Taussig, E. R. A. Seligman. — **Institutionalists:** J. A. Hobson, *Work and Wealth;* T. Veblen, *Theory of Business Enterprise, Theory of the Leisure Class;* J. Dorfman, *Thorstein Veblen and His America.* W. C. Mitchell, art. in *Trend of Economics; Business Cycles;* "Human Behavior and Economics," in *Quarterly Journal of Economics,* XXIX; J. R. Commons, *Myself, Institutional Economics.*

Jurisprudence: R. Pound, in *History and Prospects of the Social Sciences; Interpretations of Legal History;* F. Berolzheimer, *The World's Legal Philosophies;* F. Pollock, *Oxford Lectures, Essays.* — **Natural Rights:** J. J. Burlamaqui, *Principles of Natural and Political Law;* W. Blackstone, *Commentaries.* — **Historical School:** Savigny, *Vom Beruf,* usw.; H. S. Maine, *Early History of Institutions.* — **Analytical School:** J. Austin, *Jurisprudence;* T. E. Holland, *Elements of Jurisprudence.* — **Sociological School:** B. N. Cardozo, *Nature of the Judicial Process;* F. Geny, *Science of Legal Method;* R. Pound, *Law and Morals, Introduction to the Philosophy of Law, Spirit of the Common Law;* O. W. Holmes, *Collected Legal Papers.* H. Cairns, *Law and the Social Sciences.*

Political Science: *History of Political Theories, Recent Times;* H. E. Barnes, *Sociology and Political Theory;* E. Barker, *Political Thought from Spencer to To-day;* F. W. Coker, *Recent and Contemporary Political Theory;* C. E. Merriam, *American Political Ideas;* R. G. Gettel, *History of Political Thought.* C. C. Brinton, *English Political Thought in the 19th Century.* A. N. Holcombe, *The Foundations of the Modern Commonwealth;* C. Beard, *Economic Basis of Politics;* A. F. Bentley, *Process of Government.* T. H. Green, *Political Obligation;* B. Bosanquet, *Philosophical Theory of the State;* criticism in L. T. Hobhouse, *Metaphysical Theory of the State.* H. S. Maine, *Ancient Law, Popular Government;* F. Oppenheimer, *The State.* M. W. Willey, *Theory of Democracy,* in *History of Political Theories, R. T.;* M. Ostrogorski, *Democracy and the Organization of Political Parties;* R. Michels, *Political Parties;* C. E. Merriam, *The American Party System.* W. Lippmann, *Public Opinion, The Phantom Public;* A. L. Lowell, *Public Opinion and Popular Government.* H. Krabbe, *Modern Idea of the State;* H. J. Laski, *Problem of Sovereignty, Authority in the Modern State, Grammar of Politics; Rise of Liberalism, The State in Theory and Practice;* L. Duguit, *Law in the Modern State.* G. E. Catlin, *Science and Method of Politics;* E. F. Carritt, *Morals and Politics.* Merriam, *Political Power;* J. Marshall, *Swords and Symbols;* T. Arnold, *Symbols of Government.*

CHAPTER XX

RELIGION IN THE GROWING WORLD

WE left religion in the eighteenth century apparently helpless in the face of the onslaughts of the rationalistic attack. The very methods of reason, upon which men at the beginning of the century had so hopefully relied for a complete demonstration of the validity and the importance of religious beliefs, when pushed to their logical conclusion not only overthrew all faith in any supernatural revelation, but in the hands of skeptics seemed to make impossible the very religion of reason and nature itself. Every bit of the great Jewish and Christian tradition, it seemed to the leaders of the Age of Reason, had crumbled away, leaving only the appealing but fanatical figures of the prophets and saints of old, and the body of Christian ethics. When this very suicide of rational religion led to the rebirth of the religious spirit, it was upon faith and intuition that the attempt at reconstruction was based, and no compromise seemed possible with the scientific and naturalistic spirit of the day. The pietistic and evangelical movements, even the deeper poetry of the romanticists, seemed to have turned their backs squarely upon the modern world with its interests, methods, and ideals. If religion was to flourish and wax strong once more in the hearts of men, it must proceed, so it appeared, in complete disregard of all that men held dear in other fields of intellectual interest.

Naturally Catholicism, as the most complete antithesis to the spirit of the nineteenth-century world, gained most by this *volte face;* and in the Church of England the Oxford Movement, fostered by the University scholars Keble, Pusey, William Ward, and above all John Henry Newman, sought to bring that historic communion out of its Protestant wanderings into closer harmony with the spirit and doctrine of the Roman Church. The romantic reaction to all forms of rationalism, and the marked æsthetic interest among the finer spirits of the day, combined to give strength to this general tendency. When Newman's marvelously subtle mind finally convinced itself that adherence to the Church of England involved not only schism but heresy, and he joined the Roman Catholics, the movement received a temporary setback; but his following soon gathered strength once more and as the High Church party has since steadily grown in power and influence. The Catholic Church itself, strong in its faith, has with few exceptions realized that compromise is the easy descent to Avernus, and has resolutely set its face against any truce with the intellectual tendencies of the modern age. Standing like the Rock of Ages against the successive waves of unbelief and modernism, it has again and again made all the more pointed its sharp dissent from modern ideas.

But while for many souls such a complete denial of rationalism and conciliation has seemed to offer the surest buttress against doubt and disintegration, for many more it has proved impossible to keep faith and knowledge in water-tight compartments. More or less unwillingly they have made one compromise after another with the ideas of the Growing World, until the form of religion which they cherish has come to be a quite different thing from the faith of the fathers — in their eyes a better and more precious treasure, in the eyes of those who cling to the older traditions a sham and a mockery. These so-called religious liberals, who have flourished amongst the more thoughtful as well as the more indifferent in every church body, amongst Protestants and Jews and even Catholics, contend that if religion is to be a living reality, if it is to remain a permanent expression of the religious needs of the human race, it must assimilate new truth and knowledge and adapt itself to the changed conditions, intellectual and social, of the modern age. What Augustine did for the Hellenistic world, what Thomas accomplished for the Middle Ages, must be undertaken once more for the world of modern science and industry — must be undertaken again and again, in fact, so long as man's knowledge grows and his social life is transformed. To a greater or less extent the more thoughtful conservatives in all churches have realized the existence of this problem, and even the orthodoxy of to-day has been influenced in divers subtle ways by the spirit and needs of the modern age; especially is this true in the increasing shift in every communion from the older individualistic preoccupation with saving individual souls to the social conviction that, as Canon Freemantle put it in a classic work, "the world is the subject of redemption." The lines of cleavage, in fact, are drawn to-day much more sharply in matters of belief than in programs of social action; and High Churchmen and Catholics agree with liberals and modernists that it is a primary duty of organized religion to work for a social order more in accordance with Christian principles.

In the face of the modern world of science, then, men to whom the religious heritage is a precious possession of the human soul have had two alternatives: they could either cleave to the old with redoubled energy, or they could attempt the difficult and dangerous task of effecting a new harmony of knowledge and aspiration. There is, indeed, a third possibility, easier than either of the other two: they could relegate religion and religious problems more and more to the background, and find full scope for their energies in the complex activities of an industrial age. Unquestionably the last century has seen a growing indifference to the whole aim and purpose of religion, especially among two classes. The great body of industrial workers, for whose life religion has seemed increasingly to grow irrelevant, and to have no vital message, has for the most part directed its energies to making and enjoying a living; the majority without much serious questioning or searching of the heart or definite abandonment of religious beliefs, the more thoughtful minority with active antagonism, seeing little in religion but an "opiate of the people," a means of binding them to the existing social order with hypocritical promises of bliss to come. Among the professional and scientific classes it has been the inability of traditional religion to justify itself in the light of modern science, rather than its disinclination to cope with the problems of industrial society, that has led to the rapid growth of a tolerant indifference, a skeptical agnosticism, or a dogmatic atheism.

But there is much reason to doubt whether, after all, the modern age as a whole is much more indifferent to the appeal of religion than the centuries of the past. The so-called Age of Faith, when every man gave lip-service to the Church and took wise precautions against the perils of a future life, probably contained not much larger a proportion of genuinely religious souls, men to whom faith and aspiration and the service of God and man was a living reality, than are to be found in our Western world to-day. Public opinion has now made skepticism and indifference more respectable, and the old pressure for conformity is no longer so strong. The very gropings and yearnings of so many of the "unchurched" to-day, not only the rise and spread of the various cults and groups deriving their inspiration largely from Oriental sources, which make their appeal mainly to the more leisured classes, but even more the intense religious fervor with which men throw themselves into the manifold social and humanitarian movements of the day, such as socialism, and above all the strength of the most universal religion of the present, patriotic nationalism, seem to indicate the continued presence in men of the needs and the aspirations which formerly were expressed in terms of traditional religion. Men's thought upon the whole subject is sadly lacking in clarity and precision, yet amidst all the confusion and cross-currents it is dubious whether religious needs and religious satisfactions are any less intense than they were when one great body of Christ embraced the whole of Christendom.

There seem to be, then, at least five great groups and tendencies in the religious life of the last hundred years. First, there is the Catholic Church, together with the Anglican High Church party, who owe allegiance to the main traditions of Christianity. Secondly, there is the orthodox party among the Protestants, the evangelicals, finding expression in the Low Church party among the Anglicans and in the recent movement known as fundamentalism among the various Protestant denominations; this rests its faith, not upon the Catholic tradition, nor upon the doctrines of the Reformation, but upon the new evangelical orthodoxy of the eighteenth century, a quite different thing. Thirdly, there is the body of liberals or modernists amongst the Protestants, forming the Broad Church party in the Anglican fold, and even penetrating, until stamped out, into the Catholic Church. Fourthly, there are the various more radical religious movements which have broken definitely with the Christian tradition, ranging from the eighteenth-century Unitarianism through the various exotic cults to humanitarian and agnostic movements like the Positivist Religion of Humanity, the German Monists, and the Ethical Culture Societies. And finally, there are the great body of the indifferent and the skeptical, to whom no form of what they would recognize as religion makes any appeal. It might be added that a similar division to that amongst the Protestants exists in Judaism, where the line is drawn between the Orthodox and the Reformed congregations, in which latter body there flourishes a strong liberal party both in social and in theological tendencies. But before investigating the important stages in the development of these various groups, and their significant ideas, we must enumerate the chief tendencies which have influenced religious thought during the century.

Causal Factors in the Religious Development of the Present

Superficially, it would seem that in view of the protracted warfare of "religion" and "science" for the last few generations the greatest single force in bringing about contemporary religious beliefs has been the growth of scientific knowledge. But it is probable that the discovery of new facts about man and his universe has operated only indirectly. For the average man, scientific knowledge in itself appears to be in no wise incompatible with a strong religious interest, even with traditional religious ideas. Indeed, it is surprising, if one is really concerned with believing both in science and theology, how little logical conflict there is between the faith of the fathers and the acceptance of scientific truth. To be sure, such a mind is apt only to "accept" science; and it is not by such acceptance that the great discoveries have been made. But the record is full also of plenty of examples of orthodox Christians, both Catholic and Protestant, who have been pathfinders in scientific truth. It is only when to the passive acquiescence in the results of science is added an active scientific faith — faith, that is, in the power and the method and the assumptions of science — that a genuine conflict appears. Even such a faith is not necessarily irreligious, but it is undeniably disturbing. It brings with it new attitudes, new viewpoints, new loyalties, and it is bound also to bring new conceptions of the nature and function of religion. Where this scientific faith is so strong as to seem sufficient unto itself, it may easily lead to a diminishing of all religious interest.

It is neither science nor this scientific faith, but rather the reflection of a changing social experience in new philosophies, that has been the chief intellectual factor in forming modern religious thought. By the eighties alert leaders felt the need of reconstructing the religious tradition, both to circumvent the disintegrating effects of the growing science on literal-minded orthodoxy, and, more significantly, to embody better the humanistic values and progressive temper of the age. They found the already developed idealistic systems, and the more romantic of the newer evolutionary faiths, admirable instruments for these ends. As a result, the major liberal reinterpretations were worked out in terms of idealism, and deeply bound up with its patterns of thought; and most of what passed for "modern theology" in liberal circles down to our generation exhibited far more of the ethical values and monistic feeling of romanticism than of any scientific temper.

This is still largely true to-day. Though the original idealistic inspiration has been reinforced and given a scientific coloring by the speculative theology of certain recent physicists, it is the most romantic of our interpretations of science, like creative or emergent evolution, or Whitehead's philosophy of organism, that have appealed most to religious thinkers. Even the widespread resort to "religious experience," and the attempts to make of theology an "empirical science," owe far more to romantic ideas of experience than to any of our scientifically critical empiricisms. Only very recently have a few pioneers, chiefly in this country, tried to give a religious application to our more experimental and naturalistic philosophies.

But such intellectual factors have naturally operated only with the minority. The major influence affecting religious beliefs and attitudes has been the growth of our manifold secular faiths and interests. These new ways of life have corrupted orthodox and liberal alike; they have caused not so much an intellectual dissatisfaction with the faith of the fathers, as an unconscious but profound crowding aside of that faith as irrelevant in the modern world. Though men repeat the old phrases their real concern has turned elsewhere. To many observers there even seemed for a time a genuine waning of the religious need; the forces in human nature that had formerly demanded a religious faith now found sufficient expression in humanitarian activities and social idealism. The rapid rise abroad of powerful social faiths and cults has reminded us that the demand for a supreme and unifying loyalty is not so easily eradicated, but merely changes its object with a changing social experience. Still it is clear that a growing preoccupation with the secular life of this world has pushed the traditional forms of religion further and further into the background, and that this shifting of men's concerns has been the basic force at work behind the modern religious scene. Organized religion, even where vigorous, has become more and more this-worldly; the appeal of a social gospel, often felt most deeply in theologically orthodox communities, has led men to lose interest in theoretical questions and turn to some form of moral and social idealism. And the strongest and most fanatically zealous religions in our world are those new secular faiths most narrowly focused on a social goal. All in all, the outstanding religious phenomenon of the century has been not so much the fading of faith, as its transfer from a theological and cosmic to a human and social object.

It is true that the mood of disillusionment and despair of man's moral powers that accompanied defeat in Central Europe, that reached even America with the depression, and that has been made well-nigh universal by the threatened collapse of our whole accustomed world in the present great revolution, has had a striking religious repercussion in sending Protestants back to new and sophisticated versions of Reformation orthodoxy. The pre-war humanistic liberalism is dead on the Continent, it has been losing ground in Britain, and is sharply challenged in America. It is hardly possible to speak with confidence to-day of realizing the Kingdom of God on earth; the kingdoms that are being realized are too clearly of this world. In times of failure and frustration and the apparent doom of ideals the more sensitive crave something beyond the goal of any human and social program. In the light of to-day's experience, the doctrines of St. Augustine, formulated to meet the decay of another civilization, no longer need drastic reinterpretation to make them convey our vision of man's estate; they once more express what men deeply feel, as they have recurrently in the past. Theologically speaking, many have come to realize afresh the transcendence of God. But it is after all a new conception of and concern with human nature that this Neo-orthodoxy expresses: it is a moral protest against the intolerable evils of modern life in time of crisis. And in America at least it has been coupled with renewed interest in radical social programs. It bids men pursue them with greater vigor, but with a more critical temper and in the light of a purer spiritual ideal.

Opposition to the New World as Conflicting with Religious Traditions

These new forces were destined to lead to marked hostility as well as to assimilation. The orthodox and conservative groups, who may even be called reactionary in comparison with the general attitude during the eighteenth century, found themselves throughout the century in ever-increasing opposition to whatever in the newer conceptions seemed to conflict with the time-honored religious traditions. In the Protestant churches, this led to a reaffirmation of the dogmatic and precise theologies and creeds of the Reformation and Puritanical era, as modified and transformed by the eighteenth-century evangelical revival. During the first part of the century there was, amongst the more educated members of these bodies, a carrying-on of eighteenth-century supernatural rationalism, expressing itself in much concern with the scientific "evidences of Christianity." The *Analogy* of Bishop Butler, despite its double-edged argument, enjoyed a great vogue in university and college circles, in England and America, where it was long used as a textbook in Christian apologetics. It vied in popularity with William Paley's *Natural Theology* (1802), which in the manner of Tillotson and Clarke a century earlier sought by appeals to the perfect adaptations of animals and man to their environment, notably by an analysis of the intricate structure of the eye, to prove that such evidence of design in the world was explicable only in terms of a Divine Creator. This argument, cogent in the Newtonian world, lost its force in the world of nineteenth-century science, and with the theory of evolution, rightly or wrongly, seemed exploded. A similar school of rationalistic supernaturalists existed far into the century in Germany. With this group may be placed the more radical and Deistic early Unitarians, greatest among whom was the founder of the American movement, William Ellery Channing; he was a high supernaturalist who insisted upon miracles as the chief proof of Christianity, but tempered his faith with a conviction of the fundamental dignity and worth of human nature.

By the side of this rational supernaturalism existed a pious and unintellectual evangelicalism, expressing itself in great emotional "revivals" emphasizing conversion and personal salvation in the Wesleyan fashion; such waves of religious feeling swept the

American colonies in the eighteenth century, captured the new West in the early nineteenth, and have lingered on to the present in the Southern and Western States. This is the type of religion with which we are familiar as involving "camp-meetings," "the sawdust trail," and the various other appurtenances of popular religion in the rural districts and small towns of the great American hinterland. In the form of the Salvation Army it has invaded the industrial centers of England and America, devoting itself to the conversion and rehabilitation of the lowest strata of the slums.

The growth of mechanistic science, of scientific Biblical criticism, and the bursting of the bombshell of evolution in 1859, brought the conflict between evangelical traditions and the modern world to a head. In all the churches the first reaction was one of bitter hatred and fierce denunciation of Darwin's ideas in any form. Saintly Bishops grew excited in calling men like Huxley and Darwin the worst names they could think of, and proclaiming their unalterable opposition to the idea that man is a monkey and to "science falsely so-called." Ministers arose in every pulpit to denounce the impious and ungodly books which they would not disgrace themselves to read, and to announce their undying adherence to a literal interpretation of the first chapters of Genesis. "Free-thinking" opponents denounced in turn superstition and antiquated obscurantism; and men like Robert Ingersoll toured the country, maliciously pointing out the "mistakes of Moses" and the cussedness of parsons in general. Theology and science seemed to thoughtful men to be in unalterable and eternal conflict.

Protestant Fundamentalism

When the first shock had passed into history, and the smoke of battle cleared away, men commenced to wonder whether after all the opposition were really so complete, and whether the acceptance of the main facts of modern science were so incompatible with the essentials of the Christian tradition. It took over a generation to make the adjustment, but by the end of the century most thoughtful Protestants, either by reinterpreting Genesis in the light of evolutionary ideas, or by returning to the older Christian tradition of pre-Protestant days and not attempting to interpret the Bible as literal scientific truth at all, had reached the point where they had no difficulty in reconciling faith and science. But the majority of uneducated church members, who had no means of assimilating what the scientific viewpoint really means, were content to remain oblivious to the advance of mechanism and evolution and historical research; and when the liberals, especially in the theological seminaries supported by the various denominations, seemed to be too radically transforming the faith of the fathers, they lent themselves to the support of a renewed attack upon the modern tendencies. The movement known as Fundamentalism to-day came into being just before 1914, as an attempt of certain ministers to counteract the effect of the liberal teachings of the theological seminaries. Powerfully stimulated by the partisan bitternesses of the post-war period, it has gained at least passive support among great bodies of church members in all the denominations. It represents primarily a reaction against modernizing tendencies, which to its leaders seem to be taking liberals into positions which involve not only much intellectual confusion, but also the definite abandonment of the central doctrines of the evangelical faith, the depravity of human nature, the need of supernatural grace for salvation, and the attendant faith in the literal miracle of the incarnation. In these contentions the Fundamentalists are correct: it is precisely the abandonment of such doctrines which the Modernists desire to effect in the Protestant churches; and to an impartial observer there does seem, in the liberal positions, much confusion and lack of precise thinking, as well as the appearance at least of a lack of frankness and a fondness for esoteric "reinterpretation" that may approach in its effects actual hypocrisy. The cleavage, however, seems to be more basic: the Fundamentalists do not, and the Modernists do, accept present-day philosophies, and without agreement upon these basic assumptions of thinking, it seems difficult to see how the two parties can even hope to understand each other. It is but natural that men who are sincerely convinced that the doctrines of evangelical Protestantism and the literal authority of the Scriptures are supremely needful, should make every effort in their power to prevent the teaching of such secondary matters as biological science and its consequent and very real winning away and "corruption" of the minds of the young from the truth in the possession of their elders. As was pointed out in connection with the medieval inquisition, those who believe themselves possessed of absolute and necessary truth have no *right* to permit the dissemination of error, whatever laxity the kindness of their hearts may permit them.

Catholic Opposition to Modern Tendencies

The reaction of the Catholic Church to nineteenth-century beliefs was in some ways more and in some ways less pronounced than that among Protestants. The Church, for example, while maintaining that certain dogmas, as defined in the Tridentine Confession of Faith, are divinely revealed and authoritatively imposed upon all communicants, has never insisted with the orthodox Protestants upon a literal interpretation of the Bible. Hence while the latter found their sole authority seemingly absolutely opposed to evolutionary ideas, the Church has so far made no dogmatic and authoritative interpretation of the Book of Genesis, and Catholics are free to take the story of creation in whatever sense seems to them most rational. The only point upon which Catholic dogma directly opposes biological views is in insisting that at a definite point in the process of evolutionary creation the body of man was informed with an immortal soul — a belief obviously incapable of biological disproof. It is true that many individual priests have taken the same position of complete opposition that has been held among orthodox Protestants, but these views have never had any binding power upon the faithful. It cannot be seriously contended that in the last century the clergy as a whole have warmly welcomed modern science, whatever they may have done during the Middle Ages or the Renaissance; but there is a long line of devout Catholic scientists, foremost among whom are Pasteur and Mendel and the Jesuit astronomers and mathematicians, who furnish a sufficient refutation of the charge that Catholic piety and scientific discovery are necessarily incompatible.

On the other hand, the Church has insisted on its absolute and divinely appointed authority in whatever it judges touches faith and morals; and the last century has seen a strengthening and a precise definition of these powers. Among Protestants there is nothing corresponding to this authority of an existing ecclesiastical institution. For the Protestant, the Scriptures constitute the sole authority, and in theory at least he is free to interpret them in accordance with his individual reason. In many communions, notably the large body of the Baptists and the Congregationalists, there has never been any binding creed whatever; while even those churches founded upon a creedal confession in practice admit very wide variations in interpretation. In those churches with a congregational polity, like the Baptists, even the ministers are held only to the theological doctrines insisted upon by a majority of the members of an individual church; while even in those with a presbyterian or episcopal organization, there is no claim of an authoritative and divinely right interpretation of either Bible or creed. The central body which ordains ministers and can dismiss them for heresy is only using its powers of human reason to interpret the Scriptures aright, and is in theory always open to conviction by better reason. This amounts in practice to almost complete liberty of interpretation for the ordinary Protestant, and to very wide liberty for the ministers. In other words, if the Fundamentalists are strong to-day, it is because they voluntarily believe that their views are right, not because they are authoritatively told that they are.

The Reaction of Pius IX

The conservative movement in the Catholic Church dates from the pontificate of Pius IX (1846-1878). Elected as a liberal, to bring the Church up-to-date, he was so frightened by the revolutions of 1848 and the temporary loss of his sovereignty over the Papal States that he became, under Jesuit influence, a confirmed conservative. He promulgated two new dogmas, the first since the Council of Trent, and did all in his power to oppose the contemporary tendencies in thought and action. In 1854, alone and without the aid of a council, he issued the bull proclaiming the doctrine of the Immaculate Conception of the Virgin (which has nothing whatever to do with the ancient doctrine of the Virgin Birth) a binding dogma — the first time a Pope alone had promulgated a dogma. In 1864 he issued his Syllabus of Errors, occasioned by the recognition of the Kingdom of Italy by the Powers, which explicitly condemned almost all the tendencies of the age, and concluded with the ringing words: "It is an error to believe that the Roman Pontiff can and ought to reconcile himself to, and agree with, progress, liberalism, and contemporary civilization." In 1869 Pius called the first œcumenical council since Trent, which in the next year, at the very moment that the Italian troops were thundering at the gates of Rome, proclaimed the new dogma of Papal Infallibility.

This dogma represents the irrevocable commitment of the Church against liberal tendencies. It was not a new doctrine, having been taught by Thomas and the Jesuits, but it had, strangely enough, never before been made binding. It is the logical consequence of the ancient dogma of the infallibility of the Church taken in connection with the actual monarchy of the Pope; and if there is to be infallibility anywhere in a religious system, the Pope seems the best place in which to seat it. It marked the final triumph of the Papacy over the episcopal and conciliar tendencies in the Church.

The exact significance of this dogma is not usually recognized. It does not claim that the Pope's opinions are infallible, nor that he is sinless.

Faithfully adhering to the tradition received from the beginning of the Christian faith, for the glory of God our Saviour, the exaltation of the Catholic religion, and the salvation of Christian people, the sacred Council approving, we teach and define that it is a dogma divinely revealed: that the Roman Pontiff, when he speaks *ex cathedra*, that is, when in discharge of the office of pastor and doctor of all Christians, by virtue of his supreme Apostolic authority, he defines a doctrine regarding faith or morals to be held by the universal Church, by the divine assistance promised to him in blessed Peter, is possessed of that infallibility with which the divine Redeemer willed that his Church should be endowed for defining doctrine regarding faith or morals; and that therefore such definitions of the Roman Pontiff are irreformable of themselves, and not from the consent of the Church.[1]

Thus infallibility is limited to matters of faith and morals, and to official decrees addressed to the Church at large and intended to bind the Church; only such decrees can become dogmas, and be absolutely final, irrevocable, and irreformable.

As a matter of fact, Catholics have found it very difficult to determine whether any given pronouncement is infallible or not. It is agreed that only two decrees in the whole history of the Papacy have been infallible, that on the Immaculate Conception, and the Syllabus of Errors; and there is much doubt about the latter's inclusion. The fears expressed in 1870 that the Pope would promulgate new dogmas have proved groundless; indeed, the careful definition of infallibility has made many doctrines clearly not within its scope much less binding, and has naturally resulted in great caution on the part of succeeding Popes in view of their tremendous responsibility.

Still, in matters of faith and morals the Catholic Church had set its face resolutely against modern tendencies. To run over the Syllabus of errors condemned by Pius IX in 1864 is very instructive. Some of the errors are as follows:

I. *Pantheism, Naturalism, and Absolute Rationalism.* 3. Human reason, without any regard to God, is the sole arbiter of truth and falsehood, of good and evil; it is its own law to itself, and suffices by its natural force to secure the welfare of men and of nations. 5. Divine revelation is imperfect, and, therefore, subject to a continual and indefinite progress, which corresponds with the progress of human reason. 6. Christian faith contradicts human reason, and divine revelation not only does not benefit, but even injures the perfection of man.

II. *Moderate Rationalism.* 12. The decrees of the Apostolic See and of the Roman Congregations fetter the free progress of science. 13. The method and principles by which the old scholastic doctors cultivated theology are no longer suitable to the demands of the age and the progress of science.

III. *Indifferentism, Latitudinarianism.* 15. Every man is free to embrace and profess the religion he shall believe true, guided by the light of reason. 16. Men may in any religion find the way of eternal salvation, and obtain eternal salvation. 17. We may entertain at least a well-founded hope for the eternal salvation of all those who are in no manner in the true Church of Christ. 18. Protestantism is nothing more than another form of the same true Christian religion, in which it is possible to be equally pleasing to God as in the Catholic Church.

IV. *Socialism, Communism, Secret Societies, Biblical Societies, Clerico-Liberal Societies.*

VI. *Errors about Civil Society.* 42. In the case of conflicting laws between the two powers, the civil law ought to prevail. 47. The best theory of civil society requires that popular schools open to the children of all classes, and, generally, all public institutes intended for instruction in letters and philosophy, and for conducting the education of the young, should be freed from all ecclesiastical authority, government, and interference, and should be fully subject to the civil and political power, in conformity with the will of rulers and the prevalent opinions of the age. 48. This system of instructing youth, which consists in separating it from the Catholic faith and from the power of the Church, and in teaching exclusively, or at least primarily, the knowledge of natural things and the earthly ends of social life alone, may be approved by Catholics.

X. *Errors having reference to Modern Liberalism.* 77. In the present day, it is no longer expedient that the Catholic religion shall be held as the only religion of the State, to the exclusion of all other modes of worship. 78. Whence it has been wisely provided by law, in some countries called Catholic, that persons coming to reside therein shall enjoy the public exercise of their own worship. 79. Moreover, it is false that the civil liberty of every mode of worship, and the full power given to all of overtly and publicly manifesting their opinions and their ideas, of all kinds whatsoever, conduce more easily to corrupt the morals and minds of the people, and to the propagation of the pest of indifferentism.[2]

Catholic Modernism

But in spite of this official opposition, modern ideas could not be prevented from filtering into the more thoughtful minds in the Catholic hierarchy. Leo XIII, the successor of Pius IX, while not differing greatly from Pius in his own beliefs, possessed a much more liberal and tolerant spirit; he felt that error was to be combated with reason rather than with mere authority. He fostered a renewed study of the works of Thomas Aquinas in all Catholic seminaries, the upshot of which was to spread abroad that great rationalist's doctrine that between true science and true religion there can be no conflict. The very vigorous activity of the Neo-Thomists, in rejecting a mere blind appeal to faith, and setting men to effect some kind of an intellectual reconciliation between science and Catholic doctrine, greatly eased the strain. The Jesuits took the lead in their intellectual center at Louvain in restating scholastic philosophy in the light of modern knowledge, and in pursuing the sciences on Thomistic principles. Leo also, in his famous encyclical *Rerum Novarum*, issued in 1891, laid the foundations for a social program of the Church; we shall return to this later.

Encouraged by these liberal tendencies, there grew up in the Church a group of thinkers known as "Modernists," who followed the liberal Protestants in a number of their modifications of traditional doctrine in the light of recent science. The Abbé Loisy, Blondel, Labertonnière, and Leroy in France, Murri and Fogazzaro in Italy, Schell in Germany, and von Hügel and Father George Tyrrell in England, agreed in accepting the results of the historical criticism of the Bible, in accepting the principle of evolution, even as applied to dogma itself, in favoring the psychological approach to religion through experience and personal faith, and in taking many ideas from the German romanticists, such as immanence, agnosticism, and mysticism. Above all, they were united in demanding more of liberty and less of external and absolute authority within the Church. They were not, however, Protestants: they clung to the social sense and the solidarity of the Church against what they conceived to be the individualism of Protestantism. This movement had attained large proportions among the younger priesthood when Pius X, in many ways returning to the methods of Pius IX, determined to extirpate it. In the encyclicals *Lamentabile* and *Pascendi Gregis*, in 1907, modernism was summarized and specifically condemned, a new and effective censorship was set up, Loisy and Tyrrell were excommunicated; and in a few years whatever modernism still existed in the Church was driven underground. The Modernists had attempted to combine solidarity and liberty within the Church; the latter was not prepared to give up its cardinal principle of authority.

It was in vain that the Modernists sought to appeal to the example rather than the authority of Saint Thomas:

Saint Thomas was the true Modernist of his time, the man who strove with marvelous perseverance and genius to harmonize his faith with the thought of that day. And we are the true successors of the scholastics in all that was valuable in their work — in their keen sense of the adaptability of the Christian religion to the ever-changing forms of philosophy and general culture.[3]

The Pope, impressed by his responsibility "of guarding with the greatest vigilance the deposit of the faith delivered to the saints, rejecting the profane novelties of words and the gainsaying of knowledge falsely so-called," [4] declared that

were any one to attempt the task of collecting together all the errors that have been broached against the faith and to concentrate into one the sap and substance of them all, he could not succeed in doing so better than the Modernists have done.[5] It is pride which fills Modernists with that self-assurance by which they consider themselves and pose as the rule for all. It is pride which puffs them up with that vainglory which allows them to regard themselves as the sole possessors of knowledge. . . . It is pride which rouses in them the spirit of disobedience and causes them to demand a compromise between authority and liberty. It is owing to their pride that they seek to be the reformers of others while they forget to reform themselves, and that they are found to be utterly wanting in respect for authority, even for the supreme authority.[6]

The Catholic Renaissance

Since the official suppression of this attempt to reinterpret the Catholic faith in terms of nineteenth-century romantic ideas, Catholic thinkers have tried to work with rather than against the classic tradition of European rationalism. The post-war years of confusion and disintegration saw a rapid growth in the appeal and the intellectual prestige of the Church, in France as well as in Central Europe. It seemed the one great Western institution that still attempted to oppose the corrosions of nationalism, the one bulwark of the older values of the European heritage in a rapidly dissolving world. Politically, this conservatism has involved it in bitter hostility to revolutionary movements, as in Mexico and Spain; in compromising concordats with the Fascists and the Nazis; and when it held power, as in Austria and Portugal, in clerical forms of the corporative state.

Intellectually the Church has been committed to the Thomistic synthesis, the most impressive achievement of rational integration in the Western tradition; and many in search of some clear pattern in the midst of relativities and confusion have turned to it, in the hope that principles once successful might prove so again. A generation of active study has borne fruit. Scholars like Pierre Duhem and Gilson have revealed the richness and variety of the medieval currents of thought that synthesis was able to embrace. Constructive thinkers like Jacques Maritain — originally a Protestant disciple of Bergson — have shown how to effect a present-day philosophic synthesis, retaining the old values and not running after the new gods of Moscow or Berchtesgaden, by reconstructing and expanding the rationalism of St. Thomas. In France this Catholic renaissance, all the more impressive in that its leaders have been largely lay scholars and writers, has been one of the most vital intellectual movements of recent years, well suited to express the enduring standards and principles of a stable and integrated culture. But Thomism has had an appeal in England and America far beyond the Catholic Church; to many, of the major unifying faiths competing to-day, it has seemed the least destructive of hard-won values. Certainly the Church has been the most vigorous defender of the older ideals of personal relationships, against the shifting pattern of sexual morality and the claims of political totalitarianism alike.

In pursuing its policy the Church has found itself in Catholic lands involved in a long series of conflicts with the increasingly nationalistic State. The *Kulturkampf* in Germany in the seventies, the long deadlock between the Papacy and the Italian State over the question of temporal sovereignty, adjusted in the concordat of 1929, and the pre-war crises between French ultramontanism and anti-clerical "radicalism," were dramatized as the struggle of patriotism against internationalism; the so-called Catholic "black international" has been as bitterly hated as the Socialist "red international." The rise of the new secular religions has only intensified the conflict. It has centered about the control of education and the youth, a point on which neither Church nor totalitarian State will admit compromise. In France the last generation saw the lines drawn between secular education on scientific and patriotic lines, and "freedom of instruction," which meant the freedom of the Church to control the schools. Even in America the Church has tended, where it had the power, to exert a veto over moral teachings. Where the liberal state has been overthrown, the struggle between two rival religions has proceeded nakedly, and so far no compromise, even in Italy, has proved more than temporary. The future of Catholicism in its ancient strongholds will depend on its ability to come to some kind of terms with the new faiths.

Liberal Protestantism

Turning now to the other main movement in religious thought during the century, the gropings of those who were willing to attempt a new reconciliation between tradition and modern life, we find that there has been, as an inevitable result of the contemporary scientific and philosophic thought and the new industrial conditions, a more or less conscious development of what seems to be virtually a new form of religion, "Liberal Christianity" or "Modernism." In the Protestant churches, in spite of the seeming present-day strength of Fundamentalism, there is little question but that the majority of Christians have entered upon this difficult path. Whether or not this new expression of the religious life is so different from that of the past as no longer to deserve the name of Christianity at all, is a moot question which cannot be here decided; it is precisely the basic point of conflict between the conservatives and the liberals. It is certainly a far more radical break with the medieval tradition than anything produced by the Reformation; but it is no more complete a change than was the rational supernaturalism that passed as sound orthodoxy in the eighteenth century. It is obviously a development of Christianity; and those who think in evolutionary terms are profoundly convinced that it is the present-day heir of the past. There is a great deal to be said for preserving historical continuity even when much that is new is assimilated; and if it be once admitted that the primitive Christian communities, the Medieval Church, and the various Protestant churches, are all forms of a common Christianity, it is difficult to see just where to draw the line between development and transformation.

Definite Abandonment of Parts of the Religious Tradition

The effects of the newer nineteenth-century ideas seemed to be at first primarily negative; they meant the destroying of traditional beliefs and religious philosophies. But men later began to see that the leaders in the liberal movement were justified in asserting that they came to liberate rather than to destroy, that in dispensing with some beliefs they were fostering the vital growth of others. There are thus two sides to the liberal religious development of the century: it meant first the definite abandonment of parts of the old tradition, and their final rejection, and secondly a new approach and emphasis capable of supporting a strong religious life. Many have accepted the first alone, and have joined the swelling numbers of the indifferent or skeptical; but many have also given expression to a newer and freer religious faith unhampered by the constricting bonds of outgrown ideas.

The historical attitude, inspired by the romantic movement, was the first of the ideas of the age to make its way into religious thought. In eighteenth-century Germany there grew up a school of historically minded theologians who applied the newer methods of historical study, based on the assumption of the principle of uniformitarianism, to the Bible and to religious history. When these were judged by the same canons of investigation that were being applied to the study of Virgil, of Homer, of the medieval chronicles and records, the conviction was forced upon men that the Scriptures embodied the experience and the early myths and the later spiritual discoveries of the Hebrew people over a long period of time, and that to attempt to look upon Holy Writ as all of one piece, and as all equally inspired and valuable, was impossible. A careful study of the texts to determine the authorship and date of the various parts — the so-called "higher criticism" — revealed fundamental discrepancies with traditional beliefs. Differences in style, contradictory accounts of the same event, conflicting commandments purporting to come from God, made the older Protestant view that every word and every point was divinely inspired and literally true, exceedingly difficult to reconcile with faith in the wisdom and rationality of God. On the other hand, if the Scriptures were taken as the work of human minds profoundly moved by a sense of divine things, all difficulty vanished; and the sacred books became the record of early mythological and imaginative attempts to understand the world and its meaning, of sacred poetry, of religious and civil laws, and of the prophetic messages of noble souls. A more comprehensive view of comparative religions and of anthropology seemed to indicate that in all respects the Christian Bible was analogous to the early literature, and the sacred books of other peoples and religions.

For example, present-day Biblical scholars are agreed that the first five books of the Old Testament, instead of being all written by Moses, are really the selected literature of an ancient, developing people; the selective criterion, used more or less subconsciously, being that of religious and patriotic value. They have distinguished various sources from which the Pentateuch was compiled: the oldest being songs, such as those of Miriam, of Moses, and of Deborah, embodied in at least four distinct documents that can be traced in our present text. In the main the Pentateuch is a synthesized and edited collection of parts of three historical writings, parts selected by a fourth and later hand, a hand which added no little material of its own and thus became the final editor of the Pentateuch as a whole. These sources are known as the Elohist, or E, the Jehovist, or J — the first a chronicle, the second prophetic in tone — Deuteronomy, largely legalistic, and the work of the Priest-editor, P, who lived much later, in the fifth century B.C. Fundamental contradictions exist between the writings from these four sources. No one can read with an open mind, for instance, the two accounts of the Creation, that of P, Genesis I, 1, to II, 3, and that of J, Genesis II, 4 to 25, without realizing that, judged by human logic at least, *both* could not possibly be true.

The effect of this historical viewpoint was to make it impossible for those who accepted it to retain the belief that the Bible is literally and verbally inspired, in the sense that God dictated it to the scribes who wrote it down — the traditional view. Taken in connection with the nineteenth-century romantic theory of the immanence of God, however, that man and God are not two distinct substances — the Platonic philosophy at the foundation of Christian theology — but that the life of God indwells the universe and expresses itself in the souls of noble men, this meant, not that the Scriptures are not inspired, but that divine inspiration is a different kind of thing from such a "dictation-theory." It is rather a thing to be judged by its moral and spiritual fruits, as we say that Shakespeare or Goethe is inspired. For those who clung to the traditional dualism, the Scriptures seemed to lose their value; for those who believed in the newer philosophy, they took on added significance and worth. Men could now disregard the horrible bloodthirsty cruelties of much of the Old Testament, and learn from it rather the lofty morality of the prophets; its divine message could be discerned by ethical criteria rather than by a literal following out of unrighteous commandments.

This view, in fact, while it seemed very radical to orthodox Protestants, is really far more in line with the main body of Catholic interpretation of the Bible than the verbal inspiration theory. All the fathers of the Church, from Augustine down, turned to the Scriptures primarily for their spiritual and ethical value, and had no hesitation, as we saw when we were considering medieval beliefs, in quite disregarding the literal meaning of texts that in themselves seemed unimportant. Hence the Catholics have found it, on the whole, more easy to accept the results of Biblical scholarship than have orthodox Protestants, and have made important contributions to such study.

Historical study meant the abandonment of many beliefs; mechanistic science destroyed still more. Since Hume's critique of miracles in the eighteenth century, religious liberals have refused to believe in any such interferences with the order of natural law. The records they explain as the product of the natural causes of human credulity, imagination, and legend; while even those who have some doubts about abandoning all belief in these supernatural events seek religious truth in the validity of its doctrines themselves, rather than in any external buttressing by miracles. In the eighteenth century, miracles were the chief support of faith; in the next, they became the chief problem to be explained.

Modern geological and biological accounts of the world's past have of course meant giving up any literal belief in the events recorded in the first chapters of Genesis. This does not mean that, for liberals, the world was not created by God; it means only that the process was much longer and more complex than the simple tales of Genesis. This is, incidentally, the orthodox Catholic view, expressed even in Thomas himself. Genesis takes its place, with the Greek and other primitive legends, as a beautiful and poetic mythology.

Finally, the nineteenth century definitely abandoned the belief in God as a scientific principle. The watch-maker Creator of the Enlightenment has vanished, with the advance of rational scientific accounts of how the world came into being; and if religious men still believe in a Creator behind those long processes, they do it on religious rather than on scientific grounds. To them, evolution is merely a more exact description of the way in which God's creative acts took place.

The New Faith of the Liberals

While modern ideas were forcing the liberals to give up these old beliefs, they were also leading them to a new approach and a new emphasis upon the enduring verities of the religious life. Instead of seeking the object of religious aspiration and worship in another realm, in some distant heaven beyond the stars, quite remote from and external to the universe, they sought God rather in the very life of the universe itself, in the world and its processes. Natural law was no longer for them an exclusion of God from his world, it was the fundamental expression of his power and will. While the eighteenth century had seen the harmony and order of the universe as a proof of its being God's handiwork, the shift from a purely mechanical nature to one that was alive, that developed and grew and passed from one form to another, seemed to make it much more easy to regard the world-process as inherently divine in its own right. On one point all the romantic and idealistic philosophers agreed: they rejected the traditional dualism of the natural and the supernatural, and united in the monistic belief that the world is the expression of one great principle permeating all its parts and including all events in its cosmic process. Man is one with nature, and man and nature are one with God — not, perhaps, the whole expression of the divine life, but existing as essential parts of it. It was easy for religious souls to see in the whole long story of evolution itself the unfolding of the hand of Providence, and in its goal of a perfected human society "the one far-off divine event to which the whole creation moves."

Indeed, there can be no scientific objection to interpreting the course of nature as a divine process, provided that does not lead to a falsification of the specific parts of that process. The one great objection to such an interpretation, the age-old problem of evil: how, then, can the ways of God to man be justified? how, if nature be red in tooth and claw with the blood of the struggle for existence, can men without blasphemy call the work of nature the work of God? has not been made more difficult by anything modern science has discovered. It existed as acutely for Job of old as it does to-day; and if the ancient Hebrew faith could still affirm that God is the mystic union of power and goodness, in spite of the pressing evils of existence, religious faith can even yet make that bold assertion, in the very face of common-sense. Indeed, if evolutionary conceptions lead men to look on all things as the working out of some great purpose, it is perhaps even easier to-day to make an intellectual adjustment by explaining how an all-powerful and all-good God can bring good to pass from evil.

If God is to be sought in the processes of nature, and not apart from them, then in man himself is to be found the divine spark. Human nature at its best can rise to the highest manifestations of God in his universe; in the search of the scientist for truth is God's mind, in the yearning of the artist for beauty is God's longing for perfection, in the love of man for man is God's love at its highest. If the heavens proclaim his majesty, and the everlasting hills his steadfast power, if the splendor of the sunset reveals his loveliness, and the night his mystery and awe, surely in the depths of the soul of man, in his never-ending striving and aspiration after a good dimly glimpsed from afar, in his devotion to an ideal cause and his sacrifice for his fellow man, there dwells a haunting suggestion of the perfection the universe can bring forth that is unmatched by circling planet or stupendous thunderbolt. What matters it that the scientists can analyze into electrons and describe in terms of mechanics? If this be the goal of the processes of nature, if man himself is the child of natural forces and the individualization of universal power, then those forces and that power must be divine, must be God's very will; and faith in God is faith that man will go forward, will attain the unutterable blessedness of creating the Kingdom, of seeing God at last face to face.

A typical expression of this modernist faith that God is in his universe and that all will be right with the world, can be found in the pages of Father Tyrrell:

If the love of God comprehends and unifies, it also endlessly transcends and is uniquely distinct in kind from every sort of personal affection towards our fellow men and fellow creatures individually or collectively; from all devotion to, and enthusiasm for, the Ideal — for the Good, the Fair, and the True; even from the love of God's will and kingdom upon earth. For it is the love of That which is the *prius*, the source, the explanation, the end of such affections; the root of all values, the foundation of all realities, the complement of all imperfections; of That which alone possesses what they singly and collectively lack, and by lacking are unsatisfying apart from It — infinitude, eternity, sovereign independence and reality. As an affection, our love of the Absolute is more than generically distinct from all our other loves; for it is not "one of them," it is not alongside, but over and through and behind them all, implicit from the very first, explicit only at the very last. On its negative side it might be described as a sense of incurable dissatisfaction with anything that is less than infinite and eternal, with the utmost conceivable extension of finite good; a sense that is deepened and enriched just in the measure that we push out experimentally in all directions vainly seeking the Absolute in the plane of the Relative, the equivalent of the Creator in terms of the creature.... For, the sense of the Absolute is given not *beside*, but *in* and *with* and *through* the sense of the Ideal in every department: it is the sense of That over against which every conceivable Ideal is felt to be infinitely inadequate, since something greater must always be thinkable; of That which draws us to the center of a sphere whose surface we must traverse forever in pursuit of the Ideal; of That which is the source of an incurable spiritual restlessness till we learn to rest in It. It is the sense of that ultra-reality which lies behind all finite reality as an ever invisible Sun whose form and splendor is hid from us by cloud-barriers of varying density, and whose light is known to us only as luminous mist. In the Ideal, in the True, the Good and the Fair, we have the Finite variously transfused and transfigured by the rays of the Infinite, forcing upon us the conception of an illuminating source beyond, whose precise form and nature lies shrouded in mystery.[7]

If this faith be accepted, it means that the approach to religion and to God is to be made primarily through the soul of man. There is to be found the most divine thing in human experience, there is the pathway to faith in an even larger and more cosmic divinity. In a host of ways the last century has seen a complete shift from the Enlightenment's approach to God through the order of external nature, to the contemporary human approach. These facts of aspiration and love and vision, the best man knows, are the key to that in life which is most real. The whole of nature is to be judged, not in its origins, but in its fruits in man at his highest, and in the still higher things which he can foreshadow. Religion, with its striving and its worship and its conviction of an unseen reality, in adjustment to which lies man's highest blessedness, is thus an entirely natural thing, rooted in the deepest and most enduring experiences of human nature. What that reality is, whether it be the Ideal man sees, or the still further Ground of that ideal; whether it govern the course of nature independently, or impinge upon the world only through the spirit and energies of man — these are all in a sense secondary. Man's rational interpretation of these facts of experience, his successive theological beliefs, his definitions of God, have developed and changed with all else in the world; but this attitude, this feeling, these experiences, are permanently rooted in human nature. Man has worshiped God under many symbols and striven to do his will in many ways; in ages to come he will grow still further in wisdom and understanding. But religion, as an enduring aspect of human life, and God, as the object of man's aspirations and vision, cannot but remain amidst all changing forms so long as human nature itself is unaltered.

Psychologists have studied these religious experiences and recorded them; romanticists have based their faiths upon them,

[7] *Lex Orandi*, by George Tyrrell. Reprinted by permission of the publishers, Longmans, Green & Co.

mystics have through them come face to face with God. Interpretations vary, symbols conflict; but in some such way many have come to rebuild their religious life upon the firm foundation of human experience and human nature.

Monistic Evolutionary Theologies

This fundamental change in philosophy and attitude has found expression in a great variety of new monistic and evolutionary theologies. Some of the more radical of these have broken entirely with the Christian tradition, and attempted to formulate the relation of man to man and to God, and of God to the world, in an entirely fresh and new reliance upon the pure facts of the religious experience. But for the most part the Modernists have not been willing to wipe the slate clean and start afresh; they have preferred to take the fundamental concepts and doctrines of traditional Christianity, which grew up in the Neo-Platonic philosophy and are only intelligible in the terms of that philosophy, and reinterpret them in the light of the newer evolutionary and monistic philosophy. Retaining the old words and the old phraseology, they have sought to penetrate behind these intellectual symbols by which the past represented its religious experience, to the enduring experience itself, and to reinterpret the old symbols in terms of the modern Growing World. It is this process of reinterpretation that has made the Modernists appear insincere to their opponents; for they use the traditional language without always making it plain that they are taking it in a quite different sense from that in which, say, Augustine, or Thomas, or Calvin, or Wesley, took it. Their justification for this lies in the contention that each one of these men took it in a quite different interpretation; that the meaning of the ancient doctrines has been continually undergoing a change and an adjustment to the new intellectual world; and that not only in theology, but in every branch of human knowledge, from physics to economics, terms and expressions have been defined and redefined in the light of the newer knowledge. Such basic concepts in mechanics as force, motion, and power, have been progressively reinterpreted for each new generation from Thomas down; psychology is full of the use of older terms in newer senses. The Modernists contend that theology too must pour the new wine of modern knowledge into the old bottles of the classic creeds.

These new theological reinterpretations have taken many forms. Some have emphasized the notion of immanence in the relations between God and man and the world. Some have stressed the idea of creative evolution, that the whole evolutionary process has been a working upward to man and his divine nature. Some have emphasized the humanistic approach, that God and the divine are to be sought and found primarily in the soul of man. Whatever their form, however, they have involved a radical break with the traditional theological conceptions. The monistic doctrine of divine immanence has obliterated the old distinction between the natural and the supernatural. Every event that occurs, and the whole order of nature, is divine, for it is an expression of God; yet there are no miracles in the sense of isolated instances of divine power. "Miracle," says Schleiermacher, "is only the religious name for event. Every event, even the most natural and common, is a miracle if it lend itself to a controllingly religious interpretation. To me all is miracle. In your sense of the word only something inexplicable and strange is a miracle, which to me is none. The more religious you are the more miracles you will find everywhere." [8] Life, aspiration, love, are the supreme miracles, and the supremely natural events in the world. To be natural is to be real; and to be real is to be divine and hence supernatural at once. This means, of course, that the Modernist has accepted the present-day humanistic emphasis on the inherent dignity and worth of this life.

Applied to the idea of revelation, immanence makes all noble words and lofty messages, from whatever man they come, alike revelations of the divine nature. The difference, if difference there be, between the Bible and other sacred books, indeed the very difference between sacred and profane literature itself, lies in the value of its insight rather than in any distinction of origin. Isaiah, the Sermon on the Mount, Plato, Marcus Aurelius, Carlyle, Goethe — all have been alike vehicles of the divine revelation.

Applied to the idea of immortality, this attitude obliterates the older spatial distinction between earth and heaven, and makes it one of the spirit only. This is God's world, and in man's heart can dwell God's heaven. Immortality is not a continuation of existence beyond the grave, but a deathless quality of life men may achieve here and now — a reversion to the original Platonic conception, incidentally. "Not immortality outside of time and behind it, or rather in time but only after the present; but the immortality which we can have immediately and now in this temporal life, and which is a problem in whose solution we are always engaged. In the midst of the temporal to be one with the everlasting, and to be eternal every moment, this is the immortality of religion." [9]

The old theology had looked upon man as a fallen and corrupt creature, whose nature had to be radically transformed by supernatural grace. To be human was to be undivine, to be divine was to be unhuman. The conception of divine immanence makes man's very nature in itself divine, at least in its human possibilities; man needs for salvation, not a regeneration of substance — the Neo-Platonic idea — but an awakening to his potential divinity. God is in human nature, not external to it; man needs no magical or sacramental grace, but simply the determination, born of his recognition of his divine sonship, to live as a son of God should.

Perhaps the most striking change is the reinterpretation involved in the conception of the person of Christ. The orthodox doctrine, adopted at the Council of Chalcedon in 451, meant that the one person, Jesus Christ, possessed two wholly distinct and alien natures, the divine and the human. With the identification of divinity and humanity, all point in the ancient controversies over the supernatural origin of Jesus, the Incarnation and the Virgin Birth, is lost; Christ is recognized as divine, just as all men are divine, and his leadership rests on the completeness of his consciousness of his expression of God. He was no more divine than other men, but he was more fully awake to his own divinity, and brought his life more completely under its control. Hence the Modernists' abandonment of the Virgin Birth as a crude though poetical attempt to account for Jesus' preëminence in terms of his origin rather than in terms of the awakened divinity of his life and teachings.

ÆSTHETIC NATURALISM

This fundamental point of view, with its attendant theological reconstruction, has stimulated two main tendencies in present-day liberal Christianity. On the one hand, it has led to an æsthetic naturalism: religion is an imaginative and poetical embodiment of man's relations to the universe, and God is the symbol for the unified human ideal. On the other, it has found expression in an ethical theism: God is conceived as the Ideal or final cause of man, religion as "morality tinged with sentiment," and the essence of the performance of one's obligations to God consists in making his will to prevail and laboring to realize his Kingdom upon earth. The one tendency is exemplified by men who find the religious experience and the religious feelings primarily a matter of appreciation of and communion with the great religious leaders and systems of the past; they see in religion the highest of the arts, the noblest imaginative embodiment of human ideals, and seek in the great religious traditions, in their rich fruitage in storied cathedral and ancient ritual and poetic doctrine, the satisfaction of their natural yearning for beauty and piety and æsthetic adjustment to human life. The other tendency is rooted rather in the moral life, and in the struggle to make righteousness prevail in the social order; for it religion is the inspiration and the driving power of progress in moral ideals, both in their revision and criticism and in their application to the life of man. The one group makes worship central, and is priestly in its general attitude: it looks toward the past, finding there elements of the spiritual life so precious that it cannot bear to suggest any alteration. It reverences primarily the fundamental aspirations of human nature as they have been beautifully clothed in the great traditions. The other makes moral inspiration central, and is fundamentally prophetic in outlook: it is impatient of the past, the dead hand of tradition, and views the spiritual life as a thing of continued progress and endeavor for the future. The one finds satisfaction in the beautiful symbolism of ritual and religious services, the other in the moral striving to make all things new. Both tendencies relegate theology and doctrine, that is, rational interpretation of the significance of the religious experiences and of man's place in the universe, to a secondary position: the one regarding creeds as poetic hymns, and doctrines as mythological symbols, the other viewing them more literally as mixtures of outworn science and primitive superstition, and concentrating upon programs of social and humanitarian action. The one tendency leads naturally to an esoteric Catholicism and High Church Anglicanism, the other to a new Puritanism of ethical endeavor; both more or less fully admit that the main outlines of the picture of the world as pieced together from modern science are a sufficient philosophic basis for human life. The one tendency in practice is exemplified by the men who attend church for the beauty of the music and the ritual and the feelings it inspires, the other by those to whom religion is a stimulus and a motive for various attempts to secure social justice.

Both interests have, of course, united in the past of Christianity, the one to build the cathedrals and paint the pictures of the saints, the other to flower in the Isaiahs and Francises and Savonarolas of the moral life. But with the disintegration of the bond of doctrinal belief that has held them together, they seem to-day to be diverging more and more, until each group finds it increasingly difficult to sympathize with or even to understand the other. On the whole, the æsthetic tendency seems backward-looking and conservative, while the moral and social emphasis seeks to imbue society with a more humane spirit and proclaims the visions of the prophets of old to the present day and generation. The former can degenerate into a sentimental and complacent attachment to old achievements that remains indifferent to present needs; the latter, into a no less complacent faith in social "service" and social reform as an end in itself, with no more ultimate sense of direction or spiritual vision. The æsthetic attitude appeals to a small and selected class, while ethical religion has behind it generations of American faith. The latter is unquestionably the most vital force to-day in liberal Protestantism and Judaism. But a religion of consolation and security is deeply rooted in human nature. Our social crisis promises to lend it new strength. It may be that the eternal vision of ultimates will once more bind priest and prophet together in the service of the living God.

Æsthetic naturalism in religion has found its best expression in the writings of Catholics who have abandoned a literal belief in the historic dogmas. It is to be found in its more radical form in Comte's Religion of Positivism, dubbed rather unkindly by Huxley "Catholicism minus Christianity"; and in varying degrees in artists like Renan and Santayana. The latter well expresses its spirit:

The only truth of religion comes from its interpretation of life, from its symbolic rendering of that moral experience which it springs out of and which it seeks to elucidate. Its falsehood comes from the insidious misunderstanding which clings to it, to the effect that these poetic conceptions are not merely representations of experience as it is or should be, but are rather information about experience or reality elsewhere — an experience and reality which, strangely enough, supply just the defects betrayed by reality and experience here. Thus religion has the same original relation to life that poetry has. ... Like poetry, it improves the world only by imagining it improved, but not content with making this addition to the mind's furniture — an addition which might be useful and ennobling — it thinks to confer a more radical benefit by persuading mankind that, in spite of appearances, the world is really such as that rather arbitrary idealization has painted it. This spurious satisfaction is naturally the prelude to many a disappointment, and the soul has infinite trouble to emerge again from the artificial problems and sentiments into which it thus plunged. The value of religion becomes equivocal. Religion remains an imaginative achievement, a symbolic representation of moral reality which may have a most important function in vitalising the mind and in transmitting, by way of parables, the lessons of experience. But it becomes at the same time a continuous incidental deception; and this deception, in proportion as it is strenuously denied to be such, can work indefinite harm in the world and in the conscience. ...

We may therefore proceed to analyze the significance and the function which religion has had at its different stages, and, without disguising or in the least condoning its confusion with literal truth, we may allow ourselves to enter as sympathetically as possible into its various conceptions and emotions. They have made up the inner life of many sages, and of all those who without great genius or learning have lived steadfastly in the spirit. The feeling of reverence should itself be treated with reverence, although not at a sacrifice of truth, with which alone, in the end, reverence is compatible. Nor have we any reason to be intolerant of the partialities and contradictions which religions display. Were we dealing with a science, such contradictions would have to be instantly solved or removed; but when we are concerned with the poetic interpretation of experience, contradiction means only variety, and variety means spontaneity, wealth of resource, and a nearer approach to total adequacy.[10]

Ethical Religion and the Social Gospel

Ethical religion, on the other hand, is found at its best among those Protestants and Jews in whom the prophetic Puritan and Hebraic strain is prominent. Its chief exponents have been, among the Protestants, the great German theologian Ritschl,

[10] From *Reason in Religion*, by George Santayana. Reprinted by permission of the publishers. Charles Scribner's Sons.

and in America Walter Rauschenbusch; and in more radical form the outstanding moral leader Felix Adler, founder of the ethical culture movement. Its central interest is the Kingdom of God, the vision of an ideal society which man shall strive to realize upon earth. Ritschl, following Kant, abandons the attempt to obtain theoretical knowledge of reality; we can only know how that reality acts in our experience. What God may be in himself must remain for ever unknown; this divine reality in our experience acts like a Father toward his children. Religion is not theoretical, dealing with knowledge; it is an intensely practical endeavor. Man discovers himself as a part of the world, but also as in a sense above it, capable of controlling it to his purposes. The essential religious problem is to win a victory over the world, to assert ourselves as free spiritual beings who can bring better things to pass. In this striving we need a higher religious principle to which we can appeal for help: we need to merge ourselves into some larger force, in oneness with which we can conquer and control the world. This force man inevitably symbolizes as personal; and for him it is in truth a larger self of which he can make himself a part, with whose purpose and will he can bring his own strivings into line. Man is consciously religious if he has a moral purpose to which he commits himself; by adhering to the hypothesis of a God working with him, he can make the world a means to his own spiritual growth, thus verify that hypothesis, and actually find God.

For Ritschl, Christ embodied the highest expression of this moral victory. We must make his will, which is the embodiment of God's purpose, our very own; we too must work for the reign of the divine purpose on earth, for the Kingdom of God. In seeking to realize the sway of Christian love on earth we become one in purpose with Christ and with God, and thereby attain here and now to eternal life. God is that power which brings the victory to pass, and since we find such a principle and power in Christ's gospel, for us he is divine, is very God. To know God is to work with him for the Kingdom.

This basic attitude is familiar in Matthew Arnold's faith in that "something not ourselves which makes for righteousness"; in various forms it has become widespread to-day, as the "social gospel of Christianity." In laboring for the Kingdom, in striving with Christ to bring about the reign of justice and love, we veritably create God. Religion becomes a matter of moral aspiration, of the divine will; all problems of the relation of this will to nature are unimportant compared with the fundamental reality that it can and does work through the social purposes of men.

At the turn of the century a number of socially-minded leaders, most notably Rauschenbusch, had a powerful influence in spreading this conception of the aims of religion in this country. Through the work of their disciples most liberal Protestants have come to identify Christianity itself with "the religion of Jesus," interpreted as a force for realizing a society built upon individual worth, human brotherhood, service, and love of mankind.

Christianity was pure and unperverted when it lived as a divine reality in the heart of Jesus Christ. But in his mind its purpose was summed up in one great word: the Reign of God. To this he dedicated himself in baptism. This set him the problems which he faced in the wilderness temptations. This was the center of his parables and prophecies. This explains the ethical standards which he set up in the Sermon on the Mount. It was the Reign of God on earth for which he consumed his strength, for which he died, and for which he promised to return. The Kingdom of God is the first and the most essential dogma of the Christian faith. It is also the lost social ideal of Christendom. No man is a Christian in the full sense of the original discipleship until he has made the Kingdom of God the controlling purpose of his life, and no man is intellectually prepared to understand Jesus Christ until he has understood the meaning of the Kingdom of God. The Reformation of the sixteenth century was a revival of Pauline theology. The present-day Reformation is a revival of the spirit and aims of Jesus himself.[11]

The Kingdom of God is a collective conception, involving the whole social nature of man. It is not a matter of saving human atoms, but of saving the social organism. It is not a matter of getting individuals to heaven, but of transforming the life on earth into the harmony of heaven. . . . That was the faith of Jesus. Have his followers shared it? The Church has never been able to get entirely away from the revolutionary spirit of Jesus. It is an essential doctrine of Christianity that the world is fundamentally good and practically bad, for it was made by God, but is now controlled by sin. If a man wants to be a Christian, he must stand over against things as they are and condemn them in the name of that higher conception of life which Jesus revealed. If a man is satisfied with things as they are, he belongs to the other side. For many centuries the Church felt so deeply that the Christian conception of life and the actual social life are incompatible, that any one who wanted to live the genuine Christian life, had to leave the world and

---

[11] From *Christianizing the Social Order*, by Walter Rauschenbusch. Copyright, 1912, by the Macmillan Co. Reprinted by permission.

live in a monastic community. Protestantism has abandoned the monastic life and settled down to live in the world. If that implies that it accepts the present condition as good and final, it means a silencing of its Christian protest and its surrender to "the world." There is another alternative. Ascetic Christianity called the world evil and left it. Humanity is waiting for a revolutionary Christianity which will call the world evil and change it. . . . For fifteen hundred years those who desired to live a truly Christian life withdrew from the evil world to live a life apart. But the principle of such an ascetic departure from the world is dead in modern life. There are only two other possibilities. The Church must either condemn the world and seek to change it, or tolerate the world and conform to it. In the latter case it surrenders its holiness and its mission. The other possibility has never yet been tried with full faith on a large scale. All the leadings of God in contemporary history and all the promptings of Christ's spirit in our hearts urge us to make the trial. On this choice is staked the future of the Church.[12]

The creed of this social gospel is all summed up in the words of Bernard Shaw, so widely and so approvingly quoted by liberal Christians, "The only trouble with Christianity is that it has never yet been tried."

Beyond Modernism and Liberalism

As the attempt to interpret the religious tradition in terms of prevailing ideas and social experience, modernism is inevitably unstable and ever-changing. Nothing seems so completely outmoded as the modernities of yesterday. The religious compromise worked out in the pre-war generation, and spreading rapidly in America in the first post-war decade — both now so incredibly remote — has not escaped the demand for further reconstruction. The liberal movement in German Protestantism which in the nineteenth century showed the way succumbed after 1918 to other ventures in faith; symbolically enough, its last great leader, Ernst Troeltsch, died of starvation. In America Protestant modernism, thrown on its own resources, has shown little consistency in thought, but a sensitivity remarkable even for a mediating movement to the passing winds of doctrine and currents of feeling. The waning of the idealistic systems of the last generation removed the support of the integrated philosophy in terms of which its central doctrines had been formu-

[12] From *Christianity and the Social Crisis*, by Walter Rauschenbusch. Copyright, 1907, by The Macmillan Co. Reprinted by permission.

lated. Without abandoning these convictions, alert liberals have eagerly and indiscriminatingly turned to whatever tendencies in the welter of contemporary thought gave promise of satisfying the practical and emotional requirements of moral and religious living. Thus they have drawn on mysticism, on the various theories of religious experience, on each new philosophy as it rose into prominence, from James to Whitehead, on the new psychology, on the new physics, especially the religiously reassuring if theologically heretical pronouncements of the more speculative of its popularizers — often all at the same time. The result has doubtless been practically helpful and satisfying, but intellectually it represents an open-minded confusion. Convinced that Martha chose the better part, American Protestantism has directed its energies to an amazing number of practical social enterprises. In its deep and sincere devotion to the possibilities of associated living and to coöperative striving for a better world, it has turned away from interest in doctrine and theology. It is little wonder that its leaders have been content to rest with the older intellectual reformulations by which their fathers gained entrance into this busy modern world.

This lack of intellectual clarity has naturally provoked in critical minds the attempt to go beyond the nineteenth century idealism in terms of which most liberal religion is still rationalized, and to restate its common faith more consistently in the light of present-day scientific philosophies. Naturalistic philosophers like M. C. Otto, R. W. Sellars, and John Dewey have sketched the main outlines of such an enterprise; a group of religious teachers, E. S. Ames, A. E. Haydon, and H. N. Wieman, have tried to work out the details. These men differ philosophically in their precise interpretation and evaluation of traditional religious concepts, like "God"; in their literal-minded devotion to an experimental method in religious knowledge, or their willingness to admit imaginative and symbolic ways of thought; and most significantly, in whether they limit religion to man's social concerns, or include his relations to his natural environment as well — that is, in whether their philosophy is humanistic or more broadly naturalistic. But all would view religion as devotion to the ideals discoverable in human experience, and all would rely solely on man's efforts, in coöperation with the natural resources in his world, to bring them into existence.

Such an interpretation puts the ethical devotion to moral and social values on an intellectually consistent and philosophically tenable basis. It represents that real coming to terms with science and scientific philosophies of nature and human experience at which liberal religion has always aimed; and in that sense it can be fairly called its logical outcome. But as yet it has proved too drastic a reinterpretation of the Christian tradition even for hardened liberals. Its chief practical application has been with the radical Humanists among the Unitarians and Universalists. Though it may point to a future synthesis of knowledge and aspiration, so far its appeal has been limited to those whose religious interests are severely intellectual and philosophical. From a living religion most men continue to want other things more than intellectual clarity. Far more widely felt is the need to reconstruct liberal religion's central faith itself in man and his moral powers, in the face of the present collapse of his most cherished efforts and hopes.

That faith was hardly challenged in America until the depression years. For the main body of educated Protestants religion had come to be a comfortable middle-class social and ethical idealism, with a cosmic sanction guaranteeing the ultimate success of all forward-looking movements. Sensitive spirits, especially among the younger religious leaders, went further in pushing the social gospel into a mildly socialistic opposition to the "unchristlike" character of capitalistic civilization; just after the war, and again in more radical if no less sentimental form after 1929, this Christian socialism enlisted many of the more earnest and militant. Its best-known leaders have been Sherwood Eddy, Kirby Page, Harry F. Ward, Jerome Davis, and Reinhold Niebuhr. With the exception of the last, none of these high-minded social idealists has attempted to add much to the earlier theoretical foundations of the social gospel. Most of them threw themselves into practical work in secular social movements, like labor organization and the drive for peace, some into great enthusiasm for the achievements and promise of Communist Russia. Indeed, the uncritical ease with which many earnest liberals identified the winning of such temporal goals with the establishment of the Kingdom of God has been a prime cause of the growing dissatisfaction with so truncated a form of religion.

With the collapse of optimistic hopes in Germany after 1918, the reaction began, under the leadership of Karl Barth — a prophetic figure, a liberal by training, and a Christian Socialist. In the disillusionment and despair of the war, and inspired by the salvation found by the tortured souls of Kierkegaard and Dostoievsky, he rediscovered the transcendent God of Calvin and His liberating Word — the message of man's impotence in the face of Supreme Righteousness. God is not the indwelling divinity in man, the goal of human thinking and striving. He is the stern Judge condemning all human works, all human thought and morality, all man's most earnest social efforts, as not enough. The Eternal is infinitely different from all things temporal and human. His Word is wholly other than our labored reading of the Bible, dogmatic or critical; yet, in one of those insoluble paradoxes that is the highest Christian truth, He speaks in the Bible as the living God.

Barth is a prophet bringing the conviction of sin to modern man and modern civilization: man in his crisis needs repentance in fear and trembling. The liberal religion of the Ritschlians was the expression of the prosperous bourgeoisie of the Bismarckian empire; that of Troeltsch, the ethic of the new German economic civilization hurtling to its doom. Man cannot hope to "follow Jesus," or to achieve a better world by his own efforts. The Christian can only follow attentively what is done by God.

Few even of his own disciples have been able to accept this stern condemnation of all human works, even of the intellect; the less extreme dualism of Emil Brunner and the Swedish "theologians of crisis" has proved more influential. Yet so well does the condemnation of man's self-sufficiency suit these disillusioned times, so obvious is it that the social manifestations of human nature to-day are neither Christlike nor divine, that forms of this "crisis theology" or neo-orthodoxy have for some years dominated Continental Protestantism, and have introduced a tragic note into the former complacency of British theology.

Naturalism with Vision

The first stirrings of this same temper, appearing in America during the depression and growing by leaps and bounds of late, have already dissipated the uncritical optimism of the earlier liberalism. Many professed liberals now mark this change by insisting on their "realism" in facing the problem of evil. European Barthianism is still alien to the American temper. But a small group of religious leaders, led by Reinhold Niebuhr and the former German Christian Socialist Paul Tillich, have crystallized the growing dissatisfaction with the original sentimental liberalism in terms of a similar tragic and pessimistic view of modern society, and a similar insistence on the transcendence of God, the Unconditioned. Many of the more sensitive and thoughtful of the younger ministers and teachers are "bearing theologically to the right and politically to the left."

This militant post-modernism attacks the older liberalism at its weakest point, its naïve faith in man and his capacity by collective moral effort to realize the Kingdom of God on earth. It represents in truth another of those recurrent swings of the pendulum from Christian humanism to Christian pessimism as to the potential goodness of man. Its vision is centered on human nature, on man's pride and weakness. Especially does it proclaim the eternal contrast between the Christian ideal of a society of perfect love, and the inherent compulsions and immoralities, the inevitable passions and resort to brute force which every social effort of collective man must exhibit. With only too abundant illustrations at hand, it bears witness to the sins, not only of the relatively evil forms of collective life, like capitalism and nationalism, but also to those of the relatively good movements to change and revolutionize them. The corruption of the better is indeed the worst; and the worst of sins is to rest content in the goodness of any finite and human goal. This reaches its height and depth when religion itself sets up some human ideal, some social reform or utopia, some possible form of existence, as the supreme objective of aspiration and devotion. True religion passes judgment on all such self-sufficient finitude, all such "demonic" living and "demonic" religion, in the light of the transcendent Unconditioned; the Infinite is forever beyond human grasp and comprehension, beyond all possibility of existence, and yet forever calls to the spirit of man, bidding his reach exceed his grasp. The aim of religion is just this eternal striving for the vision of perfection, this divine discontent, stronger in frustration and failure than in demonic success. In this vision of the Unconditioned men gain absolute perspectives on historical relativities, attain an objectivity and detachment which enables them to criticize the limitations of every finite goal, impels them to work valiantly for that which is relatively better, yet gives them a sustaining reality above all the vicissitudes of time when efforts are doomed to frustration and failure and even the virtues of the saints are corrupted by power. History is no scene of progress: every increase in human knowledge brings greater evil as well as the possibility of greater good. The Christian ideal is always relevant, but never reached; how far society will ever approximate it we cannot tell, but we shall never reach more than an approximation.

This vision of man's estate, despite its claim to "realism," is patently as much the emotional expression of a current temper as was the earlier faith in man's potential divinity. Disillusionment bred of revulsion from former illusions hardly affords objective truth. Above all, this return to an Augustinian conception of human nature is content with crude symbols for certain aspects of man's behavior under certain historical conditions; it cares little for the hard work of closer analysis that might reveal something of the causes — and the cure. Yet it has a salutary freedom from sentimentality that suits the temper of the times, and it does not blink the more disagreeable facts — only the brighter ones. In insisting on the relativity of all human values and ideals, in sternly criticizing all pretended moral absolutes, it incorporates much of the wisdom of our scientific philosophies of human experience; and in interpreting Christian doctrines not literally but as myths with symbolic value, it maintains nothing such philosophies would reject. Indeed, Niebuhr recognizes three main conceptions of human nature, the naturalistic, the humanistic and liberal, and the Christian; and while scornfully rejecting the second, he defines the third as naturalism with a vision of the Eternal — a conception close to that of the naturalistic critics of liberal religion already mentioned.

Yet this vision of life set forth by Tillich and Niebuhr, with its infinite striving toward an unattainable goal, is the very quintessence of romantic pessimism; and it is rooted in an ultimate irrationalism, both intellectual and practical. The myths of religion are symbolic expressions, but of higher truths too transcendent for human science and reason to grasp. Rational discourse is incompetent to deal with God and human destiny; on such themes one can speak only in "dialectical" paradoxes. Whatever one says is true and yet it is not true, for its contradictory can also be said. And practically these romanticists distrust any appeal to reason. Passion and self-interest must be met, not by education and enlightenment, but by conviction, faith, and ultimately by the naked force that can alone settle social problems. As always, the confidence that while human they possess a knowledge, however dim and paradoxical, of absolute standards properly reserved to angels tends to reconcile men to the supposed necessity of acting like the devil. The genuine religious insights of these pioneers leading modernism beyond its humanistic limitations will doubtless be incorporated. But unless the whole course of American religion is destined to a sharp reversal, it is difficult to imagine it expressing itself for long in such an irrational and pessimistic form of romanticism. We still await further formulation of the saner, less sentimental, and more intelligent temper of the times.

Effects of Religious Changes on the Churches

The attempt to reinterpret the Christian tradition in the modern world of science and industry followed two major types of religious expression, æsthetic naturalism and social religion, with or without its overtones of transcendent vision. Sometimes both are combined; usually the emphasis is laid heavily on the one or the other. The effect of such modernist ideas in Protestantism has been to cause a realignment of religious groups. The traditional sectarian lines, based on earlier theological controversy, are practically gone with the theological interest that caused them; the various denominations linger on largely for historic reasons alone. The real divisions among Protestants are between the philosophies of fundamentalism and modernism, between social conservatism and social radicalism. There is consequently a growing trend toward church union through the acceptance of common programs of action rather than common theological beliefs. In many a town and village the various Protestant churches, often under economic pressure, have pooled their interests in community churches which minimize sectarian beliefs; while many urge an organic union between the national organizations of Protestant churches, the better to further the common task of the Christian in these troubled times. The outstanding denominational union already effected is that in Canada between the Methodists, the Presbyterians, and the Congregationalists; various others are under consideration.

The suppression of "modernism" in Catholicism redirected but did not destroy in the Church the spirit of conciliation with the modern world. Its vigorous devotion to a rationalistic critique and synthesis of modern ideas is aimed at a need increasingly felt to-day. Practically, it has given renewed attention to its own Christian social program for modern problems. In almost every country of Europe the Catholic or clerical party contained a large group committed to Social Catholicism and specific programs of social reform. Opposition to the newer social faiths has provoked a positive emphasis on the Catholic alternative. This in fact seems the one ground of agreement between all the religious groups in the Western world to-day; and if the dream of a reunited Christendom, which in the face of modern assaults fills many an earnest soul, is ever to take place, it will probably occur through such a common labor in the Lord's vineyard. Whether, with the religious æsthetes, men will unite on common symbols for what are intellectually different conceptions, ranging from orthodox supernaturalism through humanism to a realistic naturalism, or whether such an attempt will be frankly abandoned, and a common program of social action made the connecting bond, present tendencies seem to be bringing together the members of each of the major religious groups, Catholics, Protestant Fundamentalists, Modernists, and free religious organizations.

The religious adjustment to the Growing World is still far from completion; and the outcome of our social crisis now hangs in the balance. The present pessimistic temper will doubtless wax in strength in the bitter conflicts of the near future; and many will seek escape into some realm of absolute security above the battle, finding emotional strength and personal salvation in the confident possession of the Word of God or of insight into the Unconditioned. There will be much religious concern with the problem of adjustment to the tensions and hardships of social transition, of achieving emotional stability in the midst of change. The danger is that this genuine demand will result merely in the provision of a religious refuge and consolation.

So long, however, as men experience religious emotions and religious aspirations, it is clear that some form of organized expression for the religious life will find a place. And so long as men are living in the world, and have faith in intelligence and science, it is to be expected that they will try in some way to harmonize and synthesize their knowledge and their aspiration. In an age of social conflict, such a synthesis may well take a fundamentally social form. It is to be hoped that all the insights and the values of the past will not be forgotten in the face of some new, crude, raw and uncriticized secular faith. But if the masses of men are ever given the opportunity to develop their latent powers of mind and spirit, if a democratic society, in other words, ever comes into existence, it is at least safe to expect that it will contain a religious life on a naturalistic basis in which scientific knowledge, æsthetic feeling, and moral aspiration are blended in one whole. If such a state of affairs ever comes to pass, then and only then will the modern age have achieved a spiritual unity comparable to the heights of the thirteenth-century synthesis.

REFERENCES

1. *Dogmatic Decrees of the Vatican Council concerning the Catholic Faith and the Church of Christ*, 1870, in P. Schaff, *Creeds of Christendom*, II.
2. *The Papal Syllabus of Errors*, 1864, in the same.
3. Father George Tyrrell, *The Programme of Modernism*, ch. 5.
4. *Ibid.*, Encyclical Letter *Pascendi Gregis* of Pius X, 149.
5. *Ibid.*, 215.
6. *Ibid.*, 220.
7. George Tyrrell, *Lex Orandi*, Introduction.
8. Schleiermacher, quoted in A. C. McGiffert, *Rise of Modern Religious Ideas*, 203.
9. *Ibid.*, 205.
10. G. Santayana, *Reason in Religion*, 11, 13.
11. Walter Rauschenbusch, *Christianizing the Social Order*, ch. II.
12. Rauschenbusch, *Christianity and the Social Crisis*, 65, 90, 342.

SELECTED READING LISTS

Catholicism: Joseph McCaffrey, *Hist. of the Catholic Church in the 19th Cent.*; W. Barry, *The Papacy and Modern Times*; *Camb. Mod. Hist.*, XI, xxv; Michael Williams and Julia Kernan, *The Catholic Church in Action*; the *Catholic Encyclopedia* is a mine of material. — **Papal Encyclicals:** *On the Immaculate Conception, The Syllabus of Errors, Dogmatic Decrees of the Vatican Council concerning the Christian Faith and the Church of Christ*, in P. Schaff, *Creeds of Christendom*, II. *Rerum Novarum* in F. Nitti, *Catholic Socialism*. — **Modernism:** G. Weill, *Hist. du catholicisme libéral en France, 1828–1908*; *The Programme of Modernism*, containing *Pascendi gregis*; P. Sabatier, *Modernism*. A. Loisy, *The Gospel and the Church, My Duel with the Vatican, La Religion*. G. Tyrrell, *Lex Credendi, Lex Orandi, A Much-Abused Letter*. A. Fogazzaro,

The Saint. — **Neo-thomism:** É. Gilson, *Spirit of Medieval Phil.*, *Unity of Phil. Experience;* J. Maritain, *Freedom in the Modern World, Degrees of Knowledge, True Humanism;* M. C. D'Arcy, *Thomas Aquinas, Nature of Belief.* — **Social Programs:** F. Nitti, *Catholic Socialism;* P. T. Moon, *The Labor Problem and the Social Catholic Movement in France;* G. Metlake, *Christian Social Reform: von Ketteler;* G. P. McEntee, *The Social Catholic Movement in G. Britain;* J. A. Ryan, *A Better Economic Order.*

The Protestant World: J. T. Shotwell, *The Rel. Revolution of To-day;* E. Troeltsch, *Protestantism and Progress;* H. P. Douglass and E. de S. Brunner, *The Prot. Church as a Social Institution;* C. S. Braden, *Varieties of Amer. Rel.;* Randall and Randall, *Rel. and the Modern World.* A. C. McGiffert, *Rise of Mod. Rel. Ideas;* E. C. Moore, *Christ. Thought since Kant;* O. Pfleiderer, *Ges. d. Religionsphil.;* Wellhausen, etc., *Ges. der christl. Rel.;* J. Hunt, *Rel. Thought in England in the 19th Cent.;* J. Tulloch, *Movements of Rel. Thought in Britain during the 19th Cent.;* Benn, *English Rationalism.* E. A. Burtt, *Types of Rel. Philosophy;* G. B. Smith, ed., *Rel. Thought in the Last Quarter-Cent.;* Wieman and Meland, *Amer. Phils. of Rel.;* W. M. Horton, *Cont. British Theol.;* E. Boutroux, *Science and Rel. in Cont. Phil.;* P. Sabatier, *L'Orientation religieuse de la France actuelle.*

The Persistence of the Old: A. D. White, *H. of the Warfare of Science with Theology;* T. Huxley, *Science and Hebrew Tradition, Life and Letters.* **The Oxford Movement:** F. W. Cornish, *H. of the Ch. of England in the 19th Cent.;* R. W. Church, *The Oxford Movement;* J. H. Newman, *Apologia pro sua Vita, Development of Chr. Doctrine;* lives by W. Ward, G. G. Atkins; W. G. Peck, *Soc. Implications of the Ox. Movement.* **Protestant Fundamentalism:** S. G. Cole, *Hist. of Fundamentalism;* J. G. Machen, *Christianity and Liberalism, What is Faith?* F. L. Patton, *Fundamental Christianity.*

Criticism of the Tradition — Biblical Criticism: E. R. Trattner, *Unravelling the Book of Books;* J. E. Carpenter, *The Bible in the 19th Cent.* Introductions to the Old Testament by G. F. Moore, J. A. Bewer, J. Moffatt, S. R. Driver; A. Duff, *H. of Old Test. Criticism;* T. K. Cheyne, *Founders of Old Test. Criticism.* Intro. to the New Test. by J. Moffatt, E. C. Moore; F. C. Conybeare, *Myth, Magic, and Morals, Hist. of New Test. Criticism;* A. Schweitzer, *Von Reimarus zu Wrede, eine Ges. d. Leben-Jesu Forschung.* See Ch. III. **Psychological Approach:** W. James, *Varieties of Religious Experience;* psychologies of religion, by E. D. Starbuck, J. H. Leuba, G. A. Coe, J. B. Pratt, R. H. Thouless, W. B. Selbie, J. C. Flower, K. R. Stolz. R. Otto, *Idea of the Holy;* S. Freud, *Future of an Illusion;* E. D. Martin, *Mystery of Religion;* H. M. Kallen, *Why Religion?* G. van der Leeuw, *Religion in Essence and Manifestation.* — **Sociological and Anthropological:** H. L. Friess and H. W. Schneider, *Rel. in Various Cultures;* C. Kirkpatrick, *Rel. in Human Affairs.* E. Durkheim, *Elementary Forms of the Rel. Life;* H. Bergson, *Two Sources of Morality and Religion.* Max Weber, *Gesammelte Aufsätze zur Religionssoziologie;* J. Wach, *Einf. in die Religionssoz.* R. Lowie, *Primitive Religion;* P. Radin, *Primitive Religions.* V. F. Calverton, *Passing of the Gods.*

Liberal Religion: Philosophic Basis: See Romanticism, Ch. XVI, esp. Kant, Fichte, Schleiermacher, Hegel. A. Ritschl, *Justification and Atonement.* In England, John Caird, *Int. to the Phil. of Rel.;* E. Caird, *Evolution of Rel.;* T. H. Green, *Works,* esp. "Faith" and "The Witness of God"; R. L. Nettleship, *Life of Green;* see Mrs. H. Ward, *Robert Elsmere.* Benjamin Jowett, *Life,* by E. Abbott and L. Campbell. **Popularizers of German Philosophy:** In England, Carlyle; M. Arnold, *Literature and Dogma, St. Paul and Prot.;* A. N. Fairbairn, *Phil. of the Christ. Rel.;* J. Martineau, *Seat of Authority in Rel., Study of Rel.* In America, Emerson, Theodore Parker, *Discourse of Rel., Sermons of Theism,* and H. Bushnell, *The Spirit in Man, Nature and the Supernatural, God in Christ,* early introduced idealistic ideas. Evolutionary immanence spread from John Fiske, *The Destiny of Man Viewed in the Light of his Origins* (1884), *The Idea of God as Affected by Mod. Knowledge,* and *Through Nature to God.* See W. H. Drummond, *Ascent of Man;* B. P. Bowne, *Immanence of God, Theism, Personalism.* It was given wide hearing by Ly-

man Abbott, *Evol. of Christianity, Theology of an Evolutionist, Christianity and the Social Problem;* Washington Gladden, *How Much is Left of the Old Doctrines?* H. C. King, *Reconstruction in Theol., Theol. and the Social Consciousness,* gave it a Ritschlian emphasis; W. N. Clarke, *Outline of Christ. Theol.,* grounded it in religious experience. M. J. Savage, *The Passing and the Permanent in Rel.,* T. R. Slicer, *The Great Affirmations of Rel.,* Unitarians. **The Liberal Faith:** A. Harnack, *What is Christianity?;* W. Herrmann, *Communion of the Christian with God;* A. Sabatier, *Rels. of Authority and the Rel. of the Spirit.* A. C. McGiffert, *Christ. as Hist. and Faith;* G. B. Foster, *Christ. in its Modern Expression, The Finality of the Christ. Rel.;* W. A. Brown, *Beliefs that Matter, God at Work;* Shailer Mathews, *Faith of a Modernist;* H. E. Fosdick, *As I See Rel.;* W. Lawrence, *Fifty Years;* K. Lake, *Rel. of Yesterday and Tomorrow.* **Cosmic Theism:** A. N. Whitehead, *Religion in the Making, Process and Reality;* A. S. Eddington, *Science and the Unseen World;* J. E. Boodin, *Cosmic Evolution, God;* W. P. Montague, *Belief Unbound, Ways of Being;* E. W. Barnes, *Scientific Theory and Rel.* **Contemporary "Modernism":** F. R. Tennant, *Phil. Theology;* W. Temple, *Nature, Man, and God;* J. Baillie, *Interp. of Rel.;* A. E. Taylor, *Faith of a Moralist.* E. S. Brightman, *Personality and Rel., Phil. of Rel.;* D. C. Macintosh, *Theology as an Empirical Science, Religious Realism;* W. M. Horton, *Theism and the Mod. Mood, Theism and the Scientific Spirit, Realistic Theol.;* J. S. Bixler, *Rel. for Free Minds.* **The Aesthetic Tendency:** Schleiermacher, *Speeches on Rel., Der christliche Glaube;* Selbie, *Schleiermacher;* Cross, *The Theol. of Schl.* J. R. Seeley, *Natural Religion.* A. Comte, *Positive Politics.* E. Renan, *Life of Jesus. Études d' Hist. Rel.* G. Santayana, *Reason in Religion, Poetry and Religion, Winds of Doctrine.* B. Brownell, *Earth is Enough.*
The Ethical and Social Tendency: A. Garvie, *The Ritschlian Theol.;* G. B. Stevens, *Christ. Doctrine of Salvation.* The social gospel enunciated in W. H. Fremantle, *The World as the Subject of Redemption* (1885). W. Rauschenbusch, *Christianity and the Social Crisis, Christianizing the Social Order, A Theol. for the Social Gospel.* Harry F. Ward, *The New Social Order, Our Economic Morality, Which Way Religion?* R. Niebuhr, *Does Civilization Need Religion?* E. B. Chaffee, *The Prot. Churches and the Industrial Crisis;* C. C. Morrison, *Soc. Gospel and the Christ. Cultus;* W. M. Horton, *Realistic Theol.;* J. Bennett, *Social Salvation.* See also Felix Adler, *Ethical Phil. of Life, Reconst. of the Spiritual Ideal.*
Beyond "Modernism": Humanism and Naturalism: E. A. Burtt, *Rel. in an Age of Science;* H. E. Barnes, *Twilight of Christianity;* J. H. Leuba, *God or Man?* R. W. Sellars, *Rel. Coming of Age;* M. C. Otto, *Things and Ideals, The Human Enterprise;* A. E. Haydon, *Quest of the Ages;* C. W. Reese, *Humanist Religion.* E. S. Ames, *Religion;* John Dewey, *Quest for Certainty, Common Faith;* H. N. Wieman, *Rel. Experience and Scientific Method,* (with W. M. Horton) *Growth of Religion;* H. A. Bosley, *Quest for Rel. Certainty.* — **The New Orthodoxy:** Karl Barth, *The Word of God and the Word of Man, The Doctrine of the Word of God, The Knowledge of God and the Service of God;* studies by W. Pauck, P. H. Monsma, R. B. Hoyle. E. Brunner, *Phil. of Rel., Man in Revolt, The Divine Imperative;* N. F. S. Ferré, *Swedish Contribs. to Mod. Theol.;* A. Schweitzer, *Decay and Restoration of Civilization, Christianity and the Religions of the World;* N. Berdyaev, *Fate of Man in the Modern World.* Paul Tillich, *Kairos, Das Dämonische, The Rel. Situation, The Kingdom of God and History, The Interp. of Hist.* Reinhold Niebuhr, *Moral Man and Immoral Society, Reflections on the End of an Era, An Interp. of the Christ. Ethic, Beyond Tragedy, Gifford Lectures.* H. R. Niebuhr, etc., *The Church against the World.*

CHAPTER XXI

PHILOSOPHIC REACTIONS TO THE GROWING WORLD OF MECHANISM AND NATURALISM

It has been pointed out that for the last century the fundamental philosophy of life which a man shall adopt, which shall color his thinking and guide him in discerning what in life is of chief worth, has become primarily an individual and a personal matter. No longer can it be said, as it could during the Middle Ages and again in the Age of Reason, that all thoughtful men share a common view of the universe and a common judgment of what constitutes the good life. At the present day practically every one of the great intellectual adjustments which man can effect with his total environment, painfully worked out by outstanding thinkers or whole generations, enjoys a considerable body of adherents; truly the modern age is the philosophic heir of all the past! Nevertheless, one thing remains a matter of common property, an irreducible datum with which all thinking upon these ultimate problems of human life must begin: in some fashion or other every modern-day philosophy must recognize the existence of the vast body of scientific knowledge that has been accumulated about man and the universe in which he finds himself. Some, to be sure, merely recognize science to combat or transcend it, while others glorify it and adore; but whether it be by way of whole-hearted acceptance, or by relegating it to an unimportant place, or by complete rejection and opposition, every thinker who hopes to gain a wide adherence for his gospel of deliverance must start with the picture of the world that can be put together from the various fragmentary views of the different sciences. It is from a common scientific knowledge that men set out, and it is only on a common scientific method that men can hope to agree as the object of a genuinely inclusive social faith.

Nineteenth-century philosophy is primarily the story of varying reactions to this new science. Other groupings are possible: present perspectives would suggest economic alignments. But it was a revolutionary science that first forced the revision of the

Romantic faiths. The century began with all human interests and values deeply bound up with an anthropocentric world-view that gave them cosmic significance. Steadily and surely the advance of science was undermining that view, and making the older theological sanctions for man's ideals seem untenable. Hence to the century's end it was the religious issue that furnished the starting-point for most philosophizing, and the characteristic problem remained the old conflict between familiar faith and new knowledge. How were men to defend their religious faith against a hostile science? or how were they to find a new faith that would need no such defense? On the one hand stood the apologists for the hopes and aspirations of tradition; on the other stood militant denial. Most thinkers tried compromise; but none of the brave attempts can be said really to have succeeded. Hence while the eighteenth century found its keynote in hope, the nineteenth expressed, in its philosophy at least, either disillusionment and pessimism, or a hectic whistling to keep its courage up. It was too soon to realize that, in adjusting the precious human values of their heritage to the new world of science, men were facing merely another reconstruction of their cultural tradition.

The emotional reaction to the scientific world as a whole was not the only problem that drove men to philosophy. Science itself was rapidly changing its character; profoundly influenced by the critiques of the Romanticists, it was becoming far more concrete and rich, and for the first time adopting a genuinely experimental method. How were men to understand this new kind of science? How were they to interpret the implications of the idea of evolution, of the biological attitude? How are they now to grasp the significance of the revolution in physical theory? Here is a type of philosophic problem that will persist so long as science grows and alters its methods. The vast majority of evolutionary philosophers were so busy trying to find in the evolutionary process a new religious faith, a substitute for God and His providence, that they failed to inquire seriously what evolution and biology might really imply. They accepted and elaborated the idea of evolution because it seemed to help in their basic problem of religious compromise. But the nineteenth century also worked out new philosophic analyses of the nature and function of science itself which are the direct forebears of our own present-day naturalisms. They have given us the tools for the critical understanding of science with which our more technical philosophies are approaching the new concepts of relativity and quantum theory.

If nineteenth-century philosophers were so busy trying to adjust men's religious and moral beliefs to the new world of evolutionary science, why were they not equally concerned with the harder adjustment to industrial society? Why were not social rather than religious issues more central, as they have become in our present perspective? As compared with the eighteenth century, when political interests dominated even science, and the characteristic philosophies of rationalism and empiricism had so direct a social motivation, it is indeed surprising how little the profound economic changes affected philosophic thought. Of course, men had social philosophies, and social considerations did color the adoption of general viewpoints. But for practical guidance men went mostly to the older philosophies, not to the new evolutionary gospels. Liberalism found its official philosophy in Utilitarianism, a continuance of eighteenth-century empiricism; while collectivism, both conservative and radical, found idealism congenial, especially some form of Hegelian rationalism.

But in that complacent age social views were more or less irrelevant to the central religious problem; and at best their philosophic expressions were woefully inadequate makeshifts for dealing with the complex problems of the industrial era. Witness the fact that the three most popular philosophies of the century, those of Auguste Comte, Herbert Spencer, and Karl Marx, held completely divergent social programs. Comte preached the enlightened despotism of the old order, Spencer, a business man's individualism, and Marx an industrial socialism. Yet all three agreed on the burning issue of accepting science; and each stood, in France, England, and Germany, as the great exponent of the negative answer to the religious problem — or rather, for finding a religious faith in science itself, and taking evolution as a new and up-to-date providence working for man.

Only in the last decades have the social questions raised by the industrial revolution replaced the religious problem as the major incentive to philosophizing. This need surprise only those who forget that philosophy is primarily a means of criticism, a leverage for attacking, defending, or reconstructing tradition; its attention is first turned to problems when a bitter conflict has already arisen. Till the last generation industrial society seemed to demand opportunity for growth and expansion rather than criticism; it is only to-day that insistent maladjustments have made its organization the central intellectual issue. Now that the cosmic religious problem — as contrasted with that of the philosophic understanding of the nature and function of religion — is no longer central and dominating, and philosophers largely accept the naturalistic position, industrialism has at last begun to influence philosophy seriously. The center of attention is shifting from the cosmic problems of the nineteenth century to the human and social problems of industrial civilization; and it is clear that in the future social rather than religious issues will be the basis of philosophic divisions. The task has broadened from the adjustment to science to the larger adjustment to all the cultural and institutional changes forced upon us by our allegiance to technology.

But this shift could take place only after men had already made their peace with the scientific picture of the world. This was in itself a tremendous task, and its accomplishment remains the outstanding philosophic achievement of the century.

The Picture of the Mechanistic World Generalized from Science

What was this picture which science purported to give? The idea of evolution, its most novel and revolutionary concept, has come to stand as a symbol of the scientific faith. But it was really not so important in forcing that faith as the patient working out of mechanistic explanation; the latter seemed less of a shock because it had been in the world since Descartes. Science was advancing and filling in the details of the Cartesian picture; by the 1860's the results were so impressive they could no longer be disregarded. The fundamental dogmas of the scientific faith now served to organize a vast body of facts that could not be gainsaid. In the nineteenth century they took the form of sweeping generalizations: the conservation of energy, the laws of thermo-dynamics, natural selection, the mechanistic theory of life, above all an unyielding mechanical determinism. The laboratory had not yet unearthed so many facts that no generalization could embrace them all; the recent breakdown of traditional physical theory had not yet occurred. The idea that all such general statements are leading principles of scientific investigation, instruments to guide inquiry rather than laws governing the universe, had as yet little support. The Newtonian framework was not yet burst asunder; the most speculative assumptions, either abandoned or modified to-day, were seized upon to complete a "scientific world-view." With this framework, with these dogmas and assumptions, shaken believers felt they must come to terms.

This "scientific world-view" of the turn of the century was of course a faith, a negative faith, not to say an obsession. The dark picture fascinated our fathers. They loved to paint the alien elements as black as possible, even as they shuddered in delicious horror before it. It struck terror because they had just left the warm affection of the Christian tradition and the optimism of the Romantic faiths. Many believed it because it was so dreadful; they prided themselves on their courage in facing facts. More fled from it as from a nightmare, and used it as a springboard for a faith *quand même*. It surely needed little of the will to believe to maintain that it could not be the whole story: it was so obviously a work of sheer faith, an imaginative rendering of men's gloomiest forebodings. That "alien world" has vanished to-day; the speculative assumptions of nineteenth-century physics on which it was based have given way to others more astounding if less hostile to man's interests. Our newer naturalisms have annulled that divorce of man from nature.

One such picture of the mechanistic and evolutionary world of the last generation, from the master pen of Anatole France, has already been introduced to serve as a striking contrast to the world of the Middle Ages. Another is from the hand of that conservative sceptic, Lord Balfour:

Man, so far as natural science by itself is able to teach, is no longer the final cause of the universe, the Heaven-descended heir of all the ages. His very existence is an accident, his story a brief and transitory episode in the life of one of the meanest of the planets. Of the combination of causes which first converted a dead organic compound into the living progenitors of humanity, science, indeed, as yet knows nothing. It is enough that from such beginnings famine, disease, and mutual slaughter, fit nurses of the future lords of creation, have gradually evolved, after infinite travail, a race with conscience enough to feel that it is vile, and intelligence enough to know that it is insignificant. We survey the past, and see that its history is of blood and tears, of helpless blundering, of wild revolt, of stupid acquiescence, of empty aspirations. We sound the future, and learn that after a period, long compared with the individual life, but short indeed compared with the divisions of time open to our investigation, the energies of our system will decay, the glory of the sun will be dimmed, and the earth, tideless and inert, will no longer tolerate the race which for a moment has disturbed its solitude. Man will go down into the pit, and all his thoughts will perish. The uneasy consciousness, which in this obscure corner has for a brief space broken the contented silence of the universe, will be at rest. Matter will know itself no longer. "Imperishable monuments" and "immortal deeds," death itself, and love stronger than death, will be as though they had never been. Nor will anything that *is* be better or be worse for all that the labor, genius, devotion, and suffering of man have striven through countless ages to effect.[1]

Lord Balfour does not believe that this is the final story; but Bertrand Russell does:

That Man is the product of causes which had no prevision of the end they were achieving; that his origin, his growth, his hopes and fears, his loves and his beliefs, are but the outcome of accidental collocations of atoms; that no fire, no heroism, no intensity of thought and feeling, can preserve an individual life beyond the grave; that all the labor of the ages, all the devotion, all the inspiration, all the noonday brightness of human genius, are destined to extinction in the vast death of the solar system, and that the whole temple of Man's achievement must inevitably be buried beneath the debris of a universe in ruins — all these things, if not quite beyond dispute, are yet so nearly certain, that no philosophy which rejects them can hope to stand. Only within the scaffolding of these truths, only on the firm foundation of unyielding despair, can the soul's habitation henceforth be safely built.[2]

These pictures are, to be sure, but the expression of moods rather than of scientific verities; and all the gloomy predictions of a few decades ago, seeing the ultimate extinction of our sun as the inevitable deduction from the second law of thermodynamics, have been sadly shaken, both by the discovery of radio-activity, and by the reflection that a universe which has existed from all eternity should have run down ere this if that was destined to be its final goal. But without reflecting on this ultimate cosmic death, the picture science presents of man and his destiny is

---

[1] From *Foundations of Belief*, by Arthur Balfour. Reprinted by permission of the publishers, Longmans, Green & Co.

[2] From *A Free Man's Worship*, by Bertrand Russell. Reprinted by permission of the publishers, Longmans, Green & Co.

PHILOSOPHIC REACTIONS TO MECHANISM

sufficiently different from that of his earlier hopes to give ground for pause. Turn to the astronomer, and he answers:

> The Universe itself may be only another single unit, among a multitude of other universes; and if at this point we cease to speculate, it is not because there is no further scope for speculation, but because we have already far outstripped the last shred of solid evidence that our instruments can provide for us. Complete and absolute darkness reigns beyond. If we learn nothing else for certain, we learn at least this: that the farther we travel, the more obscure and insignificant does Man appear. And three points also emerge. Firstly, the uniformity of natural "law" remains as absolute in these regions of infinite greatness as in our own world of human dimensions. Secondly, no sign of purpose can be detected in any part of the vast Universe disclosed by our most powerful telescopes. Thirdly, this great new sphere of experience affords not the smallest trace of evidence for the existence of any spiritual entity. We find nothing but unimaginable tracts of space and time, in which move bodies by fixed laws towards ends which are wholly fortuitous, and have not the smallest relation to the advantage or requirements of Man.[3]

Turn to the psychologist or biologist, and he answers that man is a complex physico-chemical organism, the lineal descendant of some bit of primordial slime; all his hopes and aspirations, all his loves and fears, all his self-sacrifice and knowledge, are the result of the peculiar laws governing the chemical reactions that ultimately go to produce his behavior. Turn to the physicist, he who investigates these fundamental units out of which man and his universe are composed in their entirety, and he answers:

> Penetration into the secrets of atomic structure has opened up to us a vast new sphere of phenomena whose very existence was previously unsuspected, and which differ *toto cælo* from all kinds of phenomena with which we were previously acquainted. Yet throughout this new continent of knowledge we find the axioms of materialism as unquestioned as ever. The electrons and the positively charged nuclei of atoms have their unchangeable laws, and illustrate afresh the inviolable relation of cause and effect. Nor, as we approach the very foundations of existence, do we see any more signs than elsewhere of a *purpose* at the basis of the universe. Harmony and order, certainly; that arises from the universality of natural law; it is the same kind of harmony and order that prevails in the larger material masses of the Universe. Even if the Universe is running down to a final doom of extinction, there is no suggestion of purpose there. A clock also runs down, but not by previous intention — not for what we understand by a purpose. Finally,

---

[3] From *Modern Science and Materialism*, by Hugh Eliot. Reprinted by permission of the publishers, Longmans, Green & Co.

in this new field of discovery, there is no place for any kind of spiritual agency. We know at length what is the basis of matter: it is not spirit, it is energy, a factor exclusively objective in character, and residing on the materialistic, not on the spiritualistic plane.... Furthermore, one thing is certain. Whatever matter may ultimately be resolved into, it certainly cannot be resolved into spirit. The wildest speculator in science has never suggested *that* possibility.[4]

Following, then, the methods and the principles of scientific investigation, the modern philosopher can arrive at nothing in the universe aside from man that appears to have human interests and human aspirations at heart. In all the reaches of our telescopes and our microscopes there is nowhere discoverable the slightest trace of anything like man, any Friend behind phenomena, any God who cares, any principle that guarantees man success in his struggles and endeavors. So far as the eye of science can see, man is alone, absolutely alone, in a universe in which his very appearance is a kind of cosmic accident. How, then, if this be the very truth, has it come about that he has always, to the present day, in some form or other felt himself at home in his universe, felt that he was the child of the watchful forces of nature, the Son of God whom the Father lovingly cared for? To even this question the scientist has a devastating answer. Turn to the anthropologist, and he will calmly reply:

It is very important in this matter to realize that the so-called belief is not really an intellectual judgment so much as a craving of the whole nature. It is only of late years that psychologists have begun to realize the enormous dominion of those forces in man of which he is normally unconscious. We cannot escape as easily as these brave men dreamed from the grip of the blind powers beneath the threshold. Indeed, as I see philosophy after philosophy falling into this unproven belief in the Friend behind phenomena, as I find that I myself cannot, except for a moment and by an effort, refrain from making the same assumption, it seems to me that perhaps here too we are under the spell of a very old ineradicable instinct. We are gregarious animals; our ancestors have been such for countless ages. We cannot help looking out upon the world as gregarious animals do; we see it in terms of humanity and fellowship. Students of animals under domestication have shown us how the habits of a gregarious creature, taken away from his kind, are shaped in a thousand details by reference to the lost pack which is no longer there — the pack which a dog tries to smell his way back to all the time he is out walking, the pack he calls to for help when

---

[4] From *Modern Science and Materialism*, by Hugh Eliot. Reprinted by permission of the publishers, Longmans, Green & Co.

danger threatens. It is a strange and touching thing, this eternal hunger of the gregarious animal for the herd of friends who are not there. And it may be, it may very possibly be, that, in the matter of this Friend behind phenomena, our own yearning and our own almost ineradicable instinctive conviction, since they are certainly not founded on either reason or observation, are in origin the groping of a lonely-souled gregarious animal to find its herd or its herd-leader in the great spaces beyond the stars.[5]

The Friend is gone, and man is alone in a cold and alien universe.

That is the sting of it, that in the vast driftings of the cosmic weather, though many a jewelled shore appears, and many an enchanted cloud-bank floats away, long lingering ere it be dissolved — even as our world now lingers, for our joy — yet when these transient products are gone, nothing, absolutely *nothing* remains, to represent those particular qualities, those elements of preciousness which they may have enshrined. Dead and gone are they, gone utterly from the very sphere and room of being. Without an echo; without a memory; without an influence on aught that may come after, to make it care for similar ideals. This utter final wreck and tragedy is of the essence of scientific materialism as at present understood. The lower and not the higher forces are the eternal forces, or the last surviving forces within the only cycle of evolution which we can definitely see.[6]

No scientist, of course, can claim that he has *proved* that this is the whole story, and that the vast edifice man has built for his spirit, with its foundations of Godhead, its walls of a loving Providence, and its airy pinnacles of human immortality, may not dwell somewhere beyond the reach of his instruments. On the other side of the moon, indeed, there may stand the Heavenly City with its golden gates and pearly walls and alabaster turrets; and there the saints may be gathered in glory, chanting never-ending hymns to the Eternal Father upon his throne. But, so far as the scientist can discern, there is not one shred of evidence that it is aught but a dream-castle in the clouds; and his knowledge of the mythopœic faculty in man is such as to make him strongly suspect that such is indeed the case. If man continues to believe to-day in what his forbears trusted, it is by faith, and by faith alone, that he can justify himself. And by the side of the solid edifice of scientific verity, such faith seems, and cannot but seem, a slender reed upon which to rest such momentous

---

[5] From *The Stoic Philosophy*, by Gilbert Murray. Reprinted by permission of the publishers, G. P. Putnam's Sons of New York and London.

hopes. The more man actually learns of himself and his universe, the less prone he is to trust to such an unaided faith. If he have faith, it is a faith *quand même*, a faith that can remove mountains, a faith stronger than knowledge, stronger than reason, strong as life itself.

By the middle of the last century this seemed so clear to men that they were convinced that they must take it as a fundamental, an irreducible datum. Only on such a firm foundation could they build a habitation for the human spirit; only in a world set in such terms could they hope to achieve whatever measure of the good life was destined to fall to their lot. For those not willing to rest in traditional beliefs, for those who felt that human reason and human intelligence must work out its own destiny and salvation, the great problem was presented, what shall man do about it? What possibilities does such a world offer? How may a good life be led in such a world? Three general types of answer may be distinguished; together they make up the body of modern philosophies. When this realization came like a cold shock to men, the first reaction was one of disillusionment and despair. Mindful of their past hopes, they either lamented their lost dreams in lugubrious measures, or took refuge in the ivory tower of art, where for a while at least the soul might dwell amidst beauty; or, refusing to recognize the picture as more than partially and inadequately true, they retreated to a perfection elsewhere, and in some structure of philosophic idealism found consolation for the emptiness of the world of science. Stronger souls, unable still to envisage humanity as utterly alone in the wind-swept wastes of the universe, turned with pathetic eagerness to the one great process and purpose that science seemed to leave in the world. For them, evolution took the place of Providence; and, reflecting that after all man has been the outcome of the cosmic forces, they sought in the very worship and deification of evolution, in the vigorous acceptance of and rejoicing in the ends of nature, a worthy ideal for human life, and a guarantee that, if man but made his own the ends of cosmic power, he could still triumph with the course of nature. A third group, from the generation that had no longer cherished the fond hopes of the past, and hence had never experienced disillusionment, looked about itself upon the world depicted by science, and saw it neither as an alien world, nor as a great process to be glorified as realizing ideals to which man must adhere; but rather as the natural scene of human life and human striving, a dwelling-place in which man can accomplish his human purposes and bend the materials that are given him to his own will. The various reactions to the alien world — complete pessimism, Promethean defiance of nature, retreat to an idealistic faith behind and beyond the world of science; — the evolutionary faiths in the cosmic process, Progress, Creative Evolution, Pragmatism, the revaluation of values; and a Greek or a Baconian naturalism — these are the main philosophies of the modern world, together with such philosophies as have persisted, like Thomism, relatively untouched by the scientific viewpoint. The mass of mankind, uneasy but unwilling to follow out any viewpoint to its logical conclusion, have more or less successfully adopted portions of some or all these philosophies, combining them with whatever of the traditional beliefs it still seemed possible to adhere to. But every man, whatever his intellectual beliefs, who lives in the modern world, has been influenced by one fundamental notion: whatever may be man's ultimate destiny, his life is to be lived and his salvation worked out in this life and this world, and with the materials it places at his disposal. All modern philosophies are this-worldly, rather than other-worldly; they are humanistic in their emphasis, and social in their ideals.

Disillusionment — Pessimism in the Face of the Alien World

Many were the attitudes bred of the initial disillusionment with the mechanistic world of science, and the conviction that man's true interests and ideals find no place or scope in the universe. There was, first of all, a wave of pessimism that swept over tender souls. Men stood, like Matthew Arnold, upon the shore of the sea of faith, that

> Was once, too, at the full, and round earth's shore
> Lay like the folds of a bright girdle furled.
> But now I only hear
> Its melancholy, long, withdrawing roar,
> Retreating, to the breath
> Of the night-wind, down the vast edges drear
> And naked shingles of the world.[7]

Like Tennyson, they paced the Dover cliffs in agony of mind over the question of a future existence, crying aloud, "If there is no immortality, I shall hurl myself into the sea!" The long vacillation of the laureate's mind, so irritating to the modern reader, expressed the very essence of the struggle through which many passed, as traditional beliefs first crumbled.

> How sweet to have a common faith!
> To hold a common scorn of death!
> Thrice happy state again to be
> The trustful infant on the knee.
> O weary life! O weary death!
> O spirit and heart made desolate!
> O damned vacillating state! [8]

The world with Tennyson passed through the long and bitter travail of *In Memoriam:*

> O, yet we trust that somehow good
> Will be the final goal of ill,
> To pangs of nature, sins of will,
> Defects of doubt, and taints of blood. . . .
> Behold, we know not anything;
> I can but trust that good shall fall
> At last — far off — at last, to all,
> And every winter change to spring.
> So runs my dream; but what am I?
> An infant crying in the night;
> An infant crying for the light,
> And with no language but a cry.
> Are God and Nature then at strife,
> That Nature lends such evil dreams?
> So careful of the type she seems,
> So careless of the single life. . . .
> I falter where I firmly trod,
> And falling with my weight of cares
> Upon the great world's altar-stairs,
> That slope thro' darkness up to God,
> I stretch lame hands of faith, and grope
> And gather dust and chaff, and call
> To what I feel is Lord of all,
> And faintly trust the larger hope. [9]

Evolution seemed to men at first a dull despair:

> Not only cunning casts in clay:
> Let Science prove we are, and then
> What matters science unto men,
> At least to me? I would not stay.

> Let him, the wiser man who springs
> Hereafter, up from childhood shape
> His actions like the greater ape,
> But I was *born* to other things.[10]

Clough is the very epitome of this nineteenth-century disillusionment:

> To spend uncounted years of pain,
> Again, again, and yet again,
> In working out, in heart and brain
>   The problem of our being here;
> To gather facts from far and near,
> Upon the mind to hold them clear,
> And, knowing more may yet appear,
> Unto one's latest breath to fear,
> The premature result to draw —
> Is this the object, end, and law,
>   And purpose of our being here?[11]

Only a despairing Stoicism kept such minds in the struggle:

> It fortifies my soul to know
> That, though I perish, Truth is so.
>
> Say not the struggle naught availeth,
>   The labor and the wounds are vain,
> The enemy faints not, nor faileth,
>   And as things have been they remain.
> If hopes were dupes, fears may be liars;
>   It may be, in yon smoke concealed,
> Your comrades chase e'en now the fliers,
>   And, but for you, possess the field.[12]

In Thomson's *City of Dreadful Night* is perhaps the deepest expression of this pessimism in the face of the alien world:

> The chance was never offered me before;
> For me the infinite Past is blank and dumb:
> This chance recurreth never, nevermore;
> Blank, blank for me the infinite To-come.
> And this sole chance was frustrate from my birth,
> A mockery, a delusion: and my breath
> Of noble human life upon this earth
> So racks me that I sigh for senseless death.[13]

The philosophic expression of this pessimism in the face of the utter aimlessness of nature and the futility of human striving is to be found in Schopenhauer. For him, the essence of Nature and of life alike is a dumb, blind, restless activity, an utterly irrational force whose gropings have produced the world and all that lives therein. This cosmic force — too meaningless, indeed, to merit the name of "process" — Schopenhauer called "Will," and saw in its very nature the necessary and inevitable defeat of all human striving after happiness.

All Will springs from need, that is, from lack, that is, from suffering. Fulfillment puts an end to this; but for every wish that is fulfilled there are at least ten denied. Furthermore, craving lasts long, demands are infinite; fulfillment is short and finite. But finite satisfaction itself is only apparent: one wish fulfilled gives way to another: the one is a recognized, the other a still unrealized error. Lasting satisfaction that will not vanish no wished-for object of the Will can give: it is like the alms thrown to the beggar, that sustain life to-day only to increase his torture to-morrow.... Therefore, so long as our minds are filled with Will, so long as we are the prey of the press of desires with their unceasing hopes and fears, so long as we are the subjects of Will, we shall never find lasting happiness nor peace. Whether we pursue or flee, whether we fear impurity or strive for enjoyment, is in essence the same: care for the everlasting demands of the Will, in whatever form the same, fills and endlessly moves the mind; but without peace there can be no true well-being. Thus the subject of the Will lies ever bound to the revolving wheel of Ixion, fills forever the sieve of the Danaïds, is the ever thirsty Tantalus.... The inner being of nature is a striving without rest and without respite, a willing and a striving that may well be compared to an unquenchable thirst. But since the basis of all willing is need, deficiency, and thus pain, the nature of brute and man alike is originally and of its very essence subject to pain. If on the other hand it is deprived of objects of desire through too easy satisfaction, such void and ennui fills the heart that existence becomes an unbearable burden to it. Thus life swings like a pendulum from pain to ennui, from ennui to pain.... Life is a sea full of rocks and whirlpools which man avoids with the greatest care and solicitude, although he knows that even if he succeeds in getting through with all his efforts and skill, he comes thus but the nearer at every tack to the greatest, the total, the inevitable shipwreck, death.... Thus, between desiring and attaining all human life flows on. The wish is in its nature pain, the attainment satiety: the end is an illusion and possession takes away charm. The wish, the need, presents itself under a new form, or when it does not, follows desolateness, emptiness, ennui against which the conflict is just as painful as against want. Every human being and his course of life is but another short dream of the endless spirit of nature, the persistent will to live; is only another fleeting form which nature carelessly sketches in its infinite pages, allows to remain for a time so short it vanishes into nothing, and then obliterates to make room for others.[14]

In science, in art, in devotion to his fellow sufferers, man can indeed find temporary solace in self-forgetfulness; but these oases are at best not worth the suffering involved in reaching them.

If we compare life to a course which we must unceasingly run — a path of glowing coals, with a few cool places here and there; then he who is entangled in illusion is consoled by the cool places, on which he now stands or which he sees near him, and sets out to run the course. But he who sees through the illusion and thus recognizes the whole for what it is, is no longer capable of such consolation; he sees himself at all places at once, and withdraws.[15]

The only remedy is by asceticism and mortification of the flesh and spirit to still the restless striving of the will.

If we turn our glances from our own needy and embarrassed condition to those who have overcome the world, then instead of the useless striving and effort, instead of the never satisfied and never-dying hope which constitutes the life of the man who wills and desires, we shall see that peace which passeth understanding, that perfect calm of the spirit, that deep rest, that inviolable confidence and serenity, the mere reflection of which in the countenance as Raphael or Correggio has represented it is an entire and certain gospel; only knowledge remains, the Will has vanished.... What remains after the abolition of the Will is for all those who are still full of desires certainly nothing; but to those in whom the will has denied itself, this world which is so real, with all its suns and milky ways — is nothing.[16]

Such a cosmic pessimism is familiar to English readers through the pages of Thomas Hardy.

> What of the Immanent Will and Its designs?
> IT works unconsciously, as heretofore,
> Eternal artistries in circumstance,
> Whose patterns, wrought by rapt æsthetic rote,
> Seem in themselves Its single listless aim,
> And not their consequence.
>   Still thus?   Still thus?
>   Ever unconscious!
>   An automatic sense
>   Unweeting why or whence?
> Be, then, the inevitable, as of old,
> Although that SO it be we dare not hold!
>
>   "O Immanence, That reasonest not
>   In putting forth all things begot,
>   Thou build'st Thy house in space — for what?

> O Loveless, Hateless! — past the sense
> Of kindly eyed benevolence,
> To what tune danceth this Immense?"
> "For one I cannot answer. But I know
> 'Tis handsome of our Pities so to sing
> The praises of the dreaming, dark, dumb Thing
> That turns the handle of this idle Show!
> As once a Greek asked I would fain ask too,
> Who knows if all the spectacle be true,
> Or an illusion of the gods (the Will
> To wit) some hocus-pocus to fulfill?"
> "Last as first the question rings,
> Of the Will's long travailings;
> Why the All-mover,
> Why the All-power
> Ever urges on and measures out the chordless chime of Things." [17]

Consolation Sought in Art and Beauty

To many for whom science thus seemed to establish the essential meaninglessness of all existence and all striving, the ivory tower of art furnished the only solace and refuge. Only in discerning beauty in the passing show, since all action is beyond our power, and we must do as the eternal laws of nature bid us, can man find that which will make his existence worth while and lift him above the brute. For many a despairing soul during the last few generations, it has seemed that man's hopes can rest only in the ideal world of beauty; and æstheticism has proved the natural way of life in the Alien World. Says Walter Pater, in the creed of his new Cyrenaicism:

> This at least of flamelike our life has, that it is but the concurrence, renewed from moment to moment, of forces parting sooner or later on their ways. . . . Every moment some form grows perfect in hand or face; some tone on the hills or the sea is choicer than the rest; some mood of passion or insight or intellectual excitement is irresistibly real and attractive to us — for that moment only. Not the fruit of experience, but experience itself, is the end. A counted number of pulses only is given to us of a variegated, dramatic life. How may we see in them all that is to be seen in them by the finest senses? How shall we pass most swiftly from point to point, and be present always at the focus where the greatest number of vital forces unite in their purest energy? To burn always with this hard, gem-like flame, to maintain this ecstasy, is success in life. . . . Not to discriminate every moment some passionate

---

[17] From *The Dynasts*, by Thomas Hardy. Reprinted by permission of the publishers, Macmillan & Co. Ltd., London.

attitude in those about us, and in the very brilliancy of their gifts some tragic dividing of forces on their ways, is, on this short day of frost and sun, to sleep before evening. With this sense of the splendor of our experience and of its awful brevity, gathering all we are into one desperate effort to see and touch, we shall hardly have time to make theories about the things we see and touch.... We are all *condamnés*, as Victor Hugo says: we are all under sentence of death but with a sort of indefinite reprieve: we have an interval, and then our place knows us no more. Some spend this interval in listlessness, some in high passions, the wisest, at least among "the children of this world," in art and song. For our one chance lies in expanding that interval, in getting as many pulsations as possible into the given time. Great passions may give us this quickened sense of life, ecstasy and sorrow of love, the various forms of enthusiastic activity, disinterested or otherwise, which come naturally to many of us. Only be sure it is passion — that it does yield you this fruit of a quickened, multiplied consciousness. Of such wisdom, the poetic passion, the desire of beauty, the love of art for its own sake, has most. For art comes to you proposing frankly to give nothing but the highest quality to your moments as they pass, and simply for those moments' sake.[18]

Ernest Renan in France preached the same gospel to the artists and the poets of his day.

The pearl-bearing oyster seems to me the best image of the universe and of the degree of consciousness we may suppose in things. At the bottom of the abyss, obscure germs create a mind singularly ill-served by organs, and yet prodigiously able to attain its ends. What we may call a disease of this little living cosmos brings about a secretion of ideal beauty, which men value as fine gold. The general life of the universe is, like that of the oyster, vague, obscure, singularly troubled, and hence sluggish. Suffering creates spirit, intellectual and moral motion. The disease of the world, if you will, in truth the pearl of the world, spirit, is the end, the final cause, the last and certainly the most brilliant result of the world in which we live.

The government of things here below belongs to forces quite other than science and reason; the thinker can claim but a very feeble right to direct the affairs of his planet, and, satisfied with his lot, he accepts his impotence without regret. A spectator in the universe, he knows that the world belongs to him only as an object of study; and even if he could reform it, he would perhaps find it so curious an object that he would lose all desire to do so.[19]

To-day the philosopher of this æsthetic naturalism is Santayana. For him, the mind and the soul of man and all their aspirations are but a lyric cry in a world of relentless and blind matter. Consciousness itself is like the rainbow playing on the fountain, a beautiful iridescence; but the drops rise and fall in mechanical order, with no heed to the wishes of the mind. The part of wisdom, then, is to play the critic, the connoisseur.

> Sweet are the days we wander with no hope
> Along life's labyrinthine trodden way,
> With no impatience at the steep's delay,
> Nor sorrow at the swift-descended slope.
> Why this inane curiosity to grope
> In the dim dust for gems' unmeaning ray?
> Why this proud piety, that dares to pray
> For a world wider than the heaven's cope?
> Farewell, my burden! No more will I bear
> The foolish load of my fond faith's despair,
> But trip the idle race with careless feet.
> The crown of olive let another wear;
> It is my crown to mock the runner's heat
> With gentle wonder and with laughter sweet.[20]

He who does not seek thus to discriminate life's golden moments, and enters whole-heartedly into the conflict, is but the rustic at the play.

> Our youth is like a rustic at the play,
> That cries aloud in simple-hearted fear,
> Curses the villain, shudders at the fray,
> And weeps before the maiden's wreathèd bier.
> Yet once familiar with the changeful show,
> He starts no longer at a brandished knife,
> But, his heart chastened at the sight of woe,
> Ponders the mirrored sorrows of his life.
> So tutored too, I watch the moving art
> Of all this magic and impassioned pain
> That tells the story of the human heart
> In a false instance, such as poets feign;
> I smile, and keep within the parchment furled
> That prompts the passions of this strutting world.[21]

This æstheticism, no matter how refined, is but the part of wisdom applied to the old cry, "Let us eat, drink, and be merry, for to-morrow we die." This Epicureanism, whether of the scholar and critic or of the humble daily toiler and the tireless business man, has entered deeply into the very spirit of to-day. In a sense, all our modern philosophies, from Socialism to the

---

[20] From *Sonnets*, by George Santayana. Reprinted by permission of the publishers, Charles Scribner's Sons.

[21] From *The Hermit of Carmel and Other Poems*, by George Santayana. Reprinted by permission of the publishers, Charles Scribner's Sons.

worship of business success, are but elaborations of the means for eating, drinking, and being merry in the most satisfactory way. Whether we acknowledge it or no, the modern age has been in fundamental agreement with the Omar who so captured the imaginations of the last generation.

> Come, fill the Cup, and in the fire of Spring
> Your Winter-garment of Repentance fling;
> The Bird of Time has but a little way
> To flutter — and the Bird is on the Wing.
> Then to the Lip of this poor earthen Urn
> I lean'd, the Secret of my Life to learn:
> And Lip to Lip it murmured — "While you live,
> Drink! — for, once dead, you never shall return."[22]

The highest reaches of such a wise and tolerant Epicureanism, that is yet alive to the pathos of human aspiration, are perhaps to be met in the pages of Anatole France. Life is meaningless for him, too.

It resembles a vast workshop of pottery where some one is fashioning all sorts of vases for unknown purposes and where many, broken in the mould, are rejected as vile potsherds without ever having been used. The others are employed only for absurd or disgusting uses. The pots are ourselves.[23] The mystery of destiny completely envelops us in its powerful shades, and it is necessary to avoid thinking altogether if one is not to resent the tragic absurdity of living. It is there, in the absolute ignorance of our reason for being, that the root of our sadness and of our disgust is to be found.[24] Ignorance is the necessary condition, I do not say of happiness, but of existence itself. If we knew all we could not support life an hour. The sentiments which make it sweet, or at least tolerable for us, spring from a lie and nourish themselves on illusions.[25]

Yet with wisdom even disillusionment is bearable.

Irony and Pity are two counselors: the one in smiling makes life amiable; the other in weeping makes life sacred. The Irony which I invoke is not cruel. It does not mock either love or beauty.... As believers who have attained to a high degree of moral beauty taste the joys of renunciation, so the sage, persuaded that all about us is only appearance and deceit, is intoxicated with this philosophic melancholy and loses himself in the delights of a calm despair.[26]

[23–26] From *The Garden of Epicurus*, by Anatole France. Reprinted by permission of the publishers, Dodd, Mead & Co.

Promethean Defiance of the Mechanistic World

Yet such renunciation and acceptance of the Alien World could not be the only reaction to the scientific cosmos. The will to live and struggle is too strongly rooted in human nature to be stilled forever by the contemplation of human beauty and human folly. More stalwart souls gritted their teeth and, by sheer pluck and courage, engaged in the Promethean task of defying the universe and all its works. If man's birth took place in the mud and dust, he nevertheless can build for himself a heaven; and even if he fails, it is enough that he has so nobly striven. Let us fight the good fight;

> 'Tis better to have fought and lost,
> Than never to have fought at all.[27]

For many a man, the essence of humanity seemed to be its self-imposed task of creating a worthy life, though all the forces of nature beat relentlessly upon man and his endeavors. In a famous essay, *Evolution and Ethics*, Huxley, the great popularizer of Darwinism, voiced this heroic creed. Civilization may be compared to a garden created by man in the midst of a forest wilderness. Only by constant care and foresight can man keep the garden from being over-run by the weeds which nature causes to spring to life, and from being killed by the infinite parasites which nature contains. Just so, all man's endeavor must be directed to counteracting the forces of nature, and turning them to his own purposes. Man's standards of good and evil have nothing in common with the course of nature; they are discoveries or achievements which he alone in all the universe has made.

Cosmic evolution may teach us how the good and the evil tendencies of man may have come about; but, in itself, it is incompetent to furnish any better reason why what we call good is preferable to what we call evil than we had before.[28]

Man may have come into being through the struggle for existence; the heart of civilization consists in eliminating that struggle between men.

The practice of that which is ethically best — what we call goodness or virtue — involves a course of conduct which, in all respects, is opposed to that which leads to success in the cosmic struggle for existence. In place of ruthless self-assertion, it demands self-restraint; in place of thrusting aside, or treading down, all competitors, it requires that the individual shall not merely respect, but shall help his fellows; its influence is directed, not so much to the survival of the fittest, as to the fitting of as many as possible to survive. It repudiates the gladiatorial theory of existence. . . . Laws and moral precepts are directed to the end of curbing the cosmic process, and reminding the individual of his duty to the community, to the protection and influence of which he owes, if not existence itself, at least the life of something better than a brutal savage. . . . Let us understand, once and for all, that the ethical progress of society depends, not on imitating the cosmic process, still less in running away from it, but in combating it. It may seem an audacious proposal thus to pit the microcosm against the macrocosm and to set man to subdue nature to his higher ends; but I venture to think that the great intellectual difference between ancient times and our own day lies in the solid foundation we have acquired for the hope that such an enterprise may meet with a certain measure of success. The history of civilization details the steps by which men have succeeded in building up an artificial world within the cosmos. Fragile reed as he may be, man, as Pascal says, is a thinking reed: there lies within him a fund of energy, operating intelligently and so far akin to that which pervades the universe, that it is competent to influence and modify the cosmic process. In virtue of his intelligence, the dwarf bends the Titan to his will.[29]

The same attitude is expressed by Matthew Arnold:

"In harmony with Nature?" Restless fool,
Who with such heat dost preach what were to thee,
When true, the last impossibility, —
To be like Nature strong, like Nature cool!
Know, man hath all which Nature hath, but *more*,
And in that *more* lie all his hopes of good.
Nature is cruel, man is sick of blood;
Nature is stubborn, man would fain adore;
Nature is fickle, man hath need of rest;
Nature forgives no debt, and fears no grave;
Man would be mild, and with safe conscience blest.
Man must begin, know this, where Nature ends;
Nature and man can never be fast friends.
Fool, if thou canst not pass her, rest her slave![30]

Most Promethean of all, Bertrand Russell confesses *A Free Man's Worship*.

The world of fact, after all, is not good; and in submitting our judgment to it, there is an element of slavishness from which the thoughts must be purged. For in all things it is well to exalt the dignity of Man, by freeing him as far as possible from the tyranny of non-human Power. When we have realized that Power is largely bad, that man, with his knowledge of good and evil, is but a helpless atom in a world which has no such knowledge, the choice is again presented to us: Shall we worship Force, or shall we worship Goodness? Shall our God exist and be evil, or shall he be recognized as the creation of our own conscience?

The life of Man, viewed outwardly, is but a small thing in comparison with the forces of Nature. The slave is doomed to worship Time and Fate and Death, because they are greater than anything he finds in himself, and because all his thoughts are of things which they devour. But, great as they are, to think of them greatly, to feel their passionless splendor, is greater still. And such thoughts make us free men: we no longer bow before the inevitable in Oriental subjection, but we absorb it, and make it a part of ourselves. To abandon the struggle for private happiness, to expel all eagerness of temporary desire, to burn with passion for eternal things — this is emancipation, and this is the free man's worship. And this liberation is effected by a contemplation of Fate; for Fate itself is subdued by the mind which leaves nothing to be purged by the purifying fire of Time. . . .

Brief and powerless is Man's life; on him and all his race the slow, sure doom falls pitiless and dark. Blind to good and evil, reckless of destruction, omnipotent matter rolls on its relentless way; for Man, condemned to-day to lose his dearest, to-morrow himself to pass through the gate of darkness, it remains only to cherish, ere yet the blow falls, the lofty thoughts that ennoble his little day; disdaining the coward terrors of the slave of Fate, to worship at the shrine that his own hands have built; undismayed by the empire of chance, to preserve a mind free from the wanton tyranny that rules his outward life; proudly defiant of the irresistible forces that tolerate, for a moment, his knowledge and his condemnation, to sustain alone, a weary but unyielding Atlas, the world that his own ideals have fashioned despite the trampling march of unconscious power.[31]

Escape from the Alien World into Philosophic Idealism

All such men accepted the scientific picture of the Alien World as in the main true; but many were not prepared to abandon so easily their traditional beliefs and hopes. They turned to those theories that had been developed by the romanticists to get behind Newtonian science, discredit its rational scientific method, and substitute some other principles for the interpretation of the reality of the world. Various systems of philosophical idealism grew greatly in popularity during the century: they seemed the sole intellectual weapon whereby to prove that

---

[31] From *A Free Man's Worship*, by Bertrand Russell. Reprinted by permission of the publishers, Longmans, Green & Co.

science does not tell the whole story, and that somewhere, somehow, the world is like man, is working for what man is working for and cares for the objects of his care. Men unwilling to give up what was dear to them, yet also unwilling to appeal to blind faith or authority, eagerly grasped at idealism as a prop and a stay. The idealist had the advantage that, like Kant, he could freely admit that everything the scientist discovers is true in its own realm, while at the same time he possessed in addition a method of proving that that world of science is a mere show world, and that behind it, underneath it, permeating it, lies the real world, a very different kind of thing. The real world is not mechanical, not a blind and aimless process; it is spiritual and moral, and guarantees the outcome of man's endeavors. This was to many a man a very comforting doctrine; and philosophy, indeed, became so overwhelmingly idealistic in color that to many it means, to the present day, a way of proving God, freedom, and immortality in the face of negative scientific evidence. Such idealism was, on the whole, as we have pointed out in connection with the romantic movement, a conservative force, both religiously and socially: it sought to prove that there really is a God, though science cannot find him, and that society really is serving the highest ends, although it certainly does not seem to. In the last years of the century, various types of neo-Kantianism dominated German thought, and a modified form of Hegelianism served in England as the orthodox religious and social apologetic; while in this country idealism was taught in all the colleges and theological seminaries, and became what has been called "the genteel tradition in American philosophy."

As has been pointed out, when once faith in scientific methods has been displaced by faith in either speculative reason, uncontrolled by reference to the world of experience, or by faith in pure faith alone, such speculative reason and such faith will be apt to reach any conclusions desired. Hence idealism, while agreeing in disregarding science as "merely empirical," or "merely relative and phenomenal," has found the real world to be a great many different things. Men with a fierce passion for logic and consistency, like F. H. Bradley, relentlessly pursued it with dialectic until it vanished, through a maze of logical contradictions, into thin air, leaving only the pale ghost of the Absolute endlessly crooning, "In me all things are made perfect,

In me it is seen how all evil is necessary for my good." Others found the real world a more pleasant and substantial place, somewhat like the last act of a play in which everything is explained and accounted for, the hero and heroine reunited after hardships, and the villain turns out to be no villain at all, but only the hero's father trying to develop his character through opposition. More technically, this is stated "the reality known in experience is not something that merely is or possesses bare existence, but, as existing concretely, it forms part of a permanent system of relations and values." [32]

Carlyle and Emerson popularized these idealistic views during the last century. "Then sawest thou that this fair Universe," rhapsodized Carlyle, "were it in the meanest province thereof, is in very deed the star-domed City of God: that through every star, through every grass-blade, and most through every Living Soul, the glory of a present God still beams. But Nature, which is the Time-Vesture of God, and reveals Him to the wise, hides Him from the foolish." [33] "We live in succession," wrote the confident Emerson, "in division, in parts, in particles. Meantime within man is the soul of the whole; the wise silence; the universal beauty, to which every part and particle is equally related; the eternal ONE. And this deep power in which we exist and whose beatitude is all accessible to us, is not only self-sufficing and perfect in every hour, but the act of seeing and the thing seen, the seer and the spectacle, the subject and the object, are one. We see the world piece by piece, as the sun, the moon, the animal, the tree; but the whole, of which these are the shining parts, is the soul." [34]

Here is an absolute optimism to confront the pessimism of the disillusioned; and it numbered its many adherents and does today. The universe is not only divine, it is perfect here and now, could we but understand it aright.

On the view here accepted, finiteness, pain, and evil are essential features of Reality, and belong to an aspect of it which leaves its marks even on perfection.... If we knew everything and could feel everything we should see and feel what finiteness, pain and evil mean, and how they play a part in perfection itself.[35]

Applied to a social ideal, this means, we should understand how this is the best of all possible worlds.

The social process is greater than any one's formula; and what we have to think of is how causation is working, and how we can throw ourselves into it in union with the real forces of the day. . . . We shall, as a great writer has said, remember "What the world is, and what we are." We shall try to understand it, and coöperate with it, rather than to remould it. We shall seek for what is deepest in it, knowing we shall find there a power which will respond to what is deepest in ourselves. And by taking these things as our guide and criterion, we shall always be working in a direction which will at once be practicable and good.[36]

To many, such wholesale acceptance of evil as a necessary and therefore justified part of perfection seems an even greater violation of the moral conscience than the somewhat similar doctrine, flourishing in Christian Science and similar cults, that evil is non-existent.

In justice to such idealism, however, it should be pointed out that it is not necessarily a wholesale justification of existence. To Fichte, reality was the moral will struggling to overcome evil, and man's salvation consisted in flinging himself wholeheartedly into the never-ending fight. In our own day Josiah Royce, with the deep moral sense of his Puritan forbears, combined faith in a spiritual principle in the universe with a profound realization of finite evils.

A genuine synthesis of optimism and its opposing pessimism, a spiritual idealism that does not deny the reality and the gravity of evil, a religion that looks forward to the day of the Lord as to something very great and therefore very serious, and that accepts life as something valuable enough to be tragic — that is what we need. . . . If I find in myself an evil impulse, I find what in itself considered is, indeed, something hateful, lamentable, possibly horrible, something which regarded for itself can apparently form no part of a good order. If I tolerate the impulse, if I declare it to be just the nettle of sin, if I call its evil illusory, then my moral optimism is indeed open to condemnation. But suppose I resist the evil impulse, hate it, hold it down, overcome it, then, in this moment of hating and condemning it, I make it a part of my larger moral goodness. The justification of the existence of my evil impulse comes just at the instant when I hate and condemn it. Condemning and conquering the evil will makes it part of a good will. . . . There are elements in a good world which, individually regarded, ought not to be there, which are in themselves hateful, regrettable, the just object of wrath. Yet they become part of the world of the good will just in so far as they are in fact hated, condemned, subdued, overcome. The good world is not innocent. It does not ignore evil; it possesses and still conquers evil.[37]

Yet such idealism is by no means so widely held as it was a generation ago. The men who first experienced the plunge into the chill Alien World have gone; their successors no longer feel that they have to justify a cherished faith against science. Not behind, but in this scientific world of naturalism, are to be found our present-day faiths. This generation has grown up in the world of evolution, and it feels at home there; it can carry on its enterprises without fleeing for refuge to another realm. Yet idealism emphasized things of great value; and its position, if honestly followed out without religious bias and in the scientific spirit, leads directly to a naturalistic metaphysics. It found the world intelligible once more, and possessed of a logical structure accessible to mind; from "objective idealism" to present-day logical and functional realisms was an easy step. And it maintained also the reality and objectivity of values; sensitivity to values was always idealism's strongest point. All these positions are basic in our enlarged naturalisms.

Glorification of the Growing World

In these various ways men sought to adjust themselves to the vision of the Alien World. But not to all men did it come as a nightmare: to many it seemed a veritable creed of hope and promise. The disillusioned were disheartened because nature no longer offered them what they demanded; the stronger souls were willing to take what it did offer and make it their own. If the forces of nature are otherwise than has been thought, if the cosmic processes are working for other than traditional ends, then we must revise our ideals and bring them into harmony with the forces and possibilities of nature. Men in the past have worshiped the Creator and Sustainer of the Universe in ignorance of his true ends; these have at last been discovered, and man can take his proper place in the van of evolution, rather than continue to oppose his petty ideas to the cosmic sweep of things.

Faith in the Inevitability of Progress

Those liberals whose faith in Progress was unlimited naturally saw in Evolution a cosmic guarantee of human perfectibility. A few, like Gladstone, remained blind; others, like Tennyson, after many a struggle accepted it, and sang:

> One God, one law, one element,
> And one far-off divine event,
> To which the whole creation moves.[38]

Still others, like Spencer, found their earlier faith in progress but confirmed and strengthened by Darwin's discoveries. Spencer believed that human pleasure is the ultimately worth while thing in life, and that a society representing a maximum of life and development for each one of its members will contain the greatest amount of pleasure — that is, a society organized upon free competition and *laisser-faire* and individual initiative. To him, evolution meant that the whole process of the universe is working to achieve just such a society. The future evolution of society, in accordance with the great cosmic law of evolution, will be toward a more and more complete adaptation of human institutions to the natural and biological environment of man; and of every man's pleasure to every other's.

> From the laws of life it must be concluded that unceasing social discipline will so mould human nature, that eventually sympathetic pleasures will be spontaneously pursued to the fullest extent advantageous to each and all. The scope for altruistic activities will not exceed the desire for altruistic satisfactions.... An ideal social being may be conceived as so constituted that his spontaneous activities are congruous with the conditions imposed by the social environment formed by other such beings.[39]

Such a society will be completely evolved, and, *ipso facto*, perfect.

Spencer welcomed the cosmic process because he read it as bringing about the individualistic society he wanted; Karl Marx approved of it for a similar reason. But Marx read the cosmic law somewhat differently from Spencer: for him society was evolving, not toward individualism, but toward collectivism and socialism. Orthodox or "scientific" socialism, springing from Marx, has glorified the mechanistic universe and evolution because it believed that it was bringing about inevitably the day of revolution, when the workers should capture the instruments of production and administer them for their own interests. Marx, whose conception of evolution was materialistic and Hegelian, rather than biological, saw the process as the successive struggle of classes for dominance and control, and closed his outline of past social development with the dogmatic hope:

> The development of modern industry cuts from under its feet the

very foundation on which the bourgeoisie produces and appropriates products. What the bourgeoisie therefore produces, above all, are its own grave-diggers. Its fall and the victory of the proletariat are equally inevitable.[40]

The significance of the fact that both the individualist Spencer and the collectivist Marx read the evolutionary process as favoring their respective ideals, is the light it sheds on the way in which men could convince themselves that the growing world of mechanism was not bad but good, and that belief in it led not to despair but rather to infinite hope.

Confidence in Creative Evolution

After a generation, however, men came to see that acceptance of the world of science and approbation of its ends involved, not identifying those ends with preconceived notions of their own, but seeking new aims and goals by a further analysis of the process itself. Various thinkers have come to the conclusion that the only end actually revealed in the course of nature is change and growth itself, and they have therefore made of growth their own ideal. The world is a process of development, a continual growth towards diversification and variety; hence richness of life, multiplication of its forms and possibilities, is both the law of nature and the goal of man. Life is its own excuse for being, and a world that produces the rich pageantry we see about us and promises an even more variegated future to human society, must be inherently good. Nature is ever producing novelty and variety; evolution, in a word, is creative, and man, standing at the summit, possesses in his intelligence the most creative factor in the world. Let him then live, act, produce, create; in devoting himself to action for action's sake and growth that there may be more growth, he will be at once most natural, most human, and most divine.

Such a philosophy well accords with the restless and unceasing activity of modern industrial society; it idealizes just that aspect of the present Western world that sets it off most from the Middle Ages and from the ancient civilizations of the East. In countless forms men seek productivity, energy, expansion, growth; the very word "business" which best characterizes our social ideal reveals what it at bottom is. We desire above all to be busy, and for the most part we rarely question the ends of our activity; one form of business will lead to another, and so on into the glorious future. In a sense all the great spiritual movements in Western history, like the Renaissance and Romanticism, have embodied some form of this restless ever-striving Faust-spirit, so different from the finitude of Greece and the very definite aspirations of the Middle Ages. Modern literature is full of this note. Freedom, the joy of life, self-expression and self-development, fullness of life, progress — these are the dominant notes of our age. And the idea of evolution has powerfully reinforced this our native bent. Peer Gynt in his exuberance cries:

> This is life! Every limb grows as strong as a bear's.
> (Strikes out with his arms and leaps in the air.)
> To crush, overturn, stem the rush of the foss!
> To strike! Wrench the fir-tree right up by the root!
> This is life! This both hardens and lifts one high![41]

The superabundance and fecundity of life, as an adequate ideal in itself, has been well stated by the poet of evolution, Guyau:

Life has two faces: by the one it is nutrition and assimilation, by the other production and fecundity. The more it acquires, the more it must give: this is its law.... Life, like the flame, is preserved only by giving of its substance. And this is true of the intelligence no less than of the body; it is as impossible to restrict the intelligence to itself as the flame: it is made to give light. The same force of expansion is in our emotions: we must share our joy, we must share our sorrow.... It is our nature to be social; we are not sufficient for ourselves, we have more tears than we need for our own sorrows, more joy in reserve than our own happiness justifies. We must go out to others, multiply ourselves by the communion of thought and feeling.... Life is fecundity, and reciprocally fecundity is life at its fullest, it is true existence. There is a certain generosity inseparable from existence, without which we die, we dry up inside. We must flower; morality, disinterestedness, is the flower of human life.... The ideal does not indeed oppose the world, but simply surpasses it: it is at bottom identical with our thought itself which, while springing out of nature, goes before it, foreseeing and preparing perpetual progress. The real and ideal are reconciled in *life;* for life, as a whole, both is and becomes. Whoever says life, says *evolution.*[42]

In another form this ideal of growth has been adopted by John Dewey and the instrumentalists.

Growth is regarded as *having* an end, instead of *being* an end.... In reality there is nothing to which growth is relative save more growth.... In any social group whatever, even in a gang of thieves, we find some interest held in common, and we find a certain amount of interaction and coöperative intercourse with other groups. From these two traits we derive our standard. How numerous and varied are the interests which are consciously shared? How full and free is the interplay with other forms of association? ... The second means not only freer interaction between social groups but change in social habit — its continuous readjustment through meeting the new situations produced by varied intercourse.... These more numerous and more varied points of contact denote a greater diversity of stimuli to which an individual has to respond; they consequently put a premium on variation in his action. They secure a liberation of powers which remain suppressed as long as the incitations to action are partial.[43]

In the words of J. H. Tufts,

Moral progress involves both the formation of better ideals and the adoption of such ideals as actual standards and guides of life. If our view is correct we can construct better ideals neither by logical deduction nor solely by insight into the nature of things — if by this we mean things as they are. We must rather take as our starting-point the conviction that the moral life is a process involving physical life, social intercourse, measuring and constructive intelligence. We shall endeavor to further each of these factors with the conviction that thus we are most likely to reconstruct our standards and find a fuller good.[44]

But the most complete expression of this ideal of growth for growth's sake is the philosophy of Creative Evolution, in which Bergson has taken the basic idea of modern science and from it created a new romanticism. The world itself is a process of infinite growth in time; evolution is not a mere mechanical process, but life itself, a cosmic life that embraces all. It is forever giving rise to that which is supremely good, because supremely spontaneous, supremely alive and growing.

Let us imagine a vessel full of steam at a high pressure, and here and there in its sides a crack through which the steam is escaping in a jet. The steam thrown into the air is nearly all condensed into little drops which fall back, and this condensation and this fall represent simply the loss of something, an interruption, a deficit. But a small part of the jet of steam subsists, uncondensed, for some seconds; it is making an effort to raise the drops which are falling; it succeeds at most in retarding their fall. So, from an immense reservoir of life, jets must be gushing out unceasingly, of which each, falling back, is a world. The evolution of living species within this world represents what subsists of the primitive direction of the original jet, and of an impulsion which

---

[43] From *Democracy and Education*, by John Dewey. Copyright, 1916, by The Macmillan Co. Reprinted by permission.

continues itself in a direction the inverse of materiality.... There is a center from which worlds shoot out like rockets in a fire-works display — provided, however, that I do not present this center as a *thing*, but as a continuity of shooting-out. God thus defined, has nothing of the already made; he is unceasing life, action, freedom. Creation, so conceived, is not a mystery; we experience it in ourselves when we act freely.... From our point of view, life appears in its entirety as an immense wave which, starting from a center, spreads outwards, and which on almost the whole of its circumference is stopped and converted into oscillation: at one single point the obstacle has been forced, the impulsion has passed freely. It is this freedom that the human form registers. Everywhere but in man, consciousness has had to come to a stand; in man alone it has kept on its way. Man, then, continues the vital movement indefinitely, although he does not draw along with him all that life carries in itself....

On flows the current, running through human generations, subdividing itself into individuals. This subdivision was vaguely indicated in it, but could not have been made clear without matter. Thus souls are continually being created, which, nevertheless, in a certain sense preexisted. They are nothing else than the little rills into which the great river of life divides itself, flowing through the body of humanity. Such a doctrine gives us more power to act and to live. For, with it, we feel ourselves no longer isolated in humanity, humanity no longer seems isolated in the nature that it dominates. As the smallest grain of dust is bound up with our entire solar system, drawn along with it in that undivided movement of descent which is materiality itself, so all organisms, from the humblest to the highest, from the first origins of life to the time in which we are, and in all places as in all times, do but evidence a single impulsion, the inverse of the movement of matter, and in itself indivisible. All the living hold together, and all yield to the same tremendous push. The animal takes its stand on the plant, man bestrides animality and the whole of humanity, in space and in time, is one immense army galloping beside and before and behind each of us in an overwhelming charge able to beat down every resistance, and clear the most formidable obstacles, perhaps even death.[45]

A New Evolutionary Ethics — Worship of the Future

One great thinker of the last generation, really assimilating the new conception of evolution, and not content with reading into its goal the traditional ideals of the past, or of taking from it merely the vague and formless aim of growth and development, that so easily lends itself to a myriad of interpretations as the habit-ridden mind sees growth as growth towards what it instinctively feels to be good, Friedrich Nietzsche, realized that

[45] From *Creative Evolution* by Henri Bergson. Reprinted by permission of the publishers, Henry Holt & Co.

if we take evolution seriously as furnishing a moral standard for life, we must develop a whole new set of specific ideals and values. The traditional aims inherited from Christendom cannot endure unchanged in the growing world of to-day. We must advance beyond our past standards of good and evil, and set about a complete revaluation of all values. What was good in the world in which Providence ruled for the salvation of every human soul, can, to the emancipated mind that sees the bitter travail of evolution, the fierce struggle to bring about higher types of life, no longer appeal as good at all. Our ideals must be adjusted to the newly revealed conditions of their fulfillment; and if we are to bring about upon this earth a nobler race of men and a society more able to cope with the forces of nature and bring a worth-while life to pass, we must abandon the meek and docile codes of the past, with their glorification of submission and weakness. We must labor and fight for the future, we must be strong, and, if need be, ruthless, lest the other forces in the cosmic combat gain the day. We cannot rest in the idle dream that mere change, mere novelty, mere submission to the play of instinct, will of itself automatically produce a noble humanity. That task involves iron discipline and stern self-direction, else will man never rise to be a God, but instead will sink back to the dull monotonous level of the ant and the bee; we must adapt ourselves, not, like those blind insects, to our present environment, but to the conditions of further success and power over nature.

Almost alone in his age, Nietzsche abandoned, with the Christian scheme of the universe, the Christian scheme of human life as well. Such a morality is well enough for slaves, content to live for the present alone; but for the free man who has resolved that the future shall surpass the present, only the utmost of assertion against the weak, only the strong self-reliant will to power, will avail to lift man to new heights of nobility. Hence Nietzsche sought to pit himself against the whole moral tradition of the Western world, and to become, in the truest sense, the Anti-Christ. Naturally he was misunderstood; naturally his fiery idealism and devotion to the future seemed to his contemporaries a mere justification of brutality, rather than the prerequisite of future divinity. Yet his ideals are sufficiently in accord with the underlying spirit of the modern age, however it may conceal itself under lip-service to the Christian virtues and their modern democratic embodiment, to be fraught with great significance.

Nietzsche started with the philosophy of Schopenhauer, nor was he ever able to emancipate himself from that thinker's gloomy picture of nature and life. To the end, the world for him was a scene of unceasing struggle, of the never-ending assertion of the will to live. His originality lay in his refusal to flee in disgust from that struggle, in his brave conviction that in the struggle itself must be found the enduring values for the present and the hope of loftier things to come. "I preach the Superman," he proclaimed; and the Superman will come, not through any craven renunciation of the fight, but through throwing oneself with zest into the struggle itself. The army of humanity must steel itself, grasp sword and buckler, and disregarding the wails of the wounded and the cries of the disheartened, march onward into the glorious future. Its virtues must be those of the fighter, the hero; tender compassion and humility and love will never win the promised land. Not to the past, not to the present, but to the future we must give whole-souled devotion, be the sacrifice what it will. Life for the pessimist is meaningless, the sooner over the better; for the optimist, whose ideal is guaranteed, it is also without essential significance. For Nietzsche, it is hard, it is cruel, it is tragic; but in its very tragedy he found supreme joy. To fight, to lose, perhaps, against great odds, to win for our children; that is the lesson of Nature and Nature's processes.

One who like me [he writes] has long busied himself with curious interest in thinking out pessimism to its bitter end, has probably in this very pursuit — without precisely having willed it — turned his eyes toward the opposite ideal: toward the ideal of the most domineering, the most living, the most aggressive of men, toward him who has not merely reconciled and adjusted himself to things as they are and have been; but who wants more of them, just as they are and have been — more in all eternity, crying insatiably *da capo* not to his own life only, but to the whole scene and all the play.[46]

If life is tragic, it at least has a human goal.

I bring you a goal [cries his mouthpiece Zarathustra]. I preach to you the Superman. Man is something to be overcome. What have you done to overcome him? All things before you have produced something beyond themselves, and would you be the ebb of this great flood? Would you rather go back to the animal than transcend man? What is the ape to man? A jest or a bitter shame. And just that shall man be to the Superman, a jest or a bitter shame. You have traveled the way from worm to man, and much in you is still worm.... Lo, I preach to you the Superman. The Superman is the meaning of the earth.[47]

If we set out seriously to realize the Superman, that loftier race, we must abandon all pity and all compassion, and find joy in the struggle and the heroic virtues. "I sit," says Zarathustra, "with old shattered tables of the law around me — and with new tables, too, half made out." [48] Christian love is a slave-morality, a code of submission and weakness and disease. The modern world has imposed it even upon its strong men, and with it stifled their strength and all further strength to come. If life is a fight for the future race, the meaning of good and bad must change.

What is good? All that heightens in man the feeling of power, the desire for power, power itself. What is bad? All that comes from weakness. What is happiness? The feeling that our strength grows, that an obstacle is overcome. Not contentment, but more power; not universal peace, but war; not virtue, but forcefulness. The weak and ineffective must go under; first principle of *our* love of humanity. And one should even lend one's hand to this end. What is more harmful than any vice? Pity for the condition of the ineffectives and weak — Christianity.[49]

Many misunderstood Nietzsche; they thought he was deifying the commercial greed, the warring nationalism and patriotisms, the strife of combat between country and country. Nothing was further from his thought. Above all he despised the captain of industry, the statesman and the clanking general. Patriotism and national commercial expansion he thought the worst of evils; not through them will the future be made more bright. With the Supermen of the future, our children who, thanks to our struggles, have far surpassed us, the free souls who know and create and live — there lies our true Fatherland. Let the strong men of to-day abandon their internecine struggles, and work together for the true aristocracy of the future, which shall be world-wide, the very flower of humanity. "Let us fearlessly style ourselves good Europeans, and labor actively for the amalgamation of nations." [50] Only thus shall the world know in the ages to come a select band of heroes who by their excellence can justify humanity's never-ending struggle, a veritable society of gods like Nietzsche's great passions, the Siegfried of Wagner, the Brand of Ibsen, and, highest of all, the great cosmopolitan and aristocratic intellect of Goethe.

If life offers this promise to the strong man, it is worth all its cost. Forward, into the battle! "Tied to the wheel of things," said India and Schopenhauer and all the disillusioned, "therefore, let us give up." "Tied to the wheel of things," bravely cries Nietzsche, "therefore, let us keep on." [51] "Courage is the best of them that kill. Courage kills even pity. Now, pity is the deep abyss: deep as one sees into life, just so deep does one see into pain. But courage is the best of them that kill; courage that lays hold on things; courage puts even Death to death, for it says to life: 'Was that Life? Forward, then! Once more!'" [52]

The New Naturalism

With Nietzsche, the acceptance of life and evolution means turning their opportunities to use in a great romantic struggle for the better days to come, and in that struggle itself finding the very zest of living. Less impassioned and more reflective, present-day thinkers have come to feel that in the world as science now displays it man can yet achieve through intelligence a worthy individual and collective life. The world of science is not to be wept over, nor rejected, nor blindly glorified. It is to be accepted, with all its compulsions and all its promise, soberly, but with ever-renewed hope, as the natural setting within which human life must be lived if it be lived at all, and as the material out of which man can with sweat and tears construct a human habitation. If man be a very part of nature and the product of its activity, then his life is a natural life, in fruitful as in bitter interaction with nature's sustaining and imperative forces. His vital interests and ideals are as much the natural flowering of the nature that gave them birth as are his criminal follies and his ruthless passions; and he can hope to turn those forces to his own advantage through his nature-sent gift of intelligence. It is equal folly to think man the darling of the gods, and to think him a homeless outcast wandering on the face of an earth that provides nothing to sustain his cherished enterprises. A sound naturalism eliminates the need of such a choice. Nature does permit us to work and struggle; it is not irrelevant to our ideals and values. They are not idle dreams, but are rooted in the very conditions that nature — and human nature — imposes. This is an alternative alike to the complacent confidence of the supernaturalist, with his egoistic assertion of human power, doomed to early disillusionment and defeat; and to the paralysing despair of the "moral atheist," who sees no possible perfectings of things as they are, no values implicit in nature and human nature that human striving can hope to realize.

What are the problems for philosophies which in some sense accept this naturalistic attitude? There is first the development of an adequate philosophy of nature and of natural science, drawing on all we have learned about both in our generation. A nature of which life and human experience are integral parts is far different from the mechanical "alien world" of the nineteenth century: it is a nature which a chastened and revolutionized physics no longer forbids us. That alien world has gone, and the naturalistic philosophies of to-day bear little resemblance to those travesties, founded on a reductive analysis and the mechanical dogmas of an earlier physics, which went by the name a generation ago. And a science which is essentially a human method of inquiry, an institutionalized technique by which a society deals with its problems, is vastly unlike the simple discovery of the laws governing nature — the terms in which men read the scientific enterprise before their new sophistication.

Secondly, there is the problem of developing an adequate philosophy for industrial society; and this means a philosophy of cultural change. For in industrial society, cultural change is the ultimate challenge to philosophic thought, the ultimate context and subject-matter of all our thinking. We sorely need an understanding, an intellectual attitude and technique, to replace the emotional reactions which now prevail. This involves an exploration of the possibilities of industrial civilization — a clarification of the content of the good life in a technological age — and a formulation and criticism of the techniques of social control. Our greatest intellectual need to-day is for a genuinely experimental philosophy as the background and drive, a philosophy that will emphasize investigation and inquiry into the actual materials of our society, both technological and human. What can be done, and by what means? What are the obstacles?

Which are too hard to remove, and must be accepted? which are most easily controlled? In particular, such a philosophy would foster an experimental attitude toward the problem of enlisting the coöperative support of men in doing what has to be done; of determining what can be accomplished with men, and how to get them to accomplish it. It would regard this all-important political problem as itself a matter for scientific inquiry and technological invention. It is childish to convert what is an intellectual problem into a mere fight, especially in America, where the very lag behind Europe, as well as the freedom from intolerable pressure, gives an opportunity to learn the bitter lessons of European experience. Such a philosophy would teach the patience of the experimenter, willing to try and try again, not cast down by a few failures, not demanding that every problem be solved overnight. And like all genuine experimentation, such a philosophy would have the courage to act, would have a faith in intelligence, and a willingness to fight, intelligently, if need be, to enable it to function.

The religious problem is still present, but in the changed form of the adjustment of the values of the philosophies of human experience, of the great cultural traditions and the religions that clarified and expressed them, to the critical knowledge of our scientific naturalisms. Romanticism has persisted, even among physicists, because so far those naturalisms have been so meager and bare, have failed to include important elements in experience. Till we have a naturalism as rich as the idealistic philosophies, because it provides a place for their visions, romanticism in some form will keep alive its eternal call back to the wealth and variety of imaginative experience. As a part of this adjustment, we can perhaps look forward to a further *rapprochement* between Western and Oriental thought.

New Philosophies of Nature and of Science

The development of an adequate philosophy of nature and of science is to-day of central concern, for we are in the midst of the most fundamental scientific revolution since the seventeenth century. The concepts and methods involved in the actual procedures of the sciences have been so basically altered, and our psychological and sociological knowledge of the processes and function of science is so extensive, that the very notions of reason and of experience, and of their relations, on which all modern philosophy has been based, are no longer tenable. Present-day naturalistic philosophies seem split on technical questions, ultimately, on which of the sciences are to furnish the basic categories and methods. Those that start from physics and mathematics make the logical structure of scientific knowledge fundamental; those that start from biology, psychology, and the social sciences emphasize the further context of the process of inquiry within which that structure is discriminated.

Yet both sides seem to be drawing closer together: the concepts developed by the philosophers of mathematical physics, like Whitehead, are approaching those of biology and the sciences of man. Face to face with its world of radiant energy, it is physics to-day that is suggesting the novel ideas; but they in turn are finding application to the sciences of life. There is, first, the common adoption of time as a basic category; both are now taking time and temporal process seriously. The biological and social philosophies have worked out temporal concepts which physics is now deriving from its own subject-matter. The older emphases in physics on structure and in biology on activity and process are being merged in a new synthesis of both. There is a tendency to employ a new language — many call it a new logic — the space-time continuum, events, processes, and activities, rather than things or substances; the subject-attribute relation has given place to functional series and correlations.

Secondly, there is a common emphasis on systematic structure, on the organic wholes and patterns within which simpler processes are discriminated. Those elements have been found by analysis, and when found are discovered operating from the start in an interrelated system. This change we have traced in physics, in biology, and in psychology; in each case the concept of a field, organism, or situation has assumed basic importance.

Thirdly, there is an emphasis on knowing and science as itself an activity, a process — ultimately, an institutionalized way of acting. The data of science are no longer passive sensations, but measurements, activities performed, depending on complicated space-time systems of coördinates and schemes of measurement. Science involves creation, the invention and employment of elaborate theoretical constructions. Knowing is no longer taken as an immediate seeing, either intellectual or sensible; it is mediate and instrumental, not inherently, in its values — men still find it good to know — but in its nature and character. This functional conception is supported by psychology, by the history of science, and by all analyses of the techniques of scientific procedure and of the actual formation of scientific hypothesis and theory. From the side of the process or functional philosophies, Dewey has elaborated this most clearly; from the structural side the logical positivists, working with the mathematical formulations and procedures of physics, have reached the same conclusion.

The major practical issue still left between the two types of naturalism concerns the treatment of values. The philosophies starting from physics tend to exclude all questions of value from the field of science and the scope of scientific method. They either leave them to traditional non-scientific treatment, handing them over, with Russell, to the poet and mystic; or else with the logical positivists they dismiss the whole matter as "meaningless," maintaining, with Ayer, that any judgment of value is an expression of mere personal feeling. The philosophies of human experience — all the heirs of Hegel, from dialectical materialism to Dewey — subject them to the same scientific methods of criticism and testing as other beliefs; and thus offer the hope of using all we have learned of scientific procedure to erect at last a science of values comparable to the science that was the glory of Greek thought.

Naturalism — Greek and Baconian

Two ages in the past have in their leaders stood for the frank and honest acceptance of man's natural environment as furnishing the materials for a good life. In classic Greece, men spoke who believed that the world was primarily a thing to be enjoyed; and that this enjoyment was to be ordered and harmonized and enlarged through the intelligent direction and control of the natural tendencies and feelings of man. In the dawn of modern science, Bacon preached a gospel not of enjoyment, but of achievement; of bending the forces of nature to the service of human desires, and creating an environment in which man could build through science an empire of power over nature. This Greek and this Baconian naturalism have been revived and blended in the present day; and in spite of the incurable romanticism of the Western peoples, it seems not unlikely that with this faith lies the future. The modern world takes what nature offers it, and builds a structure in which it may hope to find enjoyment and power. A frank acceptance of the goods of life, and an intensification and multiplication of them through scientific knowledge — this is, perhaps, what is already emerging from the welter of conflicting faiths and pathways of salvation incidental to so profound an intellectual readjustment as the West has been making, since the Renaissance, to science and to industry. What enjoyments are most enduring, and what power will most truly attain them, is a problem to be worked out still; but in countless ways, however reluctantly, men seem to have set about the task. They are blundering, and long will blunder; but they are gradually realizing the conditions of their achievement, and the instruments of its furthering. For the critic, the connoisseur, the scholar, the Greek aim of enjoyment, as illustrated in a Renan or a Santayana, will still be the part of wisdom; for others is the dust and grime of toil and labor. But for those who cannot rest content with past achievements, nor with the exclusion of the mass of mankind from the satisfactions that they crave, the task and the joy of humanity must lie in the working for the further empire of man over nature and over his own passions and lusts. The modern expression of this widespread ideal of power through science, and the good life for all through the intelligent exercise of power, is the philosophy of pragmatism or instrumentalism — intelligence is the instrument of social well-being and advancement. For the gifted individual, perhaps, such a philosophy offers no such heights of ecstasy and self-abandonment as the ways of deliverance that have flourished in the past; but for humanity in its painful toil and struggle, it may well offer the sanest and surest road to greater satisfactions. And in the labor of bringing it to pass there is surely enough scope for whatever of sacrifice and fervor men may demand.

This change of human disposition [writes John Dewey] toward the world does not mean that man ceases to have ideals, or ceases to be primarily a creature of the imagination. But it does signify a radical change in the character and function of the ideal realm which man shapes for himself. In the classic philosophy, the ideal world is essentially a haven in which man finds rest from the storms of life; it is an asylum in which he takes refuge from the troubles of existence with the calm assurance that it alone is supremely real. When the belief that knowledge is active and operative takes hold of men, the ideal realm is no longer something aloof and separate; it is rather that collection of imagined possibilities that stimulates men to new efforts and realizations. It still remains true that the troubles which men undergo are the forces that lead them to project pictures of a better state of things. But the picture of the better is shaped so that it may become an instrumentality of action, while in the classic view the Idea belongs ready-made in a noumenal world. . . .

When the identity of the moral process with the processes of specific growth is realized, the more conscious and formal education of childhood will be seen to be the most economical and efficient means of social advance and reorganization, and it will also be evident that the test of all institutions of adult life is their effect in furthering continued education. Government, business, art, religion, all social institutions have a meaning, a purpose. That purpose is to set free and to develop the capacities of human individuals without respect to race, sex, class or economic status. And this is all one with saying that the test of their value is the extent to which they educate every individual into the full stature of his possibility. Democracy has many meanings, but if it has a moral meaning, it is found in resolving that the supreme test of all political institutions and industrial arrangements shall be the contribution they make to the all-around growth of every member of society.[53]

Santayana thus sums up the intellectual temper of the age.

The present age is a critical one, and interesting to live in. The civilization characteristic of Christendom has not disappeared, yet another civilization has begun to take its place. We still understand the value of religious faith; we still appreciate the pompous arts of our forefathers; we are brought up on academic architecture, sculpture, painting, poetry, and music. We still love monarchy and aristocracy, together with that picturesque and dutiful order which rested on local institutions, class privileges, and the authority of the family. We may even feel an organic need for all these things, cling to them tenaciously, and dream of rejuvenating them. On the other hand the shell of Christendom is broken. The unconquerable mind of the East, the pagan past, the industrial socialistic future confront it with their equal authority. Our whole life and mind is saturated with the slow upward filtration of a new spirit — that of an emancipated, atheistic, international democracy.

These epithets may make us shudder; but what they describe is something positive and self-justified, something deeply rooted in our animal

---

[53] From *Reconstruction in Philosophy*, by John Dewey. Reprinted by permission of the publishers, Henry Holt & Co.

nature and inspiring to our hearts, something which, like every vital impulse, is pregnant with a morality of its own. In vain do we deprecate it; it has possession of us already through our propensities, fashions, and language. Our very plutocrats and monarchs are at ease only when they are vulgar. Even prelates and missionaries are hardly sincere or conscious of an honest function, save as they devote themselves to social work; for willy-nilly the new spirit has hold of our consciences as well. This spirit is amiable as well as disquieting; liberating as well as barbaric; and a philosopher in our day, conscious both of the old life and of the new, might repeat what Goethe said of his successive love affairs — that it is sweet to see the moon rise while the sun is still mildly shining.[54]

Continuing with Dewey,

As the new ideas find adequate expression in social life, they will be absorbed into a moral background, and will the ideas and beliefs themselves be deepened and be unconsciously transmitted and sustained. They will color the imagination and temper the desires and affections. They will not form a set of ideas to be expounded, reasoned out and argumentatively supported, but will be a spontaneous way of envisaging life. Then they will take on religious value. The religious spirit will be revivified because it will be in harmony with men's unquestioned scientific beliefs, and their ordinary day-by-day social activities. It will not be obliged to lead a timid, half-concealed and half-apologetic life because tied to scientific ideas and social creeds that are continuously eaten into and broken down. But especially will the ideas and beliefs themselves be deepened and intensified because spontaneously fed by emotion and translated into imaginative vision and fine art, while they are now maintained by more or less conscious effort, by deliberate reflection, by taking thought. They are technical and abstract just because they are not as yet carried as a matter of course by imagination and feelings.

While it is impossible to retain and recover by deliberate volition old sources of religion and art that have been discredited, it is possible to expedite the development of the vital sources of a religion and an art that are yet to be. Not indeed by action directly aimed at their production, but by substituting faith in the active tendencies of the day for dread and dislike of them, and by the courage of intelligence to follow whither social and scientific changes direct us. We are weak to-day in ideal matters, because intelligence is divorced from aspiration. The bare force of circumstance compels us onwards in the daily detail of our beliefs and our acts, but our deeper thoughts and desires turn backwards. When philosophy shall have coöperated with the course of events and made clear and coherent the meaning of the daily detail, science and emotion will interpenetrate, practice and imagination will embrace.

---

[54] From *Winds of Doctrine*, by George Santayana. Reprinted by permission of the publishers, Charles Scribner's Sons.

PHILOSOPHIC REACTIONS TO MECHANISM

Poetry and religious feeling will be the unforced flowers of life. To further this articulation and revelation of the meanings of the current course of events is the task and problem of philosophy in days of transition.[55]

REFERENCES

1. Arthur Balfour, *Foundations of Belief*, 29–31.
2. Bertrand Russell, *Free Man's Worship*.
3. Hugh Eliot, *Modern Science and Materialism*, 39.
4. *Ibid.*, 68, 69.
5. Gilbert Murray, *The Stoic Philosophy*, 64–66.
6. William James, *Pragmatism*, 105.
7. Matthew Arnold, *Dover Beach*.
8. Tennyson, *Supposed Confessions of a Second-Rate Sensitive Mind*.
9. Tennyson, *In Memoriam*.
10. *Ibid*.
11. Arthur Hugh Clough, *Perchè Pensa? Pensando s' invecchia*.
12. Clough, "*With Whom is no variableness, neither shadow of turning*" and "*Say not the struggle naught availeth.*"
13. James Thomson, *The City of Dreadful Night*.
14. Schopenhauer, *Die Welt als Wille und Vorstellung*, Frauenstädt ed., 367, 379.
15. *Ibid.*, 448.
16. *Ibid.*, 486, 487.
17. Thomas Hardy, *The Dynasts*, 1919, 1, 524.
18. Walter Pater, Conclusion to *The Renaissance*.
19. E. Renan, *Examen d'un conscience philosophique*, in *Feuilles détachées*.
20. G. Santayana, Sonnet XIII.
21. Santayana, *The Rustic at the Play*, in *The Hermit of Carmel and Other Poems*.
22. Omar Khayyam, Fitzgerald tr.
23. Anatole France, *Le Jardin d'Épicure*, 97.
24. *Ibid.*, 66, 67.
25. *Ibid.*, 33.
26. *Ibid.*, 122, 136.
27. Clough, *Peschiera*.
28. Thomas Huxley, *Evolution and Ethics*, 80.
29. *Ibid.*, 81, 84.
30. Matthew Arnold, *In Harmony with Nature*.
31. Bertrand Russell, *Free Man's Worship*.
32. J. E. Creighton, "Two Types of Idealism," *Philosophical Review* (1917), 516.
33. Thomas Carlyle, *Sartor Resartus*, ch. 8.
34. R. W. Emerson, *The Over-Soul*.
35. B. Bosanquet, *The Principle of Individuality and Value*, 240.
36. Bosanquet, *Social and International Ideals*, 244, 246.
37. Josiah Royce, *Spirit of Modern Philosophy*, 448, 459.
38. Tennyson, *In Memoriam*.
39. H. Spencer, *Data of Ethics*, 250–54.
40. Marx, *Communist Manifesto*, ch. 1.
41. Henrik Ibsen, *Peer Gynt*, Act II, Scene 3.
42. J. M. Guyau, quoted in *Pages choisis*, 123–25; *L'Irreligion de l'Avenir*.
43. John Dewey, *Democracy and Education*, 60, 96, 100, 101.
44. J. H. Tufts, in *Creative Intelligence*, 404.
45. Henri Bergson, *Creative Evolution*, 247, 248, 266, 269 ff.
46. Nietzsche, quoted in E. Singer, *Modern Thinkers and Present Problems*, 190.

---

[55] From *Reconstruction in Philosophy*, by John Dewey. Reprinted by permission of the publishers, Henry Holt & Co.

47. Nietzsche, *Thus Spake Zarathustra.*
48. Nietzsche, quoted in Singer, 194.
49. *Ibid.,* 204.
50. Nietzsche, *Human, All-too Human,* par. 475.
51. Nietzsche, quoted in Singer, 209.
52. *Ibid.*
53. John Dewey, *Reconstruction in Philosophy,* 118, 186.
54. G. Santayana, *Winds of Doctrine,* 1.
55. Dewey, *Reconstruction in Philosophy,* 210, 211.

SELECTED READING LISTS

General: G. H. Mead, *Movements of Thought in the 19th Cent.*; J. T. Merz, *H. of Eur. Thought in the 19th Cent.*, III, IV. R. B. Perry, *Present Phil. Tendencies, Present Conflict of Ideals* (esp. valuable). Ueberweg, *Ges. der Phil.*, Bde. IV, V, full bibliog. H. Höffding, *H. of Modern Phil., Mod. Philosophers;* E. Bréhier, *H. de la Phil.* Hists. of phil. by B. A. G. Fuller, W. T. Marvin, G. Boas; Falckenberg, Weber-Perry, Windelband. R. Eucken, *Main Currents of Modern Thought;* L. Stein, *Phil. Strömungen d. Gegenwart;* A. Rey, *La Phil. Moderne;* G. de Ruggiero, *Modern Phil.* W. T. Jones, *Cont. Thought of Germany;* W. Brock, *Cont. German Phil.* J. A. Gunn, *Mod. French Phil.*; D. Parodi, *La Phil. Cont. en France;* I. Benrubi, *Cont. Thought of France, Phil. Strömungen d. Gegenwart in Frankreich.* A. K. Rogers, *English and American Phil. since 1800;* R. Metz, *Hundred Years of British Phil.*; hists. by J. M. Forsyth, W. R. Sorley, J. Seth; J. H. Muirhead, ed., *Cont. British Phil.* V. L. Parrington, *Main Currents of American Thought;* Adams and Montague, eds., *Cont. American Phil.*; Kallen and Hook, eds., *American Phil. Today and Tomorrow.*

The Mechanistic World: H. Spencer, *First Principles;* L. Büchner, *Force and Matter;* E. Haeckel, *Riddle of the Universe;* Carl Snyder, *The World-Machine;* H. Eliot, *Modern Science and Materialism;* W. Ostwald, *Natural Philosophy;* Karl Pearson, *Grammar of Science.* For implications, see Bertrand Russell, *Free Man's Worship, What I Believe, Scientific Method in Philosophy,* ch. VIII; Anatole France, *Garden of Epicurus;* G. Santayana, *Reason in Common Sense.*

Pessimism: Arthur Schopenhauer, *World as Will and Idea, Essays in Pessimism;* E. Singer, *Modern Thinkers and Present Problems,* ch. VI; works by W. Wallace, T. Whittaker; G. Simmel, *Schopenhauer und Nietzsche.* E. von Hartmann, *Philosophy of the Unconscious.* Tennyson, esp. *In Memoriam;* Arnold; A. H. Clough; J. Thomson, *City of Dreadful Night;* Thomas Hardy, *Dynasts,* poems, novels.

Æstheticism: Walter Pater, *Marius the Epicurean, Renaissance;* Swinburne, Aldous Huxley. E. Renan, *Dialogues et Fragments Philosophiques; Drames Philosophiques;* see Faguet, *19ᵉ Siècle,* L. F. Mott, *Renan.* Anatole France, *Garden of Epicurus,* etc. R. Lalou, *Contemporary French Literature.* G. Santayana, *Life of Reason, Scepticism and Animal Faith, Hermit of Carmel, Sonnets.*

Defiance: T. H. Huxley, *Evolution and Ethics;* W. R. Sorley, *Ethics of Naturalism;* B. Russell, *Free Man's Worship.*

Glorification of Nature: J. B. Bury, *Idea of Progress;* Herbert Spencer, *First Principles, Progress, Its Law and Cause, Data of Ethics.* A. Comte, *General View of Positivism, Positive Philosophy,* tr. Martineau; J. S. Mill, *A. Comte and Positivism.* John Fiske, *Outlines of Cosmic Philosophy;* Karl Marx.

Creative Evolution: J. M. Guyau, *Non-Religion of the Future; Morals without Obligation or Sanction; Vers d'un Philosophe.* H. Bergson, *Creative Evolution, Time and Free Will;* works by H. W. Carr, E. LeRoy. M. Blondel, *L'Action;* K. Gilbert, *The Philosophy of Blondel.* W. James, *Pluralistic Universe;* John Dewey, *Democracy and Education, Creative Intelligence.* C. Lloyd Morgan, *Emergent Evolution; Life, Mind and Spirit;* S. Alexander, *Space, Time, and Deity;* J. E. Boodin, *Cosmic Evolution, Three Ints. of the Universe.*

PHILOSOPHIC REACTIONS TO MECHANISM

Nietzsche: *Works*, O. Levy ed. esp. *Thus Spake Zarathustra, Genealogy of Morals, Beyond Good and Evil.* Singer, *Modern Thinkers and Present Problems*, ch. VII; works by W. Salter, R. Richter, C. Andler.

The Protest of Idealism: A. Aliotta, *The Idealistic Reaction against Modern Science.* J. Ward, *Naturalism and Agnosticism;* G. P. Adams, *Idealism and the Modern Age.* H. Lotze, *Microcosm, System of Philosophy* (most scientific in spirit); F. Paulsen, *Introduction to Philosophy;* R. Eucken, *Value and Meaning of Life, Life of the Spirit, Life's Basis and Life's Ideal.* B. Croce, *Practical Philosophy, Æsthetics.* T. H. Green, *Prolegomena to Ethics;* F. H. Bradley, *Appearance and Reality;* A. E. Taylor, *Elements of Metaphysics;* R. B. Haldane, *Pathway to Reality;* B. Bosanquet. J. Royce, *Religious Aspect of Philosophy, Spirit of Modern Philosophy, World and the Individual, Philosophy of Loyalty;* H. Münsterberg, *Eternal Values;* F. Adler, *An Ethical Philosophy of Life;* R. F. A. Hoernle, *Idealism.* G. W. Cunningham, *Idealistic Argument in Recent Brit. and Amer. Phil.*; W. M. Urban, *Intelligible World, Language and Communication;* B. Blanshard, *Nature of Thought.* C. Barrett, ed., *Cont. Idealism in America.*

The Emergence of Naturalism: G. Santayana, *Life of Reason; Selections*, ed. I. Edman. F. J. E. Woodbridge, *Purpose of History, Realm of Mind, Nature and Mind, Essay on Nature.* John Dewey, *Democracy and Education, Reconstruction in Philosophy, Human Nature and Conduct, Ethics, Experience and Nature, Quest for Certainty, Philosophy and Civilization, Art as Experience, Common Faith, Freedom and Culture.* M. R. Cohen, *Reason and Nature.* R. W. Sellars, *Evolutionary Naturalism, Phil. of Physical Reality;* R. B. Perry, *Gen. Theory of Value.* S. Alexander, *Space, Time, and Deity;* A. N. Whitehead, *Science and the Modern World, Process and Reality, Nature and Life.*

Late 19th Century Philosophies of Science: J. S. Mill, *Logic;* E. Mach, *Pop. Scientific Lectures, Analysis of Sensation;* Karl Pearson, *Grammar of Science.* W. Ostwald, *Natural Philosophy;* H. Helmholtz, *Pop. Lectures;* E. Cassirer, *Substance and Function.* H. Poincaré, *Science and Hypothesis, Science and Method, Value of Science;* P. Duhem, *La Théorie Physique.* C. S. Peirce, *Chance, Love, and Logic; Collected Papers;* study by J. Buchler. William James, *Princ. of Psychology, Meaning of Truth, Pluralistic Universe, Radical Empiricism;* R. B. Perry, *Thought and Character of W. James.*

Contemporary Philosophies of Science: Bertrand Russell, *Outline of Phil., Scientific Outlook; Principles of Math., Our Knowledge of the External World, Int. to Math. Phil., Mysticism and Logic, Analysis of Mind, Anal. of Matter.* G. E. Moore, *Principia Ethica, Phil. Essays.* S. Alexander, *Space, Time, and Deity;* C. Lloyd Morgan, *Emergent Evolution, Emergence of Novelty.* C. D. Broad, *Scientific Thought, The Mind and its Place in Nature.* A. N. Whitehead, *Princ. of Natural Knowledge, Concept of Nature, Science and the Mod. World, Symbolism, Process and Reality, Nature and Life.* M. R. Cohen, *Reason and Nature.* E. Nagel, "Logical Empiricism," in *Amer. Scholar,* 1939; C. W. Morris, *Logical Positivism, Pragmatism, and Scientific Empiricism;* O. Neurath, ed., *Foundations of the Unity of Science;* R. Carnap, *Phil. and Logical Syntax, Logical Syntax of Language;* P. Frank, *Interps. and Misinterps. of Mod. Physics;* H. Reichenbach, *Experience and Prediction.* John Dewey, *How We Think, Essays in Experimental Logic, Experience and Nature, Quest for Certainty; Logic, the Theory of Inquiry.* G. H. Mead, *Phil. of the Present; Mind, Self, and Society; Phil. of the Act.* C. I. Lewis, *Mind and the World-Order.* P. W. Bridgman, *Logic of Mod. Physics.* On values: John Dewey, *Theory of Valuation;* R. B. Perry, *Gen Theory of Values.* B. Russell, *Outline of Phil.*; M. Schlick, *Problems of Ethics;* A. J. Ayer, *Language, Truth and Logic.*

CHAPTER XXII

SOCIAL IDEALS IN THE GROWING WORLD

How are we going to bring a workable organization into our economic life? And how are we to adapt our whole liberal, humanistic, democratic heritage of Western culture to the harsh demands and the eventual promise of industrialism? In the nineteenth century men feared that science would undermine the church. To-day we tremble lest the measures we must take to meet the insistent call of our industrial machine for a more efficient integration destroy our whole legacy of painfully acquired intellectual and moral values, as they seem to be doing in many lands to-day; to say nothing of forcing fundamental revolutions in our political and social structure if the possibilities of our technology are to be realized, if it is even to continue functioning, or indeed if it is to remain ours at all. So pressing is the need for economic reconstruction that we often forget we are really facing the problem of reconstructing our entire culture. But however important the former task may seem to-day, however basic the economic organization we work out in determining the limits and the conditions of the eventual rebuilding of our culture, the latter will prove far more important, difficult, and complex. Even in its own terms it is hard enough; it is made well-nigh insoluble if it be wholly subordinated to the problem of economic organization. The experience of Central Europe has made it clear that the method of getting men to agree to a necessary economic integration can easily effect a total cultural revolution. While there is still time for us to choose, we must be sure that the method by which we meet our economic problems will bring a cultural reconstruction we can live with.

After the depression of the thirties, and in the midst of the present struggle between two rival political methods, these facts should be clear to any reflective man. But for several generations it has been apparent that the industrial revolution of the last century has altered the complexion of human society far more radically than anything else since the beginning of recorded history. To find a comparable disruptive force, we must turn back to the invention of fire in the dim ages when man was just becoming man, or to the change from a hunting and nomadic pastoral life to a settled existence founded on agriculture. More rapid social changes now take place in a single decade, or in a single year, than in whole centuries in the past; and this continual acceleration is swifter to-day than ever.

The effect upon man's mind and man's beliefs has naturally permeated every fiber of his intellectual being. Yet for all the rapid changes in his institutions, they have by no means kept pace with the growth of his industrial system. Never did the ideas and beliefs upon which men attempt to order their actions reveal so wide a discrepancy with the demands of their situation. In view of the appalling need to adjust their social structure to its technological basis, men have been driven to devote more and more of their intellectual energies to the problems of human and social relationships. Those who in another century would have taken their particular social order as a matter of course now bring all their problems to the focus of the maladjustments between group and group. We are still perplexed and confused when we find we can no longer order our political life through beliefs and institutions conceived in terms of the problems of the rural and frontier colonial civilization. Multitudes would still like to direct an economic society in which the giant corporation and centralized finance are the chief features, by ideas developed to meet the needs of eighteenth-century commercial and agricultural England and France. We still feel we ought somehow to adjust our conduct and our human relationships by an ethical code that originated in ancient Palestine over two thousand years ago. In our international relations we have fallen back on the naked power that four centuries ago won emancipation from another outgrown and constricting system, the universal dominion of the Church. Small wonder that these beliefs and institutions have proved inadequate, and have led to mutual confusion and destruction.

This, at bottom, is why religion and philosophy have to-day set themselves primarily a social task; this is why man's deepest reflection is concerned with social ideals and methods. Long before the present crisis became acute, the cardinal and characteristic expression of the mind of the present age had come to be its preoccupation with the ends of human activities and the aims of human institutions. And for men to-day, social ideals are preëminently ideals of change, ideals in the light of which society is to be transformed. In the Middle Ages, in the great Oriental civilizations, such goals were primarily idealizations of the existing order, statements of the values to be obtained in it and served by it; even in classic Greece, where social change was likewise an inescapable fact, the ideals men set up were expressions of the best life that might be lived in the existent city state. To-day every statement of the good life for society involves reconstruction, reform, reorganization, perhaps revolution. Social ideals are either Utopian visions or programs of practical change. Of conservatism, as known in the past, there are now few advocates: no one is prepared to crystallize the recent present. There are reactionaries aplenty, who look longingly backward to the past. There are revolutionaries in great numbers, who wish to make all things new. But no one wants a return to yesterday's travail: the demand of our growing world for organization is too insistent.

And now comes the war, to destroy so many great hopes, and to make all the social programs men have so passionately advocated seem irrelevant and meaningless. In a world ruled by military power, what other social ideal can men set themselves but naked strength? Can we do more than prepare to defend so much as proves possible of our heritage of liberal and democratic ideals, of respect for the individuality and worth of men, in a world dominated by totalitarian methods and physical might?

Assuredly the war makes many hopes impossible, and many distasteful measures imperative. The changes it has already rendered certain will remain inescapable facts to reckon with. But it is scarcely the problem of economic reconstruction it has made irrelevant. If America is to defend its heritage, in the world our worst fears foresee, that problem must be dealt with much more seriously than we have so far dared think. The luxuries of inefficiency, waste, and failure to utilize our resources, human and technological, we can no longer afford. We cannot go on debating whether the social gains of a better organized economic system would be worth the incidental losses: that question has been decided for us. The war has immensely accelerated the long process of adapting our economic controls to the needs of technology, which the depression had already revealed as so acute a problem. Whatever the outcome, the resulting economic organization of Europe will be quite unrecognizable; and the socialized control it will bring in America will make the New Deal look like a business-man's paradise.

In truth, it is not primarily the goal, an organized industrial machine, that is to-day at issue. That organization is being forced upon us whether we will or no. The expanding and aggressive powers have sacrificed more than a few short years ago we dreamed possible to build an efficient economy in support of military might. To meet the challenge, to live in the same world with them, other lands must achieve a like efficiency. The choices are rapidly narrowing as to the kind of "collectivism," of socialized control of industrial society, we must establish. The issue that still remains open, the great question at stake in the present conflict, concerns the method of its establishment. Can we make the most of the marvelous resources of technology with our present political methods? Can we adapt our social structure to the demands of the industrial machine without sacrificing completely the liberal and humane values of our long heritage? Is the democratic ideal compatible with efficient industrial organization?

Such questions cut far deeper than the mere struggle of rival national groups for power and domination — though whether even industrialism can long survive under a merely national organization, and which in the end will prove the tougher, are still doubtful issues. The future of democratic values rests upon whether democratic methods can prove as successful as their rivals in facing the inescapable task of economic integration. No mere defense of the past can prove more than a rear-guard action; only as democratic methods are strengthened and extended can they hope to survive. Hence far from being irrelevant in the present crisis, the social ideals and programs elaborated in the last few generations strike at the root of the problem. Unless we can accomplish the social reconstruction they have all aimed at, we may win the battles but we shall lose the war. We may succeed in meeting the challenge of this or that totalitarian state; but we must do it by performing better in our own way the essential economic task they have set themselves. If we fail, we shall in the end be forced to resort to totalitarianism ourselves.

Contrasting Types of Social Ideal

Of ideals of social change there are two major contrasting types. There are the absolutistic Utopias, the completely formulated pictures of the perfect society; for those who dwell longingly upon them, they become veritable heavens, capable of inspiring the soul and quickening the heart. They are fighting creeds, generated in the heat of battle or in the aftermath of defeat. But they have also all the defects to which such apocalyptic visions are subject: however inspiring and sustaining, they scarcely reveal how the millennium is to be brought about, and they may even steel the mind against measures of practical amelioration. A perfect illustration of such fervor is contained in the ideal of the I.W.W., as expressed in their preamble:

> The working class and the employing class have nothing in common. There can be no peace so long as hunger and want are found among millions of working people and the few, who make up the employing class, have all the good things of life. Between these two classes a struggle must go on until the workers of the world organize as a class, take possession of the earth and the machinery of production, and abolish the wage system.[1]

In sharp contrast to this type of social ideal, which makes a religion of social revolution and a completed millennium its heaven, is the ideal which, less ambitious but more practical, deals with specific problems in the light of general principles which are themselves constantly open to revision. It is relativistic rather than absolutistic, pragmatic rather than uncompromising, experimental rather than dogmatic. It involves not so much an ecstatic religious faith as a patient and careful scientific technique. It is thoroughly in harmony with that Baconian naturalism that is one of the fruits of the scientific discoveries of the last century. It investigates with an open mind, and carefully tests at every step; and when it advances, its faith is led by a firm knowledge of the complexity of social processes.

These two types of social ideal and social technique have always been in the world, and doubtless will always remain: each contributes much of value in the process of change, the one, the driving and sustaining power, the other, the intelligence and the point of attack. In the eighteenth century, the one was represented by Rousseau, the other by Bentham; both aimed ultimately at the same goal — though characteristically neither would have admitted it. In our own day the absolutistic attitude has enjoyed great vogue among the more radical critics of the obvious inadequacy, confusion, and contradictory character of the specific measures introduced by democratic governments — like the Hoover régime and the New Deal — to extend the sphere of social control. Its strongest argument has been the conviction, generated by the tenacity with which privileged groups have resisted even such half-way measures, and in the midst of such crises as the depression, that a genuine revolution in economic power is necessary before the drastic changes now demanded can be put through. To succeed against entrenched opposition, it has been held, the strongest kind of fighting psychology is needed in the attackers.

But what industry demands in general is now so clear, and the details, whoever be responsible, are so much a matter of inquiry, investigation, and experimental working out, that the rigidity and fixity, the dogmatism of the absolutist seem less called for than the flexibility and the adaptability of the experimentalist. And after all even revolutions are not caused by revolutionists, as they sometimes hopefully think; they are caused by circumstance, and the revolutionists, if they are lucky enough to survive responsibility, speedily learn to act like practical statesmen. Whatever the faults of Russian communism, undue rigidity of program has not been its major failing. And now the war with its drive for national defense has brought a powerful new motive to the most recalcitrant to accept drastic social change. It is likely that even congenital absolutists will forget their abstract formulas in the more pressing task of trying to push the changes that will come a little more in the direction they favor.

It is not part of our purpose here to describe the rise and development of the manifold social philosophies of the industrial age; above all, we do not intend to sketch the organized movements in which they have been embodied. We shall rather conclude our story of the formation of the mind of the Western world with a picture of some of the most important of these conflicting ideals, in the same spirit and on the same scale employed for the social ideals of the Middle Ages or the Renaissance or the Enlightenment. The student of political and economic movements must look elsewhere for the record of events; here we shall attempt rather to display the leading ideas back of those movements. What were the major beliefs and desires and ideals that have actuated men since 1848? What has been in their minds that found expression in or reflected the practical exertions to which they bent their energies? We shall deal with the major social ideals of the world of expanding technology in search of organization. We shall look first at those ideals to which an individualistic industrialism has consecrated its actual efforts. We shall then examine, in both their middle-class and working-class versions, those in which men have proposed to employ and extend the liberal and democratic methods to reform and reconstruct their society. We shall consider the authoritarian and totalitarian ideals which have impatiently rejected those methods in seeking the same economic end. And finally, we shall touch on the ideals of international relations, in which men have hoped to extend organization beyond the limits of the national state.

Middle-Class Ideals

After 1848 the world belonged to the middle class — the business men and manufacturers with their attendant servants and ministers, the professions. The older upper classes, clergy and landed nobility, who had retained their supremacy, though in places hard pressed, until the French Revolution, and who fought the losing fight from 1815 to 1848, with the spread of the industrial revolution were overshadowed by and absorbed into the commercial and industrial groups. Despite occasional efforts of the landed gentry, the Prussian Junkers or the English landlords, to assert themselves, the history of the Western world has since then been largely the story of the remarkable economic expansion of the middle class and its efforts to protect its position against the rising tide of factory workers. With the establishment of a fair measure of political democracy, and the consolidation of the large national states, consummated in the five years from 1865 to 1870, European civilization entered upon a phase in which business and industry played the dominating rôle. It was the golden age of liberal capitalism, of expanding economies whose national rivalries had not yet broken out into imperialistic war, and whose control was not yet seriously challenged by working-class revolt.

In most lands, to be sure, the farmer has remained numerically the largest class. But on the whole he has followed the ideals of the business man, and lent a passive support to whatever enterprises the middle class saw fit to undertake. There have been sporadic agrarian movements, in Europe and America; but they have hardly aimed at more than an immediate alleviation of the economic discrimination to which the farmer has been increasingly subjected. The farmer has so far remained too unorganized, perhaps too inexperienced in industrialism, to formulate a social ideal of his own; and middle-class intellectuals have sadly neglected him. In America the party system has often in times of depression linked him in uneasy alliance with the industrial workers. But his pioneer traditions have made him deeply suspicious of the methods of organized labor; he thinks of himself as an independent business man, and his way of life has always allied him with the supporters of middle-class ideals. Proud of his great political power, he has normally allowed it to be manipulated in support of business interests, convinced that commercial prosperity promised him most. In the future the tale may well be different; in the past the farmer has hardly counted intellectually, and has more or less patiently borne the brunt of the struggle between the middle and the working classes.

The middle class came into the ascendancy in England in the eighteenth century. Its philosophy and ideals were formulated by the classic economists and the liberal advocates of individual rights, individual initiative and enterprise, free competition and *laisser-faire*. In this country similar individualistic and libertarian views were first developed not by business men and millowners, but by agrarians like Jefferson. The absence of feudalism or any genuine upper class kept them from being identified with a "middle" class, and made them broadly "American." But they proved admirably suited to the temper of the expanding industry of the post-Civil War era; and to this day the business man, the manufacturer, the professional man, the hosts of Suburbia, as well as the mass of the farmers, believe in their hearts in that early nineteenth-century philosophy. To them it still seems the only "American" ideal; they regard it as written forever into the Constitution, as something to be returned to after forced departures and temporary wanderings in heresy like the New Deal. In the face of grave industrial problems, and in response to the constant pressure of the working class, they have of course reluctantly consented to all manner of modifications in practice; for there are other American traditions as well, above all the strong atmosphere of adaptability and willingness to experiment. But none of these specific measures has altered significantly the underlying ideals of the middle class. It continues to look back nostalgically to the days of normalcy when the "American way" was still possible. It still regards itself as the salt of the earth and the chosen of the Lord, and sees in its own material prosperity the source of good for the whole of society. The claims of James Mill a century ago it would enthusiastically echo to-day — though in America it would speak not of "the middle rank" but of "the business man":

> It is altogether futile with regard to the foundation of good government to say that this or the other portion of the people may at this or the other time, depart from the wisdom of the *middle rank*. It is enough that the great majority of the people never cease to be guided by that rank — and we may with some confidence challenge the adversaries of the people to produce a single instance to the contrary in the history of the world.[2]

Social Ideals of an Individualistic Industrialism

For several generations, without much serious questioning until the last decade, the social ideals of industrial civilization have been overwhelmingly directed toward business success. Those ideals have been well summed up as three in number: the Country House, Coketown, and Megalopolis. The Country House is the goal of every good business man's aspiration; it is the abode and the life which he desires for himself and his family and his friends. It is the ideal of the gentleman, coming down without much change from the Renaissance; an early picture has already been given in Rabelais' Abbey of Theleme.

We see pretty much the same outlines in the introduction to Boccaccio's *Decameron;* it is elaborately described in terms of that most complete of Country Houses, Hampton Court, in Pope's *Rape of the Lock;* it is vividly pictured by Meredith in his portrait of the *Egoist*. And it is analyzed in Mr. H. G. Wells's cruel description of Bladesover in *Tono-Bungay*, as well as by Mr. Bernard Shaw in *Heartbreak House*. Whether Mr. W. H. Mallock holds the pattern of Country House culture up to us in *The New Republic* or Anton Chekhov penetrates its aimlessness and futility in *The Cherry Orchard*, the Country House is one of the recurrent themes of literature.... Its standards of consumption are responsible for our Acquisitive Society.[3]

The Country House is concerned not with the happiness of the whole community but with the felicity of the governors. The conditions which underlie this limited and partial good life are political power and economic wealth; and in order for the life to flourish, both of these must be obtained in almost limitless quantities. The chief principles that characterize this society are possession and passive enjoyment.... In the Country House possession is based upon privilege and not upon work.... Such activities as remain in the Country House — the pursuit of game, for instance, — rest upon imitating in play activities which once had a vital use or prepared for some vital function, as a child's playing with a doll is a preparation for motherhood. The Country House ideal is that of a completely functionless existence.... In the Country House literature and the fine arts undoubtedly flourish: but they flourish as the objects of appreciation rather than as the active, creative elements in the community's life.... It does not matter very much whether the Country House is an estate on Long Island or a cottage in Montclair; whether it is a house in Golder's Green or a family manor in Devonshire: these are essentially affairs of scale, and the underlying identity is plain enough. The ideal of the Country House prevails even when quarters are taken up in the midst of the metropolis. More than ever the Country House to-day tries to make up by an abundance of physical goods for all that has been lost through its divorce from the underlying community; more than ever it attempts to be self-sufficient within the limits of suburbia. The automobile, the phonograph, and the radio-telephone have only served to increase this self-sufficiency; and I need not show at length how these instrumentalities have deepened the elements of acquisitiveness and passive, uncreative, mechanical enjoyment.

The Country House's passionate demand for physical goods has given rise to another institution, Coketown.[4]

Coketown is the sharp picture of the mill city in Dickens's *Hard Times*.

The center of Coketown's activity was the mill, set at first in the open country near falling water, and then as coal was applied to steam engines, removed to areas more accessible to the coal-fields. The factory became the new social unity; in fact it became the only social unit; and, as Dickens sharply put it, "the jail looked like the town hall, and the town hall like the infirmary" — and all of them looked like the factory, a gaunt building of murky brick that once was red or yellow. The sole object of the factory is to produce goods for sale; and every other institution is encouraged in Coketown only to the extent that it does not seriously interfere with this aim.... Coketown is devoted to the production of material goods; and there is no good in Coketown that does not derive from this aim. The only enjoyment which those who are inured to the Coketown routine can participate in is mechanical achievement; that is to say, activity along industrial and commercial lines; and the only result of this achievement is — more achievement. In the Coketown scheme of things, all that does not contribute to the physical necessities of life is called a comfort; and all that does not contribute either to comforts or necessities is called a luxury. These three grades of good correspond to the three classes of the population: the necessities are for the lower order of manual workers, together with such accessory members as clerks, teachers, and minor officials; the comforts are for the comfortable classes, that is, the small order of merchants, bankers, and industrialists; while the luxuries are for the aristocracy, if there is such an hereditary group, and for such as are able to lift themselves out of the two previous orders. Chief among the luxuries, it goes without saying, are art and literature and any of the other permanent interests of a humane life.... Coketown for the workaday week, the Country House for the weekend, is the compromise that has been practically countenanced.[5]

Megalopolis is the largest city of the National State. Its ultimate aim is to conduct the whole of human life through the medium of paper. Books, motion picture films, magazines, newspapers, reports, mortgages, securities, commercial paper of all sorts — it is by these means that the Megalopolitans live their lives and gain their experience.

By its traffic in Coketown's multifarious goods and by its command over certain kinds of paper known as mortgages or securities, Megalopolis ensures a supply of real foods and real staples from the countryside. Through incessant production of books, magazines, newspapers, boilerplate features, and syndicated matter, Megalopolis ensures that the ideal of the National Utopia shall be kept alive in the minds of the underlying inhabitants of the country. Finally, by the devices of "national education" and "national advertising" all the inhabitants of the National Utopia are persuaded that the good life is that which is lived, on paper, in the capital city; and that an approximation to this life can be achieved only by eating the food, dressing in the clothes, holding the opinions, and purchasing the goods which are offered for sale by Megalopolis. So the chief aim of every other city in the National Utopia is to become like Megalopolis; its chief hope is to grow as big as Megalopolis; its boast is that it is another Megalopolis.... What is Megalopolis, in fact, but a paper purgatory which serves as a medium through which the fallen sons of Coketown, the producer's hell, may finally attain the high bliss of the County House, the consumer's Heaven?[6]

[3-6] From *The Story of Utopias*, by Lewis Mumford. Reprinted by permission of the publishers, Boni and Liveright.

LIBERAL IDEALS OF SOCIAL LEGISLATION AND SOCIAL REFORM

From the first appearance of Coketowns in the early nineteenth century they have not lacked their critics. Opposition began with nostalgic admirers of the more picturesque poverty of the old agricultural order, outraged at the desecration of England's green and pleasant isle. But by the forties serious programs for the better use of the opportunities of technology had become a political force to reckon with. And for at least two generations there has been in all lands the growing realization that some form of "social reform" is essential. Both because it has seemed to them just and humane, and because it has appeared the part of wisdom for the safeguarding of their position and for the increase of general prosperity, the more thoughtful and enlightened of the middle class have sponsored and put into effect a large mass of so-called "social" or "welfare legislation" designed to regulate the extremes of business competition as they bear upon the less fortunate members of society, and have sought to introduce a great many alleviating elements into the actual conduct of industry. Business men, who a half-century ago honestly felt that a ruthless policy and reliance upon "salutary suffering" would ultimately be most productive of social good, are to-day aware of the follies of Coketown and of Megalopolis, and are more or less convinced that intelligence and social action are necessary checks upon too unregulated a struggle for economic existence. This feeling has taken two more or less blended forms: it has given rise to a series of political measures for utilizing the power of the government for benevolent ends, and to a great wave of primarily religious and humanitarian reform. The first began in England with the Tory reformers and their factory legislation; it was greatly elaborated and applied in Germany as "State Socialism," whence it spread into England as "Neo-Liberalism," into many of the smaller European countries, notably Switzerland and Scandinavia, and has appeared in America in the various "Progressive" movements. The second form, "Social Christianity," arose with the Catholics of France and Germany as "Catholic Socialism" or "Social Catholicism," and has been more recently adopted by the Protestant churches as the "social gospel." The specific measures advocated and enacted by these men need not concern us here; it is rather in the general social ideals lying back of these tendencies that we are interested.

State socialism began in Germany, as in England, with the conservatives and the landholders rather than with the business men. In its inception it was primarily patriotic in intent: it emphasized the activity of the State, not for the benefit of either the business men or the working-classes, but rather for the strengthening and the welfare of the nation as a whole; and throughout it has retained the suspicion of the motives of Plato's collectivism, that the State may be strong in war. Primarily with this aim Bismarck, seeking to avoid the ignorant blunders of the early Industrial Revolution in England, tried to make industry serve rather the good of the nation than the gain of the business men; industry and agriculture alike he fostered by protective tariffs, and sought to develop a healthy, able, and willing citizenry that the State might flourish and the army receive its appointed "cannon fodder." He was influenced also by the general idealistic attitude, already expressed by the patriotic Fichte in his *Closed Commercial State*, and by the Hegelian school, that true liberty can be attained only through state action, and that the State alone can make a free life possible through social reform and regulation. Bismarck was a friend of Ferdinand Lassalle, one of the founders of orthodox socialism, and from him he derived many collectivistic ideas without their complement of political democracy. Bismarck received vigorous support in his policies from economists like Rodbertus, Wagner, Schaeffle, and Schmoller, who in 1872 issued a manifesto against economic liberalism, and by their activity did much to spread the program of benevolent welfare legislation for the advantage of all classes of the nation. The social ideal of these so-called "Socialists of the Chair" is a state in which the friendly hand of the government directs such natural monopolies as the railroads, the telegraphs and telephones, and most municipal services; fosters industry and commerce through protective tariffs and subsidies; protects the working-class from accident and disease and the fear of old age by means of thoroughgoing factory legislation and by various forms of social insurance; and in general shapes economic institutions for the material and educational advance of the whole nation. It differs from liberalism and *laisser-faire* in setting the prosperity of the State consciously above that of the individual business man, in believing that enlightened self-interest must be checked and directed by intelligent social control, and in general in subordinating unlimited individual initiative to the collective wisdom and broader horizon of a trained body of experts.

Schmoller struck the keynote of this German State Socialism in his call for the formation of the Union for Social Politics, in 1873.

We are of the opinion that the unrestricted activity of partly hostile and unequally strong special interests is not in accord with the welfare of the community. On the contrary, the demands of the community and of humanity must assert themselves even in economic life, and well considered intervention of the State for protection of the threatened interests of all concerned should be promptly demanded. We do not regard this civic guardianship as a desperate expedient, as a necessary evil, but rather as the fulfilling of one of the highest tasks of our time and of our nation. In serious discharge of this task, the egoism of the individual and the immediate interests of the classes will fall into proper subordination to the permanent and higher destiny of the whole.[7]

Schmoller recognized the ethical duty of the community to look after its members.

We are bound to look into the future, in order to be sensitive to the impression that the tremendous increase of wealth must, at least in part, accrue to the advantage of the previously disinherited classes, and bring to them somewhat more participation in all the higher goods of civilization, in culture and comfort, if we are not to declare ourselves mentally and morally bankrupt. We are bound to see that the lower classes have a right to struggle for these things, that their compact agitation for a better situation is a necessary and just product of our free political life. We are bound, therefore, to perceive that a temporary increase of wages does not solve the social question, but that the kernel of the matter consists in placing the laborer within other conditions of life and work, which shall make of him another man in all respects.[8]

The success of specific measures like social insurance, factory legislation, labor exchanges, government ownership, municipal enterprises, and institutions of technical education, established chiefly with the aid of the Junker Conservatives and the Catholic Centrists, was sufficient to prove that, with the aid of a trained bureaucracy, the active rather than the passive policeman state could interfere with industry without any of the dire results feared by the liberals. Long before 1914 the successful competition of state-guided German business with the individual initiative of the British business man made it clear that directive and inventive ability did not necessarily suffer when economic life was made the conscious object of social policy, and the results of business enterprise became the concern and the responsibility of experts acting in the presumed interest of the nation as a whole. On the other hand, it seemed to many that such benevolent governmental activity lessened the individual responsibility of the mass of workers, and predisposed them to national enterprises of a questionable character; and it is to be feared that Bismarck and his supporters were working as much for a willing docility on the part of contented subjects as for the private good of those subjects themselves. The collectivistic state, administered by a bureaucracy with little democratic control, was in danger of becoming a servile state; the faults of any benevolent despotism seemed intensified when the system was applied to industrial life; and the building of such a system in the interest of an irresponsible nationalism seemed a threat to the established international order. In the case of Germany these fears were only too well justified; the state socialism begun under Bismarck, strengthened but not fundamentally altered in the tragic years of the Republic, has once more proved itself an admirable instrument for military power.

The ideas and the measures of this State Socialism spread to most European lands, promoted by the nationalistic impulse, the demands of the electorate, the adherence of the more far-sighted business men, and the teachings of representative economists. They secured wide popularity in England in particular; they were adopted by the Liberal-Unionists under Joseph Chamberlain, championed by the Liberal Party during its rebirth of power, 1905–1914, made the basis of the program of the Labour Party, and carried still further by the Conservatives. In the enactment of practical legislation elements of all these parties have coöperated, so that it may be said that for a generation the majority of the British nation has been committed to some form of State Socialism. The chief exponents of this collectivistic philosophy have been Conservatives like Joseph Chamberlain and his sons, Liberals like Lloyd George, Hobson, and Hobhouse, and Labourites like Macdonald, Henderson, and the Webbs. In contrast to Germany, British social legislation has been less benevolently handed down from above, and more a response to a democratic demand. It has not aimed at creating an efficient and docile military machine. And in the absence of acute pressure it has not undertaken those basic economic controls that have made the history of Germany a steady advance in State Capitalism. An excellent statement of the general social ideal back of a whole generation of British social politics is contained in an apology for the new State Socialism of the Neo-Liberals in 1906:

Without claiming too much for the new program which the Liberal Party has put forward, this, at least, may be asserted with confidence, that it implies a desertion of the old individualist standard and the adoption of a new principle — a principle which the Unionists call socialistic. If it be true that a positive policy of social reconstruction savors of socialism, then, of course, this contention can be justified. The main point is that the function of the State in the mind of the Liberal or Radical of to-day is much wider in scope than seemed possible to our predecessors. The State avowedly claims the right to interfere with industrial liberty and to modify the old economic view of the disposal of private property. Liberalism recognizes that it is no longer possible to accept the view that all men have an equal chance, and that there is nothing more to be done than merely to hold evenly the scales of government. As a matter of fact, the anomalies and the injustices of our present social system have compelled even our opponents to introduce ameliorative legislation. But the Liberal of to-day goes further. He asks that such economic changes shall be introduced as will make it possible for every man to possess a minimum of security and comfort. Property is no longer to have an undue claim; great wealth must be prepared to bear burdens in the interests of the whole community. Our social system must have an ethical basis.[9]

In the United States the teaching as well as the practice of an individualistic *laisser-faire* persisted much longer than in the countries of Western Europe. Down almost to 1914 leading social scientists like William Graham Sumner were still preaching a hard bright gospel of individual initiative, compounded of evolutionary doctrine and classical economics. But the social ideal of regulation and control was steadily winning adherents among economists and other social scientists, following the lead of the pioneer sociologist Lester F. Ward. In the last generation most industrial states, especially those in the West where farmers joined small business and workers to regulate first railroads and then "foreign" industries, began to pass social legislation. Aside from protective and health measures, American state inter-

[9] From *Democratic England*, by Percy Alden. Copyright, 1906, by The Macmillan Co. Reprinted by permission.

ference has always emphasized the desire of the middle class and small business to preserve "free competition" from the monopolistic tendencies it has developed. Under the leadership of La Follette Wisconsin was a successful pioneer. Theodore Roosevelt carried the ideas of "trust-busting" and social legislation into the arena of national politics, and Woodrow Wilson was the foremost statesman to expound the "New Freedom," whereby the government was to establish the conditions necessary for the economic freedom of the individual.

Human freedom consists in perfect adjustments of human interests and human activities and human energies. Now, the adjustments necessary between individuals, between individuals and the complex institutions amidst which they live, and between those institutions and the government, are infinitely more intricate to-day than ever before. Life has become complex; there are many more elements, more parts, to it than ever before. And, therefore, it is harder to keep everything adjusted — and harder to find out where the trouble lies when the machine gets out of order. You know that one of the interesting things that Mr. Jefferson said in those early days of simplicity which marked the beginnings of our government was that the best government consisted in as little governing as possible. And there is still a sense in which that is true. It is still intolerable for the government to interfere with our individual activities except where it is necessary to interfere with them in order to free them. But I feel confident that if Jefferson were living in our day he would see what we see: that the individual is caught in a great confused nexus of all sorts of complicated circumstances, and that to let him alone is to leave him helpless as against the obstacles with which he has to contend; and that, therefore, law in our day must come to the assistance of the individual. It must come to his assistance to see that he gets fair play; that is all, but that is much. Without the watchful interference, the resolute interference, of the government, there can be no fair play between individuals and such powerful institutions as the trusts. Freedom to-day is something more than being let alone. The program of a government of freedom must in these days be positive, not negative merely.[10]

The World War proved an enormous stimulus to concern with social reconstruction. For the first time multitudes of Americans became familiar with ideas and "proposed roads to freedom" known elsewhere for a generation. The leading social scientists had now definitely abandoned *laisser-faire* and the older individualism; they were eagerly exploring the possibilities of democratic methods of social control. In practical life busi-

[10] From *The New Freedom*, by Woodrow Wilson. Reprinted by permission of the publishers, Doubleday, Page & Co.

ness was still to enjoy an Indian summer of freedom; but even in those days social legislation steadily advanced in the industrial states. With the first pinch of the depression business turned to the government for help; and under the New Deal America began to catch up with Europe.

As a series of legislative measures put into effect, the New Deal has been a very mild form of the social regulation that other industrial lands have long adopted. It represents hardly more than the extension to a national scale of minimum guarantees and standards enjoyed in the industrial states of the Union for several decades, together with certain economic controls possible only on a federal basis. It has stood for the broad humanitarian ideal that society must step in to assist those who suffer most severely from the creakings of our economic system, that government can and must do something about its worst maladjustments. Beyond that, it has notoriously embodied a wide variety of hardly consistent economic programs, ranging from the old trust-busting to the corporate syndicalism of the N.R.A. Which program would come out on top in any particular legislation has depended on the strength of pressure groups and on the most insistent political demands of the moment. This multiplicity of counsel is a natural expression of the fact that in America there has been no clear-cut and crystallized body of opinion advocating an integrated program of economic reconstruction. Americans, even those convinced that such reconstruction is demanded, have not been agreed on any single plan. The result has been greater flexibility in dealing with specific problems, a flexibility consecrated in American experimental social philosophies, and almost widespread enough to be called the American social ideal. At the same time this experimental attitude, this willingness to try anything once, has exasperated all those business interests forced to make long-term commitments, and made it very difficult for them to plan for the future.

Yet if the New Deal has had no clear social vision of where it wanted to go, it has stood for certain definite ideals of how to get there. And to-day these ideals of political method are doubly important: because they are so widely shared as to be characteristically American, and because with the goals largely set by the nature of technology itself it is the methods of organizing its control that are at issue in our present crisis.

First, the New Deal mobilized in the service of the federal government the large fund of detailed knowledge amassed by a generation of careful social inquiry. Never had such a body of social scientists been collected at Washington; and on each of the specific problems an effort was made to secure the advice of much further expert opinion. Nor was this merely the technical skill of a trained bureaucracy; it was the best social intelligence of our society that was brought to bear.

Secondly, this social intelligence was translated into practical action through the political processes of compromise between various group pressures; it was not enforced from on high. The political skill was not perfect; plenty of mistakes were made; unnecessary antagonism was generated by too much talking in sweeping terms. But on the whole the New Deal was successful in carrying with it the mass of public opinion. And the very political imperfections made it clear that it was not a method that depended on a miraculous genius as a political leader. But it involved much more than the familiar devices of representative government and party and pressure politics. Many of the administrative agencies set up managed to enlist a wide coöperation among those vitally concerned. In the countless committees and boards of the agricultural administration, and to a lesser extent in the N.R.A. and other bureaus, men were called on to work out in responsible coöperation the details of solutions to their own problems. All in all, democratic methods had a chance to show what they could do, and they did not fail in the test. The resulting compromises and adjustments, the stopping short before insistent interested pressures, the necessity of bowing to an uninformed public opinion, were all intolerable to the absolutist, who could criticize quite rightly the destruction or distortion of many a program developed with admirable consistency and thoroughgoing logic; but they represented a workable democratic method.

Thirdly, the most serious question of the absolutists has been answered, and not in their favor. The "State" — which in American parlance becomes the Supreme Court — has not proved immune to influence by political methods. It has not stood permanently blocking the way to experimentation in social control, demanding a revolutionary "capture." The tactics that finally broke the dam were not particularly happy as politics, though they had good precedents in the history of representative government. But the net result was to remove the most serious obstacle in the face of democratic methods of social reconstruction.

The wisdom, the success, or the adequacy of the various devices by which the New Deal met its most unavoidable problems may seem largely irrelevant to-day. In our new crisis the important thing is that it did have a method for meeting problems. And that method — the experimental application of social intelligence to specific demands, under democratic control and with democratic responsibility — is what America has to offer as an alternative to the authoritarian and totalitarian political methods of other lands. It is at bottom close to what we mean by democracy: it is the American social ideal.

Religious and Humanitarian Ideals for an Industrial Society

Of great influence in breaking the hold of the older individualistic ideas and creating a body of public opinion willing to support the social legislation of the past generation have been the humanitarian teachings of sensitive and fore-sighted religious leaders. Catholics and Protestants alike have brought the prophetic visions of religion to bear on modern society; they have condemned the old economic order as unjust and incompatible with the ideals of Christian brotherhood and love. Such religious crusaders have tried to enlist the religious idealism of the churches in practical movements to "Christianize" the social order; the various formulations of "Social Christianity" have played an important part in getting men to realize the need for social reconstruction.

In France this tendency grew naturally out of the efforts of the liberal Catholics of the 1848 period. Under the Second Empire, so largely dominated by clerical influence, Le Play, an engineer and a pioneer sociologist, gave wide popularity to a movement for supplanting the older individualistic liberalism of the middle class by a call to the Church to perform in the modern age the earthly mission she fulfilled in the thirteenth century. Opposed on the one hand to the orthodox economic liberalism, and on the other to the various forms of socialism, he saw in intelligent coöperation under religious guidance the all-important hope of social peace. Relying somewhat on state interference, but more on the development of a coöperative spirit between masters and workmen, fostered by a new emphasis on that model of coöperation, the family group, he tried to promote under distinctively Catholic principles that benevolent industrialism that was advocated also by Saint-Simon and Comte. His ideal was completely paternalistic: the only salvation of the working classes must come from above, from some authority, some noble, landlord, employer, or local official. Its keynote is, "The master owes something to the worker beyond his mere wages."

More feasible and more influential has been the program of the Action Libérale, virtually the Catholic socialist party of France, founded by the Comte de Mun. It consciously seeks to reestablish in modern society the guild and corporative organization of the Middle Ages, under the aim and guidance of the Church — a modern version of the medieval vision of the City of God upon earth. Such a society, professing the Catholic faith, founded upon human brotherhood under the Father, in its hierarchical organization of social units would provide an equal life for all because all would be equally serving God in their industrial stations. "The corporations which would be set up under the ægis of religion would aim at making all their members contented with their lot, patient in toil, and disposed to lead a tranquil, happy life." [11] Aside from its paternalism, such a program resembles Guild-Socialism and Syndicalism, and on many occasions the Action Libérale and the French Syndicalists worked together against the individualism of the bourgeois Third Republic. This ideal of a neo-medieval order of "corporations" embracing both employers and workmen seemed in Latin lands a welcome alternative to the bitter class-conflict of proletarian syndicalism. It furnished much of the language and some of the inspiration to the Italian Fascist ideal of the "corporative state," and has provided a *modus vivendi* between the Church and secular Fascist dictatorships. In recent years, under the fear of Communism and under great political pressure, Catholic corporativism and Fascist movements have been drawing closer together. With the collapse of the Third Republic the two seem to have coalesced in France.

Similar ideas, medieval in origin and guild-socialistic in their working-out, were taught in Germany by Bishop von Ketteler, Canon Moufang, and Hitze, and in Austria by Karl Lüger, founder of the powerful Austrian Christian Socialist Party. Industry should be gradually taken over by creative guilds and regulated by them on religious principles.

> The solution of the social question is essentially and exclusively bound up with a reorganization of trades and professions. We must have the medieval régime of corporations reëstablished — a régime which offers a better solution of the social problem than any which existed either before or after. Of course times have changed, and certain features of the medieval régime would need modification. But some such corporative régime conceived in a more democratic spirit must form the economic basis.[12]

This program was actively pushed by the Austrian Christian Socialist Party, which ruled the destinies of the Austrian Republic after 1922, and endeavored to create a clerical corporative state.

In less thoroughgoing form Cardinal Manning, the great English prelate, supported social legislation and the labor movement in many a crisis. Guild Socialism received considerable attention from English and Irish Catholics, notably Chesterton and Belloc. In England and America, where the Church draws largely upon the working classes, it has naturally included strong tendencies toward social reform — though they have remained distinctly minority movements and have received little encouragement from the hierarchy.

The stamp of official approval on all these movements was given by Pope Leo XIII in his encyclical *Rerum Novarum*, in 1891. Affirming against socialism the justice of the right of private property, and the necessity of mutual coöperation in place of the class struggle, it nevertheless advocated clearly the main principles of Catholic Socialism, social legislation, and above all the formation of unions of workingmen like the older guilds.

> The State is the minister of God for good [13] [Leo quoted from Paul]. Employers and workmen may themselves effect much in the matter of which we treat, by means of those institutions and organizations which afford opportune assistance to those in need, and which draw the two orders more closely together ... Workingmen's organizations should be so organized and governed as to furnish the best and most suitable means for attaining what is aimed at — that is to say, for helping each

individual member to better his condition to the utmost in body, mind, and property.[14]

On the fortieth anniversary of *Rerum Novarum*, in 1931, Pope Pius XI reaffirmed its principles, condemning materialistic and secular socialism and calling for a fairer distribution between capital and labor.

In the hopeful post-war atmosphere of 1919 the American National Catholic War Council proclaimed this social ideal.

> The present system stands in grievous need of considerable modifications and improvement. Its main defects are three: Enormous inefficiency and waste in the production and distribution of commodities; insufficient incomes for the great majority of wage-earners; and unnecessarily large incomes for a small minority of privileged capitalists.[15]

As remedies, universal living wages, industrial education, harmonious relations between labor and capital, participation in management, and coöperative selling associations, were proposed.

> The full possibilities of increased production will not be realized so long as the majority of the workers remain mere wage-earners. The majority must somehow become owners, at least in part, of the instruments of production ... Though involving to a great extent the abolition of the wage-system, this would not mean the abolition of private ownership. The instruments of production would still be owned by individuals, not by the State.[16]

Under the able leadership of Father John A. Ryan, the National Catholic Welfare Council has continued to raise its voice in the same terms. During the depression years its criticisms and its proposals have been distinguished for their acumen and sanity. But save for a few outstanding leaders, notably the late Cardinal Mundelein, they cannot be said to have awakened the wholehearted enthusiasm of the hierarchy; the Church remains divided.

A similar "social gospel" has waxed strong among Protestants; though naturally it has not taken as definite a political and clerical form as in Catholicism. Indeed, the social gospel has come for most liberal Protestants to be the very core of religion, taught in the seminaries, preached in many a sermon, and embodied in many organizations and institutions. Most of the Protestant churches have established "social settlements" in the slums, following the pioneer example of Canon Barnes of Toynbee Hall in London in 1884. From such practical philanthropic efforts to more comprehensive proposals for a thoroughgoing "Christianizing of the social order," has been for many an easy step; nor must it be forgotten that much of the drive for liberal and progressive collectivism in Protestant lands has come from the attempt to follow the teachings of Jesus. The British Labour movement, in most of its older leaders, derived its moral inspiration from Christian ethics; and in general the Protestant social gospel has been much more radical and thoroughgoing than Catholic Socialism, if at the same time less definitely religious. In England the High Church party founded, under Bishops Westcott and Gore in 1889, the Christian Socialist Union, which has obtained a large following among the clergy in the industrial centers. In America many a voice has been raised for the Kingdom since the eighties, in the last generation notably those of Josiah Strong, Richard T. Ely, George D. Herron, and Walter Rauschenbusch, with a growing chorus since 1918. At the close of the World War many of the churches adopted extensive plans for social reconstruction. A quotation from one of these will bring out the general social ideal of liberal Protestantism.

According to the Christian conception of God He is the Lord of all life and of both worlds, the material as well as the spiritual. He is the creator of the physical universe and has made for the use of man all that it contains. Mankind in all its relations, therefore, must be organized according to the will of God, as revealed in Christ. The entire social order must be Christianized. The world as a whole is the subject of redemption.... It emphasizes the moral and spiritual factor as having its own independent contribution to make to the solution of economic problems. And it puts the problem of present industrial reconstruction in its true setting as part of the larger enterprise of the establishment of the Kingdom of God, extending beyond this world into another.[17]

Three principles are laid down for the Christian ideal of society: every personality possesses sacred worth as a child of God; brotherhood is the primary relation between man and man; loving service and mutual helpfulness is the fundamental law of Christian life. The resulting Kingdom of God upon earth

would be a coöperative social order in which the sacredness of every life was recognized and everyone found opportunity for the fullest self-expression of which he was capable; in which each individual gave himself gladly and whole-heartedly for ends that are socially valuable; in which the impulses to service and to creative action would be stronger than the acquisitive impulses, and all work be seen in terms of its spiritual significance as making possible fullness of life for all men; in which differences of talents and capacity meant proportional responsibilities and ministry to the common good; in which all lesser differences of race, of nation, and of class served to minister to the richness of an all-inclusive brotherhood; in which there hovered over all a sense of the reality of the Christ-like God, so that worship inspired service, as service expressed brotherhood.[18]

Such sentiments have inspired countless sermons, and elicited among ministers and laymen alike the most sincere and self-sacrificing devotion. They have helped to color the immense reservoir of humanitarian idealism that constitutes the core of American religion, and can be mobilized for so many a cause, both worthy and dubious. Their indirect effect in creating a temper willing to ameliorate the worst injustices and cruelties of industrial society has been inestimable. How far they have been an effective religious driving force, save in the hundreds of individuals they have contributed as leaders in practical social and economic movements, is more doubtful. Church bodies have been willing enough to endorse resolutions presented by zealous crusaders for social justice. But how seriously the mass of their membership has taken forthright and devastating religious critiques of our social disorder is open to question. In recent years there has undoubtedly spread a deep-seated and profound religious revulsion against any traffic with war. But it has been far easier to oppose war than to come to grips with the painful task of reconstructing capitalism.

The depression turned thoughtful religious leaders to a greater concern with the ills of our economic system than ever before; from them has come an increasing stream of realistic, penetrating, and thoroughgoing critiques. But it is significant that their programs had pretty well coalesced with secular efforts, and no longer showed much distinctive religious character or guidance. The social gospel was now not so much a definitely religious ideal as an emotional driving force behind secular ideals. And during the depression official religious bodies adopted few of those sweeping programs for industrial reconstruction that were so popular in the optimism of the post-war years. The issues had

[18] From *The Church and Industrial Reconstruction*, by W. A. Brown. Reprinted by permission of the publishers, Association Press.

been more tightly drawn; they had grown too practical and too serious for wide agreement. In the reaction against a too easy identification of the function of religion with the furtherance of some particular social program, many of the more radical religious leaders have come to distinguish sharply between the relative social ideals to which they are personally committed, and the transcendent Christian ideal of the Church itself. Christian idealism will not soon cease to be a major social momentum behind the drive for social reconstruction in America. But that drive is not likely to be influenced in its details by any distinctively Christian ideal.

Working-Class Ideals

We have dwelt at length upon these middle-class social ideals, because that class has been more able to express its aspirations, because it is still largely dominant in present-day society, and hence it is towards its aims that social forces have been mainly directed, and because in consequence such ideals, in every Western nation, have been shared by the great majority, whatever their class. The ideals of the large body of industrial workers have been in the main but modifications of these fundamental modern goals. What radically different social aims have been put forward by representatives of the laboring classes are diverse and conflicting, and at best seem as yet the expression of distinctly minority opinions. Nevertheless, since in the Western democracies these classes are growing rapidly in political and economic power, and unless the democracies are overwhelmed are likely to dominate the future — that pledge has already been given to British Labour, and in any event seems impossible to prevent — their aims demand the most serious consideration.

The fundamental ideal of the great body of workers, caught in the meshes of the industrial system — what corresponds in them to the ideal of material prosperity for the business man — is simple and direct: it is a living wage and security of position, getting and keeping a job. What the worker wants above all things is a secure position in society with the means to support a standard of living not markedly disproportionate to that of his neighbor; what he fears most of all is the loss of his job and the lowering of that standard, unemployment and destitution. The effect of the Industrial Revolution has been twofold; it has materially raised the real income of the masses, though middle-class optimism is not fully aware of the very large numbers still hovering around the bare subsistence level, and constantly in danger of falling below it with every disorder in the complex and easily upset industrial order. But at the same time the enormous multiplication of the material goods of life, with its rapid rise in the possible standard of living, has in effect, comparatively and psychologically speaking, made the worker seem worse off than ever before; the very uniformity of intellectual life, enforced through newspaper, magazine, and photoplay, has made the disparity between what might be and what is seem all the greater. And, above all, the modern economic régime has involved an almost complete loss of that security of position attained in an agricultural society, and has given the haunting fear of unemployment, for skilled and unskilled labor alike, a poignant and pressing immediacy. For the most part the individual worker is too preoccupied with getting a job and retaining it to look much farther into the future or much more widely around him at the body of society. Hence the readiness with which the promise of commercial prosperity, held out by the business men, secures his vote; in prosperous times at least he is more sure of a satisfactory job, and he must be fairly well off or else in desperate straits indeed before he will hazard any fundamental change against the certainty of the full dinner-pail.

With a fairly good wage and a fairly secure tenure, the next aim of the worker is to rise individually and achieve success, to lift himself or his children into the middle class, business or the professions. First to rise in Coketown, then in Megalopolis, and finally to attain a Country House of his own — this is the typical ideal of the worker still, sedulously fostered by the business man who wants able lieutenants, and who wishes to draw off the most pushing of the workers into his own circle. While the industrial machine was being created, it is probable that the ablest men did thus rise, especially in America; but the ladder has become harder and harder to climb with a class of the hereditary wealthy waxing in numbers and power. In practice, there are very few, in our society, who do not in their hearts desire to imitate the Avenue; and the self-made man is notoriously most out of sympathy with the group aspirations of the workers from which he rose.

Social Ideals of Organized Labor

Partly to gain security and a higher standard of living, partly because they have lost the hope of ever rising from their class, the workers have, in the last fifty years, increasingly sought rather to raise the general standard and position of the laboring group as a whole — or at least of their particular occupation. Labor organization, the trade-union movement, probably represents to-day the social ideal of the majority of the working-class; though nowhere is an actual majority of the workers organized, and in this country the Labor Movement includes at most a scant six million. But this is probably due primarily to the opposition of the employers: for there is no occupation in which that has been overcome that has not organized at least ninety per cent of its members. The fundamental aim of labor organization is to attain better conditions and greater security, not for the isolated individual, but for the group as a whole; and increasingly it has been forced upon the unions that the area within which individual competition must cease must be constantly widened if that organization is to achieve its ends. Hence, for example, the shift, in some way or other, from the trade to the industry as the basic unit, and the growing feeling of working-class solidarity against the business man. This means that the ideal of the workers has become more and more a genuinely social ideal, embracing the whole body of the workers, and envisaging the totality of the industrial system in its aim.

The primary aim, then, of organized labor in all lands is to get higher real wages with better working conditions; and it involves more or less of an equalizing process within the working-class itself. By collective bargaining, itself resting ultimately upon economic power, the right to withdraw labor or to strike, the unionists are seeking for more and more of the good things of life; and by bitter experience they have learned that they must act as a unit, subordinate private aims to the welfare of the group, enforce a uniformity of working conditions and a standardization of wages, and substitute coöperative endeavor for competition within the working-class. There are still great divergencies of interest between different union groups, divergencies that have long prevented the skilled craftsmen from organizing the workers in the mass production industries, and that have broken out in the bitter conflict between the A.F.L.

and the C.I.O.; but it is becoming increasingly clear that if the fundamental aims of organized labor are to be achieved, these conflicts must be harmonized.

What are these fundamental aims? For the majority of unionists, they are simply, more of what the business men have; but for a growing minority, they involve radical changes in the whole industrial ideal. The older generation of labor leaders, schooled in the bitter struggle for the very right to exist, stands for the first; but in every group men standing for the more radical aim, and the more broadly social vision, are coming to the fore. Orthodox unionists conceive their aim as the organization of a monopoly in labor and the selling of it to employers, as a business proposition, in return for a secure and improved status. Thus in 1895 John W. Sullivan welcomed the American Federation of Labor in these terms:

We run the largest local business enterprise on the American continent. This enterprise is to "bull" our labor market. We succeed. We keep wages up right along, twenty-five per cent above the level they would be were employers to have their way. In some cases we put them up fifty per cent. We thus retain for our own use half a million dollars which without our unions would go to enrich capitalists and monopolists. Twenty-six million dollars a year! That's our joint dividend, no less. We retain this wealth justly because we produce it. We retain it because we have the power to do it. We are well-organized, well-disciplined, well-led. We boast therefore in our chosen leaders the greatest Captains of Industry in this metropolitan center. Their equals in this community cannot be named.[19]

With somewhat broader social vision Samuel Gompers expressed the same basic ideal:

The American Federation of Labor is guided by the history of the past. It draws lessons from history in order to interpret conditions which confront working-people so that it may work along the lines of least resistance to accomplish the best results in improving the conditions of the working men, women, and children, to-day, to-morrow, and to-morrow's to-morrow, making each day a better day than the one which went before. This is the guiding principle, philosophy, and aim of the labor movement. We do not set any particular standard, but work for the best possible conditions immediately attainable for the workers. When these are obtained then we strive for better. The working people will not stop when any particular point is reached; they will never stop in their efforts to obtain a better life for themselves, for their wives, for their children, for all humanity. The object to attain is complete social justice.[20]

The present leadership of the A.F.L. has not departed from the aims of their founder; and though John L. Lewis differs from them on many points, most significantly in seeing the opportunity for increasing labor's power through organizing the mass production industries, he is no more concerned with the details of the eventual outcome.

But this initial aim of "more" demands the organization of economic power, which is increasingly used to exert a large measure of control over industry itself; and the very possession of this power of control makes necessary a further formulation of what "complete social justice" consists in. Hence in countless ways organized labor is taking more and more thought for the basic ends of industry, a tendency fostered on the one hand by the trend towards industrial organization, which makes possible planning in terms of an industry as a whole rather than of a mere isolated trade; and on the other, by the recognition of thoughtful employers that in order to awaken the workers to a sense of responsibility in the conduct of industry, it is necessary to enlist their direct coöperation in industrial management. The experience of the N.R.A., brief as it was, was profound in educating the labor leaders as well as the employers who took part in its counsels. Much of the success of the C.I.O. has been due to that training. From whatever causes and motives it springs, in England and America, as formerly in Germany, the aims of the labor movement have with its growing power expanded from a merely negative and limiting control over processes to a positive coöperation in the direction of those processes. It is no accident that when Britain was forced to make a serious effort to organize her economy on the most effective war basis, it was to leaders of Labour that she turned. The greater power organized labor attains, the greater its responsibility becomes, and the more prone its leaders are to set up aims for "complete social justice." For these reasons, elaborate formulations of widely social ideals are increasingly in vogue, and command much interest among the more thoughtful rank and file.

Industrial Democracy

These ideals of extensive social reorganization extend from the present type of collective bargaining to such radical programs as syndicalism and guild-socialism. Organized labor has already been the largest single body that has adopted and enacted the legislative program of State socialism; its lobbies and its votes have furnished the driving power behind the theories of middle-class liberals. The core of its more radical plans has been the conviction, however, that whatever be the function of the government, primary control over industry must be vested in large part in the organized workers themselves. This is the ideal of "industrial democracy," which by and large is the most widespread of present-day working-class ideals, exemplified in innumerable specific proposals and patiently being worked out in many experiments. The pioneers of industrial democracy, perhaps, have not always realized that it involves all the difficulties and problems which a half-century of political democracy has brought forth, on a greatly magnified scale because industry is much more complicated and much broader in scope than political government; they have been perhaps too optimistic. Yet political democrats at the outset shared these too fervent hopes, and only in practice have they realized the long and patient experimenting that must still take place before genuine democratic government can hope to be successful. The advocates of industrial democracy believe that the cure for the ills of democratic government is more democracy, democracy in all the interests of human life; and such an ideal seems at the basis of most working-class social philosophies to-day. Various detailed proposals have been worked out in both England and America in the past decades. Expressive of American experience was the Plumb plan, developed first for the railroads, and later elaborated for industry in general.

We are proposing a plan for the reorganization of industry on a basis of democracy. The principles that must govern such reorganization are the same as the principles that govern all human action and all human relations. . . . American democracy has builded into its foundations the principles upon which industry can be established upon a firm basis of economic efficiency and individual and social justice. . . . Our governments are instituted "for the common good, for the protection, safety, prosperity and happiness of the people." How can government secure to the people industrial liberty, and the right to enjoy the gains of their own industry? How can it protect the safety and happiness of the people, with regard to their industrial activities and interests? It can do these things by exercising the sovereign powers conferred upon it by the people, to provide such policy and organization for all industry as will secure to every individual the right to the free disposal of his own labor and of the fruits of his labor; that will reconcile and balance the interests of consumers and of the owners of labor and capital; and that will coördinate the several functions that are active in production, so that industry may serve its true purpose of supplying the economic wants of all the people. These purposes are industrial and economic purposes, and therefore can be achieved only by industrial organization and methods. . . . The corporation is the most efficient form of industrial coöperation that has ever been devised, and industrial corporations are public agencies, created for the performance of public services. . . . It is apparent, therefore, that if we can reorganize corporations so that there will be in coöperative industry an equal protection of rights and interests, and effective coördination of productive functions; and if we can devise a policy under which the corporation may be applied to all forms of coöperative industry, we shall have solved the problem of efficient and democratic industrial organization.[21]

The closest approach in this country to a concrete experiment with such democratic self-government of industry was the N.R.A., together with the more modest administration for bituminous coal. But the N.R.A. did not last long enough to determine whether in the struggle for control between big business and the government, anything would be left of democratic participation by the workers.

Industrial democracy, then, accepts the results of a century of large-scale industry, that the corporation is the best form for controlling the machine. But it disagrees with the business men in maintaining that the corporation must be democratically rather than oligarchically organized, and that its ends must be broadly social rather than the private interests of the controlling directors. This is an ideal that is deeply imbedded in the very function of labor organization; only the necessity of the struggle with industrial autocracy has warped and twisted this implicit aim. It must be confessed that any organization of American economic life would seem to demand a very great degree of decentralization or federalism, and a widely distributed initiative. American labor has always distrusted political control, though like business it has been free enough in demanding specific measures. But this implicit democratic syndicalism, like all the more theoretical proposals for decentralized administration of industry by the producers, has come into sharp conflict with the

[21] From *Industrial Democracy*, by Glenn E. Plumb. Reprinted by permission of the publishers, The Viking Press.

insistent practical demand for integration and planning on a national basis. Like the guild-socialism and political pluralism of the post-war decade, industrial democracy has been pushed into the background as a program by the problems of the centralized control of the industrial system as a whole. Just as the revolutionary syndicalism of Latin Europe has been incorporated in but rigidly subordinated to the totalitarian state, so the necessities of national planning have elsewhere taken precedence over concern with the democratization of industrial processes themselves.

Collectivistic Visions and Programs

For several generations strong working-class movements have set themselves, in most countries, still further social ideals of an absolutistic and millennial type. There have been those who hoped to use the power of the political State to control directly and bureaucratically the processes of production and distribution: Marxian Socialism, in its older orthodox and revisionary forms and in present-day Communism, expresses their faith. There have been those who, generalizing from the aims of organized labor, have painted pictures of a control of industry through the democratically organized groups of those participating directly in it: Syndicalism illustrates the extreme form, Guild Socialism the broader and more theoretical program. It is not part of our task to analyze these proposed roads to freedom, or to recount the story of those many social Utopias that have played so important a rôle in the thought of the last few generations. The tale is familiar, nor can we here attempt to remove the many prejudices that have gathered about them. They are, moreover, even in the minds of their adherents, rather visions of perfection than programs of action; and our concern is primarily with the latter, as depicting the goals that men to-day actually and seriously set themselves.

These programs are really embodiments of two fundamental and distinct ideals: State action for the control of industry, and group action for the self-government of industrial units. The one is the outgrowth of the rapid spread of State Socialism and collectivistic economic regulation. It is basically political in its attitude and temper, and has expressed itself in socialist parties. It thinks in terms of the industrial machine as a whole, and treats it as something to be manipulated from a center, in the interest of some political end. Neither this end nor the administration of control need be democratic at all, as the most spectacular embodiments make clear. The end may be mere economic efficiency or sheer military power, the administration may be highly centralized and authoritarian. The other ideal is the outgrowth of the organized labor movement. Its attitude is industrial rather than political, and it often distrusts state action and bureaucratic control; it prefers direct economic pressure. It thinks in terms of particular industries, pluralistically and specifically, and often neglects the problems of their coördination. But it is inherently democratic, for it springs, not from the desire to manipulate industry for some good end, but from the craving to have some voice, to count, in the work one is doing. With their diverse backgrounds these two ideals have often clashed. Politically minded socialists and communists are always irritating genuine trade unionists by trying to capture labor organizations for ulterior political ends. But both ideals emphasize important problems; and in any working program for the administration of industry, like those practically adopted by Russian Communists and by the British Labour Party, both have had to receive some solution.

In the last few years the more political ideal of socialism has received the lion's share of attention. The declining economy of the past decade, in forcing more and more actual state intervention; the rapidly increasing economic nationalism and autarchy; the impressive example of the Soviet Union — all have combined to emphasize state control. And the triumph and success of revolutionary socialism in Russia increased the appeal of the Communist method. Elsewhere on the Continent evolutionary socialism temporized until it was crushed; even the British Labour Party during its two periods of governmental administration failed to go beyond the well-worn paths of social legislation. In the midst of the chaos of the depression, the ideal of a "planned society," managed in the interests of the masses by a devoted and disciplined minority, fired the imagination. In Russia state industries were conducted by syndicates and trusts under experts; they were all directed and controlled by a hierarchy of councils and associations, culminating in the State Planning Commission (the *Gosplan*). Here at last had been realized a rationally coördinated and regulated economic system. Here the profit motive was replaced by the consecrated enthusiasm of an entire society valiantly striving to build a new social order. Here the chaotic pricing system of a market subject to all the raids and forays of irresponsible private interests had given way to intelligent allocation of resources and planning of production. So appealing was the ideal that generous minds found it easy to overlook how deeply entangled this centralized economic control was with a political dictatorship — easy, that is, for middle-class intellectuals and radicals; British and American labor were profoundly suspicious from the start, and in those lands the tiny Communist parties can scarcely be called working-class movements at all.

Whether a planned economy can succeed only under a political dictatorship, whether it is possible with democratic methods, or would in the end bring dictatorship in its wake, are much debated questions that can scarcely be settled by argument and logic. The experiment has not been tried, in Russia at least; it surely will be elsewhere. For the ideal of a planned industrial system has appealed to many who are firmly committed to democratic methods and resolutely opposed to even temporary dictatorship. In their vision of the new order British socialists differ little from the Communists; they too aim at a classless society and a centrally planned economy. The difference is not of final objective but of method — though there is great doubt whether means and ends can be so neatly dissevered, or whether non-democratic methods can ever reach a goal embodying the democratic quality of life. In Communism the emphasis is on centralization and dictatorship, in the Labour Party, on distributed and democratic control. The Labourites look forward to an industrial democracy of state-coördinated industries administered by expert boards subject to democratic control within industry, and ultimately to Parliamentary determination of policy. The basic program of the Labour Party grew out of its war experience, and was adopted in 1918:

> The first principle of the Labour Party is the securing to every member of the community, in good times and bad alike (and not only to the strong and able, the well-born or the fortunate), of all the requisites of healthy life and worthy citizenship. We are members one of another. No man liveth to himself alone. If any, even the humblest,

is made to suffer, the whole community and every one of us, whether or not we recognize the fact, is thereby injured. Generation after generation this has been the corner-stone of the faith of Labour. Thus it is that the Labour Party to-day stands for the universal application of the Policy of the National Minimum.... Secondly, it demands the full and genuine adoption of the principle of Democracy. The first condition of Democracy is effective personal freedom.... Hence the Labour Party insists on Democracy in industry as well as in government. It demands the progressive elimination from the control of industry of the private capitalist, individual or joint-stock; and the setting free of all who work, whether by hand or brain, for the service of the community, and of the community only.... What the Labour Party looks to is a genuinely scientific reorganization of the nation's industry, no longer deflected by individual profiteering, on the basis of the Common Ownership of the Means of Production; the equitable sharing of the proceeds among all who participate in any capacity, and only among these, and the adoption, in particular services and occupations, of those systems and methods of administration and control that may be found, in practice, best to promote, not profiteering, but the public interest.... Thirdly, the Labour Party stands for a revolution in national finance; for such a system of taxation as will yield all the necessary revenue to the Government without encroaching on the prescribed National Minimum Standard of Life of any family whatsoever; without hampering production or discouraging any useful personal effort, and with the nearest possible approximation to equality of sacrifice.... Finally, one main Pillar of the House that the Labour Party intends to build is the future appropriation of the Surplus, not to the enlargement of any individual fortune, but to the Common Good. It is from this constantly arising Surplus that will have to be found the new capital which the community day by day needs for the perpetual improvement and increase of its various enterprises.... From the same source must come the greatly increased public provision that the Labour Party will insist on being made for scientific investigation and original research, in every branch of knowledge, not to say also for the promotion of music, literature and fine art, which have been under Capitalism so greatly neglected, and upon which, so the Labour Party holds, any real development of civilization fundamentally depends.... Although the Purpose of the Labour Party must, by the law of its being, remain for all time unchanged, its Policy and its Program will, we hope, undergo a perpetual development, as knowledge grows, and as new phases of the social problem present themselves, in a continually finer adjustment of our measures to our ends. If Law is the Mother of Freedom, Science, to the Labour Party, must be the Parent of Law.[22]

In the immediate post-war years British Labourites were much interested in pushing the ideal of "workers' control." This was partly a result of the active propaganda of the Guild Socialists for "self-government in industry": they advocated handing over the administration of each industry to the whole body of workers engaged in it. It was due still more to the long experience of Labour in actual trade union practice, the expression of the labor movement's implicit aim. But the long slump proved unfavorable to any such demand by the unions; while political success, and more recently the growing fear of fascism, have turned them to ways and means of strengthening rather than of decentralizing the democratic state. In their detailed plans for the socialized administration of particular industries, of which many have been seriously offered, notably for coal; and still more in the various boards and authorities actually set up — like the Central Electricity Board — the general structure of existing management has been retained, with government-appointed directors instead of representatives of private shareholders. Democracy within industry has come to mean, not direct control, but the presence of advisory Works Councils — as in progressive private plants. The problems of democratic control seem at the moment to be more pressing in connection with the central planning and coördinating bodies than in the separate industries.

Non-Democratic and Authoritarian Methods

The goal an industrial society can hope to achieve is largely determined by the inherent nature and structure of technology itself. The detailed form its economic organization will take will depend on patient and critical inquiry into that structure, and on much painful experimentation, under whatever auspices. The basic issue is hence as to the methods used to attain that organization. By now we have had enough experience of collectivisms and planned economies to realize that the method whereby they are instituted is of supreme importance. For that method will profoundly color the kind of life lived under them, and the character of men they produce; it cannot easily be exchanged for another when its task is done. So far we have been examining the social ideals of men who cherish the sense of coöperative work, the give and take of human intercourse, the sense of dignity, of self-direction, of counting, that make up the democratic quality of life. We now turn to those of men who have sacrificed these values to the promise of a speedier and more effective method. It is the dictatorship of the proletariat and the totalitarian state that are challenging democratic processes to-day.

Communism stands for the socialist ideal of a planned economy and a classless society, the great objectives that have emerged out of industrial society. The achievements of the Soviet Union in its fervent devotion to these ideals are impressive and enlightening; they deserve the warmest sympathy and the most careful study. But Communist parties, in Russia and elsewhere, stand also for a certain political method, the dictatorship of the proletariat; and the consequences of that method have been continuing and permeating. The phrase is Marx's, but the development of the method in practice belongs to Lenin and his successors. Marx regarded the "State" of German political theory as essentially an organ of the capitalists in the class-struggle, the force by which they kept the exploited proletariat in subjection. By definition the "State" meant for him those functions of government that stand in the way of the interests of the proletariat, and are exercised for the benefit of the other side. The proletariat must therefore "capture" the State: when your side has won control, the government will then have no further function you do not like. Hence, as Engels put it, the State will "wither away," leaving only a good government or administration, not a hostile government or "State."

Wherever possible Marx favored constitutional methods for the capture of the capitalist State. But he accepted violent revolution when the occasion demanded, as in 1848 and again during the Paris Commune. After the capture he and Engels looked forward to a transitional period, during which the workers would control a government of almost unlimited power. Under this dictatorship of the proletariat they would consolidate their position, defend themselves against counter-revolution, and build up the institutions of a classless society. Gradually this working-class "State" would wither away; neither Marx nor Engels elaborated on what would be left. Engels's most precise statement is: "The government of persons is replaced by the administration of things and the direction of the process of production." [23]

Lenin, adapting this program to Russian conditions, and drawing on the pre-1848 writings of Marx's most revolutionary period, pushed the idea of a transitional dictatorship of the proletariat still further to the dictatorship of the Socialist — or Communist — Party on behalf of the proletariat. In his pamphlet *What is to be Done?* he laid down clearly in 1902 the functions and methods of a disciplined Marxian party. Industrial workers tend to become trade unionists spontaneously; but to be made into class-conscious socialists they must be indoctrinated with Marxist theory from outside by middle-class intellectuals.

> We said that [in the 1890's] *there could not yet be* Social Democratic consciousness among the workers. This consciousness could only be brought to them from without. The history of all countries shows that the working class, exclusively by its own effort, is able to develop only trade-union consciousness, i.e., it may itself realize the necessity for combining in unions, to fight against the employers and to strive to compel the government to pass necessary labor legislation, etc.[24]
>
> A small, compact core, consisting of reliable, experienced and hardened workers, with responsible agents in the principal districts and connected by all the rules of strict secrecy with the organizations of revolutionists, can, with the wide support of the masses and without an elaborate set of rules, perform all the functions of a trade-union organization, and perform them, moreover in the manner Social Democrats desire.[25]

The Communist Party thus becomes a picked body, absolutely devoted to Marxist principles, whose function is to gain the leadership of all working-class movements and steer them in the correct direction. "The Communist Party is the lever of political organization, with the help of which the more progressive part of the working class directs on the right path the whole mass of the proletariat and the semi-proletariat." [26] It must be subject to the most rigid discipline of action and opinion. When the Party has once reached a decision, there can be no further dissent; above all, there must be no tampering with the letter of Marx. "To belittle socialist ideology *in any way*, to *deviate from it in the slightest degree*, means strengthening bourgeois ideology." [27]

When Lenin with great skill gained control of the Russian Revolution, the Party naturally became the governing class of the new proletarian dictatorship. Its tight discipline over its members was not relaxed; all Communists — which meant all responsible government officials — were subject to the direction and the decisions of the Political Committee of the Party. The proletariat alone controls the government, the Party alone controls the proletariat — and it is little wonder that the Party control itself has become more and more centralized. Lenin was no democrat, and regarded majority-rule as a "constitutional illusion"; but with his fixed principles he combined an extraordinary gift for opportune compromise. His successor has not been so skilled in the arts of persuasion. Since the adoption of the program of "Socialism in Russia," the Soviet Union remains at class-war with the rest of the world, and will so remain till the delayed world revolution is consummated. Hence the disappearance of the class and party State has been postponed to the indefinite future. As Stalin explains:

The dictatorship of the proletariat is the weapon of the proletarian revolution, its organ, its most important stronghold, which is called into being, first, to crush the resistance of the overthrown exploiters and to consolidate its achievements; secondly, to lead the proletarian revolution to its completion, to lead the revolution onward to the complete victory of socialism ... The seizure of power is only the beginning. For a number of reasons, the bourgeoisie overthrown in one country remains for a considerable time stronger there than the proletariat which has overthrown it ... We must therefore regard the dictatorship of the proletariat, the transition ... as an entire historical epoch ... "The dictatorship of the proletariat," says Lenin, "is a persistent struggle — sanguinary and bloodless, violent and peaceful, military and economic, educational and administrative — against the forces and traditions of the old society. The force of habit of millions and tens of millions is a terrible force." [28]

The dictatorship of the totalitarian state was consciously modeled on the proletarian dictatorship. As political methods they have much in common; their present uneasy military alliance against the democratic world need have occasioned little surprise. Italian Fascism and German National Socialism also exhibit the same single-party control of all political life, the same dictatorship over the party, the same regimentation of opinion, the same inculcation of a secular political religion, the same effort at an organized economy. The striking difference is that for them the national state replaces the class as the object of supreme loyalty, and international conflict and hatred take the place of the class-struggle. In Italy, nationalism is combined with syndicalistic ideas in the ideal of the corporative state; in Germany, with developments of the indigenous state socialism.

Since the postponement of the world revolution and the soft-pedaling of the Communist International, totalitarian dictatorship has seemed the more dangerous to the outside world; the remarkable economic and military achievement of Germany has now made that danger a vivid reality. It is the curse of aggressive nationalism to be contagious; and despite its excellent record for peace, Russia, like every other nation, has at last been driven to act nakedly to protect its national interests, as the repository — also like every other nation — of the future hope of civilization.

The totalitarian state arose as the desperate answer to the breakdown of party government in the face of disruptive, long-drawn-out, and indecisive class conflict. Hence it has sought at every point to elevate the political power and the religious, moral, and emotional appeal of the national State. In support of this practical program it has drawn freely on the Hegelian doctrine of the organic totality of nation and state, already widespread in the thought of Central Europe. The Fascists, claiming that the State creates the nation (and seeking a colonial empire) have found the voluntaristic Hegelianism of Gentile and his followers congenial; the Nazis, anxious to consolidate all Germanic groups, have appealed rather to a mystical doctrine of race and racial instincts as the basis of the nation, of which the State is but the organ and agent. Both condemn the materialism alike of the Marxists and of individualistic liberalism with its defense of private freedoms. "The paradox of democracy and Marxism lies in the fact that both represent the most brutal, honorless materialism, and purposely support all the tendencies that favor anarchy, while at the same time they boast of their humanity and love for the oppressed and exploited." [29] For happiness fascism substitutes duty, for freedom, authority and discipline, for equality, hierarchy, and for numbers, quality.

Fascism, now and always, believes in holiness and in heroism; that is to say, in actions influenced by no economic motive, direct or indirect. And if the economic conception of history be denied, according to which theory men are no more than puppets, carried to and fro by the waves of chance while the real directing forces are quite out of their control, it follows that the existence of an unchangeable and unchanging class-war is also denied — the natural progeny of the economic conception of history ... Fascism denies the possibility of the materialist conception of happiness, and abandons it to its inventors, the economists of the first half of the nineteenth century: that is to say, fascism denies the validity of the equation, well-being is happiness, which would reduce men to the level of animals, caring for one thing only — to be fat and well-fed — and would thus degrade humanity to a purely physical existence.[30]

The Italian Charter of Labor of 1926 begins: "The Italian nation is an organism having ends, life, and means of action superior to those of the separate individuals or groups of individuals which compose it. It is a moral, political, and economic unity that is integrally realized in the Fascist State."[31] As Mussolini puts it: "For the fascist, all is comprised in the State, and nothing spiritual or human exists — much less has any value — outside the State. In this respect fascism is a totalizing concept, and the Fascist State — the unification and synthesis of every value — interprets, develops, and actualizes the whole life of the people."[32] In practice this conception supports whatever control the State may find necessary or desirable, whatever coordination of individuals and groups it may judge to serve its purpose. Fascism takes as its motto: "Everything for the State; nothing against the State; nothing outside the State." This opens the way for a total reconstruction of culture on a national — or racial — basis. Every value, economic, moral, or cultural, is a national value; the State, as the all-inclusive ethical end, must regulate them all in the interests of its own strength. Every organization, every institution is an organ and a creature of the State. To find one's true self in its service is the highest moral idealism. And every measure that can weld the nation into a solid monolithic block behind the single end of efficient military power bears all the momentum of a new religion.

Fascism has to be sure carried over much of the old syndicalist program: many of its leaders have been ex-syndicalists. It recognizes the reality of functional association, and the necessity of according it an appropriate place in the organized life of the nation. It has slowly worked out the institutions of the "corporative State"; the syndicates or unions of employers and of employees in each industry are united, with equal representation, into a corporation. These corporations are conceived as the next order of reality under the State; through them, under the State, the life of the nation is expressed. But even here nationalism has captured syndicalism. The corporations are not to be spontaneous and autonomous, with a life of their own; they are creatures of the State and subordinate contributors to its unitary life. In theory as in practice the corporative state is a device for securing the national control of industry rather than for industrial self-government.

For the actual government of this all-embracing State, every principle of parliamentary democracy is frankly repudiated. The State is controlled by the Party, and the Party avowedly by its Leader. For the person of the Leader expresses the collective will of the nation far better than any merely quantitative and "mechanical" device like the ballot. Human nature in politics is basically instinctive and irrational: fascists have drawn on the theories of all the voluntaristic anti-intellectualists from Nietzsche to Pareto. At best the masses of men have an instinctive sense of national welfare, enough to select and follow a leader, but not enough to judge the wisdom of his policies. They must be guided at every turn from above, by an élite, ordered in an ascending series of personalities. This principle the Fascists call "hierarchy"; the Nazis identify it still more frankly with the discipline of the old Prussian army.

> Fascism insists that the government be entrusted to men capable of rising above their own private interests and of realizing the aspirations of the social collectivity, considered in its unity and in its relation to the past and future. Fascism therefore not only rejects the dogma of popular sovereignty and substitutes for it that of state sovereignty, but it also proclaims that the great mass of citizens is not a suitable advocate of social interests, for the reason that the capacity to ignore individual private interests in favor of the higher demands of society and of history is a very rare gift and the privilege of the chosen few. Natural intelligence and cultural preparation are of great service in all such tasks. Still more valuable perhaps is the intuitiveness of rare great minds, their traditionalism and their inherited qualities.[33]
>
> In the old parliament, Authority and Responsibility were in reverse order. Responsibility went from top to bottom, and Authority went from bottom to top. That was a sin against natural law ... Here however the old principle holds good: Authority goes from top to bottom, but Responsibility always from bottom to top. Each is responsible to him who is called to stand next above him. The Leader carries final Responsibility. What the Leader wants will be done. His will is law for us."[34]

There can be no appeal to intelligent public opinion, to critical judgment. The masses live in the realm of feeling and will, not of intelligence; to govern them one must awaken fanaticism and even hysteria. And so fascist leadership employs consciously and avowedly all the devices of propaganda, from the shrewd counsels of Machiavelli to the latest techniques of modern advertising, to bend the masses to its will. Judicious terrorism has its recognized political function; for as Gentile points out: "Every force is a moral force, for it is always an expression of will; and whatever be the argument used — preaching or applying blackjacks — its efficacy can be none other than its ability finally to receive the inner support of a man and to persuade him to agree to it." [35] Even truth is an organ of the State: it is "the revelation of that which makes a people certain, clear, and strong in its action and knowledge."

The old idea of science based on the sovereign right of abstract intellectual activity is gone forever. The new science is entirely different from the idea of knowledge that found its value in an unchecked effort to reach the truth. The true freedom of science is to be an organ of a nation's living strength and of its historic fate.[36]

This unconditional devotion to the nation is an ideal of extraordinary power. It obviously makes possible whatever economic organization men may have the wit to work out, and whatever military adventures they have the strength to endure. It makes many things possible, and many others impossible. It offers the same psychological sense of security, the same sense of belonging to a great creative movement, the same emotional fusion with others, the same religious consecration and consolation, that Communism is capable of inspiring. But unlike the proletarian dictatorship, it holds out no hope for the future: it does not even pretend to be a transition to a more generous and humane world. And among the things it makes impossible are most of these goods most deeply embedded in our long moral tradition, disinterested inquiry, for instance, and democratic responsibility. Those things one must renounce to be strong.

Common to all the social ideals of our age is the conviction that modern society can no longer be left to develop and function without guidance. Intelligent control of its forces is fundamental, and such control must be devoted to the welfare of the entire community. Men must discover the best kind of life that can be lived with the resources and the compulsions of industrialism; and they must consciously plan, in the light of scientific knowledge and practice, how best to bring it nearer to man. In the hope of meeting this inescapable demand, great nations have unified themselves with fanatical faiths, and entrusted their destinies to self-appointed élites and dictators. In our troubled world, the goals are set for us. Can we advance towards them in our own way and by our own methods? No man yet knows the answer, for it depends upon ourselves.

Ideals of International Relations

In a world whose passionate hopes for peace have been so rudely disillusioned by the resurgence of sheer brute force, it may seem futile to speak of any ideal of international relations, save to have enough tanks and bombers to take on all comers. In retrospect, it appears that no group really believed in anything else but the international anarchy of military force, believed in it enough to modify their policies one iota — no one, that is, save multitudes in every land whose leaders have failed and betrayed them. But black as is the immediate future, for those with the detachment, and the courage, to take a longer view, the prospect is not wholly dark. If the failure of the last twenty years to achieve our high hopes has made anything clear, it is that our international anarchy cannot endure. It may be that sheer force itself will put an end to it, and Europe be organized under another iron *Pax Romana*. It may be that the Soviet Union will extend to the Atlantic. It may be that a new League of Nations will arise, or some other more closely integrated European union, profiting by the old mistakes and ready to make new ones. But what of Europe survives when the present conflict is concluded will be organized politically and economically; for there can be no conclusion until it is.

Looking back over the past century, we are confronted by the fact that the ideal of the sovereign and irresponsible national state, formulated by Machiavelli and Grotius in the harsh times of the break-up of medieval Christendom, has lost none of its force. The nineteenth-century wave of nationalism and economic imperialism served merely to intensify it and to carry it round the world. And to-day the totalitarian states have consecrated to it a fanaticism and a power never before equaled. Yet there have been vigorous alternatives. Eighteenth-century cosmopolitanism has been kept alive, and various forms of the internationalism of 1848 have developed growing strength. The ideal of international organization is so obviously rooted in a technological society, and so clearly demanded if our industrial machine is to function efficiently, or even to endure at all, that it cannot die: in some form it seems bound to come. Here too, as on the national scale, the method of its achievement raises the chief issues. The first great experiment, the League of Nations, begun amid such high hopes and such generous sentiment, was after all founded on force and dedicated to the forceful suppression of change. Perhaps the next will tell us whether it failed merely because its force was not strong enough.

In 1848 patriotism was primarily a liberating and progressive drive, looking forward to an international society of diversified and mutually coöperating nations. But with the achievement of independent and unified national existence, it was everywhere captured by interested economic groups, and bent to their private ends. "My country, right or wrong," came to be the creed of short-sighted business men and imperialistic greed, the chief and most potent instrument for uniting the masses behind a policy of commercial and industrial expansion reckless of its train of dissensions and wars. In those nationalities still subject to alien peoples, both before and since 1918, it retained indeed much of its earlier glamour; and here most men felt, and still feel, that its ends justify wars of liberation and defense. So strong was its appeal that the right of self-determination of small nationalities was written into the Versailles settlement; those whose oppressors had chosen the wrong side were set up as national states. The resulting Balkanization of Europe, with all its fresh oppressions, its unending dissensions, and its economic follies, has in the end merely made easy German and Russian absorption. The welter of small national states, strong enough to provoke their neighbors, yet too weak to resist and too jealous to unite, has proved an impossible principle of European organization. And the contrast in the larger powers between the earlier appeal of patriotism and its later fruits — between the Germany of 1848 and the Germany of 1914 and 1940, the Italy of Mazzini and the Italy of Mussolini, the patriotism of the Revolution and the patriotism of Poincaré, the self-sacrifice of both North and South in America in 1860 and the sad record of American imperialism in the Caribbean — has led many to conclude that, whatever its incidental spiritual and cultural values, patriotic nationalism is at present overwhelmingly a disserviceable and a sinister trait. These have come to agree with Veblen:

> The chief material use of the patriotic bent in modern populations appears to be its use to a limited class of persons engaged in foreign trade, or in business that comes in competition with foreign industry. It serves their private gain by lending effectual countenance to such restraint of international trade as would not be tolerated within the national domain. In so doing it has also the secondary and more sinister effect of dividing the nations on lines of rivalry and setting up irreconcilable claims and ambitions, of no material value but of far-reaching effect in the way of provocation to further international estrangement and eventual breach of the peace.... Into the cultural and technological system of the modern world, the patriotic spirit fits like dust in the eyes and sand in the bearings. Its net contribution to the outcome is obscuration, distrust, and retardation at every point where it touches the fortunes of modern mankind. Yet it is forever present in the counsels of the statesman and in the affections of the common man, and it never ceases to command the regard of all men as the prime attribute of manhood and the final test of the desirable citizen. It is scarcely an exaggeration to say that no other consideration is allowed in abatement of the claims of patriotic loyalty, and that such loyalty will be allowed to cover any multitude of sins. When the ancient philosopher described Man as a "political animal," this, in effect, was what he affirmed; and to-day the ancient maxim is as good as new. The patriotic spirit is at cross-purposes with modern life, but in any test case it is found that the claims of life yield before those of patriotism; and any voice that dissents from this order of things is as a voice crying in the wilderness.[37]

Patriotic Nationalism

Whatever its origin and its ultimate value, patriotism is beyond doubt the most widespread social ideal of the day; it is the modern religion, far stronger than mere Christianity in any of its forms, and to its tribal gods men give supreme allegiance. Nationalism is almost the one idea for which masses of men will still die. Commercial and industrial expansion afford it large scope, but it is in war, in devotion to military glory and heroism, that it finds its chief rituals. Nationalism has been taught in schools, emphasized in newspaper, magazine, and book, and

[37] From *The Nature of Peace*, by Thorstein Veblen. Reprinted by permission of the publishers, The Viking Press.

preached and mocked and sung into men, until to fail to feel the sweeping force of its appeal is to fail to belong to the modern world, to be an outlaw and a wanderer upon the face of the earth, that dreadful thing, a man without a country. Necessarily, so mighty a force enshrines priceless values; yet its present prostitution to unworthy and ignoble ends seems to many to counterbalance whatever of good it may include.

For many reasons this modern nationalism reached its first climax in the Germany of the Hohenzollern empire; but it numbered a majority in all other lands as well, if its exponents were not, on the whole, quite so frank and outspoken. Patriotism is, in practice at least, invidious: it lives by hatred of the foreigner. And the German chauvinists were merely consistent in seeing in war its highest expression. Many a man in every land has felt, if he has not often dared to express openly, what Treitschke said:

It is precisely political idealism that demands wars, while materialism condemns them. What a perversion of morality to wish to eliminate heroism from humanity! It is the heroes of a nation who are the figures that delight and inspire youthful minds; and among authors it is those whose words ring like the sound of trumpets whom as boys and youths we most admire. He who does not delight in them is too cowardly to bear arms himself for the fatherland. All reference to Christianity in this case is perverse. The Bible says explicitly that the powers that be shall bear the sword, and it also says: "Greater love hath no man than this, that he shall lay down his life for his friends." Those who declaim this nonsense of a perpetual peace do not understand the Aryan peoples; the Aryan peoples are above all things brave. They have always been men enough to protect with the sword what they had won by the spirit.... We must not consider all these things by the light of the reading-lamp alone; to the historian who lives in the world of will it is immediately clear that the demand for a perpetual peace is thoroughly reactionary; he sees that with war all movement, all growth, must be struck out of history. It has always been the tired, unintelligent, and enervated periods that have played with the dream of perpetual peace. However, it is not worth the trouble to discuss this matter further; the living God will see to it that war constantly returns as a dreadful medicine for the human race.[38]

The State is the people legally united as an independent power.... The State is Power for this reason only, that it may maintain itself alongside of other equally independent powers. War and the administration of justice are the first tasks of even the rudest barbaric State. But these tasks are only conceivable in a plurality of States permanently existing alongside of one another. Hence the idea of a World-State is odious;

the ideal of one State containing all mankind is no ideal at all. The whole content of civilization cannot be realized in a single State; in no single people can the virtues of the aristocracy and the democracy be found combined. All peoples, just like individual men, are one-sided, but in the very fullness of this one-sidedness the richness of the human race is seen. The rays of the divine light only appear in individual nations infinitely broken; each one exhibits a different picture and a different conception of the divinity. Every people has therefore the right to believe that certain powers of the divine reason display themselves in it at their highest. Without overrating itself a people does not arrive at knowledge of itself at all. The highest moral duty of the State is to safeguard its power. The individual must sacrifice himself for a higher community, of which he is a member; but the State is itself the highest in the external community of men, therefore the duty of self-elimination cannot affect it at all. The Christian duty of self-sacrifice for something higher has no existence whatever for the State, because there is nothing whatever beyond it in world-history; consequently it cannot sacrifice itself for anything higher. If the State sees its downfall confronting it, we praise it if it falls sword in hand. Self-sacrifice for a foreign nation is not only not moral, but it contradicts the idea of self-preservation, which is the highest thing for the State. Thus it follows from this, that we must distinguish between public and private morality. The order of rank of the various duties must necessarily be for the State, as it is power, quite other than for individual man. A whole series of these duties which are obligatory on the individual, are not to be thought of in any case for the State. To maintain itself counts for it always as the highest commandment; that is absolutely moral for it. And on that account we must declare that of all political sins that of weakness is the most reprehensible and the most contemptible; it is in politics the sin against the Holy Ghost.[39]

"War is the only remedy for ailing nations." The moment the State calls "Myself and my existence are now at stake!" social self-seeking must fall back and every party hate be silent. The individual must forget his own ego and feel himself a member of the whole; he must recognize what a nothing his life is in comparison with the general welfare. In that very point lies the loftiness of war, that the insignificant individual disappears entirely before the great thought of the State; the sacrifice of fellow countrymen for one another is nowhere so splendidly exhibited as in war. In such days the chaff is separated from the wheat.[40]

To hold the balance even, it is only fair to quote from an Englishman also; for before 1914 such passages might have been duplicated in any European country, or even in the United States. Nor can we forget that it was a brave American hero whose classic toast has so often served as the epitome of modern nationalism: "My country! In her foreign policy may she always be in the right — but my country, right or wrong!" Though set down in 1913, the following passage has especial pertinence to-day:

> One explanation of this extraordinary paradox in human history — the persistence of war in spite of what seems its unreason — is that there is something in war, after all, that is analogous to the heroism of Scott in the Antarctic zone, something that transcends reason; that in war and the right of war man has a possession which he values above religion, above industry and above social comforts; that in war man values the power which it affords of rising above life, the power which the spirit of man possesses to pursue the ideal. In all life at its height, in thought, art and action, there is a tendency to become transcendental; and if we examine the wars of England or of Germany in the past we find governing these wars throughout this higher power of heroism, or of something, at least, which transcends reason. Now for what have these wars been fought? Can one detect, underneath them, any governing idea, controlling them from first to last? I answer at once: There is such an idea, and that idea is the idea of Empire. All England's wars for the past five hundred years have been fought for empire.
> Is it possible to form any clear conception of what "Empire" has really always meant to England?... To give all men within its bounds an English mind; to give all who come within its sway the power to look at the things of man's life, at the past, at the future, from the standpoint of an Englishman; to diffuse within its bounds that high tolerance in religion which has marked this empire from its foundation; that reverence yet boldness before the mysteriousness of life and death characteristic of our great poets and our great thinkers; that love of free institutions, that pursuit of an ever-higher justice and a larger freedom which, rightly or wrongly, we associate with the temper and character of our race wherever it is dominant and secure. That is the conception of Empire and of England which persists through the changing fortunes of parties and the rise and fall of Cabinets. A government or a minister may seem to have the power arbitrarily to provoke a war which involves the suffering and deaths of thousands; but it is neither for government nor minister that the soldier falls. Lying there in agony, sinking into darkness, he has in himself the consciousness of this far greater thing, this mysterious, deathless, onward striving force, call it God, call it Destiny — but name it England. For England it is. To give all men within its bounds an English mind — that has been the purpose of our empire in the past. He who speaks of England's greatness speaks of this. Her renown, her glory, it is this, undying, imperishable, in the strictest sense of the word. And how is it thinkable that an English Shah Jehan should ever arise to imperil by bigotry the continuance of the British Raj? At moments, indeed, this empire seems to resemble a vast temple, with the vaulted skies for its dome and the viewless bounds of this planet for its walls. And within that temple

what prayers arise, in every accent, and what sound of hymns to every god that, down the long centuries, the human imagination has created or adored! But in this is one's final hope: that the English nation and race as a whole shall gradually perceive that if the task of internal organization is ever to be carried out in that tranquillity and security of spirit which is necessary for all high tasks in politics, England must take upon herself the fulfilment of her destiny, depending upon herself alone for the realization of a destiny that is *her* destiny.[41]

With two such ideals in the world, the outcome was inevitable.

And if the dire event of a war with Germany — if it *is* a dire event — should ever occur [written in 1913], there shall be seen upon this earth of ours a conflict which, beyond all others, will recall that description of the great Greek wars:

> Heroes in battle with heroes,
> And above them the wrathful gods.

And one can imagine the ancient, mighty deity of all the Teutonic kindred, throned above the clouds, looking serenely down upon that conflict, upon his favorite children, the English and the Germans, locked in a death-struggle, smiling upon the heroism of that struggle, the heroism of the children of Odin the War-god![42]

After four years of war such sentiments were no longer popular; and among the victors there have been few so bold as to speak since in the terms earlier common enough. Even in Germany for years opinion was overwhelmingly a passionate *"Nie wieder Krieg!"* But to those who were suffering from the Versailles Treaty — and this included Italians convinced that they had "won the war but lost the peace" — the successful Allies seemed to take every opportunity to convince them that they were condemned, not because their claims were not just, but because their arms had not been strong enough. And despite their sincere efforts to discourage aggression and change through the League of Nations, none of the former Allies in fact abandoned its nationalistic policies. The pressure of economic problems even drove them to a swiftly intensified economic nationalism. The Italian Fascists were the first to boast openly again of the "sacred egoism" of their national state. For their international policy has depended on bellicose threats, just as internally they have stridently appealed to all the military virtues. For years the most eloquent idealizations of war have been reiterated in Mussolini's speeches. In and out of season he has preached: "War alone brings all human energies to their highest tension and sets a seal of nobility on the peoples who have the virtue to face it." [43] Fortunately the Italians are too civilized a people to have absorbed this lesson or to have ceased to require this repeated exhortation. But the Germans have learned only too well that when they spoke of justice, they were rebuffed; when they rattled tanks and bombers, they got what they wanted. The Nazis have built on their deep sense of humiliation a more ardent military nationalism than any since the days of Napoleon; but even the Nazis could scarcely have done it without outside help.

Cosmopolitanism

What other ideals of international relations have men turned to? There is, first, the continuance of the cosmopolitanism of the Age of Reason, when the fact that "war transcends human reason" was not looked upon as a cogent argument in its favor. Such an ideal has been widely taught, and much less widely practiced, by two groups: first, the bankers and business men who have seen in national boundaries and above all in wars elements disturbing to trade; secondly, the working class, to whom all patriotism and war have seemed but the cloak of business greed and political and economic reaction. The first of these has descended from the Manchester cosmopolitanism of Cobden and Bright, with its evangelical and Quaker overtones; it has at times controlled the British Liberal Party, and such "Little Englanders" have even deprecated imperialistic expansion. This ideal has been ably represented by Thorstein Veblen and J. A. Hobson, and by a host of English liberals after 1918. Norman Angell before 1914 proved conclusively that neither imperialism nor war could bring prosperity to any but a small class of profiteers, while the nation suffered in every way. In *The Great Illusion* he tried to show that the belief that economic prosperity depends on national power "belongs to a stage of development out of which we have passed; that the commerce and industry of a people no longer depend upon the expansion of its political frontiers; that a nation's political and economic frontiers do not now necessarily coincide; that military power is socially and economically futile, and can have no relation to the prosperity of the people exercising it; that it is impossible for one nation to seize by force the wealth or trade of another — to enrich itself by subjugating, or imposing its will by force on another; that, in short, war, even when victorious, can no longer achieve those aims for which peoples strive." [44] After 1918 Angell was able to say, "I told you so"; and in spite of the business opportunities in national tariffs and in colonies, a vast number of business men, the much-abused "international bankers" at their head, came to feel that in economic coöperation rather than in rivalry lay the greatest prosperity and profits. Indeed, to many the League of Nations became a commercial ideal, in which investors of all nations could coöperate in brotherly fashion in exploiting the "backward portions of the globe." In America this cosmopolitanism of liberal capitalism reached its height during the twenties; Herbert Hoover was its leading exponent, though even he did not dare to take the consistent step of tariff reduction. Even to-day multitudes of business men and economists attribute all our evils to the breakdown of international free-trade. If only the barriers could be removed!

But the trend toward economic autarchy has been irresistible. It can be said that, broadly speaking, since economic life has had to be organized, it has had to be organized on a national basis; the multiplicity of controls set up has made impossible the old ideal of free-trade for the individual trader, and concentrated what international commerce remains under the close direction of governmental policy. Business cosmopolitanism seems to belong to a bygone stage of economic development. As yet no international economic organization has tied together the national organizations so far achieved. Even the arguments of Norman Angell are built on the presuppositions of an international order that has passed away. Mussolini says, "Political power creates wealth"; Hitler proclaims, "The German plow follows the German sword." Secretary Hull is crying in the jungle to those who follow the jungle's law.

For their part, all the more radical workers' movements have looked beyond national boundaries and seen in the "capitalist class" the only enemy; for them, loyalty and struggle run along class, not national lines. In 1848 Marx wrote:

> The working-men have no country. We cannot take from them what they have not got. Since the proletariat must first of all acquire political supremacy, must rise to be the leading class of the nation, must

constitute itself the nation, it is, so far, itself national, though not in the bourgeois sense of the word. National differences and antagonisms between peoples are daily more and more vanishing, owing to the development of the bourgeoisie, to freedom of commerce, to the world-market, to uniformity in the mode of production and in the conditions of life corresponding thereto.[45]

And Marx closed his *Manifesto* with the ringing words, "Working men of all countries, unite!" But the power of patriotism proved too much for this generous cosmopolitanism, and in 1914, with few exceptions, radicals were persuaded or forced to the colors. The fascists were quick to learn the lesson that intensified national feeling would wean the great mass of the workers away from the class-conscious minority. Their very aggressiveness has given a vital new meaning to international boundaries. With the world divided between fascist and non-fascist nations, for the democratic worker conflicts have become far more than the mere struggle of rival economic empires. The freedoms of liberal capitalism can no longer be taken for granted: they demand a passionate defense. And it is not easy to-day to hate Hitler and Mussolini and remember one's brothers, the German and Italian workers, so busily engaged in bombing and torpedoing. Indeed, the very depth and sincerity of the desire for peace in the last decade has ironically reconciled millions to the supposed necessity of waging war against fascist aggression, as the greatest threat to peace in our world.

Communists, relying on Lenin's interpretation of the World War, and on the wealth of support it brought to their position, have reiterated the Marxist principles. In "imperialist" wars the masses have no interest, save to turn them if possible into civil wars. But wars in behalf of oppressed nations — like India — wars against fascist aggression — like that of China against Japan, or the struggle against Italy in Ethiopia and Spain — and above all wars in defense of the workers' state against counter-revolution, all fall in a different category. The strength of the Soviet government has come in fact to depend more and more on Russian patriotism. And since the policy of a "united front" with the liberal parties in the democracies was abandoned, the Soviet Union has acted in defense of its own interests exactly like any other national state. In spite of all professions of world-brotherhood, the workers remain easily attracted by the patriotic appeal.

Internationalism and Pacifism

The second of the ideals opposing nationalism to-day is the heir of the internationalism of 1848, of Mazzini. It seeks not to destroy but to build upon existing national states. It was found liberal, compromising, and conciliatory in the programs for Leagues of Nations and World Courts, and the many other schemes for international organization with which the World War flooded the world; though recognizing weakness and grave defects, it continued hopefully to support the League even when all hope was gone. It has been found resolute and uncompromising among pacifists to whom war is the worst of evils and nationalism, uncoördinated in an international order, scarcely better. Such an attempt to unite the spiritual values of devotion to one's country with the higher values of devotion to all mankind has been framed by Santayana:

> A man's feet must be planted in his country, but his eyes should survey the world. What a statesman might well aim at would be to give the special sentiments and gifts of his countrymen such a turn that, while continuing all vital traditions, they might find less and less of what is human alien to their genius. Differences in nationality, founded on race and habitat, must always subsist; but what has been superadded artificially by ignorance and bigotry may be gradually abolished in view of universal relations better understood. There is a certain plane on which all races, if they reach it at all, must live in common, the plane of morals and science; which is not to say that even in those activities the mind betrays no racial accent. What is excluded from science and morals is not variety, but contradiction. Any community which had begun to cultivate the Life of Reason in those highest fields would tend to live rationally on all subordinate levels also; for with science and morality rationally applied the best possible use would be made of every local and historical accident. Where traditions had some virtue or necessity about them they would be preserved; where they were remediable prejudices they would be superseded.[46]

The liberal internationalists have wished some form of federation of nations, with no theoretical limitations upon national sovereignty. This proving quite unworkable as the League developed, they resorted to the earlier idea of a league to enforce peace, under the appealing guise of "collective security." This too has now gone down in the débâcle; its difficulties had not been unsuspected by critics since the days of Versailles. It is likely that the next attempt at international organization, whether under a *Pax Germanica*, or under a chastened Britain, will be much less solicitous of sovereign rights. Before sheer self-defense absorbed all other energies, opinion seemed to be crystallizing in favor of much closer European union. Any such European superstate would be likely to succeed in the measure that it emphasized not the mere enforcement of peace, but the peaceful administration of changes that would otherwise break out into open war.

The more uncompromising and pacifist internationalists, rejecting the idea of suppressing war and aggression by military force, have concentrated rather on making it unnecessary by providing adequate and workable substitutes. They have approached the problem of international organization in terms of developing genuine processes of government rather than of setting up a system of courts and an international police force. In 1838 William Lloyd Garrison formulated a declaration of principles that on the negative side might well stand to-day:

We cannot acknowledge allegiance to any human government.... We recognize but one King and Law-giver, one Judge and Ruler of mankind.... Our country is the world, our countrymen are all mankind. We love the land of our nativity only as we love all other lands. The interests, rights, and liberties of American citizens are no more dear to us than are those of the whole human race. Hence we can allow no appeal to patriotism, to revenge any national insult or injury. We register our testimony, not only against all wars, whether offensive or defensive, but all preparations for war; against every naval ship, every arsenal, every fortification; against the militia system and a standing army; against all military chieftains and soldiers; against all monuments commemorative of victory over a foreign foe, all trophies won in battle, all celebrations in honor of military or naval exploits; against all appropriations for the defence of a nation by force and arms on the part of any legislative body; against every edict of government, requiring of its subjects military service. Hence, we deem it unlawful to bear arms, or to hold a military office.[47]

But pacifist internationalism is not merely negative; as Jane Addams made clear, "People are not obliged to choose between violence and passive acceptance of unjust conditions for themselves and others, but moral courage and active good-will will achieve more than violence." [48] A contemporary formulation of principles puts it: "Peace is more than an absence of war. It is a vital principle which must be applied to all human relations. Peace is to be attained only by free coöperation for the common good. To achieve international and internal peace, machinery for free coöperation must be set up and expanded." [49] It is significant that from Versailles on such pacifists have pointed out the probable consequences of the structure and the policies of the League of Nations. To them, it has seemed a fatal flaw to attempt to preserve peace by threatening a collective war against the proponents of change. And in fact much of the failure of the League was due to this internal contradiction: its support came from those who, hoping that the mere threat of war would be enough to prevent it, were not prepared psychologically or materially for the war that would make that threat effective. To pacifists the path to the abolition of war depends upon renouncing war as an instrument of international as well as of national policy. But the renouncing of one instrument demands the substitution of others equally effective. It calls for the much more difficult and complex working out of methods that will accomplish what war secures in the redistribution of power. Pacifist internationalists have been in the forefront of this insistent task. But even the sheer refusal of public opinion to entertain the possibility of war can have a tremendous influence in forcing governments to face the problem.

The great pacifist internationalist Romain Rolland, during the equally tragic days of the last conflict, penned a statement that is pertinent to-day:

Humanity is a symphony of great collective souls; and he who understands and loves it only by destroying a part of those elements, proves himself a barbarian and shows his idea of harmony to be no better than the idea of order another held in Warsaw. For the finer spirits of Europe there are two dwelling-places: our earthly fatherland, and that other City of God. Of the one we are the guests, of the other the builders. To the one let us give our lives and our faithful hearts; but neither family, friend, nor fatherland, nor aught that we love has power over the spirit. The spirit is the light. It is our duty to lift it above tempests, and thrust aside the clouds which threaten to obscure it; to build higher and stronger, dominating the injustice and hatred of nations, the walls of that city wherein the souls of the whole world may assemble.[50]

In one sense, we have completed our survey of the beliefs that, coming from the past and operating in the present, go to make up the contents of the minds of men to-day. We have traced those streams of thought and aspiration which have gone to swell the flood of ideas and ideals which dominate the present.

There is no final picture, no possible harmonization of tendencies into one great symphony of the mind. Such a unity belongs, if anywhere, at the beginning of our story, in the Middle Ages; since that time, and increasingly in the last century, the tale has been rather of multiplicity and diversity. There is hardly a belief of the past that does not enter, in some form, into the modern world as the object of passionate allegiance. And to-day it is more difficult than for generations to point to any beliefs or ideals the future will surely adopt as its own. For we are convinced, and not without good reason, that our civilization is at a genuine crisis. We cannot go on evading the problems of organizing our economic life and our international anarchy. If we do not soon resolve to face them, we shall succumb to those who will. Can we succeed by democratic methods, by following the lead of experimental intelligence to the conclusions it imposes as best? Or must we too resort to authoritarian and irrational faiths, to the methods of compulsion and military force? If we must, we must say good-bye to the democratic release of the powers of human nature, and to the free and inquiring life of the mind. For democratic ends demand democratic methods for their realization, and it is not by blind submission that men can attain further truth.

Yet on the chaotic diversity of the modern mind this issue imposes its own unification. It selects what beliefs and what aims we must choose. Our science has brought us knowledge and power; our philosophy has delivered us from the search for a cosmic sanction to use that science for human ends. And we have generated a faith of our own, a faith in the efficacy of the methods of experimental intelligence, in the service of a freedom which is coöperative and a coöperation which is voluntary. The task is difficult, but even in these times it is not impossible. For we have faith, and we have intelligence, and these two will determine our future.

The world has need of a philosophy, or a religion, which will promote life. But in order to promote life it is necessary to value something other than mere life. Life devoted only to life is animal without any real human value, incapable of preserving men permanently from weariness and the feeling that all is vanity. If life is to be fully human it must serve some end which seems, in some sense, outside human life, some end which is impersonal and above mankind, such as God or truth or beauty. Those who best promote life do not have life for their purpose. They aim rather at what seems like a gradual incarnation, a bringing into our human existence of something eternal, something that appears to imagination to live in a heaven remote from strife and failure and the devouring jaws of Time. Contact with this eternal world — even if it be only a world of our imagining — brings a strength and a fundamental peace which cannot be wholly destroyed by the struggles and apparent failures of our temporal life. It is this happy contemplation of what is eternal that Spinoza calls the intellectual love of God. To those who have once known it, it is the key of wisdom. By contact with what is eternal, by devoting ourselves to bringing something of the Divine into this troubled world, we can make our own lives creative even now, even in the midst of the cruelty and strife and hatred that surround us on every hand.... Wisdom and hope are what the world needs; and though it fights against them, it gives its respect to them in the end.[51]

This is Faith; and whatever storms betide, it will remain a precious heritage of man. But there is one thing of even greater worth than Faith; and that is Thought.

Men fear thought as they fear nothing else on earth — more than ruin, more even than death. Thought is subversive and revolutionary, destructive and terrible; thought is merciless to privilege, established institutions, and comfortable habits; thought is anarchic and lawless, indifferent to authority, careless of the well-tried wisdom of the ages. Thought looks into the pit of hell and is not afraid. It sees man, a feeble speck, surrounded by unfathomable depths of silence; yet it bears itself proudly, as unmoved as if it were lord of the universe. Thought is great and swift and free, the light of the world, and the chief glory of man.[52]

REFERENCES

1. Paul Brissenden, *The I.W.W.*, 349.
2. James Mill, *Essay on Government*.
3. Lewis Mumford, *The Story of Utopias*, 201.
4. *Ibid.*, 202, 204, 210.
5. *Ibid.*, 212, 214, 215, 216.
6. *Ibid.*, 228, 230.
7. Gustav Schmoller, *Schriften*, I, 202.
8. Schmoller, *The Social Question and the Prussian State*, quoted in A. W. Small, *The Origins of Sociology*, 252.
9. Percy Alden, *Democratic England*, 5–7.
10. Woodrow Wilson, *The New Freedom*, 282–84.
11. Encyclical of Leo XIII, *Quod apostolici*, December 28, 1878.
12. Franz Hitze, *Capital and Labor*, quoted in Gide and Rist, *History of Economic Doctrines*, 496.
13. Encyclical of Leo XIII, *Immortale Dei*.
14. Encyclical of Leo XIII, *Rerum Novarum*, 1891; quoted in F. Nitti, *Catholic Socialism*, 418–20.

---

[51] [52] From *Why Men Fight*, by Bertrand Russell. Reprinted by permission of the publishers, The Century Co.

15. National Catholic War Council, *Social Reconstruction Report*, 1919; quoted in W. Hamilton, *Current Economic Problems*, 877.
16. *Ibid.*
17. W. A. Brown, ed., *The Church and Industrial Reconstruction*, 6, 7.
18. *Ibid.*, 31.
19. John W. Sullivan, in *Proceedings* of the 1895 Convention of the American Federation of Labor.
20. Samuel Gompers, *The American Labor Movement*, 1915.
21. Glenn E. Plumb, *Industrial Democracy*, 156, 157.
22. Arthur Henderson *et al.*, *Labour and the New Social Order;* quoted in P. U. Kellogg and A. Gleason, *British Labour and the War*, 375, 381, 382, 387-94.
23. F. Engels, *Anti-Dühring*, tr. E. Burns, 315.
24. N. Lenin, *Collected Works*, ed. Lenin Institute, IV, Bk. II, 114 f.
25. *Ibid.*, 194.
26. Resolution of Congress of the Communist International, 1920.
27. N. Lenin, *What is to be Done?* in *Collected Works*, IV, Bk. II, 123.
28. Joseph Stalin, *Leninism*, I, 41, 43, 96.
29. Alfred Rosenberg, *Der Mythus des 20. Jahrhunderts*, 192.
30. B. Mussolini, art. *Fascismo* in *Enciclopedia Italiana*, XIV; tr. in *International Conciliation*, No. 306.
31. Tr. in H. W. Schneider, *Making the Fascist State*, 333.
32. B. Mussolini, art. in *Enciclopedia Italiana*.
33. A. Rocco, *The Political Doctrine of Fascism*, 1925; tr. in *International Conciliation*, No. 223.
34. Hermann Goering, speech of September 15, 1935.
35. G. Gentile, *Che cosa è il fascismo*, 1925; tr. in Schneider, *op. cit.*, 347.
36. Bernard Rust, speech at Heidelberg centenary, June 30, 1936.
37. Thorstein Veblen, *The Nature of Peace*, 75, 40.
38. Heinrich Treitschke, *Selections from Politics*, Gowan tr., 24, 25.
39. *Ibid.*, 9, 31.
40. *Ibid.*, 23.
41. J. A. Cramb, *Germany and England* (1913), 60, 61, 124-28, 136.
42. *Ibid.*, 136.
43. B. Mussolini, art. in *Enciclopedia Italiana*.
44. Norman Angell, *The Great Illusion*, p. x.
45. Karl Marx, *Communist Manifesto*, ch. 2.
46. G. Santayana, *Reason in Society*, 175.
47. W. L. Garrison, *Declaration of Sentiments adopted by the Peace Convention held in Boston*, 1838.
48. Jane Addams, 1919.
49. *Declaration of Principles* of Women's International League for Peace and Freedom, U.S. Section, 1940.
50. Romain Rolland, *Above the Battle*, 54.
51. Bertrand Russell, *Why Men Fight*, 268.
52. *Ibid.*, 178.

SELECTED READING LISTS

General Background: See bibliographies under Chs. XIII and XVII. S. H. Slichter, *Modern Economic Society;* H. Taylor, *Cont. Problems in the U.S.;* A. A. Berle and G. C. Means, *The Modern Corporation and Private Property;* J. M. Clark, *Social Control of Business.* T. Veblen, *Theory of Business Enterprise, Theory of the Leisure Class.* Graham Wallas, *The Great Society.* R. H. Tawney, *The Acquisitive Society.* T. Arnold, *Folklore of Capitalism.* — **General Surveys:** Bertrand Russell, *Proposed Roads to Freedom, Freedom vs. Organization, 1814–1914;* Jerome Davis, *Contemp. Social Movements;* A. Birnie, *Ec. Hist. of Europe, 1760–1930;* F. W. Coker, *Recent Pol. Thought;* H. E. Barnes, *Hist. of W. Civ.*, ch. 24; D. O. Wagner, ed., *Social Reformers: Adam Smith to John Dewey;* G. D. H. Cole, *Mod. Theories and Forms of Pol. Organization, of Industrial Organization.*

Middle-Class Ideals: C. J. H. Hayes, *Hist. of Mod. Europe;* R. H. Gretton, *The*

Middle Class; J. Corbin, *Return of the Middle Class.* J. L. and B. Hammond, *Town Labourer,* x, xi (the mind and conscience of the rich). Lewis Mumford, *Story of Utopias.* R. Dell, *France.* N. A. Berdyaev, *The Bourgeois Mind.* Jerome Davis, *Capitalism and its Culture;* L. Corey, *The Crisis of the Middle Class;* T. Arnold, *Folklore of Capitalism.*

Social Reform under the Middle Class: Birnie, ch. 14; F. A. Ogg and W. R. Sharp, *Ec. Dev. of Mod. Europe,* chs. 17, 18; Coker, ch. 16. C. W. Pipkin, *Soc. Politics and Modern Democracy;* M. S. Callcott and W. C. Waterman, *Princ. of Social Legislation.* — **English Factory Legislation:** B. L. Hutchins and A. Harrison, *Hist. of Factory Legislation;* A. V. Dicey, *Law and Public Opinion in England during the 19th Cent.* — **German State Socialism:** Gide and Rist, *H. of Econ. Doctrines;* A. W. Small, *Origins of Sociology;* C. Andler, *Les origines du socialisme d'état en Allemagne* (bibl.); G. Richard, *La question sociale.* A. Wagner, *Grundlegung d. pol. Oekonomie* (theoretical background). K. Rodbertus, *Soziale Briefe;* F. Lassalle, *Arbeiterlesebuch;* lives of Lassalle by Brandes, Oncken. W. Rathenau, *The New Society.* T. Veblen, *Imperial Germany and the Indust. Rev.;* W. H. Dawson, *Bismarck and State Socialism, The German Workman, Social Insurance in Germany, 1883–1911;* A. Ashley, *Soc. Policy of Bismarck.* M. R. Carroll, *Unemployment Insurance in Germany.* — **British State Socialism:** C. J. H. Hayes, *British Social Politics;* P. Alden, *Democratic England;* L. T. Hobhouse, *Democracy and Reaction;* W. S. Churchill, *Liberalism and the Social Problem;* J. A. Hobson, *The Crisis of Liberalism;* H. G. Wells, *The New Machiavelli.* W. H. Beveridge, *Past and Present of Unemployment Insurance;* A. C. C. Hill and I. Lubin, *British Attack on Unemployment.* — **France:** E. Levasseur, *Hist. des classes ouvrières et de l'industrie en France de 1789 à 1870, Questions ouvrières et industrielles en France sous la 3e République;* R. Fighiera, *La protection légale des travailleurs en France.* — **U.S.A.:** H. V. Faulkner, *Amer. Econ. Hist.;* J. R. Commons and J. B. Andrews, *Princ. of Labor Legislation;* Callcott and Waterman, *Princ. of Soc. Legis.;* E. M. Burns, *Toward Social Security;* P. H. Douglas, *Soc. Security in the U.S.;* I. M. Rubinow, *Quest for Security.* Lester F. Ward, esp. *Applied Sociology* (fountain head); W. E. Weyl, *The New Democracy;* H. Croly, *Promise of Amer. Life;* W. Lippmann, *Preface to Politics, Drift and Mastery.* Woodrow Wilson, *The New Freedom.* — **The New Deal:** H. A. Wallace, *New Frontiers, New Deal in Action;* M. Ezekiel, *Jobs for All;* R. G. Tugwell, *Battle for Democracy.* L. M. Hacker, *Sh. Hist. of the New Deal;* Stolberg and Vinton, *Econ. Consequences of the New Deal.*

Religious Tendencies in Social Reform: See Ch. XX. **Catholic:** F. Nitti, *Catholic Socialism;* P. T. Moon, *The Labor Problem and the Social Catholic Movement in France.* Lamennais, *La question du travail* (1848); F. Le Play, *La réforme sociale* (1864); Comte de Mun, *La question sociale au xixe siècle;* F. Huet, *La regne sociale du Christianisme.* G. Metlake, *Christian Social Reform,* von Ketteler; Moufang, *The Soc. Question and Christianity* (1864); Hitze, *Capital and Labor.* Leo XIII, encyc. *Quod apostolici* (1878), *Rerum Novarum* (1891). National Catholic War Council, *Social Reconstruction;* J. A. Ryan, *The Church and Labor, A Better Economic Order.* — **Protestant:** C. Kingsley, *Alton Locke;* sermon, "The Church's Message to the Workers" (1851); F. D. Maurice; T. Carlyle, *Past and Present, Chartism;* J. Ruskin, *Unto this Last, Munera Pulveris, Fors Clavigera.* Fremantle, Rauschenbusch, and the social gospel, see Ch. XX. Sherwood Eddy, *A Pilgrimage of Ideas;* Kirby Page, *Living Triumphantly.* Post-war programs: The Archbishops' Fifth Committee of Inquiry, *Christianity and Ind. Problems;* Federal Council of the Churches of Christ in Amer., *Social Ideals of the Churches* (1916), *The Church and Industrial Reconstruction* (1920), *The Churches and the Internat. Crisis* (1939); *Quakerism and Industry.*

Organized Labor: Britain: S. and B. Webb, *Hist. of Trade-Unionism; Industrial Democracy.* P. Blanshard, *Outline of the Brit. Labor Movement;* R. H. Tawney, *The Brit. Labor Movement.* P. U. Kellogg and A. Gleason, *Brit. Labor and the War;* A. Gleason, *What the Workers Want;* L. T. Hobhouse, *The Labour Movement;* G. D. H. Cole, *The World of Labour, Organized Labour.* A. Henderson, *The Aims of Labour.* J. H. Richardson, *Ind. Relations in G.B.* —

SOCIAL IDEALS IN THE GROWING WORLD 683

U.S.A.: Mary Beard, *Sh. H. of the Amer. Labor Movement;* J. R. Commons and associates, *History of Labour in the U.S.; Documentary Hist. of Amer. Ind. Society* (chiefly before the A.F.L.). L. L. Lorwin and Flexner, *The A.F. of L.;* Zaretz, *The Amalgamated Clothing Workers of Amer.;* J. M. Budish and G. Soule, *The New Unionism.* Frank Tannenbaum, *The Labor Movement;* S. Perlman, *Theory of the Labor Movement.* By labor leaders: T. V. Powderly, *Thirty Years of Labor* (1890); John Mitchell, *Organized Labor* (1903); S. Gompers, *Labor in Europe and America, Autobiography.* R. R. R. Brooks, *When Labor Organizes, Unions of their Own Choosing;* E. Levinson, *Labor on the March.* — **France:** L. Levine, *Syndicalism in France;* G. Weill, *Hist. du mouvement social en France, 1854–1910;* H. Lagardelle, *Le socialisme ouvrier* (by a syndicalist); P. Louis, *H. du mouvement syndical en France, Le syndicalisme européen;* M. R. Clark, *H. of the French Labor Movement (1910–1928);* D. J. Saposs, *Labor Movement in Post-war France.*
Industrial Democracy: *Coal Industry Commission Report,* 1919 (Sanky Report); G. E. Plumb and W. G. Roylance, *Industrial Democracy.* — **Guild Socialism:** G. D. H. Cole, *Self-Government in Industry, Social Theory, Guild Socialism.* S. G. Hobson, *National Guilds and the State;* Reckitt and Bechhofer, *Meaning of National Guilds.* Niles Carpenter, *Guild Socialism* (critique); see B. Russell; Coker, ch. 9; H. W. Laidler, *H. of Socialist Thought,* ch. 23.
Socialism: Histories by socialists: T. Kirkup, *H. of Socialism;* H. W. Laidler, *H. of Soc. Thought;* M. Beer, *H. of Brit. Socialism;* J. Longuet, *Le parti socialiste en France;* M. Hillquit, *H. of Soc. in the U.S.;* by non-socialists: J. Rae, *Cont. Socialism* (1884); W. Sombart, *Socialism and the Socialist Movement;* F. Mehring, *Ges. d. deutschen Sozialdemokratie.* Marx and Engels, see Ch. XVII. K. Kautsky, *The Social Revolution;* R. C. K. Ensor, *Mod. Socialism.* Revisionists: E. Bernstein, *Evolutionary Socialism;* J. R. Macdonald, *The Soc. Movement; Socialism, Critical and Constructive; Parliament and Revolution. Fabian Tracts;* E. R. Pease, *H. of the Fabian Society.* S. and B. Webb, *Decay of Capitalist Society, A Constitution for the Socialist Commonwealth of Great Britain. The Labour Party's Aim: a Criticism and a Restatement.* M. Hillquit, *Present-Day Socialism;* Norman Thomas; H. W. Laidler.
Economic Planning: F. MacKenzie, *Planned Society;* G. Soule, *A Planned Society, The Coming Amer. Revolution.* H. Loeb, *Life in a Technocracy;* J. G. Frederick, ed., *For and Against Technocracy.* — **Critiques of planning and socialism:** A. C. Pigou, *Socialism vs. Capitalism;* W. H. Beveridge, *Planning under Socialism;* L. von Mises, *Socialism;* O. Lange and F. M. Taylor, *On the Economic Theory of Socialism;* L. Robbins, *Econ. Planning and International Order;* F. von Hayek, etc., *Collectivistic Econ. Planning;* W. Lippmann, *The Good Society.*
Communism: *Handbook of Marxism;* Lenin, *What is to be Done? The State and Revolution;* Stalin, *Leninism.* J. Strachey, *The Coming Struggle for Power, Nature of Capitalist Crisis.* H. J. Laski, *Communism;* S. and B. Webb, *Soviet Communism: A New Civilization.* L. Trotsky, *H. of the Russian Revolution;* W. H. Chamberlin, *H. of the Russian Rev.; Soviet Planned Econ. Order; Russia's Iron Age.* A. Rosenberg, *H. of Bolshevism;* F. Borkenau, *The Communist International.* J. Freeman, *The Soviet Worker;* C. B. Hoover, *Econ. Life of Soviet Russia.* S. H. M. Chang, *Marxian Theory of the State;* H. Kohn, *Nationalism in the Soviet Union.* K. Kautsky, *Dictatorship of the Proletariat* (critique).
Totalitarianism: Sabine; Coker. G. S. Ford, *Dictatorship in the Modern World;* L. Rogers, *Crisis Governments.* M. Ascoli and A. Feiler, *Fascism: For Whom?* H. B. Ashton, *The Fascist: His State of Mind.* — **Fascism:** H. W. Schneider, *Making the Fascist State,* (with S. B. Clough) *Making Fascists, The Fascist Government of Italy.* H. Finer, *Mussolini's Italy;* F. Pitigliani, *Italian Corporative State;* C. T. Schmidt, *The Corporative State in Action;* C. Haider, *Capital and Labor under Fascism.* A. Rossi, *Rise of Italian Fascism;* G. Salvemini, *Under the Axe of Fascism.* Mussolini, art. "Fascism" in *Enc. Italiana,* XIV; A. Rocco, *Political Doctrine of Fascism;* G. Gentile, *Che cosa è il fascismo.* — **National Socialism:** K. Heiden, *H. of Nat. Socialism, Hitler;* F. Ermarth, *The New Germany: N.S. Government in Theory and Practice;*

R. Brady, *Spirit and Structure of German Fascism;* E. Fränkel, *The Dual State;* F. L. Schuman, *The Nazi Dictatorship;* C. W. Guillebaud, *Economic Recovery of Germany, 1933–39.* Hitler, *Mein Kampf;* A. Rosenberg, *Der Mythus des 20. Jahrhunderts;* A. Kolnai, *War against the West.*

Democratic Methods: John Dewey, *Liberalism and Social Action, Freedom and Culture.* T. V. Smith, *Democratic Way of Life, Promise of Amer. Politics.* G. S. Counts, *Prospects for Democracy.* C. A. Beard, *America in Midpassage.* M. Lerner, *It's Later than you Think.* A. D. Lindsay, *Essentials of Democracy;* C. D. Burns, *Democracy: Its Defects and Advantages; Challenge to Democracy;* H. J. Laski, *Liberty in the Modern State, Democracy in Crisis, The State in Theory and Practice.*

International Ideals: W. C. Langsam, *World since 1914;* F. L. Schuman, *International Politics.* F. S. Marvin, ed., *Unity of Western Civilization;* C. D. Burns, *H. of Int. Intercourse.* C. Plater, *Primer of Peace and War: the Princ. of Int. Morality* (clear Catholic view). Veblen, *Nature of Peace.*

Nationalism and Militarism: See Ch. XVII. J. A. Hobson, *Imperialism;* P. T. Moon, *Imper. and World Politics;* L. S. Woolf, *Econ. Imperialism, Empire and Commerce in Africa.* H. C. Engelbrecht and F. C. Hanighen, *Merchants of Death.* Hayes, *Essays on Nationalism, Hist. Evol. of Mod. Nationalism;* C. E. Merriam, *Making of Citizens.* F. Delaisi, *Pol. Myths and Econ. Realities;* E. M. Patterson, ed., *World Trend towards Nationalism;* C. A. Beard, *Idea of National Interest, Open Door at Home.* F. H. Hankins, *Racial Basis of Civilization.* H. von Treitschke, *Politics;* F. von Bernhardi, *Germany and the Next War.* J. A. Cramb, *Origins and Destiny of Imperial Britain, Germany and England* (British chauvinism); Homer Lea, *Day of the Saxon, Valor of Ignorance* (American). Karl Pearson, *National Life from the Standpoint of Science* (biological defense of war). Criticisms of pacifism: A. T. Mahan, *Armaments and Arbitration: or the Place of Force in International Relations* (1912); J. K. Jones, *Econ. of War and Conquest* (1915; refutation of Angell); G. G. Coulton, *Main Illusions of Pacifism* (1916); R. Niebuhr, *Moral Man and Immoral Society;* P. H. K. Lothian, *Pacifism is not Enough.* See under Fascism and National Socialism, esp. Mussolini, Hitler, Rosenberg.

Liberal Internationalism: J. B. Scott, *Peace Conferences of 1899 and 1907;* N. M. Butler, *The International Mind;* J. A. Hobson, *Towards International Government* (1915), *Democracy after the War;* H. N. Brailsford, *A League of Nations* (1917); G. L. Dickinson, *The European Anarchy, The Choice before Us.* S. P. Duggan, ed., *The League of Nations;* T. Marburg, *Dev. of the League of Nations Idea;* J. S. Bassett, *League of Nations;* F. Morley, *Society of Nations.* J. T. Shotwell, *War as an Instrument of National Policy;* F. G. Tuttle, *Alternatives to War;* P. C. Jessup, *Internat. Security;* Clarence Streit, *Union Now.* P. B. Potter, *Int. to Study of Internat. Organization;* H. M. Vinacke, *Internat. Organization;* J. H. Randall, *A World Community.* G. Santayana, *Reason in Society;* Felix Adler, *Ethical Phil. of Life, Reconstruction of the Spiritual Ideal;* H. G. Wells.

Pacifist Internationalism: Devere Allen, *The Fight for Peace;* A. C. F. Beales, *Hist. of Peace;* B. F. Trueblood, *Dev. of the Peace Idea;* M. E. Curti, *The Amer. Peace Crusade, 1815–1860; Bryan and World Peace; Peace or War: the Amer. Struggle, 1636–1936.* Charles Sumner, *True Grandeur of Nations,* in *Addresses on War;* Tolstoy; J. S. Bloch, *Future of War* (military viewpoint); Norman Angell, *Great Illusion, Fruits of Victory* (economic); F. W. Hirst, *Pol. Econ. of War.* David Starr Jordan, *War and Waste, Aftermath of War* (biological); F. Nikolai, *Biology of War;* J. Novicow, *Les luttes entre les sociétés humaines* (refutation of social Darwinism); G. Nasmyth, *Social Progress and the Darwinian Theory.* Romain Rolland, *Above the Battle;* Bertrand Russell, *Justice in War-Time, Why Men Fight, Which Way to Peace?* Jane Addams, *Peace and Bread in Time of War, The Second 20 Years at Hull House;* M. L. Degen, *Hist. of the Women's Peace Party.* D. Allen, ed., *Pacifism in the Modern World.* M. K. Gandhi, *Great Thoughts of M. Gandhi, Speeches and Writings;* C. F. Andrews, *M. Gandhi's Ideas;* K. Shridharani, *War without Violence.* L. Richards, *Realistic Pacifism;* Canon Raven, *War and the Christian;* W. W. Van Kirk, *Religion Renounces War.*

INDEX

Abelard, 93, 94, 96
Absolutism, political, 181–85, 190; in Calvinism, 151; in 18th century, 334; scientific, 336 ff.
Action Libérale, 642
Adam of St. Victor, 94
Adams, John, 347–49
Addams, Jane, 677
Adelard of Bath, 209
Adler, Felix, 564
Aestheticism, and pessimism, 592
A.F. of L. (American Federation of Labor), 649, 651
Age of Reason, shortcomings of, 396 ff.
Agnosticism, 271, 535
Agrarian problems, 629
Agricola, Rudolf, 132
Agriculture in Middle Ages, 82, 83
Albert of Saxony, 212, 216
Alberti, L. B., universal man, 136
Albertus Magnus (Albert the Great), 80
Alfonso of Naples, 120
Alhazen, 210
Allegorical method in scholasticism, 97
Althusius, 189, 190
American Constitution, theory of, 345 ff.
Ames, E. S., 567
Amos, 40
Ampère, J. J., 471
Anarchism, philosophic, 453
Angell, Norman, 673, 674
Anselm, Saint, 93
Anthony, Saint, and Oriental dualism, 63, 64
Anthropology, 507, 520 ff.
Anti-clericalism, 549
Apollonius, 217
Aquinas, Saint Thomas, 31, 59, 80, 94 ff., 117
Arabian science, 208 ff.
Archimedes, 217, 238
Aristarchus, 218
Aristotle, astronomy, 32; in scholasticism, 93, 96; in Arabian science, 208; and medieval science, 211, 213; and early modern science, 216, 217, 228, 232, 235, 237.

Arminians, 285
Arnold, Matthew, 564, 587, 597
Art, Italian Renaissance, 124 ff.; Flemish, 127; in Romanticism, 438
Asceticism, in Plato, 47; in East, 47; in Christianity, 48; 62 ff.; rejected by Reformation, 155
Ashley, W., 525
Association, Laws of, 314, 315
Astronomy, medieval, 23, 24, 32, 228 ff.; Aristotelian, 233, 469; in 17th century, 226 ff.; in 19th century, 469, 484
Athanasian creed, 45
Atheism, 268, 298 ff., 535; not tolerated, 375
Atomic theory, 458, 470, 471, 474, 475
Augustine, Saint, 19, 96; on nature of God, 34; on grace, 48; and Reformation, 146, 149; and Protestant neo-orthodoxy, 539, 571
Austin, John, 380, 501
Authoritarian methods of economic organization, 658 ff.
Avencebrol, 210
Averroistic Aristotelians, 216
Avicenna, 209
Ayer, A. J., 615

Bacon, Francis, typical of Renaissance, 130, 204; and Roger Bacon, 210, 211; attack on scholasticism, 213–15; and scientific method, 222, 230; and Diderot, 266
Bacon, Roger, 210, 211; attack on scholasticism, 214
Baconian spirit, 223, 616, 626
Bagehot, Walter, 506
Baldi, Bernardino, 216
Balfour, Lord, 581
Banking in Renaissance, 113
Baptists, 544
Barbarian invasions, 11
Barberini, Cardinal (Pope Urban VIII) 234
Barclay, Robert, 410
Barnett, Canon Samuel Augustus, 644
Barth, Karl, 569, 570

INDEX

Bartholomew the Englishman, 22, 26 ff.
Basedow, Johann Bernhard, 415
Basil, Saint, 64
Baur, F. C., 464, 503
Baxter, Richard, 160
Bayard, Chevalier, 136
Bayle, Pierre, 167, 298, 373, 374
Beccaria, C. B., 372
Becquerel, Antoine Henri, 473
Behaviorism in psychology, 481 ff., 512 ff.
Belloc, H., 643
Bembo, Cardinal, 122
Benedetti, Giambattista, 217
Benedict, Saint, rule of, 65
Bentham, Jeremy, 310, 311, 317, 359 ff., 381, 441, 500, 501, 626
Bergson, Henri, 399, 459, 549, 606 ff.
Berkeley, George, 310
Bernard of Clairvaux, Saint, 68 ff., 94
Bernard, Claude, 479
Bernoulli, Daniel, 260
Bessel, Friedrich Wilhelm, 229
Beza, Theodore, 189
Bible, in Lutheranism, 149, 150; in Calvinism, 152; higher criticism of, 552, 553
Bill of Rights in American Constitution, 348
Biology, 479 ff., 491, 497; influence on sociology, 504 ff.
Bismarck, 634–36
Blanc, Louis, 453–55
Blondel, Maurice, 547
Bluntschli, J. C., 447, 505
Boas, Franz, 522
Bodin, Jean, 182, 184 ff., 188, 190, 193
Bohr, Niels, 474
Bonald, Vicomte de, 435, 439
Boniface, Saint, 65
Boniface VIII, 162
Borgia, Alexander, 124, 125
Bossuet, 18, 286
Boucher, Jean, 189
Boyle, Robert, 256
Bradley, F. H., 599
Brahe, Tycho, 229–32
Brandon, Saint, 33
Bright, John, 443, 452, 675
British Labour Party, 636, 645, 647, 651, 655 ff.
Broad Church Party, in Anglican Church, 536
Broglie, Louis de, 458, 473, 474
Bruni, Leonardo, 119
Brunner, Emil, 569
Bruno, Giordano, 111, 130, 220, 242 ff.
Bryce, James, 321, 527
Buchanan, George, 189

Buchez, P. B. J., 450, 453
Buffon, 264, 279, 308, 461, 462, 484, 486
Bullionism, 192
Bunyan, John, 158, 159
Buridan, John, 212
Burke, Edmund, 371, 410, 430, 432 ff., 437
Bury, Arthur, 291
Butler, Joseph, 298, 299, 368, 540
Byron, 411

Cabet, Étienne, 453
Cajetan of Thiene, 216
Calculus, 258
Calvin, 148 ff.
Calvinism, 150 ff.; predestination in, 150; and absolute monarchy, 151; and nationalism, 151, 152; and Bible, 152; and constitutionalism, 189; and religious rationalism, 283 ff.
Camoëns, Luis de, 207
Capitalism, in Renaissance, 113; and Reformation, 152; and Puritan ethic, 161
Cardano, Girolamo, 216, 223
Carlyle, Thomas, 414, 415, 450, 600
Cartesian Revolution, 217, 218, 226, 235 ff.
Cartesianism and religion, 286
Castiglione, B., 136
Catholic Democrats, in 1848, 453, 641
Catholic Reformation, 144, 153 ff.; and nationalism, 163; and education, 165
Catholic Renaissance, 549, 550
Catholic Socialism, 453, 643, 644
Catholicism, and absolutism, 190; revival of in 19th century, 438, 535 ff.; conservatism in, 545; renaissance in 20th century, 549, 550
Cattell, James M., 512
Cavendish, Henry, 264
Celestine IV, Pope, 62
Cellini, Benvenuto, 125
Chalcedon, Council of, 48
Chamberlain, Joseph, 636
Channing, William Ellery, 540
Charter of Labor, Italian, 663
Chartist Movement, 452
Chartres, School of, 209
Chateaubriand, 438
Chaucer, 87
Checks and balances, system of, 348
Chemistry, 264, 468 ff., 479
Chesterton, G. K., 643
Chivalry, 84, 85. *See* Knighthood
Christendom, ideal of united, 102 ff.
Christian epic, 18 ff.; preserved in Reformation, 144, 148
Christian Science, 601
Christian socialism, 452, 643, 645, 646

INDEX

Christian Socialist Union, 645
Christianity, effect on Western civilization, 38; conservative influence, 44; and Neo-Platonism, 46; dualism in, 47, 48; theology of, 48; medieval ideals, 52 ff.; Lutheran ideals, 137 ff., 149; Calvinistic ideals, 151; 18th-century conception, 366, 404 ff.; 19th-century, 533 ff.
Chromosomes, 489
Chrysoloras, 119
Chubb, Thomas, 291
Church, beginnings of system, 14; institution of, 50; and power of grace, 50; regular and secular clergy, 61; organization in Middle Ages, 61 ff., 75; and lay society in Middle Ages, 76; sacraments, 50, 76; inquisition, 79; conflict with State, 104; church union today, 572; and social reconstruction, 645–47
Cicero, 115, 121, 133; 218, 228; pacifism, of, 195
C.I.O. (Congress of Industrial Organization), 650, 651
City of God, 19
Civilization, Western, definition of, 10; origin, 11, 12
Clark, John Bates, 523
Clarke, Samuel, 286, 290, 367, 540
Classics in Renaissance, 118, 121
Class struggle, 675
Clergy, medieval, 21; regular, 61
Clericalism, 549, 550
Clough, Arthur Hugh, 589, 596
Cluny, 14
Cobden, Richard, 443, 444, 673
Coketown, 630–32, 648
Colbert, Jean Baptiste, 193
Cole, G. D. H., 528
Coleridge, Samuel Taylor, 403, 411, 414
Colet, John, 121
Collective security, 676
Collins, Anthony, 292
Columba, Saint, 65
Commerce, in Middle Ages, 89; in Renaissance, 113
Commercial Revolution, 192, 206
Communism, 528, 549, 568, 627, 642, 654–56, 659–61, 665, 675
Community churches, 573
Complexity, intellectual, 389 ff., 679
Comte, Auguste, 266, 450, 463, 500, 506, 510, 519, 562, 579, 642
Concordat of Bologna, 162
Condillac, 310
Conditioned reflex, 482, 513
Condorcet, 371, 382, 383, 422, 463
Congregationalists, 544

Conservation of energy, 470, 472, 475, 476
Conservatism, influence of Saint Paul on, 44; and *laisser-faire*, 331; and Romanticism, 403; philosophy of, 428 ff.
Constantine the African, 209
Constantinople, 11, 14, 15
Constitutionalism, 189 ff.; in Holland, 190 ff., 335; theory of, 339 ff.
Coöperative movement, 452
Copernican revolution, 226 ff.
Copernicus, 212, 218, 227–29, 234
Corporative state, clerical, 549; Fascist, 642, 661, 663, 664
Cosimo de' Medici, 124
Cosmopolitanism, 277, 370, 377 ff., 443, 667, 673–75
Coulomb, C. A., 471
Counter-Reformation, 144, 153 ff. *See* Catholic Reformation
Country House, ideal of, 630, 631, 648
Courtier, ideal of, 136
Cousin, Victor, 464
Cramb, J. A., 671, 672
Cremonini, Cesare, 216
Criminology, 372
Crisis theology, 569
Criticism of Bible, by Humanists, 147; in 19th century, 551–53
Cromwell, Oliver, 189, 193
Crusader, ideal of, 88
Crusades, 15, 205
Cunningham, W., 525
Cuvier, 486
Cyrenaicism, new, 592

Dalton, John, 264
Dante, world-view of, 32; and principles of interpretation, 97; and absolutism, 104, 181; 232
Dark Ages, 12, 13
Darwin, Charles, 458, 461, 485, 487 ff.
Darwin, Erasmus, 486
Darwinism, social, 507
Davenport, H. J., 525
Davis, Jerome, 568
Davy, Humphry, 470
Declaration of Independence, American, 346
Defiance of Mechanism, philosophy of, 596
Deism, 285; attack on revelation, 291; criticised, 294 ff.
Democracy, Rousseau's theory of, 349 ff.; Jeffersonian, 355; Jacksonian, 355, 357 ff.; social, 453 ff.; modern, 528; industrial, 652 ff.
Democratic methods, 393, 625, 640, 641, 658, 666, 679

Descartes, 211, 212; criticism of scholasticism, 215; and scientific method, 222; goal of science, 224; influence of, 239 ff.; mechanistic theory, 240 ff., 255, 256, 268
Dewey, John, 491, 494, 514, 518, 519, 567, 605–06, 615, 616, 618
Diderot, 264–66, 278, 283, 291, 292, 336, 337, 370
Dietrich of Freiberg, 210
Diophantus, 217
Dismal science, 328
Disraeli, 452
Dissipation of energy, 470
Divine Right of Kings, 181. *See* Political theory
Dodwell, Henry, 299
Dogmas, Catholic, 544
Dominic, Saint, 80
Dostoievsky, F. M., 569
Dualism, in Christian tradition, 47, 63
Duguit, Léon, 528
Duhem, Pierre, 549
Du Plessi-Mornay, 189
Dupont de Nemours, 323
Dürer, Albrecht, 127
Dynamics, 212, 216, 217, 237, 238

Eckhart, Master, 145
Economic determinism, 465
Economic nationalism, 192, 674. *See* Mercantilism and Neo-mercantilism
Economic theory, medieval, 89–92; in Renaissance, 192–94; in 18th century, 321–32; in 19th century, 500, 501, 523–26
Eddy, Sherwood, 568
Educated classes in Middle Ages, 20–22, 31
Education, in Middle Ages, 20–22, 31; in Renaissance, 120; in Reformation, 155, 165, 168; in Catholic Reformation, 165; in Humanism, 168; in democratic theory, 353; in Romanticism, 401, 402
Einstein, Albert, 458, 474–78
Electrons, 470, 473–75, 478
Elijah, 40
Elisha, 40
Ely, Richard T., 645
Emerson, R. W., 411, 414, 415, 600
Empiricism, 266 ff., 271–73. *See* Locke and Hume
Encyclopedia, The Grand, 264 ff.
Engels, Friedrich, 659
Enlightened despots, 335
Enlightenment, 226, 254
Environment, influence of, 315, 316, 489, 513
Epicureanism, 594

Equality, ideal of, 316
Erasmus, 121, 132 ff.; attack on medievalism, 147; philosophy of Christ, 156; pacifism, 195; disdain of natural science, 213, 216
Eternal life, ideal of, 55
Ethical culture movement, 536
Ethical reilgion, 563–66
Ethics, founded as a science, 365 ff.
Euclid, 209
Evangelicalism, 408, 540, 541
Evolution, changed conception of, 394; and Romanticism, 422 ff., 458, 459, 461, 463–65; mechanistic theory of, 465 ff.; in biology, 486–89; significance of, 489–95; and liberal religion, 554; philosophic reactions to, 588, 589, 602 ff.; creative, 604; 624
Expansion of Europe, in Crusades, 15; in commercial revolution, 205 ff.
Experience, conception of, 268 ff.
Experimental method, in natural science, 262, 264 ff.; in social sciences, 507 ff.; and analysis of origins, 483 ff.
Ezekiel, 40

Factory system, 327
Faith, revival of in 18th century, 404 ff.; Kant's apologetic for, 411 ff.; as a conservative apologetic, 430; in science, 468, 585; in religious tradition, 533
Faraday, M., 471, 472
Fascism, 528, 549, 642, 651 ff., 672
Faust spirit, 129, 605
Fechner, G. T., 511
Federalism, origin of, 191
Federalist, The, 348
Fénelon, 286
Feudalism, 83 ff.; ideal of loyalty, 86 ff.; idealized, 438
Feuerbach, Ludwig, 464, 465
Fichte, Johann Gottlieb, 379, 415, 417, 446, 601, 634
Ficino, Marsiglio, 122
Fielding, Henry, 403
Fogazzaro, A., 547
Fontenelle, 240, 254; idea of progress, 382
Fourier, Charles, 316, 449, 450, 463, 500
Fox, George, 410
France, Anatole, 17, 581, 595
Franchise, in American colonies, 347
Francis, Saint, 72 ff., 100
Franklin, Benjamin, 161, 347
Frazer, J. G., 507, 521
Fremantle, Canon W. H., 534
Fresnel, A. J., 471
Freud, Sigmund, 516 ff
Freudians, 508

INDEX

Froebel, Friedrich, 415
Fuggers, 113
Functional ideal of society, 58
Fundamentalism, Protestant, 408, 541–43

Galen, 209
Galileo, and his predecessors, 211, 212, 216–18; scientific method of, 220 ff.; astronomical discoveries, 232 ff.; opposition to, 233–35; dynamics, 237, 238, 255, 268
Galton, Francis, 507
"Garden of Epicurus," 17
Gargantua, 125
Garrison, William Lloyd, 677
Gaston de Foix, 122
Genes, 489
Genetic theory, 488, 489
Gentile, Giovanni, 662, 665
Gentleman, Renaissance ideal of, 134–36
Geography, medieval, 24; in Renaissance, 205
Geology, 264, 485, 486
Geometry, 210, 212; practical, 217, 218, 237; analytic, 212, 241
Gerard of Cremona, 209
Gerry, Elbridge, 347
Giddings, F. H., 508
Gierke, O., 528
Gilson, Étienne, 549
Gladstone, W. E., 443, 602
Godfrey of Bouillon, 187
Godwin, William, 450
Goering, Hermann, 664
Goethe, 377–79, 397; a Romanticist, 400 ff., 411, 415, 416; "Faust," 416, 417, 423, 486
Gompers, Samuel, 650
Gore, Bishop Charles, 645
Gospel ideal of love, 43
Gothic art, revival of, 438
Grace, doctrine of, in Catholicism, 48, 50; in Lutheranism, 149; in Calvinism, 151
Graebner, F., 521
Gravitation, law of, 258 ff.; and relativity theory, 475 ff.
Greek ideals, in Western civilization, 44 ff.; revived in Renaissance, 119 ff.; and the new naturalism, 615, 616
Greek science, principles of, 99 ff.
Gregory the Great, 29
Gregory VII, 77
Grosseteste, Robert, 209, 210
Grotius, Hugo, 188, 190, 195, 197 ff., 666
Guild socialism, 453, 642, 643, 654, 657, 658

Guilds, medieval, 89–92, 114, 192
Gumplowicz, Ludwik, 506
Gutenberg, Johann, 120
Guyau, J. M., 605

Haeckel, Ernst, 458
Hall, G. Stanley, 512
Hamilton, Alexander, 347
Hamilton, Walton H., 625
Hancock, John, 346
Hanseatic League, 89
Hardy, Thomas, 431, 591
Harrington, Thomas, 189
Hartley, David, 310, 314, 315, 481, 510
Hastings, Warren, 371
Haydon, A. E., 567
Hayek, F. A. von, 625
Heaven and Hell, in Middle Ages, 30, 33
Hebrew element in Western civilization, 39 ff.
Hebrew moral ideals, 42
Hegel, Georg Wilhelm Friedrich, 414, 416, 422, 435
Hegelianism, 464, 579, 599, 615, 662
Hegius, Alexander, 132
Heisenberg, W., 458, 475
Hellenistic culture, 11, 14
Helmholtz, H. L. F. von, 296, 470, 471
Helvetius, 310, 316–18, 352, 381
Henderson, Arthur, 636
Henry IV of France, 181, 201, 380
Herbert of Cherbury, 285, 291
Herder, Johann Gottfried von, 414, 419, 422, 463
Heredity, laws of, 489
Heresy, 167
Hero, 217
Herron, George D., 645
Hertz, Heinrich Rudolf, 471, 472
High Church Party, in Anglican Church, 534, 536, 561 ff.
Higher criticism of Bible, 464, 552
Hiketas, 218, 228
Hildebrand, 77. *See* Gregory VII
Hildebrand, B., 525
Hippocrates, 209
History, nature of, 4, 9; in Romanticism, 421 ff.; method of critical investigation, 464
Hitler, Adolf, 674, 675
Hitze, Franz, 450, 643
Hobbes, Thomas, 182, 185 ff., 311 ff., 528
Hobhouse, L. T., 636
Hobson, J. A., 525, 636, 673
Holbach, 265, 276, 300–03, 338, 370, 397
Holy Roman Empire, 104
Hooch, P. de, 127

INDEX

Hoover, Herbert, 627, 674
Hosea, 40
Hotelling, Harold, 625
Howard, John, 372
Hügel, Baron Friedrich von, 547
Hugo of Saint Victor, 35
Hugo, Victor, 441
Huguenots and absolutism, 190
Hull, Cordell, 674
Human nature, science of, in 18th century, 311; in 19th and 20th centuries, 497 ff.
Humanism, forerunners of, 22; growth of in Renaissance, 111, 114; in Middle Ages, 115 ff.; ideals of life, 124; in Northern Europe, 127 ff.; ideals of in Elizabethan literature, 128, 129; contrast between Northern and Italian, 131, 132; opposed by Reformation, 145; factor in Reformation, 146 ff.; attack on asceticism, 155; factor in rise of national cultures, 176; opposition to science, 212; contribution to new science, 217; cause of rational religion, 282 ff.; and evolution, 459, 493; and new physical theory, 460
Humanism, contemporary religious, 567, 568
Humanitarianism, 56, 370 ff.
Humboldt, Wilhelm von, 445
Hume, David, 96, 264, 272, 273, 292, 293, 300, 301, 310, 369, 404, 411
Hus, John, 146
Huskisson, William, 429
Hutcheson, Francis, 369
Hutchinson, Col. John, 158
Hutten, Ulrich von, 132
Hutton, James, 264, 485
Huxley, Thomas, 296, 297, 458, 596
Huygens, Christian, 256

Idealism, post-Kantian, 417, 418; philosophic, in late 19th century, 598 ff.; and liberal religion, 538
"Image of the World," 22
Immaculate Conception, dogma of, 544
Immanence, theory of divine, 419, 559
Indeterminacy, principle of, 475
Index, The, 154
Individualism, in Renaissance, 111, 134, 159 ff., 166, 172; in 18th century, 321 ff.; in Romanticism, 415 ff., 420; 19th-century philosophy of, 439, 629, 633
Industrial democracy, 652 ff.
Industrial revolution, 10; and Wesleyanism, 161; effects of, 327 ff., 622, 623, 647
Industrial unionism, 649, 651

Industrialism, ideal of, in Reformation, 127, 136 ff., 153; in Puritanism, 159 ff.; theory of benevolent, 451; effect on religion, 538, 539; effect on philosophy, 579, 580; philosophy of, 612, 613; social ideals of, 622–25
Infinity of worlds, 242
Ingersoll, Robert G., 541
Innocent III, 77 ff., 106
Inquisition, 79, 154; and Galileo, 234. See Church
Instincts, in psychology, 512 ff.
Instrumentalism, ideals of, 605, 606, 616–19
International ideals, in Renaissance, 194 ff.; in 18th century, 379; in 19th and 20th centuries, 446 ff., 666, 676 ff.
International law, 197 ff. See Grotius
Isaiah, 40
I.W.W. (Industrial Workers of the World), 625

Jacobi, F. J., 414
James I of England, 181
James, William, 400, 481, 511, 567
Jansenism, 160
Jefferson, Thomas, 318, 346, 355 ff.
Jesus, ideals of, 42 ff.
Jesus, Company of, 154, 168
Jevons, W. S., 523
John of Salisbury, 117
Johnson, Samuel, 377
Joinville, Sire de, 87
Joule, J. P., 470
Judaism, 39 ff., 536, 537, 562, 563
Julius II, 124
Jung, C. G., 517
Jurisprudence, 501, 526 ff.

Kant, Immanuel, 96, 266, 270, 300, 304, 305, 380, 405, 411, 417, 599
Kantor, J. R., 515
Keble, John, 438, 533
Kelvin, Lord, 470, 471
Kepler, 230, 231, 236, 256, 258
Ketteler, Bishop W. E. von, 450, 643
Kierkegaard, S., 569
Kinetic theory, 469, 471, 472, 473, 477
Kingsley, Charles, 450, 452
Knies, K., 525
Knighthood, 84, 85; ideals of, 85, 87, 88
Knights Templars, 85
Knowledge, problem of, 266 ff., 459, 478
Knox, John, 189
Koffka, K., 515
Köhler, W., 515
Kroeber, A. L., 522
Kulturkampf, 550

INDEX

Laberthonnière, Abbé L., 547
La Boëtie, 189
La Follette, Robert M., 638
Lagrange, Joseph Louis, 258, 295
Laisser-faire, 194, 277, 322, 637, 638
Lamarck, 264, 486, 487
Lamartine, 453
Lamennais, 347, 450, 453
Lang, Andrew, 507
Langen, Rudolf von, 132
Language, in Middle Ages, 21, 103; rise of national, 175, 176
Laplace, Pierre Simon, Marquis de, 295, 484
Laski, H. J., 528
Lassalle, F., 634
Latimer, Hugh, 156
Latini, Bruneto, 22
Lavoisier, 264
Law, William, 298
Law of Nature, 198
Law, method in, 500
League of Nations, 666, 672, 676, 678
Le Bon, Gustave, 508
Lefèvre d'Étaples, 121, 147
Leibniz, 258, 297
Lenin, N., 659–61, 675
Leo X, 124
Leo XIII, 547, 643
Leonardo da Vinci, 123, 125, 135, 216, 220, 235
Le Play, F., 450, 641, 642
Le Roy, Édouard, 547
Lessing, 422, 462, 491
Lewis, John L., 651
Liberal Party, British, 637
Liberalism, philosophy of, 439 ff., 579
Liberalism, religious, 536, 539, 542; Protestant, 550 ff.; 566 ff.
Liebig, Justus von, 479
Life, origin of, 479
Lilienfeld, Paul von, 506
Linnaeus, 264, 486
List, Friedrich, 449
Literature, of Middle Ages, 22; vernacular, 116
Little Englanders, 673
Lloyd-George, David, 636
Locke, John, 167, 191, 253 ff., 269, 272, 286–88, 310, 311, 314, 339 ff., 373–75, 381, 528
Loeb, Jacques, 479, 480
Logical positivism, 459, 478, 614, 615
Loisy, Abbé A. F., 547, 548
Lorentz transformation, 476
Louis IX of France, 87
Louis d'Orléans, 189
Low Church Party, in Anglican Church, 536
Lüger, Karl, 643

Luther, 137 ff., 148 ff., 156 ff., 230
Lutheranism, 148 ff.; and Calvinism, 148, 152, 153; predestination, 149; the gospel in, 149, 150; salvation in, 149; Bible in, 149, 150; and absolute monarchy, 182
Lyell, Charles, 264, 485

Macdonald, J. Ramsay, 637
Machiavelli, 176, 182 ff., 186, 195 ff., 666
Mackenzie, Henry, 403
Madison, James, 347
Magic, 223
Maine, Henry Sumner, 526
Maistre, Joseph de, 410, 430 ff., 436, 437, 463
Maitland, F. W., 526, 528
Malebranche, 286
Malthus, T. R., 323, 328, 381, 487
Manchester School, 443, 501, 673
Mann, Horace, 415
Manning, Henry Edward, Cardinal, 643
Manorial system, 83
Marco Polo, 205
Maricourt, Pierre de, 210
Maritain, Jacques, 549
Marlowe, Christopher, 129
Marx, Karl, 330, 453, 465, 579, 603, 654, 659, 662, 674, 675
Materialism, 300 ff., 467
Mathematical interpretation of nature, 210, 215, 220 ff., 227 ff., 231 ff., 239 ff., 255, 259 ff.
Mathematics, Alexandrian, and 17th-century science, 217
Maurice, F. D., 450, 452
Maxwell, James Clerk, 258, 471, 472
Maxwell's equations, 472, 476, 477
Mayer, Robert, 470
Mayow, John, 257
Mazzini, Giuseppe, 446–48, 667, 676
McCulloch, J. R., 443
McDougall, William, 508, 512 ff.
Mechanism, theory of, 239 ff., 255 ff.; universal, 466–68; in biology, 479–81; in psychology, 481–83; ideal of, in social sciences, 499 ff.; in 19th-century philosophy, 580 ff.
Mechanistic analysis, method of, defined, 466; broadened, 467, 480, 481, 483, 614
Medici, Lorenzo de', 120
Medicine, in Middle Ages, 209
Medieval world-view, 17 ff., 22, 32
Megalopolis, ideal of, 630, 632, 648
Melanchthon, Philipp, 148, 230
Mendel, Gregor, 489, 543
Menger, Karl, 523

Mercantilism, 192, 322
Mercier de la Rivière, 279
Method, of scholasticism, 95 ff.; of 17th-century science, 219 ff.; of Newtonian science, 261 ff.; rise of experimental, 262 ff.; in the social sciences, 18th-century, 308 ff., 340; 19th-century, analytical school, 499 ff.; historical school, 501 ff.; evolutionary school, 502, 504 ff.; biological school, 504 ff.; comparative, 504
Metternich, 429, 438
Micah, 40, 41
Michelangelo, 125
Michels, R., 527
Michelson-Morley experiment, 476
Middle class, in Renaissance, 114; and nationalism, 174, 394; ideals of, 628 ff.
Mill, James, 314, 371, 510, 630
Mill, John Stuart, 363, 441, 443, 501
Milton, John, 158, 189, 373
Mirabeau, 376
Miracles, 28–30, 289, 292, 559
Mitchell, Wesley C., 525
Modernism, in 14th century, 211, 212; religious, in 19th century, 536, 542 ff.; Catholic, 547 ff.; Protestant, 550 ff.; faith of, 554 ff.; beyond modernism, 566 ff.
Monasticism, 61 ff.; rule of, 64 ff.; ideals of, 66, 68 ff.; revolt from in Renaissance, 123, 124
Monism, German, 536
Monistic evolutionary theologies, 558 ff.
Montaigne, 167, 218
Montalembert, Charles Forbes René de, 441
Montchrétien, Antoine de, 193
Montesquieu, 311, 319, 345, 352, 366
Moore, H. L., 525
Morality, science of, 366 ff.
Moravian Brethren, 407
Morgan, Lewis H., 507, 521
Morgan, Thomas, 291
Morgan, Thomas Hunt, 489
Morley, John, 439
Mosca, Gaetano, 528
Moslem culture, 14, 208
Moufang, Christoph, 450, 643
Müller, Johannes, 479
Mun, A. A. M., comte de, 642
Mun, Thomas, 193, 194
Murri, R., 547
Mussolini, 448, 662, 663, 667, 672–75
Mutations, 488, 489
Mysticism, 35, 97, 145 ff., 236, 405

Napoleon, 381
National cultures, rise of, 175 ff.

National Socialism, 661–64, 673
Nationalism, beginnings of, 131, 132; in Renaissance, 114; and Calvinism, 151, 152; and Catholic Reformation, 155, 163; growth of, 173; and Christendom, 172; in 18th century, 376 ff.; and Romanticism, 394, 429, 434, 440; liberal philosophy of, 446 ff.; contemporary, 666 ff.
Natural history, 264
Natural law, 198, 244 ff.
Natural religion, 286 ff.
Natural rights, 340, 343, 362
Natural selection, in biology, 487, 488; in social sciences, 506
Natural theology, 294 ff.
Naturalism, Greek, in Renaissance, 122, 123; opposed by Reformation, 145; in 18th century, 282 ff.; and recent science, 459, 460; and evolution, 493; aesthetic, in religion, 560 ff.; in religious philosophy, 567, 568; with vision, 569 ff.; in philosophy, the new, 611 ff.; Greek, 615 ff.; Baconian, 615 ff., 626
Nature, ideal of, in Newtonian science, 274 ff., 366; in Romanticism, 401, 417
Neo-Liberalism, 633, 637
Neo-Mercantilism, 449
Neo-Orthodoxy, Protestant, 539, 569 ff.
Neo-Platonism, 46, 63, 122, 208, 210, 227
Neo-Thomism, 547, 549
New Deal, 625, 627, 639–41
New Freedom, 638
Newman, J. H., Cardinal, 438, 533
Newton, Isaac, 98, 229, 242, 253 ff., 257 ff., 260, 287, 295, 461, 469, 471, 473, 476, 477
Nicaea, Council of, 48
Nicholas of Oresme, 212, 216
Niebelungenlied, 86
Niebuhr, Barthold Georg, 464, 503
Niebuhr, Reinhold, 568, 570–72
Nietzsche, Friedrich, 507, 607 ff., 664
N.R.A. (National Recovery Administration), 639, 640, 651, 653
Nuremberg school of astronomy, 228

Ockham, William of, 211, 212
Ockhamite school, 212, 216, 217
Ohm, Georg Simon, 471
Oken, Lorenz, 486
Omar Khayyam, 595
Optimism, philosophic, 600
Oresme, Nicholas of, 212, 216
Organization, of economic life, 391, 622 ff., 679; of intellectual life, 392–94, 679
Organized labor, ideals of, 649 ff.

INDEX

Origen, 63
Orthodoxy, intellectual origin of, 45
Ostrogorski, M. Y., 527
Otto, Max C., 567
Owen, Robert, 453
Oxford movement, 438, 533
Ozanam, Antoine Frédéric, 450, 453

Pachomius, 64
Pacifism, of Cicero, 195; Erasmus, 195; 18th century, 370, 376, 377; 19th and 20th centuries, 676 ff.
Padua, school of, 210, 216, 217
Paganism in Renaissance, 124 ff.
Page, Kirby, 568
Paine, Thomas, 376
Paley, William, 287, 296, 540
Papacy, 178, 197, 545
Papal infallibility, dogma of, 163, 545
Pappus, 217
Paracelsus, 223
Pareto, Vilfredo, 528, 664
Paris, Masters of, 212, 216
Pascal, 256, 258, 286
Pasteur, Louis, 543
Pater, Walter, 592
Paternalism, 449 ff., 641, 642
Patriotism, 377, 429, 434, 666 ff.
Paul, Saint, 42, 44, 47, 48, 59, 63
Paul of Venice, 216
Pavlov, I. P., 482, 512
Peace and War, ideals of. *See* International ideals
Peace projects, 201, 380 ff.
Pearson, Karl, 507
Peasant class, lot of, 88
Peel, Robert, 429
"Peer Gynt," 605
Penology, 372
Periodic law of atomic weights, 470, 474
Perry, W. J., 521
Personality, Romantic ideal of, 415 ff.; in psychology, 514 ff.
Pessimism, philosophic, 587 ff.
Pestalozzi, 415
Petrarch, 118 ff., 213
Peurbach, Georg, 228
Phenomenalism, 266, 271
"Philosophy of Christ," 367
Photons, 473
Physical theory, recent revolution in, 458, 459, 472-78; and biology, 480; effect on philosophy, 613, 614
Physico-mathematical method, 261
Physiocrats, 262, 322 ff., 325, 338
Pico, Earl of Mirandola, 122, 123, 223
Pietism, German, 290, 304, 405 ff.
Pinel, Philippe, 372
Pisano, Leonardo, 209
Pius IX, 544 ff.

Pius X, 548
Pius XI, 644
Planck, Max, 458, 473
Planned economy, ideal of, 655, 656
Plato, 208, 237, 633
Platonism, 46, 47, 60, 121, 237, 238
Playfair, John, 485
Plotinus, 47, 63
Plumb plan, 652, 653
Pluralism, political, 528, 654
Political economy, 321 ff. *See* Economic theory
Political science, 526 ff.
Political theory, in Middle Ages, 102 ff., 178-81; in Renaissance, 179 ff.; absolutism, 181 ff., 334 ff.; of 18th century, chapter 14 *passim*; of 19th century, chapter 17; of Traditionalists, 435; contemporary, 526 ff.
Pope, Alexander, 275
Positivism, 266, 271, 450; logical, 459, 478, 614, 615
Positivist religion, 536, 562
Pragmatic sanction, 162
Predestination, 149, 150
Priestley, Joseph, 264
Primitive mentality, 31
"Principia Mathematica" of Newton, 260
Printing, invention of, 119, 120
Probability, in wave mechanics, 475
Progress, idea of, 381, 382, 440, 453 ff., 461, 603
Progressivism, political, in U.S., 633, 637, 638
Proletariat, philosophies of, 449 ff., 647 ff.
Property, rights of, in Middle Ages, 44, 90; in Locke, 342; in American Constitution, 346; in The Federalist, 348
Protestantism, 52, chapters 7, 12, 20
Proudhon, P. J., 450, 453
Psycho-analysis, 483, 516 ff.
Psychological method, 311 ff.
Psychology, associationalist, 314, 481 ff., 510; influence on social sciences, 507 ff.; Romanticist, 510; behaviorism, 481 ff., 512 ff.; Gestalt school, 483, 515; organismic school, 515; psycho-analysis, 483, 516 ff.
Ptolemy, 32, 209, 228, 229
Purgatory, 51
Puritanism, 143 ff., 155, 157 ff.
Purpose in universe, 34, 35; opposed, 235 ff.
Pusey, E. B., 438, 533
Pythagoreanism, 209, 238

Quakers, 410, 673
Quantum theory, 458, 473

Quesnay, 323
Quetelet, 500, 509

Rabelais, 125, 215 ff., 630
Radio-activity, 472, 473
Ramus, Peter, 214, 220
Randolph, John, 347
Ranke, L. von, 464, 503
Raphael, 125
Rational supernaturalism, 288, 540
Rationalism, geometrical, in the 18th century, 262
Rationalism, religious, 282 ff.
Ratzenhofer, Gustav, 506
Rauschenbusch, Walter, 564–66, 645
Raynal, Abbé, 371
Reactionary movements after 1815, 439, 440
Reason, ideal of, in Newtonian science, 274, 366
Reformation, 111; a compromise, 143, 145; religious changes, 144 ff.; and capitalism, 152; and industrialism, 153; moral changes, 155 ff.; political changes, 161 ff.; compared with Renaissance, 163 ff.; significance of, 163 ff., 165 ff., 206
Regiomontanus, 228
Relativity, principle of, 458, 474–78
Rembrandt, 128
Renaissance, 111 ff.; compared with Reformation, 163 ff., 206
Renan, Ernest, 562, 593, 616
Reuchlin, 121, 132
Revelation in religion, 288
Revolution, right of, 343
Ricardo, David, 323, 328 ff., 523
Richardson, Samuel, 403
Ritschl, Albrecht, 563, 564, 569
Rivers, W. H. R., 521
Robbins, Lionel, 525
Robespierre, 305
Rodbertus, Karl Johann, 634
Roemer, Ole, 256
Rogers, Thorold, 525
Roland, Song of, 85
Rolland, Romain, 678
"Romance of Sidrach," 22
Romantic idealism, 418, 430, 434, 501
Romanticism, in Renaissance, 129; and classicism, 382; reaction against reason, 395 ff.; and conservatism, 403, 404; ideals of, 415 ff.
"Romaunt of the Rose," 22
Röntgen, Wilhelm Konrad von, 473
Roosevelt, Theodore, 638
Roscher, Wilhelm, 524
Rosenberg, Arthur, 662
Rousseau, Jean Jacques, 253, 262, 350 ff., 370, 401, 410, 415, 626

Royal Society, 256
Royce, Josiah, 601
Rubens, 127
Rubianus, Crotus, 132
Rumford, Benjamin, Count, 470
Ruskin, John, 450
Russell, Bertrand, 582, 597, 615, 679, 680
Russian Communists, ideals of, 654–56, 659–61, 665
Rutherford, Daniel, 264
Rutherford, Ernest, 474
Ryan, John A., 644

Sacraments, 50 ff., 76. *See* Church
Sadler, Michael, 452
Saint-Hilaire, Geoffroy, 264, 486
Saint-Pierre, Abbé de, 201, 380
Saint-Simon, Claude Henri, Comte de, 451, 500, 642
Saintly ideal, 62, 67. *See* Monasticism
Salerno, 209
Santayana, George, 18, 400, 401, 562, 593, 594, 616, 617, 676
Savigny, Friedrich Karl von, 423, 424, 436, 526
Say, J. B., 429
Scaliger, Julius Caesar, 216
Schäffle, A., 506, 525, 634
Schell, H., 547
Schelling, F. W. J. von, 414, 486
Schiller, 411, 422
Schlegel, Friedrich, 415
Schleiermacher, F. D. E., 414, 420, 559
Schmoller, Gustav von, 525, 634, 635
Scholars, medieval, 92
Scholasticism, 92 ff.; attacked by humanists, 213 ff.
Schopenhauer, Arthur, 418, 590, 609
Schrödinger, E., 458, 473, 474
Science, 10; popular, in Middle Ages, 22 ff.; and superstition, 28; scholastic, 31, 92, 96 ff.; Greek, 44, 99 ff.; and Renaissance, 164; rebirth of natural, 203; Arabian, 208 ff.; natural, in high Middle Ages, 209–12; experimental, 210, 211, 262; opposition of Humanism, 212 ff.; Alexandrian, revived, 217, 218, 235; Baconian spirit, 223; conflict with Aristotelian thought, 214, 236, 238, 268; Newtonian, 253 ff.; experimental method, 262, 529; problem of certainty, 269; ideals of Nature and Reason in, 274 ff.; and religion, 18th century, 282 ff.; 19th century, 537 ff.; limitations of, in Kant, 411; and faith, 585; of individual, 420; in 19th and 20th centuries, 458 ff.

INDEX

Science, new philosophies of, 459, 478, 480, 481, 483, 578, 579, 612, 613 ff.
Science, social, and geometrical method, 262; in 18th century, 308 ff., 334 ff.; in 19th and 20th centuries, 497 ff.
Scientific method, in Middle Ages, 96 ff.; in Renaissance, 219 ff.; Newtonian, 261 ff.; rise of experimental, 262 ff.; in 19th and 20th centuries, 465-68, 483
Scott, Walter, 438
Sellars, R. W., 567
Senior, Nassau, 443
Sensationalism, 313 ff.
Separation of powers, theory of, 345
Serfs, 88
Serra, Antonio, 193
Shaftesbury, 3rd Earl of, 369
Shaftesbury, 7th Earl of, 452
Shakespeare, 128, 129, 177
Shaw, George Bernard, 566
Shelley, 411
Sicily, 209
Sidney, Sir Philip, 136
"Sidrach," 24
Simeon Stylites, Saint, 63, 64
Simplicity of Nature, 227 ff.
Single tax, 325
Sismondi, J. C. L. de, 449
Skepticism, 218, 286, 298 ff., 404, 494, 535, 536, 595
Smith, Adam, 194, 322, 325, 369, 429
Smith, G. Elliot, 521
Smith, William, 264, 485
Smollett, 403
Social Christianity, 633, 641 ff.
Social contract theory, 185, 342, 350 ff.
Social gospel, 534, 535, 563 ff., 568, 570, 573, 644-47
Social legislation, 633 ff.
Social science. See Science, social
Socialism, seeds of in Rousseau, 354, 355; Tory, 452; Christian, 452, 641 ff.; Catholic, 453, 641 ff.; of the Chair, 634; State, 453, 634 ff., 652, 654, 655; Marxian, 603, 654-56, 659-61, 665, 674, 675; guild, 453, 642, 643, 651, 654, 657
Society, organization of, in Middle Ages, 13, 58 ff., 102 ff.; 1815-1848, 427; need of organization today, 391, 622 ff., 679
Socinianism, 284
Sociology, modern, 519 ff.
Solar system, development of, 484 ff.
Sombart, Werner, 526
Soto, Domenico de, 216
Sovereignty, in Middle Ages, 178, 179; popular, 189; national, 194 ff.; in Rousseau, 355; theories of, 380; and pluralism, 527; and internationalism, 676, 677
Spain, 14, 154
Spencer, Herbert, 331, 444, 445, 459, 493, 500, 506, 511, 519, 521, 579, 603
Spener, P. J., 405, 406
Spenser, Edmund, 122, 123
Spinoza, 244 ff.; 269, 297, 303, 304, 419
Spiritual power, medieval ideal of, 77, 79; attacked, 146
Stalin, Josef, 661
State, theories of. See Political theory
State vs. Church in Middle Ages, 104
State of Nature, 341 ff.
State Socialism, 453, 634 ff., 652, 654, 655
Statistics, 500, 509; in quantum mechanics, 475
Steele, Richard, 161
Storm and Stress movement, 411
Strauss, David Friedrich, 414, 464
Strong, Josiah, 645
Sullivan, John W., 650
Sully, M. de Béthune, Duc de, 201
Sumner, William Graham, 637
Superman, in Nietzsche, 609, 610
Superstition, medieval, 28
Supreme Court, U.S., 640, 641
Suso, Henry, 145
Sutherland, Alexander, 508
Swift, Jonathan, 382
Syllabus of Errors, 544 ff.
Symbolism, medieval, 35, 36
Syndicalism, 625, 642, 654, 655, 661, 663

Tarde, G., 508
Tartaglia, N., 216, 217, 237
Tauler, Johann, 145, 204
Taylor, Jeremy, 373
Tennyson, 421, 444, 587, 588, 602, 603
Theleme, Abbey of, 126
Theologia Germanica, 145, 146
Thermodynamics, laws of, 470
Thierry of Chartres, 209
Thomas Aquinas, Saint, 31, 59, 80, 94 ff., 117
Thomas à Kempis, 132
Thomism, 209, 212, 213. See Neo-Thomism
Thomson, James, 589
Thoreau, Henry David, 411
Thorndike, E. L., 512
Tiberius, Emperor, 374
Tillich, Paul, 570
Tillotson, John, 286, 289, 540
Time, in Newtonian science, 275; in theory of relativity, 476, 614
Tindal, Matthew, 288, 291, 298

INDEX

Toland, John, 289
Toledo, 209
Toleration, 133, 168, 370, 372 ff.; Act of, 283
Tools and instruments, effect of on science, 217–19
Tories, 429
Torricelli, 256
Tory socialists, 452
Town life, medieval, 89
Trade, medieval, 205; in commercial revolution, 205 ff.
Trade union movement, 649 ff., 655, 657, 658
Traditionalism, 404, 410, 423, 430 ff., 436, 437
Transcendentalism, 411
Treitschke, Heinrich von, 669, 670
Trent, Council of, 52, 154, 163
Trinity, doctrine of, 45, 98
Troeltsch, Ernst, 566, 569
Truce of God, 85
Tufts, James Hayden, 606
Turgot, 323
Tylor, E. B., 507, 521
Tyrrell, George, 547, 556

Ultramontanism, 163, 436, 550
Uncertainty, principle of, 475
Uniformitarianism, doctrine of, 465 ff., 485
Uniformity of Nature, 227 ff.
Unitarianism, 284, 540, 568
Unity in Middle Ages, 78, 106
Universal man, Renaissance ideal of, 135, 136
Universal monarchy of Dante, 104 ff.
Universities in Middle Ages, 21, 209; in Reformation, 169
Urban VIII, 234
Utilitarianism, 336, 358 ff., 369, 441 ff., 579
Utopian ideals, 626 ff.

Valla, Lorenzo, 124
Veblen, Thorstein, 525, 668, 673
Vermeer, 127
Vernaculars, in Renaissance, 116
Via moderna of Ockham, 211
Vices, in Middle Ages, 53
"Vindiciae contra Tyrannos," 189
Virtues, seven cardinal, 52
Vitalism, 467, 480

Vives, Luis, 216, 220
Voltaire, 134, 264, 272, 283, 287, 292, 296, 297, 304, 311, 335, 336, 337, 375, 377, 378
Vries, Hugo de, 488

Wages, Iron law of, 330
Wagner, Adolf, 525, 634
Wallace, Alfred Russel, 458, 487
Walras, A. Auguste, 523
Wandering clerks, in Middle Ages, 116
War, and nationalism, 174, 669 ff.
War and peace, ideals of. *See* International relations
Ward, Harry F., 568
Ward, Lester F., 500, 519, 637
Ward, William, 533
Watson, John B., 481, 482, 512
Wave mechanics, 458, 473, 474
Webb, Sidney, and Beatrice, 526, 636
Weber, E. H., 511
Weismann, A., 488
Wellington, Duke of, 433
Wells, H. G., 462
Werner, A. G., 264
Wertheimer, Max, 515
Wesley, John, 405, 407
Wesleyanism, 161, 290, 304, 407
Westcott, Bishop B. F., 645
Whitefield, George, 407
Whitehead, Alfred North, 480, 538, 567, 614
Wieman, Henry Nelson, 567
W.I.L. (Women's International League for Peace and Freedom), 677, 678
William of Conches, 209
Williams, Roger, 372, 373
Wilson, Woodrow, 527, 638
Wimpfeling, 161
Wolf, A. F., 503
Woolston, Thomas, 292
Wordsworth, 403, 411, 418, 425
Working class, ideals of, 647 ff.
Worms, R., 506
Wundt, Wilhelm, 481, 511
Wyclif, John, 146, 181

Yeomen, in Middle Ages, 88
Young, Thomas, 471

Zinzendorf, Count von, 161, 407
Zwingli, 148